REV. HENRY WARD BEECHER.

PLYMOUTH CHURCH

AND ITS PASTOR,

OR

HENRY WARD BEECHER AND HIS ACCUSERS.

"Give me good proofs of what you have alleged:
'Tis not enough to say—in such a bush
There lies a thief—in such a cave a *beast*,—
But *you must show him to me* ere I shoot,
Else I may kill one of my *straggling sheep:*
I'm fond of no man's person but his virtue."
CROWN'S 1ST. PART OF HENRY VI.

COMPILED BY
J. E. P. DOYLE.

HARTFORD, CONN.:
THE PARK PUBLISHING COMPANY.
1874.

PREFACE TO THE FIRST EDITION.

It was not without many misgivings that the undersigned accepted a commission from the publisher to prepare a history of the great religious scandal that for so many months has excited a nation, caused Christians to blush for the cause of religion, and unbelievers to scoff and rejoice that the light of the most brilliant star in the pulpit firmament was likely to be extinguished, and his usefulness terminated for all time. The compilation of a work of this magnitude under ordinary circumstances would be a perplexing and thankless task, but when the reputations of two of the first men of the country, and a modest, christian wife and mother are involved, the task becomes more difficult and painful. It is more so in a case like this where no competent tribunal has been organized to compel witnesses to testify *under oath,* that all the facts may be elicited. In the compilation of the work, the undersigned has endeavored conscientiously to present the case as fairly as possible for all the parties to the unfortunate difficulty. Care has been taken to exclude all matter irrelevant to the issue, except such as may be calculated to preserve the thread of the narrative. Another difficulty—and, perhaps, the most stupendous of all—was to avoid all disgusting details likely to shock the refined sensibilities of the reader. In this particular the compiler may have partially failed. His apology is that had he shorn the testimony and documents of all these objectionable passages the reader would be unable to understand the character of the offences charged. Yet he recollects that the religious as well as the secular press have opened their columns for the admission of the deplorable story, and that in an interview with a representative, of a Chicago journal, Rev. Dr. Beecher, of that city, is credited with the use of more indelicate language than any that will be found in this compilation —language that the undersigned has carefully refrained from reproducing. With no bias in the matter, and unacquainted with the parties to the scandal, the undersigned does not desire to express any individual opinion as to the guilt or innocence of the distinguished Pastor of Plymouth Church ; and should time vindicate him no one will rejoice more than he will. Whether or not that vindication ever comes, the American people can never forget the great services Mr. Beecher has rendered his country and they will ever retain for him the same feelings of affection and love that his congregation does in this hour of trial. In the compilation of the biographies the undersigned has availed himself of extracts from a work by Mr. Leon Oliver, published in Chicago, to whom he presents his acknowledgments.

J. E. P. Doyle.

New York, August, 1874.

CONTENTS.

CHAPTER V.

CHAPTER VI.

CHAPTER VII.

CHAPTER VIII.

CHAPTER IX.

CHAPTER X.

CHAPTER XI.

CHAPTER XII.

CHAPTER XIII.

CHAPTER XIV.

CHAPTER XV.

CHAPTER XVI.

CHAPTER XVII.

CHAPTER XVIII.

CHAPTER XIX.

CHAPTER XX.

CHAPTER XXI.

CHAPTER XXII.

CHAPTER XXIII.

CHAPTER XXIV.

CHAPTER XXV.

CHAPTER XXVI.

CHAPTER I.

THE ORIGINAL CHARGES AS MADE BY MRS. WOODHULL.—HOW MR. BEECHER'S SECRET CAME INTO HER POSSESSION THROUGH MRS. PAULINE WRIGHT DAVIS.—MRS. STANTON AND MR. BEECHER'S OWN SISTER MIXED UP IN THE SCANDAL AS CIRCULATORS OF IT. —THE SCENE IN TILTON'S HOUSE WHEN HE DISCOVERED HIS WIFE'S INFIDELITY, AS WOODHULL ALLEGES TILTON DESCRIBED IT TO HER.

IN entering upon the duty of preparing a faithful narrative of this great social sensation of the nineteenth century, the author is not unmindful of the fact that much of the information—in the form of published statements, letters and other documents, may be found in the future to be in some particulars inaccurate, but as a faithful historian he proposes to give the entire case as nearly as possible in chronological order. Long before the publication of the original charges against Mr. Beecher in *Woodhull and Claflin's Weekly*—an organ devoted to advance ideas of social reform and universal love—rumors of Mr. Beecher's " irregularities " had been circulated not only in the city of Brooklyn, where Plymouth Church is situate, but within various coteries of the women suffragists. Nobody, however, placed much reliance upon the " slanders," as they were very generally designated, until in the issue of *Woodhull and Claflin's Weekly*, of November 2d, 1872, there were explicit and detailed charges made. The author proposes to copy the charges in Mrs. Woodhull's own words, the more especially as she signs them as an evidence of their truth and her responsibility in the matter of publication. The following is her statement:—

"I propose, as the commencement of a series of aggressive moral warfare on the social question, to begin in this article with ventilating one of the most stupendous scandals which has ever occurred in any community. I refer to that which has been whispered broad-cast for the last two or three years through the cities of New York and Brooklyn, touching the character and conduct of the Rev. HENRY WARD BEECHER in his relations with the family of THEODORE TILTON. I intend that this article shall burst like a bomb-shell into the ranks of the moralistic social camp.

"I am engaged in officering, and in some sense conducting, a social revolution on the marriage question. I have strong convictions to the effect that this institution, as a *bond* or *promise* to love another to the end of life, and forego all other loves or passional gratifications, has outlived its day of usefulness; that the most intelligent and really virtuous of our citizens, especially in the large cities of Christendom, have outgrown it; are constantly and systematically unfaithful to it; despise and revolt against it, as a slavery, in their hearts; and only submit to the semblance of fidelity to it from the dread of a sham public opinion, based on the ideas of the past, and which no longer really represent the convictions of anybody. The doctrines of scientific socialism have profoundly penetrated and permeated public opinion. No thought has so rapidly and completely carried the convictions of the thinking portions of the community as stirpiculture. The absurdity is too palpable, when it is pointed out, that we give a hundred times more attention to the laws of breeding as applied to horses and cattle and pigs, and even to our barn-yard fowls, than we do to the same laws as applied to human beings. It is equally obvious, on a little reflection, that stirpiculture, or the scientific propagation and cultivation of the human animal, demands free love or freedom of the varied union of the sexes under the dictates of the highest and best knowledge on the subject, as an essential and precedent condition. These considerations are too palpable to be ignored, and they look to the complete and early supercedure of the old and traditional institution of marriage, by the substitution of some better system for the maintenance of women as mothers, and of children as progeny. All intelligent people know these facts and look for the coming of some wiser and better system of social life. The supercedure of marriage in the near future, by some kind of socialistic arrangement, is as much a foregone conclusion with all the best thinkers of to-day as was the approaching dissolution of slavery no more than five or ten years before its actual abolition in the late war.

"But, in the meantime, men and women tremble on the brink of the revolution and hesitate to avow their convictions, while yet partly aware of their rights, and urged by the legitimate impulses of nature, they act upon the new doctrines while they profess obedience to the old. In this manner an organized hypocrisy has become the tone of our modern society. Poltroonery, cowardice and deception rule the hour. The continuance, for generations, of such utter falsity, touching one of the most sacred interests of humanity, will almost eradicate the sense of honesty from the human soul. Every consideration of sound expediency demands that these days be shortened; that somebody lead the van in announcement of the higher order of life.

"Impelled by such views, I entered the combat with old errors, as I believed them to be, and brought forward, in addition to the wise and powerful words which others have uttered on the subject, the arguments which my own inspiration and reflection suggested. No sooner had I done so than the howl of persecution sounded in my ears. Instead of replying to my arguments, I was assaulted with shameful abuse. I was young and inexperienced in the business of reform, and astounded to find what, as I have since learned from the veterans in the cause, is the usual fact, that the most persistent and slanderous and foul-mouthed accusations came from precisely those who, as I often happened to know, stood nearest to me in their convictions, and whose lives, privately, were a protest against the very repression which I denounce. It was a paradox which I could not understand, that I was denounced as utterly bad for affirming the right of others, to do as they did; denounced by the very persons whom my doctrines could alone justify, and who claimed, at the same time, to be conscientious and good men. My position led, nevertheless, to continuous confidences relating to people's own opinions and lives and the opinions and lives of others. My mind became charged with a whole literature of astoishning disclosures. The lives of almost the whole army of spiritualistic and social reformers, of all the schools, were laid open before me. But the matter did not stop there. I found that, to a great extent, the social resolution was as far advanced among leading lights of the business and wealthy circles, and of the various professions, not excluding the clergy and the churches, as among technical reformers.

"It was, nevertheless, from these very quarters that I was most severely assailed. It was vexatious and trying, I confess, for one of my temper, to stand under the galling fire of personalities from parties who should have been my warmest advocates, or who should, else, have reformed their lives in accordance with a morality which they wished the public to understand they professed. I was sorely and repeatedly tempted to retort, in personalities, to these attacks. But simply as personality or personal defense, or spiteful retort, I have almost wholly abstained during these years of sharp conflict from making any use of the rich resources at my command for that kind of attack.

"But, in the meantime, the question came to press itself upon my consideration: Had I any right, having assumed the championship of social freedom, to forego the use of half the weapons which the facts no less than the philosophy of the subject placed at my command for conducting the war—through any mere tenderness to those who were virtual traitors to the truth which they knew and were surreptitiously acting upon? Had not the sacred cause of human rights and human well-being a paramount claim over my own conduct? Was I not, in withholding the facts and conniving at a putrid mass of seething falsehood and hypocrisy, in some sense a partaker in these crimes; and was I not, in fact, shrinking from the responsibility of making the exposure more through regard for my own sensitiveness and dislike to be hurt than from any true sympathy with those who would be called upon to suffer?

"These questions once before my mind would never be disposed of until they were fairly settled upon their own merits, and apart, so far as I could separate them, from my own feelings or the feelings of those who were more directly involved. I have come slowly, deliberately, and I may add reluctantly, to my conclusions. I went back to and studied the history of other reforms. I found that GARRISON not only denounced slavery in the abstract, but that he attacked it in the concrete. It was not only 'the sum of all villainies,' but it was the particular villainy of this and that and the other great and influential man, North and South, in the community. Reputations

had to suffer. He bravely and persistently called things by their right names. He pointed out and depicted the individual instances of cruelty. He dragged to the light and scathed and stigmatized the individual offenders. He made them a hissing and a by-word, so far as in him lay. He shocked the public sensibilities by actual and vivid pictures of slaveholding atrocities, and sent spies into the enemies' camp to search out the instances. The world cried shame! and said it was scandalous, and stopped their ears and blinded their eyes, that their own sensibilities might not be hurt by these horrid revelations. They cast the blanket of their charities and sympathies around the real offenders for their misfortune in being brought to the light, and denounced the informer as a malignant and cruel wretch for not covering up scenes too dreadful to be thought upon; as if it were not a thousand times more dreadful that they should be enacted. But the brave old cyclops ignored alike their criticisms, their protests, and their real and their mock sensibilities, and hammered away at his anvil, forging thunderbolts of the gods; and nobody now says he was wrong. A new public opinion had to be created, and he knew that people had to be shocked, and that individual personal feelings had to be hurt. As Bismarck is reported to have said: 'If an omelet has to be made some eggs have to be broken.' Every revolution has its terrific cost, if not in blood and treasure, then still in the less tangible but alike real sentimental injury of thousands of sufferers. The preliminary and paramount question is: Ought the revolution to be made, cost what it may? Is the cost to humanity greater of permitting the standing evil to exist? and if so, then let the cost be incurred, fall where it must. If justice to humanity demand the given expenditure, then accepting the particular enterprise of reform, we accept all its necessary consequences, and enter upon our work, fraught, it may be, with repugnance to ourselves as it is necessarily with repugnance to others.

"I have said that I came slowly, deliberately and reluctantly to the adoption of this method of warfare. I was also hindered and delayed by the fact that if I entered upon it at all I saw no way to avoid making the first onslaught in the most distinguished quarters. It would be cowardice in me to unearth the peccadillos of little men, and to leave untouched the derelictions and offences of the magnates of social and intellectual power and position. How slowly I have moved in this matter, and how reluctantly it may be inferred, will appear from these little points of history.

"More than two years ago these two cities—New York and Brooklyn—were rife with rumors of an awful scandal in Plymouth Church. These rumors were whispered and covertly alluded to in almost every circle. But the very enormity of the facts, as the world views such matters, hushed the agitation and prevented exposure. The prèss, warned by the laws of libel, and by a tacit and in the main honorable *consensus* to ignore all such rumors until they enter the courts, or become otherwise matters of irrepressible notoriety, abstained from any direct notice of the subject, and the rumors themselves were finally stifled or forgotten. A few persons only knew something directly of the facts, but among them, situated as I was, I happened to be one. Already the question pressed on me whether I ought not to use the event to forward the cause of social freedom, but I only saw clear in the matter to the limited extent of throwing out some feelers to the public on the subject. It was often a matter of long and anxious consultation between me and my cabinet of confidential advisers.

"In June, 1870, *Woodhull and Claflin's Weekly* published an article in reply to HENRY C. BOWEN'S attack on myself in the columns of the *Independent*, the editorship of which had just been vacated by THEODORE TILTON. In this article the following paragraph occurred: 'At this very moment awful and herculean efforts are being made in a neighboring city to suppress the most terrific scandal which has ever astonished and convulsed any community. Clergy, congregation and community will be alike hurled into more than all the consternation which the great explosion in Paris carried to that unfortunate city, if this effort at suppression fail.'

"Subsequently I published a letter in both *World* and *Times*, in which was the following sentence: 'I know a clergyman of eminence in Brooklyn who lives in concubinage with the wife of another clergyman of equal eminence.'

"It was generally and well understood among the people of the press especially, that both of these references were to this case of Mr. BEECHER'S, and it came to be generally suspected that I was better informed regarding the facts of the case than others, and was reserving publicity of my knowledge for a more convenient season. This suspicion was heightened nearly into conviction when it transpired that THEODORE TILTON was an earnest and apparently conscientious advocate of many of my radical theories, as appeared in his far-famed biography of me, and in numerous other publications in the

Golden Age and elsewhere. Mr. TILTON'S warmest friends were shocked at his course, and when he added to his remarkable proceedings, his brilliant advocacy of my Fourteenth Amendment theory, in his letters to HORACE GREELEY, CHAS. SUMNER and MAT. CARPENTER, they considered him irremediably committed to the most radical of all radicals. Assurance was made doubly sure when he presided at Steinway Hall, when I, for the first time, fully and boldly advanced my free-love doctrines. It was noted, however, that this man who stood before the world so fully committed to the broadest principles of liberty, made it convenient to be conspicuously absent from the convention of the Women Suffragists at Washington last January. All sorts of rumors were thereupon rife. Some said he had 'gone back' on his advocacy of free-love; some said that a rupture had taken place between him and the leaders of the suffrage movement, and many were the theories brought forward to explain the facts. But the real cause did not transpire until Mr. TILTON was found at Cincinnati urging as a candidate the very man whom he had recently so severely castigated with his most caustic pen. It was then wisely surmised that political ambition, and the editorial chair of the *Tribune*, and his life-long personal devotion to Mr. GREELEY, were the inducements which had sufficed to turn his head and heart away, temporarily at least, from our movement.

"About this time rumors floated out that Mrs. WOODHULL, disgusted at the recent conduct of Mr. TILTON and the advice given him by certain of his friends, was animadverting in not very measured terms upon their conduct. An article specifying matters involving several of these persons, obtained considerable circulation, and with other circumstances, such as the definite statement of facts, with names and places, indicated that the time was at hand, nigh even unto the door, when the things that had remained hidden, should be brought to light, and the whole affair made public.

"Some time in August last there appeared in the *Evening Telegram* a paragraph which hinted broadly at the nature of the impending *exposé*. About this time, a gentleman from abroad, to whom I had related some of the facts in my possession, repeated them to a member of Mr. BEECHER'S church, who denounced the whole story as an infamous libel; but some days later he acknowledged both to his friend and me that he had inquired into the matter and had learned that it was 'a damning fact.' This gentleman occupies a responsible position, and his word is good for all that he utters. Such was the facility with which confirmations were obtained when sought for. When, therefore, those who were conversant with the case, saw in the *Boston Herald* and other papers that I had made a public statement regarding the whole matter, they were not in the least surprised. It shows that the press had concluded that it was time to recognize the sensation which, whether they would or not, was destined soon to shake the social structure from its foundation.

"A reporter was then specially detailed to interview me in order, as he said, that the matter might be published in certain of the New York papers. Why that interview has been suppressed is not possible to affirm with certainty, but it is easy to guess. An impecunious reporter can be bought off with a few hundred dollars. And there are those who would readily pay thousands to shut the columns of the press against this exposure. Fortunately I have a nearly verbatim copy of the report, as the interviewer prepared it, and in this shape I shall now present it to the public.

"But before proceeding to the main matter, let me relate, more in detail, the facts which finally determined me to enter upon this adventurous and responsible method of agitation.

"In September, 1871, I was elected, at the annual convention at Troy, President of the National Association of Spiritualists. I had never consociated with the Spiritualists, although for many years both a Spiritualist and a medium myself, with rare and wonderful experiences of my own from my childhood up. I went to this convention merely as a spectator, with no previous concert or machinery of any kind, and was myself as absolutely taken by surprise by my nomination and election as could have been any one present. It was said editorially in our paper, September 30, 1871, and said truly: 'Her surprise at her reception, and her nomination to the Presidency of the Society was equaled only by the gratitude which she felt, and will ever feel, at the unexpected and tumultuous kindness with which she was then and there honored beyond her desert.'

"In *Woodhull and Claflin's Weekly*, of Nov. 11, 1871, I addressed a President's message to the American Association of Spiritualists. In that document I made use of these words: 'A new and mightier power than all the rings and caucuses, than all the venal legislatures and congresses, has already entered the arena. Not only are all the reform parties coalescent in the reform plane, but they have *already* coalesced in spirit, under the new lead, and 'a nation will be born in a day.' They have already taken possession of the public conviction. Somewhat unconsciously, but really, all the people look to the coming of a new era; but all of them are not so well aware as we are that the spirit world has always exerted a great and diversified influence over this, while it is not till quite recently that the spiritual development of this world has made it possible for the other to maintain real and continuous relations with it.

"'Your enthusiastic acceptance of me, and your election of me as your President, was, in a sense, hardly your act. It was an event prepared for you and to which you were impelled by the superior powers to which both you, and I are subject. It was only one step in a series of rapid and astounding events, which will, in a marvellously short time, change the entire face of the social world.'

"This and similar to this was the complete avowal which I then made of my faith, in the spiritual ordering of human events, and especially of a grand series of events, now in actual and rapid progress, and tending to culminate in the complete dissolution of the old social order, and in the institution of a new and celestial order of humanity in the world. And let me now take occasion to affirm, that all the, otherwise viewed, terrible events which I am about to recite as having occurred in Plymouth Church, are merely parts of the same drama which have been cautiously and laboriously prepared to astound men into the consciousness of the possibilities of a better life; and that I believe that all the parties to this *embroglio* have been, throughout, the unconscious agents of the higher powers. It is this belief, more than anything else, which finally reconciles me to enact my part in the matter, which is that of the mere *nuncia* to the world of the facts which have happened, and so of the new step in the dissolution of the Old and in the inauguration of the New.

"At a large and enthusiastic National Convention of the reformers of all schools, held in Apollo Hall, New York, the 11th and 12th of May, 1872, I was put in nomination as the candidate of the Equal Rights Party for the presidency of the United States. Despite the brilliant promise of appearances at the inception of this movement, a counter current of fatality seemed from that time to attend both it and me. The press, suddenly divided between the other two great parties, refused all notice of the new reformatory movement; a series of pecuniary disasters stripped us, for the time being, of the means of continuing our own weekly publication, and forced us into a desperate struggle for mere existence. I had not even the means of communicating my condition to my own circle of friends. At the same time my health failed from mere exhaustion. The inauguration of the new party, and my nomination, seemed to fall dead upon the country; and, to cap the climax, a new batch of slanders and injurious innuendoes permeated the community in respect to my condition and character.

Circumstances being in this state, the year rolled round, and the next annual convention of the National Association of Spiritualists occurred in Sept., 1872, at Boston. I went there—dragged by the sense of duty—tired, sick and discouraged as to my own future, to surrender my charge as President of the Association, feeling as if I were distrusted and unpopular, and with no consolation but the consciousness of having striven to do right, and my abiding faith in the wisdom and help of the spirit world.

"Arrived at the great assemblage, I felt around me everywhere, not indeed a positive hostility, not even a fixed spirit of unfriendliness, but one of painful uncertainty and doubt. I listened to the speeches of others and tried to gather the sentiment of the great meeting. I rose finally to my feet to render an account of my stewardship, to surrender the charge, and retire. Standing there before the audience, I was seized by one of those overwhelming gusts of inspiration which sometimes come upon me, from I know not where; taken out of myself; hurried away from the immediate question of discussion, and made, by some power stronger than I, to pour out into the ears of that assembly, and, as I was told subsequently, in a rhapsody of indignant eloquence, with circumstantial detail, the whole history of the BEECHER and TILTON scandal in Plymouth Church, and to announce in prophetic terms something of the bearing of those events upon the future of Spiritualism. I know perhaps less than any of those present, all that I did actually say. They tell me that I used some naughty words upon that occasion. All that I know is, that if I swore, *I did not swear profanely*. Some said, with the tears streaming from their eyes, *that I swore divinely*. That I could not have shocked or horrified the audience was shown by the fact that in the immense hall, packed to the ceiling, and as absolutely to my own surprise as at my first election at Troy, I was re-elected President of the Association. Still impressed by my own previous convictions, that my labors in that connection were ended, I promptly declined the office. The convention, however, refused to accept my declinature.

"The public press of Boston professed holy horror at the freedom of my speech, and restricted their reports to the narrowest limits, carefully suppressing what I had said of the conduct of the great clergyman. The report went forward, however, through various channels, in a muffled and mutilated form, the general conclusion being, probably, with the uninformed, simply that *Mrs. Woodhull had publicly slandered Mr. Beecher.*

"Added, therefore, to all other considerations, I am now placed in the situation that I must either endure unjustly the imputation of being a slanderer, or I must resume my previously formed purpose, and relate in formal terms, for the whole public, the simple facts of the case as they have come to my knowledge, and so justify, in cool deliberation, the words I uttered, almost unintentionally, and by a sudden impulse, at Boston.

"I accept the situation, and enter advisedly upon the task I have undertaken, knowing the responsibilities of the act and its possible consequences. I am impelled by no hostility whatever to Mr. BEECHER, nor by any personal pique toward him or any other person. I recognize in the facts a fixed determination in the Spirit world to bring this subject to the light of day for high and important uses to the world. They demand of me my co-operation, and they shall have it, no matter what the consequences may be to me personally.

"The following is the re-statement from notes, aided by my recollection, of the interviewing upon this subject by the press reporter already alluded to:

"*Reporter.*—'Mrs. WOODHULL, I have called to ask if you are prepared and willing to furnish a full statement of the BEECHER-TILTON scandal for publication in the city papers?'

"*Mrs. Woodhull.*—'I do not know that I ought to object to repeating whatever I know in relation to it. You understand, of course, that I take a different view of such matters from those usually avowed by other people. Still I have good reason to think that far more people entertain views corresponding to mine than dare to assert them or openly live up to them.'

"*Reporter.*—'How, Mrs. WOODHULL, would you state in the most condensed way your opinions on this subject, as they differ from those avowed and ostensibly lived by the public at large?'

"*Mrs. Woodhull.*—'I believe that the marriage institution, like slavery and monarchy, and many other things which have been good or necessary in their day, is now *effete*, and in a general sense injurious, instead of being beneficial to the community, although of course it must continue to linger until better institutions can be formed. I mean by marriage, in this connection, any *forced* or *obligatory tie* between the sexes, *any legal intervention* or *constraint* to prevent people from adjusting their love relations precisely as they do their religious affairs in this country, in complete personal freedom; changing and improving them from time to time, and according to circumstances.'

"*Reporter.*—'I confess, then, I cannot understand why you of all persons should have any fault to find with Mr. BEECHER, even assuming everything to be true of him which I have hitherto heard only vaguely hinted at.'

"*Mrs. Woodhull.*—'*I* have no fault to find with him in any such sense as you mean, nor in any such sense as that in which the world will condemn him. I have no doubt that he has done the very best which he could do under all the circumstances—with his demanding physical nature, and with the terrible restrictions upon a clergyman's life, imposed by that ignorant public opinion about physiological laws, which they, nevertheless, more, perhaps, than any other class, do their best to perpetuate. The fault I find with Mr. BEECHER is of a wholly different character, as I have told him repeatedly and frankly, and as he knows very well. It is, indeed, the exact opposite to that for which the world will condemn him. I condemn him because I know, and have had every opportunity to know, that he entertains, on conviction, substantially the same views which I entertain on the social question; that, under the influence of these convictions, he has lived for many years, perhaps for his whole adult life, in a manner which the religious and moralistic public ostensibly, and to some extent really condemn; that he has permitted himself, nevertheless, to be over-awed by public opinion, to profess to believe otherwise than as he does believe, to have helped to maintain for these many years that very social slavery under which he was chafing, and against which he was secretly revolting both in thought and practice; and that he has, in a word, consented, and still consents to be a hypocrite. The fault with which I, therefore, charge him, is not infidelity to the old ideas, but unfaithfulness to the new. He is in heart, in conviction and in life, an ultra socialist reformer; while in seeming and pretension he is the upholder of the old social slavery, and, therefore, does what he can to crush out and oppose me and those who act and believe with me in forwarding the great social revolution. I know, myself, so little of the sentiment of fear, I have so little respect for an ignorant and prejudiced public opinion, I am so accustomed to say the thing that I think and do the thing that I believe to be right, that I doubt not I am in danger of having far too little sympathy with the real difficulties of a man situated as Mr. BEECHER has been, and is, when he contemplates the idea of facing social opprobrium. Speaking from my feelings, I am prone to denounce him as a poltroon, a coward and a sneak; not, as I tell you, for anything that he has done, and for which the world would condemn him, but for failing to do what it seems to me so clear he ought to do; for failing, in a word, to stand shoulder to shoulder with me and others who are endeavoring to hasten a social regeneration which he believes in.'

"*Reporter.*—'You speak very confidently, Mrs. WOODHULL, of Mr. BEECHER's opinions and life. Will you now please to resume that subject, and tell me exactly what you know of both?'

"*Mrs. Woodhull.*—'I had vaguely heard rumors of some scandal in regard to Mr. BEECHER, which I put aside as mere rumor and idle gossip of the hour, and gave to them no attention whatever. The first serious intimation I had that there was something more than mere gossip in the matter came to me in the committee room at Washington, where the suffrage women congregated during the winter of 1870, when I was there to urge my views on the Fourteenth Amendment. It was hinted in the room that some of the women, Mrs. ISABELLA BEECHER HOOKER, a sister of Mr. BEECHER, among the number, would snub Mrs. WOODHULL on account of her social opinions and antecedents. Instantly a gentleman, a stranger to me, stepped forward and said: '*It would ill become these women, and especially a Beecher, to talk of antecedents or to cast any smirch upon Mrs. Woodhull, for I am reliably assured that Henry Ward Beecher preaches to at least twenty of his * * * * every Sunday.*'

"'I paid no special attention to the remark at the time, as I was very intensely engaged in the business which had called me there; but it afterward forcibly occurred to me, with the thought also that it was strange that such a remark, made in such a presence, had seemed to have a subduing effect instead of arousing indignation. The women who were there could not have treated me better than they did. Whether this strange remark had any influence in overcoming their objections to me I do not know; but it is certain they were not set against me by it; and, all of them, Mrs. HOOKER included, subsequently professed the warmest friendship for me.'

"*Reporter.*—'After this, I presume you sought for the solution of the gentleman's remark.'

"*Mrs. Woodhull.*—'No, I did not. It was brought up subsequently, in an intimate conversation between her and me, by Mrs. PAULINA WRIGHT DAVIS, without any seeking on my part, and to my very great surprise. Mrs. DAVIS had been, it seems, a frequent visitor at Mr. TILTON'S house in Brooklyn—they having long been associated in the Woman's Rights movement—and she stood upon certain terms of intimacy in the family. Almost at the same time to which I have referred, when I was in Washington, she called, as she told me, at Mr. TILTON'S. Mrs. TILTON met her at the door and burst into tears, exclaiming: 'Oh, Mrs. DAVIS! have you come to see me? For six months I have been shut up from the world, and I thought no one ever would come again to visit me.' In the interview that followed, Mrs. TILTON spoke freely of a long series of intimate, and so-called criminal relations, on her part, with the Rev. HENRY WARD BEECHER; of the discovery of the facts by Mr. TILTON; of the abuse she had suffered from him in consequence, and of her heart-broken condition. She seemed to allude to the whole thing as to something already generally known, or known in a considerable circle, and impossible to be concealed; and attributed the long absence of Mrs. DAVIS from the house to her knowledge of the facts. She was, as she stated at the time, recovering from the effects of a miscarriage of a child of six months. The miscarriage was induced by the ill-treatment of Mr. TILTON in his rage at the discovery of her criminal intimacy with Mr. BEECHER, and, as he believed, the great probability, that she was *enciente* by Mr. BEECHER instead of himself. Mrs. TILTON confessed to Mrs. DAVIS the intimacy with Mr. BEECHER, and that it had been of years' standing. She also said that she had loved Mr. BEECHER before she married Mr. TILTON, and that now the burden of her sorrow was greatly augmented by the knowledge that Mr. BEECHER was untrue to her. She had not only to endure the rupture with her husband, but also the certainty that, notwithstanding his repeated assurance of his faithfulness to her, he had recently had illicit intercourse, under most extraordinary circumstances, with another person. Said Mrs. DAVIS: 'I came away from that house, my soul bowed down with grief at the heart-broken condition of that poor woman, and I felt that I ought not to leave Brooklyn until I had stripped the mask from that infamous, hypocritical scoundrel, BEECHER.' In May, after returning home, Mrs. DAVIS wrote me a letter, from which I will read a paragraph to show that we conversed on this subject.'

A LETTER.

"'DEAR VICTORIA: I thought of you half of last night, dreamed of you and prayed for you.

"'I believe you are raised up of God to do a wonderful work, and I believe that you will unmask the hypocrisy of a class that none others dare touch. God help you and save you. The more I think of that *mass of Beecher corruption* the more I desire its opening.

"'Ever yours, lovingly,

PAULINA WRIGHT DAVIS.

"'PROVIDENCE, R. I., May, 1871.''

"*Reporter.*—'Did you inform Mrs. DAVIS of your intention to expose this matter, as she intimates in the letter?'

"*Mrs. Woodhull.*—'I said in effect to her, that the matter would become public, and that I felt that I should be instrumental in making it so. But I was not decided about the course I should pursue. I next heard the whole story from Mrs. ELIZABETH CADY STANTON.'

"*Reporter.*—'Indeed! Is Mrs. STANTON also mixed up in this affair? Does she know the facts? How could the matter have been kept so long quiet when so many people are cognizant of it?'

"*Mrs. Woodhull.*—'The existence of the skeleton in the closet may be very widely known, and many people may have the key to the terrible secret, but still hesitate to open the door for the great outside world to gaze in upon it. This grand woman did indeed know the same facts, and from Mr. TILTON himself. I shall never forget the occasion of her first rehearsal of it to me at my residence, 15 East Thirty-eighth street, in a visit made to me during the Apollo Hall Convention in May, 1871. It seems that MR. TILTON, in agony at the discovery of what he deemed his wife's perfidy and his pastor's treachery, retreated to Mrs. STANTON's residence at Tenafly, where he detailed to her the entire story. Said Mrs. STANTON, 'I never saw such a manifestation of mental agony. He raved and tore his hair, and seemed upon the very verge of insanity.' 'Oh!'

said he, 'that that damned lecherous scoundrel should have defiled my bed for ten years, and at the same time have professed to be my best friend! Had he come like a man to me and confessed his guilt, I could perhaps have endured it, but to have him creep like a snake into my house leaving his pollution behind him, and I so blind as not to see, and esteeming him all the while as a saint—oh! it is too much. And when I think how for years she, upon whom I had bestowed all my heart's love, could have lied and deceived me so, I lose all faith in humanity. I do not believe there is any honor, any truth left in anybody in the world.' Mrs. STANTON continued and repeated to me the sad story, which it is unnecessary to recite, as I prefer giving it as Mr. TILTON himself told it me, subsequently, with his own lips.'

"*Reporter.*—'Is it possible that Mr. TILTON confided this story to you? It seems too monstrous to be believed!'

"*Mrs. Woodhull.*—'He certainly did. And what is more, I am persuaded that in his inmost mind he will not be otherwise than glad when the skeleton in his closet is revealed to the world, if thereby the abuses which lurk like vipers under the cloak of social conservatism may be exposed and the causes removed. Mr. TILTON looks deeper into the soul of things than most men, and is braver than most.'

"*Reporter.*—'How did your acquaintance with Mr. TILTON begin?'

"*Mrs. Woodhull.*—'Upon the information received from Mrs. DAVIS and Mrs. STANTON I based what I said in the *Weekly*, and in the letters in the *Times* and *World*, referring to the matter, I was nearly determined—though still not quite so—that what I, equally with those who gave me the information, believed, but for wholly other reasons, to be a most important social circumstance, should be exposed, my reasons being, as I have explained to you, not those of the world, and I took that method to cause inquiry and create agitation regarding it. The day that the letter appeared in the *World* Mr. TILTON came to my office, No. 44 Broad street, and, showing me the letter, asked: 'Whom do you mean by that?' 'Mr. TILTON,' said I, 'I mean you and Mr. BEECHER.' I then told him what I knew, what I thought of it, and that I felt that I had a mission to bring it to the knowledge of the world, and that I had nearly determined to do so. I said to him much else on the subject; and he said: 'Mrs. WOODHULL, you are the first person I have ever met who has dared to, or else who could, tell me the truth.' He acknowledged that the facts, as I had heard them, were true, but declared that I did not yet know the extent of the depravity of that man—meaning Mr. BEECHER. 'But,' said he, 'do not take any steps now. I have carried my heart as a stone in my breast for months, for the sake of ELIZABETH, my wife, who is broken-hearted as I am. I have had courage to endure rather than to add more to her weight of sorrow. For her sake I have allowed that rascal to go unscathed. I have curbed my feelings when every impulse urged me to throttle and strangle him. Let me take you over to ELIZABETH, and you will find her in no condition to be dragged before the public; and I know you will have compassion on her.' And I went and saw her, and I agreed with him on the propriety of delay.'

"*Reporter.*—'Was it during this interview that Mr. TILTON explained to you all that you now know of the matter?'

"*Mrs. Woodhull.*—'Oh, no. His revelations were made subsequently at sundry times, and during months of friendly intercourse, as occasion brought the subject up. I will, however, condense his statements to me, and state the facts as he related them, as consecutively as possible. I kept notes of the conversations as they occurred from time to time, but the matter is so much impressed on my mind that I have no hesitation in relating them from memory.'

"*Reporter.*—'Do you not fear that by taking the responsibility of this *exposé* you may involve yourself in trouble? Even if all you relate should be true, may not those involved deny it *in toto*, even the fact of their having made the statements?'

"*Mrs. Woodhull.*—'I do not fear anything of the sort. I know this thing must come out, and the statement of the plain ungarnished truth will outweigh all the perjuries that can be invented, if it come to that pass. I have been charged with attempts at blackmailing, but I tell you, sir, there is not money enough in these two cities to purchase my silence in this matter. I believe it is my duty and my mission to carry the torch to light up and destroy the heap of rottenness, which, in the name of religion, marital sanctity, and social purity, now passes as the social system. I know there are other churches just as false, other pastors just as recreant to their professed ideas of morality—by their immorality you know I mean their hypocrisy. I am glad that just this one case comes to me to be exposed. This is a great congregation. He is a most eminent man. When a beacon is fired on the mountain the little hills are lighted up. This exposition will send inquisition through all the churches and what is termed conservative society.'

"*Reporter.*—'You speak like some wierd prophetess, madam.'

"*Mrs. Woodhull.*—'I am a prophetess—I am an evangel—I am a saviour, if you would but see it; but I too come not to bring peace, but a sword.'

"Mrs. WOODHULL then resumed, saying: 'Mr. TILTON first began to have suspicions of Mr. BEECHER on his own return from a long lecturing tour through the West. He questioned his little daughter, privately, in his study regarding what had transpired in his absence. 'The tale of iniquitous horror that was revealed to me was,' he said, 'enough to turn the heart of a stranger to stone, to say nothing of a husband and father.' It was not the fact of the intimacy alone, but in addition to that, the terrible orgies—so he said—of which his house had been made the scene, and the boldness with which matters had been carried on in the presence of his children—'These things drove me mad,' said he, 'and I went to ELIZABETH and confronted her with the child and the damning tale she had told me. My wife did not deny the charge nor attempt any palliation. She was then *enciente*, and I felt sure that the child would not be my child. I stripped the wedding ring from her finger. I tore the picture of Mr. BEECHER from my wall and stamped it in pieces. Indeed, I do not know what I did not do. I only look back to it as a time too horrible to retain any exact remembrance of. She miscarried the child and it was buried. For two weeks, night and day, I might have been found walking to and from that grave, in a state bordering on distraction. I could not realize the fact that I was what I was. I stamped the ring with which we had plighted our troth deep into the soil that covered the fruit of my wife's infidelity. I had friends, many and firm and good, but I could not go to them with this grief, and I suppose I should have remained silent through life had not an occasion arisen which demanded that I should seek counsel. Mr. BEECHER learned that I had discovered the fact, and what had transpired between ELIZABETH and myself, and when I was absent he called at my house and compelled or induced his victim to sign a statement he had prepared, declaring that so far as he, Mr. BEECHER, was concerned, there was no truth in my charges, and that there had never been any criminal intimacy between them. Upon learning this, as I did, I felt, of course, again outraged and could endure secrecy no longer. I had one friend who was like a brother, Mr. FRANK MOULTON. I went to him and stated the case fully. We were both members of Plymouth Church. My friend took a pistol, went to Mr. BEECHER and demanded the letter of Mrs. TILTON, under penalty of instant death.'

"Mrs. WOODHULL here remarked that Mr. MOULTON had himself, also since, described to her this interview, with all the piteous and abject beseeching of Mr. BEECHER not to be exposed to the public.

"'Mr. MOULTON obtained the letter,' said Mrs. W., 'and told me that he had it in his safe, where he should keep it until required for further use. After this, Mr. TILTON'S house was no house for him, and he seldom slept or ate there, but frequented the house of his friend MOULTON, who sympathized deeply with him. Mrs. TILTON was also absent days at a time, and, as Mr. TILTON informed me, seemed bent on destroying her life. I went as I have said to see her and found her, indeed, a wretched wreck of a woman, whose troubles were greater than she could bear. She made no secret of the facts before me. Mr. BEECHER'S selfish, cowardly cruelty in endeavoring to shield himself and create public opinion against Mr. TILTON, added poignancy to her anxieties. She seemed indifferent as to what should become of herself, but labored under fear that murder might be done on her account.

"'This was the condition of affairs at the time that Mr. TILTON came to me. I attempted to show him the true solution of the imbroglio, and the folly that it was for a man like him, a representative man of the ideas of the future, to stand whining over inevitable events connected with this transition age and the social revolution of which we are in the midst. I told him that the fault and the wrong were neither in Mr. BEECHER, nor in Mrs. TILTON, nor in himself; but that it was in the false social institutions under which we still live, while the more advanced men and women of the world have outgrown them in spirit; and that, practically, everybody is living a false life, by professing a conformity which they do not feel and do not live, and which they cannot feel and live any more than the grown boy can re-enter the clothes of his early childhood. I recalled to his attention splendid passages of his own rhetoric, in which he had unconsciously justified all the freedom that he was now condemning, when it came home to his own door, and endeavoring, in the spirit of a tyrant, to repress.

"'I ridiculed the *maudlin sentiment* and *mock heroics* and '*dreadful suzz*' he was exhibiting over an event the most natural in the world, and the most intrinsically innocent; having in it not a bit more of real criminality than the awful wickedness of negro-stealing' formerly charged, in perfect good faith, by the slaveholders, on every one who helped the escape of a slave. I assumed at once, and got a sufficient admission, as I always do in such cases, that he was not exactly a vestal virgin himself; that his real life was something very different from the awful 'virtue' he was preaching, especially for women, as if women could 'sin' in this matter without men, and men without women, and which, he *pretended*, even to himself, to believe in the face and eyes of his own life, and the lives of nearly all the greatest and best men and women that he knew; that the 'dreadful suzz' was merely a *bogus sentimentality*, *pumped* in his imagination, because our sickly religious literature, and Sunday-school morality, and pulpit pharaseeism had humbugged him all his life into the belief that *he ought to feel and act* in this harlequin and absurd way on such an occasion —that, in a word, neither Mr. BEECHER nor Mrs. TILTON had done any wrong, but that it was he who was playing the part of a fool and a tyrant; that it was he and the factitious or manufactured public opinion back of him, that was wrong; that this babyish whining and stage-acting were the real absurdity and disgrace—the unmanly part of the whole transaction, and that we only needed another Cervantes to satirize such stuff as it deserves to squelch it instantly and forever. I tried to show him that a true manliness would protect and love to protect; would glory in protecting the absolute freedom of the woman who was loved, whether called wife, mistress, or by any other name, and that the true sense of honor in the future will be, *not to know even* what relations our lovers have with any and all other persons than ourselves—as true courtesy never seeks to spy over or to pry into other people's private affairs.

"'I believe I succeeded in pointing out to him that his own life was essentially no better than Mr. BEECHER'S, and that he stood in no position to throw the first stone at Mrs. TILTON or her reverend paramour. I showed him again and again that the wrong point, and the radically wrong thing, if not, indeed, quite the only wrong thing in the matter, was *the idea of ownership in human beings, which was essentially the same in the two institutions of slavery and marriage.* Mrs. TILTON had in turn grown increasedly unhappy when she found that Mr. BEECHER had turned some part of his exuberant affections upon some other object. There was in her, therefore, the same sentiment of the real slaveholder. Let it be once understood *that whosoever is true to himself or herself is thereby, and necessarily, true to all others*, and the whole social question will be solved. *The barter and sale of wives stands on the same moral footing as the barter and sale of slaves.* The God-implanted human affections cannot, and will not, be any longer subordinated to these external, legal restrictions and conventional engagements. *Every human being belongs to himself or herself by a higher title than any which, by surrenders or arrangements or promises, he or she can confer upon any other human being. Self-ownership is inalienable.* These truths are the latest and greatest discoveries in true science.

"'Perhaps Mr. BEECHER knows and feels all this, and if so, in that knowledge consists his sole and his *real* justification, only the world around him has not yet grown to it; institutions are not yet adapted to it; and he is not brave enough to bear his open testimony to the truth he knows.

"'All this I said to Mr. TILTON; and I urged upon him to make this providential circumstance in his life the occasion upon which he should, himself, come forward to the front and stand with the true champions of social freedom.'

"*Reporter.*—'Then Mr. TILTON became, as it were, your pupil, and you instructed him in your theories.'

"*Mrs. Woodhull.*—'Yes, I suppose that is a correct statement; and the verification of my views, springing up before my eyes upon this occasion, out of the very midst of religious and moral prejudices, was, I assure you, an interesting study for me, and a profound corroboration of the righteousness of what you call 'my Theories.' Mr. TILTON's conduct toward Mr. BEECHER and toward his wife began from that time to be so magnanimous and grand—by which I mean simply just and right—so unlike that which most other men's would have been, that it stamped him, in my mind, as one of the noblest souls that lived, and one capable of playing a great *role* in the social revolution, which is now so rapidly progressing.

"'I never could, however, induce him to stand wholly, and unreservedly, and on principle, upon the free-love platform; and I always, therefore, feared that he might for a time vacillate or go backward. But he opened his house to Mr. BEECHER, saying to him, in the presence of Mrs. TILTON: 'You love each other. Mr. BEECHER, this is a distressed woman; if it be in your power to alleviate her condition and make her life less a burden than it now is, be yours the part to do it. You have nothing to fear from me.' From that time Mr. BEECHER was, so to speak, the slave of Mr. TILTON and Mr. MOULTON. He consulted them in every matter of any importance. It was at this time that Mr. TILTON introduced Mr. BEECHER to me, and I met him frequently both at Mr. TILTON's and at Mr. MOULTON's. We discussed the social problem freely in all its varied bearings, and I found that Mr. BEECHER agreed with nearly all my views upon the question.'

"*Reporter.*—'Do you mean to say that Mr. BEECHER disapproves of the present marriage system?'

"*Mrs. Woodhull.*—'I mean to say just this—that Mr. BEECHER told me that marriage is the grave of love, and that he never married a couple that he did not feel condemned.'

"*Reporter.*—'What excuse did Mr. BEECHER give for not avowing these sentiments publicly?'

"*Mrs. Woodhull.*—'Oh, the moral coward's inevitable excuse—that of inexpediency. He said he was twenty years ahead of his church; that he preached the truth just as fast as he thought his people could bear it. I said to him, 'Then, Mr. BEECHER, you are defrauding your people. You confess that you do not preach the truth as you know it, while they pay for and persuade themselves you are giving them your best thought.' He replied: 'I know that our whole social system is corrupt. I know that marriage, as it exists to-day, is the curse of society. We shall never have a better state until children are begotten and bred on the scientific plan. Stirpiculture is what we need.' 'Then,' said I, 'Mr. BEECHER, why do you not go into your pulpit and preach that science?' He replied: 'If I were to do so I should preach to empty seats. It would be the ruin of my church.' 'Then,' said I, 'you are as big a fraud as any time-serving preacher, and I now believe you are all frauds. I gave you credit for ignorant honesty, but I find you all alike—all trying to hide, or afraid to speak the truth. A sorry pass has this Christian country come to, paying 40,000 ministers to lie to it from Sunday to Sunday, to hide from them the truth that has been given them to promulgate.''

"*Reporter.*—'It seems you took a good deal of pains to draw Mr. BEECHER out.'

"*Mrs. Woodhull.*—'I did. I thought him a man who would dare a good deal for the truth, and that, having lived the life he had, and entertaining the private convictions he did, I could perhaps persuade him that it was his true policy to come out and openly avow his principles, and be a thorough consistent radical, and thus justify his life in some measure, if not wholly, to the public.'

"*Reporter.*—'Was Mr. BEECHER aware that you knew of his relations to Mrs. TILTON?'

"*Mrs. Woodhull.*—'Of course he was. It was because that I knew of them that he first consented to meet me. He could never receive me until he knew that I was aware of the real character he wore under the mask of his reputation. Is it not remarkable how a little knowledge of this sort brings down the most top-lofty from the stilts on which they lift themselves above the common level?'

"*Reporter.*—'Do you still regard Mr. BEECHER as a moral coward?'

"*Mrs. Woodhull.*—'I have found him destitute of moral courage enough to meet this tremendous demand upon him. In minor things, I know that he has manifested courage. He could not be induced to take the bold step I demanded of him, simply for the sake of truth and righteousness. I did not entirely despair ot him until about a year ago. I was then contemplating my Steinway Hall speech on Social Freedom, and prepared it in the hope of being able to persuade Mr. BEECHER to preside for me, and thus make a way for himself into a consistent life on the radical platform. I made my speech as soft as I conscientiously could. I toned it down in order that it might not frighten him. When it was in type, I went to his study and gave him a copy and asked him to read it carefully and give me his candid opinion concerning it. Meantime, I had told Mr. TILTON and Mr. MOULTON that I was going to ask Mr. BEECHER to preside, and they agreed to press the matter with him. I explained to them that the only safety he had was in coming out as soon as possible an advocate of social freedom, and thus palliate, if he could not completely justify, his practices by founding them at least on principle. I told them that this introduction of me would bridge the way. Both the gentlemen agreed with me in this view, and I was for a time almost sure that my desire would be accomplished. A few days before the lecture, I sent a note to Mr. BEECHER asking him to preside for me. This alarmed him. He went with it to Messrs. TILTON and MOULTON asking advice. They gave it in the affirmative, telling him they considered it eminently fitting that he should pursue the course indicated by me as his only safety; but it was not urged in such a way as to indicate that they had known the request was to have been made. Matters remained undecided until the day of the lecture, when I went over again to press Mr. BEECHER to a decision. I had then a long private interview with him, urging all the arguments I could to induce him to consent. He said he agreed perfectly with what I was to say, but that he could not stand on the platform of Steinway Hall and introduce me. He said, 'I should sink through the floor. I am a moral coward on this subject, and I know it, and I am not fit to stand by you, who go there to speak what you know to be the truth; I should stand there a living lie.' He got upon the sofa on his knees beside me, and taking my face between his hands, while the tears streamed down his cheeks, begged me to let him off. Becoming thoroughly disgusted with what seemed to me pusilanimity, I left the room under the control of a feeling of contempt for the man, and reported to my friends what he had said. They then took me again with them and endeavored to persuade him. Mr. TILTON said to him: 'Mr. BEECHER, some day you have got to fall; go and introduce this woman and win the radicals of the country, and it will break your fall.' 'Do you think,' said BEECHER, 'that this thing will come out to the world?' Mr. TILTON replied: 'Nothing is more certain in earth or heaven, Mr. BEECHER; and this may be your last chance to save yourself from complete ruin.''

"'Mr. BEECHER replied: 'I can never endure such a terror. Oh! if it must come, let me know of it twenty-four hours in advance, that I may take my own life. I cannot, cannot face this thing!'

"'Thoroughly out of all patience, I turned on my heel and said: 'Mr. BEECHER, if I am compelled to go upon that platform alone, I shall begin by telling the audience why I am alone, and why you are not with me,' and I again left the room. I afterward learned that Mr. BEECHER, frightened at what I had said, promised, before parting with Mr. TILTON, that he would preside if he could bring his courage up to the terrible ordeal.

"'It was four minutes of the time for me to go forward to the platform at Steinway Hall when Mr. TILTON and Mr. MOULTON came into the ante-room asking for Mr. BEECHER. When I told them he had not come they expressed astonishment. I told them I should faithfully keep my word, let the consequences be what they might. At that moment word was sent me that there was an organized attempt to break up the meeting, and that threats were being made against my life if I dared to speak what it was understood I intended to speak. Mr. TILTON then insisted on going on the platform with me and presiding, to which I finally agreed, and that I should not at that time mention Mr. BEECHER. I shall never forget the brave words he uttered in introducing me. They had a magic influence on the audience, and drew the sting of those who intended to harm me. However much Mr. TILTON may have since regretted his course regarding me, and whatever he may say about it, I shall always admire the moral courage that enabled him to stand with me on that platform, and face that, in part, defiant audience. It is hard to bear the criticisms of vulgar minds, who can see in social freedom nothing but licentiousness and debauchery, and the inevitable misrepresentation of the entire press, which is as perfectly subsidized against reason and common sense, when social subjects are discussed, as is the religious press when any other science is discussed which is supposed to militate against the Bible as the direct word of God to man. The editors are equally bigots, or else as dishonest as the clergy. The nightmare of a public opinion, which they are still professionally engaged in making, enslaves and condemns them both.'

"Mrs. WOODHULL concluded by saying that since her Steinway Hall speech she had surrendered all hope of easing the fall of Mr. BEECHER, that she had not attempted to see him, and had not in fact seen him. She only added one other fact, which was, that Mr. BEECHER endeavored to induce Mr. TILTON to withdraw from his membership in Plymouth Church, to leave him, Mr. BEECHER, free from the embarrassment of his presence there; and that Mr. TILTON had indignantly rejected the proposition, determined to hold the position with a view to such contingencies as might subsequently occur.

"So much for the interviewing which was to have been published some months ago; but when it failed or was suppressed, I was still so far undecided that I took no steps in the matter, and had no definite plan for the future in respect to it, until the events as I have recited them, which occurred at Boston. Since then I have not doubted that I must make up my mind definitely to act aggressarily in this matter, and to use the facts in my knowledge to compel a more wide-spread discussion of the social question. I take the step deliberately, as an agitator and social revolutionist, which is my profession. I commit no breach of confidence, as no confidences have been made to me, except as I have compelled them, with a full knowledge that I was endeavoring to induce or force the parties to come to the front along with me in the announcement and advocacy of the principles of social revolution. Messrs. BEECHER and TILTON, and other half-way reformers, are to me like the border States in the great rebellion. They are liable to fall, with the weight of their influence, on either side in the contest, and I hold it to be legitimate generalship *to compel* them to declare on the side of truth and progress.

"My position is justly analogous with that of warfare. The public, Mr. BEECHER included, would gladly crush me if they could—will do so if they can—to prevent me from forcing on them considerations of the utmost importance. My mission is, on the other hand, to utter the unpopular truth, and make it efficient by whatsoever legitimate means; and means are legitimate as a war measure, which would be highly reprehensible in a state of peace. I believe, as the law of peace, *in the right of privacy*, in the sanctity of individual relations. It is nobody's business but their own, in the absolute view, what Mr. BEECHER and Mrs. TILTON have done, or may choose at any time to do, as between themselves. And the world needs, too, to be taught just that lesson. I am the champion of that very right of privacy and of individual sovereignty. But, that is only one side of the case. I need, and the world needs, Mr. BEECHER's powerful championship of this very right. The world is on the very crisis of its final fight for liberty. The victory may fall on the wrong side, and his own liberty and mine, and the world's, be again crushed out, or repressed for another century for the want of fidelity in him to the new truth. It is not, therefore, Mr. BEECHER as the individual that I pursue, but Mr. BEECHER as the representative man; Mr. BEECHER as a power in the world; and Mr. BEECHER as my auxiliary in a great war for freedom, or Mr. BEECHER as a violent enemy and a powerful hindrance to all that I am bent on accomplishing.

"To Mr. BEECHER, as the individual citizen, I tender, therefore, my humble apology, meaning and deeply feeling what I say, for this or any interference on my part, with his private conduct. I hold that Mr. TILTON himself, that Mrs. BEECHER herself, have no more right to inquire, or to know or to spy over, with a view to knowing, what has transpired between Mr. BEECHER and Mrs. TILTON than they have to know what I ate for breakfast, or where I shall spend my next evening; and that Mr. BEECHER's congregation and the public at large have just as little right to know or to inquire. I hold that the so-called morality of society is a complicated mass of sheer impertinence and a scandal on the civilization of this advanced century, that the system of social espionage under which we live is damnable, and that the very first axiom of a true morality, is for the people *to mind their own business*, and learn to respect, religiously, the social freedom and the sacred social privacy of all others ; but it was the paradox of Christ, that as the Prince of Peace, he still brought on earth, *not peace* but *a sword*. It is the paradox of life that, in order to have peace, we must first have war ; and it is the paradox of my position that, believing in the right of privacy and in the perfect right of Mr. BEECHER socially, morally and divinely to have sought the embraces of Mrs. TILTON, or of any other woman or women whom he loved and who loved him, and being a promulgator and a public champion of those very rights, I still invade the most secret and sacred affairs of his life, and drag them to the light and expose him to the opprobrium and vilification of the public. I do again, and with deep sincerity, ask his forgiveness. But the case is exceptional, and what I do, I do for a great purpose. The social world is in the very agony of its new birth, or, to resume the warlike simile, the leaders of progress are in the very act of storming the last fortress of bigotry and error. Somebody must be hurled forward into the gap. I have the power, I think, to compel Mr. BEECHER to go forward and to do the duty for humanity from which he shrinks ; and I should, myself, be false to the truth if I were to shrink from compelling him. Whether he sinks or swims in the fiery trial, the agitation by which truth is evolved will have been promoted. And I believe that he will not only survive, but that when forced to the encounter he will rise to the full height of the great enterprise, and will astound and convince the world of the new gospel of freedom, by the depth of his experiences and the force of his argument.

"The world, it seems, will never learn not to crucify its Christs, and not to compel the retractation of its Galileos. Mr. BEECHER has lacked the courage to be a martyr, but, like Galileo, while retracting, or concealing and evading, he has known in his heart *that the world still moves;* and I venture to prophesy, as I have indeed full faith, that he and the other parties to this social drama will yet live to be overwhelmed with gratitude to me for having compelled them to this publicity. The age is pregnant with great events, and this may be the very one which shall be, as it were, the crack of doom to our old and worn out, and false and hypocritical social institutions. When the few first waves of public indignation shall have broken over him, when the nine days' wonder and the astonished clamor of Mrs. Grundy shall have done their worst, and when the pious ejaculations of the sanctimonious shall have been expended, and he finds that he still lives, and that there are brave souls who stand by him, he will, I believe, rise in his power and utter the whole truth. I believe I see clearly and prophetically for him in the future a work a hundred times greater than all he has accomplished in the past. I believe, as I have said, a wise Providence, or, as I term it, and believe it to be, the conscious and well calculated interference of the spirit world, has forecast and prepared those very events as a part of the drama of this great social revolution. Of all the centres of influence on the great broad planet, the destiny that shapes our ends, bent on breaking up an old civilization and ushering in a new one, could have found no such spot for its vantage ground as Plymouth Church, no such man for the hero of the plot as its reverend pastor, and, it may be, no such heroine as the gentle cultured, and, perhaps, hereafter to be sainted wife of Plymouth Church's most distinguished layman. Indeed I think that Mrs. TILTON has had, at least at times, a clearer intuition guiding her, a better sense of right, and more courage than her reverend lover; for, on one occasion, Mr. TILTON told me that he took home to her one of my threatening notices, and told her that that meant her and Mr. BEECHER, and that the exposure must and would come; and he added that she calmly replied: 'I am prepared for it. If the new social gospel must have its martyrs, and if I must be one of them, I am prepared for it.'

"In conclusion, let us again consider, for a moment, the right and the wrong of this whole transaction. Let us see whether the wrong is not on the side where the public puts the right, and the right on the side where the public puts the wrong. The immense physical potency of Mr. BEECHER, and the indomitable urgency of his great nature for the intimacy and the embraces of the noble and cultured women about him, instead of being a bad thing as the world thinks, or thinks that it thinks, or professes to think that it thinks, is one of the noblest and grandest of the endowments of this truly great and representative man. The amative impulse is the physiological basis of character. It is this which emanates zest and magnetic power to his whole audience through the organism of the great preacher. Plymouth Church has lived and fed, and the healthy vigor of public opinion for the last quarter of a century has been augmented and strengthened from the physical amativeness of HENRY WARD BEECHER. The scientific world know the physiological facts of this nature, but they have waited for a weak woman to have the moral courage to tell the world such truths. Passional starvation, enforced on such a nature, so richly endowed, by the ignorance and prejudice of the past, is a horrid cruelty. The bigoted public, to which the great preacher ministered, while literally eating and drinking of his flesh and blood, condemned him, in their ignorance, to live without food. Every great man of Mr. BEECHER's type has had, in the past, and will ever have, the need for, and the right to, the loving manifestations of many women, and when the public graduates out of the ignorance and prejudice of its childhood, it will recognize this necessity and its own past injustice. Mr. BEECHER's grand and amative nature is not, then, the bad element in the whole matter, but intrinsically a good thing, and one of God's best gifts to the world.

"So again, the tender, loving, womanly concessiveness of Mrs. TILTON, her susceptibility to the charm of the great preacher's magnetism, her love of loving and of being loved, none of these were the bad thing which the world thinks them, or thinks that it thinks them, or professes to think that it thinks them to be. On the contrary they are all of them the best thing—the best and most beautiful of things, the loveliest and most divine of things which belong to the patrimony of mankind.

"So again, it was not the coming together of these two loving natures in the most intimate embrace, nor was it, that nature blessed that embrace with the natural fruits of love which was the bad element in this whole transaction. They, on the contrary, were good elements, beautiful and divine elements, and among God's best things for man.

"The evil and the whole evil in this whole matter, then, lies elsewhere. It lies in a false and artificial or manufactured opinion, in respect to this very question of what is good or what is evil in such matters. It lies in the belief that society has the right to prohibit, to prescribe and regulate, or in any manner to interfere with the private love manifestations of its members, any more than it has to prescribe their food and their drink. It lies in the belief consequent upon this, that lovers own their lovers, husbands their wives and wives their husbands, and that they have the right to complain of, to spy over, and to interfere, even to the extent of murder, with every other or outside manifestation of love. It lies in the *compulsory hypocrisy and systematic falsehood* which is thus enforced and inwrought into the very structure of society, and in the consequent and wide-spread injury to the whole community.

"Mr. BEECHER knows all this, and if by my act he is compelled to tell the world that he knows it, and to force them to the conviction that it is all true, he may well thank God that I live, and that circumstances have concurred to emancipate him, despite of himself, from his terrible thralldom, and to emancipate, through him, in the future, millions of others.

"Still in conclusion, let me add, that in my view, and in the view of others who think with me, and of all, as I believe, who think rightly on the subject, Mr. BEECHER is to-day, and after all that I have felt called upon to reveal of his life, as good, as pure and as noble a man as he ever was in the past, or as the world has held him to be, and that Mrs. TILTON is still the pure, charming, cultured woman. It is, then, the public opinion that is wrong, and not the individuals, who must, nevertheless, for a time suffer its persecution.

"Mrs. ISABELLA BEECHER HOOKER has, from the time that I met her in Washington, stood my fast friend, and given me manifold proofs of her esteem, knowing, as she did, both my radical opinions and my free life. I have been told, not by her, but upon what I believe to be perfectly good authority, that she has for months, perhaps for years past, known the life of her brother, and urged on him to announce publicly his radical convictions, and assured him that if he would do so she, at least, would stand by him. I know, too, by intimate intercourse, the opinions, and, to a great extent, the lives of nearly all the leading reformatory men and women in the land; and I know that Mr. BEECHER, passing through this crucial ordeal, retrieving himself and standing upon the most radical platform, need not stand alone for an hour, but that an army of glorious and emancipated spirits will gather spontaneously and instantaneously around him, and that the new social republic will have been forever established.

VICTORIA C. WOODHULL."

As Mrs. Hooker's name appears frequently in this work, we may state that during the excitement attending the labors of the Committee, G. H. Beecher wrote a letter to the *Brooklyn Eagle* in which he says:—

On the occasion of Mrs. Hooker's visit to New York, and threatened invasion of Plymouth pulpit, (it was at the time of the funeral of Horace Greeley), Dr. Edward Beecher called to see her in New York, and as he can testify, she did not pretend to have evidence from Mrs. Tilton nor from Mr. Beecher, except that he refused to deny the charge and talk with her about it, (the course which, with few exceptions, he pursued with every one), but her sole reliance was upon the testimony of Mrs. Woodhull, Mrs. Stanton and Miss Anthony. Upon this testimony, coupled with the refusal of her brother to discuss the subject with her, she based her belief of his guilt, and wished to ascend Plymouth pulpit and read a confession which she had prepared for him, to the Plymouth people, and then she would plead in his behalf. She also desired that he would place himself at the head of a new woman's movement, and she would stand by and uphold him. Far be it from me to speak against this loving sister; for her letters, several of which I have read, breathe the tenderest, noblest sympathy and love toward her brother, and if ever they are published they will touch the hearts of all in this respect. Her views on the marriage relation are somewhat similar to those of Mrs. Woodhull, though not so gross. She does not believe in promiscuous free love as does Mrs. Woodhull, but the law should not bind man and wife together when they have ceased to love one another. She also believes that having separated on such grounds, they should be at liberty to marry again if they find mates that they truly love. She was devotedly attached to Mrs. Woodhull, and has never withdrawn from her. The strange fascination which this remarkable woman possessed over her is evinced, among other things, by the letter which she wrote to Mrs. Woodhull, about the time of her nomination by the free love wing of the Woman's Suffrage Convention as candidate for the Presidency of the United States, commencing as follows:—"My darling Queen," and proceeding in the same rhapsodical language. I wish the letter could be reproduced. It was published in the papers at the time. In her interview with her brother Edward she seemed in a wild and excited state of mind. The interview of Henry with her, as he stated to his brother, was to soothe and quiet her and induce her to return home. He said he refused for her sake to enter upon the subject, and his refusal to deny the stories, or say anything about them, was because if he did so it would bring up the whole subject for discussion between them, and she would bring forward her evidence from these women, which he could not enter into or explain without making her a confidant of the whole matter, and, as she was in constant communication with these women, he did not judge it best for him to do so in any shape or manner.

14 Ringgold St. Providence, R. I.
September 16, 1872.

My Dear Victoria:

My husband and myself called on Friday evening, accompanied by Mrs. Colonel Pope, of Harrison street, on Mrs. J. H. Conant, and found her at home; Dr. Pyke was with her. He, the doctor, entered into conversation with me concerning your attack upon Beecher, as he termed it, which I defended, whereupon Theodore Parker controlled Mrs. Conant, and spoke in substance as follows:

"When Henry Ward Beecher, knowing spiritualism to be true, stood in his own pulpit and denounced it as 'one of the most dangerous humbugs of the day,' the spirit world felt that it had pleaded and borne with him long enough, and that they would unmask and show him to the world a hypocrite as he is. This it has done, and it mattered little whether Mrs. Conant, Victoria Woodhull or Laura Cuppy Smith was the instrument used. The spirit world has not yet completed its work. Other canting hypocrites remain to be proclaimed to the public in their true colors, and the Scripture shall be verified, 'There is nothing secret that shall not be made known, nothing hidden that shall not be revealed.' If I could have divested my medium of the *influence of persons in the form* I should have proclaimed this through her lips on the platform of John A. Andrews' hall on Wednesday afternoon."

"I think I have given you Theodore Parker's words verbatim.

"The same evening I was conversing with E. B. Beckwith, a prominent lawyer of Boston, who remarked that there seemed to him to be a retribution following the Beechers, and that you could use in your own behalf the same argument in vindication of your exposure of Beecher that Mrs. Stowe and her family had used in her defence with regard to the Byron affair, with this addition, that you had not accused the living, who could defend themselves, of half so base a crime as she had laid to the charge of the poet and a sister woman, the dead who could not reply. I thought the suggestion too good to be lost, shall use it myself freely, and send it to you.

Laura Cuppy Smith.

The publication of this article, as may well be supposed, struck everybody, who was not familiar with the cool audacity of the author of it, with astonishment. The paper was in great demand, and within a few hours not a copy could be obtained, except at exhorbitant prices. The author, the following day, paid two dollars for a copy, from which the above is extracted, and as high as ten dollars were paid for copies. In Brooklyn, and especially among the congregation of Plymouth Church, the most alarming consternation was caused by it, and, as a matter of course, gossip became at once busy with the names of the Plymouth pastor and some ladies of the congregation to whom Mr. Beecher had shown little attentions. The public outside of the church directly affected, had come to look upon the "female brokers" as blackmailers who would not stop at any unscrupulous means, nor spare the most sacred hearthstones, to secure money, and the press very generally ignored it as a nasty scandal, unfit to be even referred to.

But when Mrs. Woodhull reiterated the scandal in her paper and on the platform, people began to enquire:—

"Why does not Mr. Beecher cause the arrest of these vile women?"

But he still remained silent, and still retained the confidence of the people who had so long loved him for his nobleness of character and spotless life. A little later, however, when, through the instrumentality of Anthony Comstock, of the Young Men's Christian Association, the women were arrested for circulating obscene literature, their office and paper confiscated, and leading friends of Mr. Beecher appeared as prosecuting counsel, suspicions were aroused that there was something in the story after all, and that Plymouth Church was stationed in the shadow of the Criminal Court, to prosecute them. Sympathy was enlisted in their behalf, and as will be seen by a reference to the trial, in another part of this work, the "brokers" were acquitted.

CHAPTER II.

"THE REPUBLIC THREATENED!—THE BEECHER-TILTON SCANDAL AND THE BEECHER-BOWEN-COMSTOCK CONSPIRACY—THE SEAL BROKEN AT LAST—WOODHULL'S 'LIES' AND THEODORE TILTON'S 'TRUE STORY'—THE ACCOUNT HORRIBLE AT BEST—'NO OBSCENITY,' BUT GOD'S TRUTH—THE THUNDERBOLT SHATTERS A BAD CROWD AND PLOUGHS UP THE WHOLE GROUND."

THE arrest of the brokers and the suppression of their paper, however, did not deter them from their warfare upon Mr. Beecher, and society generally, which did not accept of them as the true teachers of a new social system. Theodore Tilton, it is believed, himself added fuel to the flame by spreading broadcast among his friends his version of the case. The publication of Woodhull's charges, however, was a mere bombshell, compared with what was to follow. The community had now become excited,—so much so, that people eagerly read everything published on the subject—and in May following there was issued simultaneously in Albany, Troy and New York a review of the case in a paper called *The Thunderbolt*, established by Edward H. G. Clark, editor of the Troy *Whig*, for the special purpose of exposing the Plymouth pastor to greater shame. In the editorial accompanying the statement the editor says:—

"This is a special paper issued to defy conspirators, beat free speech, and rouse a nation. It will be published as occasion may demand. * * * As a mere scandal the affairs of

Mr. BEECHER would be of no consequence. But the terrible violations of justice and law that have grown out of that scandal, make it the most momentous question of American rights since the days of Garrison and the abolitionists. And this alone is the interest in it held by Mr. EDWARD G. H. CLARK, the writer of our leading article—[The True Story—AUTHOR] and one of the editors of the *Thunderbolt.* * * * Mr. CLARK has, therefore, assumed by name the direct responsibility of his article. *He is too well known among Mr. Beecher's own friends to be charged with any nonsense of 'black-mail,' and he is ready to step into court and prove his assertions,* if any one dares to take him there."

This publication, introduced as above to the public really proved what its name implied. It was a Thunderbolt—a discharge of red-hot shot upon the Plymouth Church,—*yet, to this day, no one has accepted Mr. Clark's challenge to take him into court, and compel him to prove his accusations!* It was generally believed that this volley was discharged by Mr. Tilton, and although he has frequently been accused of its authorship, he has not publicly denied it. It is "The True Story," often referred to in the discussion of the great case. But we will proceed to give the "True Story" to the reader.

It may be stated in this connection that the headings to this chapter are those attached to the original article, as it appeared in *The Thunderbolt,* and not those of the author:—

"Christianity is the highest world of civilization, and the spirit of Jesus is the true Religion of humanity. But to-day the orthodox pulpit is a menace to forty millions of people. To save one powerful preacher from deserved shame its retainers have raped the goddess of American liberty. And to accomplish this outrage they have resorted to fraud, and have not scrupled at a monstrous conspiracy. 'Tis the purpose of this paper, the *Thunderbolt,* to stun the nation into a knowledge of these crimes. The 'Evangelical Church' with its Young Mens Christian Association, shall no longer cheat the government, brow-beat the courts and subsidize the press, with impunity. When a republic is crucified between its priests and its editors, honest patriots should speak out. It is time that theological plotters be thrown upon the defensive, and be made to beg of common sense a further lease of their own life. The *Thunderbolt* has power to effect much of this purpose through the very 'forbidden fruit' that has tempted the present quacks of conventional piety to become liars, perjurers and law-breakers. By this forbidden fruit, I mean the Greatest Social Drama of modern times, The BEECHER-TILTON Scandal! This scandal as reported by VICTORIA C. WOODHULL is at once truth and a falsehood; or as THEODORE TILTON has himself explained, a 'true story' underlies the false one. Three months after the WOODHULL account had been published, and no one had given the public a direct, authentic denial of it—three months after the country had been insulted in connection with it by the moral and legal fraud of obscene literature, I was stung into writing a full account, analysis and criticism, of the BEECHER and TILTON scandal. In that article (published in the *Troy Daily Press* of February 11th, and since reproduced in other journals), the WOODHULL account was given in condensed form as follows:

"'The BEECHER-TILTON scandal case,' is this, Mrs. WOODHULL declares there has been a long, continued liaison between Mr. BEECHER and Mrs. TILTON; that it first came to Mr. TILTON'S knowledge through the revelation of one of his children; that he accused Mrs. TILTON of it, and received her acknowledgment of her guilt; that he was driven nearly to insanity at the moment and treated Mrs. TILTON so severely that she miscarried a child, which was considered the offspring of Mr. BEECHER. Mr. TILTON kept his grief secret, however, as Mrs. WOODHULL asserts, until Mr. BEECHER went again to his house during his absence, and extorted a letter from Mrs. TILTON to the effect that he had never been guilty of the wrong she had acknowledged to her husband. Then Mr. TILTON doubly outraged, confided his grief to a bosom friend, Mr. FRANK MOULTON, who went to BEECHER'S house and forced him at the mouth of a pistol to give up the letter. This story, in whole or in part Mrs. WOODHULL says was first revealed to her by Mrs. PAULINA WRIGHT DAVIS, who received it from Mrs. TILTON and then by Mrs. ELIZABETH CADY STANTON, who received it from Mr. TILTON. The knowledge of it came to Mrs. WOODHULL in the early part of 1870, and she refers to an allusion which she made to it in *Woodhull and Claflin's Weekly* at that time. 'Subsequently,' continues Mrs. WOODHULL, I published a letter in both *World* and *Times* in which was the following sentence:

"'' I know a clergyman of eminence in Brooklyn, who lives in concubinage with the wife of another clergyman of equal eminence.' Mrs. WOODHULL affirms that the day when this letter appeared in the *World*, Mr. TILTON came to her office, No. 44 Broad St., and showing Mrs. WOODHULL the letter, asked her whom she meant. 'Mr. TILTON,' she replied, 'I mean you and Mr. BEECHER.' According to Mrs. WOODHULL'S statement, Mr. TILTON then acknowledged that the account was true and worse than she had heard it. But he said that he was broken-hearted and his wife was broken-hearted, and that she especially was then in no condition to be dragged before the public. Mr. TILTON took her to see Mrs. TILTON, and both imparted to her the whole story. The same thing was again detailed to her by Mr. TILTON'S friend, Mr. FRANK MOULTON, and finally by HENRY WARD BEECHER himself.''

"Mrs. WOODHULL'S declared purpose in publishing the BEECHER-TILTON Scandal was to create a 'Social Revolution.' She wished to show that the foremost minds of the age had outgrown the institution of marriage rendering to it only the outward homage of hypocrites, not the adherence of conscience or the practice of life. There is no danger that any social revolution will grow to proportions beyond the actual truth and common-sense contained in it. But in one thing WOODHULL & CLAFLIN instantly succeeded: they created a social panic that turned New York into a mob. Their scandal, as they have since boasted, was indeed 'a bombshell' that carried dismay on every hand an infernal machine of letters so terrific that many even feared to read it,' while others cursed and prayed, laughed and cried as if in the presence of the 'crack of doom.'

"The plans of this Social Revolution it seems were somewhat deeply laid. The issue of *Woodhull and Claflin's Weekly* containing the bombshell was dated Nov. 2d 1872. But anticipating that some steps might be taken to suppress the entire issue when its contents should become known, the paper was dispatched to its subscribers a week in advance, and, (if the word of its social revolutionist" can be trusted in anything) to the entire list of newspapers in the United States, Canada and Great Britain." Then on Monday morning the 28th of October it was put on sale at the WOODHULL headquarters. Before night the demand grew to a rush." During the week it increased to a crush needing even the regulation of the police. 'Tis said the sales reached a hundred and fifty thousand copies, and promised two millions. For several days newsmen retailed the paper as high as fifty cents. On the day of its suppression two dollars and a-half was a common price for it. In some instances single copies brought ten dollars and one extraordinary lover of literature is reported to have invested forty dollars in a copy. Owners of the paper then leased it to other readers at a dollar a day.'

"But by Saturday Nov. 2d the general panic of good society in New York had so far subsided that some steps were indeed taken and with a vengeance to suppress the BEECHER-TILTON scandal. And 'tis these steps alone that make the scandal of sufficient importance to claim the interference of persons 'in no way connected with it, and to heed the unfaltering scrutiny of the public.' These 'steps,' then were nothing less than a daring conspiracy not merely against the audacious and hated women WOODHULL and CLAFLIN, but against the whole people of the United States. In no other terms will I ever consent to describe that bastard New York monstrosity, begotten of lust, fear and guilt—the arrest of WOODHULL and CLAFLIN for publishing obscene literature.'

"If I had myself been situated like THEODORE TILTON on the day of that arrest, and the darlings of my household had been so cruelly belied as his true story claims of his own, I don't know but I could have gone into Broad St. and cut the throats of WOODHULL, CLAFLIN and BLOOD, with as little compunction as I would shoot a mad dog. But that would have been a business and a risk confined to three or four persons. It would not have been a national fraud endangering every great principle at the bottom of human liberty. The special friends however, of HENRY WARD BEECHER the skulkers of Plymouth Church and the Young Men's Christian Association—preferred to deflour the laws of their country and the freedom of its people by a gigantic performance of bigotry and chicanery. In the shadow of their false pretences, the WOODHULL slanders, however atrocious have grown comparatively dim and insignificant. The question of the mere rake, whom the moralist might pity and forgive, sinks in the question of the conspirator and traitor, whom the patriot must hate.'

"A law of the United States passed June 8. 1872 makes a very proper provision in aid of public morals by branding the transmission of obscene literature through the mails as a misdemeanor. The act is this :—

"'No obscene book, pamphlet, picture, print, or other publication of a vulgar or indecent character, or any letter upon the envelope of which, or postal card upon which, scurrilous epithets may have been written or printed, or disloyal devices printed or engrossed, shall be carried in the mail; and any person who shall knowingly deposit, or cause to be deposited, for mailing or delivery, any such obscene publication shall be deemed guilty of a misdemeanor, and on conviction thereof shall for any such offence be fined not more than five hundred dollars, or be imprisoned at hard labor not exceeding one year, or both, at the discretion of the courts.'

"Whatever sins WOODHULL and CLAFLIN had committed in issuing their *Weekly* of Nov. 2d, 1872, they had carefully avoided any violation of this statute against obscene literature. Their paper contained a harrowing account of seduction—an instance of such diabolical heartlessness that the noted philanthropist, PARKER PILLSBURY, has since declared that if its revelations were true, 'no matter though Mrs. Woodhull were an imp of hell, she should have a monument of polished Parian marble as high as Trinity steeple, and every father and mother of daughters should be proud to contribute a stone.' In addition to that nightmare of horrors the paper contained several bold articles on social, religious and financial themes, in the midst of which was the BEECHER-TILTON Scandal—a sad, unexpected story of adultery, but differing little in its detail from scores of such stories reported in hundreds of newspapers. There is only one test of obscene literature—the purpose of the publication; and any other test a free people should resent, if necessary, with battle and blood. Any other test would overturn the Bible, destroy the classics, and exclude physiology from human knowledge. It would insult the grave of every great thinker and poet, from Plato to Shakspeare and Burns. It would steal the bread and meat of letters, and leave only the baby sugar-tits of a Sunday school library. The purpose of obscene literature is to pamper lust, and no fact, no fiction is obscene without this purpose. But the expressed intent of the WOODHULL articles was to destroy lust, and whether this intent was real or feigned, the articles were so written as almost to stop the breath and freeze the soul. In a word, they were ghastly, sickening *libels* if false, but no more *obscene* than a picture of the crucifixion.

"WOODHULL and CLAFLIN were, however, two women regarded almost as outlaws. They had become feared as "blackmailers," and unfragrantly notorious as 'free-lovers.' For such reasons, undoubtedly, the special guardians of Mr. BEECHER's reputation thought that the worst of means might be good enough to sweep 'female nuisances' out of Broad Street. *Public sentiment was exasperated, not quite enough for a direct mob, but an indirect mob, slinking behind a pretence of law, might crush its victims with safety.* In this position, the legal subterfuge was found in the act of Congress passed to punish the venders of obscene prints. Then Mr. ANTHONY J. COMSTOCK, *backed by the Young Men's Christian Association*, stepped up to manage the dangerous *fraud*. Mr. COMSTOCK is generally credited with 'good intentions,' and as hell, also, is said to be paved with the same materials, I have never doubted their presence in the man. God seems to have made him partly a fool in order that the fellow could do a good work as long as he could be kept from getting above his business. The dirty wretches who corrupt young minds by feeding them on licentious books need some little man, by nature a spy and hypocrite, to check their villainous trade. A full-grown, honest soul could neither sell the books nor dodge and lie to catch those who do. In such a dilemma the earth has a COMSTOCK.

"Mr. COMSTOCK declares that, in prosecuting WOODHULL and CLAFLIN, he has never moved in collusion with Mr. BEECHER. In spite of the habit of tongue necessary to his vocation, he probably tells the truth: Mr. BEECHER has acted, from the first, through his friends. But one of the affidavits on which the arrest of the two women was procured, was made by one TALIESIN WILLIAM REES, a clerk in the office of the *Independent:* and that Mr. HENRY C. BOWEN, the proprietor of that journal, might be trusted to act for Mr. BEECHER, (when he could *save himself* by the same industry,) will be quite evident by-and-by to the 'gentle reader' of the *Thunderbolt*. Is it not known that the scheme was planned in Mr. BOWEN'S office—spies being thence dispatched to WOODHULL and CLAFLIN to buy papers and order them sent to certain persons by post? On receipt of the papers Mr. A. J. COMSTOCK made his complaint before Commissioner OSBORN, and the women were arrested. They were in a carriage at the time, and claimed to have been hunting up the officials who had come for them.

"As the charge against them was a fraud, born of a plot, and as they, if no one else, had brains enough to know it, they naturally supposed it could soon be broken. But in this opinion they measured only the justice of law itself, not the powers of a mob, called 'public opinion,' which renders American law useless on so many important occasions. The United States Government, however, treated WOODHULL and CLAFLIN with endearing familiarity. It sat in their lap on the way to court, through the supreme gallantry of Marshall COLFAX or BERNHARD—one of the two Chesterfields who had them in charge. It then hurried them, not into open court, but into a side room where the 'examination' might be *private*. In this 'star chamber' they met five persons—District Attorney NOAH DAVIS, 'a member of Plymouth Church and a family connection of Mr. BEECHER;' Assistant District Attorney Gen. DAVIES, Commissioner OSBORN, and two other gentlemen, one of these being also a member of Plymouth Church. But the 'brazen sisters' sent for counsel; and, insisting on being conducted to the proper court-room, their examination was finally held in public. In this examination the prosecuting blunderer, Gen. DAVIES, let out the secret that WOODHULL and CLAFLIN were not merely guilty of 'circulating obscene literature,' but of a 'gross libel' on a 'gentleman' whose character it was 'well worth the while of the government of the United States to vindicate.' Interpreted, this lingo meant that a United States Court had been procured to convict, on the pretense of *obscenity*, two women who had *libeled a man*—this man declining to protect himself, except through a conspiracy of his friends and lackeys.

"This 'holy show' of American jurisprudence took place on Saturday the 2d of Nov., 1872, and was finally adjourned to the ensuing Monday, the prisoners being held to bail in eight thousand dollars each, with two sureties. But when Monday came the BEECHER tools of the United States Courts *dodged a further examination altogether.* By an unheard-of proceeding, the grand jury had pushed in an indictment which took the case out of Commissioner OSBORN's jurisdiction. The motive was evident; Mr. BEECHER's Gen. DAVIES had found that his owner could never be persuaded or dragged into court to pursue WOODHULL for her 'gross libel,' and that the charge of 'obscenity' was a most ruinous one to try, if Plymouth Church had any further desire to save its Bible. For by far the most 'indecent passage' in *Woodhull and Claflin's Weekly* had been cut out of the divinely inspired book of Deuteronomy. By this indictment, however, the prisoners were remanded to jail in utter disgrace, the mob of piety and fashion was appeased, and the Young Men's Christian Association was sustained in fraud!

"So much done, it was only necessary to muzzle the New York newspapers, (some of whose editors had strong personal reasons for dreading 'black-mailers' if not 'free-lovers,') and to bribe or cheat the Associated Press into sending lies by lightning throughout the country. Both feats were performed. A consultation of leading quills *adopted darkness and falsehood as a deliberate policy;* and as for our 'country press,' that never dares to sneeze unless the metropolitan nose is crammed with snuff. The telegraph even prated about the finding of 'immodest cartoons;' and on the 4th of November the credulous public actually supposed that two women, claiming to be 'reformers,' were guilty of the meanest offence in the calendar of shame. The ablest lawyer in the United States has since given an opinion scouting the whole arraignment, and of course the parties will never be tried, much less convicted. But, on a second arrest, they were taken before another United States Commissioner,—DAVENPORT,—who was obliged to make some appearance of a 'decision.' And that fearful and wonderful thing was this:—

"As to the intention of Congress in the framing and passage of the statute under which these proceedings were instituted, I am clear that a case of this character was never contemplated. * * However * * I am disposed to, and shall hold, the prisoners.

"And for this "decision," the Commissioner declared there was no American precedent, but that an "English case" furnished one.'

"From Commissioner Davenport's ruling there is just one logical deduction:—that this faithful servant of Her Majesty, the Queen of Great Britain, should be swiftly retired from the American Bench, and sent where his English decisions may be rendered in English courts.'

"I have dwelt upon the dry details of law, and in the miserable company of its New York expounders, to show beyond a doubt that the ridiculous proceedings against WOODHULL and CLAFLIN were simply the work of a virtual mob. And in our "commercial metropolis"—the great city of this BEECHER-COMSTOCK rabble—there was only one notable man with brains and pluck enough to care nothing about persons, and to look only at principles. In an age of Daniel Drew, "Jim" Fisk, and Phelps, Dodge & Co., that man is naturally deemed "insane." I refer to GEORGE FRANCIS TRAIN. This "lunatic" instantly perceived the vast public dangers that loomed up in a conspiracy by which the Church might shut the mouth of slanderers or truth-tellers alike, disembowel literature, and stay the march of humanity itself.

"BEECHER must have justice," said TRAIN: "So must Mr. TILTON—so must the sisters CLAFLIN."

To these women he said:—

"'Never approving your doctrine of Free Love, I fought you out of the Woman-Suffrage movement and the International when you were in prosperity: but now you are in adversity I am your friend."

"From his hotel (the St. Nicholas) he instantly wrote them a note:—

"'I will go your bail. I am satisfied the cowardly christian community will destroy you, if possible, to cover up the rotten state of society."

"Events have since proved that the "mad cap," GEORGE FRANCIS TRAIN, was the one greatly sound mind in New York. In spite of the momentous principles at stake, it soon became evident (as I have already shown) that the great "churches of commerce" and the Young Men's Christian Association were in league with the greedy, corrupt press of the city, and that all had joined hands to deceive the nation. Not even a public hall could be secured by Mr. TRAIN, to speak in. He, too, was gagged! It was in this exasperating state of affairs that he took desperate measures, and issued a newspaper of his own—*The Train Ligue*. He rung a score of changes on the expressions called "obscene" in *Woodhull and Claflin's Weekly*. He flung them into the streets of the city, and dared the authorities to arrest him. *He demanded the prosecution of the Bible Publishing Company for printing "disgusting slanders on Lot, Abraham, Solomon and David."* But the Government footboys of Mr. A. J. Comstock had become timid and wary. They let TRAIN alone, while the cords were drawn more tightly still around WOODHULL and CLAFLIN. In unspeakable disgust Mr. TRAIN then issued his *Second Train Ligue*, in which he scattered about the most shocking parts of the Old Testament, under the most audacious of sensational heads, but used no doubtful words except those having the authority of the Bible itself. The work was a coarse one. Only a thorough "Pagan Preacher" could have done it. It seemed revolting and blasphemous; and my own first impression was that TRAIN should be punished for it. But better aware now of the provocation, I have no doubt that history will justify the *Train Ligue* as the natural reaction of COMSTOCK'S idiocy, and as a last democratic test of absolute religious equality. Mr. TRAIN was finally arrested by the State, not the United States authorities, and after the latter had declined to touch him. He was thrown into the Tombs. He pleaded guilty to "quoting obscenity from the Bible," and refused to leave the Tombs on bail. The Church and the Young Men's Christian Association, again, dared not risk a trial—which would either justify WOODHULL and TRAIN or else convict the Bible. In such straits, the BEECHER-BOWEN-COMSTOCK traitors have attempted at last to end their conspiracy by sending GEORGE FRANCIS TRAIN to a "lunatic asylum."

To oppose these assassins of liberty is now the highest duty that God gives me to see. I would help do it, if necessary, with battle and blood. I will first do what I can with ink and types—going back to the cause of the struggle, the BEECHER-TILTON Scandal. I said that VICTORIA C. WOODHULL'S account of it is "at once a truth and a falsehood." As for THEODORE TILTON'S "true story," long since promised to the public, that also shall now be judged.

In a criticism of my own, from which I have already quoted, I said, two months ago, that Mrs. WOODHULL'S statement must be accepted as substantially true; for, of the six persons on whose authority it was told, not one had uttered a word of direct denial. I have now in my possession two letters from Mrs. PAULINA WRIGHT DAVIS—both dated at Paris, one the 20th of November and the other the 28th—showing that I was mistaken. But a mere extract from one of these letters had been set afloat in the newspapers, and had at last become so tortured by a change of names that, as I saw it, I knew it must be either a falsehood or a forgery. Mrs. DAVIS first letter is this :—

PARIS, Nov. 20th.

To Judge———

Dear Friend :—Yours, with its astounding contents, is just received. Thanks for your consideration.

In relation to the TILTON versus BEECHER affair I have only this to say; I was *never* on any terms of intimacy in the family of either party. I never visited at Mr. TILTON'S but once in my life, and that was *ten years* ago, in company with Mr. and Mrs. Johnson. A year or two since I called at Mr. TILTON'S house for some books I had lent Mr. TILTON. I then saw Mrs. TILTON for ten or fifteen minutes. I have met Mrs. TILTON two or three times at the houses of mutual friends, but at no time has there ever been the slightest approach to a *confidential conversation between us.* Nor have I ever even insinuated that there had been. If Mrs. T. has ever, in my presence, spoken of Mr. BEECHER, it has been in terms of respect as a man of honor and her pastor.

I did believe that V. C. WOODHULL was going to do a great work for woman. I am grieved that she has failed in what she gave promise of doing.

I am writing in great haste, and must be very brief, that my letter may go to England to-night by a friend, and so reach you at the earliest hour, and set your mind at rest that I could never have originated or spread this scandal.

Yours very truly,

P. W DAVIS.

"According to 'the WOODHULL,' she received a letter from Mrs. DAVIS in May, 1871, in which Mrs. D. said:

"'I believe you are raised up of God to do a wonderful work, and I believe you will unmask the hypocrisy of a class that none others dare touch. God help you and save you. The more I think of that *mass of Beecher corruption* the more I desire its opening.'

"In Mrs. DAVIS' second note from Paris, she refers to her letter from which Mrs. WOODHULL claimed to have taken this extract, and says:

"'The reference in my letter I do not remember; but, if there, it was in allusion to *statements made by them to me*. But I think it was not there.'

"As far, then, as WOODHULL has given Mrs. PAULINA WRIGHT DAVIS for authority in the BEECHER-TILTON Scandal, she is fairly and flatly denied.

"The position, however, of Mrs. ELIZABETH CADY STANTON is quite different. At Lewiston, Me., she undoubtedly '*denounced*' Mrs. WOODHULL's story, as the newspapers declared at the time; and THEODORE TILTON holds a letter from her, in which she declines to stand in the precise attitude portrayed by Mrs. WOODHULL. Yet an excellent lady, whose letter I have traced to its source, declared in the Hartford *Times* soon after Mrs. STANTON was interviewed in Maine, that she 'had charged Mr. BEECHER, to parties residing in Philadelphia and known to the correspondent, with *very much the same offence* of which Mrs. WOODHULL speaks.' This testimony is confirmed by EDWARD M. DAVIS, Esq., the disciple and son-in-law of the venerable LUCRETIA MOTT, and by Mrs. AMELIA BLOOMER, who asserts that Mrs. STANTON whispered the scandal to her 'a year and a half ago,' and said 'the WOODHULL knew all about it.' At Rochester, not long since, Mrs. STANTON publicly refused to deny *anything;* and, last of all, she has recently sent to me, through a mutual friend, this word: 'Assure Mr. CLARK that I care more for justice than for BEECHER.' Mrs. STANTON, in short, has been somewhat *perverted* by WOODHULL, and *denies the perversion*. And now, THEODORE TILTON's letter to his 'complaining friend:'—one of the strangest epistles on record, and one which every careful reader was immediately obliged to regard as *a negative confession of much that Mrs. Woodhull had asserted.*

"'174 Livingstone Street, BROOKLYN, Dec. 27th, 1872.—*My Complaining Friend:* Thanks for your good letter of bad advice. You say, 'How easy to give the lie to the wicked story, and thus end it forever.' But stop and consider. The story is a whole library of statements—a hundred or more,—and it would be strange if some of them were not correct, though I doubt if any are. To give a general denial to such an encyclopedia of assertions would be as vague and irrelevant as to take up the *Police Gazette*, with its twenty-four pages of illustrations, and say, 'This is all a lie.' So extensive a libel requires (if answered at all) a special denial of its several parts; and, furthermore, it requires, in this particular case, not only a denial of things mistated, but a truthful explanation of other things that remain unstated and in mystery. In other words, the false story (if met at all) should be confronted and confounded by the true one. Now, my friend, you urge me to speak; but when the truth is a sword, God's mercy sometimes commands it sheathed. If you think I do not burn to defend my wife and little ones, you know not the fiery spirit within me. But my wife's heart is more a fountain of charity, and quenches all resentments. She says: 'Let there be no suffering save to ourselves alone,' and forbids a vindication to the injury of others. From the beginning she has stood with her hand on my lips saying 'Hush!' So when you prompt me to speak for *her*, you countervail her more Christian mandate of silence. Moreover, after all, the chief victim of the public displeasure is myself alone; and so long as this is *happily* the case, I shall try, with patience, to keep my answer within my own breast, lest it shoot forth like a thunderbolt through other hearts.

Yours truly,

THEODORE TILTON.'

"Mr. TILTON'S 'thunderbolt' has come! I have tapped the mysterious cloud in which it lay sheathed; and if it now 'shoots' through any 'hearts,' let their owners remember the danger of conspiring against the most sacred rights of an American citizen!

"I will remark, at this point, that the defense which Mr. TILTON prepared against Mrs. WOODHULL,—which he indirectly promised to the public, and then 'concluded to withhold,'—is a thick, heavy pile of manuscript, written on foolscap, and bound in flexible black leather. It has every appearance of elaboration,—being erased in parts and rewritten,—and is very circumstantial. How this 'true story' came into my possession is of no consequence to the public, but can easily be ascertained in the courts, if any of the specially interested parties should have the temerity to press an investigation. I shall give the substance of it, but as briefly as possible, and chiefly, though not wholly, in my own language. Here, then, is THEODORE TILTON'S 'true story.'

"He asserts that, in the fall of 1870,—Mrs. TILTON having just returned to her home from a watering-place,—she was visited by Mr. BEECHER; and that on this occasion the pastor of Plymouth Church unbridled his fiery passions, and besought of Mrs. TILTON the most intimate relationship accorded by sex. Such warmth of pastoral attention was declined by Mrs. TILTON—not with the loud anger of ostentatious virtue, but with the mature sadness of common sense. The good lady was surprised, and the true wife reported the occurrence to her husband. Greatly angered and grieved, he requested her to make a memorandum of it. She did so:—and I give her own words, literally, as they were written.

"'Yesterday afternoon my friend and pastor, HENRY WARD BEECHER, solicited me to become *his wife in all the relations which that term implies.*'

"In his manuscript-book Mr. TILTON comments, with some evidence of pride, upon the delicate and skillful manner in which Mr. BEECHER'S hideous overtures were here expressed. Mrs. TILTON'S language *is striking*, and is apt to impress itself on the reader's memory.

"At the time Mrs. TILTON'S memorandum was written, Mr. TILTON was the editor of the New York *Independent* and of the Brooklyn *Union*, receiving $5,000 a year from each of these sources, and about $5,000 more from still another source, and was in most intimate business relations with Mr. HENRY C. BOWEN, the eminent publisher, and a fellow-member of Plymouth Church. As Mr. TILTON was writing his 'true story,' he could hardly be blamed for a yearning look backward at those halcyon days of the BOWEN flesh-pots.

"About six weeks after Mr. BEECHER'S pastoral interview with Mrs. TILTON, the nature of it was explained by Mr. TILTON to his friend and patron, Mr. BOWEN. The confidence was natural; for Mr. TILTON affirms that, during a whole previous year, Mr. Bowen had been denouncing Mr. BEECHER as 'a corruptor of Brooklyn society,' and charging him, in unmistakable terms, with 'numerous adulteries and rapes.' Mr. TILTON justifies his own terrible statement, at this juncture, by the affidavit of another gentleman, (whose name has thus far been kept out of the scandal,) but who swears that on two occasions he had heard Mr. Bowen impute these crimes to Mr. BEECHER. Again, during a Summer respite at his country-seat in Woodstock, Conn., Mr. Bowen had written a letter to Mr. TILTON, condemning Mr. BEECHER more severely than ever, and bitterly accusing himself of infidelity to his own conscience in having so long delayed an exposure of so base a scoundrel. He added that he should publish BEECHER's guilt on returning to the city. Mr. Bowen failed to keep the promise; but he still vented his indignation in private to Mr. TILTON, who finally unbosomed the story of his own household.

"Thereupon Mr. Bowen became unusually excited. He said the time had come to *act*. He urged Mr. TILTON to write instantly to Mr. BEECHER, demanding his retirement from Plymouth Church and his withdrawal from Brooklyn. '*Write that letter*,' exclaimed Mr. Bowen, '*and let* ME *carry it to the scoundrel for you*.' Impelled by such eloquent friendship, Mr. TILTON says he wrote the following note:

"'HENRY WARD BEECHER, *Sir:*—For reasons which you will understand, and which I need not therefore recite, I advise and demand that you quit Plymouth pulpit forever, and leave Brooklyn as a residence.

THEODORE TILTON.'

"The note was then handed to Mr. Bowen, according to his vehement solicitation, for delivery to Mr. BEECHER.

"In Mrs. Woodhull's account of the BEECHER-TILTON Scandal, she cites a Mr. Frank Moulton as one of her witnesses. This gentleman's name appears also in Mr. TILTON'S manuscript-book. He is a member of Plymouth Church. He has long been Mr. TILTON'S most intimate friend. He was called into the difficulty at the very first step. A day or two after Mr. BEECHER'S visit to Mrs. TILTON in the coveted light of a 'wife,' Mr. TILTON consulted Mr. Moulton, it appears, and placed Mrs. TILTON'S memorandum in his hands. And now, after sending the note of 'advice and demand' to Mr. BEECHER, Mr. TILTON imparted the circumstance to Mr. Moulton.

"'But, TILTON,' said Mr. Moulton at once, '*did Bowen sign that letter with you?*'

"'No,' replied Mr. TILTON, 'I signed it alone.'

"'*Then you are a ruined man!*'

"How Mr. Frank Moulton acquired 'the gift of prophecy,' we need not pause to inquire. But that he understands the 'pillars' of Plymouth Church, was soon proved. For when

Mr. TILTON's friend, Bowen, reached Brooklyn Heights with the letter which he had so earnestly requested him to bear to 'that scoundrel, BEECHER,' he certainly delivered it with remarkable suavity, under the circumstances. Said he,

"'Mr. BEECHER—a letter from TILTON. TILTON is your implacable enemy, Mr. BEECHER, but I will be your friend.'

"It is unnecessary, perhaps, to explain Mr. H. C. Bowen's motive in this unparalleled act of 'strategy,' not to say treachery. But not long afterward it became known to the 'newspaper world' that Mr. Bowen had concluded to dispense with the services of Mr. TILTON on the *Independent*. To kill off a useless friend, and at the same time grapple a useful enemy with 'hooks of steel,' is sometimes an object to a shrewd man of business.

"Some eight months after the commencement of the BEECHER-TILTON differences, an investigation and a storm were thought to be brooding over Plymouth Church; and Mr. BEECHER, fearing that Mrs. TILTON's memorandum (which he had heard of) might be brought to light, made bold to visit her in Mr. TILTON's absence. Although informed that she was sick in bed, he insisted on seeing her, and was finally admitted to her room. Mr. TILTON's 'true story' declares that the great preacher drew a doleful picture of his troubles. He pleaded with Mrs. TILTON that he was on the brink of ruin, and that she alone could save him. Mrs. TILTON finally sat up in bed, with book and paper in hand, and wrote at Mr. BEECHER's dictation a few lines, the point of which is that in all his intercourse with her he '*had conducted himself as a gentleman and a Christian.*' Flushed with success, the Plymouth shepherd then pressed her to add that the troublesome memorandum in Moulton's hands had been wrested from her when she was '*ill*,' and in '*an irresponsible condition.*' She gave an oral promise also, as Mr. TILTON adds, that she would not appear against Mr. BEECHER in any coming investigation, unless her husband should move in the matter. In 'the Woodhull's scandal, she speaks of Mrs. TILTON's 'sweet concessiveness.' Much of it seems also evident in Mr. TILTON's 'true story.'

"On Mr. TILTON's return home, Mrs. TILTON again told him what had happened. He assures the reader that he would now have borne the humility of his wife's merciful retraction, had it not been for the concluding portion, which apparently placed him in the position of having *compelled her to indite her first memorandum.* Mr. TILTON's proud spirit, outraged at the possibility of this appearance of vulgar malice on his part—or even black-mail itself—had resource at once to his unfailing social strategist, Mr. Moulton. He urged Mr. Moulton to hasten to Mr. BEECHER, and force him to give up Mrs. TILTON's last paper.

"Mr. Moulton went; and he had a long private conference with his beloved pastor. He requested and insisted that the document should be given up. Among other things, he reminded Mr. BEECHER that the statement which he had just worried out of Mrs. TILTON was *false on its face*—as the lady was known to have been *not 'ill'* and '*in an irresponsible condition*' when her original memorandum was made, *but uncommonly well*, as Mr. BEECHER remembered,—she *having just returned home from a summer resort.* Mr. Moulton further elucidated to his minister that Mrs. TILTON was *now 'ill' and in an 'irresponsible condition,' instead of on the former occasion.*

"Mr. Moulton's persuasions were not easily answered, though Mr. BEECHER still held on to the paper. As the discussion sharpened, however, and Mr. Moulton evinced that he was not to be trifled with, Mr. BEECHER finally asked him what he would do with the paper if it should be placed in his hands. '*I will keep the first memorandum and this one together,*' said Mr. Moulton, '*and thus prevent you and Tilton from harming each other.*'

"'But,' said Mr. BEECHER, imploringly, 'Frank, can I, *can I* confide in you? Will you protect the paper?'

"'Yes,' was the reply; 'nobody shall have it; I will take care of it.'

"'How?' asked Mr. BEECHER.

"'In every way,' answered Mr. MOULTON; and then, *putting his hand on a pistol in his vest pocket*, he added; '*with this, if necessary.*'

"Mr. BEECHER thereupon gave up the document, and Mr. MOULTON has faithfully kept his promise. But he returned at once to Mr. TILTON, and made a full, circumstantial record of the conference with Mr. BEECHER. This record was written in short-hand, but was afterwards rendered into ordinary English, and it now occupies several pages of Mr. TILTON's 'true story,' and is highly dramatic reading.

"In due time Mr. TILTON became acquainted with Mrs. WOODHULL. He says he had previously declined an introduction to her; but met her accidentally one day in company with a mutual friend, and was presented to her. He afterward visited her at times, as did most of the other men and women in New York who were connected with the Woman Suffrage movement. On one occasion of a visit at her office she suddenly seized a copy of the *World*, and, thrusting it before him, pointed to this passage in a letter she had written to that journal:—

"'I know a clergyman of eminence in Brooklyn, who lives in concubinage with the wife of another clergyman of equal eminence.'

"Mr. TILTON,' said WOODHULL, 'do you know whom that means?' 'No.' 'It means you and Mr. BEECHER.'

"Mr. TILTON claims that he said nothing, or almost nothing in reply; but was simply thunder-struck. He instantly perceived that the woman had heard, in an exaggerated form, rumors that had been traveling about for a year or two, and he feared that, in her possession, they might become very dangerous. He soon left Mrs. WOODHULL, and sought, of course, the Napoleonic MOULTON. The result was the deliberate plan of a campaign to get thoroughly on the right side of WOODHULL, keep there, and thus close her mouth. He then called upon her frequently—sometimes in company with MOULTON, sometimes alone, took her part publicly, and defended her character. He sometimes saw her in such exaltations as he considered states of trance, and her husband in affinity, Col. BLOOD, used to read him extracts from the heavens, which VICTORIA was said to have received (often the night before) from the 'spirits.' Mr. TILTON does not deny that he honestly considered Mrs. WOODHULL a remarkable woman, with a 'mission;' and, if mistaken, he naturally contends that Mr. BEECHER, his sister, Mrs. HOOKER, Mrs. STANTON and many others 'trained in the same regiment' of erring mortality.

"On statements furnished by Mrs. WOODHULL and Col. BLOOD, Mr. TILTON finally made the last bold stroke to win the undying gratitude of 44 Broad Street, by giving his name and the literary finish of his pen to the 'Biography of VICTORIA C. WOODHULL.' He was mistaken, he now thinks, in that person. With 'the WOODHULL' 'gratitude' is nothing, 'principle' everything; and principle, in her case as in VANDERBILT'S, is to 'carry a point.' Mr. TILTON had a terrible warning of this phase of her character, when some of his lady-acquaintances and special friends deemed it necessary, in the early part of 1872, to disown Mrs. WOODHULL in the arena of

Woman's Rights, on account of her social doctrines. The WOODHULL instantly flanked the movement by sending the ladies printed slips of their own private histories, (in an article called 'Tit for Tat'), declaring that if they should disgrace her for *teaching* '*social freedom*,' she would print the article in her *Weekly*, and they should sink *with her* for *practicing the theory*. This generalship may be defended by the old proverb that 'any thing is fair in love and war;' but such a blow 'under the belt' was severely rebuked by Mrs. STANTON, and was regarded with reasonable terror by Mr. TILTON. He now became fully conscious of Mrs. WOODHULL'S capacity of destruction, and retired completely from her circle. The impending 'crack of doom' was not to be hushed up with 'gratitude.' Mr. TILTON had himself confided the substance of his 'true story' toMrs. WOODHULL, and knew that so much of his fate was in her hands. Still, he affirms that he was astonished beyond measure when she at last magnified it into the unearthly proportions of the BEECHER-TILTON Scandal.

"Such is a careful summary of that 'true story' which THEODORE TILTON said he should try to keep within his own breast.

"As far as Mr. BEECHER is concerned, it will instantly be seen that his virtue, at best, is not always the inclination of his own will. If Mrs. WOODHULL has misrepresented him, and Mr. TILTON has turned her falsehood into truth, still it was only through Mr. BEECHER'S *failure in carrying out an immoral purpose* that Mrs. WOODHULL'S story is not correct. A correspondent of the Cincinnati *Commercial*—who has evidently been admitted into some of the secrets of Mr. TILTON'S foolscap volume, and at the same time employed to whitewash Mr. BEECHER —declares that the 'true story' embraces 'a period of ten years,' implicates 'persons who have not publicly figured in it,' and 'elucidates some things not likely to be known till the Day of Judgment.'

"These stilted phrases have some foundation, though it would not be difficult for so plain a man as myself to bring that 'Day of Judgment' close to hand, if necessary. I have no wish, however, to drag any cringing mortal before the public in mere wantonness,—especially any *woman*. I regard Mr. HENRY C. BOWEN as Mr. BEECHER'S chief 'supe' and conspirator, in combining with that wretched Jesuit of Protestantism, Mr. ANTHONY J. COMSTOCK, to violate American liberty. From my position, Mr. BOWEN deserves no mercy beyond the bare truth. In regard to other persons, I think the public have no special interest in them, with one exception. As I view the whole case, in all its bearings, I deem it right to say that Mr. TILTON claims that he has always been violently hated by his wife's mother, Mrs. MORRIS—a lady who is definitely represented to me as insane.

"This poor lady is said to have circulated, for many years, the most damaging reports against the character of her daughter, and against Mr. BEECHER and Mr. TILTON. The earliest scandals concerning Mrs. TILTON and the Plymouth pastor are said to have proceeded from her. I must add, also, that a long time ago there were *rumors*, among the special acquaintances of the parties, that Mrs. TILTON was subject to the *hallucination* that some of Mr. BEECHER'S children were those of her own household. (But Mr. TILTON'S narrative affords me no hint of this rumor.)

"And now what conclusion is to be drawn from Mr. TILTON'S 'thunderbolt' on one hand, and Mrs. WOODHULL'S vaunted 'bombshell' on the other? I am sorry to say I have little confidence in the strict veracity of either account.

"As for 'the Woodhull,' there can be no doubt that she has belied Mrs. Paulina Wright Davis completely. This excellent lady did believe, to use her own language, 'that V. C. Woodhull was going to do a great work for woman,' and in that belief Mrs. Davis encouraged her by word and deed. About a year ago Mrs. Davis went to Europe; and as late as May of 1872, she seems to have retained an affectionate regard for Mrs. Woodhull. It is supposed that when 'the Woodhull' printed her slips to use against those select advocates of Woman's Rights who wished to push her aside, one of the slips was sent abroad to Mrs. Davis; for Mrs. Woodhull has since published a letter (thought to be genuine) which can only be explained by some such cause. Here it is:

"'*My dear Victoria:* Driven to bay at last, you have turned, poor hunted child, and dealt a cruel blow on the weak instruments of men—such men as the editors of the *Herald*, *Tribune*, *Sun*, etc. Every one of the women you name has been hounded by these men, and now that it suits them, they make cat's-paws of them to hunt you. The first time I ever saw Mrs. Phelps I was told by a man that she was a woman of damaged reputation. T. W. Higginson said the same thing of Mrs. Blake in a meeting of ladies in Providence. I was urged to avoid these women, but it was not for me to make war on any one who would work for woman's freedom. They have not stood by me in my faith in you. But, dear child, I wish you had let them pass, and had taken hold of those men whose souls are black with crimes and who set up to be the censors of morality. They should be torn from their throne of the judgment of woman's morals, and made to shrink from daring to utter one word against any woman as long as they withhold justice from her. Men are the chief scandal-mongers of the age: it is they who import all the vile scandals of New York here, and so make society detestable. You are not *befooled* by them, hence you must be *crucified.* God in His mercy pity you and give you grace, strength and wisdom, to do your work aright. But do not again take hold of the "cat's-paws:" excoriate the monkeys, the scandal-mongers, the base-hearted, cowardly betrayers of woman's confidence and honor. Give woman a fair field of equality, and then if she is weak, wicked and mean, let her bear her share of the odium.

Ever yours,

PAULINA WRIGHT DAVIS.

FLORENCE, ITALY, May, 1872.

This letter,—which I consider worthy the head and heart of any woman that ever lived,—commits Mrs. DAVIS to the cause of social fair-play in the broadest sense. She has no fear, surely, for the "face of man;" and, as *one* man, I always take off my hat to such a woman. Yet Mrs. DAVIS flatly contradicts Mrs. WOODHULL, and declares that if she ever spoke to her of the "BEECHER-TILTON Scandal," she relied simply on Mrs. WOODHULL'S own declarations.

Mrs. STANTON, again, has now said enough to show that she considers her conversation with WOODHULL to have been warped, if nothing more, and stuffed out for dramatic effect. Then THEODORE TILTON denies "the WOODHULL"—that is, when the letter to his "complaining friend" finds interpretation at last in the *Thunderbolt.*

"This complaining friend is Col. James B. Mix, a well-known journalist long connected with the *Tribune*—a gentleman who has undoubtedly read Mr. TILTON'S "true story," and who has since rebuked him severely for not fulfilling his declared intention to publish it. In the Chicago *Times* of February 28th, Col. Mix has the one remarkable letter, as far as any hint of hidden facts is concerned, that the BEECHER-WOODHULL excitement has thus far produced. The rest are either thick lamp-black or else thin whitewash. First explaining his position in connection with Mr. TILTON, Col. Mix says:—

"We never expected again to put pen to paper in this matter. But since you, Theodore Tilton, stand trembling with your written statement in your hand, we deem it an act of friendship to give you that spur which shall start you on the stern path of duty. * * * * One would suppose that the Christian Church was founded with the birth of the reverend gentleman who is principally concerned, so mealy-mouthed are the blind idolators who worship at the shrine of Plymouth. * * * For years the sword of Damocles has been suspended above his platform, and yet he has never flinched. One miscreant among his congregation has, figuratively speaking, been shaking the finger of guilt at him for years. * * People ask why has Mr. BEECHER not said, 'This is all a lie.' It is only a little band of dear friends who know of the efforts that have been made during the past winter to shield Mr. BEECHER from the parasites that have surrounded him, and who now feel that every honorable effort having availed nothing, he must meet the blow.

Col. Mix—impersonating Diogenes, out with his lantern to look for an honest man—next addresses Mr. BEECHER directly:

"Why was it that you desired that your protege should read you his written statement, which he did but a few nights since at the house of a mutual friend? Why was it necessary for you to correspond with 'the Woodhull?' If she is the vile wretch they say she is; and if the letters you have from her contain any thing but the woman's inmost thoughts; any thing that can be construed into a threat; any thing that will bear the construction of black-mail, why not give them to the world, so that those who love you for your great talents and the good you have accomplished in the world, may breathe freer? Why was it that she and you were together on the Heights, Nov. 19th, 1871, except it was that she then expected you to make your 'new departure,' and become the high priest of that peculiar sect of which she is the champion? *What mysterious influence was it that she then possessed over you, that you allowed her to dare to propose that you should introduce her at Steinway Hall.* Was it her pure unadulterated cheek, or *did she know 'who was who?'* Certain it was that she was not dismayed; and she nerved your pupil to do that from which you shrank.

"Did not one of the noblest of men * open wide for you another field of usefulness? * * But, alas! Mammon again claimed you. * * The auctioneer was again on hand, and one by one the most conspicuous spots were secured. * * Why was it that your sister, Harriet, Sunday after Sunday, sat at your feet? Was it that another sister, more impulsive, had threatened to mount your platform and plead your cause?

"Come to the front and center, Henry Ward Beecher. You are but human. * * You have a constituency outside of Plymouth Church, to which they are but a drop in the bucket. In your proper element you can unmask the cold-blooded varlets that flaunt their piety on 'Change and in the mart. * * Society was organized on a substantial basis, and no man or woman can overthrow it. Let us have the truth though the heavens fall. *Shall it be? Or must a desperate woman be allowed an excuse,* THROUGH THE COWARDICE OF THOSE WHO HAVE COMMUNED WITH HER, *to give to the world that which may sear other hearts, and tear open, afresh, wounds that are almost healed?*

The immense suggestiveness of this letter, taken in connection with *its source*, supplies all need of excuse for quoting it so liberally. It is the only article from the BEECHER-TILTON circle that the WOODHULL herself has deigned to notice. And what remarkable notice! She says :—

"This is but another attempt on the part of the defense, many others of different bearing having failed to draw our fire before the turning-point. And it will fail, as all others before have failed. * * We shall neither be surprised, annoyed or driven into a showing of our hands until the right time comes. But when that time shall come, the 'Manricoes, 'Brooklyns,' 'Vidies'—the curs who bark at our heels behind *nom de plumes*—* * these, we say, all these will have good reason to think the last trump has sounded; *for we shall then tell the whole truth though the heavens do fall, and though,* WITH THE REST, WE GO DOWN IN THE GENERAL RUIN.

"It is this close, deadly fire, and then the locking of bayonets, between Col. Mix and the WOODHULL, that gives me pause over Mr. TILTON's "true story."—This, and one thing more: from Brooklyn I am asked this question :—

"'How can Tilton deny even what you say he does? Mrs. Stanton has not been his only confidant. My friend,———, long ago received from him a story that did not so spare his hearthstone. It was Woodhull's account, or much like it.'

"I have greatly admired Mr. TILTON. I have thought him a hero, erring, perhaps, but loving, forgiving and abused on many sides. But was that "true story" written, after all, *on purpose to be hidden*, and to be sprung, by and by, as a trap, on history? Is it another book by a Bolingbroke, who "loaded his gun," as Dr. Johnson said, "but dared not fire it, and so hired a beggarly Scotchman to pull the trigger after he was dead?"

"But Col. Mix, in his article, makes no scruple of describing Mr. Beecher as "The modern Arbaces"—insatiate luxury masked in the idol of a god! The picture is either very careless or else very frightful. He tells 'Arbaces' that Mrs. Woodhull knew 'who was who,' and 'nerved his pupil to do' that from which he 'shrank.' Mr. Tilton's 'complaining friend' fears, too, that Mrs. Woodhull may 'sear other hearts, and tear open, afresh, wounds that are almost healed.' Then Mrs. Woodhull herself assures him that she shall yet 'tell the whole truth, though the heavens do fall,' and though she 'goes down with the rest in the general ruin.' Very well: but when those heavens crack and tumble, will the Woodhull 'go down' in the arms of 'Arbaces,' or of the 'pupil,' or of both? I have so little faith in the chastity of Plymouth Church that the two brethren may 'toss up a cent' for the benefit of the doubt.

And now let us glance over the whole field of the Woodhull-Beecher battle, pick up the wounded, bury the dead, and look all the results straight in the face.

As far as Mr. Beecher is concerned, the most direct, though interested witness, Mr. Tilton, affirms that he is not an adulterer, as charged; but that, in spite of his eager intentions to become one, his virtue was preserved by Mrs. Tilton.

But Mr. Beecher's method of magnetizing a sick person into writing down lies for his temporal salvation, is itself as bad as a breach of the Seventh Commandment. It marks at once the perfidious conspirator. It is the old spirit of David, putting Uriah in the 'fore front of the battle.' It justifies every suspicion that leagues Beecher with Bowen and Comstock, their raid on American law and the necessities of human progress. No: Plymouth Church may cling to Henry Ward Beecher, asking no questions, and both may go to the devil together. But he is henceforth on the retired list of great names and honest men. 'The Woodhull' has always claimed that his dead silence, as to her, is a 'masterly system of tactics'—a waiting until public sentiment can tide up to his justification in 'social freedom.' She may bottle her soothing-syrup. The man has no self-sacrifice, much less a bit of aggressive heroism. He is not fit to stand even with her in 'reform.' He will rot away in a dead church.

"But he can easily be spared in all other connections. The Beecher family has been great in American history. Forty years ago Lyman Beecher had power to make even Wendell Phillips a Calvinist, though *he prudently excused himself, as a shrewd Christian, from joining Garrison and the Abolitionists, on the plea that he already had 'too many irons in the fire.'*

When the battle for freedom had grown warm, and the ranks were pretty well filled, Harriet Beecher Stowe wrote 'Uncle Tom's cabin,' and Henry Ward Beecher stood vigorously up for old John Brown. A grateful country can never forget such services. The younger Mr. Beecher, too, has made Puritanism as broad as the sons of Puritans would let him; *but he has always been very careful not to step an inch ahead of assured support.* Theodore Parker—the one great thinker of the recent American pulpit—once spoke of Mr. Beecher's 'deep emotional nature, so devout and so humane,' and his 'poetic eloquence that is akin to both the sweet-briar and the rose, and all the beauty which springs up wild amid New England hills.' No thoroughly trained scholar has ever given Mr. Beecher credit for any thing more than Theodore Parker described.

"His mind is loose and uncertain. He has borrowed a great deal of 'originality' from Emerson, mixed it with sentiment and theology, and fed it to Plymouth Church. But a profound, systematic thinker, like Kant or Hegel, would give him the lock-jaw. He is like the recent book '*Ecce Homo*,' which furnished the crude average mind of the day with a new conception of Jesus, but was only a pretty toy to real scholars. As an orator and actor, however, Henry Ward Beecher has few equals; and like Butler at the bar, or Phillips on the platform, Beecher can always bring instantly to the pulpit all that is in him. His greatness is his readiness. But when he combines with Bowen and Comstock to save a name by endangering a nation, it is evident that he has been petted and pampered into counting himself a god. When Harriet Beecher Stowe—after digging up Byron to brand 'incest' on the corpse,—holds back Isabella Beecher Hooker from admitting her brother's faults, the further usefulness of Mrs. Stowe to the world may also be questioned. And when at last the author of 'Catharine Beecher's Cook Book' demands that some defunct law shall be unburied to imprison Woodhull without the appearance in court of a prosecuting witness, the end has come to an illustrious line. '*Assez de Bonaparte*,' said France in 1814. America is just ready to say: '*Enough of the Beechers!*'

"In estimating Theodore Tilton, I scarcely know what to think. *He has several letters from Beecher, exalting him as the most magnanimous of men and Christians.*' He would have earned these on the supposition that his 'true story' is not a false one, and he would have doubly earned them, certainly, on the supposition that the worse version of Woodhull has any truth at all in it. Mr. Tilton has been the most brilliant young editor in the United States, though he, too, seems dependent on the inspiration of the moment, rather than on any very deep centre of thought. He may yet be pushed into showing that he has not become rotten before getting ripe. But his silence with Beecher, and his patience with Bowen and Comstock, fill many who would like to love him with doubt and distrust.

"And how, finally, shall the thunderbolt fall on 'the Woodhull' herself? I have never seen the dreaded ogress of Broad Street but once—a year or two ago—when I conversed with her a few minutes in a public hall. Her sister, Miss Claflin, I have never seen at all. But having taken a deep interest in great principles victimized through these two women, and having honestly sought nothing but truth in scrutinizing the Beecher-Tilton Scandal, this attitude has drawn to me many people, and has opened various sources of information on all sides. I know persons who admire Mrs. Woodhull, those who hate her, those who think her nature distorted but her work necessary, and those who have watched and studied her, with the care of detectives, for both public and private purposes.

On seeing her myself, I said (in the Troy *Whig* of September 25th, 1871,) that she struck me as a rapt idealist—"out of her head" in the sense of "enthusiasm;" a nature "so intense that she might see visions of angels or devils," and as many as St. John or Luther. "Had she been carefully trained from childhood," I added, "I must think she would have been a wonderful scholar, poet, and thinker. As it is, she is an abnormal growth of democratic institutions, thoroughly sincere, partly insane, and fitted to exaggerate great truths." As precisely this opinion has been reflected back to me by several very acute minds—both men and women—I have no doubt today, that it describes the "Woodhull," in one mood, pretty closely. But I know, from facts in my possession, that she has other moods, in which she loses her remarkable sweetness of voice and all touch of the heavens, to swagger like a pirate and scold like a drab.

This phase of her character has been so conspicuous at times, before close judges of human nature, that they regard her as an ingrained liar and a complete quack. At one time she sinks every vestige of egotism in the absorbed expression of ideas; and at another she would steal the genius of a friend to aid her in "putting on airs." It seems as if she loves notoriety more than any other being on earth; yet she loves her notions of duty even more than notoriety. She is ignorant; and her strong signatures in letters and on the backs of photographs, is commonly the handiwork of Col. Blood. It is probable that she never wrote, unaided and alone, any of her "great speeches" or her stirring editorials—the "Beecher-Tilton Scandal" being no exception. Yet she is the inspiration, the vitality and the mouthpiece of her clan and "cause." Her organ, *Woodhull and Claflin's Weekly*, has voices from the "seventh heaven" and the gabbling of a frog-pond. Its advertisements are gratuitous "blinds;" and its proprietors have lately had the kindness to publish my own circular without request or leave; yet the amazing journal is crowded with thought, and with needed information that can be got nowhere else. And to-day it stands as the test of a free press, and the possibility of a better breed of men than now make the city of New York a vast *immoral improvement* on Sodom and Gomorrah. Mrs Woodhull, in short, is like Daniel O'Connell, as judged by "Bobus Smith": She ought to be hanged, and then have a monument erected to her memory at the foot of the gallows.

Does all this seem like a contradiction or a joke? Very likely—to the puny-souled babes, suckled on the dish-water that is now-a-days called "religion," "theology," "morality." The Sunday-school and the Young Men's Christian Association divide mankind into two classes—the good and the bad. But their Jesus said: "There is none good but one—the Father; and the Son went down to sympathize with publicans and harlots.

The world should have done, once for all, with *expecting* to find a saint who is all sanctity, or a sinner who is all sin. The conception is an old humbug, clasped to the bosom of snobs to double their natural hypocrisy. God made the world—every thought and every thing—out of two opposites. Philosophy, in a Hegel, analyzes them into abstracts, calls them "being" and "nothing," poses these abstracts in necessary evolution, and then synthesises the whole solid world back again. Common sense sees the same thing in every human being, and calls it good and evil. In strong people, especially, it is stiffly mixed. "Every literary man," said Landor, "has the spice of a scoundrel in him." The most useful American writer, during four or five years of our "Great Rebellion," is a natural miser and bummer, and "dead-beat:" —and he is my friend, and I love him heartily. If Beecher himself *would only be honest*, and *not try to garrote the prospects of his race to cover his own frailties*, I could hug him in ten minutes. But he prefers the "orthodox" embraces of "twenty mistresses" and a few millions of fools.

But of all incarnate mixtures of Manna and Helebore that are now going "to and fro on the earth and walking up and down in it," the Woodhull appears to be the most extreme. According to her own story (Tilton's biography) she was conceived in the frenzy of a Methodist revival, and born in a treacherous nest of human catamounts. She was marked from the womb with preternatural excitement. The baby played with ghosts. She dug in the garden with the devil's foot on her spade, to hurry her up. The child of fourteen married to please a rake's whim, and lived fifteen years with a man she ought to have left in a week. She was a little of every thing to earn hard bread—handmaid and shop-girl, actress and clairvoyant healer of general aches. What else, poor soul, they tell me, is not down in the book. She was crushed and cursed in motherhood with an idiot-boy. She was taunted with marital fidelity by a husband who was himself the popinjay of strumpets.

This poor, imp-ridden, heart-burnt woman turned at last against the social fate that had crushed her; and, having been its manifold victim, she knew all its sores and all its weapons. Her treatment of its diseases are new: SHE CURES SEDUCTION BY KILLING REPUTATION, AND LANCES ADULTERY WITH A "SOCIAL REVOLUTION."

She is accused of levying black mail, and special detectives of Wall street claim to hold indictments against her, hidden in their safes. But if such papers were of any effect, when New York would pay a million dollars for a legal pretext to send the woman to Sing Sing, the detectives must have blackmailed somebody for two millions in the interest of burning the indictments up. That Mrs. Woodhull is at all "nice in business honor, I doubt. If she would use the name of Mrs. Paulina Wright Davis falsely, to strengthen even an essential truth, she would suborn a friend's purse to carry out some other "mission."

But that holy horror should gripe the bowels of the whole New York press at the two-penny corruptions of the Woodhull and Claflin, is enough to make the memory of Bennett wink with its cock-eye. The *Herald* was born in smut and libel, and now keeps a regular assignation-house in its columns.

4

Yet perhaps 'tis the most manly of all the great city dailies. How many times was the *World* blatent with threats at the Tammany Ring, and then sopped into silence. Whitelaw Reid has lately elected himself editor and publisher of the *Tribune*, with half a million dollars behind him. Who owns the dog now that nosed Greeley into the grave? When the *Tribune* truckles to Jay Gould, calls for the hanging of Stokes, and plays into the hands of David Dudley Field, a little black-mailing would dignify its character Faugh! the American press has been the mere skunk of the Church, bribed by its subscription-list to save Beecher in a universal stench of black-mail. But the Woodhull's doctrine of Free-Love, the one thing "beastly and abominable" that now inhabits the earth!

Well, I praise the Lord that I have never had any personal use for this doctrine. The "effete system of marriage," as Woodhull and Claflin sometimes call it, has always been good enough for me in spirit and in letter. And there can be no possibility that the love of average human beings will ever fall into chaotic license—the common misunderstanding of "free-love—and which the poet Wordsworth once described to Emerson as "the crossing of flies in the air." But for even the earnest opponents of a theory, it is well to know *what the theory is.*

Such, however is not the current method of opposing "social freedom." The rule in this case is to shut both eyes, strike out with all your might, and hit—nothing. That is, the fops and dolls—the nincompoops in general—who make up what is called "society," are without the mental capacity to understand what free-love means. The whole world is a big brothel—that is their conception. And they can't be cured of it. The true idea would burst open their little heads. With them too "free love" is now the last rotten egg they can find to throw at people who *do know* something. Though enlisted for the war against free-love in the sense of unchained lust, and though distrusting and opposing any departure from monogamy in marriage, I have no desire to stand in an infant-class of idiots, who answer our argument, first by misconceiving it, and then by turning up the end of a pug nose.

Besides, there is much in the movement called "social freedom" that should be admitted at once, as simple justice, in the practical application of rights and morals.

In a recent article, for instance, by Tennie C. Claflin (to take an authority sufficiently obnoxious) she claims this:—

"If the loss of purity is disgrace to unmarried women, then the same should be held of men; if the mother of a child out of legal wedlock is ostracized, then the father should share the same fate. If a life of female prostitution is wrong, a life of male prostitution is equally wrong. If Contagious Diseases Acts are passed, they should operate equally on both sexes."

The *Young Men's Christian Association, of New York*, have endeavored to present the equal chastity of the sexes by suppressing Miss Claflin's article as "obscene." But there is more of the Christian religion in it, and more good sense, than in Dodge and Comstock's entire band of theological Hessians.

But directly in regard to the doctrine of "free love" again, it is necessary for our *intelligent opponents* to acknowledge that 'tis not merely a Woodhull that believes in "new social relations" for men and women, but 'tis many of the most capacious minds and hearts on earth, from John Stuart Mill to Elizabeth Cady Stanton. Woodhull is only a tremendous horn, and Col. Blood is now blowing in front of Jericho.

When Mrs. Stanton stood up in New York, after the trial of McFarland for killing Richardson, and said that no brute should be the dreaded *owner* of a woman's soul and body, she stated the principle of social freedom, as understood by its own expounders. Mrs. Stanton felt no statute in a book was so sacred as that which crushed woman's right to her own individuality.

"Social freedom," then, from one view, is merely the extreme logical end of democracy—absolute individual sovereignty—simple self ownership. No bond, no custom, no law can righteously deny it. Yet this truth, after all, is only half a truth, and the other half is the duty which every individual—every self sovereign—owes to his neighbor—that is, to society.

"Love," says the Woodhull, should be "free" precisely like "worship." The world has outgrown laws to govern religion and leaves conscience unfettered. The fetters of constraint should be broken from marriage, and the parties allowed to mind their own business.

Such is the argument. But the world has not outgrown all laws concerning worship. It prevents one congregation from disturbing another, or taking possession of their church. And in regard to marriage has *society* no "undeniable rights?" Marriage is not a relation of two individuals solely, but of their children as well. And has my neighbor no right to protect himself against the enforced support of *my children?*

Undoubtedly there is no mysterious sacredness in the relation of sex; it is a human affair, amenable to human justice.

'Twould now be useless to treat it otherwise; for general liberty has become so broad that strong persons, justified to themselves, take their lives in their own hands, defying society if necessary, and conquering it by ability and success, as Mr. and Mrs. Lewes have done even in the midst of English conservatism. The sentiment of love is perhaps the most important in the happiness of life. Nor is it even *perfect* without the *expectation of permanence.* So 'tis easy enough to see that two human beings will not generally give themselves up to each other in the closest of intimacy and responsibility, without as much formality, at least, as they would take in "passing receipts" over the transfer of a horse or a pig. Still the tendency in America is doubtless to multiply the facilities of divorce; and the laws will probably end in according to all the "sovereignty" that two parties to a "civil contract" mutually desire, and that the interests of offspring will permit.

In the Beecher-Tilton scandal, however, "the Woodhull" sets up an illustration of "social freedom" that must delight the soul of Stephen Pearl Andruss, but would empty the very meaning of virtue out of the world. Claiming all she does of Beecher, she claims with it, that *no wrong was done except in the deceit of the doing and the hypocrisy of hiding the deed.* A man who feeds Plymouth Church with his soul, *needs* the magnetic sustenance of "many women." It is all lovely to Woodhull—all serene and beautiful. The only fault would be in a Tilton's monopolizing some poor woman, so that she should not be comforted by her pastor, and so that he should be deprived of elixir for new prayers and sermons.

Here is the Oneida community let loose—free love for the saints without even the advantages of material communism. Fourier himself puts Ninon de L'Enclos, Beecher, and the Woodhulls in a separate "phalanx" of their own kind, though he insists that some such people will always exist as exceptions to the race. They have got out of their "phalanx," it seems, and have gone to "reforming things."

But, as Mrs. Paulina Wright Davis says, "the Woodhull" is not to be *befooled.* The woman's bitter experience has taught her all the sickness of the times. "Free love" and "stirpiculture" are rather striking remedies for it. But in an age of Tweed, and Oakes Ames, Challis, Comstock, and God in the constitution; Oakey Hall, model artists and Rosenweig; industrious fleas and D. W. Huston; Bowen, Beecher, the Tombs, and the *Police Gazette*—in such an age the world *can't change for the worse.* Free love may be its last hope. At any rate, if a young woman of thirty-four years and another of thirty, with one Missouri Colonel behind them, can frighten the whole American people out of free speech, a free press, and an honest court house, "stirpiculture" is needed at once for the begetting of some tolerable race of men.

CHAPTER III.

TRENCHANT REVIEW OF THE "TRUE STORY" AND MR. CLARK'S ERRORS, BY THE WOODHULL—THE POEM "SIR MARMADUKE'S MUSINGS," WHICH, IT IS ALLEGED, IS INTENDED TO REFER TO THEODORE—HOW IT WAS WRITTEN IN BOSTON WHEN TILTON HAD DISCOVERED HIS WIFE'S FALL, WITH A PISTOL BEFORE HIM, AND PREPARATORY TO COMMITTING SUICIDE—MRS. PAULINA WRIGHT DAVIS' LETTER—"THE MORE I THINK OF THIS MASS OF BEECHER CORRUPTION, THE MORE I DESIRE ITS OPENING."

WHILE the author has never been an admirer of Mrs. Woodhull, and is one of the few journalists of the metropolis who has never, at this writing, laid eyes upon her, fairness to her and justice to the reader demands that she should be permitted to be heard here, in defence of the charges made in the *Thunderbolt*. Shortly after the appearance of the *Thunderbolt*, Mrs. Woodhull published in the *Weekly* the following:—

"'THE THUNDERBOLT.'—A paper bearing the above name," says Mrs. Woodhull, "has been issued from the press, simultaneously in New York, Albany and Troy, which *purports* to have been written principally by Edward H. G. Clark, of the latter city, and published by some unknown parties, who, however, are understood to be men of the first rank in social and political circles. Notice of this paper has been given in the *Weekly*, whose readers are undoubtedly expecting it, therefore I do not need to apologize for copying it entire.

THEODORE TILTON.

"It will be remembered that Mr. Clark has written several criticisms upon the various phases of the Beecher-Tilton scandal, which have been copied into the *Weekly*, not excluding his severe allusions to myself, without comment. But I shall remain silent no longer and permit this conspiracy to proceed, apparently to whitewash somebody, but really to blackwash me, to pass as current stuff without showing its true character and bringing it home to its real source. I shall, therefore, analyze this thunderbolt as severely as my crucible will admit of, notwithstanding he has been led to convey the impression that I am too ignorant to attempt any such thing, and attempting, could only expect to write myself down an ass; however, the public shall have the opportunity to judge between us as to which of us is the greater. But I shall borrow no adjectives with which to do this, as he has felt it necessary to do to accomplish the purposes of the *Thunderbolt*.

"The paper is called the *Thunderbolt*. After a careful and candid reading, however, I do not think the name it bears is justified by its contents, unless, indeed, a thunderbolt may be a general concentration of many lesser bolts which have already been expended, and are gathered together to be hurled anew and *en masse* at a given point, for a certain purpose. This paper contains no new facts; indeed no new arguments regarding existing facts. The several features of the Scandal are concentrated, and—as everyone who reads it can well surmise—with a well-defined purpose in view, which I denominate the double one of whitewashing and blackwashing.

"This will become evident when other things which do not appear upon the face of the paper itself, are shown. *It will be remembered that I recently published a letter from Mr. Clark to George Francis Train, in which he said he had stolen Theodore Tilton's 'true story.'* How the stealing of such a document was done, if what I surmise be true, is not hard to conjecture. Some three months ago a strange paper made its appearance entitled the *Rainbow*. The moment I saw it I said that is the *Golden Age* print, its types, rules, head-lines and all; and so it turned out to be. The moment I saw the *Thunderbolt* I said that is the *Golden Age* print, its types, rules, head-lines and all; and I believe it will so turn out to be. It bears the marks of Theodore Tilton too conspicuously to permit one to whom he has so often, as he has to me, pointed out the characteristic points of the *Golden Age* to doubt this. I, therefore, have no hesitation in expressing my belief, and resting upon it, that this paper was not only written by the knowledge and consent of Mr. Tilton, but that it was published by him, *or at least composed and electrotyped by him.* If any doubt this let him or her compare the *Thunderbolt* with the *Rainbow*, and both with the *Golden Age*.

"This at first blush may seem improbable, since the *Thunderbolt* is severe upon Mr. Tilton. Evidently, however, he realizes the futility of escape; indeed, that he deserves it all and more, and therefore makes a virtue of necessity and aids in the publication, perhaps even connived to bring it about.

"But what, upon its face, are the purposes of the *Thunderbolt?* Ostensibly they are to show the danger by which the Republic is threatened by the overt acts of the Federal authorities, acting under the inspiration of the Y. M. C. A. in prosecuting Woodhull, Claflin and Blood for obscenity, to protect the reputation of Mr. Beecher, and to relieve Mrs. Tilton from the position into which she was thrown by the publication of the Beecher-Tilton Scandal; but this will scarcely be held to be its real objects by the careful, analytic reader. The reasons to such will appear to be—

1. "To whitewash Mr. Tilton for the part of informer which he has played in exposing Mrs. Tilton's love for and liaison with Mr. Beecher, which it performs in a rather dubious manner.

2. "To blackwash me for having given publicity to the Beecher-Tilton Scandal, which had previously only been talked

about behind the doors, which it does not do with colors that will wash.

3. "To fix irremediably upon Mr. Beecher the fact of his private devotion to the principles of social freedom, and to brand him to the world as one of the most consummate and hypocritical villains living, which, I fear, is done only too mercilessly.

"These, I say, are undoubtedly the motives that led to the publication of the *Thunderbolt*. But all of them could not have existed in the mind of Mr. Clark; nor were they all apparent in any of his previous articles written by him and copied into the *Weekly*. But Mr. Clark himself informed me that he was in receipt of letters in which I was severely denounced, and I am informed by another, that Mr. Clark has been 'advised to treat Mrs. Woodhull in the most contemptuous manner.' Here, then, we find the source of the animus which pervades the *Thunderbolt*, and it is the same as that from which I believe the paper really issues.

"Mr. Clark, I have good reasons for believing, had no inconsiderable regard for me personally; but that has been more than overbalanced by the influence that has been brought to bear upon him since he began to write about this matter. When he informed me that he was receiving very bitter letters regarding me, I at once, and frankly replied, asking their source, and saying: 'Give these letters to me to publish in the *Weekly* for the benefit of the public.' I denounced as dishonest and cowardly those who would stab me behind my back, when they have the opportunity to meet me squarely and openly; and to those terms I now add vicious and malicious, and hurl them all in the faces of any one who has busied him or herself in writing letters about me all over the country, endeavoring to vitiate the truth of my statement of November 2d, by falsehood and malice, but failing to submit them for publication in the *Weekly*.

"Therefore, when I find emanating from the pen of a gentleman, who previously held me in esteem, the contemptuous words and the still more contemptible insinuations with which I am described in the *Thunderbolt*, I am forced to the conclusion that the real motives for them lie outside of the person over whose name they stand.

"Another conclusive reason that Mr. Clark is not the real source of the *Thunderbolt*, the responsibility of which he, however, assumes, is that of his own knowledge he would not have laid himself open to the terrible repulse he must now sustain. The *Thunderbolt* is vulnerable at every point.

"Moreover, had the statements been entirely the work of Mr. Clark, I have a sufficiently good opinion of his ability to believe it would not have been so faulty in its construction as to make it certain that, when only one of its chief corner-stones is removed, as it will be, the whole thing will tumble in an insignificant mass of ruins. Besides, it is contradictory and unreasonable in its positions, and resorts to falsehoods and unwarrantable insinuations to sustain them. I have said to the readers of the *Weekly* that Mr. Clark is a gentleman. I fear they may not be able to agree with me when they shall come to realize the true character of the *Thunderbolt*, which is supposed to represent the character of its writer, but which I hope only represents the terrible pressure to which he has been subjected by those whom he at least has honored in the past. I freely confess that the course taken by Mr. Clark in his previous articles, excepting only a few of what I thought unnecessary epithets used about me, won for him a high place in my esteem; but also I freely confess that the *Thunderbolt* has staggered me. I expected great and good things of it. I did not think it would stoop to pander either to prejudice, position or passion; but that it would be just what ought to be expected from a gentleman who is every inch a man. But if the *Thunderbolt* is found, when subjected to the crucible of stern analysis, to be based upon other than purely and highly moral motives, and to be elaborated for other purposes than the vindication of truth and the establishment of justice, and that these are promoted by falsifications and the use of unjustifiable methods, what must the conclusion be, except that the *Thunderbolt* does not sustain the reputation of Mr. Clark. If it do not, neither he nor his friends ought to censure me for showing it, since neither he nor they can possibly be more disappointed than I shall be.

"And at the very outset, before proceeding to the argument, I am compelled to call attention to a fact which I fear will cast doubt even over other portions of the *Thunderbolt* which ought to stand unchallenged. It is of little consequence to me how it may please critics to treat me personally, if their efforts carry forward the glorious cause to which I am devoted ; hence, personally, I might consistently permit the *Thunderbolt* to stand unscathed ; but its defects are too apparent to justify me in passing what I refer to without comment, or, when comment is begun, from pressing it persistently to the end. Moreover the glory of the cause of freedom and justice will not allow me to stand publicly convicted by silence, of endeavoring to promote it by fraud. Therefore, observe the following quotation from the *Thunderbolt*, and if, as I said, it vitiate the whole affair let those who resorted to a subterfuge so vulgar, bear the odium and not me:

"'SUSPICIOUS POETRY BY T. T.'"—[MEANING THEODORE TILTON.]

Published in the "Golden Age," November 12, 1872, (just after the Woodhull account of the Beecher-Tilton Scandal.)

" I clasped a woman's breast
As if her heart I knew,
Or fancied would be true,
Who proved—*alas! she too*—
False like the rest."

"Now why was this quotation made in the *Thunderbolt*—special care being taken to state the date, and to italicize the parenthetical explanation? Evidently to convey the idea that my publication of the scandal had proved me, 'too—false like the rest.' I ask again, can there be any other construction put upon this remarkable quotation? and I answer no other can be imagined.

"But what are the facts about this poem which I now copy entire from the *Woodhull & Claflin Weekly* of date December 23, 1871, where it was copied from the *Golden Age* of November 12, 1871:

SIR MARMADUKE'S MUSINGS.

BY THEODORE TILTON.

"I won a noble fame
But with a sudden frown,
The people snatched my crown,
And in the mire trod down
My lofty name.

"I bore a bounteous purse,
And beggars by the way
Then blessed me day by day;
But I, grown poor as they,
Have now their curse.

"I gained what men call friends;
But now their love is hate,
And I have learned too late,
How mated minds unmate
And friendship ends.

"*I clasped a woman's breast,*
As if her heart I knew
Or fancied would be true,
Who proved—alas she too!—
False, like the rest.

I now am all bereft—
As when some tower doth fall,
With battlement, and wall,
And gate and bridge and all—
And nothing left.

"But I account it worth
All pangs of fair hopes crossed,
All loves and honors lost,
To gain the heavens at cost
Of losing earth.

"So, lest I be inclined
To render ill for ill,
Henceforth in me instill,
Oh God, a sweet, good will
To all mankind."

SLEEPY HOLLOW, NOVEMBER 1, 1871.

"Mr. Clark is one of the editors of the *Thunderbolt*, and although the poem stood in it, below the article to which his name gives personal responsibility, he is not relieved from the general editorial responsibility. And I can, therefore, do no less than hold Mr. Clark responsible for this fraud, since a fraud of the most malicious and vicious kind I must show it to be.

"It will be seen that the poem, instead of having been published in the *Golden Age*, November 12, 1872, was really published a year before, in 1871; therefore the explanation (just after the Woodhull account of the Beecher-Tilton Scandal) bears the stamp of a vicious and malicious lie, invented to cast a reflection upon me, and to question the character of the intimacy between Mr. Tilton and me. If Mr. Clark is responsible for this, or even if he has permitted this to be done by others—he being the only one known in the *Thunderbolt*—I say he must have been insane to thus tamper with figures and dates and records, and expect it to pass the scrutiny of the world. It might, perhaps, be expected to pass the 'Damphools' of whom Mr. Train treats, but even Mr. Clark's 'ignoramus,' of 44 Broad street, ought not to be counted among so dull a crew as that. As if, however, to court the responsibility of the intentions of this falsehood, Mr. Clark apparently proceeds upon its theory, dragging them conspicuously into another portion of the *Thunderbolt,* for which he cannot escape responsibility. Therefore I see no escape for him from either, and fear he has unwittingly been betrayed into something that a calmer survey of the field, and less reliance upon the honor of those who write bitter letters about me would have saved him.

"Since, however, the inspiration of this poem has been called up and falsely stated, I may, with consistency, give the truth regarding it.

"*This poem was written by Mr. Tilton, so he informed me, in Young's Hotel, Boston, where he had gone to lecture in Tremont Temple, on 'Home, Sweet Home,' with a revolver lying beside him, with which he intended to end his misery, leaving the poem behind as an explanation of his suicide.* Returning, however, to his better sense, he desisted and returned home, called at my residence, 15 East Thirty-Eighth street, read me the poem in manuscript, and gave me this history of it. It was immediately published in the *Golden Age,* whereupon Mr. Tilton's friends complained bitterly that he had told the whole story of his wife's infidelity by that poem, which ought never to have been written, much less published.

"I therefore hurl the lie and the insinuation in the face of the manufacturer, whoever he may be, and there they shall stick as an everlasting mark of infamy. I do not do this because I would shrink from the insinuation. I have the honor of informing Mr. Tilton, Mr. Clark and the world, that I shall ever be only too happy and proud to acknowledge all the service rendered me by Mr. Tilton ; and, moreover, that I never receive or accept service of whatever kind, or contract alliances of any sort, of which I am ashamed to accept the responsibility. And I wish it to be distinctly understood if pretensions have been put forward which any one thinks an honor to himself but a disgrace to me, I shall not hesitate to correct the error into which men usually fall ; or if it requires it, to show that whatever is to their credit is also to the credit of women. I believe that the world shall come not only to know, but also to recognize that any associations between men and women cannot at the same time be honorable to the former and disgraceful to the latter; and I have permitted many a lie to go unheeded to teach the world just this fact. It is simply nobody's business what my social relations are, or what they have been, unless I am found advocating publicly one thing while living privately quite a different one.

"*But since, as I believe, through the conspiracy of Mr. Tilton, this insinuation has been publicly made in reference to himself, I think I have the right to call upon him to publish a certain letter of mine to him, written on four pages of wrapping paper, which contains a statement that will either prove or disprove what he has thus wantonly thrust before the public.* Further on I shall have reason to refer more fully to this matter and of what he has denominated the breach between us, but for which he has assigned a lie as the cause.

"*I have thus shown the character of one portion of the 'Thunderbolt' which has special reference to me, in order that all other portions may be critically considered by the reader..*"

Mrs. Woodhull after quoting the denial of Mrs. Davis having informed her of the scandal remarks:—"A letter differing somewhat from this, but evidently having the same source, went the rounds of the press in December. At that time I pronounced it, so far as it denies the truth of my statement, as false, and I now re-affirm that I have good reasons for stating that this letter has been 'doctored' by Mrs. Davis' friends since it was received. Mrs. Davis is an honorable, straightforward woman, and will not consent to lie. Had I used her name in this connection against her expressed wish, which I have not, I am sure she would not deny it. Mrs. Davis knew that I intended to use the 'Beecher corruption' to bring on the social revolution, and instead of endeavoring to dissuade, always encouraged me to do so. I therefore again repeat that I believe this letter is a forgery, and I know that at least one of the persons behind Mr. Clark believes it to be so. I shall never believe that Mrs. Davis will consent to have this stand as her letter until I either see her own handwriting to that effect or she tells me herself that it is so. I therefore call upon Mrs. Davis to state to me in writing, which I promise in advance to publish in the *Weekly,* the truth or falsity of this whole matter.

"I know that this letter has been in the hands of Mr. Tilton, as well as others from other persons whom I named as my authority: and I also know that had they contained the much-needed contradiction they would have been published authoritatively by him long since. Nevertheless, he took care to have it come to my ears that he had letters completely refuting my statements; but the perusal of the letters to and by others revealed this thin pretense. They perhaps question the language used, *but not the thing stated.* Now let this be disproved if it can be, by the publication of the *original* letters from Mrs. Davis and Mrs. Stanton; all others, as I believe, are forgeries.

"According to the Woodhull, she received a letter from Mrs. Davis, in May, 1871, in which Mrs. D. says:

"'I believe you are raised up of God to do a wonderful work, and I believe you will unmask the hypocrisy of a class that none others dare touch. God help you and save you. The more I think of that mass of Beecher corruption the more I desire its opening.'

"In Mrs. Davis' second note from Paris, she refers to her letter from which Mrs. Woodhull claimed to have taken this extract, and says:

"'The reference in my letter I do not remember; but, if there, it was in allusion to statements made by them to me. But I think it was not there.'

"Now, says Mrs. Woodhull, if Mrs. Davis wrote the above, which I do not believe she did, the following may refresh her memory:

HOME, Wednesday.

"'*Dear Victoria:*—I have prepared the manuscript and returned it to Mr. Wood. There is a sentence missing at the end of Mrs. Stanton's address, which I have written in pencil.

I think if the appendix was begun in the middle of the page it would look better. I wish that a dozen could be sent at once to Mrs. Emily Pitt Stevens, *Pioneer*, San Francisco, California. Pray ask Mr. Andrews, Col. Blood—any one who has time, to see that it comes out right this time. If he would send me a copy before the edition is struck off it would be a good thing.

"'It seems to me, on the whole, that it will not be best to send the platform out in this edition—that is to bind it up with it. The appendix closes properly with the winter's work. The platform belongs to another season.

"'How I wish, dear, you could be here a little while, it is so quiet and peaceful. I wonder I ever want to go anywhere—into the turmoil and strife of life.

"'I thought of you half of last night, dreamed of you and prayed for you.

"'I believe you are raised up of God to do a wonderful work, and I believe you will unmask the hypocrisy of a class that none others dare touch. *God help you and save you. The more I think of that mass of Beecher corruption the more I desire its opening.*

"'I wish you would send me the names of the two kept women on the platform of Boston. I will not use them till you give me leave, but it will help me to act as I must.

"'I suppose you have seen the scrap I enclose· at all events. it's best you should be armed at all points.

"'If Mr. Andrews will give an hour or two to that book it will give me rest. Kind regards to him and Tennie.

"'Ever yours lovingly,

"'PROVIDENCE, May 29, 1871. "'P. W. DAVIS.'"

"Immediately after the Washington Convention in January, 1871, Mrs. Davis begun the preparation of 'The Twenty Years' History of the Woman Suffrage Movement,' which was published under the supervision of Woodhull & Claflin by their printer. This letter refers to that work and was written in May, after the Convention in Apollo Hall, and if I remember rightly, was the first one received from her on her return home after that convention.

"Who can read this letter, the original of which in her own handwriting and bearing her own signature, I happen still to have, and believe that Paulina Wright Davis ever wrote the first letter in the *Thunderbolt,* pretending to be from her. I will not attempt here to show the inconsistencies of the several statements contained in the letter dated Paris, November 20, 1872, which that of May, 1871, does not refute, since I have no excuse to review Mrs. Davis until I am satisfied that she has denied something. But I may consistently show the disparity between such points of the two letters as their own language involves. 'I did believe that V. C. Woodhull was going to do a great work for woman; I am grieved that she has failed in what she gave promise of doing.' Now, what was this work? Her letter to me fully explains. 'I believe you are raised up of God to do a wonderful work; and I believe that you will unmask the hypocrisy of a class that none other dare touch. God help and save you. The more I think of that mass of Beecher corruption the more I desire its opening.' It seems clear that she conceived the great work that I was to do was the very thing I have done and the very thing that Mrs. Davis desired should be done. Where, then, have I failed to do what she believed I was raised up of God to do? And can Mrs. Davis be grieved because I have opened just what she desired should be opened, which 'none other dare touch?'

"And she was thinking more and more of 'that mass of Beecher corruption.' Now, what did that mass consist of? A mass means more than one thing of one kind, and Mrs. Davis is a careful writer, never writing one thing and meaning another. When she said 'that mass of Beecher corruption' she meant just what I have stated that she said to me she learned from Mrs. Tilton, not only about herself, but all that has more recently come to the light of day, by the publication of Tilton's letter to Bowen regarding a member of his own family, which is the foundation for the statement by Mrs. Tilton, that she had recently learned that Mr. Beecher had had * * * * * * * under most extraordinary circumstances with another person. What those extraordinary circumstances were, may be learned by referring to Tilton's letter to Bowen. * * *

"I repeat that the first knowledge I had of the Beecher-Tilton matter was imparted to me by Mrs. Davis at my office, 44 Broad street, where she called on her way over from Mrs. Tilton's, and related to me what she had just heard from her. But she told me nothing of Mr. Bowen. Whatever I know of him I learned much later, from Mr. Tilton himself. Neither did Mrs. Stanton say anything to me about the Bowen affair, and when I published my first intimation in the *World* and *Times* that 'I knew a clergyman of eminence in Brooklyn who lives in concubinage with the wife of another clergyman of almost equal eminence,' I meant Mr. Beecher and Mr. Tilton. Had I known at that time that Bowen was mixed up in the muddle I should have used it, because he had just made a furious and unwarrantable assault upon me in a leading editorial in the *Independent.* Mrs. Davis, I am certain, did not originate this scandal, but that I first heard some of the particulars from her I have ample proof, which will be advanced should a denial from her ever make it necessary. But I wish parenthetically again to state my position regarding Mrs. Tilton. I conceive that Mrs. Tilton's love for Mr. Beecher was her true marriage, and that her marriage to Mr. Tilton, while loving Mr. Beecher, is prostitution. If I have any cause to criticise her, it is for consenting to remain the legal wife of Mr. Tilton, As I said in the original article, Mrs. Tilton is really far advanced in the principles of social freedom, as I learned from Mr. Tilton himself.

"In view of all this, can anybody believe what Mr. Clark infers from the pretended letters to Mrs. Davis that 'Mrs. Woodhull is flatly denied.' If there is a denial, it is Davis against Davis. Besides this, I have a recent letter from Providence, from one who knows some of Mrs. Davis' friends, which says: 'There are not a few of her friends who do not credit the authority of the letter.'

"As far, then as Woodhull has given Mrs. Paulina Wright Davis for authority in the Beecher-Tilton Scandal, she is fairly and flatly denied. The position, however, of Mrs. Elizabeth

Cady Stanton is quite different. At Lewiston, Maine, she undoubtedly 'denounced' Mrs. Woodhull's story, as the newspapers declared at the time; and Theodore Tilton holds a letter from her, in which she declines to stand in the precise attitude portrayed by Mrs. Woodhull. Yet an excellent lady, whose letter I have traced to its source, declared in the Hartford *Times* soon after Mrs. Stanton was interviewed in Maine, that she 'had charged Mr. Beecher, to parties residing in Philadelphia, and known to the correspondent, with very much the same offense of which Mrs. Woodhull speaks.' This testimony is confirmed by Edward M. Davis, Esq., the disciple and son-in-law of the venerable Lucretia Mott, and by Mrs. Amelia Bloomer, who asserts that Mrs. Stanton whispered the scandal to her 'a year and a half ago,' and said 'the Woodhull knew all about it.' At Rochester, not long since, Mrs. Stanton publicly refused to deny anything; and, last of all, she has recently sent to me, through a mutual friend, this word: 'Assure Mr. Clark that I care more for justice than for Mr. Beecher.' Mrs. Stanton, in short, has been somewhat perverted by Woodhull, and denies the perversion.

"Why, asks Mrs. W., has the part played by Mrs. Stanton been so niggardly treated by Mr. Clark? It seems to me that she is of sufficient importance to have received much greater consideration. Or does Mr. Clark know that too many people have learned the same facts from her that I learned? People in California and Chicago, as well as in Philadelphia and Iowa, testify to the same things. Mr. Clark says I have lied. In what, Mr. Clark? pray inform me. And if I have lied, do you mean to also say that Mrs. Stanton has lied? But why does Mr. Clark say, 'At Lewiston, Maine, she undoubtedly denounced Mrs. Woodhull's story,' when he knows that she has denied that telegraphic statement of 'two clergymen.' "The following was published in the *Weekly* of Feb. 15th. The following we clip from the *Springfield Republican's* Boston letter:

"'Mrs. Stanton, by the way, has disclosed a curious fact about the dispatch from Lewiston, Maine, sent all over the country, some months since, to contradict Mrs. Woodhull's Beecher slander on Mrs. Stanton's authority. She never authorized such a dispatch, and asserts that the two clergymen at Lewiston, who called on her to talk about the matter, quite misrepresented what she said to them. Without going into the general question of fact, it is understood that Mrs. Stanton's correction of Mrs. Woodhull's account referred only to some expressions of her own there quoted, and she expressly disclaims any statement that Mrs. Woodhull's story was 'untrue in every particular,' which the Lewiston dispatch made Mrs. Stanton say, but which she never has said.'

"There has been, says Mrs. Woodhull, a great deal said by the members of Plymouth Church about a letter from Mrs. Stanton in the hands of Mr. Tilton, which they claim is parallel with the Lewiston telegraph despatch. Now that Mrs. Stanton has said that 'two clergymen' stated untruth in the Lewiston dispatch, will the above-mentioned members please publish the letter, so that the public may see if they too have not, in their zeal for Mr. Beecher, gone as far beyond the truth as their Lewiston friends? It will also be remembered that in the 'Justitia' letter published in the Hartford *Times*, and dated November 25, 1872, the writer, in speaking of the reason that this alleged denial could not have been written by her, said: 'I will tell you, Mr. Editor; simply because Mrs. Stanton dare not imperil her own reputation for veracity; for she has herself charged Mr. Beecher to parties residing in this city and known to me, the writer, and elsewhere, with very much the same offenses of which Mrs. Woodhull speaks.'

"In direct connection with the above, we find the following in the *Patriot*, of Chariton, Iowa:

"'In the Council Bluffs *Nonpareil* Mrs. Amelia Bloomer says: In the general condemnation of Mrs. Woodhull for publishing the scandal told to her, the question of its truth or falsity is in a great measure lost sight of. A. B. does not believe that Mrs. Woodhull manufactured these stories; and now that the thing is out, she would like to see "the Beecher-Tilton Scandal" tried on its merits. One year and a half ago this scandal was whispered in the ears of A. B. by one of the parties given as authority, by "the Woodhull," and the one so whispering gave Mr. Tilton himself as her authority. She further said that "the Woodhull" knew all about it, and threatened its publication. This agrees, as far as it goes, with the statement of Woodhull, and proves she did not get up the story for the purpose of "blackmailing." A. B. has kept this scandal to herself, and never would have revealed her knowledge if it had not come so fully before the public. While deploring, for the sake of all parties concerned, for the sake of the church, for the sake of decency and good morals, that it has ever come to light, she hopes, now it is out, that truth will be elicited and justice done—that the chief actors may receive their share of punishment, instead of being shielded from censure, while the talebearer alone is condemned.' It is useless to add more to this. Neither of these refer in the slightest manner to the solution of the matter by the Bowen affair; nor are they based upon 'rumors' or 'hallucinations.' It is preposterous simply, to attempt to evade the fact that Mr. Tilton is the authority to more than me for the details of the Beecher-Tilton, not the Beecher-Bowen, Scandal. I have only to ask if Mrs. Stanton could have denied the truth of my statement regarding Mrs. Tilton, would she not have done it long ago? Everybody must unhesitatingly answer yes. But instead of this, her letter to Laura Curtis Bullard, which Mr. Tilton has in his possession, only qualifies the language used, but not the thing said. I believe she claims she did not say that Mr. Tilton called Mr. Beecher a *damned* lecherous scoundrel.

"I am satisfied to let it remain as Mr. Clark concluded, 'Mrs. Stanton in short, has been somewhat perverted by Woodhull, but denies the perversion.'

Referring to the story of the *Thunderbolt* as to the manner in which Mrs Tilton was dishonored, Mrs. W. says:—"As a correction to this introduction to the 'true story,' I ask Mr. Tilton to publish to the world a certain letter received from Mrs. Tilton, during her absence from Brooklyn at a 'watering-place,' in the summer of 1871, and refresh his own memory somewhat about the facts therein treated of. I remember them very distinctly. Perhaps he will accommodate Mr. Clark with the loan of that letter. Will Mr. Clark please manage to *steal* that letter if Mr. Tilton will not loan it? I assure you it will give a great deal of light as to my truth or falsity; and if Mr. Tilton will not loan you the letter, and you cannot manage to steal it, please ask him if that letter did not state that *Mrs. Tilton said she had been reading 'Griffith Gaunt,' and that night, while on her knees till midnight, she had awakened to the horrible crime she had committed against her husband. I am sorry to be obliged to jog Mr. Tilton's memory on these points; but Mr. Clark might also ask him if, in that letter, she did not state that she felt that she had been divorced from him, and that she should never live with him again unless they were remarried.* Again, it may not be invidious to inquire, what was the cause of the misunderstanding between Mr. and Mrs. Tilton, which could cause Mrs Tilton to feel divorced? Surely the refusal to accept Mr. Beecher's kind proposals could not have been a cause for divorce! Such faithfulness is generally repaid by other treatment than this. But let us have the letter. Do not let this rest upon my word merely when so good proof exists. If Mr. Tilton prepares a 'true story and permits it to be 'stolen' let it be a 'true one,' not a partly true one, but a wholly true one—a half-truth always being a lie.

Commenting upon the *Thunderbolt's* account of how Beecher obtained his vindication from Mrs. Tilton, Mrs. Woodhull says:—

"Here we have as tangled a web as was ever unraveled. But does it explain away the original statement upon these facts? Read both carefully and then consider the following which I purposely omitted stating at the time, as I had no desire to introduce Mr. Beecher to the public, in any light other than was necessary for my purpose. But the above is given to the public, as will be believed, by Mr. Tilton's consent. and I am therefore justified in saying that what is here called his 'true story' differs in some material points from the story he told me, which was this:

"He said after he had learned of the facts, and while Mrs. Tilton was still dangerously ill from the premature birth of a child induced by his treatment, that he met Mr. Beecher at Frank Moulton's and there confronted him; that they endeavored to compel Mr. Beecher to terms, and that the interview was suddenly terminated by Mr. Beecher begging to be excused for a few moments until he could consult a friend. This was granted. He left them, returning in an hour or so, his manner entirely changed. His suing for mercy was turned into defiance. He simply rang the door bell and said; 'Gentlemen. I do not see fit to prolong this interview; I have got my vindication in my pocket,' and turned upon his heel and incontinently left.

"He said both he and Frank were utterly astonished at the conduct of Mr. Beecher, but it was fully explained when he returned to his home, where Mrs. Tilton, in deep distress, stated that Mr. Beecher had been there, and that she had signed some paper she scarcely knew what, but she was afraid it was something that might do harm. It was then that Mr. Moulton went to Mr. Beecher, and in the manner I have already described, demanded the document. No such rendition as the one given in the 'true story' was ever given to me either by Mr. Moulton or Mr. Tilton, and it is entirely inconsistent with his conduct toward Mrs. Tilton, and his grief and rage before me, and especially his conduct when he took me to ride to the grave where was buried, as he said, the fruits of Mr. Beecher's intimacy with his wife, at which time sitting on the Battle Hill Monument, he went anew over the whole story, including the stamping of the wedding ring into the soil of the grave. It is also utterly inconsistent with the sentiment of the poem in which is 'She, too, false like the rest.' And what was the great grief that caused him to walk the streets of Brooklyn the whole night inconsolable, as he has done night upon night either alone or with Mr. Moulton; and his constantly expressed desire 'to die as he had nothing to live for in this world?' The purported faithfulness of Mrs. Tilton in saving Mr. Beecher from becoming an adulterer ought to have made Mr. Tilton extremely happy in her possession. Or was he distracted because she did resist the persuasions of Mr. Beecher? But I have no desire at this time to call attention to the other discrepancies between Mr. Tilton's statements to me and his 'true story,' except to say that my statement stands, made by me as I received it, fact after fact from Mr. Tilton himself, most of which were also confirmed by the several witnesses whom I have mentioned. Had Mr. Tilton never told the same story to others than to me, I might feel called upon to go into a detailed proof of the whole matter; but since he has so repeated it to a half dozen persons whom I know, I do not think it necessary to refute his later and amended statement. The public will place it side by side with mine, and give due weight to the fact that the amended statement was prepared under the bias of an emergency which, perhaps, he did not contemplate when he made the former and unbiased statement to me and Elizabeth Cady Stanton, Col. Mix and others; although I ought to say that Mr. Tilton always gave me to understand that he should be glad when the matter was out, but that he should not want to be the one to first move in it.

Next Mrs. W. reviews the manner in which she made Theodore's acquaintance and says:—

"Mr. Tilton did not meet me accidentally in company with a mutual friend, but he came to my office with Stephen Pearl Andrews and was introduced to me, and this was the only time I ever saw him previous to that when he called with the *World.* To others he has said that upon that occasion I sent for him to come to see me. In his 'true story' he has neglected to do this, and he does so because he knows it is not true. I neither sent for him nor thrust the *World* before him when he did come. He came of his own accord with the article in question from the *World,* and asked me: 'Whom do you mean by that?' But the idea that an exaggerated rumor that had been travelling about for a year or two, which he could have instantly corrected if false, but which he did not even attempt to do, might become very dangerous in my hands, would be preposterous if it were not ridiculous. I do not think any logical mind can read this part of the 'true story' and not conclude, if it be true, that there is still another true story which he at least has not told, and that the magnified proportion of the campaign which was planned to capture me is only to be believed upon the theory that what I knew, which it was necessary should be kept quiet, was not exaggerated rumors merely.

"It must be remembered that this occurred in the spring of 1871, soon after the May Convention in Apollo Hall. It will also be seen by reference to the 'true story,' that this imbroglio with Mrs. Tilton began 'in the fall of 1870;' that it was 'six weeks' thereafter that Mr. Tilton explained the matter

5

to Mr. Bowen, after which the other facts occurred. But it was 'eight months after the commencement of the Beecher-Tilton differences' that Mr. Beecher visited Mrs. Tilton and got the letter from her. Now this would carry the time forward at least to August 1871, and yet I am found possessed of 'exaggerated rumors' regarding it in May of the same year, before they happened, which 'had already been travelling about for a year or two.' Figures are dangerous things with which to attempt a lie, because they always mean definite things and the same things to all people. In constructing a 'true story,' Mr. Tilton should have made more careful use of such a dangerous agent. Of course he presumes that he can place his own word in opposition to mine, and be believed; but he is not egotist enough to imagine he can arrange figures to suit himself, and be able to palm them off as correct when any one is liable to prove them. The failure to keep his time correctly, to my mind, will invalidate his 'true story' to no inconsiderable extent, in the minds even of those who may wish to accept and believe his false one. Mr. Clark ought to have been clear enough to have detected this discrepancy in the 'True' Statement."

"'On statements furnished by Mrs. Woodhull and Colonel Blood, Mr. Tilton finally made the last bold stroke to win the undying gratitude of 44 Broad street by giving his name and the literary finish of his pen to the "Biography of Victoria C. Woodhull." He was mistaken, he now thinks, in that person. With the Woodhull "gratitude" is nothing, "principle" everything; and principle in her case, as in Vanderbilt's, is to "carry a point." Mr. Tilton had a terrible warning of this phase of her character, when some of his lady acquaintances and special friends deemed it necessary, in the early part of 1872, to disown Mrs. Woodhull in the arena of Woman's Rights on account of her social doctrines. The Woodhull instantly flanked the movement by sending the ladies printed slips of their own private histories (in an article called "Tit for Tat,") declaring that if they should disgrace her for teaching 'social freedom,' she would print the article in her *Weekly*, and they should sink with her for practicing the theory.'

"I scarcely know," says Mrs. Woodhull "in what manner justly to characterize the misconstruction contained in the above paragraph. To properly show all the circumstances involved would require an entire paper, which is impossible here, but as it refers to circumstances that have been variously and widely commented on, and in a manner most prejudicial to me, I feel that I ought not to pass them without the notice they deserve.

"Mr. Tilton, upon several public occasions, long before my publication of the scandal, regretted that he had written my biography, in a manner and with explanations that perhaps ought at the time to have received notice. The statement here, however, is very guarded, compared with some others he has made. Just previous to the writing of that biography. The Victoria League had been formed, and it was found necessary to put some authoritative statement before the world regarding my past life in the form of an autobiography. I put Col. Blood in possession of the material, and requested him to arrange it for me. While he was doing this, Mr. Tilton came forward with the proposition that this must be his work, and he insisted so strenuously on performing it that I consented, and he did it. But he did not take the manuscript prepared by Col. Blood as his only authority. All the important or seemingly extravagant statements he took special pains to verify by other authority, while all the 'finish,' and that which upon its face is his own, and which really gives it all its importance, was the result of his own observation and was his own judgment. He may, for aught I know, have written that biography for some motive unknown to me; but it is absurd to pretend that it was to keep me from publishing the scandal, the basis for the whole of which, as I have already shown according to his figures, did not at that time exist.

"But what, as early as the Cincinnati Convention, had occurred to cause him to change his judgement of me? He had found me a 'truthful person,' and one with whom he was proud to be known or connected. Something must have compelled a change. He has stated on some occasions that it was the 'Tit for Tat' above referred to. What was that article? I will state just what it was, and thus at one and the same time correct the erroneous version given above, and show that it was not the cause of the breach between Mr. Tilton and me. A number of women, all of whom belonged to 'one set,' had for two years taken every occasion to let their long and loose tongues wag in defaming me. I determined to stop it. I grouped them together in an article which I had put in type, sending a proof of it to each of the persons involved. In the next issue of the *Weekly* I wrote an editorial, in which I faithfully promised them if the blackguarding of me did not cease I should publish the article.

"Not one of these, however, was 'some of his lady acquaintances and special friends,' who disowned me 'in the arena of Woman's Rights' 'on account of my social theories,' since none of them had ever taken any part with the wing of suffragists in which I labored. Nor was it because they disowned me as a suffragist that I prepared the article, as Mr. Tilton's 'true story relates? And nobody knows this better than Mr. Tilton himself. He knows it was because I was constantly belied by them as to what Free Love meant to me in practice. The editorial to which I refer sufficiently explains this, and it was not misunderstood by any of them at whom it was written. I have had no occasion to publish it."

"'This generalship may be defended by the old proverb that "anything is fair in love and war;" but such a blow "under the belt" was severely rebuked by Mrs. Stanton, and was regarded with reasonable terror by Mr. Tilton. He now became fully conscious of Mrs. Woodhull's capacity of destruction, and retired completely from her circle. The impending "crack of doom" was not to be hushed up with "gratitude." Mr. Tilton had himself confided the substance of his "true story" to Mrs. Woodhull, and knew that so much of his fate was in her hands. Still, he affirms that he was astonished beyond measure when she at last magnified it into the unearthly proportions of the Beecher-Tilton Scandal.'

"What does Mr. Tilton mean," asks Mrs. W., "when he says, 'I was severely rebuked by Mrs. Stanton?' I have Mrs. Stanton's letter to me regarding it; but when he says it in the form of a rebuke he only again wilfully perverts it. I never received a kinder note from Mrs. Stanton than that one, and I therefore hurl this utter disregard for truth in his teeth as another evidence that he has 'a constitutional disregard for truth which is ever showing itself when an opposite course would serve him better.

"Now, as to the 'terror' it inspired in Mr. Tilton, and 'the terrible warning' it was to him, and his 'retiring completely from her circle,' I am perfectly conscious that he was terrified by it, since he came with it to me, and said Laura Curtis Bullard had just left his office, having come there with the article which he held in his hand. He said, 'Strike out this portion,' pointing to a part of it, 'and I will help you kill the rest.' But he played none of the 'heroics' with which he has been in the habit of relating this interview, which he says occurred in his office instead of mine—only another evidence of his constitutional defect. Theodore Tilton never attempted heroics with me but once, and he found they did not have the desired effect and he at once and forever abandoned their use; but he has become so accustomed to them when others are involved, that when I am not present he forgets himself and assumes them in things which involved me.

"'He had become fully conscious of Mrs. Woodhull's capacity for destruction and retired completely from her circle, and this he presents as the cause of the breach between us to which I refer in the opening of this case. But before proceeding to perform a disagreeable task, I must premise by saying I had hoped that selfish personal considerations on the part of Mr. Tilton, if no higher motive, would have for ever saved me from the necessity of doing this; but since he seems to court distinction, let him have it to his heart's content.'

"I therefore state, as emphatically as I can, that it was not 'Tit for Tat' that caused him to 'retire from her circle.' At the time he came to me with that article I had not seen him for six weeks, and I should not have seen him then had it not been for 'reasonable terror' that something regarding a particular friend of his which it contained was going to be made public.' But he did call quite frequently after that, during the interval until the Cincinnati Convention. The day before he left to attend that Convention he called upon me for the last time.

'He said he was 'going to the Convention to report it for the *Tribune*.'

"I said, "Theodore you are lying again. You are going to Cincinnati to nominate Mr. Greeley, and I see, clairvoyantly, a coffin following you, in which you will be responsible for putting him, because it will result in his death.'

"He sat looking and listening to me, and for a long time never said a word; but finally, with a sad tenderness I shall never forget, rose and left me, and I have never spoken with him since. Up to that time he had never even hinted that he regretted his associations with me; but, on the contrary, always expressed a deep satisfaction regarding it, the reasons for which I have no desire to make public, unless compelled, when I shall not hesitate to do so to the fullest extent.

"But to return to the time prior to the 'Tit for Tat' article. A goodly time before that I was forced to the conclusion, in spite of all his efforts in behalf of reform, that his inspirations and mine were entirely dissimilar. I was absolutely absorbed in reform projects, and was indifferent to any and all who were not the same; and I could no longer afford to be annoyed in the manner in which I was annoyed by him. As he would not accept a verbal communication from me as meaning anything, I was finally compelled deliberately to write a formal letter, which I know was delivered to him, and a copy of which I now have before me, instructing him that his visits to me, both at my house and office, must be discontinued, plainly stating the reasons for so doing. They were not for any want of esteem and kind regard, because I had a regard amounting almost to affection for him. Besides, I had been his teacher in the principles of the new social dispensation, and I found elements in him that I was hopeful might make him the hero of that dispensation. That hope I never finally abandoned until a few days after the appearance of his letter to 'my complaining friend.' On Christmas day last I wrote him a final appeal, endeavoring to rouse him to a sense of what he was losing, and to stimulate him, even in that late moment, to come forward and be the hero:—

"'CHRISTMAS DAY, NEW YORK CITY, 1872.

"'THEODORE:—The spirit saith unto me, "Write:" "And the truth shall make you free,"—while anything less than that will add to the bondage of the present.

"'I told you, a year ago, that within six months you would fall away from me. "By all that's good, never!" you replied. Nevertheless the fall came!

"'I told you that you were going to lead your friend to his grave; you thought it would be to the Presidential chair. He lies buried—a victim to the ill-starred movement led off by you.

"'You became a champion of advanced freedom in your support of me; and your name was on the lips and treasured in the heart of every Radical in the world. You repudiated the course that had won this love, and neither Radical nor Conservative stands by you.

"'And now I say: There is a single course of redemption left you; and for your own sake I pray you heed it. Accept the situation. Stand by principle, and be not affrighted by public opinion.

"'You have the most glorious opportunity ever vouchsafed to man. Strike the hypocrite (if you will) the blow you have at your service; but put your loving, protecting arm about the angel whom he deceived. Dare to defend her freedom, and stand by her, not to the death, but to the new life.

"'Think not to gain what you desire, by catering to the hypocrisy, the poltroonery, the cowardice of the present; but strike for the glorious and redeemed souls of the near future, and become their hero. VICTORIA.

"Since then I am grieved to confess I have believed him lost, lost to the cause, lost to himself, and lost to all sense of honor and truth. I believed firmly that he would come forward as he had so often said he would, when the time should arrive, and stand by the cause. He knew that the statement of November 2d was to be published, and that I only wanted to receive the command of him, whom I serve, to publish it. Well do I remember an evening when he and I were discussing this very subject, that Col. Blood turned from the desk at which he was writing, and said:

"'Theodore, do you think you will have the courage to stand in the gap with us when that time shall come?'

"He replied with the most extraordinary asservations in the affirmative; and when the whole history of the incipiency of this scandal shall come to be known, as it soon will, if justice cannot be forced without it, I fear that the once glorious spirit of Theodore Tilton will set in the mud. Nobody, not even those who are now apparently his best friends, will mourn for him more sincerely than I shall; and whatever they may pretend to him now, not one of them more deeply regrets his position than I do, and none would do more to save him than I would do, short of the sacrifice of truth, honor and justice. And in his soul Theodore Tilton knows this to-day; but he also knows that my sense of outraged justice could not be swerved to save my own life; and here I again say, there is still an avenue of escape for him. He knows what it is, but he will not avail himself of it. 'Whom the gods would destroy they first make mad.' Theodore Tilton rests under their ban. I know whereof I speak when I say that his affirmations 'that he was astonished beyond measure' when the scandal appeared, were of the same unapproachable acting, in which long practice has made him perfect, with which he received the announcement that the *Thunderbolt* had appeared; and the inspiration in both instances was the same—knowledge and expectation. Mr. Tilton did confide all the details of the Beecher-Bowen-Proctor Scandal to me, besides a dozen others equally astonishing and confounding; but those that I obtained from him in this way I have not used in my war upon social rottenness, neither shall I unless compelled; but what I have used I was not indebted to his confidence for, since I wrung it from him, perhaps not so skillfully as he did the Bowen Scandal from the lady involved, nevertheless with sufficient adroitness to become fully possessed of it without being under any obligations to not disclose it.

"Mr. Tilton having disclosed to me, 'knew so much of his fate was in her hands.' Mr. Tilton could not have considered the force of those few words, otherwise he never would have used them. If his 'true story' is really a true one, and the only true one, what had I to do with fate to him? How could I possibly have been able to do him harm by any use which I might make of the so-called facts of that story? It is one of the most difficult of *roles* to maintain to endeavor to tell a consistent stream of lies about any grave thing. A lie once told needs continual lies to sustain it; and people forget lies, and neglect to always tell the same one. The truth will sometimes slip out unwittingly. This instance is a singularly forcible illustration. My possession of the really true story he might consistently have considered as so much of his fate in my hands; but with his true story only he should have said so much of Mr. Beecher's fate in my hands. I have no doubt every person will at once perceive this. And with this I may close the analysis of the matter very nearly in the language of Mr. Clark with which he closes the presentation of his *resume* of the 'true story:'

"Such is a careful summary of that 'true story' which Theodore Tilton said he should try to keep within his own heart.

"Changed, however, in this wise:

"[Such is the result of a hasty analysis of the whole story which, if Theodore Tilton did not desire made public, he should from the outset, have confined within his breast.]

"'As far as Mr. Beecher is concerned, it will instantly be seen that his virtue, at best, is not always the inclination of his own will. If Mrs. Woodhull has misrepresented him, and Mr.

Tilton has turned her falsehood into truth, still it was only through Beecher's failure in carrying out an immoral purpose that Mrs. Woodhull's story is not correct. A correspondent of the Cincinnati *Commercial*—who has evidently been admitted into some of the secrets of Tilton's foolscap volume, and at the same time employed to whitewash Beecher—declares that the 'true story' embraces 'a period of ten years,' implicates 'persons who have not publicly figured in it' and 'elucidates some things not likely to be known till the Day of Judgment."

"'These stilted phrases have some foundation, though it would not be difficult for so plain a man as myself to bring that "Day of Judgment" close to hand, if necessary. I have no wish, however, to drag any cringing mortal before the public in mere wantonness—especially any woman. I regard Henry C. Bowen as Beecher's chief "supe" and conspirator, in combining with the wretched Jesuit of Protestantism, Anthony J. Comstock, to violate American liberty. From my position, Bowen deserves no mercy beyond the bare truth. In regard to other persons, I think the public have no special interest in them, with one exception.'

"Now here the cause, says Mrs. W., which makes the case hang fire in Brooklyn, is at last reached. Clark could, if he saw fit, bring the day of judgment close to hand, but he has no wish to drag a cringing woman before the public. Had it been my desire, as the act has been generally interpreted, to destroy the usefulness of Beecher and to drive him from Plymouth Church, I could have made such use of the material in my possession as to have accomplished it. He could not have escaped under having me prosecuted on an impossible charge of obscenity. He would either have had to throw himself upon the church and confessed or prosecuted me for libel, which I know very well he would never attempt to do so long as three witnesses now living should live. But such was not any part of my motives, and I only used such facts as I had good reasons for believing would not be very objectionable to any of the parties involved, Beecher alone excepted. And I know that, should he be compelled, as he would have been, had

Tilton acted well his part, to have acknowledged the whole matter, that Plymouth Church would be compelled to sustain or fall with him. Beecher did not hesitate to say that he knew of fifty members of his congregation who would stand by him in any event.

"But the suppression policy cannot succeed. Everything will eventually be made public. It has gone too far. All the facts are in possession of too many persons, some of whom, I think, do wish to kill Beecher, and who will not hesitate to drag even a 'cringing woman' before the public to do it. The only method of salvation, as I frankly informed Beecher, was to come at once to the front and say: 'Well this is true, and now what are you going to do about it?'

"But I frankly confess that I believe the ultimate fate of the now distressed woman, who every hour of her life stands in mortal dread of the facts coming before the public, would be much better if she were herself to come out and solve this whole matter. It will come some time, and the indications now are that it is not far off. There should be no more real disgrace attached to her about the affair, than there should be had she personally been injured in some other manner. No honest person could condemn her for any part she was compelled to play, and for the judgment of the dishonest none should trouble themselves. Therefore, the wise part is to at once ventilate this whole affair before its attempted suppression drags a half dozen other families into its yawning vortex.

"'As I view the whole case, in all its bearings, I deem it right to say that Tilton claims that he has been violently hated by his wife's mother, Mrs. Morris—a lady who is definitely represented to me as insane.

"'This poor lady is said to have circulated, for many years, the most damaging reports against the character of her daughter, and against Beecher and Tilton. The earliest scandals concerning Mrs. Tilton and the Plymouth pastor are said to have proceeded from her. I must add, also, that a long time ago there were rumors, among the special acquaintances of the parties, that Mrs. Tilton was subject to the hallucination that some of Beecher's children were those of her own household (But Tilton's narrative affords me no hint of this rumor.)

"I think it was very unwise in Tilton to attempt to drag his mother-in-law into the controversy. But what must be said of the 'rumors' among the special acquaintances of the parties about Mrs. Tilton's 'hallucination?' Those strange rumors remind me at once of the finding of Moses in the bulrushes of the Nile, and of the immaculate conception of Jesus; and I have no doubt if Tilton's 'true story' stands, that this last hallucination will pass into history and be accounted by the future as an equally marvelous example of the special providences of the God of the Christians.

"But this hallucination, as I happen very well to know, did not extend to Tilton's brain, but in him it rather assumed the form of madness, venting itself in violence, especially upon the picture of one of the persons involved in the hallucination. Whatever milder forms it may now have assumed in him, I fear its former violence may cast as serious doubts upon the future divinity of this last manifestation as the skeptics of to-day throw around that of eighteen centuries ago.

"What, however, must be the judgment of the future should it come to know that this paper, this *Thunderbolt*, was prepared in the rooms of the *Golden Age*, and when it shall come to be known that the letter of 'my complaining friend,' which called out the reply contained in the *Thunderbolt*, was actually written by the dictation of Theodore Tilton, and that at the time it was written he was preparing the way to publish in the *Golden Age* the whole of the 'true story.' I do not think I overstate it when I say that no such combination of hypocrisy, duplicity, falsehood and social irregularities ever existed as the future will show the Beecher-Tilton-Bowen-Proctor Scandal to have been: and I am ready to stake my future upon its being so.

"'And now what conclusion is to be drawn from Tilton's "thunderbolt" on one hand and Mrs. Woodhull's vaunted "bombshell" on the other? I am sorry to say I have little confidence in the strict veracity of either account.'

"But Clark, apparently unwittingly, has let the cat out of the bag, since does he not say, 'Tilton's *Thunderbolt?* That is sufficient. It cannot be Clark's *Thunderbolt* if it be Tilton's; and, moreover, does he not say that he has very little confidence in the strict veracity of it? And if he has as little in my bombshell, I can afford to wait yet a little longer. I know the truth will come out uppermost, and I court its coming. Almost everybody else who is concerned in the affair seems to be using the most superhuman exertions to 'squelch' the whole thing. So much, at all events, would appear at present to stand in my favor; and those who have seen fit to daub me all over with contemptous epithets, will have more cause to be ashamed of them in the future than I have now. I can afford to stand under the implication of having 'belied Mrs. Davis,' and of having 'warped and stuffed out' Mrs. Stanton, because I know that

> "'Ever the right comes uppermost,
> And ever is justice done."

Of that part of the *Thunderbolt* devoted to Mrs. Woodhull, this gifted, but singular woman says:—

"Were it not for a single point, I should pass without notice 'The fall of the *Thunderbolt* on Woodhull herself,' and as that is the special one that—more than all others—causes me to doubt the thorough honor and consistency of Mr. Clark, I will touch it first, although in order of succession it should be last. He says: 'Its proprietors have lately had the kindness to publish my circular without request or leave. Its advertisements are gratuitous blinds.' Mr. Clark must surely have forgotten himself to have made this fling at me, to which I make bold to say, the most debauched Bohemian in New York would not have stooped. Even had I published his circular without request or leave, he ought, as a gentleman, to have accepted it as a journalistic courtesy, and refrained from dragging it into this controversy. Besides, what has it to do with the question at issue? Does that have any bearing upon the truth or falsity of the Scandal? I confess I cannot see that it does. My 'ignorance' may, however, prevent me from seeing it. What business had Mr. Clark to do this thing? But it happens that I did not publish his circular without request or leave. Mr. Clark, in a letter to me, sent a dozen of his circulars, and in the letter requested me to notice their contents. Instead, however, of writing any notice, I ordered the circular, or parts of it, published. It may barely be possible that this may have slipped his memory; but on no other ground can I forgive so outrageous a breach of courtesy.

"And, pray, what have my 'other moods' to do with the effect of 'The *Thunderbolt* upon Woodhull;' and what, pray, upon the truth or falsity of the Scandal, which Mr. Clark has taken specific pains to assert, 'as having honestly sought nothing but truth in scrutinizing the Beecher-Tilton Scandal?' Suppose I am 'out of my head;' that I am an enthusiast;' that I see 'angels' or 'demons;' that 'I swagger like a pirate,' and 'scold like a drab,' what has all that to do with arriving at the truth of the Scandal? Can Mr. Clark inform me? Perhaps he may be cajoled into furnishing me the facts in his possession about this swaggering and scolding. If he can, I will make all possible haste to publish them. Come, Mr. Clark, you have said this; now send on the facts, because I am anxious to be well informed regarding myself upon these points as you seem to be.

"And why does he seek to belittle me by saying I am 'ignorant,' that I never write my 'great speeches' or 'stirring editorials? How can he know all this? The resort to this contemptible meanness by my enemies to endeavor to injure me in the esteem of those who can only know me by repute, is the best possible evidence that they can find no better means by which to attempt it. For two years I have stood before the world, almost alone, as the pronounced advocate of social freedom, and I have been the butt of ridicule, of abuse and of censure from almost everybody who writes for the public press, and now, at this late day, when, still almost alone, I am fighting the battle of a free press and free speech against the combined powers of state and church, it was entirely uncalled for on the part of Mr. Clark to enter the arena, and attempt to destroy any part of my strength, and to stab me in the back in the house of my friends. Perhaps this act of unkindness may be the very one to make it impossible to withstand the immense odds pitted against me, and I go a martyr to the Infernalism of the Christianity of the nineteenth century. But I do not intend that it shall accomplish this. I intend that Mr. Clark's effort to aid the enemies of reform in their crusade against it in my person shall fall dead upon the ears and hearts of every lover of freedom in the country. Had I been strong financially, and backed up by powerful friends; had I been a man even lacking these, the reformatory world might have forgiven Mr. Clark this ungenerous aid to the enemy; but lacking all these, having to struggle personally against all sorts of obstacles, and with few friends who have the moral courage to stand pronouncedly and boldly with me, it was a most cowardly attack, and I am sorry, for Mr. Clark's sake, that the bitterness of Theodore Tilton or of any body else should have been so potent with him as to induce him to stoop so ungenerously; and so on to the end, through all the rest of his presentation of me personally; but I refrain from following him. The judgment of the reformers of the world will, however, do so, and it will be inexorable, since they will come, sooner or later, to know that Mrs. Woodhull is not 'only a tremendous horn that Col. Blood is now blowing in front of Jericho,' but that she, of all persons, insists on blowing her own horn."

Mrs. Woodhull having noted, as above some of the "misrepresentations," as she styles them, of the *Thunderbolt*, thus sums up her case:—

SUMMING UP.

"It is desirable that a thorough summing up of the whole case should be made, a careful and just review of all that has transpired regarding it up to the present time, so that a just judgment of it, as it stands to-day, may be arrived at. This, however, is a task that time makes it impossible for me to perform to present in this week's issue of the *Weekly*.

"But next week I shall do this. I shall go back to the starting point of this scandal to fasten its source were it belongs. I shall trace it from that source through all its ramifications up to date. I shall compare the various statements and facts which appeared previously to November 2nd with those that have been put forth since, and endeavor to find a solution for their discrepancies. And I think I am not presuming too greatly to say, that if any now have doubts as to the substantial truth of all that I said November 2nd, they will be removed when the reviews shall have been read.

"This will be done, however, with no view to the conviction if it must be so regarded, of Mrs. Tilton. I should have been glad never to have mentioned her name in the affair, but some one of the several I had at command had to be used. It was useless simply to charge Mr. Beecher with an offense. It was necessary to give the specifications upon which the charge was founded. I am glad, however, that in all the discussion that has grown out of it, her name has been seldom mentioned, and I have yet to hear her condemnation from the lips of any one.

"Had Mr. Tilton, or his friends for him, been satisfied to let the matter rest there, I should never have written another word as to the truth or falsity of the charge, so far as Mrs. Tilton is concerned. I was perfectly satisfied to have accomplished what I aimed at—to establish the fact that Henry Ward Beecher, notwithstanding his professions, is at heart and in practice just as much a Free Lover as I am; and that

Plymouth Church is a Free Love Church, and ought to stand, as it will have ultimately to do, side by side with me in the advocacy of social freedom. Of this, since the appearance of the *Thunderbolt,* no sensible person can entertain a doubt. Mr. Beecher stands before the world as one who believes it his right as an individual to administer his social relations as pleases himself, and Plymouth Church as upholding him. This was all I desired, and the attainment of it has been made much sooner than I had any hope it would be.

"But they have made the attempt to cast me into the lie, and this my own sense of right compels me to repel, and I shall do it with all the ability I can command in the use of facts already before the public; but as I have often said before, I shall not be betrayed into a full showing of my case unless the course against me shall be such as to force me to it; and I repeat, if that time ever come, there will be 'good reason to think the last trump has sounded, for I shall tell the whole truth though the heavens do fall, and though, with the rest, I go down in the general ruin.' And those who would be involved in it know me too well to even imagine I will not keep my word to the very letter.

"VICTORIA C. WOODHULL."

CHAPTER IV.

THE DEVELOPMENTS DURING THE SUMMER AND FALL OF 1873—PLYMOUTH CHURCH CHARGES MR. TILTON WITH SLANDERING MR. BEECHER — MR. TILTON'S DEFENCE SUMMARIZED — THE ACTION OF THE CHURCH — MR. BEECHER'S DECLARATION THAT HE HAD NO COMPLAINT TO MAKE AGAINST MR. TILTON—ACTION OF THE SISTER CHURCHES THROUGH REV. DRS. STORRS AND BUDINGTON — THE CORRESPONDENCE BETWEEN THEM AND MR. BEECHER, THAT LED TO THE ASSEMBLING OF THE CONGREGATIONAL COUNCIL.

DURING the summer of 1873, the damaging stories of the Woodhull and Claflin women traveled rapidly, until the "scandal" became a reproach to the Church and its pastor, and an annoyance to all Congregational Churches of the country. Many damaging additions were made to the original charges, and when there was surreptitiously published, what is known as the "Tripartite Covenant," signed by Beecher, Bowen and Tilton, which will appear in full further on, the interest in the case was increased. The author does not deem it essential to dwell at length upon the action of Plymouth Church, in October of that year. Suffice it to say that charges were preferred by a member against Theodore Tilton, to discipline him for slandering the pastor of the church, of which it was supposed he was still a member. Mr. Tilton appeared, and offered to answer personally to Mr.

PLYMOUTH CHURCH, ORANGE STREET BROOKLYN.

Beecher for any wrong he had done him. Mr. Beecher openly declared before the Church authorities that he had no complaint to make against Mr. Tilton. The latter gentleman declared that he had not for some time considered himself a member, having voluntarily withdrawn from attendance upon the services of the pastor; yet, he was willing to waive this point, and answer any charge of slandering Mr. Beecher. Mr. Beecher, in the meantime, had caused to be published in the Brooklyn *Eagle*, the first denial of the allegations made :—

To the Editor of the Brooklyn Eagle :

Sir,—In a long and active life in Brooklyn it has rarely happened that the Eagle and myself have been in accord on questions of common concern to our fellow-citizens. I am for this reason compelled to acknowledge the unsolicited confidence and regard of which the columns of the Eagle of late bear testimony. I have just returned to the city, to learn that application has been made to Mrs. Victoria Woodhull for letters of mine supposed to contain information respecting certain infamous stories against me. I have no objection to have the Eagle state in any way it deems fit, that Mrs. Woodhull or any other person or persons who may have letters of mine in their possession, have my cordial consent to publish them. In this connection, and at this time, I will only add that the stories and rumors which have for some time past been circulated about me are untrue, and I stated them in general and in particular as utterly untrue.

Respectfully,

HENRY WARD BEECHER.

The result of this action of the church, briefly stated, was the dropping of Mr. Tilton's name from the rolls and the declaration by the church that a member could at any time voluntarily sever his connection from the Society, and as Mr. Tilton had done so, and was no longer a member of the Plymouth Society, he could not be placed on trial for slander, and, therefore, the church had no jurisdiction in the matter. This course, on the part of the church, caused much concern to sister churches, and especially to Rev. Drs. Budington and Storrs. It has been charged against these distinguished divines that their subsequent action in corresponding with Plymouth Church, and calling a council of all the churches, was dictated by a desire to tear Mr. Beecher down from the high position he had attained in Congregationalism, and get rid of a rival whose popularity they envied. The author must confess that he can find no justification for this charge, or the subsequent one, that Rev. Dr. Bacon was prompted from similar motives to make the attacks in his New Haven address, and *his* articles in the *Independent* upon Mr. Tilton, and thus secure the publication of Tilton's story in self defence.

But to return to the record of the events in the order in which they presented themselves to the public. This action of Plymouth Church regarding Mr. Tilton occurred in October. In the following January, Drs. Storrs and Budington held a private conference with Mr. Beecher, which was thought at the time to be of great importance, and likely to result in a settlement of the questions at issue, but which closed with a lively and argumentative correspondence, settling nothing, and leaving affairs in a more hopeless condition than before. The following are the essential parts of that correspondence, minor details being omitted:—

The first is a letter from Drs. Storrs and Budington to Mr. Beecher:

BROOKLYN, Jan. 7, 1874.

REV. H. W. BEECHER:—Two principles are, in our view, essential to Congregationalism. The first is, that the local church is a brotherhood of believers, confessing Christ, in common, as their Supreme Lord and Savior, and covenanting not only to worship together, but to watch over each other in the divine life and service. It follows, then, according to our view, that as one does not enter such a brotherhood by his own act alone, but also by the consent of the body, discerning in him the temper of Christ, so neither does he leave it by his own act alone; but only as the brotherhood consents. It further follows, according to our view, that if one member of such a brotherhood is formally and publicly charged by another with grave offenses, directly impeaching his Christian character, such accusation must be considered, until it is ascertained either that he is innocent, and so may be retained with his honor vindicated, or that he is guilty, and so must, if possible, be reclaimed; and that if, in the latter case, he prove unrepentant, he must be excluded from the brotherhood, as not being a believer, and therefore not properly one of its members. The second principle is, that each local church, while properly and entirely independent in the management of its own affairs, so long as it maintains the evangelical faith, and this mutual watchfulness among its members, is still in responsible fellowship with other such churches; so that, if its faith should cease to be evangelical, or its assiduous care for the purity of its members should be given up, these churches may properly remonstrate with it; and if it should persist, may withdraw from it the fellowship which had been pledged and maintained only on these essential conditions. Both these principles appear to us Scriptural, Congregational, and indispensable to be maintained for the welfare of our churches, and for the honor of Christ. And both these principles have seemed to us to be overlooked and imperiled, in the recent action of Plymouth Church; the first, in its action in the case of discipline issued by it October 31, when a member appeared to us to be released, without trial or censure, in the face of grave accusations; the second, in the resolutions adopted by it December 5, affirming its entire independence of all other churches, in regard to its faith, order, and discipline. Our recent conversation with you has led us to infer that you do not regard these principles as denied by Plymouth Church, in its recent action; that, in your view, the difference between that church and other Congregational churches is largely, if not wholly, one of methods and means, instead of principles. Will you let us know your views more fully on these points?

To make the points specific:—Suppose a member of the Plymouth Church to have been absent from the communion for a year, while still residing in the city, and then to have been formally charged by a brother in the church with having led a licentious life during that year, and when thus accused, to plead his voluntary withdrawal from the communion bar of investigation, would it be according to the customary methods and policy of Plymouth Church to accept that plea, to suspend inquiry as to the facts, and to drop his name from the roll without censure? Suppose, further, if you will allow the supposition, that the church itself should omit from its Articles of

Faith that one which affirms the inspiration of the Scriptures, or that which declares the Divinity of our Lord, would it still, in its own judgment or in yours, be entitled to claim that the churches before in fellowship with it should make no remonstrance, but should continue in the fellowship, without reference to its action?

WM. IVES BUDINGTON.
R. S. STORRS.

In reply to this, after full consultation with Plymouth Church, Mr. Beecher wrote:—

POSITION OF PLYMOUTH CHURCH DEFINED.

LETTER OF HENRY WARD BEECHER.

Jan. 14, 1874.

MY DEAR BRETHREN: I heartily assent to the fact that one uniting with a church does so by his own voluntary act, and with the consent of the brotherhood; and that when, in his judgment, it is his duty to leave it, it should for the sake of good order, of courtesy, and Christian kindness, be done with the assent of the church. But, I should dissent from any such view of membership as implied or asserted that in joining a church one so surrenders his personal rights that he is not at liberty to withdraw from it unless the church gives him back the right to do so. No church owns its members. No covenant is scriptural or reasonable which is in the nature of a legal contract.

No word more happily expresses the idea of a church than that which you employ—brotherhood. The church is a peculiar form of family, only it has not a legal contract between its members as there is between husband and wife, nor legal relations such as exist between parents and children. It is a voluntary brotherhood for moral ends, in which the members are held by personal, affectionate, and sympathetic influences.

In fact, it may be said that if it is not general usage among Christian churches for members to leave upon their own proper judgment and liberty, yet it is so frequent as to show the practical recognition of the right. The Covenant of Plymouth Church contemplates such facts, and does not bind men absolutely, but "so long as in the providence of God you shall continue among us."

The fathers of Congregationalism were Englishmen, and though they cleared their minds of local prejudices in a wonderful manner by going back to scripture, yet the operation of scripture to loose them from bondage is seen chiefly in regard to those points which were in controversy with Rome and those which had been instruments of oppression from civil government. It was impossible but that they should reflect the opinions and customs of their age in other things. It was, and is, the custom-law of England that persons in public trusts cannot resign. No member of Parliament can resign his seat. A legal fiction has to be used to get him out. He accepts the office, say, of Steward of The Chiltern hundreds; as no member of Parliament can hold an office of profit and trust, this act voids his membership in Parliament. Sheriffs, constables, once elected, must serve. And, in general, the English custom is, once a member always a member, except by some well-defined process. The power of an individual to leave office or position in corporate bodies was un-English. In America the very reverse doctrine and custom is universally established, and very important decisions have been rendered by our courts.

As there is absolutely no teaching in Scripture on the right of a church-member to leave a local church, even though it does not consent, either from another, or to disjoin himself from all churches, no doctrine can be insisted upon authoritatively by Congregational churches on this point.

I do not wish you to suppose that I advocate the common use of this ultimate right of the individual to exclude himself from the church. For social and moral reasons, on account of the true spirit of brotherhood, every one leaving a church should do it with respectful notice and assent. And, therefore, the ground taken by most Congregational writers of repute I should respect in practice. But if, in any extraordinary case, an individual member chooses to exercise his latent right, and goes forth into the world, or into another body, no church which professes to derive all its authority from Sacred Scriptures can make that act an offense; and no amount of consent of Congregational writers can forbid that which the Scriptures do not forbid, and which the laws of the land permit.

"The second inference which you deduce from your first principle is, 'That if one member of such a brotherhood is formally and publicly charged by another with grave offenses, directly impeaching his Christian character, such accusation must be considered until it is ascertained either that he is innocent, and so may be retained with his honor vindicated, or that he is guilty, and so must, if possible, be reclaimed; and that if, in the latter case, he prove unrepentant, he must be excluded from the brotherhood as not being a believer, and, therefore, not properly one of its members.'

"To this I would reply, that when charges have been made, and judicially entertained by the church against any recognized member of the church, and he shall then abandon the church for the sake of escaping investigation, it may be proper for the church, so far as is necessary, to vindicate its own good name, or for the relief of any who may have been wronged, to proceed with the case, and to declare its judgment. But to pursue such a one with pains and penalties, after his own withdrawal, would probably render all concerned actionable at law.'

"But if one has gone out from the church for years—has not attended its services—is known to have changed his religious views, and is known for years to have disavowed church membership, it is not the duty of the church, if charges should be made against such a one, to attempt to bring back under their jurisdiction, for the sake of trial, one whom, by long consent, they have treated as no longer a member. In Plymouth Church, express, and, as I think, wise provision is made to prevent the frequent occurrence of trials, which, in so large a membership, might naturally take place.' [The functions of the Examining Committee are here explained.]

"Any representation to you that proceedings against a member of Plymouth Church had been terminated by his withdrawal to escape investigation or withdrawal for any other reason from a recognized membership, while under judicial progress, is wide of the truth. The only fact out of which such a report could have arisen is that the Examining Committee, in investigating charges against persons long absent and long ceased to be recognized members, have reported that charges should not be entered upon with judicial process on account of the virtual non-membership of the parties.'

"The only point on which there seems likely to be a difference of principle is the inherent right of a man to leave a church when he regards it as his duty to do so. Practically, we agree. For obvious reasons the separation should be a mutual act. But at the bottom there lies a principal of individual right and liberty which no covenant should restrain and no church take away. In regard to fellowship I would say in general:

1. That I regard the fellowship of churches as highly important, and to be cherished, and to be developed by such a use of it as shall make each church feel the light and warmth of

love which God has kindled in every other. Fellowship is the interchange of love and sympathy and mutual service between neighboring churches, and it should exist among all churches, of whatever sect, but especially between those of the same faith and order. That this fellowship may develop itself in kindly suggestions, in affectionate advice, or even expostulation, I admit. For fellowship which virtually punishes, though the penalty be moral, is all the more oppressive on that very account, since in the progress of Christian civilization moral penalties are transcendently more painful, and if wrongly or unskillfully employed more oppressive, than any other punishment can be.

2. Whenever any church shall openly and avowedly change the essential conditions upon which it was publicly received into the fellowship of neighboring churches, it is their right, either by individual action or by council, to withdraw their fellowship. If any church shall, by flagrant neglect, make itself a cover for immorality, or shall exert a pernicious and immoral influence upon the community, or upon sister churches, they have a right to withdraw themselves from the contagion. Preceding disfellowship, in all such cases, there may be, and should be, such affectionate and reasonable inquiry as shall show that the evil is real—that the causes of it are within the control of the church, that the evil is not a transient evil, such as may befall any church, but is permanent. and tending to increase rather than diminish.

3. I make a distinction between a withdrawal of fellowship by the will of individual churches and the arraignment of a church, and virtually putting it upon trial before a council. There is no power on earth that can try a sovereign church. By whatever name it may be softened, and by whatever authorities justified, the denunciation or excommunication of a church by recommendation is in derogation of its local independence, and is without warrant in the Word of God. The attempt to bring churches to trial has never been productive of good. It is likely in every way to produce mischief. There was never such an occasion to employ councils and to withdraw fellowship upon their recommendation as in New-England during the Unitarian controversy. But there was never a council called. While, then, I heartily believe in the fellowship of churches, I am mindful that it was through the claims of fellowship that the churches of old learned to exercise domination, and that there is an inherent danger in the disciplinary exercise of fel-

lowship which should put every lover of the liberty of the churches upon his guard.

"You next proceed to say that, in your judgment, both of the principles which you lay down 'have seemed to us to be overlooked and imperiled in the recent action of Plymouth Church; the first in its action in the case of discipline, issued by it Oct. 31st, 1873, when a member appeared to us to be released without trial or censure, in the face of grave accusations; the second in the resolutions adopted by it Dec. 5th, 1873, affirming its entire independence of all other churches in regard to its faith, order and discipline.' In reply to the first statement, I would say that Plymouth Church never has taken the action alleged. It accepted a report of its Examining Committee, dismissing the case of one under charges, and dropping his name from the roll, on the ground that he was not and for years had not been a member of the Church, and was, therefore, not within its jurisdiction. This is simply a matter of fact. The person declared that he was not a member. The Church declared he was not a member. Is not the Church competent to determine its own membership? Does 'fellowship' allow a neighboring church to review and redetermine the action of a church in regard to a matter of fact?'

"In regard to the second point, viz: that 'resolutions were adopted by it (viz: Plymouth Church) affirming its entire independence of all other churches, in regard to its faith, order, and discipline,' you have not quoted the resolutions passed by us. You have quoted almost verbatim Rule 1 of Plymouth Manual, which was originally published in 1848. The substance of this rule was before the council which aided in organizing Plymouth Church, and the council which helped to install me as its pastor; on both of which councils Dr. Storrs took important parts. The original Rule in 1847 was this: 'This Church regards the Scriptures as the only infallible guide in matters of church order and discipline, and is therefore amenable to no other ecclesiastical body.'

"Within a year (1848) it took the form now in the Manual, and has kept it. I cannot see why, at this late day, you take exception to this rule of a quarter of a century's standing, as violating the principle of Fellowship. But if, through inadvertence, you quote the Manual, meaning, rather, to point attention to our resolutions explanatory of these words, will you explain wherein you think that these resolutions differ from the doctrine laid down by Dr. Dexter in his excellent work on

Congregationalism, quoted in the last answer of Plymouth Church to your letter?'

["Mr. Beecher then refers to the hypothetical cases, drawing these conclusions.] In short, I hold that a church should care for its erring members, and restore them if possible by moral influence; that when they are incorrigible they be dropped from the roll, if no crime or glaring sin be imputed to them; that if convicted of crime, they be expelled; that if they go out, meantime, of their own accord while under trial, that the church drop their name from the roll, with such other action as may in the circumstances seem needful for the vindication of the church, or of any of its members.'

"I would, in reply to the other case proposed, say, that when any church has essentially changed those conditions on which fellowship was originally extended, it is the right of the churches to withdraw from it, as it is undoubtedly their right by arguing, preaching, or writing, first to endeavor to convert them to sounder views. But experience has, thus far, taught that it is wise to do this by associated ecclesiastical action; the experience of the churches in Massachusetts with reference to the Unitarians having shown that the end can be quietly reached by each church acting for itself, thus escaping these liabilities to the usurpation of authority and the domination of the churches, which always attend large convocations of ministers, and the consciousness, on their part, that they represent and wield the moral convictions of large bodies of men. Ecclesiastical history reveals not a single instance of beneficial results from an attempt to discipline a church by associated ecclesiastical action. H. W. BEECHER.

This was not at all satisfactory to Rev. Drs. Storrs and Budington, who were believed to represent the sentiment of sister Congregational churches, and they replied as follows, suggesting the council that was subsequently held:—

BROOKLYN, N. Y., Jan. 26, 1874.

Rev. H. W. BEECHER:—On the subject of church-membership, you hold, as we understand you, that every member has the right to leave a church, at any time, for another church, or for the world; that the exercise of this right is not conditioned upon the consent of the church; that the covenant into which he entered, in joining the church, was only the expression of his then present intention and purpose; and that his separation from the church is completed with his own act or volition in retiring, the church having simply to drop his name, in accordance with his will. This seems to us a principle wholly unknown to Congregationalism, and contradicted by its history from the beginning; the admission of which would render impossible the administration of Christian and orderly discipline; the prevalence of which would absolutely dissolve the bands of church association.

We say we should be content with a deliverance upon these two questions; for what you say in your letter on the subject of fellowship seems to us so far just and comprehensive as to warrant the belief of a substantial accordance between us. We differ from you widely, it is true, in regard to special points connected with your expression of your views—as, for example, in regard to the argument which you derive from the action and experience of the churches in Massachusetts in the Unitarian controversy. But it is aside from the purposes of this correspondence to consider the history and results of that case and we refrain from giving the reasons why we think a council expedient when serious divergencies take place between our churches. You seem to us, however, to lay down the essential principle involved in the communion of churches where you say, "Whenever any church shall openly and avowedly change the essential conditions upon which it was publicly received into the fellowship of neighboring churches, it is their right, either by individual action, or by council, to withdraw their fellowship." Upon this we gladly unite, as well as upon what you say as regards the necessity of "affectionate and reasonable inquiries preceding disfellowship." As respects, therefore, this question of the independency or fellowship of the churches, we have only to ask if you will favor the introduction into your new church-manual of some declaration similar to the above quotation from your letter? The resolution adopted by your church, December 5th, seems to make a corporate declaration of this kind important and needful. This would leave only two subjects upon which we do not find in your letter any basis of agreement. Would you be willing, therefore, to use your influence with your church to unite with our churches in asking the advice of a council, mutually called, upon these two questions namely:

1. Does the order and usage of Congregational churches permit a member who has entered into public covenant with a church, to terminate his relations with that church, by his own

volition or act, so that no action on the part of the church is requisite to such termination of membership?

2. Was the action of Plymouth Church on the 31st October, 1873, in dropping a member against whom grave and specific charges had been formally presented, an action in accordance with the usages of Congregational churches, and with their understanding of the rule of Christian discipline?

WM. IVES BUDINGTON.
R. S. STORRS.

The above called forth from Mr. Beecher the following reply, showing his willingness for a council of the churches, but expressing the opinion that Plymouth Church would not assent to it.

BROOKLYN, Feb. 8, 1874.

MY DEAR BRETHREN:—I am gratified that you find in my letters so much that you approve. The kind tone of your reply leads me to hope that a basis of mutual agreement may be found. I proceed at once to the points which you have made. With only a single addition, I accept the first article to be submitted to a mutually called council (should our three churches conclude to call one). As it now reads it is, "Does the order and use of Congregational Churches permit a member who has entered into public covenant with a church, to terminate his relations with that church by his own volition or act, so that no action on the part of the church is requisite to such termination of membership?" I would suggest that the question read, "Does the Word of God, and the order and usage of Congregational Churches," etc. You are aware that I regard the right to withdraw on the part of an individual as a latent right, not ordinarily to be used, and like the right of self-defense, to be used only in extreme cases. I would therefore suggest that "in any case," be inserted, thus: "to terminate, in any case, his relations," etc.

"In regard to the second point: I would suggest that the thing aimed at be stated as a question of usage, and not as a historical question. If it can be put into a form which shall leave out the particular case of Plymouth Church, and be made general, I shall, for myself, be heartily glad to hear the opinions of a Council upon it. But as it stands, it would be very difficult to induce the Plymouth Church to assent to it. I would suggest something like the following: "May a Church according to the Word of God and the usages of the Congregational Churches, exercise its own discretion in dropping from its roll the name of one against whom serious charges are preferred, but who declares himself not to be a member of the Church; or must the Church, according to the Word of God and Congregational usage, go forward with the trial of charges, to a final issue.

I will mention two points in which we regard your internal economy as unwise, and which could be easily corrected by the insertion in the respective manuals of your Churches of some such rule as this:

1. That at every business meeting of the church a Chairman be chosen by the brethren.

2. That no action involving the interest of other churches shall be taken, except at a meeting publicly called from the pulpit on the Sunday preceding the meeting.

These changes, or some equivalent, would take away from the minds of our people the impression that you are attempting a legislative authority, and will bring our churches together in such amicable consultation as could not but restore the cordiality which once existed between us. In all this letter I have given you my own view and not that gathered by conference with the brethren of the church.

HENRY WARD BEECHER.

Despairing of settling the questions of church discipline involved in the correspondence, the Rev. Drs. Storrs and Budington closed the correspondence as follows:—

BROOKLYN, N. Y., Feb. 10, 1874.

The Rev. H. W. BEECHER—*Dear Brother*:—It was the aim of our last letter to reduce the points of difference between us to the minimum, and to meet you, as far as we could, without surrendering principles dear to us and, as we think, to all our churches. We are disappointed, consequently, to find that you cannot unite with us upon either of the three propositions submitted.

Your proposition that our churches should change their manuals in certain particulars, as an inducement to Plymouth Church to adopt your statement on the subject of fellowship between churches, concerns matters which have never been in discussion between us, and appears to us wholly irrelevant.

The matter of fellowship with other churches is a matter

directly concerning those churches. Plymouth Church has adopted a resolution designed expressly to declare its relations to other churches. You have interpreted this resolution in a sense materially different from its obvious import, as it appears to us. Inasmuch, however, as this is only a private statement of your personal opinion, it seemed to us legitimate, indeed necessary, to inquire if the Plymouth Church would accept and affirm the doctrine which you lay down? If not, or if it will do this only on some impossible conditions, then the expression of your personal views on the subject does not alter or affect the public attitude of your church toward ours and others.

We should feel constrained, consequently, to add a third question to the two we propose, for the advice of a council, a question concerning the proper relations of our churches to yours, in view of its resolution of December 5th; and it seems to us indispensable that some declaration be made on the subject of Fellowship, as on the others.

We regret that the three propositions, submitted to you in our letter of the 26th inst., as a possible basis of agreement, are not satisfactory to you; and as we cannot surrender them, or modify them in any important particular, there is probably no occasion, in view of your many engagements and ours, for further protracting our correspondence.

WM. IVES BUDINGTON,
R. S. STORRS.

This correspondence clearly established the fact that Plymouth Church would not recede from the rules it had laid down in the case of Mr. Tilton's withdrawal from the church, and rendered necessary the convening, a few weeks later, of the Congregational Council which took full cognizance of the facts in dispute, as will be seen by a perusal of the ensuing chapter.

CHAPTER V.

THE ASSEMBLING OF THE COUNCIL OF CONGREGATIONAL CHURCHES—THE INVITATION TO PLYMOUTH CHURCH TO EXPLAIN ITS ACTION IN DROPPING MR. TILTON'S NAME FROM THE ROLLS—THE DECLARATION BY PLYMOUTH CHURCH OF ITS INDEPENDENCE—THE VERDICT OF THE COUNCIL—A REVIEW BY REV. DR. BACON.

THE Council of Congregational Churches assembled March 24th, in the Clinton-ave. Church, Brooklyn. It was no ordinary gathering, but was noteworthy on account of its unusual size and the distinguished character of a large number of the delegates present. The permanent organization of the Council resulted in the election of the Rev. Dr. Leonard Bacon of New Haven, and the Hon. C. I. Walker of Detroit, as the Moderators, and the Rev. Dr. Alonzo H. Quint of New Bedford, Mass., and the Rev. I. C. Meserve of Brooklyn, as Scribes. Immediately upon the completion of the organization, the question of inviting Plymouth Church to a mutual council, or to sit in the Council, was raised. Prof. E. C. Smythe, of Andover Theological Seminary, presented resolutions favoring the representation of that church by pastor and committee, for the purpose of making such statements as they might wish, and of answering such questions as the Council might have to ask; in other words, to have the same opportunities in the Council as the other two churches. This opened a hearty but good-natured discussion, which continued for two hours, and in which the question as to the exact nature of the Council was raised. The Rev. Dr. Storrs set this at rest by stating that neither an ecclesiastical, mutual, nor *ex parte* council had been called, and if this was not an advisory Council it was nothing. The discussion then turned upon the kind of invitation to be extended to Plymouth Church. Substitute after substitute was offered to Prof. Smythe's resolution, and when brought to a vote were successively defeated; and it became apparent that the good sense of the assembly favored the fullest courtesy to Plymouth Church, and when Dr. Storrs advocated such a course it became certain that Plymouth Church would have an opportunity to be fully and freely heard. Warm speeches were made on both sides; questions of order were raised, and at times a dozen delegates were on their feet at once. But the ease of the chairman, Dr. Bacon, and his familiarity with Congregational usage, of which some of the delegates seemed to have little conception, kept the delegates in good humor, and helped dispatch the business of the meeting, which had otherwise threatened to be well-nigh interminable. Prof. Smythe's resolution was finally carried by a very decisive vote. The author does not wish to inflict upon the reader a long report of the deliberations of this eminent body, but will merely quote the action and correspondence bearing upon the case. The following is the summons to Plymouth to answer:—

In Ecclesiastical Council convened by letters from the Church of the Pilgrims and Clinton Ave. Congregational Church, Brooklyn, N. Y., March 24, 1874, in the house of worship of the Clinton Ave. Church, it was

Resolved, That the Plymouth Church be invited, with the consent of the committees of the churches, to present its views orally before the Council on the questions presented in the Letter Missive by its pastor and such committee as it may appoint, and by the same committee to furnish such information concerning the action referred to in these questions as the Church may request.

It was voted that the Rev. Egbert C. Smythe, D. D., and the Scribe of the Council be a committee to present this resolve to Plymouth Church. ALONZO H. QUINT, Scribe of the Council.

Brooklyn, N. Y., March 24, 1874.

To this exhortation, after mature deliberation, Plymouth Church made the following response.

Reverend and Beloved Brethren and Fathers in God: Having been notified by the Church of the Pilgrims and the Clinton Avenue Congregational Church of your assemblage, under their call, for purposes specified in their Letters Missive, and having received from those churches an invitation to appear before you by our pastor and a committee, simply for the purpose of correcting any statements of fact which might seem to us erroneous, and furnishing any further and specific information which you might request; and having declined this invitation on the ground that these churches thus called us before a council in the convening of which we had been permitted to take no part, in which we had never been offered the rights of equal members, in which it was not proposed now to give us the rights even of ordinary defendents, we nevertheless desire, out of our respect and love for you, beloved brethren and venerable fathers, to make a brief statement of our position, and to lay this our solemn protest before you.

"It is not against your convening or organizing as a council that we desire to remonstrate. So far as the Letters Missive, under which you have assembled, state matters which do not relate to any other church than the two churches issuing those Letters, we make no complaint. We do not even object to the consideration in your body of the question whether those two churches have made a mistake in their manner of approaching us, and therefore owe us an apology, instead of our owing them an explanation. [Applause.] Although this is a question in which we, as a church, have some interest, yet an *ex parte* discussion of that point, for the sole enlightenment of those brethren, may be of great profit to them, and cannot seriously encroach upon the rights of Congregational churches at large.'

"Neither do we object to the consideration of the abstract questions submitted to your body. Bearing as these questions doubtless do upon the internal economy of the two churches which have called you, it is for you to decide whether there are difficulties arising, or likely to arise, within those churches of sufficient importance to justify their asking for advice upon those points, in the light of which they may judge of their own past acts, and guide their future course. We are bound to presume that such is the case. [Applause.]

"But when they call upon you to examine into our action

for their edification, a far different issue is presented. You have been called to determine whether the action of Plymouth Church, in a specified case, was justifiable, whether our pastor's name was left without proper vindication, and whether we are to be retained in the fellowship of Congregational churches.'

"Brethren, we approach this part of your duties, if we know anything of our own hearts, in a spirit free from all personal motives. We will not pretend that, at all times past, we have felt unconcerned for ourselves as a church, or for that member of our church who, by reason of long and faithful service, and of his signal success in bringing home to our hearts a living and ever-present Savior, has become to us the best beloved of men. [Repeated applause.] But these things are of the past. The Lord hath given us peace and strength, and we rest in Him, with absolute confidence, and absolute content.'

"But we still owe a duty to our weaker brethren. [Laughter.] Not every church could pass through such a storm in safety. Not every church could withstand the decrees of a council so worthy of respect as yours, even though the council were known to have been called *ex parte*, and informed erroneously. Lest, therefore, our silence should leave the way open for the oppression of other churches, less powerful and less united than our own, we speak.'

"In the name of our Congregational policy—in the name of our feebler brethren—in the name of justice, even as administered by those who know not God—but above all, in the name of that God—whose throne is seated in justice and judgment, we protest against any action whatever by this Council, upon any issue relating to Plymouth Church.

"(Long and hearty applause followed the reading of the sentence, and caused Mr. Beecher to say, 'Brethren, you'll wear out your hands before you get through;' Mr. Halliday broke in with, 'and the Council too.')

"And this we do for the reasons following, as well as for others, to set forth which, time would fail.'

"*First:* This is an *ex parte* council, convened without any regular and sufficient steps to obtain a mutual council—without any refusal upon our part to join in such a council—called to consider our affairs for the sole instruction of two other churches, and carefully fettered, so as to make it impossible, by the terms of its call, for the Council to alter itself into a mutual council. Yet it is a well-known and fundamental rule of Congregational polity that no *ex parte* council can be called until a mutual council has been distinctly offered and clearly refused, and that every *ex parte* council should be at liberty, and should offer to make itself a mutual one.

"*Second:* If it is claimed that one or more churches, acting on the pretext that they are not in controversy with a sister church, and desire instruction only for themselves, may call a council to instruct them as to their relations with that church-free from the rules governing the call of ordinary *ex parte*, councils, this claim appears to us subversive of the whole system of mutual councils. If this Council has been regularly called and is competent to advise the churches calling it as to their duty toward us, then our pastor can call a council, without consulting us, to advise him publicly what is his duty toward his church. We have inquired in vain for a precedent of this kind, and have every reason to believe that none can be found. The present case is a most dangerous innovation, which, if sanctioned by the churches, will do more to disorganize Congregational polity than all the alleged errors of Plymouth Church could do, if ten times repeated.

"*Third:* This Council is summoned to advise, precisely as we were originally summoned to take advice, under distinct menace and moral coercion. Just as Plymouth Church was in one breath requested to explain the facts, and informed that it must be cut off unless the facts had been misreported, so this Council is called upon to advise whether the action of Plymouth Church has been conformable to Congregational usage, and is at the same moment informed that, if such is indeed Congregational usage, the two churches 'cannot sustain such a position,' that it would be 'entirely unreasonable to expect it from' them, that 'even if they could continue to hold it in view of the past, they should feel it indispensable to be extricated from it in forecast of what may occur in the future,' that 'such a position is simply insupportable,' and that 'if this is to be Congregational practice, many churches [clearly meaning their own] will certainly prefer to identify themselves with some other communion.'

"While we do not for a moment assume that such threats will intimidate you, any more than the threats, which for nearly a year past have been uttered from the same quarter, intimidated us, yet we conceive it possible in the future that a combination of large powerful churches might select a council of weak and dependent ones for the purpose of crushing one still weaker; and in such a case, menaces like these would have a controlling and disastrous effect. We resist them now, when they seem to us idle and vain, lest they should be left by our silence to be drawn into a precedent fatal to the liberty of other churches.

"*Fourth:* Officers of the great institutions to which Congregationalists have been accustomed to contribute most liberally—the Home Missionary Society, the Congregational Union, the Board of Commissioners for Foreign Missions, and others—having been invited to attend this Council, in which their wisdom, experience, and devotion to the great work of the Church make them distinguished and valuable members, are singled out for special and almost personal dictation, and are warned in most pointed language that the callers of this Council do not intend to contribute any more funds to the support of these Christian enterprises, if their theories of Congregational fellowship and discipline are not indorsed by this Council.

"This attempt to pervert great missionary organizations into engines of ecclesiastical power, to stop the fountains of Christian benevolence, and to overawe members of councils by appeals to their fears for the special branch of the Lord's work in their charge, tends to destroy the moral force of all councils, and constitutes an assault on the independence of both the churches and the societies, entirely without parallel in the history of Congregationalism. [Applause.]

"*Fifth:* In so far as this Council is called to consider the points of conflict between Plymouth Church and neighboring churches, the whole frame of the Council, in its widespread constituency and national character (so appropriate and admirable if called only to deal with large and general questions) is directly in opposition to the genius of Congregational polity, one great aim of which is to confine local troubles to their own locality, and to settle them in the neighborhood, by the aid of neighboring churches, without spreading the tale of local dissensions over the whole land.

"*Sixth:* The charges brought against this church are partly based upon the reported speeches of its pastor, although it is well known that Plymouth Church, with the hearty concurrence of its pastor, has from the beginning of its history declared that no man, however beloved and revered, may usurp the rights of the brotherhood, and has always insisted, and does now insist, that by its own acts and declarations, and by these only, it will be judged. And the maintenance of this rule with respect to all churches, we hold to be an essential part of Congregational polity.

"*Seventh:* It is proposed virtually to arraign this church for alleged violations of Congregational usage. But Congregational usage itself derives its sole authority from the Word of God; and no Council may call to account a Congregational church for the alleged violation of principles not declared by the Word of God.

"Nor can we assent to any action by which the tradition of the elders shall be placed upon even equal grounds with the commandment of God, nor agree to receive for doctrines the commandments of men. And we therefore protest against any attempt to formulate the usages of churches into a code of ecclesiastical law, to be placed on an equality with the Word of God, as binding upon the conscience of the churches. [Applause.] In the presentation of the case to you, it happens naturally enough, from the fundamental error of the whole proceeding, that our views and practice in cases of discipline are not correctly stated. We shall not correct these errors of detail. Nevertheless, for the purpose of informing you frankly, as brethren beloved in the Lord, what are our views and practice concerning church discipline, although not recognizing your power to act upon this subject, we append to this paper our past and present rules of discipline, and a declaration of our practice under them, adopted unanimously by this church, and representing not merely the course we have marked out for the future, but that which has been followed in the past.

"Our doctrine of church fellowship is in like manner gravely misinterpreted. We have never claimed (as asserted) that 'fellowship binds to silence the churches which have pledged it.' We have never denied the right of churches to offer to each other advice in a Christian spirit, nor the duty of churches to receive such an offer in the spirit of brotherhood. We have asserted the right of every church, acting in the like spirit of fraternal love, while receiving the offer, to decline the advice and to judge for itself when, according to the laws of Christ, an occasion has arisen for exercising this right. And, having received an offer of advice which seemed to us to be tendered in a spirit not according to the mind of Christ, we did decisively exercise our right, by declining to listen to advice conceived in such a spirit. Nor can we ever assent to any doctrine of church fellowship which shall be destructive of the liberty of the local church, or which shall convert that which the

Lord ordained as a safeguard and an instrument of sympathy, into an irritating espionage and an instrument of oppression.

"But we rejoice to live in affectionate fellowship with all churches of the Lord Jesus, and especially with those who are in all things like-minded with us, holding to the same faith and order, not only in things fundamental, but in things less essential, yet dear to us by conviction or association. In asserting that this church was not responsible for the doctrine, order, or discipline of other churches, we never for a moment intended to cut ourselves off from relationship to them. There is a certain vague and general sense in which all Christians are responsible for one another. But this is not the sense in which the word is generally used. The responsibility of members of the same church for one another is the mildest form in which the word is commonly understood. And it was just that degree of responsibility between churches which we meant, and still mean, to deny. Members of a church can put each other on trial before the Church. We deny the right of any church to put another church upon trial before any ecclesiastical body whatever. [Applause.]

"Yet we cheerfully admit that whenever any church shall openly and avowedly change the essential conditions upon which it was publicly received into the fellowship of neighboring churches, or shall, by flagrant neglect, exert a pernicious and immoral influence upon the community or upon sister churches, it is their right, either by individual action or by council, to withdraw their fellowship.

"We hold that preceding fellowship, in all such cases, there should be such affectionate and reasonable inquiry as shall show that the evil is real—that the causes of it are within the control of the church, that the evil is not a transient evil such as may befall any church, but is permanent and tending to increase rather than diminish.

"It was with this meaning, and reasoning from this point of view, that we used the word 'responsibility.' We do maintain that we are responsible for no other church and to no other church. But we use these words in their ordinary and popular sense, and not with reference to all those shadowy grades of meaning which may possibly be attached to them. In short, we used this language for the purpose of repelling dictation, and of relieving the conscience of other churches from a sense of any such responsibility as necessarily implied the right to dictate. The responsibility of affection we gladly accept; the responsibility of authority, even in its lightest touch, we utterly repudiate. [Applause.]

"We pray for the divine blessing upon you and your deliberations. We commit you and ourselves to the care of the great Master, in whose service we are all united here, and who will, out of perplexities, conflicts, and doubts, bring us all into an eternal unity of love, and through love to peace.

"This much, brethren and fathers, it was in our minds to say to you before receiving any other invitation than that of the two churches; but having now received your invitation to appear before you by our pastor and a committee, we are constrained to decline, lest by our acceptance we should seem to renounce our conscientious convictions and to withdraw our solemn testimony against the violation of Christian liberty, courtesy, and equity which have characterized the calling of this Council and the steps which led to it, and lest we should establish a precedent full of danger to smaller churches, as encouraging irregular and unwarrantable proceedings on the part of strong churches, which the weaker party might afterward, by the force of our example, be compelled to condone. We are not responsible for the errors which have been committed in the treatment of this Church and in the calling of this Council, and we are not willing to cover them with our consent.

By order of Plymouth Church.

F. M. Edgerton, Moderator.
Thomas G. Shearman, Clerk.

Brooklyn, March 25th, 1874.

Mr. Theodore Tilton sent, on March 27, a letter to the Council giving his position in the controversy. The following are the chief points of the communication:

To the Congregational Council.—Gentlemen, Clerical and Lay: As your honorable body are discussing a case in which I am made to appear a principal actor, you will accord to me the courtesy of contributing to your official records a correct statement of my own position; a privilege which I ask because my position has been misrepresented in your body, to my grievous injury.

This misrepresentation touches two vital points: *first:* my attitude toward Plymouth Church; *second:* my action toward its pastor. I will make a plain statement of the facts bearing on both points.

First: In 1850 I became a member of Plymouth Church. In 1869 I terminated my connection with that church. In 1873 my name, which still lingered on the roll, was officially erased. My retirement from the church was executed by me in strict conformity with a rule of the church; and the validity of my act has since been signally and repeatedly ratified by the unanimous vote of the church, affirming and reaffirming the principle on which that act was based. That principle, as I hold it, is the free right of a free man to sever his connection with a church by his free will; and I shall never become a churchman in any church in which this is not a rule. On the part of Plymouth Church, this same principle has been similarly stated as follows :

Every man has an indefeasible right to separate himself from the church by his own sole act.

It was this right, thus held and now championed by Plymouth Church, that I exercised in that church four years ago by that act, and on that principle I have ever since stood, and still stand; and I believe that if the discussion arising from this case shall result in stamping this principle into currency as a canon law among any considerable number of churches, I shall thereby have contributed by an accidental example, to further not a little the religious liberty of mankind. The affectionate loyalty which I bear to my father and my mother evermore reminds me that they belong to the church of whose liberty Roger Williams was the early champion in this country; and it is the native blood within me that makes me jealous, to an extreme degree, of sacerdotal authority and ecclesiastical bonds. No action of Plymouth Church, growing out of my case, could have been more in consonance with my traditional convictions, or more gratifying to my ancestral pride, than that this church should have unanimously followed me into my retirement and invested my individual act with the moral majesty of a public precedent for the further enfranchisement of the human mind from church bonds and priestly powers. But whether you agree or disagree with this view, I request you to take special notice of the fact that whatever doubts your honorable body may cast upon this method of voluntary retirement, or whatever such doubts may have existed in Plymouth Church at the time when I assumed and exercised this right four years ago, yet this assumption has since been ratified by that church on several signal occasions, and is now put forth by Plymouth Church as a cherished principle of its ecclesiastical polity.

Second: Four years after I had thus terminated my connection with Plymouth Church, I was charged by a member of that body with "having circulated and promoted scandals derogatory to the Christian integrity of the pastor, and injurious to the reputation of the church." A widespread impression overshadowed good men's minds that whatever other points were in doubt, there could be no doubt that I had slandered the pastor of Plymouth Church. I hereby declare that I had not then, nor have I since, nor at any time in all my life have I ever uttered a slander against any human being. (Mr. Tilton then proceeds to quote, in support of his position, the letter of Mr. Beecher, published on the 2d of June, denying that Mr. Tilton was the author of the calumnies against him.)

He then quotes his own letter sent to the Examining Committee of Plymouth Church, explicitly denying that he had ever spoken against Mr. Beecher falsely, and asking for an examination. He then refers to his statement in Plymouth Church to the effect that if he had slandered Mr. Beecher he was ready to answer for it, and calling upon Mr. Beecher to speak, if he had any accusation to make against him. After alluding to Mr. Beecher's declaration that he had no charges to prefer against him, he concludes as follows:

In conclusion, let me repeat the two points which the above statements prove, namely:

First: That my voluntary retirement from Plymouth Church was wholly in accordance with the rule and spirit of that church; and

Second: That my action toward the pastor has always been prompted by an honorable sense of what constitutes fair dealing between man and man. Yours, with respect,

THEODORE TILTON.

Brooklyn, Thursday, March 26, 1874.

The following are the Declarations of Principles and Rules of Discipline referred to in the report:

Plymouth Church, believing that care in the admission of members is of more value in maintaining the purity of the church, than severity in dealing with them after admission, attaches great importance to the evidence given by candidates for membership of vital faith in Christ and of spiritual life begun. The Examining Committee must be satisfied upon these points before recommending the candidate to the church, and letters from other churches are not accepted as substitutes for personal examination. All persons who enter Plymouth Church are, in effect, admitted upon profession of their faith.

The active membership, numbering about two thousand three hundred souls, is so organized that a systematic watch and care is extended over all, in the form of visitation, inquiry, fraternal advice, encouragement, and assistance, and, in the case of non-resident members, by regular correspondence. We recognize it also as our privilege and duty to reprove and admonish one another with all fidelity, provided it be in love; and all these duties, while not neglected by the members of the church as individuals, are moreover laid upon special officers of the church, and so distributed and discharged that no single member is omitted from this fraternal vigilance.

"By the assiduous use of personal, social, and spiritual influences, by preventing or healing disputes and reclaiming wanderers, we seek to avoid the necessity of judicial discipline; and this we hold to be not only wise policy but Christian obligation. Nevertheless, when these means fail, the discipline of this church is express and energetic. If any member of our body brings dishonor upon the Christian profession, we hold it our duty to reclaim him if possible, with all long-suffering and patience, but, if unsuccessful in this, to make it known that we are no longer responsible for the dishonor which he has brought or may bring upon the name of Christ.'

"If any one desires no longer to be known as a member of this church, or as a professed follower of Christ, we hold that, while we cannot release him from the special obligations to Christ which he has assumed by the public profession of his faith, we may, and should, after having endeavored to change his purpose, release ourselves from our responsibility to and for him, in whatever method the circumstances of the case may require, regard being had to the best good of the individual, the well-being of the church, and the honor of the Master.'

"While we are ready at all times to receive suitable inquiry and to give to sister churches every reasonable explanation concerning our action in cases of public interest, we hold that it is our right, and may be our duty, to avoid the evils incident to a public explanation or a public trial; and that such an exercise of our discretion furnishes no good ground for the interference of other churches, provided we neither retain within our fellowship, nor dismiss by letter, as in regular standing, persons who bring open dishonor upon the Christian name.

RULES OF DISCIPLINE.

I, As adopted April, 1848.

RULE 5. No member can be deprived of church privileges except by regular process. The presentation of complaints may be first made to the Examining Committee, who shall, upon sufficient cause, prefer charges to the whole church, or the complainant may present his complaint in person to the church. When a member is accused he shall be seasonably furnished with a copy of the complaint, and shall have a full hearing.

RULE 6. The censures which may be inflicted on offending members are, according to the aggravation of the offense, either (1) private reproof, (2) public admonition, (3) suspension, or (4) excommunication. In cases of excommunication notice thereof must be given from the pulpit on the Sabbath.

II. As amended in 1865.

RULE. 4. *Discipline.*—Members cannot be censured by the church, except by the process herein stated. A complaint may be made, either to the Examining Committe, or the whole church. In the former case, the clerk of the committee, and, in the latter case, the clerk of the church must reduce the complaint to writing, if it is entertained, and must use due diligence to forward a copy to the accused, and to give him personal notice of the time and place of hearing. The accused must have a full opportunity to be heard in his own defense. An accusation presented to the church must always be heard, either by the church or by the Examining Committee, unless the application for a hearing is rejected at a meeting of the church by a three-fourths vote.

RULE 5.—[Same as Rule 6 above.]

RULE 7. [Adopted, 1859; amended 1871.]—Members may be dropped from the roll of the church, with or without notice to them, as may be deemed just, by a two-thirds vote of the church, upon the recommendation of the Examining Committee, either upon their own application, or in case they have abandoned their connection with the church by prolonged absence or otherwise, upon the application of any other person.

III. As amended in 1874.

RULE 4. *Discipline.*—Members cannot be censured except by the process herein stated.

1. Complaints must be made in writing either to the Examining Committee or the whole church.

2. If the complaint is made to the Examining Committee, the facts must first be investigated by it, so far as to determine whether there is reasonable probability that the charges can be sustained by proof.

3. If the complaint is made to the church, it may order a similar inves-

tigation by the Examining Committee, or by special committee, before deciding to proceed.

4. If the Examining Committee or church decide to proceed with the case, the clerk of the church must use due diligence to forward a copy of the complaint to the accused, and, if practicable, to give him personal notice of the time and place of hearing.

5. The accused must, in all cases, when a trial is had, have a full opportunity to be heard in his own defense.

6. The church may refer any case of discipline to a committee to hear the evidence, and report its opinion on the whole case, or any part thereof.

7. When a complaint is made to the Examining Committee, the accused, at his first appearance, may require the committee to submit to the church the question, whether the complaint shall be taken out of the committee for trial, and the committee cannot proceed meantime.

8. Proceedings before the Examining Committee shall be kept private until otherwise ordered by the church; and the committee, unless the complaint is sustained, or unless it desires instructions, or unless a report is ordered by vote of the church, shall make no report upon the case.

9. No member of a committee can vote upon its final report in case of discipline, unless he has heard and read the evidence and arguments in the case, except by consent of both the complainant and the accused.

10. If the evidence has been taken by a committee, the church is not bound to hear evidence on either side.

11. Final censure can be inflicted only by the church, and by concurrence of two-thirds of all present and voting.

Rules 5 and 7 unchanged.

"On motion the Moderator and Clerk by a vote of four hundred and eighty to nothing were directed to sign and transmit the documents to the Council, and Dr. Edward Beecher. H. W. Sage, and R. W. Raymond were appointed messengers, when the meeting adjourned.

This was not accepted by the Council and spread upon the minutes for the reason that it was the sense of the Council that it was a matter of which they could not take cognizance. Mr. Tilton then said:

GENTLEMEN, CLERICAL AND LAY: I received yesterday the courteous note of your Moderator informing me of the technical reasons why my communication to your honorable body could not be officially put on the minutes. I respectfully offer you this present brief letter as a substitute in the hope that it may be within the possibility of your acceptance for record. Among the five points which you are asked to decide concerning my case with the Plymouth Church the second will pass into permanent statement on your journal as follows:

During the voluntary absence of a member from the ordinances, if specific charges of grossly unchristian conduct are presented against him by a brother in the church, to which charges he declines to answer, &c.,

The above statement, which has been constantly reiterated during your proceedings, implies that gross charges were made against me, and that these charges I declined to answer.

Gentlemen of the Council, every man among you knows that I did not decline to answer.

I ask you, therefore, as an act of justice to me, to permit the true record to accompany the false. Respectfully yours,

THEODORE TILTON.

Brooklyn, Saturday, March 28.

The deliberations of the Council covered several days, and resulted in the verdict given below:—

The Council has listened carefully to the Committees of the churches by which it was convened, and has received from them a clear and earnest statement of the aims and principles which have determined the action of these churches in the proceedings which they ask us to review.

We have also received from the Plymouth Church a communication declining an invitation from this Council, as well as from the two churches, to appear by its pastor and the Committee and assist in the presentation and discussion of the questions before us, but at the same time offering suggestions and arguments which we have carefully and candidly considered.

We cannot doubt the right of these two churches to ask advice of us concerning the regularity and Christian character of what they have done in their dealings with the Plymouth Church. No church is beyond the reach of the public opinion of other churches, expressed either directly or through an ecclesiastical council.

Any church in its essential and inalienable independence may in the exercise of a reasonable discretion consider any public action of any other church; may, in proper methods, express its approval or disapproval, and may make that public action the subject of friendly correspondence and remonstrance, or if need be, the ground of a temporary or permanent cessation of acts of intercommunion.

There has been laid before us a series of letters that have passed between these two churches and the Plymouth Church. On that correspondence it is our unquestionable right to have an opinion and to express it, though we have no right to try the Plymouth Church as a party before us. We have to say, then, that the letter of remonstrance and admonition with which the correspondence began was not uncalled for.

The churches throughout the United States, and the general public also, felt a painful anxiety on a question imminent and urgent in this city of Brooklyn, and involving the honor, not of the Congregational churches only, but of Christianity itself.

Without any explicit reference to that question, it will suffice to say that in the Plymouth Church a complaint was brought against a member that he had "circulated and promoted scandals derogatory to the Christian integrity of the pastor and injurious to the reputation of the church." The person complained of appeared in the church meeting and declared that four years before that time he had by his own volition terminated his connection with the church; and thereupon his name was by a vote of the church dropped from the catalogue of its members. That action of the Plymouth Church was the occasion on which these two churches interposed, and with a request for a friendly conference.

In this act they represented the interests of the fraternity of Congregational Churches, whose principles of discipline and whose fair Christian fame were endangered by the course which Plymouth Church seemed to be pursuing.

For this moral heroism they deserve thanks, even should errors of judgment be traceable in some of the details of their procedure. In our consideration of the letter then addressed to the Plymouth Church, we find that the impression made by it was in some measure different from what was intended by its authors. Written under the pressure of apprehensions and anxieties long suppressed, it seems to have impinged more faithfully than was intended on the sensibilities of those to whom it was addressed. To many the letter seems entirely unexceptionable in matter and in manner, and entirely appropriate to the occasion; while to others it seems unnecessarily severe in the tone of its condemnation of the proceedings complained of. In their second letter the complaining churches having found what impression they had made by their remonstrance offered an explanation, which, we trust, was not unacceptable. Concerning the reply of Plymouth Church to that letter, we say nothing more than that an ingenuous explanation of the reasons which had prompted Plymouth Church to rid itself of an offending member by an exceptional method might have brought the correspondence to an early and happy determination. We can see no sufficient reason why the request of the complaining churches for a fraternal conference should not have been granted.

In the subsequent correspondence we see on the part of the complaining churches an expression of their desire to unite with the Plymouth Church in referring the points of difference to the advice of a Council.

We find on the part of Plymouth Church no definite expression either of consent or refusal. Yet, inasmuch as the Plymouth Church did not distinctly refuse to unite on a reference to a Council, we cannot but regret that the complaining churches did not urge their request till a refusal or an evasion should have become unequivocal.

We are not invited nor do we take it upon ourselves to advise the Plymouth Church concerning its methods of dealing with offenders. But we are invited to advise these two churches on certain questions.

Therefore, we say distinctly that the idea of membership in a Congregational Church is the idea of a covenant between the individual member and the church; that by virtue of that covenant the member is responsible to the church for his conformity to the law of Christ, and the church is responsible for him; and that this responsibility does not cease till the church, by some formal and corporate act, has declared the dissolution of the covenant. The covenant may be broken by the member. He may offend, and when duly admonished, may give no satisfactory evidence of repentance. In that case, he is cut off from communion; the Church having given its testimony is no longer responsible for him, and he can be restored only by the removal of the censure. Voluntary absence of a resident member from the Communion of the Church, and from its public worship, does not dissolve the covenant, but is a reasonable ground of admonition and, if persisted in, of final censure.

When a regular complaint is made against such a member, that in some other respect he violates the laws of the Church, and especially when the complaint is that he has circulated and promoted scandals derogatory to the Christian integrity of the pastor and injurious to the reputation of the Church, the consideration that he has long ago forsaken the Church is only an aggravation of his alleged fault.

In regard to the future relations between these churches and Plymouth Church, we express our hope that the very extraordinary proceeding which gave occasion for the correspondence and for this Council will not be a precedent for the guidance of that Church hereafter. Could we suppose that such proceedings will be repeated, we should feel that the disregard of the first principles involved in the idea of church membership, and the idea of the fellowship of churches with each other, would require the strongest possible protest. But the communication from the Plymouth Church to this Council makes professions and declarations which justify the hope that such deviation from the orderly course of discipline will not be repeated.

The accused person in that case has not been retained in the church nor commended to any other church.

We recite some of those declarations from the Plymouth Church which encourage the hope we have expressed: "We rejoice," says the Plymouth Church, to live in affectionate fellowship with all churches of the Lord Jesus, and especially with those who are in all things like-minded with us, holding to the same faith and order, not only in things fundamental but in things less essential yet dear to us by conviction or association." "We cheerfully admit that whenever any church shall openly and avowedly change the essential conditions upon which it was publicly received into the fellowship of neighboring churches, or shall by flagrant neglect exert a pernicious and immoral influence upon the community, or upon sister churches, it is their right either by individual action or by counsel to withdraw their fellowship. We hold that preceding disfellowship in all such cases there should be such affectionate and reasonable inquiry as shall show that the evil is real, that the causes of it are within the control of the church, that the evil is not a transient evil, such as may befall any church, but is permanent and tending to increase rather than diminish."

While it is not to be forgotten that this communication from Plymouth Church is entirely subsequent to the case as it stood upon the convening of this Council, when the Plymouth Church, by its action of December 5th, had declared itself responsible for no other church, and no other church for it, in respect to doctrine, order and discipline, which action, as interpreted in the circumstances then existing, implied a withdrawal to the ground of total independency, yet that church is to be fraternally judged by its latest utterance.

These professions on the part of Plymouth Church may be accepted by other churches as indicating its intention to maintain an efficient discipline, and to regard the mutual responsibility of churches. At the same time, the Council feels constrained to declare that these declarations seem to us inconsistent with the resolution of interpretation adopted by Plymouth Church, December 5th, 1873, and with other acts and statements appearing in the published documents. We think that the action of that church, as presented in these documents, if unmollified, would justify these churches in withdrawing fellowship. Yet, inasmuch as the Plymouth Church seems to us to admit, in its communication to us, the Congregational principles of discipline and fellowship, we advise the churches convening this Council to maintain with it the relations of fellowship as heretofore, in the hope that Plymouth Church may satisfy these churches of its acceptance of the principles which it has been supposed to disavow.

We also desire in this connection to reaffirm and emphasize the doctrine laid down in all our platforms of the obligations of Fellowship. This duty applies to all Christian churches. In the case of those instituted and united in accordance with the Congregational polity, it involves that more intimate communion which is exercised in asking and giving counsel, in giving and receiving admonition, and other acts relating to doctrine, order and discipline.

This mutual responsibility of the Congregational churches has characterized their system from the beginning, distinguishing it from simple independency.

With the autonomy of the local church it is one of the formative and essential principles of Congregationalism. Without it we have no basis in our polity for that system of coöperative effort to which our churches are pledged. We regard, therefore, the principles of Fellowship which the pastors and churches convening us have so earnestly maintained to be those which we have received from our Father and the word of God.

We appreciate and honor their fidelity to those principles under circumstances of peculiar and severe trial, and we offer our earnest prayer to the great Head of the Church that He may bestow upon them and the pastor and Church with which they have been in correspondence wisdom and grace; that He may guide them in all their actions, and that He may quicken in all our churches, through these painful trials, a spirit of renewed fidelity to the sacred obligations of our covenants and our church communion, and we pray that He to whom all power in heaven and on earth is given, and who has promised to be with His church always, even to the end of the world, and who, under the inspiration of His spirit and His truth has joined these churches in a grand and memorable past, standing shoulder to shoulder in the great moral and spiritual battles of the age, may again unite them in the future conflicts and victories of His kingdom.

LEONARD BACON,
C. L. WALKER, } Moderators.

A. H. QUINT,
J. C. MESERVE, } Scribes.

Clinton Avenue Congregational Church,
Brooklyn, March 28th, 1874.

In April following the adjournment of the Council, Rev. Dr. Bacon delivered a lecture in New Haven before the middle class of Yale College upon the action of the Council. We extract it:

I have been giving to the Senior Class a series of lectures, as they might be called by courtesy—more properly familiar talks—about the theory and practice of the Congregational Church polity. Having been requested by the Middle Class to interpose among my talks to them on American church history an account of the Council which was held last week at Brooklyn, I propose to make use of that conspicuous example as an illustration of what I have been teaching more abstractly in general statements of the principles and usages which regulate either the self-government of our churches or their intercommunion.

Remember the two principles, which, taken together and carried out into all their applications, are the Congregational polity.

1. Every stated and organized assembly of Christian disciples and worshipers is a church full and complete, self-governed under the law of Christ, and having in itself all church power.

2. There is an intercommunion of churches, and there are mutual duties which that intercommunion involves. As there is intercourse between independent States, each asserting its own sovereignty, so there is intercourse between churches mutually independent, and each maintaining its own self-government under Christ. As political sovereignties are responsible one to another, so churches are mutually responsible. As there are principles of justice and comity which regulate the intercourse of nations and which are international law, so there are principles which ought to regulate the intercommunion of all churches, and which our churches profess to recognize.

So much for preliminaries. We come now to our particular subject, the Brooklyn Council of 1874:

I. What is a Council as understood and practiced by Congregationalists? (Platform of 1865, Part III., Chapters 1, 2.)

1. Not a permanent organization like a Presbytery or a Methodist Conference. It comes into existence for a special occasion, performs its work well or ill, and exists no longer.

2. Not a governing body. It can inflict no censures in the technical sense. Its judgment on whatever subject takes effect only as it is freely accepted and made effectual by the churches.

3. Its function is to consult, to give light, to form and express opinions concerning a given statement of facts, or concerning facts, which it ascertains by testimony—in a word, to advise.

II. On what occasion and by what right was this council convened?

1. A certain proceeding in the Plymouth Church was public and (taken in connection with foregoing circumstances) scandalous, *i. e.* causing offense, an occasion of stumbling. It was a proceeding in which other churches had an interest.

2. The two nearest churches—nearest in the intimacy of their relations to the Plymouth Church—interposed with united remonstrance. (Ought they not rather to have interposed in a closer analogy with the rule concerning personal offenses? first one, then two or three?)

3. A correspondence ensued, with no satisfactory result—no explanation of the questionable proceedings. A proposal for a mutual council was made by the complaining churches, but was not accepted.

4. The complaining churches thought they needed advice and therefore sought advice through this Council. (Platform

1865, P. III, ch. ii., sec. 7 (3), f. 52.) This was their right.

III. What were the powers of the Council, and the limitations under which it acted?

1. It had not the power of a mutual council. There were no two parties before it.

2. It had not the power conceded by Congregational usage to an *ex parte* Council. An aggrieved member or minority in a church may, under certain conditions (one of which is that a mutual Council shall have been distinctly refused by the other party, namely the church), invite the neighbor churches to review the action complained of, and to give advice concerning it. This was not at all a Council of that sort. The Plymouth Church had an interest in the case, but it was not a party to the proceedings. The Council could give it no advice, still less arraign it for trial.

3. The Council had just so much power as the constituent churches had committed to it, by sending their delegates in answer to the letter "Missive." That letter, with the subsequent action of the churches invited by it, was its charter.

4. Therefore it had no power to put the pastor of Plymouth Church on trial, directly or indirectly. It had as little power to vindicate him as to condemn him. It had no right to assume any other theory than that of his Christian integrity. Any statement that the result of the Council was in some way a vindication of that eminent minister is absurd. It was for the Plymouth Church to vindicate its pastor against a damaging imputation from one of its own members. But with great alacrity—the pastor himself consenting—it threw away the opportunity of vindication.

IV. What were the points on which advice was sought from the Council?

In essence there were only two, presented under various aspects in a series of questions, which the Council carefully considered, voting upon most of them with great unanimity in their private session, though they did not think it necessary to answer those several questions, one by one, in their result.

1. That act just referred to, in which the Plymouth Church threw away the opportunity of vindicating its pastor, was what gave occasion for remonstrance from neighboring churches. As stated in the Result of the Council it was this: "In the Plymouth Church a complaint was brought against a member that he had 'circulated and promoted scandals derogatory to the Christian integrity of the pastor, and injurious to the rep-

utation of the Church.' The person complained of appeared in the church-meeting, and declared that four years before that time he had, by his own volition, terminated his connection with the Church; and thereupon his name was, by vote of the Church, dropped from the catalogue of its members." The regularity of this proceeding, that is, the consistency of it with the true idea of the relation between a Christian Church and its individual members, was the first point submitted to the Council for its advice.

2. The advice of the Council on that point might be such as would make advice on another point necessary for the guidance of the complaining churches. If the action of the Plymouth Church in the case referred to was inconsistent with the true idea of the relation between a church and its members, what more ought these two complaining churches to do in the matter? Should they continue to interchange with the Plymouth Church those acts of inter-communion which constitute the special fellowship of the Congregational Churches? This question was the more serious because the action complained of was not apologized for as exceptional and unlikely to be repeated, but was defended as normal—an instance of the responsibility to which the members of that church are held by their covenant; and because by a published note it had interpreted its rules as relieving "all other churches from responsibility for the doctrine, order, and discipline of [that] church, and [that] church from all responsibility for those of other churches." Advice was therefore desired by the two complaining churches on the question of withdrawing from special communion with the Plymouth Church.

V. What was done by the Council.

To give a general answer, I may say, not much, for the reason that there was little to be done. In such a case, so large a body must take a long time to do a little—to enunciate the case, to find out what can be done and what cannot be done. I have mentioned the fact that the case was before the Council in the form of published and official documents. These documents were supplemented by a communication which the Plymouth Church sent in reply to an invitation from the Council, and which made such professions and declarations as might justify a hope that the exceptional and very exceptionable action complained of would not be repeated. The Result, then, of the Council affirms:

1. That the complaining churches had a right to ask advice

concerning the regularity and Christian character of what they had done in their dealings with the Plymouth Church.

2. That in their remonstrance they acted in the interest of the entire fraternity of Congregational churches, and deserved thanks for their "moral heroism."

3. That their first letter made an impression in some measure different from what was intended, and wounded the sensibilities of those to whom it was addressed, for which they had made in a subsequent letter all necessary explanation.

4. That an ingenuous explanation from the Plymouth Church of the reasons which had moved it to rid itself of an offending member by an exceptional method might have brought the correspondence to an early and happy termination.

5. That the complaining churches would have done wisely if they had urged their request for a mutual council till refusal or evasion on the part of the Plymouth Church should have become unequivocal.

6. That without obtruding upon the Plymouth Church any advice concerning its method of dealing with offenders, the principles maintained by the complaining churches in regard to responsibility of church members are sound.

7. That in view of the latest utterance from the Plymouth Church concerning its method of discipline and its regard for the intercommunion of the Congregational churches, the complaining churches are advised to maintain with it the relations of fellowship as heretofore, in the hope that the Plymouth Church may satisfy them of its acceptance of those principles which it has been supposed to disavow.

And now, some of you may think that what has been said has been dictated by suspicion of Mr. Beecher's purity. My theory of all these transactions and troubles proceeds on a belief in the highest Christian integrity of Mr. Beecher. I believe that the infamous women who have started this scandal have no basis for it. [Applause.] If it were their testimony alone, it would not be worth kicking a dog for. But I doubt not that he has his infirmity, which is to let unprincipled men know too much of him. I object not to his being a friend to publicans and sinners. Our Lord was. But the harlot who washed his feet with her tears, and wiped them with her tresses, was a repentant harlot. So one must hedge himself in a little. And you, as you go out to preach, be on your guard, lest in your anxiety to do good to the low you become liable to be charged with their sins.

Another part of my theory is that Mr. Beecher's *magnanimity is unspeakable. I never knew a man of a larger and more generous mind. One who was in relations to him the most intimate possible, said to me, "If I wanted to secure his highest love, I would go into a church-meeeting and accuse him of crimes." This is his spirit. But I think he may carry it too far. A man whose life is a treasure to the Church Universal, to his country, to his age, has no right to subject the faith in it to such a strain.* Some one has said that Plymouth Church's dealing with offenders is like Dogberry's. The comparsion was apt: "If any one will not stand, let him go, and gather the guard and thank God that you are rid of such a knave." So of Lance, who went into the stocks and the pillory to save his dog from execution for stealing puddings and geese. I think he would have done better to let the dog die. And I think Mr. Beecher would have done better to have let vengeance come on the heads of his slanderers.

But he stands before his Master, and not before men. I hope ever to feel the fullest confidence in his character, and to see his influence enlarge and round out more and more. No one could give such a course of lectures as this last one of his here —which was the best—and show unconsciously such a reach of spiritual experience and growth, without being pure and noble. [Applause.] And in this feeling the Council shared. Dr. —— himself said to me as we went out of the church after Dr. Storrs' address, in which he paid his high tribute to Mr. Beecher's character and work. "That passage should be saved to be Mr. Beecher's funeral eulogy, for it could never be excelled."

This address of the Ex-Moderator of the Council was supplemented by several articles in the *Independent* published by Mr. Henry C. Bowen, from the pen of Dr. Bacon. These articles severely criticised the action of Mr. Tilton and were written in such language as was well calculated to goad that gentleman into a defence of his position.

CHAPTER VI.

MR. TILTON'S CELEBRATED REPLY TO DR. BACON'S CRITICISMS. —HIS DECLARATION THAT OWING TO THE EFFORTS MADE BY MR. BEECHER'S FRIENDS TO CRUSH HIM HE FELT CALLED UPON TO SHOW THAT HE WAS NOT THE CREATURE OF MR. BEECHER'S MAGNANIMITY.—THE LETTER OF BEECHER ASKING THEODORE TILTON'S FORGIVENESS.—"I HUMBLE MYSELF BEFORE HIM AS I WOULD BEFORE MY GOD."—THE OFFENSE COMMITTED AGAINST TILTON BY BEECHER, WHICH THEODORE FORBEARS TO NAME.—TILTON SPURNS A PROPOSITION FROM BEECHER'S FRIENDS TO PAY HIS EXPENSES IF HE WILL RETREAT TO EUROPE WITH HIS FAMILY.

UPON the congregation who worship at Plymouth Church there had settled the conviction that the great majority of the distinguished divines and laymen who formed that celebrated council were dissatisfied with the result of the conference, that failed to re-open the case, and compel Mr. Beecher's church to force him to answer before it the charges so explicitly made, and while many hoped that—to use an expressive but unlicensed word—that body having been "bluffed" by the Plymouth society, there was likely to be an end of the effort in behalf of an investigation. Others saw clearly that grave complications were likely to arise in the future. They argued that the declared independence of Plymouth of sister Congregational churches was likely to aggravate instead of allaying the excitement, and result in a combined movement on the part of the disappointed and defeated council, and its distinguished moderator, Dr. Bacon, to force an investigation by some more summary means. The publication of Dr. Bacon's address and essays on the subject, referred to in the preceding chapter, convinced these gentlemen that their suspicions were well founded, and they intuitively came to the conclusion that these articles by the moderator were prepared specially to pave the way for a response from Mr. Tilton that would compel the church to act promptly in the premises. It was well known within the corporation of the church and especially to the more confidential friends of the pastor, that the celebrated gentlemen who formed that council keenly felt the slight given them by the course the society of Plymouth Church had followed on the advice of Mr. Beecher, and none of them were surprised when Mr. Tilton spoke in the able review of the case a few days later. As this document is of so great importance that no history of the scandal would be complete without it, it is here given in full. It is in the following words, as published in Mr. Tilton's *Golden Age*, June 24th.

The Rev. Leonard Bacon, D. D., L. L. D., ex-Moderator of the Brooklyn Council:—SIR—I have carefully read your New Haven address concerning the late Council, and also your five essays on the same subject, just concluded in the *Independent*.

The numerous and extraordinary misrepresentations of my position which these writings of yours will perpetuate to my injury, if not corrected, compel me to lay before you the data for their correction—misrepresentations which, on your part, are of course wholly unintentional, for you are incapable of doing any man a willful wrong.

In producing to your inspection some hitherto unpublished papers and documents in this case, I need first to state a few facts in chronological sequence, sufficient to explain the documentary evidence which follows:

I. After I had been for fifteen years a member of Plymouth Church, and had become meanwhile an intimate friend of the Pastor, knowledge came to me in 1870 that he had committed against me AN OFFENSE WHICH I FORBEAR TO NAME OR CHARACTERIZE. Prompted by my self-respect, I immediately and forever ceased my attendance on his ministry. I informed him of this determination as early as January, 1871, in the presence of a mutual friend, Mr. Francis D. Moulton.

The rules of Plymouth Church afforded me a choice between two methods of retirement: One, to ask for a formal letter of dismissal; the other to dismiss myself less formally by prolonged absence. I chose the latter. In so doing, my chief desire was to avoid giving rise to curious inquiries into the reasons for my abandoning a Church in which I had been brought up from boyhood; and therefore I did not invite attention to the subject by asking for a dismissory letter, but adopted the alternative of silently staying away,—relying on the rule that a prolonged absence would finally secure to me a dismissal involving no publicity to the case.

Several powerful reasons prompted me to the adoption of this alternative, among which were the following: The Pastor communicated to me in writing an apology, signed by his name. He also appealed to me to protect him from bringing reproach to the cause of religion. He alleged that an exposure WOULD FORBID HIM TO REASCEND HIS PULPIT. These, and other similar reasons, I had no right or disposition to disregard; and I acted upon them with a conscious desire to see Mr. Beecher protected rather than harmed.

II. At length my absence from the Church—an absence of which not three members of the congregation, beside the Pastor, knew the cause—began to excite comment in private circles.

Some of the members hinted that I had lapsed into a lamentable change of religious views; whereas my views continued to be the same as they had been for many years previous, and, though they had long before ceased to find their honest expression in the formal creed which I had professed in my childhood at the altar of Plymouth Church, yet my religious faith had not changed from that early original more than the views of some of the most honored members and officers of the same Church had changed within the same time.

Other persons insinuated that I had adopted unchristian tenets concerning marriage and divorce: whereas, touching marriage, I have always held, and still hold, with ever-increasing firmness, the one and only view common to all Christendom; and touching divorce, the substance of what I held was, and still is, the needful abrogation of our unjust New York code, and the substitution of the more humane legislation of New England and the West.

Other persons fancied that I had become a Spiritualist of an extravagant type; whereas I have never yet seen my way clear to be a Spiritualist at all,—certainly not to be so much a Spiritualist as some of the most prominent members of Plymouth Church are known to be.

All these suppositions,—and many others,—but never the right one,—became current in the Church (and still are) to explain my suddenly-ended membership,—the true reason for which has been understood always by the Pastor, but never by his flock.

III. At length, after many calumnious whisperings near and far (since evil tales magnify as they travel), a weekly paper in New York, in November, 1872, published a wicked and horrible scandal,—a publication which some persons in the Church ignorantly attributed in its origin and animus to me; whereas I had previously spent many months of CONSTANT AND UNREMITTING ENDEAVOR TO SUPPRESS IT,—an endeavor in which, with an earnest motive, but a foolish judgment, I made many ill-directed sacrifices of my reputation, position, money, and fair prospects in life; for all which losses of things precious, since mine alone was the folly, let mine alone be the blame.

IV. In May, 1873, occurred the surreptitious publication of a tripartite agreement signed by H. C. Bowen, H. W. Beecher, and myself,—an agreement which, so far as I was concerned, had for its object to pledge me to silence against using or circulating charges which Mr. Bowen had made against Mr. Beecher. This covenant, as originally written, would have bound me never to speak, not only of Mr. Bowen's, but also of my own personal grievances against Mr. Beecher. I refused to sign the original paper. My position in the amended paper was this: Mr. Bowen had made grave charges against Mr. Beecher. These charges Mr. Bowen had been induced to recall in writing. I cheerfully agreed never to circulate the charges which Mr. Bowen had recalled.

V. In August, 1873, Mr. William F. West, a member of Plymouth Church, hitherto a stranger to me, came to my residence, accompanied (at his request) by my friend, Mr. F. B. Carpenter, and told me that, when the summer-vacation was over he (Mr. W.) meant to cite me before the Church on the charge of circulating scandals against the Pastor,—declaring, in Mr. C.'s presence, that Mr. Beecher had acted as if the reported scandalous tales were true rather than false, and urging that I owed it to myself and the truth to go forward and become a willing witness in an investigation. I peremptorily declined to join Mr. West in his proposed investigation, and declared that, as I had not been a member of Plymouth Church for several years, I could not be induced to return to that Church for any purpose whatever, least of all for so distasteful a purpose as to participate in a scandal. Mr. West had meanwhile discovered that my name still remained on the Church-roll; from which circumstance he determined to assume that I was still a member, and to FORCE ME TO TRIAL. Accordingly, a few weeks later, he brought forward charges which were nominally against myself, but really against the Pastor,—charges which, if I may characterize them by the recently published language of the present Clerk of Plymouth Church, were "an indirect and insincere method of investigating one man under the false pretense of investigating another."

Some leading members, including especially the Pastor, desired my coöperation in defeating Mr. West, and I cheerfully gave it. To this end, I wrote—with their pre-knowledge and at their urgent desire—a letter declining to accept a copy of the charges addressed to me as a member, on the ground that I had, four years previously, ceased my connection with the Church. For this letter, I received, on the next day after sending it, the pastor's prompt and hearty thanks. An understanding was then had between Mr. Beecher and myself, in an interview at the residence of Mr. Moulton, that Mr. West's indictment against me was to be disposed of in the following way, namely: by a simple resolution to the effect that, whereas I had four years previously, terminated my membership; and whereas by inadvertence my name still remained on the roll: therefore, resolved that the roll be amended in accordance with the fact. This was to put Mr. West's case quietly out of court without bringing up the scandal. *To my surprise and indignation*, I learned on the morning of October 31st, 1873, that the report which was to be presented at the Church-meeting to be held on that evening would not be in the simple form already indicated, but would declare that, whereas I had been charged with slandering the Pastor; and whereas I had been cited before the Church to meet the charge; and whereas I had pleaded non-membership as an excuse for not appearing for trial; therefore resolved, that I should be dropped, etc.

This gross imputation, thus foreshadowed to me, led me to appear in person at the Church on that evening, there to await the reading of the forthcoming report. This report, when it came to be read, brought me the following novel intelligence, namely: "Whereas a copy of the charges was put into the hands of the said Tilton on the 17th of October, *and a request made of him that he should answer the same* by the 23d of October," etc.

I do not know to this day whose hand it was that drew the above report, and therefore I am happily saved an offensive personality when I say that the statement which I have here quoted is diametrically the opposite of the truth; for, instead of my having been requested to answer the charges, I had been requested *not* to answer them.

After the public reading of the above report, I arose in the meeting, and said, in Mr. Beecher's presence, that, if I had slandered him, I would answer for it to his face; to which he replied, in an equally public manner, that he had NO CHARGE WHATEVER TO MAKE AGAINST ME.

IV. Next, growing out of the Church's singular proceedings in the case, came the Congregational Council of which you were Moderator.

The above facts and events—which I have mentioned as briefly as possible, omitting their details—will serve as a sufficient ground-work whereon to base the correction of the unjust and injurious statements which you have unwittingly given of my participation and responsibility in the case. With the Congregational theories and usages which you have so ably discussed, I have no concern; you are probably right about them. But, as to all the essential facts growing out of my relationship to Plymouth Church, you have been wholly misinformed, as you will see by the following proofs.

I. You say that I retired from the Church, giving no announcement of my so doing to any proper officer; in other words, that I stole out secretly, letting no one in authority know of my purpose. Your language concerning me is as follows:

> His position was that he had terminated his membership four years previously,—*not by requesting the Church* (as by its rules it might have done) *to drop his name from its roll* etc.

You then ask:

> Is this the beautiful non-stringency of the covenant which connects the members of that Church with the body, and with each other? What sort of covenant is that which can be dissolved at any moment, not by mutual

consent, nor by either party giving notice to the other, but by a silent volition in the mind of either?

The above is *a thorough mistatement* of the manner in which I left Plymouth Church.

On the very first occasion of my meeting the chief officer of the Church after my retirement, I gave notice to him of that retirement. At a late period, I repeated this notice to other officers of that body. In evidence of this fact, I adduce the following extract from a recent card by Mr. Thomas G. Shearman, Clerk of Plymouth Church, published in the *Independent* of June 18th, 1874. He says:

> Long before any charges were preferred against him, Mr. Tilton distinctly informed the Clerk of the Church, and various other officers and members (myself included), *that he had withdrawn, and that his name ought to be taken off the roll.*

II. You say that I have either "a malicious heart or a crazy brain." I know the fountain-head of this opinion. While the Council was in session in Brooklyn, the following startling paragraph appeared in the Brooklyn *Union* of Saturday, March 28th, 1874:

> At the close of the services a *Union* reporter approached Mr. Beecher for the purpose of getting his views as to the Council, but he declined to be interviewed. Mr. Shearman, the Clerk, of the Church, however, was communicative. He said he had received no intimation, as yet, what course the Council would pursue. In regard to the scandal on Mr. Beecher he said, so far as Tilton was concerned, he (Tilton) was out of his mind, off his balance, and did not act reasonsbly. As for Mrs. Tilton, she had occasioned the whole trouble while in a half-crazed condition. she had mediumistic fits, and while under the strange power that possessed her often spoke of the most incredible things, declared things possible that were impossible, and, among the rest, had slandered Mr. Beecher. Mr. Tilton himself had acknowledged that all the other things she had told him in her mediumistic trance were false and impossible; then why, asked Mr. Shearman, should the scandal on Mr. Beecher be the only truth in her crazy words?

My attention was not called to the above paragraph until after the Council had adjourned and its members had gone to their homes. At first I was not willing to believe that the Clerk of Plymouth Church—the same officer whose name had been officially signed to all the documents which the Church had just been sending to the Council—*could have been guilty of so great an outrage against truth and decency* as the above paragraph contained—particularly against a lady whose devout religious faith and life are at the farthest possible remove from Spiritualism or fanaticism of any kind. Accordingly I procured the following sworn statement by the reporter, certifying to the accuracy of his report:

KINGS COUNTY, ss.

Edwin F. Denyse, reporter of the Brooklyn *Union*, being duly sworn, deposed as follows:

At the close of the Friday evening meeting in Plymouth Church, March 27th, 1874, I, in company with another member of the press, requested Mr. Thomas G. Shearman, Clerk of the Church, to communicate to us for publication any facts, or comments, or opinions, which he might wish to make concerning the Congregational Council then in session; whereupon Mr. Shearman stated in our hearing, and for the purpose for which we asked him to do so, the allegations contained in the previous paragraph. And I do swear that this paragraph is a correct and moderate report of Mr. Shearman's statement, both in letter and spirit. And I further testify, that I solicited as a reporter the above statement from Mr. Shearman because he was the Clerk of the Church, whose name had been affixed in that capacity to the documents that Plymouth Church had sent to the Council, and because an opinion from such a high officer would have an official authenticity and importance. EDWIN F. DENYSE.

Sworn to before me this 1st day of April, 1874.

FRANK CROOKE, Justice of the Peace.

Shortly after the appearance of Mr. Shearman's reported interview in the *Union*, that gentleman sent to me, through Mr. F. D. Moulton, a letter, the substance of which was that he (Mr. S.) had referred in the above conversation, not to *me* or *my* family, but to other persons. This letter I declined to receive, and returned it to the writer, with a demand upon him to retract his untrue and unjust statements. Furthermore, I required,as a condition of my accepting from Mr. Shearman any apology at all, that this apology should be presented to me in writing in the presence of the Rev. Henry Ward Beecher. This was promptly done. At Mr. Moulton's house, in Mr. Beecher's presence. Mr. Shearman's apologetic letter was as follows:

BROOKLYN, April 2, 1874.

DEAR SIR:—Having seen a paragraph in the Brooklyn *Union* of Saturday last, containing a report of a statement alleged to have been made by me concerning your family and yourself, I desire to assure you that this report is seriously incorrect, and that I have never authorized such a statement.

It is unnecessary to repeat here what I have actually said upon these subjects, because I am now satisfied that what I *did* say was erroneous, and that the rumors to which I gave some credit were without foundation.

I deeply regret having been misled into an act of unintentional injustice. and am glad to take the earliest occasion to rectify it. I beg, therefore, to withdraw all that I said upon the occasion referred to as incorrect (although then believed by me), and to repudiate entirely the statement imputed to me as untrue and unjust to all parties concerned.

T. G. SHEARMAN.

Theodore Tilton, Esq.

The above-named calumny which Mr. T. G. Shearman thus retracted is but one of several falsehoods against my wife and myself which have been fostered by interested parties to explain the action of Plymouth Church—falsehoods which, in some instances, have been corrected in the same way, and which, in others, still await to be corrected, either in this way, or a court of justice.

III. You ask, "When did Mr. Tilton cease to be responsible to the Plymouth Church?" I answer that I first ceased my responsibility to that church when I terminated my membership, four years ago. I afterwards voluntarily renewed my responsibility to the church on the evening of October 31st, 1873, by appearing in person at one of its public meetings, and offering to answer then and there, in the pastor's presence, the charge that I had slandered him. Less than two months ago, I still further renewed my responsibility to Plymouth Church, as will appear by the following correspondence:

BROOKLYN, May, 4 1874.

The Rev. Henry Ward Beecher, Pastor of Plymouth Church; the Rev, S. B. Halliday, Associate Pastor; and Mr. Thomas G. Shearman, Clerk:

GENTLEMEN:—I address, through you, to the Church of which you are officers, the following statement, which you are at liberty to communicate to the church through the Examining Committee, or in any other mode, private or public.

The Rev. Leonard Bacon D. D., L. L. D., Moderator of the recent Congregational Council, has seen fit since the adjournment of that body, to proclaim, publish and reiterate, with signal emphasis, and with the weight of something like official authority, a grave declaration which I here quote, namely:

"It was for the Plymouth Church," he says, "to vindicate its Pastor against a damaging imputation from one of its members. But with great alacrity—the Pastor himself consenting—it threw away the opportunity of vindication."* * * "That act," he continued, "in which the Plymouth Church threw away the oppo tunity of vindi ating its Pastor, was what gave occasion for remonstrance from neighboring Churches." * * * "There are many," he says also, "not only in Brooklyn, but elsewhere, who felt that the Church had not fairly met the question, and by evading the issue had thrown away the opportunity to vindicate its Pastor."

The Moderator's decla ation is thus made three times over, that the Plymouth Church, in dealing with my case, threw away its opportunity of vindicating the Pastor.

This declaration, so emphatically repeated by the chief mouth-piece of the Council, and put forth by him apparently as an exposition of the Council's views, compels me, as the third party to the controversy, to choose between two alternatives.

One of th se is to remain contentedly in the dishonorable position of a man who denies to his former Pastor an opportunity for vindication of that Pastor's character,—an offense the more heinous because an unsullied character and reputation are requisites to his sacred office.

The other alternative is for me to restore to his Church their lost opportunity for his vin ication by presenting myself voluntarily for the same trial to which the Church would have power to summon me if I were a member,—a suggestion which (judging from my past experience) will subject me afresh to the unjust imputation of reviving a scandal for the suppr ssi n of which I have made more sacrifices than all other persons.

Between these two alternatives,—which are all that the Mod rator leaves to me, and which are both equally repugnant to my feelings,—duty requires me to choose the second.

I, therefore, give you notice that, if the Pastor, or the Examining Committee, or the Church as a body, desire to repossess the opportunity which the Moderator laments that you have thrown away, I hereby restore to you this lost opportunity as freely as if you had never parted with it.

I authorize you (if such be your pleasure) to cite me at any time within the next thirty days to appear at the bar of Plymouth Church for trial on the charge heretofore made against me, namely: that of circulating and promoting scandals derogatory to the Christian integ ity of the Pastor, and injurious to the reputation of the Church.

My only stipulation concerning the trial is, that it shall not be held with closed doors, nor in the absence of the Pastor.

I regret keenly that the Moderator has imposed upon me the necessity for making this communication, but nothing but necessity would extort it.

The practical good which I seek to achieve by this proposition is, that, whether accepted or declined, it will in either case, effectually put an end forever to the Moderator's grave charge that Plymouth Church has been deprived through me of an opportunity to vindicate its Pastor, or that its Pastor has been by any act of mine deprived of an opportunity to vindicate himself.

Truly yours,

THEODORE TILTON.

To the above communication I received the following reply from the Clerk of the Church:

BROOKLYN May 18th, 1874.

DEAR SIR:—Your note of the 4th inst., inclosing a letter addressed to Mr. Beecher, Mr. Halliday and myself, was duly received.

This letter has been received by Mr. Halliday, with whose concurrence it has been submitted to the Examining Committee: and we all deem its contents to present a question which should be decided by that Committee, and which should not be submitted to the Pastor of the Church, to whom, therefore, the letter has not been shown, though he has been advised of its substance.

Having consulted the members of the committee, I am informed by them that they *see no reason for accepting your proposition*, or even for laying it before the Church.

Whatever view may be taken of the case by others, the Examining Committee and the Church have seen no necessity for vindicating any member of the Church from charges which no one has made, and the Church has never, in the twenty-seven years of its history, adopted such a course. No one can, therefore, hold you responsible for the loss of an opportunity to the Church to do that which it never yet has done, and probably never will do.

We do not understand your letter as implying that you have any charge to make, but to the contrary. If the Committee had so understood it, they would have readily entertained and fully investigated it.

It is proper to add that your name was dropped from the roll, not simply because of the statements made by you *after* charges had been preferred against you, but because months, if not years, *before* any charges were made, you distinctly stated to various officers and members of the Church that you had permanently abandoned your connection with it, thus bringing yourself expressly within the terms of our rule upon this subject.

Yours truly

THOMAS G. SHEARMAN.

MR. THEODORE TILTON.

As the above communication by Mr. Shearman seemed to bear no official, but only a private signature, I addressed to him the following communication:

174 LIVINGSTON STREET, BROOKLYN,
May 23d, 1874.

Mr. Thomas G. Shearman, Clerk of Plymouth Church—SIR:—My recent communication, addressed to the Pastor, Associate Pastor, and the Clerk of Plymouth Church, is acknowledged by you in a note which you seem to have signed merely as a private individual, and not as an officer of the Church.

I call your attention to the fact that I did not address you in your private capacity, but solely as the Clerk of Plymouth Church.

I therefore respectfully request to be informed by you definitely in writing, whether or not I am at liberty to regard your letter an official reply to mine. Truly yours,

THEODORE TILTON.

Mr. Shearman's reply was as follows:

81 HICKS STREET, BROOKLYN, May 29, 1874.

DEAR SIR:—In reply to your inquiry whether my letter of the 18th inst. was an official answer to yours of the 4th inst., I beg to say that I did not feel at liberty, without the express authority of the Church itself, to sign that letter as its Clerk.

In so far as the letter stated that your proposition of May 4th, was declined, it was official: since, as Clerk of the Church, I declined then, and decline now, to lay the proposals before the Church itself, holding myself responsible to the Church for so doing.

The remainder of the letter of 18th inst. must be regarded as my individual statement of what I believe to be the unanimous opinion of the officers of the Church. Your obedient servant,

THOMAS G. SHEARMAN.

MR. THEODORE TILTON.

It will thus be seen that Mr. Shearman, in answer to my inquiry, characterizes his previous letter to me as partly official and partly unofficial,—though how he could originally have expected me to draw the dividing line between its two parts without the subsequent explanation, I am at a loss to understand. But the official portion of his letter (now that it has been pointed out to me) is sufficient to answer your query: "When did Mr. Tilton cease to be responsible to the Plymouth Church?" I respectfully submit that, setting aside all previous cavils and technicalities concerning the Church-roll, I may be fairly said to have ceased my responsibility to Plymouth Church when the Clerk of that Church officially informed me that my voluntary offer to return and be tried was officially declined.

IV. In your five essays, you were led, through ignorance of the facts, to make several other erroneous and injurious statements concerning my case; but the corrections and explanations which I have already given will of themselves correct the others.

It now remains for me to give you some reasons why I have been prompted, after years of reticence, to lay before you the grave matters contained in this communication. Nothing could induce me to make my present use of the foregoing facts, except the conviction which the events of the last year, and particularly the last half-year, have forced upon my mind, that Mr. Beecher, or his legal and other agents, acting in his interest and by his consent, have shown themselves willing to sacrifice *my* good name for the maintenance of *his*. I have come slowly to this judgment,—more slowly than my personal friends have done; but that I am not mistaken in it, you shall see by a few illustrative instances:

I. I have already shown you how the Church, at a public meeting, on Friday evening, October 31st, 1873, by an official document which was published the next morning in every leading journal in New York, gave the public falsely to understand that I had been cited to answer charges, when I had really been requested *not* to answer them—a piece of ecclesiastical misrepresentation which was the more grievous to me because it was subsequently accepted by the Council as authentic, and because it is still widely believed by the public.

II. Mr. Beecher's journal, the *Christian Union*, published this official falsehood to a wide circle of readers, and took no notice of the correction which I addressed at the time in a brief note to the Council. Let me ask you to weigh the peculiar gravity of this omission by that journal. My case, as presented to the Council by the two protesting Churches, was based by them, not on any private or accurate knowledge of facts, but solely on the published misstatements of those facts by Plymouth Church. I was described by the two Churches to the Council as follows:

> Specific charges of grossly un-Christian conduct are presented against him by a brother in the Church, *to which charges he declines to answer*, etc.

You will remember that I promptly addressed to you a reply to the above, in which I used the following explicit words:

> Gentlemen of the Council, every man among you knows I did *not* decline to answer.

You, as Moderator of the Council, courteously gave me the ecclesiastical reasons why my letters could not be officially laid before that body; but can you give me any honorable reason why my defense should not have been published in the *Christian Union!* If every other American journal should be destroyed, and only the files of the *Christian Union* should remain, that journal's report of my case would represent me as a culprit, first who had slandered a clergyman; next, who had been summoned before the Church to answer for this calumniation; next, who had evaded this summons by resorting to the safe shelter of non-membership; and last, who, on account of his moral poltroonery, had been dropped from the roll. Such is the record which Mr. Beecher's journal contains of my case up to date.

III. During the Council, and when there seemed a probability that Plymouth Church would receive condemnation and be disfellowshiped by the neighboring Churches, Mr. Beecher inspired a message from his Church to the Council, closing with these words:

> We hold that it is our right and may be our duty, to avoid the evils incident to a public explanation or a public trial, and that such an exercise of our discretion furnishes no good ground for the interference of other Churches, *provided we neither retain within our fellowship nor dismiss by letter, as in regular standing, persons who bring open dishonor on the Christian name.*

This adroit insinuation against me is what you, as Moderator of the Council, know to have been the turning point in the fortunes of Plymouth Church before that tribunal. The Council's verdict borrows almost these identical words. It says: "The accused person has not been retained in the Church, nor commended to any other Church." You, too, quote these words,—borrowed thus doubly from the Church's plea and from the Council's verdict,—and you then logically say: "Therefore, the abnormal method in which the charges against him [me] were disposed of was overlooked." In other words, the Council, on reading the above excusatory petition sent up to it by Plymouth Church, found in it the one and only ground for retaining that Church within the Congregation fellowship; and this one and only ground was because Mr. Beecher's final appeal to the Council represented me as a person who had neither been retained in his Church, nor been recommended to any other, but was dropped from the roll for bringing "dishonor on the Christian name." This document —constituting Plymouth Church's ungenerous defense before the Council—was accepted by you in good faith, and has since led you to point against me the following cruel words:

The Plymouth Church [you say] made it known that they were no longer responsible for the dishonor which he has brought, or may bring, on the name of Christ. They dropped him from the roll of the Church. In one word, they excommunicated him, for such a dropping from the roll was excommunication from the Church.

You could never have uttered the preceding injurious words against me, had not Mr. Beecher and his Church-Agents given you the materials for so doing by ingeniously putting before the Council a document which you, as Moderator, interpreted as being only another way of Plymouth Church's saying that I had brought dishonor on the Christian name, and had therefore been excommunicated.

Do not misunderstand me. I will not say that, in my unsuccessful management of this unhappy scandal, I have brought no "dishonor on the Christian name"—the one which, of all others, I most seek to honor. With infinite sorrow I look back through the last few years, and see instances in which, by the fatality of my false position, I have brought peculiar "dishonor on the Christian name"—all of which I freely acknowledge and hope yet to repair. But I solemnly aver —and no man shall gainsay me—that the reason why Plymouth Church avoided an investigation into the scandal with which I was charged was not because *I, but another man*, had "brought dishonor on the Christian name." And yet this other person, a clergyman, permitted his Church to brand me before the Council with an accusation which, had I been in his place and he in mine, I would have voluntarily borne for myself instead of casting on another.

III. I will adduce a further instance by a quotation from a letter which I had occasion to address to Mr. Beecher, dated May 1st, 1874:

Henry Ward Beecher:—SIR—Mr. F. B. Carpenter mentions to me your saying to him that, under certain conditions, involving certain disavowals by me, a sum of money would or could be raised to send me, with my family, to Europe for a term of years.

The occasion compels me to state explicitly that, so long as life and self-respect continue to exist together in my breast, I shall be debarred from receiving either directly or indirectly *any pecuniary or other favor at your hands.*

The reason for this feeling on my part you know so well that I will spare you the statement of it.

Yours truly,

THEODORE TILTON.

IV. Take another instance. You will perceive that in Mr. Shearman's letter, given above—the letter officially declining my offer to return to the Church to be tried,—he says, under date May 18th, 1874:

Your note of the 4th inst., inclosing a letter addressed to Mr. Beecher, Mr. Halliday, and myself, was duly received. *This letter has been read by Mr. Halliday with whose concurrence it has been submitted to the Examining Committee.*

And yet, a month and a half after Mr. Halliday saw this letter, and a month after Mr. Shearman had officially replied to it, the Brooklyn *Union*, of June 19th, contained the following singular statement by a reporter who visited Mr. Halliday:

In an extract [says the *Union*] from a letter written to the Chicago *Tribune*, it stated that Mr Tilton had addressed a note to the "Trustees of Plymouth Church." The *Tribune's* correspondent declares that Mr. Tilton "not only expresses his willingness, but desires, to answer any summons as a witness during the next thirty days." A *Union* reporter (Mr. Tilton not being accessible) called on the Rev. Mr. Halliday to-day, and, upon presenting the extract to him, was assured that the person who corresponded with the Chicago *Tribune* must have been misinformed. The very fact of his stating that the letter was addressed "to the Trustees of the Church," he said, "was an absurdity." The Trustees only attended to temporalities of the Church. *If Mr. Tilton had written such a letter—of which, however, he had no knowledge, it would have either been addressed to the Church, to its Pastor, or to some member or members.* At the last Friday evening meeting no such letter had been presented for consideration, and he was certain none had since been received, although he must say he had been absent in Massachusetts about a week. *He added that he had reason for believing that Mr. Tilton felt "a little sore about what the Rev. Mr. Bacon had said of him. But whether he would take to writing about it, he couldn't say."*

And yet Mr. Halliday, according to Mr. Shearman's testimony, above given, had read my letter forty days before thus denying that he had ever seen or heard of it.

A similar statement to the above appeared in the Brooklyn *Eagle* at the same time (June 20th), as follows:

The Trustees of Plymouth Church deny that Theodore Tilton has addressed a letter to them offering himself as a witness, and expressing a desire to answer certain charges against Mr. Beecher, during the next thirty days. They say that the whole story is false from beginning to end.

The above are recent specimens—not solitary or unique—of the manner in which Mr. Beecher's agents have not hesitated to use the Brooklyn press, on numerous occasions, to misrepresent and pervert my case to the community in which I reside, and to the public at large.

V. Furthermore, I regret to point you to the evidence that Plymouth Church, or rather the attorney who now acts as its Clerk, is attempting to make up a false but plausible record concerning this case, for the purpose of appealing to it in future to my disadvantage. It was to this end that Mr. Shearman ingeniously incorporated in his letter to me, dated May 18th, 1874, the following words:

We do not understand your letter as implying that you have any charges to make, but the contrary. *If the Committee had so understood it, they would have readily entertained and fully investigated them.*

The manifest object of the above record is to enable the Church to say, a year or five years hence, that, if I ever had any charges to make against Mr. Beecher, the Church had long ago given me an abundant opportunity to make them. Mr. Shearman is still more bold in his communication to the *Independent*, dated June 18th, 1874. He therein says of the Church:

Its officers have in the proper way, without parade *given every facility for investigation that could reasonably be desired, even by the most captious critics.*

The above statement by Mr. Shearman is made in a letter which was put forth by him ostensibly in my interest, and which I am already accused of having inspired. This leads me to disavow the declaration which I have last quoted, as insincere and at variance with the truth.

VI. Not to multiply instances needlessly, there is one other to which my self-respect compels me to allude with painful explicitness. In your New Haven speech, you characterized Mr. Beecher as the most magnanimous of men, and in the context referred to me as a knave and a dog. You left the public to infer that I had become, in some despicable way, the creature of Mr. Beecher's magnanimity. Early in April last, I called Mr. Beecher's attention to the offensiveness and injuriousness of your statement, and informed him that *I should insist on its correction*, either by him or me. In order to provide an easy way for him to correct it, involving no humiliation to his feelings, I addressed to you the following letter:

BROOKLYN, April 3d, 1874.

The Rev. Leonard Bacon, D. D.—My dear Sir:—I have just been reading the *Tribune's* report of your Yale speech on the Brooklyn Council, in which occurs the following paragraph:

"Another part of my theory is, that Mr. Beecher's magnanimity is unspeakable. I never knew a man of larger and more generous mind. One who was in relations to him the most intimate possible said to me. 'If I wanted to secure his highest love, I would go into a church-meeting and accuse him of crimes.' This is his spirit. But I think he may carry it too far. A man whose life is a treasure to the Church Universal, to his country, to his age, has no right to subject the faith in it to such a strain. Some one has said that Plymouth Church's dealings with offenders is like Dogberry's. The comparison was apt: 'If any one will not stand, let him go and gather the guard and thank God that you are rid of such a knave.' So of Lance, who went into the stocks and the pillory to save his dog from execution for stealing puddings and geese. I think he would have done better to let the dog die. And I think Mr. Beecher would have done better to have let vengeance come on the heads of his slanderers."

* * * * * * * * * * * *

Setting aside the satire and mirth, if there be any criticism directed toward me in these words of sobriety and earnestness, then I beg you to do me the following act of justice:

Please forward to Mr. Beecher the letter which I am now writing, and ask him to inform you, on his word of honor, whether I have been his slanderer; whether I have spoken against him falsely; whether I have evaded my just responsibility to Plymouth Church; whether I have treated him other than with the highest possible fairness; and whether he has not acknowledged to me in large and ample terms, that *my* course towards *him* in this sorrowful business has been marked by the magnanimity which you apparently intimate has characterized *his* towards me.

If you will write to Mr. Beecher as I have indicated, I will thank you for a line as to the words or substance of his reply. With great respect I am truly yours,

THEODORE TILTON.

In reply to the above letter, you sent me the following:

NEW HAVEN, April 10th, 1874.

Theodore Tilton, Esq.—DEAR SIR:—Not being in Mr. Beecher's confidence, I have doubted what I ought to do with your letter written a week ago. I was not—and am not—willing to demand of him that he shall admit me to his confidence in a matter on which he chooses to be reticent. But, as the letter seems to have been written for *him* quite as much as for *me*, I have now sent it to him, without asking or expecting any reply.

* * * * * * * * * * * *

With the best wishes for your welfare, I am yours truly,

LEONARD BACON.

It is now between two or three months since I received from you the foregoing letter; and, as I have not heard that Mr. Beecher has made a reply, either to you or to me, I am at last forced to the disagreeable necessity of borrowing a reply in his own words, as follows:

BROOKLYN, Jan. 1, 1871.

I ask Theodore Tilton's forgiveness, and *humble myself before him as I do before my God.* He would have been a better man in my circumstances than I have been. I can ask nothing except that he will remember all the other breasts that would ache. I will not plead for myself. I even wish that I were dead.

* * * * * * * * * * * *

H. W. BEECHER.

The above brief extract from Mr. Beecher's own testimony will be sufficient, without adducing the remainder of the document, to show that I have just ground to resist the imputation that I am the creature of his magnanimity.

In conclusion, the common impression that I have circulated and promoted scandals against Mr. Beecher is not true. I doubt if any other man in Brooklyn, during the whole extent of the last four years, has spoken to so few persons on this subject as I have done. A mere handful of my intimate friends —who had a right to understand the case—are the only persons to whom I have ever communicated the facts. To all other persons I have been dumb,—resisting all questions, and refusing all explanations.

If the public have heretofore considered my silence as inexplicable, let my sufficient motive be now seen in the just forbearance which I felt morally bound to show to a man who had sent me a written and absolute apology.

But my duty to continue this forbearance ceased when the spirit of that apology was violated to my injury by its author or his agents. These violations have been multitudinous already, and they threaten to multiply in the future—forcing me to protect myself against them in advance—particularly against the cunning devices of the Clerk of the Church, who, acting as an attorney, appears to be conducting this business against me as if it were a case at law.

Had the fair spirit which I had a right to expect from Plymouth Church—at least for its Pastor's sake—been shown toward me, I would have continued to rest in silence on Mr. Beecher's apology, and never during the remainder of my life would I have permitted any public word of mine to allude to the offense or the offender.

But the injurious measure which the author of this apology has since permitted his Church to take against me, without protest on his part—measures leading to the misrepresentation of my case and character by the Church to the Council, and by the Council to the general public—involving gross injuries to me, which have been greatly aggravated by your writings—all these indictments, conjoining to one end, have put me before my countrymen in the character of a base and bad man—a character which, I trust, is foreign to my nature and life. Under the accumulating weight of this odium—unjustly bestowed on me—neither patience nor charity can demand that I keep silent.

In your capacity as ex-Moderator of the Council, and as its chief expositor, you have labeled the theme of your animadversions, "the celebrated case of Theodore Tilton." You have declared that "the transaction, with all its consequences, belong to history, and is in every way a legitimate subject of public criticism." If, therefore, your estimate of the historic importance of the case is true (though I hope it is not), I now finally appeal to you as its chief historian, not to represent me as playing an unmanly or dishonorable part in a case in which, so far as I can yet see, I have failed in no duty save to myself.

Truly yours, THEODORE TILTON.

DOCT. LEONARD BACON.

CHAPTER VII.

A SCATHING REVIEW OF TILTON, BEECHER AND WOODHULL'S PERNICIOUS DOCTRINES FROM THE PEN OF PROFESSOR V. B. DENSLOW. —THE "RECORD OF THESE THREE REFORMERS THE OUTCROPPINGS OF UNCLEANLINESS."—TILTON'S BIOGRAPHY OF "THAT UNBLUSHING APOSTLE OF PROSTITUTION" SEVERELY CRITICISED. —TILTON'S AMBITION AND HIS MARTYRDOM.—HIS ANALYZATION OF BEECHER'S CHARACTER.—HENRY WARD IS A VOLUPTUARY AND VERY SELFISH.—TILTON BEING A "FREE LOVER" COULD VERY PROPERLY ACCEPT AN APOLOGY FROM BEECHER FOR INVADING HIS HOME, INSTEAD OF RESORTING TO THE COWHIDE OR PISTOL.—THE INNER-LIFE OF PLYMOUTH CHURCH.

THE publication of Tilton's response to the Moderator, had the effect that both he and the members of the Council who had been so politely invited by Plymouth Church to "mind their own business," anticipated; it called attention to the subject that Beecher's friends had labored so long to ignore and stifle, and set not only the religious communities of New York and Brooklyn, where Mr. Beecher was so well and universally esteemed for his great talents, and bold and eloquent utterances, but the whole country, canvassing the pastor's guilt or innocence. The secular and religious journals alike published it, and commented thereon in such an unmistakable tone, that from the Kennebec to the Pacific the universal cry came up and was echoed and re-echoed, "*Mr. Beecher must now speak! He cannot: he dare not be silent!*" That letter: "*I humble myself before Theodore Tilton,*" etc., in the judgment of the entire nation demanded a prompt explanation. With Plymouth Church congregation the article in the *Golden Age* created intense alarm. Had a sixty-four pound shell dropped and exploded in the midst of one of Mr. Beecher's eloquent discourses no greater consternation could have been created.

And when some of the ablest writers of the country placed their opinions on paper their alarm was intensified an hundred fold. Among the reviews of the case that attracted general attention was the following supplied to the *Northwestern Christian Advocate* by Professor V. B. Denslow :—

"Those three persons," he says, referring to Tilton, Beecher and Woodhull, "whose names are now associated in the crowning scandal of the age, by a coincidence more logical than many will admit, are all, or have been, presidents of national women's rights associations. They have all entertained and advocated certain advanced notions of women's freedom, very like those advanced nearly a century ago by Mary Wolstoncraft and Charles Fourier, and more recently by John Stuart Mill. How remarkable the outcroppings of uncleanness in the record of those reformers! Mary Wolstoncraft teaches her sex to abhor marriage as a form of slavery; and not until her third illegitimate child brings upon the domicile of herself and her paramour the indignation of a British mob does she consent to convert her lover into a husband—not for the sake of decency, but that she might obtain for him the protection of the law. Fourier in one sentence defines lust in a manner that would have pleased the crude devotees of Isis and Osiris, and in the next teaches that the secret of the future progress of the race lies in so enlarging the freedom of man and woman that the fact of chastity shall disappear and the thought of it become ridiculous. A disciple of Fourier, Robert Dale Owen, procures, as a member of the Indiana legislature, the passage of the 'easiest' divorce law yet enacted, except in Wisconsin. Tilton advocates the Wisconsin law, whereby the bond of marriage may be severed by the mere consent of the parties who make it. Mrs. Woodhull scorns marriage, and procures a divorce from the husband she professes to love, in order that she may live with two divorced husbands under the same roof, in that freer relation which Fourier advocates, called the harmonial or complex marriage. Beecher marries the wife of

McFarland to the dying body of her legal seducer, the man who had ventured to address her 'My darling wife' while she was still living with her lawful husband, as if the mummery of the marriage ceremony could cleanse their guilt. John Stuart Mill, the foremost apostle of woman's freedom, takes to himself the wife of another, who had not been even accused of unkindness toward her, for no other reason than that she in her 'woman's freedom' preferred a metaphysical seducer to a Christian husband.

"Doubtless there are thousands of well-meaning ladies in the woman's rights movement who conscientiously deny that it has any affinity with licentiousness. It may tend, perhaps to correct this error when they observe the three publicly elected exponents of the woman's rights movement cowering together under the burden of a common shame, the legitimate result of an erroneous conviction as to the relations of the sexes to each other.

"Whoever has read Tilton's pamphlet life of Mrs. Woodhull, wherein he extols that unblushing apostle of prostitution as a woman the 'spotless whiteness of whose character' was above encomium, must have become satisfied that however silly a man must be to write in praise of the party of one who advocates strumpetry in the name of freedom, yet Tilton, with all his brilliant powers, had shown himself to be just as silly. He could only have done so, with any sincerity, by adopting a new definition of purity. This new definition Mrs. Woodhull's lectures, Tilton's articles on divorce, and Beecher's example in marrying Mrs. McFarland to the dying Richardson, all furnish. It is that that woman is chaste whose relations with men never violate the course of her free inclination, either by continuing with one of whom she is tired, or by failing to go to one of whom she is newly enamoured. Accepting this as the new definition of chastity, Mr. Tilton's praise, Mr. Beecher's liberality and Mrs. Woodhull's 'chastity' are alike accounted for.

"But with these convictions, what is likely to be their practice? In all this exposure, let not Mr. Tilton for one moment suppose that he is to be vindicated. Avenged he may be. No more.'

"He would never have placed it in the power of Mrs. Woodhull to so employ an equivocal and darkly-hinted scandal as deeply to affect the reputation of his own wife, had not his own relations with his revelator been as unguarded as his life of Mrs. Woodhull and Mrs. Woodhull's tale of scandal, combined, compel us to believe. There his drama of perdition begins. He has so often taught that if Cæsar's wife must be above suspicion, so also must Cornelia's husband, that he need feel no surprise if the world is slow to sympathize with him when the adventuress whom he has publicly commended to the world as of 'stainless purity' charges the wife whom he knows to be so, with dishonor. Again: Mr. Tilton, as an advocate of 'freedom for woman' in its most odious sense, has been too sincere to feel, and too logical to express, that just indignation which one not professedly a free-lover would have felt upon being made the victim of so blasting an infamy as this would have been to one who believed in the religious sanctity of marriage as a divine ordinance. A conservative man of honor would have probably shot Beecher—certainly would have cow-hided and exposed him. But Mr. Tilton, as an apostle of 'free-love' and woman's rights, was logically bound to regard the so-called 'crime' as an appeal to his wife's sovereign rights over her own person in the exercise of his pastor's sovereign rights to believe and practice what Tilton taught, viz: the purity of perfect freedom. Hence the secret written apology of Beecher, and the long and 'chivalrous' silence of Tilton.'

"Apart from the weak and corrupt views entertained by all these parties concerning the marriage relation, its divine sanction and its perpetuity, how has this scandal come about?'

"Eight years ago Theodore Tilton had the finest position and reputation, for a young man, in this country or age. He is an orator of first-class power, a poet of real merit, an editor of various talent. He is handsome, socially proud, and the husband of a lovely, petite, modest, accomplished wife. Mrs. Tilton is highly and most honorably connected—her father, the reverend Judge N. B. Morse of the supreme court, conservative on all moral and religious questions, and who was, we believe, a brother to the eminent Sydney E. Morse and Prof. S. F. B. Morse. Their children are of a style of beauty at once spiritual, striking and rare. Whoever in those years had the pleasing fortune to accept the hospitality of this brilliant man and of his beautiful wife, must have retained forever the delightful image of that home. All that could conduce to make home lovely was there. Reputation, converse with noble minds, such as fame draws around the hearthstone of its fortunate possessor, a charming companion, whose very soul kindled each moment in pure worship of her admired husband, children whose smiles were like the radiance of angel's eyes when turned toward the throne of God, and the rustle of whose garments was graceful as the silent movements of forest birds when bathing in the holy Sabbath dawn—what more could Theodore Tilton have sought or wished?

"Yet, in his profound egotism, he sought martyrdom. The martyrs only were truly great; he would link his name with some cause to-day odious, to-morrow glorified, and so after the cross wear the crown—as did Garrison, Wilberforce, Howard, and the rest. He advocated miscegenation, but nobody mobbed him. He boasted in every speech of having been mobbed in anti-slavery days. Few remembered that mob. Now, if he could but render himself odious by attacking the marriage relation, by striking a stalwart blow for woman's freedom, somebody, he sincerely hoped, would persecute him, and he would be immortal. This was his ambition. And now his martyrdom has come—all he ever sought, and directly, by the means he used, but of a character far more logical than he expected, the inexorable penalty due to false doctrine, the eternal cross that bears no crown save one of thorns. During those years the writer, on one occasion, by a chance question, turned the conversation upon Beecher, who was then among the daily visitors at Mr. Tilton's house. 'Is Mr. Beecher's inward life that which it seems to those who hear him? I have been at a loss to conceive how one whose conscience is so sensitive as Mr. Beecher's seems, should boast himself to be the happiest man living. Deep moral sensitiveness more often makes men sad.'

"Mr. Tilton answered, greatly to the writer's surprise: 'Mr. Beecher has a keen, intellectual discrimination on moral questions, but he is personally an epicure, a voluptuary, though of the most refined sort, who does nothing—not even his preaching and praying—from a sense of duty, but only for the pleasure it affords him. It happens to make him happier to preach than to race horses; but if it made him happier to follow any other form of amusement he would pursue it. Doubtless, when you heard him declare himself the happiest man living, he felt so, but scores of times has he come to this house as to a den of refuge, thrown himself down on that sofa and groaned in misery. You would have thought him the veriest wretch alive.'

"Indeed; what was the cause of his trouble?"

"It is chiefly domestic! His wife has no sympathy with his pains. She is a common-place, matter-of fact woman, who ought to have wed a merchant—not 'the great Beecher.' I have had my own difficulties with her, but these do not color my judgment. She has even followed me to the front door and ordered me out of her house, while Beecher stood at the top of the stairs and said: 'Theodore, whatever Mrs. Beecher says to you, remember that I am always your devoted friend!'"

"But I am surprised that you speak of Beecher as a voluptuary. I had thought him too unselfish and laborious for that."

"No; Beecher has no unselfishness. His tastes are æsthetic and cultivated, and he is a busy man because his capabilities for joyous activity are various. He enjoys preaching, editing, art, society, amusement, labor of certain kinds, and so on. But he is a voluptuary; he does everything that he enjoys, and only because he enjoys it. Greeley is self-sacrificing. If I want an article for the *Independent*, Greeley will sacrifice his own ease to write it; not because it is anything he wants to say, but because I, his friend, need his help. Beecher never writes on that principle. He would promise the article, and, if he found nothing more agreeable to do, he would write it; not otherwise."

"But Beecher is certainly industrious."

"No! He is lazy. He accomplished a vast amount of what from many would require work. But he does it because in his case it only requires the vigorous play of his versatile powers. He prepares for his sermons on Sunday morning and afternoon. It is not work to muse for an hour over what one shall say for the next hour."

"But is he not charitable and generous?"

"All in the epicurean sense. He enjoys doing good, and gives as giving yields him pleasure."

Mr. Tilton was then the warm and enthusiastic friend of the great preacher whom he thus criticised. We believe he had never formed the acquaintance of the wierd sister whose utterances are "inspired by Demosthenes." He had committed but the single error of adopting the theory that the reciprocal relations of men and women can be adjusted on the basis of equality and right, whereas nature intended them to rest on a basis of mutual inequality, interdependence and affection. In the very act of attempting to prove that boiling pitch is a very clean substance, snowy white and pure, he fell into the cauldron. If his catastrophe shall enable any to see in time that there is no "spotless whiteness" in those who would emancipate man or woman from that just subjection which is implied in Christian marriage as distinguished from Fourieristic infidelity, that intersexual love, to be chaste, must be exclusive; that its so-called "freedom" is its desolation and ruin, his martyrdom will not have been in vain.

Right here we will embody some correspondence which has an important bearing upon the subject in dispute, and which is frequently referred to in this work. It shows the connection of Mr. Henry C. Bowen with the case, and will perhaps, in a measure explain the cause for that gentleman's forced silence during the excitement attending the revelations that were subsequently made. Mr. "Suffolk" who supplied these letters for publication is generally supposed to be Mr. Frank Moulton, the confidential friend of all the parties to the controversy. The reader will note that the letter of Mr. Tilton is dated immediately after his dismissal from Bowen's service, when excited over the treatment he had received, while the triparte agreement being dated more than a year after, shows that a long time elapsed before the effort was successful in binding the parties to secrecy. The following is the correspondence:

TO THE EDITOR OF THE NEW YORK TIMES:—It is high time that the torrent of slander against Henry Ward Beecher be arrested. I have in my possession a copy of a disavowal of all the charges and imputations against Mr. Beecher ever made by Henry C. Bowen, which was executed on the 2d of April, 1872. Without Mr. Beecher's knowledge, I have held this in my hands from that time to this, and now, without his knowledge, I give this document to the world and estop and convict the principal offender against truth, public decency and the rights of reputation.

My inducement to do this is the fact that Mr. Bowen has of late repeatedly declared that he had never disavowed his charges against Mr. Beecher, but that he yet insisted on their truth. And now the public can understand the brave silence which the great preacher has kept under this protracted storm of slander. He had covenanted to bury the past and to maintain peace and brotherhood. The violation of that agreement by Henry C. Bowen unseals my mouth if it does not open the lips of the pastor of Plymouth Church. SUFFOLK.

NEW YORK, May 29th, 1873.

BROOKLYN, Jan. 1st, 1871.

MR. HENRY C. BOWEN:—SIR—I received last summer your sudden notices breaking my two contracts, one with the *Independent*, the other with the Brooklyn *Union*. With reference to this act of yours I will make a plain statement of facts. It was during the early part of the rebellion, if I recollect aright, when you first intimated to me that Rev. Henry Ward Beecher had committed acts of adultery for which, if you should expose him, he would be driven from the pulpit. From that time onward, your references to the subject were frequent and always accompanied with deep seated injury to your heart. In a letter which you addressed to me from Woodstock, June 16th, 1863, referring to this subject, you said:—"I sometimes feel that I must break silence; that I must no longer suffer as a dumb man and be made to bear a load of grief most unjustly. One word from me would make a rebellion throughout Christendom, I had almost said, and you know it. You have just a little of the evidence from the great volume in your possession. I am not pursuing a phantom, but solemnly brooding over an awful reality."

Subsequent to this letter and on frequent intervals from this till now you have repeated the statement that you could at any moment expel Henry Ward Beecher from Brooklyn. You have reiterated the same thing not only to me, but to others. Moreover, during the year just closed, your letters on the subject were marked with more feeling than heretofore, and were not unfrequently coupled with your emphatic declaration that Mr. Beecher ought not to be allowed to occupy a position as Christian teacher and preacher.

On the 25th of December, 1870, at an interview in your house, at which Mr. Oliver Johnson and I were present, you spoke freely and indignantly against Mr. Beecher as an unsafe visitor in the families of his congregation. You alluded by name to a woman, now a widow, whose husband's death you did not doubt was hastened by his knowledge that Mr. Beecher had maintained with her an improper intimacy As if to leave no doubt on the minds of either Mr Johnson or myself, you informed us that Mr. Beecher had made to you a confession of guilt, and had with tears implored your forgiveness. After Mr. Johnson retired from this interview, you related to me the case of a woman of whom you said (as nearly as I can recollect your words) that "Mr. Beecher took her in his arms."

* * * * * * *

During your recital of this tale you were filled with anger toward Mr. Beecher. You said, with terrible emphasis, that he ought not remain a week longer in his pulpit. You immediately suggested that a demand should be made upon him to quit his sacred office. You volunteered to bear to him such a demand in the form of an open letter, which you would present to him with your own hand, and you pledged yourself to sustain the demand which the letter should make—namely, "that he should, for reasons which he explicitly knew, immediately cease from his ministry at Plymouth Church, and retire from Brooklyn." The first draft of this letter did not contain the phrase "for reasons that he explicitly knew," and these words, or words to this effect, were incorporated in a second, at your motion. You urged, furthermore, very emphatically, that the letter should demand not only Mr. Beecher's abdication of his pulpit, but the cessation of his writing for the *Christian Union*, a point on which you were overruled. This letter you presented to Mr. Beecher at Mr. Freeland's house. Shortly after its representation you sought an interview with me at the editorial office of the Brooklyn *Union*, during which, with unaccountable emotion in your manner, your face livid with rage, you threatened with loud voice that if ever I should inform Mr. Beecher of the statements which you made concerning his adultery, or should compel you to adduce the evidence on which you agreed to sustain the demand for Mr. Beecher's withdrawal from Brooklyn, you would immediately deprive me of my engagement to write for the *Independent* and to edit the Brooklyn *Union*, and that in case I should ever attempt to enter the offices of those journals you would have me ejected by force. I told you that I should inform Mr. Beecher or anybody else, according to the dictates of my judgment, uninfluenced by any authority from my employers. You then excitedly retired from my presence. Hardly had your violent words ceased ringing in my ears when I received your summary notices breaking up my contract with the *Independent* and the Brooklyn *Union*. To the foregoing narrative of fact I have only to add my surprise, and regret at the sudden interruption by your own act of what has been on my part a faithful service of fifteen years.

Truly yours. THEODORE TILTON.

We three men, earnestly desiring to remove all causes of offence existing between us, real or fancied, and to make Christian reparation for injuries done or supposed to be done, and to efface the disturbed past and provide concord, good will and love for the future, do declare and covenant each to the other as follows:—

1. I, Henry C. Bowen, having given credit, perhaps, without due consideration to tales and inuendoes affecting Henry Ward Beecher, and, being influenced by them, as was natural to a man who receives impressions suddenly, to the extent of repeating them (guardedly, however, and within limitations, and not for the purpose of injuring him, but strictly in the confidence of consultation), now feel that therein I did him wrong. Therefore, I disavow all the charges and imputations that have been attributed to me as having been by me made against Henry Ward Beecher; and I declare fully and without reserve that I know nothing which should prevent me from extending to him my most cordial friendship, confidence, and Christian fellowship. And I expressly withdraw all the charges, imputations and inuendoes imputed as having been made and uttered by me and set forth in a letter written to me by Theodore Tilton on the first day of January, 1871 (a copy of which letter is hereto annexed), and I sincerely regret having made any imputations, charges, or inuendoes unfavorable to the Christian character of Mr. Beecher. And I covenant and promise that for all future time I will never, by word or deed, recur to, repeat, or allude to any or either of said charges, imputations and inuendoes.

2. And I, Theodore Tilton, do of my own free will and friendly spirit toward Henry C. Bowen and Henry Ward Beecher, hereby covenant and agree that I will never again repeat by word of mouth or otherwise any of the allegations or imputations or inuendoes contained in my letter hereunto annexed, or any other injurious imputations or allegations suggested by or growing out of these; and that I will never again bring up or hint at any cause of difference or ground of complaint hereunto existing between the said Henry C. Bowen and myself or the said Henry Ward Beecher.

3. And I, Henry Ward Beecher, put the past forever out of sight and out of memory. I deeply regret the causes of suspicion, jealousy and estrangement which have come between us. It is a joy to me to have my old regard for Henry C. Bowen and Theodore Tilton restored, and a happiness to me to resume the old relations of love, respect and reliance to each and both of them. If I have said anything injurious to the reputation of either, or have detracted from their standing and fame as Christian gentlemen and members of my church, I revoke it

all, and heartily covenant to repair and reinstate them to the extent of my power.

H. C. BOWEN,
THEODORE TILTON.
H. W. BEECHER.

BROOKLYN, April 2d, 1872.

While on this subject of the Tripartite covenant it is proper to add the testimony given subsequently before the Investigating Committee by Mr. Samuel Wilkerson. The substance of this testimony is as follows, as supplied by that gentleman to the *New York Herald:*

In the last week of March, 1872, Theodore Tilton came to my office in New York and took out of his pocket a worn press proof of a letter which he said he purposed to publish in the next issue of his paper, the *Golden Age*, unless Henry Ward Beecher did him justice, and handed it to me to read. He said that he came to me because I had an interest in its publication through my property in the *Christian Union* newspaper, of which Mr. Beecher was editor, and through my partnership in the house which published his books, and because I was the common friend of himself and Mr. Beecher. The letter was as follows:

[These followed the above letter from Tilton to Bowen.—AUTHOR.]

I was shocked at the mischievousness of the matter he threatened to publish. I remonstrated with him against its publication. A discussion ensued, on his part passionate and noisy. He complained, first, that Henry C. Bowen had without cause dismissed him from the editorship of the *Independent* and of the Brooklyn *Union*, and ruined him in fame, prospects and estate; that he had crowned this wrong by refusing to pay him a large debt for editorial services, of which he was in pressing need, and compelling him to bring a suit to collect the amount. His next plaint was that Mr. Beecher had not helped him in his troubles. He said that he was lying crushed on the sidewalk in Brooklyn under the misfortunes of losing his positions on the two papers, and the incomes derived from them, with the accompanying loss of the public respect and confidence—the loss, in a word, of the entire stored-up capital for his life career, and that Mr. Beecher, who had such power that with his little finger he could have lifted him up and reinstated him, saw him in his agony and ruin, and passed by in silence and indifference on the other side of the way. Rising into a dramatic rage, and tramping my room from corner to corner, and speaking with intense passion, he declared "I will have revenge on him. I will pursue him into his grave."

It was clear to me that what Mr. Tilton wanted was money. and that his purpose in coming to me was to raise money Omitting further details of this interview he left my office calm and happy, in the prospect of an arrangement I outlined that should immediately give him in hand, without the delays of a contested lawsuit, the money Mr. Bowen owed him and. that would restore his old relations to Mr. Beecher and Mr Bowen and procure for him restorative and flattering mention in the editorial columns of the *Independent* and cause to be inserted editorially in the *Christian Union* such handsome notice of his newspaper enterprise as should at once gratify and profit him. What is somewhat well known as the "Tripartite Agreement" came from the negotiation initiated after this interview. Before it was drafted, but after its terms were settled, Mr. Bowen agreed to pay Mr. Tilton forthwith the amount of unpaid salary for which he had brought suit. He likewise promised to publish a card in the *Independent*, over his own signature, that should repair as fully as it could the injury done to Mr. Tilton by dismissing him from that paper. On the night of the 2d of April, 1872, when the tripartite agreement was ready for signature, Mr. Tilton was in a happy frame of mind. In conversation he especially overflowed with love and admiration Beecher-wards.

This tripartite agreement, which I intended to be an estoppel to two of the parties to it, and a concordat all around, was in the words:—

[These followed the above agreement, dated April 2d, 1872. —AUTHOR.]

This paper was read at a meeting of four gentlemen, of whom Mr. Tilton was one, at a house in Brooklyn. He was more than satisfied with the paragraph concerning himself. He was charmed with it. He said he could conscientiously and heartily subscribe his name to every word of it. He said he would sign it twelve times over if that would induce Mr. Bowen to sign it once; and in his eagerness he took up a pen to sign. But he was restrained by the suggestion of a wise and influential party to the conference that Mr. Bowen might be less willing to sign the paper if Mr. Tilton should sign first. It was carried away without Mr. Tilton's signature.

In a full and kind conversation between me and Mr. Tilton, after the meeting on the night of April 2d, broke up, he replied to a clear cut question I put to him, that *the only wrong Mr. Beecher had ever done him had been to address improper language to his wife, and that for that he held in his hands an ample and satisfactory written apology.* I repeated to him mention of a graver injury than that made to me by a person whose information was alleged to be derived, in part directly from himself, in part at second hand, from a confession of his wife. With great spirit he denied the truth of both these statements. He called the informant at second hand a sexually morbid monomaniac, who had imagined every word she uttered. He scornfully said that there was not a shadow of truth in her story. He expressed amazement that the other person should state that he had ever said that there was anything criminal in Mr. Beecher's conduct, and denied in the fullest and most energetic manner that he had ever said so, or said anything that could be so construed by a truthful and healthy mind. And he returned to his previous declaration that Mr. Beecher's sole offence was improper language to his wife, and repeated it anew, and again repeated that the written confession and apology he had in keeping was ample atonement for that wrong.

The next morning, on the 3d of April, Mr. Tilton came to my office, in the Equitable Insurance Company's building. He was flushed and sullen. There was a hitch in the money payment. He said abruptly that he would not sign the agreement; that it would have to be altered before he would sign it. Kindling in anger as he talked, he said that in the negotiation Mr. Bowen had been well taken care of by Mr. Claflin and Mr. Beecher well taken care of by me, but he had been left out in the cold with the money due from Bowen unpaid. I combated this fancy kindly and tried to soothe him and hold him to the arrangement he had made, but he flew out wild and declared with the utmost passion that he would never while he lived sign a paper that should disable him from pursuing Henry Ward Beecher, and he demanded a copy of his paragraph in the tripartite agreement, that he might alter it. I made a copy for him, and he sat down at a table and began to scratch and interline it; but he rose up and carried his work away uncompleted. Before he left I gathered from what he said that Mr. Bowen had refused to pay the full amount of his claim, and that his lawsuit would have to go on.

But the full amount was paid within a day or two thereafter, and the tripartite agreement was executed—not the one I drafted, and which was accepted by all the parties, but a modification of that. I used my last copy of this instrument in my testimony before the committee, and I cannot show the changes of the original by a comparison of the two. I can now only say that all the portions of the agreement (above set forth in full) which are italicized were omitted from the agreement finally executed.

The efficacy of the covenants I aimed at was lost and the compact was defeated. Tilton, in modifying his paragraph, backed out of his disavowal of his imputations on Mr. Beecher and his admissions that they were untrue, and carefully secured to himself the largest liberty to pursue the great preacher forever with innuendoes. My testimony before the committee shows the changes in the tripartite agreement as originally drawn, and which all the parties to it had heartily approved and had promised to sign. It also shows my earnest remonstrances against permitting these changes to be made and my warnings of the mischievous consequences that would inevitably follow."

CHAPTER VIII.

A GRAPHIC DESCRIPTION OF MR. BEECHER'S FIRST CHURCH, AND REMINISCENCES OF HIM AND HIS CONGREGATION AT LAWRENCEBURG, INDIANA, AND HIS LABORS AMONG THE COLORED PEOPLE OF THE CINCINNATI SUBURBS.—HIS MARRIAGE TO THE AMBITIOUS EUNICE LEIGHTON OF HILL FARM.—MRS. BEECHER'S BOOK, "FROM DAWN TO DAYLIGHT," AND THE MYSTERIOUS MUTILATION OF THE CHURCH RECORDS.—DEPARTURE OF THE BEECHERS FROM LAWRENCEBURG IN A BUGGY.—HIS CAREER IN INDIANAPOLIS, AND HOW HE PLAYED THE ROLE OF JOSEPH IN RESISTING THE ADVANCES OF THE FAIR MRS. POTIPHARS OF HIS CONGREGATION.—A ROMANCE OF TILTON.—HOW HE SECURED BEECHER'S LOVE.—IN THE ROLE OF A GOVERNOR OF A STATE.—HIS FIRST MEETING WITH BEECHER AND HIS INFLUENCE ON HIS AFTER LIFE.—"WALKING ON STILTS WITH HIS FACE HEAVENWARD."—ANECDOTE OF BEECHER'S SON.

WHILE the excitement in New York was at its height and the great dailies in every issue devoted columns to the deeply interesting and exciting theme, the western journals partook of the excitement, and dispatched correspondents to the scenes of Mr. Beecher's early administrations to gather such incidents of his life as would add to the interest centering around the principal figures in the unrivaled scandal. One of these journals, the Chicago *Times*, as a result, gave on July 27th a highly entertaining letter from Lawrenceburg, Indiana, from which extracts are here made:—

Henry Ward Beecher preached the first sermon of his life in this little city on the north bank of the Ohio river.

A hundred miles by rail, mostly over the popular I. C. and L.,—what is known as the "Kankakee," Cincinnati and Chicago Through line—under the able management of President Ingalls, brought me to this very old and very quiet little Indiana town. It is among the oldest in this state, and was for years the menacing rival of Cincinnati. Legendary chronicles inform us that but for the accidental death of an enterprising man widely connected with Ohio river commerce, in all probability impetus would have been given to Lawrenceburg progress in preference to Cincinnati, and the result might have been that Cincinnati to-day would boast her 5,000 population while Lawrenceburg would put in her successful claim to a quarter of a million. For a commercial metropolis the site of Lawrenceburg is far superior to that of the queen city, the latter being a pent-up Utica under the cliffs on which the truly good Deacon Richard Smith lives, while this village is finely situated, with a "second-bottom" plain stretching back from the beautiful and dreamy Ohio river like the plains of Troy from the Ægean sea beneath the glories of a soft and seductive Mysian sky. But Cincinnati, half a century ago, got the start of modest little Lawrenceburg, and their relative relations are reversed forever.

Forty-five years ago, when Lawrenceburg was the chiefest commercial town in this commonwealth, when she boasted the best and largest buildings, the most enterprising and richest men, the handsomest women, the prospect of the first railway west of the Alleganies (a charter having been granted about that period for the "Lawrenceburg and Indianapolis railroad," two miles of which were constructed before your correspondent was born), and when her people had "made up their minds" to lead the advance guard of western development, fourteen of her citizens, Presbyterian in belief, organized themselves into "the first Presbyterian Church" of Lawrenceburg. They proceeded immediately to erect a neat and substantial brick and stone church building, certainly one of the best edifices of that character in any village of the west at that time. It was finished and dedicated in 1829. The course of the Ohio at this place being southwardly, streets leading from it extend westwardly. This Presbyterian church, which is now invested with so much historic importance, in connection with Beecher and the scandal, stands here to-day precisely as erected, precisely as young and handsome and luxurious Henry Ward entered upon his eventful career in it, and is assuredly as unique and interesting an architectural link coupling the past and faded generation with the present, as the west can show. On a thoroughfare bearing the not very pleasingly suggestive name of "Short" street, extending from the river west toward the distant hills, two squares from the water's edge, stands this cosy little old building. It is not precisely a "wart of an edifice on a wrinkle of a hill," but reminds you, in its cob-webbed and grimy appearance of a wrinkled and decrepit old man, one foot in the grave, and the other going speedily hence. When erected, it loomed up two full, strong stories high—the first story of rough stone, laid in mortar; the second, of brick, nicely and neatly primed, and not by any means an unattractive structure. A broad 50-foot gable-end fronted on the street; the depth was 60 feet; and as there was no vestibule, but an entrance by two outside stairways leading directly up to the two front doors of ingress, the auditorium was 50x60, or 3,000 square feet—not a backwoods hut in any respect. The basement was used for Sabbath school and for "sessions," while the more stylish and large hall above was devoted, as now, to the uses of the congregation in divine worship. The exigencies of city improvement have wrought no change in the substantial old church itself, but have materially metamorphosed the contour of the approaches, by filling up the street and the whole surroundings to within five or six feet of the floor of the second story. This simple fact of the old building being half buried from sight, (in spite of our rage for cremation) and but a few feet of the moss-covered and ragged stone work of the first story at the *front* remaining visible, suggests age, death, interment, and fading forever from memory. Yet, stepping to one side and glancing over a short picket fence adown a path in the grass leading to a side entrance at the back of the building to the basement story, the actual and symmetrical proportions of the aged edifice loom up to the vision. My friend, Mr. Sparks, unlocked the old door, and it creaked on its rusty hinges as he swung it back to admit us. I found a plain, airy, cleanly hall, 50x60, occupied by the cushioned pews, a Mason & Hamlin organ, a bookless new book-case, and a graceful modern reading-stand in the center of a dais, upon which lay a handsome copy of the bible. I found the dais neatly but unpretentiously carpeted. The only internal change since the days of Beecher was substituting this slightly elevated dais for the old-fashioned coop in the air, from which elevated box young and handsome Henry made his ministerial début thirty-seven years ago.

The name and fame of Henry Ward Beecher are just now abroad in the land. Four million readers desire to know something of the introduction of this intellectual comet into the galaxy of eccentric orbs. Your correspondent came here purposely to investigate upon the ground, and come face to face with the ancient living witnesses. In Mr. Beecher's famous Friday evening lectures he has, throughout his remarkable career in Plymouth Church, made the reading world familiar with "that obscure little pioneer town in Indiana." A multiplicity of domestic details have fallen from his eloquent lips sandwiched between chunks of wisdom and pathos. They sound and read like fiction, yet have been ingeniously utilized to illustrate the sympathetic sermonizing of the great orator of Plymouth Church. Given as bits of hardship and personal experience in his own life, conquered by holy devotion and Christian perseverance, they carried all the force of a direct personal appeal to his hearers, and the contrasts between then and now in his personal affairs were ever present to the mind of the devoted admirer of Beecher. Under the circumstances of the attitude of fame reached by Brother Beecher and of the great scandal hanging over him like an avenging Nemesis, it may prove interesting to turn to Beecher's beginning.

In 1837, Henry was twenty-four years old, and about to graduate from Lane theological seminary (under the direction of his father, the eminent Lyman Beecher), and go out into the gospel work of the wide world. This town was regarded as a "choice spot" of beginning by graduates of that college. Situated but an hour or two by boat from the Queen city, youthful aspirants to the pulpit could run down here, try their hand, and go back to their dormitory or their sweetheart in a brief time. Whenever the pulpit of this church became vacant, all that was necessary was to send up to the "Lane," and ask for a "cadet." Sometimes for six successive weeks the pulpit would be occupied by as many different young men, either full-fledged graduates seeking a location, or those about to graduate and enter upon a career. Sometimes these experimenters upon the ears and credulity of hapless humanity proved anything but acceptable or agreeable. As an illustration, the story told of an old darkey will suffice. When a holy fledgling desired to air his wings, theologically speaking, and test his flights of fancy, if no better opportunity offered he was directed to the "missions" amongst the colored population in the outskirts of Cincinnati. One old "cullud brudder" was prevailed on to go and "heah de gospil" one sweltering Sabbath. The following Sunday the same person sought out the "old cullud man" to accompany him again to "divine punishment," (as a Washington friend of mine always called divine worship). "Cum go an' heah de gospel ob Jesus to-day, Uncle Abraham!" "No, sah, no sah! nebber!" sternly answered Uncle Abraham, "dis niggah is no gwine down dar fur dem young chickens to practice darsels on *meah!* No, sah!"

At all events, the Presbyterian church of Lawrenceburg was minus a minister in 1837. A call on Lane seminary was made. Successive Sabbaths several young graduates came down, young Beecher among the rest. He preached two or three times; was liked; proposed to become their regular preacher, and finally was accepted. In a contest like that, where the church took "pick and choice" from a dozen, it was regarded an honor to win the prize—an honor conferred by the intelligent congregation and membership. And young men were considered peculiarly fortunate to walk directly into a substantial old community, and into a large and paid-for church edifice, commodious, and elegant for the age, instead of going to some home or foreign mission, to preach on the street, or in log-cabins, or in the woods—

"The groves were God's first temples."

In fact, in this precise way, the *present* pastor of "the First Presbyterian church "of Lawrenceburg, young and gentlemanly Rev. Mr. Little, came here, while contemplating missionary work in the wilds, and among the heathen of Mexico.

Thus, thirty-seven years ago, young Beecher came, and entered upon his work in the ministry. He soon became popular, and started on his career of world-wide fame. I spent several hours to-day hunting up old church books. I thought by consulting them, and all the records and entries made by Henry Ward, way back there in the dim past, I might obtain a better impression of his two years' occupancy of this pulpit, first as "stated supply," and secondly as the regular pastor, than from any other source. At least such impressions would have the merit of accuracy, springing from so authentic a fountain as 'record evidence.' A diligent search, assisted by Mr. Sparks, Jr., a former journalist (whose kindness I wish hereby to acknowledge), discovered the real, genuine, original, yellow, musty records, in the safe care of a leading member and officer of the church, Dr. Vance. In a most agreeable way, the Doctor and his good lady received your correspondent; and from a quantity of brown old record books, dusty, and cobwebbed, with the rich smell of antiquity hovering about them like a halo, the little brown and worn *first* record book of this church, five by seven inches in surface, containing perhaps about one hundred and fifty pages of yellow-stained paper, was brought forth. It contained not only the record of the organization of the church, but covered the years of young Beecher's pastorate and many beyond. I turned to 1837, in search of the record, in Beecher's own handwriting, of his first "session." Ah! me! I was doomed to disappointment. Some vandal hand had ruthlessly torn out the *first two leaves* of his records. Upon a further examination, the surprising, and, to the members of the church present, unaccountable fact was revealed to us that in addition to the leaves torn from the first of Mr. Beecher's records, *fifteen leaves of the last* of his own records were cut out, leaving but a meagre three remaining! What this singular mutilation signifies no one could precisely tell, but by one of the gentlemen present (a Sabbath-school pupil of Mr. Beecher's and present communicant of the church) "an opinion as is an opinion" was unhesitatingly expressed. He remarked:

"There is no doubt in *my* mind that Mr. or Mrs. Beecher has sent some one to perform this piece of vandalism and tear out these pages, as the facts they would disclose might possibly be very unsavory in contrast to such autobiography as Mrs. Beecher issued in her volume entitled 'From Dawn to Daylight,' and also in connection with such history as Mr. Beecher is now so speedily making."

The little volume of musty records proved interesting; and no mutilations of any other part appeared. The six pages so kindly left to posterity by the vicious vandal, every word and line in Beecher's own handwriting, are not freighted with any very alarming manuscript,—not a word about Mrs. Tilton,—not a line of the rampant, cuckolded, and ambrosial Theodore,—and not even a prophetic sentence of the coming Victoria Claflin Woodhull. Yet, notwithstanding these grave oversights, I extract a few excerpts from his entries, which I here insert:

"LAWRENCEBURG, Nov. 19th, 1837.—Session was constituted with prayer by Rev. George Beecher, moderator. Mr. Thomas Hunt of Elizabethtown sat as corresponding elder. The following persons were received into communion of the church by letter (here follow the names of five persons named Gage) from the Central Presbyterian Church of New York City. * * * The session then adjourned.

H. W. BEECHER.
"Stated supply."

"Jan. 13th, 1838.—* * * The following persons being examined and giving satisfactory evidence of a change of heart, were admitted to the church. * * *

"H. W. BEECHER.
"Stated supply."

"LAWRENCEBURG,——, 1838, * * * Joined about this time also: * * * Mr. Thomas Guard, by examination, *Mrs. Eunice Beecher* (by letter)."

This last lady was his then young and dashing, and present, wife. This entry follows the regular record of the session, and his name is not signed to it.

"LAWRENCEBURG, Sept. 26th, 1838,—A meeting of the church having been appointed from the pulpit the Sabbath previous, the church met and elected Mr. Basset chairman, and Mr. Thomas Guard, secretary. The following resolutions were then read and unanimously adopted.

"H. W. BEECHER.

On the same page with this last entry is pasted a clipping from a newspaper, containing a series of half a dozen or more resolutions. As indicating a characteristic of Henry Ward Beecher, permit me to quote briefly from them, under the head of Beecher's First Revolution.

* * * * * * * *

"3. *Resolved*, That this church withdraws from the presbytery of Oxford, and is from this time an Independent Presbyterian church.

4. *Resolved*, That there has occurred no change whatever in our doctrinal views and forms of worship—the only change being in dissociating ourselves from the ecclesiastical courts of the Presbyterian church.

5. *Resolved*, That this church approves or the pastoral services of the Rev. H. W. Beecher, and it is their wish that he continue their pastor."

Thus we see that within a twelvemonth after this remarkable youth had launched out for himself he rebelled from the presbytery and the "organized church," and set up shop "on his own hook." About that time he had added a rib to his anatomical economy, by taking unto himself a Miss Eunice

9

Leighton, a bright, ambitious, willful, energetic, fame-loving, gold-worshiping country girl from "Hill Farm," (her father's abode,) in Massachusetts. She had been jilted by a rich Boston *roué* named Dalton, whom she afterward denounced as "a self-conceited young man, utterly devoid of delicacy, and nothing doubting but that half a million could *buy* the *fairest lady in the land.*"

In her autobiography, "From Dawn to Daylight," Mrs. Eunice Beecher describes herself as, at that time, a very young girl, "very beautiful" in her "fond mother's eye," and who wore "rich auburn curls." Later through the book she contrasts herself to the wife of George Beecher, brother of Henry W., and, calling herself Mary, says:

"Mary's figure was larger, and not so graceful or dignified, and her educational advantages had been far inferior. She was inclined to grieve over this, fearing that she might not prove, in all things, such a wife as her loving heart believed her husband must deserve."

(Perhaps this accounts for the trouble with Mrs. Tilton.)

Mrs. Beecher further says of herself:

"Her hair was of dark chestnut, folded neatly around a well-shaped head, with a low brow, blue eyes, and clear, rosy complexion."

With his young wife, in 1838, Mr. Beecher quit boarding and went to "house-keeping" in apartments which I have inspected to-day. I only refer to this trivial matter because Mr. Beecher is so very fond of calling the attention of his millionaire and aristocratic Plymouth Church audiences to it. Mrs. Beecher in her book pictures the apartments and all the surroundings as simply terrible. The same building is standing to-day, and the apartments which the Beechers occupied more than a third of a century ago are just as they were then. They comprise a suite on the second floor, the full width of a large brick-house—not less than twenty-five feet front. Furnished as she pictures they were, after her deft and industrious Yankee hands had completed the cleaning and "fixing up," I should think any young couple who hadn't money enough to buy a cooking stove, or even a bed (as she says they had not until she sold a cloak her father gave her in Boston, for $30 in silver), would feel very comfortable in them. The front (on the street) was west, and the rear apartment, opening on to a veranda, overlooked the rolling Ohio river, with the lovely Kentucky hills for a background,—a scenic picture for an artist. The entrance to these delightful apartments was by an easy flight of stairs to the veranda. And while residing in these two rooms, with a young wife to love and a young church to preach to, Henry Ward Beecher began his clerical career. He was self-reliant, courageous, ambitious,—if as winning as described to me, he was the living, breathing impersonation of poetry, passion, grace, wit, daring, tenderness, and every other fascinating quality.

Lawrenceburg was then a thriving and interesting little city, with more good brick business buildings than any other town in Indiana. The first four-story brick block erected in the state was then standing at the corner of the very same square in which young Henry Ward and his Yankee wife occupied rooms. It stands there yet, a village hostelry conducted by old uncle 'Squire Anderson.

During my brief sojourn here, I have met numerous present members of the old Beecher church, but learned that only five or six persons who were members under his preaching thirty-seven years ago, can now be found in this community. Most of the old flock have died. I did not deem it advisable or practicable to hunt up the old cemetery and interview the grave-stones, though I had no doubt whatever that could many of those sleeping beneath them who listened to and loved Beecher young and good, see the shame which does not bring a blush to Beecher old and hypocritical, their very bones would scramble through the sod and gladly express to the world through an interview in *The Times* their sad indignation. But I found the next best thing to a cemetery, and give you the result of a talk with an octogenarian.

"I was introduced to an old gentleman who sat under the droppings of young Beecher's wisdom, and who has resided here and remained a member of that church to this hour.'

"'How did you like Mr. Beecher, when he was with you?' I asked.

"'Oh, we liked him first rate, I tell ye,' was his prompt reply.

"'I suppose you regretted it, when he left you for Indianapolis?'

"'Yes, yes, we did *that*. We could never understand why he did go, unless to please his wife. She was vain. He was ambitious, I s'pose, too.'

"'Permit me to ask how often Mr. Beecher comes back to see his first flock? I observe that he constantly parades you, or his life here, before his Brooklyn people.'

"'Oh, bless your life, he never has set foot in our town since he got into his buggy with his wife to go to Indianapolis. He has been to Cincinnati several times, an hour from here by rail, but bless your soul he never thought of us whom he claims to have loved with his young love.'

"'Why, sir, you astonish me!' I ejaculated.'

"'And is it possible Mr. Beecher ignores you? Has he never sent you a Sunday-school library or given the old church a check for five thousand dollars to reconstruct or modernize it?' I inquired.'

"'No, sir, no sir,' was the prompt and petulant answer. No, sir, never a visit, never a book, never a dollar of aid, no more than if he had never heard of us, than if we had never given him a good start on his grand career, never helped him with our means and encouragement as perhaps few communities and few churches would have done.'

"'Perhaps, my good friend, Mr. Beecher did not think he was kindly treated here, and may be you seared his heart instead of blessing it,' I suggested.

"'How can that be,' my snow-white haired old friend exclaimed, 'how can that be so, when time and again, time and again, Mr. Beecher has said in his celebrated Friday evening lectures, that 'the happiest hours of my life were those I spent in the little town in the West the first two years of my ministry?' Mr. Beecher was petted here as no one has been before or since.'

"'I am greatly surprised,' I remarked. I continued:

"'Will you give me your opinion of the general feeling in Lawrence concerning Mr. Beecher, and particularly as to his guilt or innocence of the immoralities charged?'

"'I think the general feeling is against him,' responded the old gentleman, 'and I am sure it is in our church, where he used to preach when I wasn't quite as old as I am now. I suppose people are divided in opinion as to his guilt; but most of his old friends here think he is a man of the world, who preaches for fame and gold, and then practices the very vices he denounces in the pulpit.'

"Here our interview ended, and bidding the communicative old gentleman an adieu, I called upon a younger man, who was one of Beecher's Sunday-school scholars, for many years past a member of the old church, and now nearly fifty years of of age. He gave me, substantially, the same opinion of Mr. Beecher that the elderly gentleman did; that Beecher was a hypocrite; had sacrificed Christianity for 'the world, the flesh, and the devil;' loved gold and fame above all things; was all for 'Beecher, Beecher;' was selfish and scheming; and simply preached sensational eloquence to win the world's favor and prove a 'success.'

"'Was Mr. Beecher your teacher in the Sunday school?' I asked.

"'No, sir, but Mrs. Beecher was,' answered my friend.

"'I presume you were pleased with your teacher?' I suggested.

"'I wish I could answer you in the affirmative?'

"'Of course you recollect her?'

"'Assuredly. My impressions of her are most vivid. Had I loved her I suppose I should have remembered her equally well; had I been indifferent, I might have forgotten her; but I disliked her so much that I never could forget her.'

"'Your impressions of Mrs. Beecher must have been unfortunate. What did you think?'

"'I thought she was vain and proud. In my boyish reasoning, I thought she all the time acted as if she had come from some superior part of creation down among us pitiable heathen. I was too proud and too conscious of her faults to fall into her way of thinking; and I was glad when she was gone.'

About the same time when the above details regarding Mr. Beecher's ministry were published, there appeared in the Cincinnati *Commercial* the following relative to Mr. B's ministrations at Indianapolis to which point he repaired after separating from his Lawrenceburg Charge. Writing from that city the correspondent says:—

"One of his first good works here was a revival, the like of which has never recurred in the history of the place. Young men and maidens, old men and matrons were moved by his eloquence, through the grace of God, to repentance, and for a while it seemed as if the New Jerusalem had been anticipated in this Indiana spot of earth. Among the matrons was one in her first youth, and as lovely as a peri, if one can imagine a stray angel from heaven's gates married to a pork packer and the mother of twins. Nevertheless was my heroine beautiful, and added to rare personal charms was a certain bewitching trustfulness or helplessness of manner that was calculated to make her a rather dangerous proselyte. One day in a private interview with Mr. Beecher (she told the story herself) she was so moved by his holy teachings that with face glowing with emotion, her eyes suffused in tears, and her voice broken with sobs, she threw her lovely arms around his neck and cried, 'Oh, Mr. Beecher, save me!'

"You must look to a higher power," was his brave reply, as putting both hands from about his neck, he fell on his knees and said: "Let us pray."

In spite of himself, however, Mr. Beecher was the occasion of jealousy. One gentleman in particular was supremely jealous of his wife because the night before Mr. Beecher preached his farewell sermon she had not slept for crying. He did not sleep much either, and tortured by angry fears went to church with her in the morning, determined to see if the popular preacher knew and would take advantage of the hold he had upon the fair portion of his fold. Instead of that, he beheld a man with solemn mien, like one who goes forth to death, the burden of whose prayer was forgiveness of God and man for sins and shortcomings. It was as if he craved to enter the new and untrodden fields of the vineyard of the Lord with clean hands and shriven by the blessing of his tried friends. He seemed lifted out of himself, and the hour was a consecrated one to his hearers. To none more than the self-abashed, humbled husband whose lover-like tenderness to his wife thenceforward was received with sweet surprise. It is not patent that he ever communicated his suspicions to her. It does not take a man long to learn that it is not always best to tell his wife everything.

With his great, liberal, noble nature and childlike simplicity Mr. Beecher did many things, no doubt, which wicked people with a regard to appearances could not understand. It is this class of people that are quick to say now, "He is no better than he should be." A more unconventional man, I suppose, never lived, and his friends are ready to believe that some slight disregard of the common proprieties of life has been taken advantage of by his enemies. For instance, a friend who was invited to breakfast with him on one occasion found him in a lady's parlor in his shirt sleeves while she was sewing a button on his vest. On the other hand, there are many women who are in a manner looking out for adventure, sensation, or insult, as the case may be, and it would be easy for such a one to misunderstand the innocent kindness of Mr. Beecher. It should be remembered that he was never more of a favorite of women than of children and men. Those who were children when he lived here revere his memory, and there is not a matron who was then a maiden that can recall a mean impression of him. On the contrary, it is borne in mind that not one of the few women of his acquaintance who have since been under ban, or who have dropped out of the charmed circle of society, was a favorite of his. It was not altogether accident which preserved him from their toils.

"I had spent most of the day hunting up the old members of Mr. Beecher's congregation, when on the street I was hailed by a cheery voice with, 'How do you do?'

"The face of the friend that met my view was as pleasant as his voice, and as I stopped to shake hands I asked, 'What do you think of Mr. Beecher?'

"'I think him an innocent man,' was the reply.

"My friend being a clergyman, I further asked his reason for the faith that was in him, and he said:—

"I believe in Mr. Beecher's innocence from my knowledge of him years ago, and it was only the other day my confidence was sustained by hearsay. A co-missionary laborer of mine in India was at my house on his way from the Presbyterian General Assembly in St. Louis. He told me that he met there a Kentucky clergyman who is a cousin of Mrs. Tilton, and that in conversation with him about the Beecher-Tilton scandal, Mrs. Tilton's cousin said that she had assured him there was not a particle of foundation for the charges Mr. Tilton had made against Mr. Beecher that Mr. Tilton was insanely jealous of her, in fact, and his charges had no grounds but his morbid imagination.'

"'Perhaps you'd better not put that in print,' added my friend. 'It might make trouble between man and wife—Mr. and Mrs. Tilton, you know.'

"The majority of persons interviewed in regard to Mr. Beecher were free to say that he could no longer afford to be silent—that silence would be taken for a confession of guilt, while a few were as reticent as Mr. Beecher himself—declaring their perfect confidence in his purity, and avowing their willingness to wait his own good time for an explanation of the mystery. Two or three persons accounted for his silence by saying he was 'screening somebody.' The expression struck me as peculiar, but in the delicate task of probing popular sentiment it will not do to appear inquisitive, and I waited patiently for light.

"'You see,' at length said a gentlemen, 'Mr. Beecher is evidently screening somebody. I think he is screening his wife.'

"I did not exactly understand how that could be, but I took good care not to say so, and after a pause the gentleman proceeded as follows:—

"Perhaps I had as good an opportunity of knowing Mr. Beecher in his domestic relations as any one in his charge, and I never have seen such devotion as Mrs. Beecher manifested toward her husband. Never did a woman love her husband better. It was the outpouring of the purest and holiest affection. He loved her as much as most men love their wives after the hey-day of the honeymoon is over; but she was older than he, and would likely be more watchful than a young woman. He was absorbed in his books, his work and his flowers. May it not be that as the habit of being thus absorbed grew on him she got jealous of him? I knew her to be good and true, but it is not to be supposed she kept pace with him in intellectual development or personal popularity. Seeing him surrounded by every variety of attractive women—young, accomplished, and beautiful women—it would not be unreasonable to suppose her jealousy was excited. Some time she may have dropped an inadvertent word that the scandal-mongers have interpreted into a grave accusation."

From other accounts Mrs. Beecher is quite the peer of her husband. The years that have made him the least bit puffy and inclined to corpulency, have framed her roseate complexion in a wealth of silver hair, and her deep blue eyes are as clear and pure as azure, while there is a repose in her manner that sets every one at ease, and is quite enchanting.

For the most part, however, the recollection of Mrs. Beecher is not held in high esteem in Indianapolis, and in his visits here she has never accompanied him. The trouble is, in an evil hour she was tempted to write a book, and for want of a more familiar subject indulged in a species of autobiography under the title of "From Dawn to Daylight," in which the trials and vicissitudes of her life in the West were minutely described. This could not well be done without other *dramatis personæ* than herself and family, and the mirror she held up to nature was not as flattering as that in which we are wont to see ourselves. In the then primitive condition of society the humble beginnings of fortune and influence were not as well crusted over as they are now-a-days, and the blood in our veins may not have been as blue as it was in the vicinity of Boston, but the hearts were as true, the kindness as extreme, and the appreciation as keen as could be found anywhere in the world.

In some of the comments upon the Beecher trouble I thought I could perceive a lingering pique caused by Mrs. Beecher's book, and I was at some trouble to hunt it up. It could not be found, and I was told the edition had been recalled. Those who happened to have a copy said they cared so little for possessing it that it had been mislaid. The generally expressed opinion was that it was the most slanderous production ever penned by a woman. It did violence to the good and true friends who had stood by her so faithfully in the trying hours of her pioneer life. Mrs. Beecher, it is said, wrote the book so quietly, and had it published so clandestinely, that her husband did not know of it until he found it on his table. So he told his old friends here, speaking of it with deep regret, his own heart beating with such true and fond love for the friends in his Western home.

While the author does not desire to vary materially in this narrative from the official proceedings, he feels that the reader will pardon him for embodying here a letter written from Brooklyn Heights on July 21, 1874, to the Pittsburg *Commercial*, giving as it does so much bearing upon the case, and perhaps a little romance as well.

On the first day of the year 1873, I gave you some particulars of a church scandal in which the Pastor of Plymouth Church, Henry Ward Beecher, was mentioned. It was not a pleasant topic on which to write or speculate. Since then, it has been the theme of many a plodding journalist, from the editor-in-chief to the Bohemian scribe. The culmination was reached last evening. Theodore Tilton, goaded to desperation, appeared before a committee of the leading members of Plymouth church. He was attended by two life-long friends, Frank Moulton, an old school-mate, and Frank Carpenter, the gifted artist who painted Lincoln and his Cabinet, and author of "Six Months in the White House," and a man whom Professor Fowler, in his work on Phrenology, gives as his highest type of the organic quality. He contrasts him with the idiot Emerson, and says: "He is pre-eminently fine-grained, pure-minded, ethereal, sentimental, refined, high-toned, intense in emotion, full of human nature, most exquisitely susceptible to impressions of all kinds, most poetic in temperament, lofty in aspiration, and endowed with wonderful intuition as to truth, what is right, best," etc.

With these two men at his side, Theodore Tilton probed the ulcer which has been gnawing at his heartstone for the past four years. Surrounding the house, in a drenching rain, were perched a legion of the members of the press. The committee rose at one hour past midnight. Theodore Tilton came out with his friends, and in response to a question from a dozen of the reporters as to whether the committee would furnish his statement, said: "I know not whether it is obtainable; but I know it is unanswerable." The *Tribune* of this morning says, editorially: "The reticence as to the nature of either charges or proof comes late. There has been too much promptness in seeking publicity heretofore, or there is too little now, as it is but fair to suppose that if Tilton proved nothing, the fact would have been flashed over two continents." I will imagine you, dear *Commercial,* in the city of churches, interviewing your correspondent.

Do I know Theodore Tilton? Well, yes, somewhat. We were born on the same block, within sight of Printing-House Square, and went to the same public school, but were never very intimate. His boyhood was passed among books, and he was never given to any of the rompish frivolities so natural to youth. Many a time have I sat on the fence that separates our homes and watched his wan face, from the sides of which fell a mass of golden hair. He was never without a book, and always in a pensive mood. Like a hot-house plant, he bloomed at an early age. While boys, we both drifted into journalism. Twenty years ago no youngster on the New York press gave fairer promise of a brilliant career than Theodore Tilton. Before he was out of his teens, he was one of the most reliable and rapid of phonographers, and while reporting lectures and political meetings for the *Tribune,* he attracted the notice of Horace Greeley, to whom Tilton was always warmly attached.

Why did he not stick by the *Tribune?*

Well, you see, he drifted over to Brooklyn, where every young man, to be deemed respectable, must regularly attend church. It is the *open sesame* to the social circle. The worldliness he encountered on the secular press was every way repugnant to him. No young man was more orthodox in his religious faith than Theodore. He became one of the shining lights of Plymouth Church; eschewed the secular papers entirely; delved deep into theology, and looked patronizingly down on the acquaintances of his boyhood. He was no Pharisee. His egotism was his predominating characteristic, but he was always affable and courteous. His paradise was the gilt-edged community on the Heights, and his æsthetic tastes caused him to avoid the rendezvous where Bohemians most did congregate.

He was married in 1855, by Mr. Beecher, to Miss Elizabeth Richards. who, for some time, had been one of Mr. Beecher's flock. Theodore closely identified himself with Plymouth Church, and, when but a few years past his majority, became the protege and coadjutor of his pastor. They were the closest of friends. In the year 1860 they, with Henry C. Bowen, were the Trinity of Plymouth. The Plymouth deacons were really spoony over "Theo." Some of them thought they saw in his face a resemblance to that of our Savior, and it was not long before he seemed t be walking on stilts, with his face turned heavenward. He and his pastor were inseparable. As an evidence of the friendship which existed between them, I will relate an incident that happened.

One of the first regiments formed in the City of Brooklyn for the defense of the Union was the Long Island phalanx. Among its officers was one of the sons of Beecher. While the army was being organized under McClellan, young Beecher committed some breach of discipline, and was placed under arrest. The affair greatly alarmed and agitated his father, who immediately counseled with Tilton as to the course he should take to shield his son from disgrace. Tilton asked Beecher for his (Beecher's) pocketbook, and took from it fifty dollars. He took the first train for Washington, and on reaching there, went direct to the house of Secretary of War Cameron. Mr. Cameron was dressing preparatory to entertaining a breakfast party of Governors of States. Tilton ascertained this fact from the servant, and, of course, announced himself as a Governor. He met Cameron, challenged his admiration, enlivened the table, and when the guests had departed, importuned for a commission for young Beecher in the regular army. Tilton would not be satisfied with a promise, and after an interview with President Lincoln, secured the desired commission. His subsequent inquiries at the camp of the regiment justified the wisdom of his course. He returned by the next train, handed Mr. Beecher the commission, at which his friend and patron fell on his breast and wept tears of gratitude. Theirs was no ordinary friendship, seemingly. Beecher's light reflected on Tilton, and he was happy.

Have I seen him lately? Oh, yes; we are not much further apart than we were in boyhood. We live on the same street.

Is he insane? Oh, that is only the screeching of the *Eagle* from its ærie under the Bridge.

What do I think about the scandal? Very little. I gave up thinking about it long since.

My opinion? That's of very little account. Has not Mayor Hunter, Mr. Tracy, Mr. Shearman, who was Fisk's attorney, and now clerk, of Plymouth Church, Joe Howard, and that legion of mutual friends of Mr. Beecher and Tilton, said that it amounted to nothing? You must certainly know that for the past two years it has been social ostracism for any one in this community to hazard one word that would dispel the mist that has so long covered this city like a pall. To opine that Tilton had a case was worse than sacrilege. To be seen walking with him was to encounter the gaze of thousands of angry eyes.

Think he will come out all right? Not much; he will bleach a great deal, however. He certainly could not be blacker than they have painted him.

By what process? Sunshine will do it. The mutual friend has been his curse. Their desires for the pastoral pressure of Mr. Beecher was keener than their sympathy for Theodore, and they have all cried, "Hush!"

The fact is, it has been quibble, quibble, from beginning to end. The papers have been playing the hurrah game, and, the worst of all, they have continued throwing their javelins at Tilton until he is now backed up to the wall.

Can Tilton vindicate himself in any way? I should think that if he could not he had better take a header from the ferry boat. Brooklyn may, like the ostrich, push its head into the sand, but the cyclone will sweep on just the same. Thunderbolts have been darting in every direction for the past four years, doing but little or no damage, not even clearing the atmosphere; but that bolt of Dr. Bacon's has at last struck a vital part. In fact, it was his lightning that did the mischief. The fuse it fired is burning slowly, but yet is as unquenchable as if it was trained through the lowermost confines of the infernal regions.

No proofs? Why not take a common-sense view of this matter? It has got to be done, sooner or later. What other divine in the land could stand such a racket? Trinity, in New York, had its Onderdonk, and Tremont Temple, in Boston, its Kalloch, and the Christian religion still survives.

Warm in his defense? Not a bit of it. I would rather remain dumb if I could; but when you see a man battling with a legion of foes, it makes one's blood boil to see "Tray, Blanche and Sweetheart" snapping so sharply. Why, the impudent stare of some of these curs has been cast into the face of every shapely and comely woman that crossed the Fulton ferry.

Why has he maintained silence so long? Ask Frank Moulton or Frank Carpenter. They have been his keepers. The solution of the query should be left to the man it most concerns. I am not his apologist. His was a grievous fault, and grievously hath he answered it. Tilton was always a radical —always ready to espouse some obnoxious doctrine. The sanctity of the marriage tie is not as strong in this community and some others as it should be. That mummery over the death bed of Richardson was a terrible piece of sacrilege; and ever since the mills of the Gods have been doing some crushing work under heavy pressure. Tilton is pretty thoroughly pulverized. When he found these fell destroyers had not spared his hearthstone, he became paralyzed, and then he allowed his friends to strap his cross to his back, when they pushed him into the abyss, on the side of which he has ever since been clinging. Here this drama of perdition began.

The result? Wait for the culmination, and then rush in among the mangled and dying, where you can hear their cries of anguish and despair.

Did he sign the covenant? No, not as originally drawn. You see, Tilton had been deserted by Bowen and cast adrift. They had recited to each other their grievances. Tilton had his moments of petulant decision. The mutual friends saw that Tilton must be muzzled. So Samuel Wilkeson, the veteran Washington correspondent of the *Tribune* and *Times* during the war, drew up a compact. Tilton could not swallow it all; so it was modified, and then they each signed it—Beecher, Bowen and Tilton. This was in the early part of 1872. Subsequently, "Suffolk" furnished it to the press. This was the first boiling over of the pitch. Wilkeson is part owner of the *Christian Union*, and a partner in the Christian publishing house of J. B. Ford & Co. He is a perfect Hotspur in temperament. Had any man desecrated his household, his hours would have been numbered on this earth. There would have been no covenants or compromise, or anxiety for the Christian Church, etc., etc. But in this imbroglio he became the diplomat. He was interested in Mr. Beecher's reputation in more ways than one, as is many another man. To think of Sam Wilkeson, with his keen perception, and knowledge of men and things, who has probed more mountains of corruption than tongue can tell, temporizing with this affair, is enough to make one lose all faith in the human race.

What brought about the last phase of this affair? Tilton endeavored to get a word in edge-ways at the Church Council, but the Moderator would not have it. Fate, unswering and unalterable fate, selected two instruments to carry out its decrees. These were Thomas Shearman, of Fisk and Gould notoriety, and the Rev. Dr. Bacon. Shearman managed Mr. Beecher's interests, while the Rev. Dr. Bacon, a contributor to the *Independent*, Bowen's paper, was the unwitting tool of Bowen, who, like a deer-stalker, has been crawling on his stomach with his eye on the sun for years.

These men in godliness resemble each other as much as Hyperion does the Satyr. Shearman, in an interview with an editor of the Brooklyn *Union*, pronounced Mrs. Tilton a spiritualist and expressed his doubts of Tilton's sanity. The editor was a friend and former coadjutor of Tilton, while he was chief of the *Union*. Tilton sent for him and questioned him as to the truth of the statement. The editor stated that he had not exaggerated, but on the contrary, had eliminated much that was offensive. This he put in the form of an affidavit, and then Tilton went for Shearman. He informed him by letter that he had done him (Tilton) and his family gross injustice, and offered him an opportunity to retract the offensive remarks, which was to be done in the presence of a witness, who was none other than Tilton's *Fidus Achates*, the ubiquitous Moulton. Shearman met Tilton at Moulton's house, and here the retraction was made in writing. Tilton, who, though notwithstanding he has committed the most egregious blunders in managing this unfortunate affair, is a natural diplomatist, thought he would put a bee in Shearman's bonnet, touched the messenger alarm, which was quickly answered. A message was sent to Henry Ward Beecher. It was a request that he would step over to Moulton's. He came and was informed that he was invited to be present as a witness to a retraction. The business concluded, Tilton picked up the copy of the *Tribune* which contained Dr. Bacon's address, delivered at New Haven the day before. Tilton turned to Beecher and said: "Now that we are here together, I desire to call your attention to a paragraph in which Dr. Bacon speaks of you as one of the most magnanimous of men, and characterizes me as a dog, who is the creature of your magnanimity. As you know *you* are the *creature* of *my* magnanimity, it is but right that Dr. Bacon should be disabused on this point." Shearman was the only one of that party of four that was in any way dismayed. He had from the beginning pushed himself to the front. This may account for Lawyer Shearman's desire for the bracing air of the Berkshire mountains. Mr. Beecher crossed his hands and remained silent. Tilton, seeing that there was to be no response, said: "As you are undecided what course to pursue, I will take the initiative, and will forward to Dr. Bacon a letter that he can transmit to you for an answer. He has been the Moderator of the Council, and necessarily becomes the historian of the matter. I cannot afford to stand on the record as a creature of your magnanimity." The letter was written, sent to the reverened gentleman, and by him forwarded to Mr. Beecher, and, like the Rev. Dr. Storrs' letter of condolence and sympathy, remains to the present time unanswered. Then followed Tilton's letter to Bacon, in which he mentioned an offense which he would not characterize. It is believed that it was this allegation that caused the leaders of Plymouth Church to advise their pastor that he could not longer maintain silence, whereupon Mr. Beecher named his court, and asked the members to do that which truth and justice may require, and desired that they satisfy themselves by an impartial and thorough examination of all sources of evidence, and to communicate to the examining committee, or to the church, such action as may then seem to them right and wise.

Why did Mrs. Tilton go before the committee? She never went before the committee. It was from a lady friend she first heard of the investigating committee. She sent for Mr. Beecher to meet her at the house of her friend, Mrs. Ovington. Mr. Beecher sent her word that it would not be policy for him to see her at that stage of affairs, but in his place came his lawyer. I do not know who that was, but if it was Shearman, and he has been the marplot in this affair, it can be readily understood that a man who was a match for the adventuress Mansfield in her legal tilts with Fisk, would be equal to the pettifogging required to manage a poor wife only too eager to screen her pastor, and save her husband and children from disgrace. While the lawyer was preparing her testimony, he found her in such a pliable mood that he deemed it best that her testimony should be immediately taken. Accordingly, he went in hot haste to the residence of one of the members, where the committee was in session, and informed them of the situation of affairs, whereupon there was an abrupt termination of their deliberations. The gentlemen hurried to the hat stand, grasped their hats and canes in confusion and in a body quickly repaired to the residence where Mrs. Tilton was sojourning. There, she, unknown to her husband, exonerated her pastor from the charges with which her name had been connected. On the tenth, Tilton was sent for by the committee. He was not then aware that it was a court appointed by Mr. Beecher. His suspicions were aroused, and it made him wary. There was legal counsel and a stenographer. That night, when he returned to his home, he learned for the first time, from his own wife, that it was a church court, and that she had given them her statement. Up to this moment Tilton had been on the defensive. He had merely explained his reason for writing to Dr. Bacon, but now that the gauntlet had been thrown down, he braced himself. His agonized wife saw the impending doom, and unmindful of the fact that he possessed all the proofs that would have palliated a tragedy, she fled from the house, abandoning her husband and children, and took refuge with Mr. Beecher's friends.

The statement? I have not seen its contents, nor has any one but his counsel. He requires no corroborative testimony, nor the assistance of a stenographer, and had called no witnesses. There is no longer any necessity for innuendoes. He expects no consideration from the New York or Brooklyn press. He realizes the fact that the odds are terribly against him, but says it is a day of battle and death; in fact, that he stands alone, unpitied and despised for having so long borne his cross, and now placed in a position by the refusal of others to protect him from further calumny, when he is forced to answer the demands, that the essential truth and the whole of it shall be made known. He feels keenly the bitter flings of the Brooklyn *Eagle*. Interviewers have besieged his house, (and you know how ravenous and merciless they can be in a hunt), night and day.

Those that have spoken with him have put flabby words in his mouth that he never uttered. They have described him as jolly, when he was but bland. One racy interviewer, described him as "having a merry twinkle in his eye," which when he saw in print, he remarked, in an agonizing voice, "Great Heavens! what is there now in my life to come that

will excite an expression of merriment in my eye or any feature of my face!"

How does he stand it? That I cannot tell. You see that he does; but that benign expression so natural to his face is gone. Marius amid the ruins was not more desolate and alone than is Tilton to-day in his cozy vine-clad cottage. That he is almost friendless is beyond all doubt, from the fact that, of all the dear mutual friends, not one but counseled from the beginning that he should continue to carry his burden. The precipice from which he is now hanging is one over which many a man has stumbled before; but the creepers that entangled his feet are of his own planting. He has fastened his death grip to the High Priest, and intends to fall not alone.

Have I mingled in the contest? Oh, no. I am not an "eminent respectable," and not a mutual friend. I was only a skirmisher. I was not a match for Moulton's sophistical diplomacy or Frank Carpenter's angelic sweetness. I have warned them time and time again of the danger of trifling. I have crossed bayonets with the terrible ogress Woodhull many a time. When Osborne, Comstock, and many others, in their honest indignation entangled her in the meshes of the law, I begged and beseeched those who could have done so to open her prison door. In her calmer moments she had shown me the letters that she had threatened to publish. When I saw whom she had fraternized with, and the hearts she could lacerate; when I saw that hers was the terrible fury of jealousy, I implored that she could not have the opportunity of doing any more mischief. I encountered nothing but moral cowards. Turn where I would, I met obstacles. Quibbling was then, as it is now, the rule, not the exception, and I gave up in despair, and the canker continued its gnawing. One ounce of honesty and manliness would have averted the coming storm, but it was not to be. If the fate that awaits those who desecrated the sanctity of domestic peace, will make odious the theories and sophistries of those who would emancipate husband and wife, the lesson will not be lost.

Is no compromise possible? About as possible as floating up Niagara rapids on a crowbar.

What next? It's hard to tell what the week may bring forth. Should a crowner's quest be the last act in the drama, it would not be surprising. I cannot see that Tilton has much to live for. He is as freakish as a woman, and has always courted martyrdom of some kind. Wait and see. All the clamor is but idle words. Mr. Beecher's battle is many another man's fight. There be editors who, while they would not add a pang to the misery of a brother journalist by any act of theirs, will permit some mangy cur who has returned to his vomit to do the work.

Will the statement be given to the press? I don't know. It will in time. Its immediate appearance depends entirely on the action of the committee. Yes, a seat around that committee table last evening would have been heaven to a scribe; but there was no leak there, that I can assure you. It was not a court of Tilton's choosing, nor a council of churches. It was Mr. Beecher's tribunal, composed of members of Plymouth Church, and never was the power of a king more absolute than is Mr. Beecher's over his congregation; and "The King can do no wrong."

CHAPTER IX.

A VISIT TO THE CLAFLIN SISTERS' BANKING OFFICE—A RUNNING COMMENTARY UPON THEODORE TILTON, WHO LOVES SCOTCH ALE AS HE ONCE LOVED THE MODERN DEMOSTHENES—A SPICY INTERVIEW WITH THE WOODHULL—HER RELATIONS TO TILTON AND BEECHER EXPLAINED—"THEODORE WAS MY DEVOTED LOVER."

In the same letter of the gossiping correspondent who, in the preceding chapter, describes Beecher's career at Lawrenceburg, is given some interesting facts regarding the great actors in this scandal, and interviews with them that certainly throws valuable light upon the relations existing between these free-lovers of Plymouth and New York. The writer says:

During 1872 I was a resident of New York city, and inextricably entangled in the swirl of national politics. Required to be at Greeley headquarters much of the time, I formed there the acquaintance of many persons of note and celebrity. By the 17th of June three presidential candidates were already in the field—Horace Greeley, General Grant, and Victoria C. Woodhull. On a warm June afternoon, when I had elbowed my way on the east side of crooked Nassau street from the *Tribune* office to Wall street, and failed to find my friend in, at Jay Cooke's, in sheer adventure I concluded to call on the most notorious adventuress of our country, Victoria C. Woodhull, at her broker's office, 48 Broad street, a block south of Wall. No. 48 was easily reached, after a brisk and dangerous walk past the Stock Exchange and through the throngs of bellowing bulls and roaring bears, and I tripped up three or four steps to the "parlor" office floor and entered the door of the front office. Handing Miss Tennie C. Claflin my card, she beamed upon me one of her witching smiles (the kind that wilted poor Challis, I presume), and lisped to me:

"Won't you pleathe be theated, thir, here on the thofa bethide me?"

Of course I would. I would not be so ungallant as to decline to "thit" down by so beaming and buxom a beauty as Miss Tennie, when so cordially invited. While I sat, Miss Tennie was frequently called to the telegraphic stock-and-gold-board register tick-tick-tick-a-ticking away at a great rate at the end of the apartment next the street. During her brief absence I stole a glance over the luxurious rooms of the Woodhull & Claflin brokers. They have time and again been described to you—I only need mention that Col. Blood sat at his desk in front; rich carpetry, and upholstery, and pictures furnished the apartment, which was spacious; and some thirty feet from the front, a high and richly carved walnut partition, crowned with ornamented glass, separated the public from the rear private office. Tennie fluently inflicted me for an hour, when I inquired for her more famous sister, Victoria. "Oh, yeth, of courth, you mutht the thisther, Vic.," prattled fat and sprightly Tennie; and she bounded within the private office with my card. Returning, she seated herself familiarly and in close proximity to your correspondent, and on went the chat till a voice came from an opened slat or "port-hole" in that glass, calling "Tennie!" She responded, and immediately conducted me face to face with Victoria Woodhull. My first impressions of her were agreeable. There was a bright, intelligent face, lit up by two soft, dark-blue or changeable eyes. She smiled sweetly, and greeted me in tones tender and plaintive as a flute. She was stylishly attired, and at that moment was partaking of a dish of luscious berries, a generous quantity of which had been sent in to the "sisters" by some anonymous millionaire (probably old Vanderbilt), and I was pressed to join in the refreshment while we chatted familiarly on politics, social life, her prospects for the presidency, &c. She remarked, in her animated way, that she would receive a million votes. "You look incredulous!" she went on to observe, "and I do not wonder, for it takes money to conduct a great campaign, and of that we shall have abundant supplies. Look here!" she exclaimed, as she drew forth what I at first mistook for a U. S. bond. "Here," she continued, "here is a bond we are issuing, and upon which we shall raise $200,000, or twice or thrice that sum if needed." Then, with a fascinating smile and a pensive and tender glance from her mellow eyes, she softly and confidingly whispered : "The next time you call you shall have one of these bonds. They draw 7 per cent. interest." I gracefully bowed my blushing thanks, and soon took my leave. I did not meet her again during the summer.

At Glenham hotel headquarters I frequently met Theodore Tilton. Our acquaintance sprang up informally, and progressed similarly. Millions of our countrymen have seen Theodore, yet to gratify those of you readers who have not, I may observe that he is tall, well-built, and large-boned man, with just the least perception of a stoop, and physically a success. His face is a study—a luxury—the essence of intellect and intelligence. It is not large below the forehead. Together, they present a handsome, pleasing irresistible contour. I do not wonder that feminine hearts swell and break beneath his beaming countenance. His smile is as witching as a woman's and his laugh hearty and sympathetic. What distinguishes him in general appearance is a wealth of blonde hair hanging in clustering profusion over his shoulders. Now, he is not far from 40 years of age, and in the prime of intellectual and physical vigor. I do not know that I ever had a talk with Tilton "between the sherry and champagne" *a la* Watterson, but I recollect a very entertaining lunch we had together one morning, when I was charmed with his sparkling conversation between the Scotch ale and the oysters. Tilton is a strictly temperate man, but not a teetotaler. Greeley had an abiding love for his "boy Theodore," as he often spoke of him. When Greeley went to Boston, July 4th, 1872, Tilton accompanied the party. At midnight's calm and holy hour on that night, long after Greeley was in his state-room and asleep, the press demons proceeded to explore the nether depths of the ill-fated Sound Steamer Metis, in search of the bar. Somewhat to our surprise we stumbled on to Brother Tilton and another gentleman interviewing a bottle of Scotch ale for a "night-cap." He is neither improved with or depressed without his occasional glass of ale. A shadow seemed hovering over Tilton, notwithstanding his effervescing and grandly recuperative nature. When the campaign closed disastrously (he strongly supported Greeley), Theodore Tilton was a sorrowful man. Other afflictions than political defeat weighed upon his heart. There was an impending doom. I did not meet him again for weeks.

During the summer Mrs. Woodhull had left the city. Late

in the autumn she returned, and the broker firm of Woodhull & Claflin opened out again in full blast. Their appearance among the infuriated bulls and bears of Broad street always produced a sensation; but no sensation did they ever produce equal that of the publication in *Woodhull & Claflin's Weekly* of the Beecher-Tilton scandal. Such a feeling of general distrust of the Claflin sisters prevailed that the public did not accept the astounding revelation therein made as the genuine article. How many hundred thousand copies of their *Weekly* were sold before the frail sisters were enjoying the hospitality of Ludlow street jail, I never could ascertain. Out of curiosity, on the evening of the day before their arrest, accompanied by a New York journalist, I crowded my way through the army of newsboys and newsdealers wishing to leaving orders which actually blocked up Broad street for hundreds of feet, and appeared in the presence of Victoria and Tennie at their old quarters, No. 48 Broad street. Hundreds of dollars per hour were flowing into their coffers. The conspirators were jubilant—the terrible expose had gone off like buttered hot cakes. I was cordially pressed to call at their dwelling in Fourth avenue, with my friend, that evening. We did so. We found it a first-class, English basement, four-story private house, well-furnished.

The reception was cordial and generously warm. We were ushered into a spacious parlor, at the further end of which long flowing lace curtains, gently drawn apart, half-disguised and half-disclosed a magnificent mahogany bedstead—the chief article of furniture in Tennie's perfumed boudoir. A grand piano occupied a place in the rear division of the parlor. Mrs. Woodhull, a married sister, and Tennie were the adult persons present, while the occasion was graced by the presence of two nieces of Mrs. W. and her own young daughter, the nieces being fifteen and twelve respectively, and the daughter about a dozen summers. Miss Woodhull was shy and reserved; but the two young misses, the nieces, entered upon the programme of receiving and entertaining us with a nonchalance as refreshing as a midsummer shower. The elder of the nieces was then on the boards in minor parts with Daly's company at the Fifth Avenue Theatre and she could sing ballads very attractively. She indicated, in her playing, singing, and recitations that evening, some degree of histrionic talent. During a lull in the general, ecstatic, jubilant joy which pervaded, and on that occasion spontaneously exploded from the members of that family, Mrs. Woodhull and I happened to be alone in an adjoining reception room. Without preliminaries, I opened a conversation with her concerning the terrible expositions of her Beecher-Tilton scandal article, at that hour convulsing the social life of two great cities.

I give you the interview substantially as it occurred, from notes recorded at the time:

Correspondent—Mrs. Woodhull, does our friendship entitle me to ask you confidentially for details of a private matter?

Mrs. Woodhull—Perhaps so. Proceed, You know me well enough to know that I will at least be frank.

Cor. Of course I do, madam. I have had proof positive of that. Well, then, what I wished to inquire about is, How much truth, *actual fact, is* there in the publication about Beecher and Mrs. Tilton, and her husband, Theodore Tilton, in this last issue of your *Weekly?*

Mrs. W.—My dear sir, it is every word of it true. Why, I know directly from the principal parties themselves that the greater share of it is actual fact. I have had peculiar and extraordinary proofs of its accuracy. Perhaps some of the minor details, as to dates and incidents, may be at fault, but the full sweep of the *expose*, in all its *enormity* (from the popular conventional stand-point), it is a bare statement of a fact. You see we do not allude to it to denounce it, but to show that the sectarian or Christian world *lives* the principles we advocate while denouncing *us* for their advocacy.

Cor.—You know personally both Mr. Tilton and Mr. Beecher, of course. I should suppose your opportunities for knowing the facts were superior.

Mrs. W.—Certainly they were. I ought to know Mr. Tilton, for he was my devoted lover for more than half a year, and I admit that during that time he was my accepted lover. A woman who could not love Theodore Tilton, especially in reciprocation of a generous, impulsive, overwhelming affection such as he is capable of bestowing, must be indeed dead to all the sweeter impulses of our nature. *I* could not resist his inspiring fascination.

Cor.—Do I understand, my dear madam, that the fascination was mutual and irresistible?

Mrs. W.—You will think so when I tell you that so enamored and infatuated with each other were we that for *three months* we were hardly out of each other's sight, and that during that time he rarely left my house day or night. *Pardon* *me for the statement, but you sincerely seek truth, and you shall have it first-handed * * * * * Theodore was then estranged from his wife, and undergoing all the agonies of the torture inflicted upon him by the treachery of his friend Mr. Beecher.*

Cor.—Pardon me, but I presume that it was under such circumstances and during this intimacy that Mr. Tilton unlocked the secrets and griefs of his breast to you ?

Mrs. W.—Yes, sir, we were very naturally mutually confiding. And it was during this time he so eloquently wrote of me, in the little *brochure* of a biography from his pen.

Cor.—You speak of Mr. Tilton's sorrow over his friend Beecher's treachery. You refer, I presume to the alleged seduction of Mrs. Tilton by Henry Ward Beecher.

Mrs. W.—Yes, sir, as we have stated it in the *Weekly*, giving the true relations existing at one time between Beecher and Mrs. Tilton. You observed we did not blame either. To do so would be inconsistent.

Cor.—So I understand that Mr. Tilton gave you an insight into his trouble directly from his own lips ?

Mrs. W.—As sure as God rules the spheres he did. He confided in me and won my entire sympathy, and I tried to solace him by pointing out to him that *our* teachings in the *Weekly* and our lectures were natural and not abnormal, as shown in his own family and that of Henry Ward Beecher.

Cor.—Did I understand you to say, Mrs. Woodhull, that you were personally acquainted with Mr. Beecher?

Mrs. W.—Oh, yes, sir, I know Mr. Beecher very well.

Cor.—Permit me to ask if Mr. Beecher ever exhibited toward you his especial friendship in any unmistakeable manner. I have a particular reason for making this inquiry ?

Mrs. W.—Indeed he has. His private carriage could have been seen waiting before our door every afternoon for many months, to take us riding to Central Park. You would, perhaps, call that *some* indication or evidence of personal friendship.

Cor.—Yes, madam, I would most unquestionably consider it a very practical proof of regard, if in my own case. I presume all this occurred months ago ?

Mrs. W.—Yes, months ago—before Mr. Beecher discovered that the Argus eyes of the world had detected him practicing one system and preaching another. Compelled to choose, he preferred to be open in his preaching, and, I presume, to *cloak* his practices. It *pays* better, you see.

Cor.—I will not ask you, Mrs. Woodhull, if your intimacy with Mr. Beecher extended beyond the carriage rides.

Mrs. W.—I leave you to your own inferences ; but must not be understood as suggesting that Mr. Beecher and Mr. Tilton ever occupied precisely similar personal relations toward myself. I never loved Mr. Beecher.

Cor.—Now that you have permitted (in your *expose* in your *Weekly*) the feline quadruped to escape from the amorous bag, what results other than your immense sales of *The Weekly* are visible ?

Mrs. W.—"Well, my friena, please look here, [showing me a score or more of freshly arrived letters]. This is my mail this evening. Nearly every letter conveys some point of positive proof to sustain our *expose*. Here is a letter [reading] from an eminent lawyer in Brooklyn. See what he writes. He says that in his professional capacity he has come into possession of much evidence not only similar to what we publish but in direct support of it. He says scores of such cases exist in Brooklyn and New York churches—that prominent lawyers make fortunes, not by practicing *law*, but by suppressing scandals. He is familiar with Plymouth church congregation and a regular attendant on Beecher's preaching, and affirms that it has become a kind of playful gossip among the outsiders who merely *look* on the play, as to *which one* of Mr. Beecher's score of female lovers in his flock (dames and virgins) is, at the time, basking in his smile.

Cor.—You suggest this condition of things in your *expose*, I believe?

Mrs. W.—Yes, for we are sure that it is so. I wish the parties to this particular infraction (so-called) of the seventh commandment would dare investigate. The truth would be laid bare and society elevated.

Cor.—Will your publication not precipitate a complete and formal explosion of this fermenting mass of hypocrisy and corruption?

Mrs. W.—Ah, sir, I fear not. I *know* there is a covenanted bond—a league of *silence*. But we shall see how long before it will be broken.

At that moment of our somewhat explicit interview, Tennie came dashing into our presence with:—

"Thister Vic., have you tholen ofth here by yourthelfths for the whole evening ?"

Then we returned to the parlor; and soon my friends and I

10

put on our furs and took a stage for down town. Twenty-four hours thereafter the sisters were in Ludlow street Jail. During their incarceration there, in company with my demon of the press, I frequently looked in upon them, and marveled at these curious characters midst their ringing laughter and their tears. Mrs. Woodhull's calm and sympathetic eyes, her tender and motherly voice, and her chaste manners indicated to me that she is, whatever else may be said, a *truthful woman.*

On a chill December day, long after the campaign was over and poor Greeley and the wife of his bosom were laid away under the sod in Greenwood, I had occasion to comply with a standing, written, invitation to call and see Theodore Tilton at his cottage home, 174 Livingston street, just off Fulton avenue, Brooklyn. I found No. 174 to be a neat but unpretentious wooden cottage, with an unusually wide front, two stories high, and suggesting comfort and a good degree of elegance. My ring at the door-bell was answered by a female servant with a hideous face. In view of all that had fallen on my ear, involuntarily the wicked thought came, somehow, coupling Mrs. Tilton's domestic diplomacy with that repulsive countenance. Whether Theodore could find occasion to exercise equal defensive powers as against his better half, I did not know. Admitted to the sitting-room, adjoining the parlor and at the rear of the hall, I found the handsome hero of the greatest scandal of our time, slippered and gowned and lazily lounging on a sofa before a cosy grate fire. He accosted me cordially and familiarly, and smilingly pointed to a chair near him, saying:—"Pardon my laziness. I am fatigued by overwork and came home early to lounge about in this free and easy manner.

Business soon dispatched, our conversation drifted to Greeley, and his wife, and concomitant matters. He gave a ludicrous description of his first acquaintance with Mrs. Greeley; how he went to Chappaqua to fill a lecture engagement made for another; how he pleased Mrs. Greeley so well that ever after until death she was one of his warmest friends.

As Theodore Tilton lay stretched on his sofa, I sat fronting his face. Lifting my eyes above his grand, poetic head, I could not avoid perceiving an exquisite portrait on canvas, gracing the wall. Again and again my eyes fell upon it. Something peculiarly charming, and fascinating, and tender hung about it. Musingly I thought the artist was himself a most imaginative genius and consummate creator, or, if an actual instead of fancy subject, his brush must have been inspired. A most symmetrical head, intellect and poetry predominating; a wealth of silken brown hair; soft and soulful eyes of richest hazel; a face of exquisite sweetness and tenderness, and ripe with culture and character; a mouth carved by the gods, and lips full, warm, and suggesting robustness of modest passion; a chin indicating a gentle firmness and abundant will; a shapely neck and graceful shoulders, and a finely developed bust—all harmony, all beauty, all the vigor and tenderness of young life and fascination. The witching eyes seemed to brighten when looked into; a very smile so sweet as to thrill me appeared upon that face when I involuntarily fixed my gaze upon it. Contemplating that portrait, so strange a feeling came over me that I heedlessly trespassed on propriety, and before I was aware of it I said to Mr. Tilton:

"What a charming painting you have above your head."

He turned, and looked up with a tender smile. "Why," said he, "that is a portrait of Mrs. Tilton. Wait a moment, I will call her. I desire that you shall meet her."

And Mr. Tilton briskly passed to an adjoining room, whence, shortly thereafter, he returned, bringing on his arm the original of the portrait on the wall.

Mrs. Tilton is of medium height, perfectly, voluptuously developed, modest, not very vivacious, with beautiful eyes, and a soft, charming voice. She is in the prime of life, enjoys good health (at least looked as though she did) and her manners are most winning. My visit to Mr. Tilton's was not prolonged.

The world has learned to bear no malice toward Mark Anthony for his fall before Cleopatra. Some time it may be equally generous with Beecher's fall before lovely Mrs. Tilton.

CHAPTER X.

TILTON'S LIFE OF WOODHULL WITH CUTTING COMMENTS BY A FRIEND OF H. W. BEECHER.—THE FASCINATION UNDER WHICH TILTON WROTE IT.—THE PRIESTESS OF FREE LOVE AND UNLIMITED AFFECTION AND THE VARYING PHASES OF HER PHANTASMAGORIC CAREER FONDLY PHOTOGRAPHED.—HOW SHE BURST THE FETTERS OF MATRIMONY AND FLED TO HER AFFINITY.—MRS. WOODHULL ON THE HOUSETOP COMMUNING WITH DEMOSTHENES.—HER REVELATIONS TO THEODORE.—MRS. WOODHULL RETURNS FROM THE WEST TO AID IN VINDICATING THEODORE.—AN INTERESTING INTERVIEW WITH HER.—SHE DENIES THAT MR. TILTON HELD CRIMINAL RELATIONS TO HER.—SHE AVERS THAT SHE FIRST LEARNED OF THE LIAISON BETWEEN MRS. TILTON AND MR. BEECHER FROM THE PASTOR'S SISTER AND ELIZABETH CADY STANTON.

NO history of this great subject of anxiety and conversation would be complete without giving the reader some passages from the biography of Mrs. Woodhull, written by Theodore Tilton at a period when it is alleged he was under her fascinating spell. This biography, that so shocked some of the friends of Mr. Tilton was published as a *Golden Age* Tract, and bore as a motto: "He that uttereth a slander is a fool." Proverbs x, 18. The Brooklyn *Eagle*, which during the popular clamor for an investigation, very strongly sided with the Pastor of Plymouth Church, in republishing extracts from Theodore's tribute to Victoria thus comments introductorily and severely. "Mr. Theodore Tilton, when in the first throes of that anguish which has lately found frequent if vague expression in letters and protests, turned to Mrs. Victoria C. Woodhull for comfort and moral support. The virtuous current of his life had been interrupted. The ascetic purity of

VICTORIA C. WOODHULL.

his soul had been disturbed, and for the first time in his life he found himself face to face with moral enormities of the existence of which he had scarcely been aware. He says, just at present, that his home has been shaken to its modest foundations by the act or word of Henry Ward Beecher. Of the dimensions and of the significance of that act or word Mr. Tilton has vouchsafed, so far, to say nothing exact or precise. We are forced to believe that the shock was so desperate, so tremendous, that in his agonized recoil from its contemplation, he fell into the siren's clutch of Mrs. Woodhull. How grimly that arch priestess of Priapus held on to Tilton's streaming coat tails, he has himself testified as few men of moderate common sense would like to bear witness. "The wife of his bosom had been insulted," The sanctuary of his home had been invaded by "an improper proposal." His belief in the flowery code of ethics which he himself received one hundred dollars a night for rehearsing about the country, had been shaken. What so natural, because so paradoxical, as the recourse of his original resentment to the oracle of Broad Street—to the woman whose Satanic embassy was precisely the description and extraction of those very social and marital relations, the menacing of whose stability in Tilton's own case by Beecher, was the mainspring and private cause of Tilton's despair? The proposition is simple enough in all conscience. Tilton loved his wife, and cherished his domestic purity with an enthusiasm almost frantic. Beecher's inconsiderate act revealed to him possibilities of injury and destruction to that domestic religion, which his own crystal integrity had never suspected. Naturally, in his tearful perplexity, he hied to the sorceress who trafficked in lusts and adulteries, and who, from a negative sort of personal experience, knew more —and less—about the inviolability of marriage than any other counselor to whom he could apply. Mrs. Woodhull had been fishing for souls for some time in Broad Street. She had landed half a dozen meagre spirits of the stockbroker set, but these had slipped out of her hands, and left no good behind. When Tilton blundered into the meshes of her net, we can conceive how, like a spider, she clasped the bleating victim to her ruthless breast. Here, at all events, was a good catch, plump and succulent because full of vanity and a rich store of maudlin sentimentality. Therefore she made up her mind that this, her latest gudgeon, should distil a nourishment of which, just at this crisis, she stood in sore need. The Tiltonian chastity which had shrunk in horror from confronting the spectral possibilities evoked by Mr. Beecher's alleged proposal to Mrs. Tilton, was dazzled and blinded by the moral effulgence of Mrs. Woodhull. Hovering on the edge of her fascination, at first, Tilton was finally engulfed, and three months of the time he devoted to purging his sensitive honor, were spent in the closest and nearest intimacy with the polyandrous nymph of Broad Street. In brief, if the word of that notorious drab be worth the credit which Tilton, himself, over his own signature, attaches to it, Tilton conceived the project of re-consecrating his home and re-establishing its purity, in the adulterous arms of his mistress! In exchange for the sympathy and the comfort of that woman, he devoted his remarkable genius to the creation of a monument for her. At her feet he laid a votive biography, penned at intervals during the preparation of his remedy for the wrongs which Mr. Beecher, as he complains, had perpetrated upon his honor. That biography was regarded at the time of its original publication with only the moderate interest which attaches itself to the irrational and inexplicable freak of some madman. But in view of the light it throws both on Tilton's mentalcondition and in his painfully acute moral sensibility, the *Eagle* devotes some space to that wonderful literary work."

Tilton opens his remarkable biography thus:—

"I shall swiftly sketch the life of Victoria Claflin Woodhull; a young woman whose career has been as singular as any heroine's in a romance; whose ability is of a rare and whose character of the rarest type; whose personal sufferings are of themselves a whole drama of pathos; whose name (through the malice of some and the ignorance of others) has caught a shadow in strange contrast with the whiteness of her life; whose position as a representative of her sex in the greatest reform of modern times renders her an object of peculiar interest to her fellow citizens; and whose character (inasmuch as I know her well) I can portray without color or tinge from any other partiality save that I hold her in uncommon respect.

"In Homer, Ohio, in a small cottage, white painted and high peaked, with a porch running around it and a flower garden in front, this daughter, the seventh of ten children of Roxana and Buckman Claflin, was born September 23d, 1838. As this was the year when Queen Victoria was crowned, the new born babe, though clad neither in purple nor fine linen, but comfortably swaddled in respectable poverty, was immediately christened (though without chrism), as the Queen's namesake; her parents little dreaming that their daughter would one day aspire to a higher seat than the English throne. The Queen with that early matronly predilection which her subsequent life did so much to illustrate, foresaw that many glad mothers who were to bring babes into the world during that coronation year, would name them after the chief lady of the earth; and accordingly she ordained a gift to all her little namesakes of Anno Domino 1838. As Victoria Claflin was one of these, she has lately been urged to make a trip to Windsor Castle, to see the illustrious giver of these gifts, and to receive the special souvenir which the Queen's bounty is supposed to hold still in store for the Ohio babe that uttered its first cry as if to say, "Long live the Queen!" Mrs. Woodhull, who is now a candidate for the Presidency of the United States, should defer this visit till after her election, when she will have a beautiful opportunity to invite her elder sister in sovereignty—the mother of our mother country—to visit her fairest daughter, the Republic of the West.

[The elasticity of a mind which condescends from schemes of moral crucifixion to state that "Victoria Claflin has lately been urged to make a trip to Windsor Castle to see the illustrious giver of these gifts," and come back with a present from the Queen, reminds one of the elephant's trunk, capable both of tearing up a tree or picking a pocket. We are rather at a loss to comprehend how the babe of such promise was christened "without chrism." The performance of such a feat must have been something remarkable, or Mr. Tilton would surely never have embalmed mention of the fact in a parenthesis. "Her eldest sister in sovereignty" is a very picturesque sentence. Its only fault is that, on being analyzed, it doesn't yield much meaning as a result. It looks very much as if that and the succeeding phrases were gauzy and prismatic, if very unsubstantial, devices of the Tiltonian genius, to fill out a paragraph. But let us proceed.]—*Eagle Critic.*

"It is pitiful to be a child without a childhood. Such was she. Not a sunbeam gilded the morning of her life. her girlish career was a continuous bitterness—an unbroken heart break. She was worked like a slave—whipped like a convict. Her father was impartial in his cruelty to all his children;

her mother, with a fickleness of spirit that renders her one of the most erratic of mortals, sometimes abetted him in his scourgings; and at other times shielded the little ones from his blows, In a barrel of rain water he kept a number of braided green withes made of willow or walnut twigs, and with these stinging weapons, never with any ordinary whip, he would cut the quivering flesh of the children till their tears and blood melted him into mercy. Sometimes he took a handsaw or a stick of firewood as the instrument of his savagery. Coming home after the children were in bed, on learning of some offense which they had committed, he has been known to waken them out of sleep, and whip them until morning. In consequence of these brutalities one of the sons, in his thirteenth year, burst away from home, went to sea, and still bears a shattered constitution the damning memorial of his father's wrath. "I have no remembrance of a father's kiss," says Victoria. Her mother has on occasions tormented and harried her children until they would be thrown into spasms, whereat she would hysterically laugh, clap her hands, and look as fiercely delighted as a cat in playing with a mouse. At other times, her tenderness towards her offspring would appear almost angelic. She would fondle them, weep over them, lift her arms and thank God for such children, caress them with ecstatic joy, and then smite them as if seeking to destroy at a blow both body and soul. This eccentric old lady, compounded in equal parts of heaven and hell, will pray till her eyes are full of tears, and in the same hour curse till her lips are white with foam. The father exhibits a more tranquil bitterness, with fewer spasms. These parental peculiarities were lately made witnesses against their possessors in a court of justice."

[It is hard to explain Mr. Tilton's evidently accurate acquaintance with the castigatory apparatus of the Claflin family. "The barrel of rain water" in which Claflin *père*, kept his "braided green withes made of willow or walnut twigs," is so vividly projected on our retina, that a sharp and sympathetic spasm responds, in divers portions of our anatomy, to the lurid description. "A handsaw or a stick of firewood" were occasionally substituted for "the braided green withes." No wonder that with the alternation of such regulative implements in *la famille* Claflin, one of the sons "burst away from home."

The only marvel is that the rest of the children didn't indulge in a like domestic explosion. "I have no remembrance of a father's kiss," says Victoria, to whom the fates afterward seemed to have allowed huge osculatory compensation. The portrait of old Mrs. Claflin "hysterically laughing," clapping her hands and looking as fiercely as a "cat playing with a mouse," is the work of a master hand. Nobody other than Tilton could have done so much with so little. Nor could anybody else have described the vigorous spanking powers of the old lady so neatly and so graphically.—*Eagle Critic.*]

If I must account for what seems unaccountable, I may say that with these parents, these traits are not only constitutional but have been further developed by circumstances. The mother, who has never in her life learned to read, was during her maidenhood the petted heiress of one of the richest German families of Pennsylvania, and was brought up not to serve but to be served, until in her ignorance and vanity she fancied all things her own, and all people her ministers. The father, partly bred to the law and partly to real estate speculations, early in life acquired affluence, but during Victoria's third year suddenly lost all that he had gained, and sat down like a beggar in the dust of despair.

The mother, from her youth, had been a monomaniac, a spiritualist before the name of spiritualism was coined, and before the Rochester knockings had noised themselves into the public ear. She saw visions and dreamed dreams. During the half year preceding Victoria's birth, the mother became powerfully excited by a religious revival, and went through the process known as "sanctification." She would rise in prayer meetings and pour fourth passionate hallelujahs that sometimes electrified the worshippers. The father, colder in temperament, yet equally inclined to the supernatural, was her partner in these excitements. When the stroke of poverty felled them to the earth, these exultations were quenched in grief. The father, in the opinion of some, became partially crazed; he would take long and rapid walks, sometimes of twenty miles, and come home with bleeding feet and haggard face. The mother, never wholly sane, would huddle her children together as a hen her chickens, and wringing her hands above them, would pray by the hour that God would protect her little brood. Intense melancholy—a misanthropic gloom thick as a sea fog—seized jointly upon both their minds, and at intervals ever since has blighted them with its mildew. It is said that a fountain cannot send forth at the same time sweet waters and bitter, and yet affection and enmity will proceed from this couple almost at the same moment. At times they are full of craftiness, low cunning, and malevolence; at other times they beam with sunshine, sweetness and sincerity. I have seen many strange people, but the strangest of all are the two parents whose commingled essence constitutes the spiritual principle of the heroine of this tale.

Just here, if any one asks, "How is it that such parents should not have reproduced their eccentricities in their children?" I answer, "This is exactly what they have done." The whole brood are of the same feather, except Victoria and Tennie. What language shall describe them? Such another family circle of cats and kits, with soft fur and sharp claws, purring at one moment and fighting the next, never before filled one house with their clamors since Babel began. They love and hate—they do good and evil—they bless and smite each other. They are a sisterhood of furies, tempered with love's melancholy. Here and there one will drop on her knees and invoke God's vengeance on the rest. But for years there has been one common sentiment sweetly pervading the breasts of a majority toward a minority of the offspring—namely, a determination that Victoria and Tennie should earn all the money for the support of the numerous remainder of the Claflin tribe—wives, husbands, children, servants, and all. Being daughters of the horseleech, they cry "give." It is the common law of the Claflin clan that the idle many shall eat up the substance of the thrifty few. Victoria is a green leaf, and her legion of relatives are caterpillars who devour her. Their sin is that they return no thanks after meat; they curse the hand that feeds them. They are what my friend Mr. Greeley calls "a bad crowd." I am a little rough in saying this, I admit; but I have a rude prejudice in favor of the plain truth."

[If the elder Claflin had been father-in-law and mother-in-law to their daughter's biographer, we could understand, without much difficulty, the painful minuteness of description which he lavished upon their characteristics. But we respectfully submit that his caricatures of the old lady and gentleman are really outrageous. What would be excusable, on the ground of precedent, in the case of one of their daughter's numerous husbands, is unwarrantable in that of a mere stranger and devotee at the Woodhull shrine. We are forced to believe that "the whole brood" didn't extend to Mr. Tilton that hearty welcome which he received at the hands of "Victoria and Tennie." They must have treated the eminent historian as an interloper, or he never would have drawn upon Mr. Greeley's vocabulary to call them "a bad crowd." What charming simplicity in his assertion that he "has a rude prejudice in favor of the plain truth?"—*Eagle Critic.*

Victoria's schooldays comprised, all told, less than three years—stretching with broken intervals between her eighth and eleventh. The aptest learner of her class, she was the pet alike of scholars and teacher. Called "The Little Queen" (not only from her name but her demeanor) she bore herself with mimic royalty, like one born to command. Fresh and beautiful, her countenance being famed throughout the neighborhood for its striking spirituality, modest, yet energetic, and restive from the overfullness of an inward energy such as quickened the young blood of Joan of Arc, she was a child of genius, toil and grief. The little old head on the little young shoulders was often bent over her schoolbook at the midnight hour. Outside of the schoolroom she was a household drudge, serving others so long as they were awake, and serving herself only when they slept. Had she been born black or been chained to a cart wheel in Alabama, she could not have been a more enslaved slave. During these school years, child as she was, she was the many burdened maid of all work in the large family of a married sister; she made fires, washed and ironed, she baked bread, she cut wood, she spaded a vegetable garden, she went on errands, she tended infants, she did everything. "Victoria! Victoria!" was the call in the morning before the cock crowing; when, bouncing out of bed, the "little steam engine," as she was styled, began her buzzing activities for the day, Light and fleet of step, she ran like a deer. She was everybody's favorite—loved, petted, and by some marveled at as a semi-supernatural being. * * * * *

["To comment on the above paragraph, would be to shower hot sand on a garden bed of flowers. So it shall gleam, unset, save only with a mere invitation to the reader to consider more than once the religious accuracy which tells how Victoria "made fires, washed and ironed, baked bread, spaded a vegetable garden, went on errands, did everything." Cinderella and the Prince over again—only this time, a pamphlet biography instead of a glass shoe.]—*Eagle Critic.*"

She acquired her studies, performed her work, and lived her life by the help (as she believes) of heavenly spirits. From her childhood till now (having reached her thirty-third year) her anticipation of the other world has been more vivid than her realization of this. She has entertained angels, and not unawares. These gracious guests have been her constant companions. They abide with her night and day. They dictate her life with daily revelation; and like St. Paul, she is "not disobedient to the heavenly vision." She goes and comes at their behest. * * * * * * Her writings and speeches are the products, not only of their indwelling in her soul, but of their absolute control of her brain and tongue. Like a good Greek of the olden time, she does nothing without consulting her oracles. Never, as she avers, have they deceived her, nor ever will she neglect their decrees. * * * * * Seldom a day goes by but she enters into this fairy land, or rather into this spirit-realm. In pleasant weather she has a habit of sitting on the roof of her stately mansion on Murray Hill, and there communing hour by hour with the spirits. She is a religious devotee—her simple theology being an absorbing faith in God and the angels.

Moreover, I may as well mention here as later, that every characteristic utterance which she gives to the world is dictated while under spirit influence, and most often in a totally unconscious state. The words that fall from her lips are garnered by the swift pen of her husband, and published almost verbatim as she gets and gives them. To take an illustration, after her recent nomination to the Presidency by "The Victoria League," she sent to that committee a letter of superior dignity and moral weight. It was a composition which she had dictated while so outwardly oblivious to the dictation, that when she ended and awoke, she had no memory at all of what she had just done. The product of that strange and weird mood was a beautiful piece of English, not unworthy of Macaulay; and to prove what I say, I adduce the following eloquent passage, which (I repeat) was published without change as it fell from her unconscious lips:—

"I ought not to pass unnoticed," she says "your courteous and graceful allusion to what you deem the favoring omen of my name. It is true that a Victoria rules the great rival nation opposite to us on the other shore of the Atlantic, and it might grace the amity just sealed between the two nations, and be a new security of peace, if a twin sisterhood of Victorias were to preside over the two nations. It is true, also, that in its mere etymology the name signifies *Victory!* and the victory for the right is what we are bent on securing. It is again true, also, that to some minds there is a consonant harmony between the idea and the word, so that its euphonious utterance seems to their imaginations to be itself a genius of success. However this may be I have sometimes imagined that there is perhaps something providential and prophetic in the fact that my parents were prompted to confer on me a name which forbids the very thought of failure; and, as the great Napoleon believed the star of his destiny, you will at least excuse me, and charge it to the credulity of the woman, if I believe also in fatality of triumph as somehow inhering in my name."

In quoting this passage, I wish to add that its author is a person of no special literary training; indeed, so averse to the pen that, of her own will, she rarely dips it into ink, except to sign her business autograph; nor would she ever write at all except for those spirit-promptings which she dare not disobey; and she could not possibly have produced the above peroration except by some strange intellectual quickening—some overbrooding moral help. This (as she says) she derives from the spirit world. One of her text is, "I will lift up mine eyes unto the hills from whence cometh my help—my help cometh from the Lord who made Heaven and Earth." She reminds me of the old engraving of St. Gregory dictating his homilies under the outspread wing of the Holy Dove.

It has been so from her childhood. So that her school studies were, literally, a daily miracle. She would glance at a page, and know it by heart. The tough little mysteries which bother the bewildered brains of country school dullards, were always to her as vivid as the sunshine. And when sent on long and weary errands, she believes that she has been lifted over the ground by her angelic helpers—"lest she should dash her foot against a stone." When she had too heavy a basket to carry, an unseen hand would sometimes carry it for her. Digging in the garden as if her back would break, occasionally a strange restfulness would refresh her, and she knew that the spirits were toiling in her stead. All this may seem an illusion to everybody else, but will never be other than a reality to her.

"Let me cite some details of these spiritual phenomena, curious in themselves, and illustrating the forces that impel her career.

"'My spiritual vision,' she says dates back as early as my third year.' In Victoria's birthplace, a young woman named Rachel Scribner, about twenty-five years of age, who had been Victoria's nurse, suddenly died. On the day of her death, Victoria was picked up by her departing spirit, and borne off into the spirit world. To this day Mrs. Woodhull describes vividly her childish sensations as she felt herself gliding through the air—like St. Catherine winged away by the angels. Her mother testifies that while this scene was enacting to the child's inner consciousness, her little body lay as if dead for three hours.

Two of her sisters, who had died in childhood, were constantly present with her. She would talk to them as a girl tattles to her dolls. They were her most fascinating playmates, and she never cared for any others while she had their invisible society.

In her tenth year, one day while sitting by the side of a cradle rocking a sick babe to sleep, she says that two angels came, and gently pushing her away, began to fan the child with their white hands, until its face grew fresh and rosy. Her mother then suddenly entered the chamber, and beheld in amazement the little nurse lying in a trance on the floor, her face turned upward toward the ceiling, and the pining babe apparently in the bloom of health.

[In the above paragraph it will be seen that Mr. Tilton "warms to his work," and that his enthusiastic confidence in the gifted Woodhull expands into a wider faith in each and every one of her elastic creeds. Clinging to her snowy petticoats he climbs painfully "to the roof of her stately mansion on Murray Hill," and there blissfully contemplates the sainted Victoria "communing hour by hour with the spirits." We can imagine the first consternation, afterward charging to mute surprise, of the neighbors as they descried Mr. Tilton and Mrs. Woodhull thus enthusiastically engaged in ghostly exercises.

Mr. Tilton, slowly and majestically telescoping himself through the scuttle and handing Mrs. Woodhull through the same narrow aperture as a preface to their "communing hour by hour with the spirits," must, indeed, have been a remarkable spectacle, and one doubtless much appreciated by the residents of the vicinity.

But while Mr. Tilton gloomily smoked his cigar "on the roof of her stately mansion on Murray Hill," Mrs. Woodhull, "unbeknownst to him," was holding high and lofty converse, as befitted one perched on a housetop with no less a spiritual dignity than Demosthenes. Why Demosthenes, unless because of his *quadrusyllabate*, and therefore prodigious name, we can't for the life of us make out. But the testimony of Mr. Tilton is clear enough that although he didn't see the great orator with his own eyes, yet did Mrs. Woodhull "commune with him hour by hour," a proceeding which would have been excessively monotonous and irritating to any one less patient and considerate than Mr. Tilton, who was apparently more than content to deal with Demosthenes second-hand, *per* Mrs. Woodhull, as schoolboys explore the rhetorical mysteries with the secret aid and assistance of "cribs," and "ponies."—*Eagle Critic.*]

The chief among her spiritual visitants, and one who has been a majestic guardian to her from the earliest years of her remembrance, she describes as a matured man of stately figure, clad in a Greek tunic, solemn and graceful in his aspect, strong in his influence, and altogether dominant over her life. For many years, notwithstanding an almost daily visit to her vision, he withheld his name, nor would her most importunate questionings induce him to utter it. But he always promised that in due time he would reveal his identity. Meanwhile he prophesied to her that she would rise to great distinction; that she would emerge from her poverty and live in a stately house; that she would win great wealth in a city which he pictured as crowded with ships; that she would publish and conduct a journal; and that finally, to crown her career, she would become the ruler of her people. At length, after patiently waiting on this spirit guide for twenty years, one day in 1868, during a temporary sojourn in Pittsburgh, and while she was sitting at a marble table, he suddenly appeared to her, and wrote on the table in English letters the name "Demosthenes." At first the writing was indistinct, but grew to such a lustre that the brightness filled the room. The apparition, familiar as it had been before, now affrighted her to trembling. The stately and commanding spirit told her to journey to New York, where she would find at No. 17 Great Jones street, a house in readiness for her, equipped in all things to her use and taste. She unhesitatingly obeyed, although she never before had heard of Great Jones street, nor until that revelatory moment had entertained an intention of taking such a residence. On entering the house, it fulfilled in reality the picture which she saw of it in her vision—the self-same hall, stairways, rooms, and furniture. Entering with some bewilderment into the library, she reached out her hand by chance, and without knowing what she did, took up a book which, on idly looking at its title, she saw (to her blood-chilling astonishment) to be "The Orations of Demosthenes." From that time onward, the Greek statesman has been even more palpably than in her earlier years her prophetic monitor, mapping out the life which she must follow, as a chart for the ship sailing at sea. She believes him to be her familiar spirit—the author of her public policy, and the inspirer of her published words. Without intruding my own opinion as to the authenticity of this inspiration, I have often thought that if Demosthenes could arise and speak English, he could hardly excel the fierce light and heat of some of the sentences which I have heard from this singular woman in her glowing hours.

[Mr. Tilton then returns to Victoria's marriage at the age of fourteen years, to a husband in his twenty-eighth year—a marriage that was approved by her parents, but which Tilton believes they should have prevented. He says of this event:—

"From the endurable cruelty of her parents, she fled to the unendurable cruelty of her husband. She had been from her twelfth to her fourteenth year a double victim, first to chills and fever, and then to rheumatism, which had jointly played equal havoc with her beauty and health, until she was brought within a step of "the iron door." Dr. Canning Woodhull, a gay rake, but whose habits were kept hid from her under general respectability of his family connections (his father being an eminent judge, and his uncle the Mayor of New York), was professionally summoned to visit the child, and, being a trained physician, arrested her decline. Something about her artless manners and vivacious mind captivated his fancy. Coming as a prince, he found her as Cinderella—a child of the ashes. Before she entirely recovered, and while looking haggard and sad, one day he stopped her in the street, and said, "My little chick, I want you to go with me to the picnic"—referring to a projected Fourth of July excursion then at hand. The promise of a little pleasure acted like a charm on the house-worn and sorrow-stricken child. She obtained her mother's assent to her going, but her father coupled it with the condition that she should first earn money enough to buy herself a pair of shoes. So the little fourteen-year old drudge became for the nonce an apple merchant, and with characteristic business energy sold her apples and bought her shoes. She went to the picnic with Dr. Woodhull, like a ticket-of-leave juvenile delinquent, on a furlough. On coming home from the festival, the brilliant fop, who, tired of the demi-monde ladies whom he could purchase for his pleasure, and inspired with a sudden and romantic interest in this artless maid, said to her: "My little puss, tell your father and mother that I want you for a wife." The startled girl quivered with anger at this announcement, and with timorous speed fled to her mother and repeated the tale, feeling as if some injury was threatened her and some danger impended. But her parents, as if not unwilling to be rid of a daughter whose sorrow was ripening her into a woman before her time, were delighted at the unexpected offer. They thought it a grand match. They helped the young man's suit and augmented their persecutions of the child. Ignorant, innocent and simple, the girl's chief thought of the proffered marriage was an escape from the parental yoke. Four months later she accepted the change—flying from the ills she had to others that she knew not of. Her captor, once possessed of his treasure, ceased to value it. On the third day after taking his child wife to his lodgings, he broke her heart by remaining away all night at a house of ill repute. Then for the first time she learned, to her dismay, that he was habitually unchaste and given to fits of intoxication. She was stung to the quick. The shock awoke all her womanhood. She grew ten years older in a single day. A tumult of thought swept like a whirlwind through her mind, ending at last in predominant purpose, namely, to reclaim her husband. She set herself religiously to this pious task—calling on God and the spirits to help her.

Squandering his money like a prodigal, he suddenly put his wife into the humblest quarters, where, left mostly to herself, she dwelt in bitterness of spirit, aggravated from time to time by learning of his ordering baskets of champagne, and drinking himself drunk in the company of * * * * * * *

Sometimes, with uncommon courage, through rain and sleet, half clad and shivering, she would track him to his dens, and by the energy of her spirit compel him to return. At other times, all night long she would watch at the window, waiting for his footsteps, until she heard then languidly shuffling along the pavement with the staggering reel of a drunken man, in the shameless hours of the morning.

During all this time, she passionately prayed Heaven to give her the heart of her husband, but Heaven, decreeing otherwise, withheld it from her, and for her good.

In fifteen months after her marriage, while living in a little low frame house in Chicago, in the dead of Winter, with icicles clinging to her bedpost, and attended only by her half drunken husband, she brought forth in almost mortal agony her first born child. In her ensuing helplessness, she became an object of pity to a next door neighbor who, with a kindness which the sufferer's unhomelike home did not afford, brought her day by day some nourishing dish. This same ministering hand would then wrap the babe in a blanket, and take it to a happier mother in the near neighborhood, who was at the same time nursing a new born son. In this way Victoria and her child—themselves both children—were cared for with mingled gentleness and neglect.

At the end of six days the little invalid attempted to rise and put her sick room in order, when she was taken with delirium, during which her mother visited her just in time to save her life.

On her recovery, and after a visit to her father's house, she returned to her own, to be horror struck at discovering that her bed had been occupied the night before by her husband in company with a wanton of the streets, and that the room was littered with the remains of their drunken feast.

"The biographer describes the desertion of the child-wife by the husband for an entire month, her visit to a fashionable boarding house, where Dr. W. was living with a female in the relation of husband and wife, her exposure of him, and the expulsion of the Dr. and his mistress from the house in disgrace.

Of the first fruits of this ill-assorted marriage Mr. Tilton writes:—

To add to her misery she discovered that her child, begotten in drunkness, and born in squalor, was a half idiot; predestined to be a hopeless imbecile for life; endowed with just enough intelligence to exhibit the light of reason in dim eclipse—a sad and pitiful spectacle in his mother's house to-day, where he roams from room to room, muttering noises more sepulchral than human; a daily agony to the woman who bore him, hoping more of her burden; and heightening the pathos of her perpetual scene by the uncommon sweetness of his temper which, by winning every one's love, doubles every one's pity.

Journeying to California as a region where she might inspire her husband to begin a new life freed from old associations, she there found herself and her little family strangers in a strange city—beggars in a land of plenty. Change of sky is not change of mind. Dr. Woodhull took his habits, his wife took her necessities, and both took their misery, from East to West. In San Francisco, the girlish woman, with unrelaxed energy, and as part of that lifelong heroism which will one day have its monument, set herself to supporting the man by whom she ought to have been supported.—A morning journal had an advertisement—"A cigar girl wanted." The wife, with her face of sweet sixteen, presented herself as the first candidate, and was accepted on the spot. The proprietor was a stalwart Californian—one of those men who catch from a new country something of the liberality which the sailor brings from the sea. She served for one day behind his counter—blushing, modest and sensitive, her ears tingling at every rude remark by every uncouth customer—and at nightfall her employer, who had noticed the blood coming and going in her cheeks, said to her, "My little lady, you are not the clerk I want; I must have somebody who can rough it; you are too fine." Inquiring into her case he was surprised to find her married and a mother. At first he discredited this information, but there was no denying the truth of her story. He accompanied her to her husband, and as the two men discovered themselves to each other as brother Freemasons, he gave his clerk of a day a twenty dollar gold piece and dismissed her with his blessing. And I hope this has been revisited on his own head. * * * * * * * Resorting to her needle, she carried from house to house this only weapon which many women possess wherewith to fight the battle of life. She chanced to come upon Anna Cogswell, the actress, who wanted a seamstress to make her a theatrical wardrobe. The winsome dressmaker was engaged at once. But her earnings at this new calling did not keep pace with expenses. "It is no use," said she to her dramatic friend; "I am running behindhand. I must do something better." "Then," replied the actress, "you, too, must be an actress." And, nothing loth to undertake anything new and difficult, Victoria, who never before had dreamed of such a possibility, was engaged as a lesser light to the Cogswell star. For a first appearance she was cast in the part of the *Country Cousin* in "New York by Gaslight." The text was given to her in the morning, she learned and rehearsed it during the day, and made a fair hit in it at night. For six weeks thereafter she earned fifty-two dollars a week as an actress.

"Never leave the stage," said some of her fellow performers, all of whom admired her simplicity and spirituality. "But I do not care for the stage," she said, "and I shall leave it at the first opportunity. I am meant for some other fate. But what it is, I know not."

It came—as all things have come to her—through the agency of spirits. One night, while on the boards, clad in a pink silk dress and slippers, acting in the ball room scene in the "Corsican Brothers," suddenly a spirit voice addressed her saying, "Victoria, come home!" Thrown instantly into a clairvoyant condition, she saw a vision of her young sister Tennie, then a mere child—standing by her mother, and both calling the absent one to return. Her mother and Tennie were then in Columbus, Ohio. She saw Tennie distinctly enough to notice that she wore a striped French calico frock. "Victoria, come home!" said the little messenger, beckoning with her childish forefinger. The apparition would not be denied. Victoria thrilled and chilled by the vision and voice, burst away at a bound behind the scenes, and without waiting to change her dress, ran, clad with all her dramatic adornments, through a foggy rain to her hotel, and packing up her few things that night, betook herself with her husband and child next morning to the steamer bound for New York. On the voyage she was thrown into such vivid spiritual states that she produced a profound excitement among the passengers. On reaching her mother's home she came upon Tennie dressed in the same dress as in the vision ; and on inquiring the meaning of the message, "Victoria, come home!" was told that at the time it was uttered her mother had said to Tennie, "My dear, send the spirits after Victoria to bring her home;" and moreover the French calico dress had appeared to her spirit sight at the very first moment its wearer had put it on.

This homeward trip, and its consequences, marked a new phase in her career—a turning point in her life.

Hitherto her clairvoyant faculty had been put to no pecuniary use, but she was now directed by the spirits to repair to Indianapolis, there to announce herself as a medium, and to treat patients for the cure of disease. Taking rooms in the Bates House, and publishing a card in the journals, she found herself able, on saluting her callers, to tell by inspiration their names, their residence, and their maladies. In a few days she became the town's talk. Her marvelous performances in clairvoyance being noised abroad, people flocked to her from a distance. Her rooms were crowded and her purse grew fat. She reaped a golden harvest—including, as it worthiest part golden opinions from all sorts of people. Her countenance would often glow as with a sacred light, and she became an object of religious awe to many wonder stricken people whose inward lives she had revealed. Moreover, her unpretentious modesty, and her perpetual disclaiming of any merit or power of her own, and the entire crediting of this to spirit influence, augmented the interest with which all spectators regarded the amiable prodigy. First at Indianapolis, and afterwards at Terre Haute, she wrought some apparently miraculous cures. She straightened the feet of the lame; she opened the ears of the deaf; she detected the robbers of a bank; she brought to light hidden crimes; she solved physiological problems; she unveiled business secrets; she prophecied future events. Knowing the wonders which she wrought, certain citizens disguised themselves and came to her, purporting to be strangers from a distant town, but she instantly said, "Oh, no; you all live here." "How can you tell?" they asked. "The spirits say so," she replied.

Benedictions followed her; gifts were lavished upon her; money flowed in a stream towards her. Journeying from city to city in the practice of her spiritual art, she thereby supported all her relatives far and near. Her income in one year reached nearly a hundred thousand dollars. She received in one day, simply as fees for cures which she had wrought, five thousand dollars. The sum total of the receipts of her practice, and of her investments growing out of it, up to the time of its discontinuance by direction of the spirits in 1869, was seven hundred thousand dollars. The age of wonders has not ceased!

During all this period, though outwardly prosperous, she was inwardly wretched. The dismal fact of her son's half idiocy so preyed upon her mind that, in a heat of morbid feeling, she fell to accusing her innocent self for his misfortunes. The sight of his face rebuked her, until, in brokenness of spirit, she prayed to God for another child—a daughter—to be born, with a fair body and a sound mind. Her prayer was granted, but not without many accompaniments of inhumanity. Once during her carriage of her unborn charge, she was kicked by its father in a fit of drunkenness—inflicting a bruise on her body and a greater bruise to her spirit. Profound as her double suffering was, in its lowest depth there was a deeper still. She was plunged into this at the child's birth. This event occurred at No. 53 Bond street, New York, April 23d, 1861. She and her husband were at the time the only occupants of the house—her trial coming upon her while no nurse, or servant, or other human helper was under the roof. * *
* * * * * * * * * * * *

[Here follows details too disgusting to reproduce.—The Author.]

It was this horrible experience that first awoke her mind to the question:

"Why should I any longer live with this man?" Hitherto she had entertained an almost superstitious idea of the devotion with which a wife should cling to her husband. She had always been so faithful to him, that, in his cups, he would mock and jeer at her fidelity, and call her a fool for maintaining it. At length the fool grew wiser, and after eleven years of what, with conventional mockery, was called a marriage—during which time her husband had never spent an evening with her at home, had seldom drawn a sober breath, and had spent on other women, not herself, all the money he had ever earned—she applied in Chicago for a divorce, and obtained it.

Previous to this crisis, there had occurred a remarkable incident which more than ever confirmed her faith in the guardianship of spirits. One day, during a severe illness of her son, she left him to visit her patients, and on her return was startled with the news that the boy had died two hours before. "No," she exclaimed, "I will not permit his death.' And with frantic energy she stripped her bosom naked, caught up his lifeless form, pressed it to her own, and sitting thus, flesh to flesh, glided insensibly into a trance in which she remained s ven hours, at the end of which time she awoke; perspiration started from his clammy skin, and the child that had been thought dead was brought back again to life—and lives to this day in sad half death. It is her belief that the spirit of Jesus Christ brooded over the lifeless form, and rewrought the miracle of Lazarus for a sorrowing woman's sake.

Victoria's father and mother, growing still more fanatical with their advancing years, had all along subjected her to a series of singular vexations. And the elder sisters had joined in the mischief making, out-doing the parents. Sometimes they would burst in upon Mrs. Woodhull's house, and attempt to govern its internal economy; sometimes they would carry off the furniture, or garments, or pictures; sometimes they would crown her with eulogies as the greatest of human beings, and in the same breath defame her as an agent of the devil.

But their great cause of persecution grew out of her younger sister Tennie's career.

This young woman developed, while a child in her father's house, a similar power to Victoria's. It was a penetrating spiritual insight applied to the cure of disease. But her father and mother, who regarded their daughter in the light of the damsel mentioned in the Acts of the Apostles, who "brought her masters much gain by soothsaying," put her before the public as a fortune teller. By adding to much that was genuine in her mediumship more that was charlatanry, they aroused against this fraudulent business the indignation of the sincere soul of Victoria, who, more than most human beings, scorns a lie, and would burn at the stake rather than practice a deceit. She clutched Tennie, as by main force, and flung her out of this semi-humbug, to the mingled astonishment of her money-greedy family, one and all. At this time Tennie was supporting a dozen or twenty relatives by her ill-gotten gains. Victoria's rescue of her excited the wrath of all these parasites—which has continued hot and undying against both to this day. The fond and fierce mother alternately loves and hates the two united defiers of her morbid will; and the father, at times a Mephistopheles, waits till the inspiration of cunning overmasters his parental instinct, and watching for a moment when his ill word to a stranger will blight their business schemes, drops in upon some capitalist whose money is in their hand, lodges an indictment against his own flesh and blood, takes out his handkerchief to hide a few well feigned tears, clasps his hands with an unfelt agony, hobbles off smiling sardonically at the mischief which he has done, and the next day repents his wickedness with genuine contrition and manlier woe. These parents would cheerfully give their lives as a sacrifice to atone for the many mischiefs which they have cast like burrs at their children; but if all the scars which they and their progeny have inflicted on one another could be magically healed to-day, they would be scratched open by the same hands and set stinging and tingling anew to-morrow.

There is a maxim that marriages are made in heaven, albeit contradicted by the Scripture which declares that in heaven there is neither marrying nor giving in marriage. But, even against the Scripture, it is safe to say that Victoria's second marriage was made in heaven; that is, it was decreed by the self same spirits whom she is ever ready to follow, whether they lead her for discipline into the valley of the shadow of death or for comfort in those ways of pleasantness which are paths of peace.

Col. James H. Blood, commander of the Sixth Missouri Regiment, who, at the close of the war, was elected City Auditor of St. Louis, who became President of the Society of Spiritualists in that place, and who had himself been, like Victoria, the legal partner of a morally sundered marriage, called one day on Mrs. Woodhull to consult her as a spiritualistic physician (having never met her before), and was startled to see her pass into a trance, during which she announced, unconsciously to herself, that his future destiny was to be linked with hers in marriage. Thus, to their mutual amazement, but to their subsequent happiness, they were betrothed on the spot by "the powers of the air." The legal tie by which at first they bound themselves to each other was afterward by mutual consent annulled—the necessary form of Illinois law being complied with to this effect. But the marriage law stands on its merits, and is to all who witness its harmony known to be a sweet and accordant union of congenial souls.

Col. Blood is a man of a philosophic and reflective cast of mind, an enthusiastic student of the higher lore of spiritualism, a recluse from society, and an expectant believer in a stupendous destiny for Victoria. A modesty not uncommon to men of intellect, prompts him to sequester his name in the shade rather than to see it glittering in the sun. But he is an indefatigable worker—driving his pen through all hours of the day and half of the night. He is an active editor of *Woodhull and Claflin's Weekly,* and one of the busy partners in the firm of Woodhull, Claflin & Co., Brokers, at 44 Broad street, New York. His civic views are (to use his favorite designation of them) cosmopolitical; in other words, he is a radical of extreme radicalism—an internationalist of the most uncompromising type—a communist who would rather have died in Paris than be the president of a pretended republic whose first official act has been the judicial murder of the only Republicans in France. His spiritualistic habits he describes in a letter to his friend, the writer of this memorial, as follows: "At about eleven or twelve o'clock at night, two or three times a week, and sometimes without nightly intervals, Victoria and I hold parliament with the spirits. It is by this kind of study that we both have learned nearly all the valuable knowledge that we possess. Victoria goes into a trance, during which her guardian spirit takes control of her mind, speaking audibly through her lips, propounding various matters for our subsequent investigation and verification, and announcing principles, detached thoughts, hints of systems and suggestions for affairs. In this way and in this spiritual night school, began that process of instruction by which Victoria has arisen to her present position as a political economist and politician. During her entranced state, which generally lasts about an hour, but sometimes twice as long, I make copious notes of all she says, and when her speech is unbroken, I write down every word, and publish it without correction or amendment. She and I regard all the other portion of our lives as almost valueless as compared with these midnight hours." The preceding extract shows that this fine-grained trancendentalist is a reverent husband to his spiritual wife, the sympathetic companion of her entranced moods. and their faithful historian to the world.

After a union with Col. Blood, instead of changing her name to his, she followed the example of many actresses, singers, and other professional women whose names have become a business property to their owners, and she still continues to be known as Mrs. Woodhull.

One night, about half a year after their marriage, she and her husband were awakened at midnight, in Cincinnati, by the announcement that a man by the name of Dr. Woodhull had been attacked with delirium tremens at the Burnet House, and in a lucid moment had spoken of the woman from whom he had been divorced, and begged to see her. Col. Blood immediately took a carriage, drove to the hotel, brought the wretched victim home, and jointly with Victoria took care of him with life-saving kindness for six weeks. On his going away they gave him a few hundred dollars of their joint property to make him comfortable in another city. He departed full of gratitude, bearing with him the assurance that he would always be willing to come and go as a friend of the family. And from that day to this, the poor man, dilapidated in body and emasculated in spirit, has sojourned under Victoria's roof and sometimes elsewhere, according to his whim or will. In the present ruin of the young gallant of twenty years ago, there is more manhood (albeit an expiring spark like a candle in its socket) than during any of the former years; and to be now turned out of doors by the woman he wronged, but who would not wrong him in return, would be an act of inhumanity which it would be impossible for Mrs. Woodhull and Col. Blood, either jointly or separately to commit. For this piece of noble conduct—what is commonly called her living with two husbands under one roof—she has received not so much censure on earth as I think she will receive reward in heaven. No other passage of her life more signally illustrates the nobility of her moral judgments, or the supernal courage by which she stands by her convictions. Not all the clamorous tongues in Christendom, though they should simultaneously cry out against her, "Fie, for shame!" could persuade her to turn this wretched wreck from her home. And I say she is right; and I will maintain this opinion against the combined Pecksniffs of the whole world.

This act, and the malice of enemies, together with her bold opinions on social questions, have combined to give her reputation a stain. But no slander ever fell on any human soul with greater injustice. A more unsullied woman does not walk the earth. She carries in her very face the fair legend of a character kept pure by a sacred fire within. She is one of those aspiring devotees who tread the earth merely as a stepping stone to heaven, and whose chief ambition is finally to present herself at the supreme tribunal "spotless, and without wrinkle, or blemish, or any such thing." Knowing her as well as I do, I cannot hear an accusation against her without recalling Tennyson's line of King Arthur:

"Is thy white blamelessness accounted blame?"

Fulfilling a previous prophecy, and following a celestial mandate, in 1869, she founded a bank and published a journal. These two events took the town by storm. When the doors of her office in Broad street were first thrown open to the public, several thousand visitors came in a flock on the first day. The "lady brokers," as they were called (a strange confession that brokers are not always gentlemen), were besieged like lionesses in a cage. The daily press interviewed them; the weekly wits satirized them; the comic sheets caricatured them; but like a couple of fresh young dolphins, breasting the sea side by side, they showed themselves native to the element, and cleft gracefully every threatening wave that broke over their heads. The breakers could not dash the brokers. Indomitable in their energy, the sisters won the good graces of Commodore Vanderbilt—a fine old gentleman of comfortable means, who of all the lower animals prefers the horse, and of all the higher virtues admires pluck. Both with and without Commodore Vanderbilt's help, Mrs. Woodhull has more than once shown the pluck that has held the rein of the stock market as the Commodore holds his horse. Her journal, as one sees it week by week, is generally a willow basket full of audacious manuscripts, apparently picked up at random and thrown together pell mell, stunning the reader with a medley of politics, finance, free love, and the pantarchy. This sheet, when the divinity that shapes its end shall begin to add to the rough hewing a little smooth shaping; in other words, when its unedited chaos shall come to be moulded by the spirits to that order which is Heaven's first law; this not ordinary but "cardinary" journal, which is edited in one world, and published in another, will become less a confusion to either, and more a power for both.

In 1870, following the English plan of self-nomination, Mrs. Woodhull announced herself as a candidate for the Presidency, mainly for the purpose of drawing public attention to the claims of women to political equality with man. She accompanied this announcement with a series of papers in the *Herald* on politics and finance, which have since been collected into a volume entitled "The Principles of Government." She has lately received a more formal nomination to that high office by the Victoria League, an organization which, being somewhat Jacobinical in its secrecy, is popularly supposed, though not definitely known, to be presided over by Commodore Vanderbilt, who is also similarly imagined to be the golden corner-stone of the business house of Woodhull, Claflin & Co. Should she be elected to the high seat to which she aspires (an event concerning which I make no prophecy), I am at least sure that she would excel any queen on any throne now in her native faculty to govern others.

"One night in December, 1869, while she lay in deep sleep, her Greek guardian came to her, and sitting transfigured by her couch, wrote on a scroll (so that she could not only see the words, but immediately dictated them to her watchful amanuensis) the memorable document now known in history as "The Memorial of Victoria C. Woodhull"—a petition addressed to Congress, claiming under the Fourteenth Amendment the right of women as of other 'citizens of the United States" to vote in "the States wherein they reside"—asking, moreover, that the State of New York, of which she was a citizen, should be restrained by Federal authority from preventing the exercise of this constitutional right. As up to this time neither she nor her husband had been greatly interested in women suffrage, he had no sooner written this manifesto from her lips, than he awoke from the trance, and protested against the communication as nonsense, believing it to be a trick of some evil disposed spirits. In the morning the document was shown to a number of friends, including one eminent judge, who ridiculed its logic and conclusions. But the lady herself, from whose sleeping and yet unsleeping brain that strange document had sprung like Minerva from the head of Jove, simply answered that her antique instructor, having never misled her before, was guiding her aright then. Nothing doubting, but much wondering, she took the novel demand to Washington, where after a few days of laughter from the shallow minded, and of neglect from the indifferent, it suddenly burst upon the Federal Capital like a storm, and then spanned it like a rainbow. She went before the Judiciary Committee, and delivered an argument in support of her claim to the franchise under the new amendments, which some who heard it, pronounced one of the ablest efforts which they had ever heard on any subject. She caught the listening ears of Senator Carpenter, Gen. Butler, Judge Woodward, George W. Julian, General Ashley, Judge Loughridge and other able statesmen in Congress, and harnessed these gentlemen as steeds to her chariot. Such was the force of her appeal that the whole city rushed together to hear it, like the Athenians to the market place when Demosthenes stood in his own and not a borrowed clay. A great audience, one of the finest ever gathered in the Capitol, assembled to hear her defend her thesis in the first public speech of her life. At the moment of rising, her face was observed to be very pale, and she appeared about to faint. On being afterward questioned as to the cause of her emotion, she replied that, during the first prolonged moment, she remembered an early prediction of her guardian spirit, until then forgotten, that she would one day speak in public, and that her first discourse would be produced in the Capital of her country. The sudden fulfilment of this prophesy smote her so violently that for a moment she was stunned into apparent unconsciousness. But she recovered herself, and passed through the ordeal with great success—which is better luck than happened to the real Demosthenes, for Plutarch mentions that his maiden speech was a failure, and that he was laughed at by the people.

"Assisted by Elizabeth Cady Stanton, Paulina Wright Davis, Isabella Beecher Hooker, Susan B. Anthony, and other staunch and able women whom she swiftly persuaded into accepting this construction of the Constitution, she succeeded, after her petition was denied by a majority of the Judiciary Committee, in obtaining a minority report in its favor, signed jointly by B. F. Butler, of Massachusetts, and Judge Loughridge, of Iowa. To have clutched this report from Gen. Butler—as it were a scalp from the ablest head in the House of Representatives—was a sufficient trophy to entitle the brave lady to an enrollment in the political history of her country. She means to go to Washington again next winter to knock at the half open doors of the Capitol until they shall swing wide enough asunder to admit her enfranchised sex.

"I must say something of her personal appearance, although it defies portrayal, whether by photograph or pen. Neither tall nor short, stout nor slim, she is of medium statue, lithe and elastic, free and graceful. Her side face looked at over her left shoulder, is of perfect aquiline outline, as classic as ever went into a Roman marble, and resembles the masque of Shakspeare taken after death; the same view, looking from the right, is a little broken and irregular; and the front face is broad, with prominent cheek bones, and with some unshapely nasal lines. Her countenance is never twice alike, so variable is its expression and so dependent are her moods, Her soul comes into it and goes out of it, giving her at one time the look of a superior and almost saintly intelligence, and at another dull, commonplace and unprepossessing. When under a strong spiritual influence, a strange and mystical light irradiates from her face, reminding the beholder of the Hebrew Lawgiver who gave to men what he received from God and whose face during the transfer shone. Tennyson, as with the hand of a gold-beater, has beautifully gilded the same expression in his stanza of St. Stephen the Martyr in the article of death:

"And looking upward full of grace,
He prayed, and from a happy place,
God's glory smote him on the face."

"In conversation, until she is somewhat warmed with earnestness, she halts, as if her mind were elsewhere, but the moment she brings all her faculties to her lips for the full utterance of her message, whether it be of persuasion or indignation, and particularly when under spiritual control, she is a very orator for eloquence—pouring forth her sentences like a mountain stream, sweeping away everything that frets its flood.

"Her hair, which when left to itself is as long as those tresses of Hortense in which her son, Louis Napoleon, used to play hide and seek, she now mercilessly cuts close like a boy's, from impatience at the daily waste of time in suitably taking care of this prodigal gift of nature.

"She can ride a horse like an Indian, and climb a tree like an athlete; she can swim, row a boat, play billiards, and dance; moreover, as the crown of her physical virtues, she can walk all day like an English woman.

"'Difficulties,' says Emerson, 'exist to be surmounted.' This might be the motto of her life. In her lexicon (which is still of youth) there is no such word as fail. Her ambition is stupendous—nothing is too great for her grasp. Prescient of the grandeur of her destiny, she goes forward with a resistless fanaticism to accomplish it. Believing thoroughly in herself (or rather not in herself but in her spirit aids), she allows no one else to doubt either her or them. In her case the old miracle is enacted anew—the faith which removes mountains. A soul set on edge is a conquering weapon in the battle of life. Such, and of Damascus temper, is hers.

"In making an epitome of her views I may say that in politics she is a downright Democrat, scorning to divide her fellow citizens into upper and lower classes, but ranking them all in one comprehensive equality of right, privilege and opportunity; concerning finance, which is a favorite topic with her, she holds that gold is not the true standard of money value, but that the Government should abolish the gold standard, and issue its notes instead, giving to those a fixed and permanent value, and circulating them as the only money; on social questions, her theories are similar to those which have long been taught by John Stuart Mill and Elizabeth Cady Stanton, and which are styled by some as free love doctrines, while others reject this appellation on acount of its popular association with the idea of a promiscuous intimacy between the sexes—the essence of her system being that marriage is of the heart and not of the law, that when love ends marriage should end with it, being dissolved by nature, and that no civil statute should outwardly bind two hearts which have been inwardly sundered; and finally in religion she is a spiritualist of the most mystical and ethereal type.

In thus speaking of her views, I will add to them another fundamental article of her creed, which an incident will best illustrate. Once a sick woman who had been given up by the physicians, and who had received from a Catholic priest extreme unction in expectation of death, was put into the care of Mrs. Woodhull, who attempted to lure her back to life. This zealous physician, unwilling to be baffled, stood over her patient day and night, neither sleeping nor eating for ten days and nights, at the end of which time she was gladdened not only at witnessing the sick woman's recovery, but at finding that her own body, instead of weariness or exhaustion from the double lack of sleep and food, was more fresh and bright than at the beginning. Her face, during this discipline, grew uncommonly fair and ethereal; her flesh wore a look of transparency; and the ordinary earthiness of mortal nature began to disappear from her physical frame and its place to be supplied with what she fancied were the foretokens of a spiritual body. These phenomena were so vivid to her own consciousness and to the observation of her friends, that she was led to speculate profoundly on the transformation from our mortal to our immortal state, deducing the idea that the time will come when the living human body, instead of ending in death by disease, and dissolution in the grave, will be gradually refined away until it is entirely sloughed off and the soul only, and not the flesh, remains. It is in this way that she fulfills to her daring hope the prophecy that "the last enemy to be destroyed is death."

Engrossed in business affairs, nevertheless at any moment she would rather die than live, such is her infinite estimate of the outer world over this. But she disdains all commonplace parleyings with the spirit realm such as are had in ordinary spirit manifestations. On the other hand, she is passionately eager to see the spirits face to face, to summon them at her will and commune with them at her pleasure. Twice, as she unshakenly believes, she has seen a vision of Jesus Christ, honored thus doubly over St. Paul, who saw his Master but once, and then was overcome by the sight. She never goes to any church, save to the solemn temple whose starry arch spans her housetop at night, where she sits like Simeon Stylites on his pillar, a worshiper in the sky. Against the inculcations of her childish education, the spirits have taught her that He whom the church calls the Savior of the world is not God but man. But her reverence for Him is supreme and ecstatic. The Sermon on the Mount fills her eyes with tears. The exulting exclamations of the Psalmist are her familiar outbursts of devotion. For two years, as a talisman against any temptation toward untruthfulness (which, with her, is the unpardonable sin), she wore stitched into the sleeve of every one of her dresses the second verse of the 110th Psalm, namely, "Deliver my soul, O Lord; from lying lips, and from a deceitful tongue." Speaking the truth punctiliously, whether in great things or small, she rigorously exacts the same of others, that a deceit practiced upon her enkindles her soul to a fire; and she has acquired a clairvoyant or intuitive power to detect a lie in the moment of its utterance, and to smite the liar in his act of guilt. She believes that intellectual power had its fountains in spiritual inspiration. And once when I put to her the searching question, "What is the greatest truth that has ever been expressed in words?" she thrilled me with the sudden answer, "Blessed are the pure in heart for they shall see God."

As showing that her early clairvoyant power still abides, I will mention a fresh instance. An eminent judge in Pennsylvania, in whose court house I had once lectured, called lately to see me at the office of the *Golden Age*. On my inquiring after his family, he told me that a strange event had just happened in it. "Three months ago," said he, "while I was in New York, Mrs. Woodhull said to me, with a rush of feeling, 'Judge, I foresee that you will lose two of your children within six weeks.'" This announcement, he said, wounded him as a tragic sort of trifling with life and death. "But," I asked, "did anything follow the prophecy?" "Yes," he replied, "fulfillment; I lost two children within six weeks." The Judge, who is a Methodist, thinks that Victoria, the clairvoyant, is like "Anna, the prophetess."

Let me say that I know of no person against whom there are more prejudices, nor any one who more quickly disarms them. This strange faculty is the most powerful of her powers. She shoots a word like a sudden sunbeam through the thickest mist of people's doubts and accusations, and clears the sky in a moment. Questioned by some committee or delegation who have come to her with idle tales against her busy life, I have seen her swiftly gather together all the stones which they have cast, put them like the miner's quartz into the furnace, melt them with fierce and fervent heat, bring out of them the purest gold, stamp thereon her image and superscription as if she were sovereign of the realm, and then (as the marvel of it all) receive the sworn allegiance of the whole company on the spot. At one of her public meetings when the chair (as she hoped) would be occupied by Lucretia Mott, this venerable woman had been persuaded to decline this responsibility, but afterward stepped forward on the platform and lovingly kissed the young speaker in the presence of the multitude. Her enemies (save those of her own household) are strangers. To see her is to respect her—to know her is to vindicate her. She has some impetuous and headlong faults, but were she without the same traits which produce these she would not possess the mad and magnificent energies which (if she lives) will make her a heroine of history.

In conclusion, amid all the rush of her active life, she believes with Wordsworth that

> "The gods approve the depth and not
> The tumult of the soul."

So, whether buffeted by criticism, or defamed by slander, she carries herself in that religious peace which through all turbulence, is "a measureless content." When apparently about to be struck down, she gathers unseen strength and goes forward conquering and to conquer. Known only as a rash iconoclast, and ranked even with the most uncouth of those noise makers who are waking a sleepy world before its time, she beats her daily gong of business and reform with notes not musical but strong, yet mellows the outward rudeness of the rhythm by the inward and devout song of one of the sincerest, most reverent and divinely gifted of human souls.

The above voluminous extracts from Mr. Tilton's biography of Mrs. Woodhull, clearly show the sentiments he entertained towards her when this glowing tribute to her talent and her virtues came fresh from his pen. Whether it be true, as Mrs. Woodhull alleges, that Theodore Tilton was her devoted lover is a secret probably only known to themselves; but that this biography should be reproduced in the journal that throughout the investigation championed the cause of the accused, and left the legitimate domain of journalism to traduce and bring disrepute on the accuser, is an evidence that the friends of the Plymouth pastor, feared the power held by Theodore Tilton. The *Eagle* editor in closing his criticism of the biography thus bitterly writes:

"[Little remains to be added by way of comment to the extraordinary and suicidal columns in which Mr. Tilton sought to crucify the principles in behalf of which he yearns to expire in roseate martyrdom. While his own wife was suffering at home, wrapped in the shadow of doubt and suspicion, wrung with open charges against her fidelity to him, tortured with all the ingenious refinements which accumulated until they drove her from her home and from her children, Mr. Tilton was busily engaged in glorifying a creature whose diabolical mission was the debasement and degradation of the purest and noblest of social institutions.

As if in the bitterest irony at his own expense, he sacrificed the intellectual harvest of his life, on the altar of that very licentiousness which he complains has brought havoc into his household and dishonor on his name. That sacrifice confronts the people of Brooklyn to-day, in this page, and, if there be one person who can derive pleasure from contemplating the sorrowful spectacle, that person can be none other than the vicious and fatal adventuress who lured him into her house of death and at whose feet, as Sampson at Delilah's he fell and slumbered, to his own ruin and despair.

On Friday July 26th Mrs. Woodhull and her sister Miss Claflin arrived unexpectedly in the city and were immediately interviewed by the reporters of several journals. As it bears directly upon her relations with Mr. Tilton and flatly contradicts the reported interview given with her in Chap. IX. as to criminal relations between her and her biographer, it is given here in full as it appeared in the *Argus* on the following day :—

"'I would not have granted this meeting to any but an ARGUS representative,' began Mrs. Woodhull, with a smile, 'but I saw a copy of your paper at the Fifth Avenue Hotel, last evening, and I was delighted with the straightforward statement from Mr. Tilton, which it contained. Why, sir, do you know,' said the lady, frankly, 'I have had reporters following me ever since I left San Francisco, but I did not wish to tell them anything, and I didn't.'

"'When did you leave San Francisco.'

"'Let me see—two weeks ago this morning. I stopped three or four days at Salt Lake City.'

"'Was it the Beecher-Tilton matter which prompted you to come East?'

"'Yes; I intended remaining three or four months longer, but I looked upon this as my own battle, a battle for the principles which I have advocated, and I came straight on to take my part in the fight.'

"There was little need of the reporter's propounding questions after Mrs. Woodhull had fairly opened on the subject. With that vivacity of manner and crispness of speech that have always characterized her, the lady gave her views plainly and emphatically.

"'I know very well why this great pressure has been brought to bear to hide the truth. It is because many persons are frightened to death from fear that all the facts will be made known. And yet, what have they to be frightened about? Let them come out and withstand public opinion! Eighteen hundred years ago Christ bade the woman sin no more; and after all these years of wickedness and wretchedness, are men fit, to-day, to judge their fellows?'

"'Mrs. Woodhull, you have read the Statement of Theodore Tilton"—

"I have read every word that has been printed.'

"Very good. Do you believe that Statement to be true?'

"'Every word of it is true,' and her words were spoken with marked emphasis. She continued:

"The only fault that I find is, that Theodore has told only one-third of what he ought and might have told. He wants to shield some one. Who is it? He has been a sorely-abused and injured man. He ought to speak out! See the charity which he displayed in living with his wife for years after he knew all! He has made an affidavit, and Mr. Beecher and Elizabeth deny its substance. Will the public be satisfied with simply a verbal denial? Let me tell you, the sentiment in the West—and I have had excellent opportunities for judging it aright—is turning strongly in favor of Mr. Tilton.

"Now 'here is a direct question, Mrs. Woodhull: Did Mrs. Tilton ever confess to you that she had been faithless to her marriage vows?'

"'I won't answer?' exclaimed Mrs Woodhull, impulsively. Then, after a moment's hesitation, she added: "When I first published the statement that I knew of two eminent divines who were living in concubinage and preaching from their pulpits, I was not acquainted with Theodore Tilton. I had never met him. I supposed him to be a clergyman. The day after the announcement appeared, he called upon me, showed me the extract, and asked me if it referred to him. I told him it did. In two or three days' time, he invited me to his house, and introduced me to his wife. What would he have done that for? What if not to say Elizabeth, here is one who knows all!'

"Then you did not get your first information from Mr. Tilton?'

"No; that assertion is a falsehood. Elizabeth Cady Stanton and Isabella Hooker told me. The matter had been talked over for months between these ladies, before I gave it to the public. And, understand, it was the hypocrisy of the thing I detested. If, when I had made the charges, Mr. Beecher had come out and said, 'Well sir, what are you going to do about it?' What could any one have done about it? Who was to arraign the pastor of Plymouth Church?"

"You remarked, just now, Mrs. Woodhull, that you believed Mrs. Tilton's Statement to be true. What think you of Mrs. Tilton's denial?"

"Mrs. Tilton's denial is untrue, and I know it. Had Elizabeth stopped to recall some facts, she would not have made such a statement. When Mr. Tilton found that Elizabeth loved Mr. Beecher, and when Mrs. Beecher found that her husband loved Elizabeth, it was positively wicked for either man and wife to live together longer. It is always wrong for two persons to live together when they do not love each other. Why, I have talked often with Mr. Beecher on this subject, and

I know very well what his views are. You saw the words of his brother, Thomas K., 'Henry only carries out the philosophy against which I protested twenty years ago,' which means my philosophy. And that is the philosophy of Mr. Beecher. He knows the present social system is wrong; he don't believe in it. I have asked him to preach what he practiced, but he has not had the courage to do so. Mr. Beecher sees a rottenness in the whole social world. To remedy this has been and is his philosophy. As to the Statement made by Mr. Beecher, I believe that Mr. Beecher never wrote that statement. It doesn't show it. There is nothing in it suggestive of the man."

"Your opinion of Mr. Frank Moulton is not changed, is it?"

"Not in the least. I believe Frank Moulton to be the same grand, good man that he always was. As I said last night, Frank is one of nature's noblemen. He has stood between Mr. Tilton and Mr. Beecher throughout this affair; and he has done his duty to both. I do not believe he will shirk now."

"His testimony, you think, will be important?"

"Of the utmost importance! All that Mr. Tilton has said will be proven. He has the letters in his possession, and I know he will produce them. Without Frank Moulton's evidence, I think they would crush Mr. Tilton, for so many influential members of Plymouth Church are bent on doing it."

"And you have no doubt that Mr. Moulton will speak?"

"None. Only yesterday, when I met him, he said, 'Theodore Tilton shall not be crucified,' and he meant what he said."

"Do you know more of this matter, Mrs. Woodhull, than you have given to the world?"

"Yes, I know something of the inside history. When they are all done, I shall speak. I shall give some truths which are not now known, and some facts which are not now understood. *By the way, I wish you would correct that absurd statement which appeared in some of the papers charging intimate relations between Mr. Tilton and myself. It is an atrocious falsehood.*"

"Just supposing the Committee should report adversely to Mr. Beecher's case—what do you predict the pastor of Plymouth would do? Step down and out?"

"No, indeed! I believe that he would collect about him a circle of higher minds than he ever has before. If he has nobleness enough, even now, to state things as they are, he will rise to a higher eminence than he has ever attained."

"Then you entertain no ill-feeling toward Mr. Beecher?"

"Not the slightest. It is only the hypocrisy I hate!"

CHAPTER XI.

MR. BEECHER'S CALL FOR AN INVESTIGATION BY A JURY OF HIS OWN CHOICE.—THE LONG LOOKED FOR BLOW FALLS AT LAST UPON THE PASTOR.—THE ASTOUNDING CHARGES OF TILTON.—OFT REPEATED ACTS OF CRIMINAL COMMERCE BETWEEN MRS. TILTON AND HER PASTOR.—MR. BEECHER CHARGED WITH "NEST HIDING."—A SAD TALE OF DOMESTIC INFELICITY.—A WOMAN'S DEVOTED LOVE, RELIGIOUS ZEAL, PLATONIC LOVE FOR HER PASTOR, ETC.—HER CONFESSION TO HER HUSBAND.—HOW MR. BEECHER WRUNG A DENIAL OF THE CHARGES FROM HER TO SAVE AN EXPOSURE.

THE public at once saw that the time had passed for compromise and the whole scandal was likely to be laid bare. The whole community were visibly excited over the threatened revelations, and the church especially felt that there was no longer a hope of suppression. On the 27th of June, two days after the publication of Mr. Tilton's letter to Dr. Bacon, Rev. Henry Ward Beecher asked several gentlemen of the Congregation of Plymouth Church to examine the charges against him, and to make a report in regard to them. The following is the letter, a copy of which was sent to each of the gentlemen named:—

BROOKLYN, June 27th, 1874.

GENTLEMEN: In the present state of the public feeling, I owe it to my friends and to the Church and the Society over which I am pastor, to have some proper investigation made of the rumors, insinuations, or charges made respecting my conduct, as compromised by the late publications

MRS. ELIZABETH R. TILTON.

made by Mr. Tilton. I have thought that both the Church and the Society should be represented, and I take the liberty of asking the following gentlemen to serve in this inquiry, and to do that which truth and justice may require. I beg that each of the gentlemen named will consider this as if it had been separately and personally sent to him, namely:

From the Church—Henry W. Sage, Augustus Storrs, Henry M. Cleveland.

From the Society—Horace B. Claflin, John Winslow, S. V. White.

I desire you, when you have satisfied yourselves by an impartial and thorough examination of all sources of evidence, to communicate to the Examination Committee, or to the Church, such action as then may seem to you right and wise. HENRY WARD BEECHER.

On the 6th of July, Mr. Beecher wrote the following note to the Examining Committee of Plymouth Church.

July 6th, 1874.

DEAR BRETHREN: I enclose to you a letter in which I have requested three gentlemen from the Church, and three from the Society of Plymouth Church (gentlemen of unimpeachable repute, and who have not been involved in any of the trials through which we have passed during the year), to make a thorough and impartial examination of all charges or insinuations against my good name, and to report the same to you; and I now respectfully request that you will give to this Committee the authority to act in your behalf also. It seemed wise to me that the request should proceed from me, and without your foregoing knowledge, and that you should give to it authority to act in your behalf in so far as a thorough investigation of the facts should be concerned.

HENRY WARD BEECHER.

Public opinion forced this course upon the accused pastor, and when it was published, sympathy was created for him, where before his action was viewed with grave suspicion. All hope of a compromise was not yet abandoned, however, and on the 13th of July Frank Moulton, the mutual friend of Beecher and Tilton, appeared before the Committee and presented the following statement:—

"*Gentlemen of the Committee:*—I appear before you at your invitation, to make a statement which I have read to Mr. Tilton and Mr. Beecher, which both deem honorable, and in the fairness and propriety of which, so far as I am concerned, they both concur. The parties in this case are personal friends of mine, in whose behalf I have endeavored to act, as the umpire and peacemaker, for the last four years, with a conscientious regard for all the interests involved. I regret for your sakes the responsibility imposed on me of appearing here to-night. If I say anything, I must speak the truth. I do not believe that the simple curiosity of the world at large, or even of this Committee, ought to be gratified through any recitation by me of the facts which are in my possession, necessarily in confidence, through my relations to the parties. The personal differences of which I am aware as the chosen arbitrator, have once been settled honorably between the parties, and would never have been revived except on account of recent attacks, both in and out of Plymouth Church, made upon the character of Theodore Tilton, to which he thought a reply necessary. If the present issue is to be settled, it must be, in my opinion, by the parties themselves, either together or separately before your Committee, each taking the responsibility of his own utterance. As I am fully conversant with the facts and evidences, I shall, as between these parties, if necessary, deem it my duty to state the truth, in order to final settlement, and that the world may be well informed before pronouncing its judgment with reference to either. I therefore suggest to you that the parties first be heard; that if then you deem it necessary that I should appear before you, I will do so, to speak the truth, the whole truth, and nothing but the truth. I hold to-night, as I have held hitherto, the opinion that Mr. Beecher should frankly state that he had committed an offence against Mr. Tilton, for which it was necessary to apologize, and for which he did apologize in the language of the letter, part of which has been quoted; that he should have stated frankly that he deemed it necessary for Mr. Tilton to have made the defence against Dr. Leonard Bacon which he did make, and that he (Mr. Beecher) should refuse to be a party to the re-opening of this painful subject. If he had made this statement, he would have stated no more than the truth, and it would have saved him and you the responsibility of a further inquiry. It is better now that the Committee should not report; and, in place of a report, Mr. Beecher himself should make the statement which I have suggested; or that, if the Committee does report, the report should be a recommendation to Mr. Beecher to make such a statement."

The action of Mr. Beecher in asking to be tried by a committee of his own choosing excited much criticism, and for a few days doubts were entertained whether Mr. Tilton would recognize that body as a proper tribunal to pass upon the momentous question of their pastor's guilt or innocence. But in the meantime Mrs. Tilton, without the knowledge or consent of her husband, had appeared before them, and disavowed any criminal transactions with her pastor. This action at once aroused the husband, and rendered further compromise impossible. He at once recognized the Committee in the following communication:—

No. 174 LIVINGSTON STREET, BROOKLYN, July 13th, 1874.

To the Investigating Committee:

GENTLEMEN—When, on Friday last, I met you at your invitation, the appointment of your Committee had not then been made known to the public. You sat in a private capacity.

Moreover, one of your legal advisers had previously given me a hope that if, on my appearance before you, I would preserve a judicious reticence concerning the worst aspects of the case, I might thereby facilitate, through you, such a moderate public presentation of Mr. Beecher's offense and apology as would close, rather than prolong, the existing scandal.

I rejoiced in this hope, and promptly reciprocated the kindly feeling which was reported to me as shared by you all toward myself and family.

Accordingly, when I met you in conference, my brief statement was, in substance, the two following points. First, that my letter to Dr. Bacon was written, not as an act of aggression, but of self-defense—arising, as therein set forth, from great and grievous provocation by your pastor, your Church, the Brooklyn Council, and the ex-Moderator's criticisms on my supposed conduct—all uniting to defame me before the world, and to inflict upon me an unjust punishment for acts done by another; and second, that having by that letter defended myself so far as I thought the occasion required me to carry my reply, I felt unwilling to proceed further against Mr. Beecher without farther public provocation or other necessity.

Such a necessity is now laid upon me by Mr. Beecher himself, in the publication of a direct request by him to you to inquire officially into his character as affected by his offense and apology, to which I referred. He thus offers to me a direct challenge, not only before your Committee, but before the public, which I hereby accept.

I, therefore, give you notice that I shall prepare a full and detailed statement in accordance with the terms of your Committee's invitation to me, "to furnish such facts, as are within my knowledge," touching matters "which compromise the character of Rev. Henry Ward Beecher." I shall be ready to lay this before you within a week or ten days, or as soon thereafter as I shall find myself able to set the numerous facts and evidences in such strict array as that I can cover them, each and all, with my oath to their exact truth, sworn before a magistrate.

I await the appointment of a day by you mutually convenient for my presentation of this statement in person before your Committee.

Meanwhile I shall make public my present note to you, because Mr. Beecher's letter to which this is a preliminary response has been made public by him. With great respect, I am truly yours, THEODORE TILTON.

There was a week of suspense and anxiety in Brooklyn and indeed throughout the country, not unmixed with curiosity as to the nature of the offense which Mr. Tilton would charge against Mr. Beecher. The journals daily contained columns of speculations and interviews or alleged interviews with the principal parties to the scandal, but they are not embodied here,—the object of the compiler being to adhere as closely as possible to the published record. Seven days after Mr. Tilton's recognition of the Committee he appeared before them with his charges, which Frank Moulton had assisted him to prepare,and read it to the Plymouth Church jury on the evening of July 20th. The following day the document appeared in full in the Brooklyn *Argus*. If the previous "True Story" was a thunderbolt, this was an earthquake. People read it in utter astonishment, and from that moment Mr. Beecher's reputation seemed to be doomed for all time. But we will here give the letter accompanying the statement as a preface, and the sworn charges filed:

"GENTLEMEN OF THE COMMITTEE:—In communicating to you the detailed statement of facts of evidences which you have been several days expecting at my hands let me remind you of the circumstances which call this statement forth.

"In my recent letter to Dr. Bacon I alluded to an offence and an apology by the Rev. Henry Ward Beecher. To whomsoever else this allusion seemed indefinite, to Mr. Beecher it was plain. The offence was committed by him; the apology was made by him; both acts were his own, and were among the most momentous occurrences of his life. Of all men in Plymouth Church, or in the world, the Rev. Henry Ward Beecher was the one man who was best informed concerning this offence and apology, and the one man who least needed to inquire into either.

"Nevertheless, while possessing a perfect knowledge of both these acts done by himself, he has chosen to put on a public affectation of ignorance and innocence concerning them, and has conspicuously appointed a committee of six of the ablest men of his church, together with two attorneys, to inquire into what he leaves you to regard as the unaccountable mystery of this offence and apology; as if he had neither committed the one nor offered the other; but as if both were the mere figments of another man's imagination—thus adroitly prompting the public to draw the deduction that I am a person under some hallucination or delusion, living in a dream and forging a fraud.

"Furthermore, in order to cast over this explanation the delicate glamour which always lends a charm to the defence of a woman's honor, Mrs. Elizabeth R. Tilton, lately my wife, has been prompted away from her home, to reside among Mr. Beecher's friends and to co-operate with him in his ostensibly honest and laudable inquiry into facts concerning which she too, as well as he, has for years past had perfect and equal knowledge with himself.

"The investigation, therefore, has been publicly pressed upon me by Mr. Beecher, seconded by Mrs. Tilton, both of whom, in so doing, have united in assuming before the public the non-existence of the grave and solemn facts into which they have conspired to investigate, for the purpose not of eliciting, but of denying the truth.

"This joint assumption by them, which has seemed to your committee to be in good faith, has naturally led you into an examination in which you expect to find, on their part, nothing but innocence, and on my part nothing but slander.

"It is now my unhappy duty, from which I have in vain hitherto sought earnestly to be delivered, to give you the facts and evidences for reversing your opinion on this subject.

"In doing this painful, I may say heartrending duty, the responsibility for making the grave disclosures which I am about to lay before you belongs not to me, but first to Mr. Beecher, who has prompted you to this examination, and next to Mrs. Tilton, who has joined him in a conspiracy which cannot fail to be full of peril and wretchedness to many hearts.

"I call you to witness that in my first brief examination by your committee I begged and implored you not to inquire into the facts of this case, but rather to seek to bury them beyond all possible revelation. Happy for all concerned had this entreaty been heeded. It is now too late. The last opportunity for reconciliation and settlement has passed. This investigation, undertaken by you in ignorance of dangers against which Mr. Beecher should have warned you in advance, will shortly prove itself, to your surprise, to have been an act of wanton and wicked folly, for which the Rev. Henry Ward Beecher, as its originator and public sponsor, will hereafter find no "space for repentance, though he seek it carefully and with tears." This desperate man must hold himself only, and not me, accountable for the wretchedness which these disclosures will carry to his own home and hearth, as they have already brought to mine.

I will add that the original documents referred to in the ensuing sworn statement are, for the most part, in my possession; but that the apology and a few other papers are in the hands of Mr. Francis D. Moulton. Truly yours,

THEODORE TILTON.

The charges are as follows:—

"Whereas the Rev. Henry Ward Beecher has instigated the appointment of a committee consisting of six members of his church and society to inquire and report upon alleged aspersions upon his character by Theodore Tilton; and whereas Mrs. Elizabeth R. Tilton, formerly the wife of Mr. Tilton, has openly deserted her home in order to co-operate with Mrs. Beecher in a conspiracy to overthrow the credibility and good repute of her late husband as a man and citizen; therefore, Theodore Tilton being thus authorized and required, and by the published demand made upon him by the Rev. Henry Ward Beecher, and being now and hereafter released by act of Mrs. Tilton from further responsibility for concealment of the truth touching her relations with Mr. Beecher—therefore, Theodore Tilton hereby sets forth, under solemn oath, the following facts and testimony:—

First—That on the 2d of October, 1855, at Plymouth church, Brooklyn, a marriage between Theodore Tilton and Elizabeth M. Richards was performed by the Rev. Henry Ward Beecher, which marriage, thirteen years afterward, was dishonored and violated by this clergyman through the criminal seduction of this wife and mother, as hereinafter set forth.

Second—That for a period of about fifteen years, extending both before and after this marriage, an intimate friendship existed between Theodore Tilton and the Rev. Henry Ward Beecher, which friendship was cemented to such a degree that in consequence thereof the subsequent dishonoring by Mr. Beecher of his friend's wife was a crime of uncommon wrongfulness and perfidy.

Third—That about nine years ago the Rev. Henry Ward Beecher began, and thereafter continued, a friendship with Mrs. Elizabeth R. Tilton, for whose native delicacy and extreme religious sensibility he often expressed to her husband a high admiration; visiting her from time to time for years, until the year 1870, when, for reasons hereinafter stated, he ceased such visits; during which period, by many tokens and attentions, he won the affectionate love of Mrs. Tilton; whereby after long moral resistance by her and after repeated assaults by him upon her mind with overmastering arguments, accomplished the possession of her person; maintaining with her thenceforward, during the period hereinafter stated, the relation called criminal intercourse; this re ation being regarded by her during that period as not criminal or morally wrong—such had been the power of his arguments as a clergyman to satisfy her religious scruples against such violation of virtue and honor.

Fourth—That on the evening of October 10th, 1868, or thereabouts, Mrs. Elizabeth R. Tilton held an interview with the Rev. Henry Ward Beecher at his residence, she being then in a tender state of mind, owing to the recent death and burial of a young child; and during this interview an act of criminal commerce took place between this pastor and this parishioner, the motive on her part being, as hereinbefore stated, not regarded by her at the time criminal or wrong; which act was followed by a similar act of criminality between these same parties at Mr. Tilton's residence, during a pastoral visit paid by Mr. Beecher to her on the subsequent Saturday evening, followed also by other similar acts on various occasions from the autumn of 1868 to the spring of 1870, the places being the two residences aforesaid, and occasionally other places to which her pastor would invite and accompany her, or at which he would meet her by previous appointment, these acts of wrong being on her part, from first to last, not wanton or consciously wicked, but arising through a blinding of her moral perceptions, occasioned by the powerful influence exerted on her mind at that time to this end by the Rev. Henry Ward Beecher, as her trusted religious preceptor and guide.

Fifth—That the pastoral visits made by the Rev. Henry Ward Beecher to Mrs. Tilton during the year 1858 became so frequent as to excite comment, being in marked contrast with his known habit of making few pastoral calls on his parishoners, which frequency in Mrs. Tilton's case is shown in letters written to her husband during his absence in the West, these letters giving evidence that during the period of five or six weeks twelve different pastoral calls on Mrs. Tilton were made by the Rev. Henry Ward Beecher, which calls became noticeably infrequent on Mr. Tilton's return to his home.

Sixth—That previous to the aforesaid criminal intimacy one of the reasons which Mrs. Tilton alleged for her encouragement of such exceptional attentions from the Rev. Henry Ward Beecher was the fact that she had been much distressed with rumors against his moral purity, and wished to convince him that she could receive his kindness and yet resist his solicitations; and that she could inspire in him, by her purity and fidelity, an increased respect for the chaste dignity of womanhood. Previous to the autumn of 1868 she maintained, with Christian firmness towards her pastor this position of resistance, always refusing his amorous pleas, which were strong and oft-repeated; and in a letter to her husband, dated February 3d, 1868, she wrote as follows:—"To love is praiseworthy, but to abuse the gift is sin. Here I am strong. No demonstrations or fascinations could cause me to yield my womanhood."

"*Seventh*—That the first suspicion which crossed the mind of Theodore Tilton that the Rev. Henry Ward Beecher was abusing, or might abuse, the affection and reverence which Mrs. Tilton bore towards her pastor, was an improper caress given by Mr. Beecher to Mrs. Tilton by the * * * while seated by her side on the floor of his library overlooking engravings. Mr. Tilton, a few hours afterwards, asked of his wife an explanation of her permission of such a liberty, whereat she at first denied the fact, but then confessed it, and said that she had spoken chidingly to Mr. Beecher concerning it. On another occasion Mr. Tilton, after leaving his house in the early morning, returned to it in the forenoon, and, on going to his bedchamber, found the door locked, and when, on knocking, the door was opened by Mrs. Tilton, Mr. Beecher was seen within, apparently much confused, and exhibiting a flushed face. Mrs. Tilton afterwards made a plausible explanation, which, from the confidence reposed in her by her husband, was by him deemed satisfactory.

"*Eighth*—That in the spring of 1870, on Mr. Tilton's return from a winter's absence, he noticed in his wife such evidences of the absorption of her mind in Mr. Beecher that in a short time an estrangement took place between her husband and herself, in consequence of which she went into the country earlier than usual for a summer sojourn. After an absence of several weeks she voluntarily returned to her home in Brooklyn. On the evening of July 8th, 1870, when, and then and there, within a few hours after her arrival, and after exacting from her husband a solemn promise that he would do the Rev. Henry Ward Beecher no harm nor communicate to him what she was about to say, she made a circumstantial confession to her husband of the criminal facts hereinbefore stated, accompanied with citations from Mr. Beecher's arguments and reasonings with her to overcome her long maintained scruple against yielding to his desires, and declaring that she had committed no wrong to her husband or her marriage vow, quoting, in support of this opinion, that her pastor had repeatedly assured her that she was spotless and chaste, which she believed herself to be. She further stated that her sexual commerce with him had never proceeded from low or vulgar thoughts either on her part or his, but always from pure affection and a high religious love. She stated, furthermore, that Mr. Beecher habitually characterized their intimacy by the term "nest hiding," and he would suffer pain and sorrow if his hidden secret were ever made known. She said that her mind was often burdened by the deceit necessary for her to practice in order to prevent discovery, and that her conscience had many times impelled her to throw off this burden of enforced falsehood by making a full confession to her husband, so that she would no longer be living before him a perpetual lie. In particular she said that she had been on the point of making this confession a few months previously, during a severe illness, when she feared she might die. She affirmed also that Mr. Beecher had assured her repeatedly that he loved her better than he had ever loved any other woman, and she felt justified before God in her intimacy with him, save the necessary deceit which accompanied it, and at which she frequently suffered in her mind.

"*Ninth*—That after the above-named confession by Mrs. Elizabeth R. Tilton she returned to the country to await such action by her husband as he might see fit to take, whereupon, after many considerations, the chief of which was that she had not voluntarily gone astray, but had been artfully misled, through religious reverence for the Rev. Henry Ward Beecher as her spiritual guide, together also from a desire to protect the family from open shame, Mr. Tilton condoned the wrong, and he addressed to his wife such letters of affection, tenderness and respect as he felt would restore her wounded spirit, and which did partially produce that result.

"*Tenth*—That in December, 1870, differences arose between Theodore Tilton and Henry C. Bowen, which were augmented by the Rev. Henry Ward Beecher and Mrs. Beecher; in consequence whereof and at the wish of Mrs. Elizabeth R. Tilton, expressed in writing in a paper put into the hands of Mr. Francis D. Moulton, with a view to procure a harmonious interview between Mr. Tilton and Mr. Beecher, such an interview was arranged and carried out by Mr. Moulton at his then residence on Clinton street; Mr. Beecher and Mr. Tilton, meeting and speaking then and there for the first time since Mrs. Tilton's confession of six months before. The paper in Mr. Moulton's hands was a statement by Mrs. Tilton of the substance of the confession which she had before made and of her wish and prayer for reconciliation and peace between her pastor and her husband. This paper furnished to Mr. Beecher the first knowledge which he had as yet received that Mrs. Tilton had made such a confession. At this interview between Mr. Beecher and Mr. Tilton permission was sought by Mr. Beecher to consult with Mrs. Tilton on that same evening. This permission being granted, Mr. Beecher departed from Mr. Moulton's house, and in about half an hour returned thither expressing his remorse and shame, and declaring that his life and work seemed brought to a sudden end. Later in the same evening Mr. Tilton, on returning to his house, found his wife weeping and in great distress, saying that what she had meant for peace had only given pain and anguish; that Mr. Beecher had just called on her, declaring that she had slain him, and that he would probably be tried before a council of ministers unless she would give him a written paper for his protection.

Whereupon she said he dictated to her, and she copied in her own handwriting, a suitable paper for him to use to clear himself before a council of ministers. Mrs. Tilton having kept no copy of this paper her husband asked her to make a distinct statement in writing of her design and meaning in giving it, whereupon she wrote as follows:—

DECEMBER 30th, 1870—Midnight.

MY DEAR HUSBAND:—I desire to leave with you, before going to bed, a statement that Mr. Henry Ward Beecher called upon me this evening and asked me if I would defend him against any accusation in a council of ministers, and I replied, solemnly, that I would, in case the accuser was any other person than my husband. He (H. W. B.) dictated a letter, which I copied as my own, to be used by him as against any other accuser except my husband. This letter was designed to vindicate Mr. Beecher against all other persons save only yourself. I was ready to give him this letter because he said with pain that my letter in your hands addressed to him, dated December 29th, "had struck him dead and ended his usefulness." You and I are pledged to do our best to avoid publicity. God grant a speedy end to all further anxieties. Affectionately, ELIZABETH.

"On the next day, namely, December 31st, 1870, Mr. Moulton, on being informed by Mr. Tilton of the above-named transaction by Mr. Beecher, called on him (Mr. Beecher) at his residence and told him that a reconciliation seemed suddenly made impossible by Mr. Beecher's nefarious act in procuring the letter which Mrs. Tilton had thus been improperly persuaded to make falsely. Mr. Beecher, through Mr. Moulton, returned the letter to Mr. Tilton, with an expression of shame and sorrow for having procured it in the manner he did. The letter was as follows:—

DECEMBER 30th, 1870.

Wearied with importunity and weakened by sickness, I gave a letter implicating my friend Henry Ward Beecher under assurance that it would remove all difficulties between me and my husband. That letter I now revoke. I was persuaded to it—almost forced—when I was in a weakened state of mind.

I regret and recall all its statements.

E. R. TILTON.

I desire to say explicitly, Mr. Beecher has never offered any improper solicitation, but has always treated me in a manner becoming a Christian and a gentleman. ELIZABETH R. TILTON.

At the time of Mr. Beecher's returning the above document

to Mr. Tilton through Mr. Moulton, Mr. Beecher requested Mr. Moulton to call at his residence, in Columbia Street, on the next day, which he did on the evening of January 1st, 1871. A long interview then ensued, in which Mr. Beecher expressed to Mr. Moulton great contrition and remorse for his previous criminality with Mrs. Tilton, taking to himself shame for having misused his sacred office as a clergyman to corrupt her mind; expressing a determination to kill himself in case of exposure, and begging Mr. Moulton to take a pen and receive from his (Mr. Beecher's) lips an apology to be conveyed to Mr. Tilton, in the hope that such an appeal would secure Mr. Tilton's forgiveness. The apology which Mr. Beecher dictated to Mr. Moulton was as follows:—

My Dear Friend Moulton:—I ask, through you, Theodore Tilton's forgiveness, and I humble myself before him as I do before my God. He would have been a better man in my circumstances than I have been. I can ask nothing, except that he will remember all the other breasts that would ache. I will not plead for myself. I even wish that I were dead. But others must live to suffer. I will die before any one but myself shall be inculpated. All my thoughts are running out toward my friends, and toward the poor child lying there, and praying, with her folded hands. She is guiltless, sinned against, bearing the transgression of another. Her forgiveness I have. I humbly pray to God to put it into the heart of her husband to forgive me.

I have trusted this to Moulton, in confidence.

H. W. Beecher.

In the above document, the last sentence and the signature are in the handwriting of the Rev. Henry Ward Beecher.

Eleventh—That Mrs. Tilton wrote the following letter to a friend:—

No. 174 Livingston Street,
Brooklyn, Jan. 5th, 1871.

Dear Friend:—A cruel conspiracy has been formed against my husband, in which my mother and Mrs. Beecher have been the chief actors. * * *

Yours truly,

Elizabeth R. Tilton.

Twelfth—That in the following month Mr. Moulton, wishing to bind Mr. Tilton and Mr. Beecher by mutual expressions of good spirit, elicited from them the following correspondence:—

MR. TILTON TO MR. MOULTON.

BROOKLYN, Feb. 7th, 1871.

MY DEAR FRIEND:—In several conversations with you, you have asked about my feelings toward Mr. Beecher; and yesterday you said the time had come when you would like to receive from me an expression of this kind in writing.

I say, therefore, very cheerfully, that, notwithstanding the great suffering which he has caused to Elizabeth and myself, I bear him no malice, shall do him no wrong, shall discountenance every project (by whomsoever proposed) for any exposure of his secret to the public, and (if I know myself at all) shall endeavor to act toward Mr. Beecher as I would have him in similar circumstances act toward me.

I ought to add that your own good offices in this case have led me to a higher moral feeling than I might otherwise have reached.

Ever yours, affectionately,

TO FRANK MOULTON. THEODORE.

On the same day Mr. Beecher wrote to Mr. Moulton the following:—

MR. BEECHER TO MR. MOULTON.

FEBRUARY 7th, 1871.

MY DEAR FRIEND MOULTON:—I am glad to send you a book, etc.

* * * * * * * *

Many, many friends has God raised up to me, but to no one of them has He ever given the opportunity and the wisdom to serve me as you have.

You have also proved Theodore's friend and Elizabeth's. Does God look down from heaven on three unhappier creatures that more need a friend than these? Is it not an intimation of God's intent of mercy to all, that each one of these has in you a tried and proved friend? But only in you are we thus united. Would to God, who orders all hearts, that by His kind mediation Theodore, Elizabeth and I could be made friends again.

Theodore will have the hardest task in such a case; but has he not proved himself capable of the noblest things?

I wonder if Elizabeth knows how generously he has carried himself toward me? Of course I can never speak with her again without his permission, and I do not know that even then it would be best. * * *

Mr. Moulton, on the same day, asked Mr. Tilton if he would permit Mr. Beecher to address a letter to Mrs. Tilton, and Mr. Tilton replied in the affirmative, whereupon Mr. Beecher wrote as follows:—

MR. BEECHER TO MRS. TILTON.

BROOKLYN, Feb. 7th, 1871.

MY DEAR MRS. TILTON:—When I saw you last I did not expect ever to see you again, or to be alive many days. God was kinder to me than were my own thoughts. The friend whom God sent to me, Mr. Moulton, has proved, above all friends that I ever had, able and willing to help me in this terrible emergency of my life. His hand it was that tied up the storm that was ready to burst on our heads.

You have no friend (Theodore excepted) who has it in his power to serve you so vitally, and who will do it with such delicacy and honor.

It does my sore heart good to see in Mr. Moulton an unfeigned respect and honor for you. It would kill me if I thought otherwise. He will be as true a friend to your honor and happiness as a brother could be to a sister's.

In him we have a common ground. You and I may meet in him. The past is ended. But is there no future?—no wiser, higher, holier, future? May not this friend stand as a priest in the new sanctuary of reconciliation, and mediate and bless Theodore and my most unhappy self? Do not let my earnestness fail of its end. You believe in my judgment. I have put myself wholly and gladly in Moulton's hand; and there I must meet you.

This is sent with Theodore's consent, but he has not read it. Will you return it to me by his own hand? I am very earnest in this wish for all our sakes, as such a letter ought not to be subject to even a chance of miscarriage. Your unhappy friend. H. W. BEECHER.

Thirteenth—That about a year after Mrs. Tilton's confession her mind remained in the fixed opinion that her criminal relations with Mr. Beecher had not been morally wrong, so strongly had he impressed her to the contrary; but at length a change took place in her convictions on this subject, as noted in the following letter addressed by her to her husband:—

MRS. TILTON TO MR. TILTON.

SCHOHARIE, June 29th, 1871.

MY DEAR THEODORE—To-day, through the ministry of Catherine Gaunt, a character of fiction, my eyes have been opened for the first time in my experience, so that I see clearly my sin. It was when I knew that I was loved, to suffer it to grow to a passion. A virtuous woman should check instantly an absorbing love. But it appeared to me in such false light. That the love I felt and received could harm no one, not even you, I have believed unfalteringly, until four o'clock this afternoon, when the heavenly vision dawned upon me. I see now, as never before, the wrong I have done you, and hasten immediately to ask your pardon, with a penitence so sincere that henceforth (if reason remains) you may trust me implicitly. Oh, my dear Theodore! though your opinions are not restful or congenial to my soul, yet my own integrity and purity are sacred and holy things to me. Bless God, with me, for Catherine Gaunt, and for all the sure leadings of an all-wise and loving Providence. Yes, now I feel quite prepared to renew my marriage vow with you, to keep it as the Savior requireth, who looketh at the eye and the heart. Never before could I say this. When you yearn towards me with true feeling, be assured of the tried, purified and restored love of ELIZABETH.

Mrs. Tilton followed the above letter with these:—

MRS. TILTON TO MR. TILTON.

July 4th, 1871.

Oh, my dear husband! may you never need the discipline of being misled by a good woman as I was by a good man.

[No date.]

I would mourn greatly if my life was to be made known to father. His head would be bowed indeed to the grave.

[No date.]

Do not think my ill health is on account of my sin and its discovery. My sins and life-record I have carried to my Savior. No; my prostration is owing to the suffering I have caused you.

Fourteenth—That about one year after Mrs. Tilton's confession, and about a half year after Mr. Beecher's confirmation of the same, Mrs. V. C. Woodhull, then a total stranger to Mr. Tilton, save that he had been presented to her in a company of friends a few days previous, wrote in the *World*, Monday, May 22d, 1871, the following statement, namely:—

I know of one man, a public teacher of eminence, who lives in concubinage with the wife of another public teacher of almost equal eminence. All three concur in denouncing offences against morality. I shall make it my business to analyze some of these lives.

VICTORIA C. WOODHULL.

NEW YORK, May, 20th, 1871.

On the day of the publication of the above card in the *World*, Mr. Tilton received from Mrs. Woodhull a request to call, on imperative business, at her office; and on going thither, a copy of the above card was put into his hand by Mrs. Woodhull, who said that " the parties referred to therein were the Rev. Henry Ward Beecher and the wife of Theodore Tilton." Following this announcement, Mrs Woodhull detailed to Mr.

Tilton, with vehement speech, the wicked and injurious story which she published in the year following. Meanwhile, Mr. Tilton, desiring to guard against any possible temptation to Mrs. Woodhull to publish the grossly distorted version which she gave to Mr. Tilton (and which she afterwards attributed to him), he sought by many personal services and kindly attentions to influence her to such a good will towards himself and family as would remove all disposition or desire in her to afflict him with such a publication. Mr. Tilton's efforts and association with Mrs. Woodhull ceased in April, 1872, and six months afterwards—namely, November 2d, 1872—she published the scandal which he had labored to suppress.

XV. That on the third day thereafter, the Rev. Thomas K. Beecher, of Elmira, N. Y., wrote as follows:

ELMIRA, November 5th, 1871.

Mrs. Woodhull *only carries out Henry's philosophy*, against which I recorded my protest twenty years' ago.

XVI. That in May, 1873, the publication by one of Mr. Beecher's partners of a tripartite covenant between H. C. Bowen, H. W. Beecher, and Theodore Tilton, led the press of the country to charge that Mr Tilton had committed against Mr. Beecher some heinous wrong, which Mr. Beecher had pardoned; whereas the truth was the reverse. To remedy this false public impression, Mr. Moulton requested Mr. Beecher to prepare a suitable card, relieving Mr. Tilton of this injustice.

In answer to this request Mr. Beecher pleaded his embarrassments, which prevented his saying anything without bringing himself under suspicion. Mr. Tilton then proposed to prepare a card of his own, containing a few lines from the recently quoted apology, for the purpose of showing that Mr. Beecher, instead of having had occasion to forgive Mr. Tilton, had had occasion to be forgiven by him. Mr. Beecher then wrote a letter to Mr. Moulton, which, on being shown to Mr. Tilton, was successful in appealing to Mr. Tilton's feelings. Mr. Beecher said in it, under date of Sunday morning, June 1st, 1873:

My Dear Frank:

I am determined to make no more resistance. Theodore's temperament is such that the future, even if temporarily earned, would be absolutely worthless, and rendering me liable at any hour of the day to be obliged to stultify all the devices by which we saved ourselves. It is only fair that he should know that the publication of the card which he proposes would leave him worse off than before. The agreement [viz., the "tripartite covenant"] was made after my letter through you to him [viz., the "apology"] was written. He had had it a year. He had condoned his wife's faults. He had enjoined upon me, with the utmost earnestness and solemnity, not to betray his wife, nor leave his children to a blight * * * * With such a man as T. T., there is no possible salvation for any that depend upon him. With a strong nature, he does not know how to govern it, * * * * There is no use in trying further. I have a strong feeling upon me, and it brings great peace, that I am spending my last Sunday, and preaching my last sermon.

The hopelessness of spirit which the foregoing letter portrayed on the part of its writer, led Mr. Tilton to reconsider the question of defending himself at the cost of producing misery to Mr. Beecher; which determination by Mr. Tilton to allow the prevailing calumnies against himself to go unanswered, was further strengthened by the following note received by him two days thereafter, from the office-editor of Mr. Beecher's journal: Oliver Johnson:—

128 East Twelfth Street, June 4th, 1873.

My Dear Theodore:

May I tell you frankly that when I saw you last, you did not seem to me to be the noble young man who inspired my warm affection so many years ago. You were yielding to an act which I could not help thinking would be dishonorable and perfidious; and although it is easy for me to make every allowance for the circumstances that had wrought you to such a frenzy, I was dreadfully shocked. My dear Theodore, let me as an old friend, whose heart is wrung by your terrible suffering and sorrow, tell you that you were then acting ignobly, and that you can never have true peace of mind till you conquer yourself and dismiss all purpose and thought of injuring the man who has wronged you. Of all the promises our lips can frame, none are so sacred as those we make to those who have injured us, and whom we have professed to forgive; and they are sacred just in proportion as their violation would work injury to those to whom they are made. You cannot paint too blackly the wrongs you have suffered. On that point, I make no plea in abatement; but I beg you to remember that nothing can change the law which makes forgiveness noble and God-like.

I have prayed for you night and day, with strong crying and tears, beseeching God to restrain you from wronging yourself by violating your solemn engagements. To-night I am happy in the thought that you have been preserved from committing the act which I so much dreaded.

In a letter written by Mr. Beecher, in order to be shown to Mr. Tilton, Mr. Beecher spoke as follows:—

MR. BEECHER TO MR. MOULTON.

No man can see the difficulties that environ me, unless he stands where I do. To *say* that I have a Church on my hands is simple enough, but to have the hundreds and thousands of men pressing me, each one with his keen suspicion, or anxiety, or zeal; to see the tendencies which, if not stopped would break out into a ruinous defence of me; to stop them without seeming to do it; to prevent any one questioning me; to meet and allay prejudices against T. which had their beginnings years before; to keep serene as if I was not alarmed or disturbed; to be cheerful at home and among friends when I was suffering the torments of the damned; to pass sleepless nights often, and yet to come up fresh and fair for Sunday—all this may be *talked* about, but the real thing cannot be understood from the outside, nor its wearing and grinding on the nervous system."

In still another letter, written for the same purpose as the above, Mr. Beecher said:

MR. BEECHER TO MR. MOULTON.

"If my destruction would place him (Mr. Tilton) all right, that shall not stand in the way, I am willing to step down and out. No one can offer more than that. That I do offer. Sacrifice me without hesitation, if you can clearly see your way to his safety and happiness thereby. In one point of view, I could desire the sacrifice on my part. Nothing can possibly be so bad as the power of great darkness in which I spend much of my time. I look upon death as sweeter far than any friend I have in the world. Life would be pleasant if I could see that rebuilt which is shattered. But to live on the sharp and ragged edge of anxiety, remorse, fear, despair, and yet to put on an appearance of serenity and happiness, cannot be endured much longer. I am well nigh discouraged. If *you* cease to trust me, to love me, I am alone. I do not know any person in the world to whom I could go."

Mr. Tilton yielded to the above-quoted and other similar letters, and made no defence of himself against the public odium which attached to him unjustly.

XVII. That the marriage union between Mr. and Mrs. Tilton, until broken by Mr. Beecher, was of more than common harmony, affection, and mutual respect. Their home and household were regarded for years, by all their guests, as an ideal home.

As evidence of the feeling and spirit which this wife entertained for her husband, up to the time of her corruption by Mr. Beecher, the following letters by Mrs. Tilton, written only a few months before her loss of honor, will testify:

MRS. TILTON TO MR. TILTON.

TUESDAY MORNING, January 28th, 1868.

My Beloved:

Don't you know the peculiar phase of Christ's character as lover is precious to me, because of my consecration and devotion to you? I learn to love you from my love to Him. I have learned to love Him from my love to you. I couple you with Him. Nor do I feel it one whit irreverent. And as every day I adorn myself, consciously, as a bride to meet her bridegroom, in like manner, I lift imploring hands that my soul's love may be prepared. I, with the little girls after you led us with overflowing eyes and hearts, consecrated ourselves to our work and to you. My waking thoughts last night were of you. My rising thoughts this morning were of you. God sustain us, and help us both to keep our vows.

MRS. TILTON TO MR. TILTON.

SATURDAY EVENING, Feb. 1st, 1868.

Oh! well I know, as far as I am capable, I love you. Now to keep this fire high and generous, is the ideal before me. I am only perfectly contented and restful when you are with me. These latter months I have thought, looked, and yearned for the hour when you would be at home, with longings unutterable.

MRS. TILTON TO MR. TILTON.

MONDAY, Feb. 3d, 1868.—9 o'clock A. M.

What may I bring to my beloved, this bright morning? A large, throbbing heart full of love, single in its aim and purpose to bless and cheer him? Is it acceptable, sweet one?

MRS. TILTON TO MR. TILTON.

MONDAY MORNING, February 24th, 1868.

Do you wonder that I couple your love, your presence and relation to me, with the Savior's? I lift you up sacredly, and keep you in that exalted and holy place where I reverence, respect, and love with the fervency of my whole being.

Whatever capacity I have, I offer it to you. The closing lines of your letter are these: "I shall hardly venture again upon a great friendship—your love shall be enough for the remaining days." That word "enough," seems a stoicism on which you have resolved to live your life—but I pray God he will supply you with friendships pure, and with wifely love which your great heart demands, withholding not Himself as the Chief Love which consumeth not, though it burn, and whose effects are always perfect rest and peace.

Again, in one of your letters, you close with: "Faithfully yours."

That word *faithful* means a great deal. Yes, darling, I believe it, trust it, and give you the same surety with regard to myself. I am faithful to you, have been always, and shall forever be, world without end. Call not this assurance impious; there are some things we *know*. Blessed be God!

MRS. TILTON TO MR. TILTON.

HOME, February 28th, 1868.
SATURDAY EVENING.

Ah! did man ever love so grandly as my Beloved? Other friendships, public affairs, all "fall to naught" when I come to you. Though you are in Decorah, to-night, yet I have felt your love, and am very grateful for it. I had not received a line since Monday, and was so hungry and lonesome that I took out all your letters and indulged myself as at a feast, but without satiety. And now I long to pour out, into your heart, of my abundance. I am conscious of three jets to the fountain of my soul—to the Great Lover and yourself—to whom as *one* I am eternally wedded; my children, and the dear friends who trust and love me. I do not want another long separation. While we are in the flesh, let us abide together.

MRS. TILTON TO MR. TILTON.

WEDNESDAY, MORN., March, 1868.

Oh! how almost perfectly could I minister to you, this Winter—my heart glows so perpetually! I am conscious of great inward awakening toward you. If I live, I shall teach my children to *begin* their loves, where now I am. I cannot conceive of anything more delicious than a life consecrated to a faithful love. I insist that I miss you more than you do me; but soon I shall see my beloved.

YOUR OWN DEAR WIFE.

In addition to the above, many other letters by Mrs. Tilton to her husband prior to her corruption by Mr. Beecher, served to show that a Christian wife, loving her husband to the extreme degree above set forth, could only have been swerved from the path of rectitude by artful and powerful persuasions, clothed in the phrases of religion, and enforced by strong appeals from her chief Christian teacher and guide.

XVIII. That the story purporting to explain Mr. Beecher's apology as having been written because he had offended Mr. Tilton by engaging his wife in the project of a separation from her husband, is false; as will be seen by the following letter written only three days after the date of the apology:

MRS. TILTON TO MR. MOULTON.

174 LIVINGSTON STREET, BROOKLYN,
January, 4th, 1871.

Mr. Francis D. Moulton:

MY DEAR FRIEND—In regard to your question whether I have ever sought a separation from my husband, I indignantly *deny that such was ever the fact*, as I have denied it a hundred times before. The story that I wanted a separation was a deliberate falsehood coined by my poor mother, who said she would bear the responsibility of this and other statements she might make, and communicated to my husband's enemy, Mrs. H. W. Beecher, and by her communicated to Mr. Bowen. *I feel outraged* by the whole proceeding, and am now suffering in consequence more than I am able to bear. I am yours, very truly,

ELIZABETH R. TILTON.

XIX. That during the first week in January, 1871, a few days after the apology was written, Mr. Beecher communicated to Mr. Tilton, through Mr. Moulton, an earnest wish that he (Mr. Tilton) would take his family to Europe and reside there for a term of years, at Mr. Beecher's expense. Similar offers have been since repeated by Mr. Beecher to Mr. Tilton through the same channel. A message of kindred tenor was brought from Mr. Beecher to Mr. Tilton, last summer, by Mr. F. B. Carpenter, as will appear from the following affidavit:

HOMER, N. Y., July 18th, 1874.

On Sunday, June 1st, 1873, two days after the surreptitious publication of the tripartite covenant between H. W. Beecher, H. C. Bowen, and Theodore Tilton, I walked with Mr. Beecher from Plymouth Church to the residence of Mr. F. D. Moulton, in Remsen street. On the way to Mr. Moulton's house, Mr. Beecher said to me if Mr. Tilton would stand by him he would share his fame, his fortune, and everything he possessed with him (Tilton). FRANCIS B. CARPENTER.

Sworn to and subscribed before me, this 18th day of July, 1874.

WILLIAM T. HICKOK, Notary Public.

Mr. Carpenter, in communicating to Mr. Tilton the above affidavit, says, in a letter accompanying it:—

I have no hesitation in giving you the statement, as I understood at the time that it was for me to repeat in substance to you, and I did so repeat it. It was at this interview Mr. Beecher spoke to me of his apology to you.

The charge that Mr. Tilton ever attempted to levy blackmail on Mr. Beecher, is false; on the contrary, Mr. Tilton has always resented every attempt by Mr. Beecher to put him under pecuniary obligation.

XX. Not long after the scandal became public, Mrs. Tilton wrote on a slip of paper, and left on her husband's writing-desk, the following words:—

Now that the exposure has come, my whole nature revolts to join with you or standing with you.

Through the influence of Mr. Beecher's friends, the opinion has long been diligently propagated that the scandal was due to Mr. Tilton, and that the alleged facts were malicious inventions by him to revenge himself for supposed and imaginary wrongs done to him by Mr. Beecher. Many words were spoken from time to time by Mrs. Tilton to the praise and eulogy of Mr. Beecher, which, being extensively quoted through his congregation, heightened the impression that Mr. Tilton was Mr. Beecher's slanderer, Mrs. Tilton being herself the authority for the statement. In this way Mrs. Tilton and one of her relatives have been the chief causes of the great difficulty of suppressing the scandal. They have had a habit of saying, "Mr. Tilton believes such and such things;" and their naming of these things by way of denial has been a mischievous way of circulating them broadcast. In this way, Mr. Tilton has been made to appear a defamer, whereas he has made every effort in his power to suppress the injurious tales which he has been charged with propagating. On all occasions, he has systematically referred to his wife in terms favorable to her character.

Further, Mr. Tilton would not have communicated to the Committee the facts contained in this statement, except for the perverse course of the Rev. Henry Ward Beecher and Mrs. Elizabeth R. Tilton, to degrade and destroy him in the public estimation.

XXI. That one evening, about two weeks after the publication of Mr. Tilton's letter to Dr. Bacon, Mrs. Tilton, on coming home at a late hour, informed her husband that she had been visited at a friend's house by a committee of investigation, and had given sweeping evidence acquitting Mr. Beecher of every charge. This was the first intimation which Mr. Tilton received that any such Committee was then in existence. Furthermore, Mrs. Tilton stated that she had done this by advice of a lawyer, whom Mr. Beecher had sent to her, and who, in advance of her appearing before the Committee, arranged with her the questions and answers which were to constitute her testimony in Mr. Beecher's behalf. On the next day, after giving this untrue testimony before the Committee, she spent many hours of extreme suffering from pangs of conscience at having testified falsely. She expressed to her husband the hope that God would forgive her perjury, but that the motive was to save Mr. Beecher and her husband, and also to remove all reproach from the cause of religion. She also expressed similar contrition to one of her intimate friends.

XXII. Finally, that in addition to the foregoing facts and evidences, other confirmations could be adduced, if needed, to prove the following recapitulated statement, namely, that the Rev. Henry Ward Beecher, as pastor and friend of Mr. Tilton and his family, trespassed upon the sanctity of friendship and hospitality in a long endeavor to seduce Mrs. Elizabeth R. Tilton; that by the artful use of his priestly authority with her, she being his pupil in religion, he accomplished this seduction; that for a period of a year and a half, or thereabout, he maintained criminal intercourse with her, overcoming her previous modest scruples against such conduct by investing it with a false justification as sanctioned by love and religion; that he then participated in a conspiracy to degrade Theodore Tilton before the public, by loss of place, business and repute; that he abused Mr. Tilton's forgiveness and pledge of protection by thereafter authorizing a series of measures by Plymouth Church having for their object the putting of a stigma upon Mr. Tilton before the Church, and also before an Ecclesiastical Council, insomuch that the moderator of that Council, interpreting these acts by Mr. Beecher and his Church, declared that they showed Mr. Beecher to be the most magnanimous of men, and Mr. Tilton to be a knave and dog; that when Mr. Tilton thereafter, not in malice but for self-protection, wrote a letter to Dr. Bacon, alluding therein to an offence and apology by the Rev. Henry Ward Beecher, he (Mr. Beecher) defiantly appointed a committee of his Church members to inquire into the injury done him by Mr. Tilton by the aforesaid allusion, and implying that he (Mr. Beecher) had never been the author of such offence and apology, and that Mr. Tilton was a slanderer; that to make this inquiry bear grievously against Mr. Tilton, he (Mr. Beecher) previously connived with Mrs. E. R. Tilton to give false testimony in his (Mr. Beecher's) behalf; that Mr. Beecher's course toward Mr. Tilton and family has at last resulted in the open destruction of Mr. Tilton's household and home, and in the desolation of his heart and life.

THEODORE TILTON.

Sworn to before me this 20th day of July, 1874.

THEO. BURGMYER, Notary Public.

Gentlemen of the Committee:

Having laid before you the above sworn statement, which I have purposely restricted to relations of Mr. Beecher with Mrs. Tilton only, and with no other person or persons, I wish to add an explanation due to yourselves.

In the *Golden Age*, lately edited by me, a suggestion was made, not with my knowledge or consent, that your Committee, in order to be justly constituted, should comprise, in addition to the six members appointed by Mr. Beecher, six others, appointed by myself.

To no such proposal would I have consented, for I have never wanted any tribunal whatever for the investigation of this subject. Neither your Committee, as at present constituted, nor an enlarged Committee on the plan just mentioned, nor any other Committee, of any kind, could in and of itself have persuaded or compelled me to lay before you the facts contained in the preceding statement. Distinctly be it understood that these facts had not been evoked by your Committee because of any authority which I recognize in you as a tribunal of inquiry. Nor would they have been yielded up to any other Committee or Board of Reference, however constituted (except a Court of law) ; but, on the contrary, I have divulged the above statement because of the openly-published demand for it, made directly to me by the Rev. Henry Ward Beecher, aided and abetted by Mrs. Elizabeth R. Tilton. These two parties—these alone, and not your Committee—have by their action prevailed with me. No other authorities or influences (except a Court of law) could have been powerful enough to have extorted from me the above disclosure. For the sake of one of these parties, gladly would I have continued to hide these facts in the future, as I have incessantly striven to do in the past. But, by the joint action of Mr. Beecher and Mrs. Tilton, I can withhold the truth only at the price of perpetual infamy to my name, in addition to the penalty which I already suffer in the destruction of a home once as pleasant as any in which you yourselves dwell.

Respectfully, THEODORE TILTON.

The surreptitious publication of this document that Mr. T.

had assured the committee would not be published by him, naturally created indignation on the part of Mr. Tilton, and he at once took the course indicated in the following card, published in the Brooklyn *Argus* on the 22d:

It is a time for every person connected with this scandal to take the just responsibility that belongs to him—I want to take mine. And, in order that I may take it fully, I herewith print a note which I have this morning received from my friend Theodore Tilton:

WEDNESDAY, July 22.

My Dear Maverick:

From no other person save either yourself, as my copyist, or from the committee's short-hand writer, or from some member of the committee, could my sworn statement have got into print. My heart is bowed and bleeding at seeing these facts spread before the world. Tell me how could you have taken such a fearful, dreadful, horrible responsibility without consulting me in advance? There now remains no possibility of peace or silence—nothing but everlasting woe. Explain yourself—you must do it, both to me and to the public. Yours in grief,

THEODORE TILTON.

I will answer, not only to Mr. Tilton, but to the public.

I was the groomsman of Mr. Tilton at his marriage in 1855, and I have been his friend ever since. Last Saturday, feeling that I might render him some service in the preparation of his defense to the committee, I called at his home. He was wearied and worn with copying papers, saying that he must do it himself, for he could not trust the facts to an amanuensis. I then offered to copy for him, in a clear round hand, his statement, that he might get a chance to rest and sleep. In doing this work for an old friend I became so thoroughly struck with the perfection of his defense that I felt sure it would carry the public, and told him so. He then replied that he never meant the public to see it, and it was in vain that I attempted to convince him of the necessity of its publication. As one of his stanch friends, loving and knowing him to be a long-abused man, and that he still shrunk from hurting others in order to shield himself, I resolved that this defense should be published, and I published it. I did so without his knowledge or consent. And I did right—and stand by the act, as an act of justice to a man who has been wronged, and to a community that has a right to know all the facts.

AUGUSTUS MAVERICK.

BROOKLYN, July 22d, 1874.

CHAPTER XII.

ALLEGED CROSS-EXAMINATION OF MR. TILTON AND HIS DENIAL OF THE WORDS PUT INTO HIS MOUTH—HENRY WARD BEECHER'S DEFENCE—HIS RELATIONS TO MRS. TILTON WERE ONLY SUCH AS COULD BE ENTERTAINED BY A PURE MINDED WOMAN, BUT HE DID CAUSE A SOCIAL CATASTROPHE—MRS. TILTON'S SWEEPING DENIAL—HER OWN GRAPHIC STORY OF HER DOMESTIC TROUBLE, HER RELATIONS TO AND AFFECTION FOR HER PASTOR—MR. TILTON INTERVIEWED—HIS THREAT TO DRAW A TWO-EDGED SWORD, AND OFFERS TO GO INTO COURT, EITHER AS PLAINTIFF OR DEFENDANT—GENERAL BUTLER'S ADVICE, AND A SIGNIFICANT HERALD EDITORIAL—MR. JAMES M'DERMOTT DECLARES HE HOLDS DAMAGING TESTIMONY AND DOCUMENTS—EVIDENCE IN EXISTENCE THAT THE DECEASED WIFE OF HENRY C. BOWEN WAS DISHONORED.

On July 22d, Mr. Tilton was again before the committee on cross-examination by Gen. Tracy, counsel for Mr. Beecher. The Brooklyn *Eagle*, which throughout the controversy had shown a bitter partizan hostility to Mr. Tilton, and even threatened editorially that he might be driven from the city, published the following as the cross-examination :—

Mr. Tilton was quietly asked by Mr. Tracy as to his relations with a certain woman, not Mrs. Victoria Woodhull. Had he not at certain specified times and in certain alleged places been guilty of the offense with that woman, of which Mr. Tilton alleges Mr. Beecher to have been guilty with Elizabeth Tilton.

To the asking of this question Mr. Tilton manifested the greatest indignation. He did not exactly rage, but he denounced the implication in the loftiest terms. He was dramatic. He put himself upon a very high pedestal of dignity.

Mr. Tracy then asked Mr. Tilton as to his private relations with another woman, naming her.

To this Mr. Tilton replied very calmly. He was not wounded in that place.

Mr. Tracy then asked Mr. Tilton if he had ever held any improper relation or criminal intercourse with a third woman, naming that woman.

Mr. Tilton thereupon again raged and fumed, and expressed his indignation in terms of theatrical and almost tragic import.

Mr. Tracy then asked Mr. Tilton if he had not had improper relations with another woman, the sister of the last one referred to; if he did not take her with him on one certain occasion to Winsted, Conn., when he delivered a lecture there, and if he and that woman did not then and there occupy the same room with this woman. Mr. Tracy indicated also that his question was founded upon charges to that effect, made by the clerk and proprietor of the hotel in which Mr. Tilton and this woman are alleged to have stayed.

Mr. Tilton again raged with indignation. He made, as he does in answering nearly every important question put to him, a speech. He declared that if this form of warfare was to be kept up he himself would do some talking. If names were to be called in that way he would have some names to mention. The thing should not end in that way.

In fine, Mr. Tilton put himself on the record as threatening to expose other parties, who, as he insinuated, had been guilty of improper conduct at some time or other, and in some place or other.

Mr. Tracy, said: Mr. Tilton, you have charged your wife with having committed adultery with Mr. Beecher. Now, answer this question. Did you ever commit adultery?

Mr. Tilton (running his hands through his locks, straightening them out into their longest extent)—Sir! Talk to me as one gentleman talks to another. I decline to be questioned in that way.

Mr. Tracy—I ask you the question squarely. It is a question easy to be understood, and you can see that it is a question essential to this case. You have stated that you had a beautiful home until Mr. Beecher corrupted your wife. The Committee want to know what sort of a home you made for your wife; whether or not you brought other women to your house and held improper relations there with them. You see it is essential to know what sort of a peaceful and happy home you made it for her before Mr. Beecher, as you say, corrupted her and ruined that home. Now, Mr. Tilton, I put the question squarely to you, did you ever commit adultery?

Mr. Tilton (striking a Tiltonian attitude and stretching out his finger after the manner of Nathan to David)—Mr. Tracy did you ever commit adultery?

Mr. Tracy—When I shall have charged my wife with committing adultery it will be time for you to ask that question.

Mr. Tilton—Well, sir, I decline to answer that question. It is an insult to me, sir! If I have ever had any intimacy with ladies I would be a scoundrel sir to call their names!

Mr. Tracy—Well, under that head we will suppose that you have already named your wife.

Mr. Tilton again rose to an indignation pitch, and refused to answer.

Mr. Tracy—Mr. Tilton, do you know that your intimacy with public women greatly disturbed Mrs. Tilton, and made her life unhappy?

Mr. Tilton (with another attitude)—What do you mean, sir, to talk to me about public women?

A Member of the Committee—Mr. Tilton, Mr. Tracy does not mean public women in an odious sense. He means reformers.

Mr. Tilton (coming down to his usual manner again—O, yes, Elizabeth was very much annoyed that I ever should associate with such persons. She said they were not sound in theology; they were heretics and exercised bad influence on me. She talked very much about it and always opposed it. "She hated," she said, "such women as Elizabeth Cady Stanton and Mrs. Woodhull." She said "they were on the wrong side always." She feared I was going to be led astray.

In another connection Mr. Tilton said: One great grievance of my wife was that I was not a clergyman. *Thank God*, I am not a minister! I want you to put it down, Mr. Stenographer, I despise the church, I despise creeds. Not but that I am a religious man though. I *am* a religious man. I love God, but I despise the church. I saw the cowardice of the church in the great anti-slavery fight, and it has always been false. But Elizabeth has always had a reverence for the church, and she has been greatly disturbed because I could not receive the doctrine of the divinity of the Lord Jesus Christ. I could not receive it. I had to reject it, and it disturbed her very much. It is a sort of keystone to her whole faith that Christ is divine. and my refusal to believe it has been the subject of many conversations and many of her prayers. She spends whole hours on her knees in prayer. A whiter souled woman does not live to-day than Elizabeth Tilton!

In another connection Mr. Tilton admitted that "my complaining friend," to whom one of his celebrated letters which goes under that name was addressed had no existence whatever. It was, he said, a device of his to quiet down the scandal, "although Elizabeth told me at the time that it would make it all the worse."

During the examination on Tuesday Mr. Tilton stated facts which prove incontestably that he was himself the sole inspiration of the Woodhull scandal, and that he gave Mrs. Woodhull all the alleged facts on which her exposure was founded. Among other things, in answer to the question whether he had said anything to Woodhull reflecting on the integrity of Beecher before Woodhull published her scandal Tilton said: "O yes, I gave her my opinion of him very freely."

It has also come to light that Tilton did his best to induce Beecher to preside over the Woodhull woman's meeting, and used as one inducement the necessity of conciliating Mrs. Woodhull, who, he said, was in possession of damaging rumors concerning him, and would possibly use them against him. He told Beecher that he had better look out, or Woodhull would injure him.

With reference to but one action in presiding over that meeting, Tilton says that he reached the hall only ten minutes before the meeting commenced; Woodhull was indignant because there was not a man there who dared to introduce her, and Tilton said he dared do it and would do it. He said he did not know what her utterances would be, although he might have known, as the proofs of her address were in his office; he had not read them. The most extreme things she said, however, were not in her manuscript, but were what he calls "ebullitions of the moment." The following question was put to Tilton by Mr. Tracy:

Mr. Tilton, have you any evidence of Mr. Beecher's adultery except what you say your wife told you?

Tilton—*I have none whatever.*

It also appears that one of Mr. Beecher's letters, from which Mr. Tilton extracts a few lines of doubtful meaning, is *over a column long*. Tilton has twice promised to produce it, but has not yet done so. He may produce it this afternoon, when his cross-examination will be resumed. The committee want to know what is in the whole letter. It is fair to presume that Tilton has taken from it only such parts as suit his purposes.

Simultaneous with this cross-examination the denial of Mr. Beecher to the charges appeared. It reads thus:—

I do not purpose at this time a detailed examination of the remarkable statement of Theodore Tilton, made before the Committee of Investigation, and which appeared in the Brooklyn *Argus* of July 21st, 1874. I recognize the many reasons which make it of transcendent importance to myself, the Church, and the cause of public morality, that I shall give a full answer to the charges against me. But, having requested the Committee of Investigation to search this matter to the bottom, it is to them that I must look for my vindication. But I cannot delay for an hour to defend the reputation of Mrs. Elizabeth R. Tilton, upon whose name, in connection with mine, her husband has attempted to pour shame. One less deserving of such disgrace I never knew. From childhood, she has been under my eye, and, since reaching womanhood, she has had my sincere admiration and affection. I cherish for her a pure feeling, such as a gentleman might honorably offer to a Christian woman, and which she might receive and reciprocate without moral scruple. I reject with indignation every imputation which reflects upon her honor or my own. My regard for Mrs. Tilton was perfectly well known to my family. When serious difficulties sprang up in her household, it was to my wife that she resorted for counsel; and both of us, acting from sympathy, and, as it subsequently appeared, without full knowledge, gave unadvised counsel, which tended to harm. I have no doubt that Mr. Tilton found that his wife's confidence and reliance upon my judgment had greatly increased, while his influence had diminished, in consequence of a marked change in his religious and social views which were taking place during those years. Her mind was greatly exercised lest her children should be harmed by views which she deemed vitally false and dangerous. I was suddenly and rudely aroused to the reality of impending danger by the disclosure of domestic distress, of sickness perhaps unto death, of the likelihood of separation, and the scattering of a family every member of which I had tenderly loved. The effect upon me of the discovery of the state of Mr. Tilton's feelings, and the condition of his family, surpassed in sorrow and excitement anything that

I had ever experienced in my life. That my presence, influence, and counsel had brought to a beloved family sorrow and alienation, gave (in my then state of mind) a poignancy to my suffering which I hope no other man may ever feel. Even to be suspected of having offered, under the privileges of a peculiarly sacred relation, an indecorous word to a wife and mother, could not but deeply wound any one who is sensitive to the honor of womanhood. There are peculiar reasons for alarm in this case on other grounds, inasmuch as I was then subject to certain malignant rumors, and a flagrant outbreak in this family would bring upon them an added injury derived from these shameless falsehoods.

Believing at the time that my presence and counsels had tended, however unconsciously, to produce a social catastrophe, represented as imminent, I gave expression to my feelings in an interview with a mutual friend, not in cold and cautious self-defending words, but eagerly, taking blame upon myself, and pouring out my heart to my friend in the strongest language, overburdened with the exaggerations of impassioned sorrow. Had I been the evil man Mr. Tilton now represents, I should have been calmer and more prudent. It was my horror of the evil imputed that filled me with morbid intensity at the very shadow of it. Not only was my friend affected generously, but he assured me that such expressions, if conveyed to Mr. Tilton, would soothe wounded feelings, allay anger, and heal the whole trouble. He took down sentences and fragments of what I had been saying, to use them as a mediator. A full statement of the circumstances under which this memorandum was made, I shall give to the Investigating Committee. That these apologies were more than ample to meet the facts of the case, is evident, in that they were accepted, that our intercourse resumed its friendliness, that Mr. Tilton subsequently ratified it in writing, and that he has continued for four years, and until within two weeks, to live with his wife. Is it conceivable, if the original charge had been what it is now alleged, that he would have condoned the offence, not only with the mother of his children, but with him whom he believed to have wronged them? The absurdity as well as falsity of this story is apparent, when it is considered that Mr. Tilton now alleges that he carried this guilty secret of his wife's infidelity for six months locked up in his own breast, and that then he divulged it to me, only that there might be a reconciliation with me! Mr. Tilton has since, in every form of language, and to a multitude of witnesses, orally, in written statements, and in printed documents, declared his faith in his wife's purity. After the reconciliation of Mr. Tilton with me, every consideration of propriety and honor demanded that the family trouble should be kept in that seclusion which domestic affairs have a right to claim as a sanctuary; and to that seclusion it was determined that it should be confined.

Every line and word of my private and confidential letters which have been published is in harmony with the statements which I now make. My published correspondence on this subject comprises but two elements—the expression of my grief, and that of my desire to shield the honor of a pure and innocent woman. I do not propose to analyze and contest at this time the extraordinary paper of Mr. Tilton ; but there are two allegations which I cannot permit to pass without special notice. They refer to the only two incidents which Mr. Tilton pretends to have witnessed personally—the one an alleged scene in my house while looking over engravings, and the other a chamber scene in his own house. His statements concerning these are absolutely false. Nothing of the kind ever occurred, nor any semblance of any such thing. They are now brought to my notice for the first time.

To every statement which connects me dishonorably with Mrs. Elizabeth R. Tilton, or which in any wise would impugn the honor and purity of this beloved Christian woman, I give the most explicit, comprehensive, and solemn denial.

HENRY WARD BEECHER.

BROOKLYN July 22d, 1874.

This was supplemented upon the following day by the emphatic denial of the charges by Mrs. Tilton in these words addressed to the public: —

To pick up anew the sorrows of the last ten years, the stings and pains I had daily schooled myself to bury and forgive, makes this imperative duty, as called forth by the malicious statement of my husband, the saddest act of my life. Beside, my thought of following the Master contradicts this act of my pen, and a sense of the perversion of my life-faith almost compels me now to stand aside, till God, Himself, delivers.

Yet I see in this wanton act an urgent call and privilege from which I shrink not. To reply in detail to the twenty-two articles of arraignment, I shall not attempt at present.

Yet if called upon to testify to each and all of them, I shall not hesitate to do so. Suffice it for my purpose now that I reply to one or more of the most glowing charges.

Touching the feigned sorrow of my husband's compulsory revelations, I solemnly avow that long before the Woodhull publication, I knew him, by insinuation and direct statement, to have repeated to my very near relative and friend the substance of these accusations which shock the moral sense of the entire community this day. Many times, when hearing that certain persons had spoken ill of him, he has sent me to chide them for so doing; and then and there I learned he had been before me with his calumnies against myself, so that I was speechless.

The reiteration in his statement that he had "persistently striven to hide" these so-called facts, is utterly false, as his hatred to Mr. Beecher has existed these many years, and the determination to ruin Mr. Beecher has been the one aim of his life.

Again, the perfidy with which the holiest love a wife ever offered has been recklessly discovered in this publication, reaches well nigh to sacrilege; and, added to this, the endeavor, like the early scandal of Mrs. Woodhull, to make my own words condemn me, has no parallel.

Most conspicuously, my letter quoting the reading of "Griffith Gaunt." Had Mr. Tilton read the pure character of Catherine, he would have seen that I lifted myself beside it—as near as any human may affect an ideal. But it was her character, and not the incidents of fiction surrounding it, to which I referred. Hers was no sin of criminal act or thought.

A like "confession" with hers, I had made to Mr. Tilton in telling of my love to my friend and pastor, one year before. And I now add that, notwithstanding all misrepresentations and anguish of soul, I owe to my acquaintance and friendship with Mr. Beecher, as to no other human instrumentality, that encouragement in my mental life, and that growth toward the Divine nature which enables me to walk daily in a lively hope of the life beyond.

The shameless charges in articles seven, eight and nine are fearfully false in each and every particular.

The letter referred to in Mr. Tilton's tenth paragraph was obtained from me by importunity, and by representations that it was necessary for him to use in his then pending difficulties with Mr. Bowen. I was then sick, nigh unto death, having suffered a miscarriage only four days before. I signed whatever he required, without knowing or understanding its import. The paper I have never seen, and do not know what statements it contained.

In charge eighteen, a letter of mine, addressed to Mr. Francis Moulton, quoted to prove that I never desired a separation or was advised by Mr. or Mrs. Beecher to leave my husband, I reply, the letter was of Mr. Tilton's own concocting, which he induced me to copy and sign as my own—an act which, in my weakness and mistaken thought to help him, I have done too often during these unhappy years.

The implication that the harmony of the home was unbroken till Mr. Beecher entered it as a frequent guest and friend, is a lamentable satire upon the household where he himself, years before, laid the corner-stone of Free Love, and desecrated its altars up to the time of my departure; so that the atmosphere was not only godless, but impure for my children. And in this effort and throe of agony, I would fain lift my daughters, and all womanhood from the insidious and diabolical teachings of these latter days.

His frequent efforts to prove me insane, weak minded, insignificant, of mean presence, all rank in the category of heartlessness, selfishness and falsehood, having its climax in his present endeavor to convince the world that I am or ever have been unable to distinguish between an innocent or a guilty love.

In summing up the whole matter, I affirm myself before God to be innocent of the crimes laid upon me; that never have I been guilty of adultery with Henry Ward Beecher in thought or deed; nor has he ever offered to me an indecorous or improper proposal.

To the further charge that I was led away from my home by Mr. Beecher's friends, and by the advice of a lawyer whom Mr. Beecher had sent to me, and who, in advance of my appearing before the Committee, arranged with me the questions and answers which are to constitute my testimony in Mr. Beecher's behalf, I answer, that this is again untrue, having never seen the lawyer until introduced to him a few moments before the arrival of the Committee, by my step-father, Judge Morse; and in further reply I submit the following statement of my action before the Committee, and the separation from my husband.

The publication of Mr. Tilton's letter in answer to Dr. Bacon, I had not known or suspected, when on Wednesday evening he brought home the *Golden Age*, handing it to me to read. Looking down its columns I saw, well nigh with blinding eyes, that he had put into execution the almost daily threat of his life—"that *he* lived to crush out Mr. Beecher; that the God of battles was in *him;* he had always been Mr. Beecher's superior, and all that lay in his path, wife, children or reputation, if need be, should fall before this purpose."

I did not read it. I saw enough without reading. My spirit rose within me as never before.

"Theodore," I said, "tell me what means this quotation from Mr. Beecher? Two years ago you came to me at midnight saying: 'Elizabeth, *all* letters and papers concerning my difficulties with Mr. Beecher and Mr. Bowen are burned, destroyed; now don't *you* betray me, for I have nothing to defend myself with.'"

"Did you believe that?" said he.

"I certainly did, implicitly," I said.

"Well, let me tell you—they all *live;* not one is destroyed."

If this was said to intimidate me, it had quite the contrary effect. I had never been so fearless, nor seen so clearly before with whom I was dealing.

Coming to me a little later, he said: "I want you to read it; you will find it a vindication of *yourself*. You have not stood before the community for five years as you now do.

Roused still further by the wickedness hid behind so false a mask, I replied, "Theodore, understand me, this is the last time you call me publicly to walk through this filth. My character needs no vindication at this late hour from *you*. There was a time, had you spoken out clearly, truthfully and manfully for me, I had been grateful but now I shall speak and act for myself. Know also, that if in the future I see a scrap of paper referring to any human being, however remote, which it seems to me you might use or pervert for your own ends, I will destroy it."

"This means battle on your part, then," said he.

"Just so far," I replied.

I write this because these words of mine he has since used to my harm.

The next morning I went to my brother, and told him that now *I* had decided to act in this matter; that I had been treated by my husband as a nonentity from the beginning, a play thing, to be used or let alone at will; that it had always seemed to me I was a party not a little concerned. I then showed him a card I had made for publication.

He respected the motive, but still advised silence on my part. I yielded to him thus far, as to appearing in the public prints; but counseling with myself *and no other*, it occured to me that among the brethren of my own communion, I might be heard.

Not knowing of any church committee, I asked the privilege of such an interview in the parlors of those who had always been our mutual friends. Mr. and Mrs. Ovington then learned, for the first time, that the Committee would meet that night and advised me to see *those* gentlemen, as perhaps the goodliest persons I could select. This I accordingly did.

There, *alone*, I pleaded the cause of my husband and my children, the result being that their hearts were moved in sympathy for my family—a feeling their pastor had shared for years, and for which he was now suffering.

On going home, I found my husband reading in bed. I told him where I had been, and that I did not conceal anything from him, as his habit was from me. He asked who the gentlemen were; said no more; rose, dressed himself and bade me good-bye forever.

The midnight following I was awakened by my husband standing by my bed. In a very tender, kind voice he said he wished to see me. I rose instantly, followed him into his room, and sitting on the bed side, he drew me into his lap, said "he was proud of me, loved me; that nothing ever gave him such real peace and satisfaction as to hear me well spoken of; that, meeting a member of the Committee, he had learned that he had been mistaken as to my motive in seeing the Committee, and had hastened to assure me that he had been thoroughly wretched since his rash treatment of me the night before," etc.

Then and there we covenanted sacredly our hearts and lives —I most utterly; renewing my trust in the one human heart I loved.

The next day, how happy we were! Theodore wrote a statement, to present to the Committee when they should call upon him, to all of which I heartily acceded. This document, God knows, was a true history of this affair, completely vindicating my honor and the honor of my pastor. In the afternoon he left me to show it to his friends.

He returned home early in the evening, passing the happiest

hours I had known for years; renewedly assuring me that there was no rest for him, away from me. So in grateful love to the dear Father, I slept. Oh, that the end had then come! I would not then have received the cruel blow "which made a woman mad outright."

The next morning he called upon our friends, Mr. and Mrs. Ovington, and there, with a shocking bravado, began a wicked tirade, adding with oath and violence the shameless slanders against Mr. Beecher, of which I now believe him to be the author.

This fearful scene I learned next day. In the afternoon, he showed me his invitation from the Committee to meet them that evening. I did not then show my hurt—but carried it heavily within, but calmly without, all night, till early morning.

Reflection upon this scene at Mr. Ovington's convinced me, that, notwithstanding my husband's recent professions to me, his former spirit was unchanged; that his declarations of repentance and affection were only for the purpose of gaining my assistance to accomplish his ends in his warfare upon Mr. Beecher. In the light of these conclusions, my duty appeared plain.

I rose quietly, and having dressed, roused him only to say "Theodore, I will never take another step by your side. The end has indeed come!"

He followed me to Mrs. Ovington's to breakfast, saying I was unduly excited, and that he had been misrepresented perhaps—but leaving me determined as before.

How to account for the change which twenty-four hours have been capable of working in his mind, then many years past, I leave for the eternities with their mysteries to reveal. That he is an unreliable and unsafe guide whose idea of truth-loving is self-loving, it is my misfortune in this late, sad hour to discover.

ELIZABETH R. TILTON.

JULY 23d, 1874.

The emphatic denials of both the principal actors in the alleged crime, gave the friends of Mr. Beecher a ray of hope, and the press, which had with one or two exceptions, treated the subject with generous fairness, rejoiced that he had at last spoken in defence of a woman who many considered, had been brutally maligned by one who had occupied her heart and love before her fatal visit to the Committee. Yet this was not considered sufficient. People said, it is merely the denial of persons accused, is not sworn to as are the charges. Mr. Beecher is chivalrous in thus coming to the rescue of a helpless woman, but these denials are not answers. The public in the meantime had not heard from Mr. Tilton ; but the alleged cross-examination as given above, and the manifestoes of his wife and Mr. Beecher forced him to speak in a semi-official manner through the *Argus*, which thus reports him:—

A gentleman called on Mr. Tilton on Friday, July 24th, at his residence in Livingston Street, and asked him if his examination before the Committee had been concluded. Mr. Tilton replied that he did not know. He had promised to go before the Committee as often as they sent for him. He added:—Mr. Tracy and Mr. Hill are directly responsible for the misrepresentations of my examination before the Committee. Please do not understand that I object, at this juncture, to be misrepresented either by the press or by Mr. Beecher's counsel. The more I am misrepresented, the more right I have to defend myself. Mr. Tracy and Mr. Hill, the counsel for Mr. Beecher, already have as little influence with the Committee as they have with the public. I have just ground of accusation against Mr. Tracy, and have been advised by far more eminent counsel than himself, that his course would not be sustained if submitted to the Bar. I do not wish to press it, because the Committee themselves—or, at least, a few of them—are men of too much dignity of character and moral integrity to be tossed up and down like a ball on a fountain by the gushing leakages of Mr. Tracy and Mr. Hill. The substance of the examination up to the present time, so far as I am concerned, is briefly this:—General Tracy asked me if I committed adultery. I asked General Tracy if he committed adultery. But neither General Tracy, nor Mr. Hill, nor anybody in the Committee, has yet asked me whether Mr. Beecher committed adultery. * * * * * *

"You think then that they have made blunders"

Mr. Tilton—"Yes; and they have made one hideous blunder?"

"What is it?"

Mr. Tilton—"They have diverted their examination from

the facts at issue, into an inquiry into the names and characters of my female acquaintance—particularly those who, as writers or speakers on various reforms, have attained eminence in public life. The animus of this inquiry was obvious; its design was to associate me with the extreme and radical sentiment against which the conservative class in the community are arrayed in large majority. I, myself, did not object to this inquiry, though I, myself, would not have begun any such line of policy in this case. General Tracy's supreme blunder has been, that in instituting an inquiry into the standing of the ladies of my acquaintance, he gives me the right to institute, a counter inquiry into the standing of the ladies of Mr. Beecher's acquaintance.

I informed the Committee yesterday that I deprecated such a plan of battle, but that if it was forced upon me by the Committee's counsels I could draw a sword with two edges to their one. If this new aspect which General Tracy flings upon the case like a shadow, is to characterize the remainder of the controversy, it will be the better for General Tracy's chief client that he had never been born.

Reporter—I perceive that Mr. Tracy questioned you concerning your acquaintance with Mrs. Woodhull?

Mr. Tilton—Yes; but Mr. Tracy was careful not to elicit the fact that Mr. Beecher's apology addressed to me through Mr. Moulton was written half a year before I ever saw the face of Mrs. Woodhull. He was careful also not to elicit the fact that Mr. Beecher himself had private interviews with Mrs. Woodhull, and that lady had taken far more pains to associate herself with him and he with her than ever I had done. * *

I wish you would do me the favor to say through the columns of the *Argus*, that though I have hitherto declined being interviewed concerning my appearance before the Committee, and have steadfastly remained silent concerning the proceedings in the Committee, yet the above report, coming as it does from the Committee's counsel, is an absolute fabrication. I told the Committee distinctly that Mr. Beecher had confessed his adultery to me; that he had confessed it to Mr. Moulton; that he had confessed it to other persons whom I named, and, furthermore, I give the names of several persons who for the last four years have been perfectly well aware that Mr. Moulton's entire connection with this case from beginning to end, has been based on the one and only corner-stone of Mr. Beecher's criminality. I ask that all these persons be produced before the committee. I ask, futhermore, for the privilege of being present to cross-examine Mr. Beecher and the other witnesses. I still further suggested that the case had come to be of such magnitude that it would be better for the Committee to dismiss this informal examination in which no one but myself has thus far spoken under oath, and adjourn to meet in Court. I expressed a willingness to be sued for libel, or to be put in any other way before a tribunal which could compel witnesses to testify under oath, and which could punish perjury with the State Prison. If this case, with all the facts which lie behind it, revealed and unrevealed, were now before a Criminal Court instead of a voluntary committee, and if Mr. Beecher's printed statement had been made under oath, subject to cross-questioning and overthrow, he would indeed be compelled to "step down and out." I feel at liberty to speak freely, because Mr. Beecher's counsel have falsified me to the world, and I have no recourse but to smite them in the face.

[It is proper for a due understanding of the above expressed willingness of Mr. Tilton to go into court either as a defendant or complainant, that we should say that for several days previous to this publication, General Benjamin F. Butler had been in the city as the legal adviser of Mr. Tilton, and had recommended such a course as the most effective way of settling the matter by fixing the guilt upon the accused, or vindicating him from the astounding charges made by Mr. Tilton. On the following day a significant editorial suggesting this course appeared in the *World*.] We make some extracts:—

"The time has passed for concealment, subterfuge or explation—nay even for secret investigations by irresponsible church committees. Ever since the publication of the letter of Mr. Tilton to Dr. Bacon, compromise or peace has been impossible. Mr. Beecher could never rest under that letter. That was the real challenge to war—a challenge that came from Mr. Tilton, who, by the way, has acted in this matter with a coolness, a force and a pitiless energy that render the stories of his 'insanity' the extreme of absurdity. His war upon Mr. Beecher may be regarded as a species of vivisection, and in the interest of humanity it should cease. The torture which Mr. Tilton has inflicted upon his enemy, so strongly shown in the letters of the unfortunate clergyman, should come to an end. Better that Henry Ward Beecher should be with the dead, and find that peace which his soul craved in his touching letters, than that he should live under the misery which Mr. Tilton has never ceased to force upon him since the 1st of January, 1871 Whatever the end is, let us have the end, more particularly as Mr. Tilton in a remarkable interview, reprinted elsewhere from the Brooklyn *Argus*, intimates that he 'could draw a sword with two edges.' In other words as he further shows, he will, if provoked, rake up the scandals that have been floating about Brooklyn, and introduce the names of ladies not yet named in the case, ladies who now hold good positions in society, as the alleged victims of sin and shame.

"Upon this there is one plain word to be said. Mr. Tilton has told us that this was to be a day of battle and of death. He may make war upon his own family, upon Mr. Beecher and his family, and, whatever we may say, there is probably no method of interference. But if this controversy is to be made the means of carrying misery into other families; if Mr. Tilton is to brandish his 'two-edged sword' over the households of those who have not wronged him, who are not in this controversy, he enters upon a course so extraordinary that he becomes an outlaw and the common enemy of society—a course that can no more be permitted than we would permit a band of Sioux with their scalping knives to range around Brooklyn. Much is due to vindication and the assurance of one's good name, and much may be pardoned to a man in anger, in the heat of strife and at bay before his enemy. But society also has claims, and the time has come when it must be protected against the extraordinary course which Mr. Tilton assures us he stands ready to pursue."

The week of anxiety, alarm and grief at the danger that environed America's favorite minister ended on July 25th, and it was believed that the worst had been elicited—that after the week of storm a quiet rest would settle over the central figures in the unfortunate disputes, and that the Sabbath quietude would place all in a more forgiving frame of mind. Not so, however. The Brooklyn Sunday papers appeared and they were very hostile to Mr. Beecher—the Sunday *Sun* reviewing the case and charging that Mr. Beecher was convicted of all charged by his own letters, and those of Mrs. Tilton. But the worst blow was reserved for infliction by the Sunday *Review*, and this stab came in the form of an interview with Mr. James McDermott, a journalist, who had been on confidential relations with the Free Love sisters and learned many of their secrets. We would fain pass it over in silence, but feel that our duty to give all the material evidence on both sides demands its repetition here:—

Reporter—Mr. James McDermott, I presume?

Mr. McDermott—You needn't presume anything about it. Be sure you are right, and I think you are this time.

Reporter—I am sent to see you, sir, by the Editor of the Sunday *Review*, respecting what you know of the Tilton scandal.

Mr. McD.—Tilton be d—— scandal; call it by its proper name—the Beecher scandal. If the *Review* editor sent you to talk to me about this subject, he had little respect for this weather or my capacity to endure it.

Reporter—Commence where you like.

Mr. McD.—Well, you want a sensation and I'll give you one or two. You are right in suggesting that I was one of the parties who accompanied Mr. Bowen and Mr. H. B. Claflin to the residence of Mrs. Woodhull on the afternoon of Mr. Tappen's funeral. He was, I believe, Mr. Bowen's father-in-law. But what of it?

Reporter—Oh, I merely wanted to know if you went there in the capacity of a journalist, or as a friend of Mr. Bowen's?

Mr. McD.—I confess I went there in a double capacity. I was there anyhow, all the time. Mr. Henry C. Bowen, Mr. H. B. Claflin, Mr. Bowen's nephew and son, Judge Ryer, Counselor Wood, and other gentlemen of this city were there with me. We went there for the purpose of hearing what Mrs. Woodhull and her counsel had to say, and to see what we might or could.

Reporter—What, if anything, outside of your personal relationship with Mr. Bowen, prompted you to accompany these gentlemen on that occasion?

Mr. McD.—I'll be frank with you, sir. I cultivated Mrs. Woodhull's acquaintance through a business accident. Through her I became acquainted with her family. Victoria is a woman of advanced character. I never knew her to do an injury to any one, and in this reprehensible Beecher scandal I think she is the one, above all others, who has told the most truth. She certainly never lied to me, and I'll prove it to you, sir.

Reporter—Can you do it by documentary evidence?

Mr. McD.—I can. Why here, my dear sir, is the original of the letter which made me know both Beecher and Tilton first. You see it's in Tilton's own handwriting, and does away effectually with Beecher's theory that he only knew Mrs. Woodhull through her asking him to preside at one of her meetings. Beecher falsifies, and here's the proof of it—a proof that has been in my possession for nearly two years—and this document I showed to Deacon West, of Plymouth Church, when he called upon me in relation to this matter.

Mr. McDermott then showed the reporter a letter, of which the following is a copy:—

"GOLDEN AGE.

MY DEAR VICTORIA:—I have arranged with Frank that you shall see Mr. Beecher at my house on Friday night. He will attend a meeting at the church till ten o'clock, and will give you the rest of the evening as late as you desire. You may consider this fixed. Meanwhile, on this sunshiny day, I salute you with a good morning—peace be with you.

Yours,

THEODORE TILTON.

Reporter—That letter is evidently genuine but what does it prove?

Mr. McD.—It proves Mr. Beecher a falsifier, though the letter is not dated, it is in my possession over two years—prior to the time I published the tripartite statement so often alluded to. Why, my friend, I have in my possession over one hundred letters of Mr. Tilton's, and three or four of Mr. Beecher's in connection with this matter. I have a good many of them yet; but sit down till I shock you:

In company with Mr. Bowen's son—his youngest by his first wife, I believe—and a nephew. I visited what we then considered the bed-side of a dying woman. We were accompanied by Mr. Tusch, now a reporter on the *Eagle*, who made stenographic notes of all that was said on the occasion of what I style the death-bed confession.

The record is now or was in Mr. Bowen's house. That record pronounces the dishonor of the dead Mrs. * * * * * by Mr. Beecher, and in a manner that I would blush to repeat. It implicated also the wife of a physician, and other ladies on the Heights whose names I do not feel at liberty just now to mention, but I will if I am forced to it. I admire Mrs. Beecher's course in this matter, she is a noble woman and a true wife, and

Mrs. Tilton would do well to follow her example rather than her advice. I claim to know why Mrs. Beecher was sent to Italy by her husband, and now conscientiously believe that the only way for Mr. Beecher to get out of this matter is to make a frank and open confession. The public are generous and willing to forgive him as a man; but he must retire from the ministry.

Reporter—Did Mrs. Woodhull show you the letters of Mr. Beecher?

Mr. McD.—She did, and in the presence of Mr. Horace B. Claflin and Henry C. Bowen; I know the letters to be genuine, and, as Mrs. Woodhull afterwards said to me on the steamer going to Long Branch, she would not give them up nor disclose their contents because she felt that she was being prosecuted in the Courts by Plymouth Church, or rather by individuals acting for it by proxy.

Reporter.—Could you be mistaken respecting the identity of the letters of Mr. Beecher or Mr. Tilton?

Mr. McD.—I might, but I was convinced of their genuineness by Mr. Claflin, a most upright and responsible gentleman and citizen.

RESIDENCE OF THEODORE TILTON.

CHAPTER XIII.

THEODORE ON THE RACK OF CROSS-EXAMINATION—HE ADHERES TO HIS STORIES OF "CRIMINAL COMMERCE" AND DESCRIBES "THE ANKLE SCENE," THE "BEDROOM MEETING," ETC.—A PECULIARLY BAD MEMORY—HE GIVES MR. BEECHER THE BENEFIT OF A DOUBT—"MUTUAL FRIEND MOULTON" AND A HISTORY OF ELIZABETH'S CONFESSION—DRAMATIC DENIALS, FIERCE THREATS AND DEFIANCES.

On Sunday evening, July 27th, the grand committee of Inquisition, through their chairman, supplied the press of New York with the stenographer's report of the testimony on cross-examination. It is here given in full, including Mr. Sage's letter transmitting it:—

General Tracy—Are you able to give the date of the transaction which you say you witnessed at Mr. Beecher's house at the time of the examination of the engraving? A. I cannot state the date.

Q. At the time you received the information you speak of from your wife, you were the editor of the *Independent* and of the Brooklyn *Union*, I believe? A. I was.

Q. Did your wife continue to attend Plymouth Church after that information? A. Yes, sir; that was in the summer time; she went into the country and was absent a long time; she has always continued to attend once or twice a year; she is a member of Plymouth Church.

Q. Did she attend regularly after returning from the country? A. No, sir; she attended occasionally for Communion service, and would steal in quietly at the corner of the building so as to be unobserved.

Q. Previous to announcing your discovery or pretended discovery to Mr. Beecher, you had fallen into trouble with Henry C. Bowen, had you not? A. Yes, sir.

Q. How long before? A. Two days.

Q. You had ceased to be the editor of the *Independent* when you made this announcement? A. No, sir. I ceased to be the editor of the *Independent* on the 1st day of January.

Q. Was not your valedictory published on the 22d of December? A. Yes, sir, but my engagement ended on the 31st.

Q. Had you not entered into a contract with Mr. Bowen to be the editor of the *Union* and contributor to the *Independent* before you made any announcement to Mr. Beecher of this pretended discovery, and had not Mr. Bowen discovered immoralities on your part, and did he not threaten to break the engagement? A. No, he did not.

Q. Did he not make such allegations against you, and did not you and he appoint a day of meeting at his house, when, in the presence of a mutual friend, the allegations against you should be stated, and you should make an explanation, and did not you meet in the presence of a mutual friend for that purpose? A. No, sir; Mr. Johnson wished me, about Christmas time, to see Mr. Bowen; he said there was some story afloat concerning me; I think Christmas was Sunday and I went to see him on Monday; we had a few words concerning the matter; he did not tell me what the story was; I said, "If there is any story afloat bring the author of it here and let us see what it is;" we then went on in a conversation concerning Mr. Beecher."

Q. Did not you and Mr. Bowen meet on that day, and did not Mr. Bowen begin to repeat the charges against you, and did not you, while listening to those charges, break out against the Rev. Henry Ward Beecher? A. I did not; I never heard of those charges until after that interview, when Mr. Bowen went from it to bear the letter to Mr. Beecher; I never knew that Mr. Beecher or Mrs. Beecher had anything to do with Mr. Bowen's feelings.

Q. Did not you make an allegation against Mr. Beecher? A. No, sir; after Mr. Johnson went out he made an allegation.

Q. Did not you make an allegation? A. I did toward the end of the interview.

Q. You made a very distinct allegation to Mr. Bowen, did you not, against Mr. Beecher, of the offense that he had committed against you? A. Yes.

Q. It was on that occasion, was it not, that the letter was agreed upon between you and Mr. Bowen demanding that Mr. Beecher should quit Plymouth pulpit? A. I remember a letter.

Q. Was it on that occasion that the letter was agreed upon between you and Mr. Bowen? A. Yes, it was.

Q. And was that agreement the result of his statement of the offenses against Mr. Beecher which he and you knew of? A. On the part of Mr. Bowen, yes.

Q. On your part? A. I made one statement and he made many.

Q. Will you state what offense you stated against Mr. Beecher to Mr. Bowen on that occasion? A. Mr. Johnson having introduced the subject, Mr. Bowen said to me, "Mr. Tilton, you do not say as much of Plymouth Church as a Brooklyn paper should; you do not go there; why do you not go?"

Q. I asked you what offense you stated against Mr. Beecher to Mr. Bowen? A. I must answer your question in my own way. I came to tell you the truth and not fragments of the truth. Mr. Bowen wanted me to speak more in the paper of Plymouth Church. Mr. Johnson said, "Perhaps Mr. Tilton has a reason for not going to Plymouth Church." And thereupon Mr. Bowen was curious to know the reason. I, in a solitary phrase, said that there was a personal, domestic reason why I could not go there consistently with my self-respect—that Mr. Beecher had been unhandsome in his approaches to my wife. That is the sum and substance of all I have ever said on this subject to the very few people to whom I have spoken of it.

Q. It was on that occasion that you agreed upon the letter which demanded Mr. Beecher to leave the pulpit? A. Yes, sir, that was the precise occasion.

Q. You think that was on the 26th of December? A. I have no recollection of dates; the only identification that I have in my mind is that it was near Christmas.

Q. When were you dismissed from the *Union?* A. The last night of the year, I think.

Q. The 31st, was it? A. Yes, sir.

Q. When did you first learn that Mr. or Mrs. Beecher had in any way communicated facts to Mr. Bowen which inflamed him in the matter of your dismissal? A. I learned that from Mr. Beecher himself on the day after his apology was written; it was the 2d, possibly the 3d, of January; it was in Mr. Moulton's front room; Mr. Beecher came in, it was an unexpected meeting; he burst out in an expression of great sorrow to me, and said he hoped the communication which he had sent to me by Mr. Moulton was satisfactory to me; he then and there told Mr. Moulton he had done wrong, not so much as some others had (referring to his wife, who had made statements to Mr. Bowen that ought to be unmade), and he there volunteered to write a letter to Mr. Bowen concerning the facts which he had misstated.

Q. Do you say that was the first time that you knew that Mr. Beecher or Mrs. Beecher had given Mr. Bowen any information or had any conversation with him on the subject? A. Yes, sir; I did not know that Mr. Beecher had given Mr. Bowen any such information; Mrs. Tilton had intimated to me that there was something.

Q. When did Mrs. Tilton intimate that to you? A. In December she told me of visits which Mrs. Beecher had made to her and of testimony which they wanted to get.

Q. What time in December? A. I do not know.

Q. Was it before or after the publication of your valedictory in the *Independent?* A. I do not remember; Mrs. Tilton spoke to me a number of times of the enmity which Mrs. Beecher had for some strange reason connected with Mrs. Morse (Mrs. Tilton's mother); there was a conspiracy between Mrs. Morse and Mrs. Beecher before September; the truth is that Mrs. Tilton's confession was made also to her mother, and the mother naturally wanted to protect the daughter, and she made a kind of alliance with Mr. Beecher, and Mrs. Beecher took part in it; there was a desire on their part to protect Elizabeth.

Q. You say that Mrs. Tilton referred some time in December to the fact that Mrs. Beecher had interfered in your matters? A. Not that she had interfered in my matters, but that Mrs. Morse and Mrs. Beecher were colleaguing together with reference to me.

Q. Are you able to fix that date? A. It was many times.

Q. Was any of it before the 22d of December, think you? A. Yes, I think early in the summer, but do not know.

Q. Any time in December was Mrs. Tilton separated from you with her family? A. Not that I remember; Mrs. Tilton went a few weeks to make a visit at her mother's.

Q. Do you remember the occasion of sending for your wife to come to the *Union* office while she was separated from you? A. Yes, she was at her mother's.

Q. Do you remember telling her that you were about to be dismissed from the *Union* and that she must return to you and live with you to prevent it? Did you tell her anything of that? A. Not a shadow; It would have made no difference one way or the other.

Q. Did you on that day send a letter by a servant by the name of Ellen, directing the person in whose house she was to return your children to your house in her absence? A. I do not recollect it; Mrs. Morse had the children, and I told Ellen Dennis to bring them; I do not remember the time.

Q. Did you send a note by her? A. I sent quite a peremptory message.

Q. And the children came? A. Yes, or were brought; I think there was only one.

Q. Did your wife come late in the evening after that? A. I do not remember; I think I went personally for Elizabeth, and told her she was doing wrong in staying away; I have no distinct recollection of so many details.

Q. How long after that return was it that this statement, which you say she made, and which was placed in Mr. Moulton's hands, was written? A. I do not know; I have no means of knowing; the date of her giving the letter for the interview with Mr. Beecher I think was on the 29th of December.

Q. The object of giving the letters was to bring about an interview between you and Mr. Beecher that there might be a reconciliation, and that Mr. Beecher might aid in saving you from dismissal from the *Independent?* A. No. Mrs. Tilton thought that my retirement from the papers was due in some way to Mr. and Mrs. Beecher, and she thought as I was very indignant against Mr. Bowen, unless there was some reconciliation between Mr. Beecher and myself, her secret would be exposed, and she begged me to have an interview with him, and wrote a note to that effect.

Q. Have you that note? A. I decline to answer.

Q. Will you produce it? A. I decline to answer. I decline to answer because you know the fact already.

Q. You say that note was written on the 29th day of December? A. I think there is a record on the subject here (in the statement which he had read) somewhere.

By Mr. Hill—Can you refer to a note written by you to Ellen? Do you think that had a date attached which would fix the time? A. I do not know; I remember Ellen to have had something to do with the return of one of the children; I think that note was written to Mrs. Morse.

Q. Was not the subject of the interview between you and Mr. Beecher for the purpose of inducing him to aid in preventing your dismissal? A. No more than it had with this investigation; the sole purpose of that interview was this. Mrs.

Tilton felt that Mr. Beecher and I were in danger of coming into collision: for her sake, at her request, I had this interview; it was solely in reference to Mrs. Tilton.

Q. It was two days before your final dismissal, and pending the question whether you should be retained or not? A. My dismissal from the *Union* came after that interview; it took effect the last night of the year; my interview with Mr. Beecher had nothing to do with that.

By General Tracy—It was two days before it, and pending the question of whether you would be dismissed or retained, was it not? A. No, sir; these documents themselves, I think, show that my interview with Mr. Beecher was after my dismissal from the *Union.*

Q. That interview was on the 29th, and your dismissal was on the 31st. Then that interview was before your dismissal, and pending the question whether you would be retained or dismissed, was it not? A. The question of my dismissal, was decided in the flash of an eye; I never knew that there was any such question; I, two or three days previous to the interview with Mr. Beecher, had filled up contracts, one to be editor of the *Union* for five years and the other to be chief contributor of the *Independent,* and there was no pending question.

Q. Was not your contract to be editor of the *Union* for five years, and to be chief contributor of the *Independent,* signed previous to the publication of your valedictory in the *Independent?* A. They were signed very near that time.

Q. Was not the interview at which Mr. Johnson was present at Mr. Bowen's house on the 26th of December? A. Yes, sir.

Q. The interview with Mr. Beecher was on the 29th? A. I cannot say precisely.

Q. Your final dismissal from the *Union* was on the 31st? A. I cannot say yes, unless the letters will show.

Q. Will you tell us why it was that having been possessed of this information for six months without any desire to communicate it to Mr. Beecher, you were seized with a desire to communicate that information to him on or about the 29th of December? A. Yes, sir; because Mrs. Tilton feared that Mr. Beecher, Mr. Bowen and I were in danger of such a clash and collision that the family secret would be exposed, and felt that there was a necessity for a reconciliation, and she begged and prayed me to be reconciled with Mr. Beecher; and on her account and for her sake I said I would have an interview with him.

Q. Will you explain why the difficulty you had with Mr. Bowen in regard to the *Independent* and the *Union* would involve the necessity of your exposing the family secret which you obtained from Mrs. Tilton six months before? A. It was not through fear of my exposing it; Mrs. Morse and Mrs. Beecher were sometimes in collision, and Mrs. Tilton always made me believe that Mr. Beecher knew this secret, until in December, when she told me. I took it for granted, all summer long, that she had told him what she had told me, and what she had told her mother, and I suppose that Mrs. Beecher was co-operating with Mrs. Morse.

Q. Did you complain of Mr. Beecher for not aiding you to remain in the *Independent?* A. No, sir; I would have scorned it.

Q. You have read Mr. Wilkeson's statement? A. I have not.

Q. You know Samuel Wilkeson? A. Yes.

Q. Did you say to him about that time that Mr. Beecher had not befriended you in that matter? A. I did not, and Mr. Wilkeson will not dare to say that under oath.

Q. You say you never complained of Mr. Beecher for not helping you? A. No, not for not helping me, but for being unjust to me and saying that I ought to be turned out; I understood that he said to Dr. Spear that they were going to have Mr. Tilton out of the *Independent;* Mr. Charles Briggs told me that; he said, "I know something about this; I heard some such thing."

Q. You say that Mr. Beecher apologized and that you accepted the apology? A. I read the account of that in the document.

Q. Did you, or did you not, as a matter of fact, accept the apology which Mr. Beecher made, and forgive the offence? A. I accepted the apology and forgave the offence with as much largeness as I thought it was possible for a Christian man to assume.

Q. Friendly relations continued after that between you and Mr. Beecher? A. Well, not friendly; you can understand what such relations would be; they were not hostile; they were relations which Mr. Moulton forced with an iron hand; he compelled them.

Q. Did you or not, after or about the time of the tripartite agreement, express friendly sentiments in regard to him? A. I have taken pains to make it appear in all quarters that Mr. Beecher and I were not in hostility, and I have suppressed my self-respect many times in doing it.

Q. Did you ever state this offence of Mr. Beecher as committed against you to Mr. Storrs? A. I never did.

Q. Was it ever stated in your presence to him? A. No, sir; he read a statement that Mrs. Tilton made and that I helped her to make.

Q. Did you go with her when she made that statement to Dr. Storrs? A. I did not.

Q. Did you ever state or read to Dr. Storrs any statement of the offences which you charged against Mr. Beecher? A. No; I showed Dr. Storrs a letter which Elizabeth and myself wrote and which I still preserve; Mr. Carpenter and I went to Dr. Storrs as counsellor; my intention was to have Elizabeth go, but she preferred to write a few lines.

Q. You took what she wrote and what you helped her to write to Dr. Storrs and showed it to him as the statement of the offence which you charged Mr. Beecher with? A. No. I did not charge Mr. Beecher with any offence at all.

Q. I am trying to get at what offence you stated against Mr. Beecher. A. Elizabeth stated that.

Q. And you had it and gave it to Dr. Storrs to read? A. Yes, sir.

Q. How was the offence stated? A. It began in this way, that on a certain day, in the summer of 1870, she had informed her husband that Mr. Beecher had asked her to be a wife to him together with all that this implies; she was very solicitous to make it that she did not accept his proposition, and, happily, in reading it, those who saw it, naturally inferred that she did not accept his proposition; it was a perfectly correct statement.

Q. You and she wrote it? A. She wrote it with my assistance.

Q. You took that statement to Dr. Storrs, and it was read by him in your presence? A. Yes, sir.

Q. It was read also to Mr. Beecher? A. I read it to him myself. Mr. Beecher objected to it and I made no further use of it.

Q. You prepared a document, did you not, giving a history of this case? A. No, not in this case, but of my relations to Mr. Bowen.

Q. It was stated in that document? A. Yes; this letter of Elizabeth's was quoted in it.

Q. And it was read to Dr. Storrs? A. Yes.

Q. Did you also quote the letter of apology in it? A. Just as I did in the letter to Dr. Bacon?

Q. You quoted the apology as an apology for the offence? You stated and cited it as proof that he had apologized for that offence? A. Yes, I put that in, not wishing to make the offence more than that; I was solicitous not to have the worst of the case known.

Q. You went voluntarily to Dr. Storrs, did you not? A. I did, in great distress, wanting counsel.

Q. And so as to get correct counsel you misstated the case? A. Yes, as you did in your statement in the *Union;* it was a statement necessary to be made; after Mrs. Woodhull's statement I was out of town, and the thing had filled the country, and Mr. Beecher had taken no notice of it; it was seven or eight days old, and I went to Dr. Storrs for counsel; he asked me about the story; I said, "Do not ask me for that;" he said, "Give me some facts by which I can judge; give me that which can be proved;" so I gave an account of my affairs very largely, about Mrs. Woodhull, and so on; the origin of that document was a seeking for something that would put before the public a plausible answer to the Woodhull tale, and I conceived that by a chain of facts we might, perhaps, explain it away. I read it to Mr. Beecher and he burst into a long sigh, and I saw that he would not or could not stand upon it; and Elizabeth burned it or tore it to pieces.

Q. You showed it to others did you not? A. To a few friends.

Q. To whom besides Dr. Storrs? A. I think that I showed it to George Bell; I showed it to one or two.

Q. Did you show it to Mr. Beecher? A. No; I think not; I think I showed him the document in the tripartite confession.

Q. You have known Mr. Beecher many years. A. Yes, sir.

Q. Is he your personal friend? A. I used to regard him as such.

Q. You remember showing him something on this subject? A. I remember showing him the letter in proof, which explained my going out of the *Independent* and the *Union;* whether I showed him the document, I cannot say; I showed it to a number of people, hoping that it would do good; but it did not, so it disappeared.

Q. You say Mr. Beecher refused to stand upon it? A. No; Mr. Moulton asked Mr. Beecher to come and hear me read it; I was in hopes Mr. Beecher might not feel bad at such a document, but he felt slain by it.

Q. And, just as on other occasions, he refused to stand by a statement of the offence? A. No; he drew a long sigh.

Q. You understood him as refusing? A. No; I did not understand that.

Q. Why did you abandon the document? A. Because there was no success in it.

Q. Why was there no success in it? Was it not because he did not accept it? A. Because he did not accept or reject it; he wanted that no statement should be made, and so the thing was buried.

Q. Did you ever state the offence to Dr. Budington? A. I never saw him until within two weeks; I heard that he went to see Dr. Bacon, and I went to see him.

Q. Have you not frequently asserted the purity of your wife? A. No; I have always had a strange technical use of words; I have always used words that conveyed that impression; I have taken pains to say that she was a devoted Christian woman; that necessarily carried the other; it was like the statement that I carried to Dr. Storrs; I do not think he caught the idea of that statement; as he took it I do not think that it covered the whole; I have said that Elizabeth was a tender, delicate, kindly, Christian woman, which I think she is.

Q. Have not you stated that she was pure? A. No.

Q. Have you not stated that she was as pure as an angel? A. No; Mr. Halliday says I said that; he asked me in Mrs. Bradshaw's presence whether or not I had not said that my wife was as pure as gold, "No," I said, "Mr. Halliday, because the conversation to which you allude was this:—I said 'Go and ask Mr. Beecher himself and he will say that she is as pure as gold;'" it is an expression which he used; I have sought to give Elizabeth a good character; I have always wanted to do so; I think she deserves a good character; I think she is better than most of us—better than I am; I do not believe in point of actual moral goodness, barring some drawbacks, that there is in this company so white a soul as Elizabeth Tilton.

Q. Did you not state that, in substance, to one or more of the gentlemen with whom you were lunching? A. In substance, yes; and I state it now, but I did not use the phrase that she had never violated her chastity.

Q. Did you not say that she was pure? A. No.

Q. Did you not use expressions which you intended to be understood as meaning the purity of the woman? A. I did, exactly. There are many ways in which you can produce such impressions, and I have written this document to produce the same impression.

By Mr. White—Mr. Wilkeson, in his testimony, stated in substance that he had a long conversation with you in regard to Mr. Beecher's offences, and that in answer to his inquiry as to what these offences consisted of, you said that he had made improper addresses to your wife, and that he then said to you that he had heard from another person whom he named to you that it referred to more than the implication, that it referred to adultery, which you denied. Is that true? A. No; the conversation was about Mr. Bowen: he came to me with a flushed and rose-colored eulogy on Mr. Beecher for me to sign; it was desired that Mr. Bowen's charges should be withdrawn, and it was said to me, "suppose Mr. Bowen is willing to blot this out, you have no interest to keep it afloat?" "No," I said. "Well, if Mr. Bowen will withdraw those charges, will you agree to consider them blotted out?" I said, "Certainly." I was exceedingly glad to have it done, for I thought that every charge against Henry Ward Beecher endangered my wife; I said that I would sign it twenty times over, or conveyed such an idea; but when the paper was brought to me to sign it was a compliment to Mr. Beecher, rose-colored, in which I was to look up to him with filial respect. I said, "I won't sign that to the end of the world," and I cut out a few lines and would not use them.

Q. It is not with reference to the circumstances of signing the paper that I am speaking, but with reference to the question which he put to you as to the offence. A. He did not put to me any such question; Mr. Wilkeson is too much of a gentleman to ask a man whether his wife had committed adultery.

Q. Mr. Wilkeson says you took the paper away to make such emendations as you chose before signing it, and that after, perhaps, the second night, on its return, you said to him that you never would sign anything that required you to let up on

Henry Ward Beecher? A. I said that my self-respect would not permit me to do it; I told him also, or I told other persons, that I would keep to the line of that necessary reconciliation which Mr. Moulton had planned, but that as for going to Mr. Beecher's church, or signing such a letter, I would wait to the end of the world first, and I did not think Mr. Bowen would sign it.

By Mr. Cleveland—You expressed confidence in the paper you signed in Mr. Beecher, did you not? A. No; I expressed friendliness toward him.

By Mr. White—Mr. Wilkeson says, in substance, that in speaking of your dismissal from the *Union* you spoke of Mr. Beecher as not assisting you, and said that you would follow him to his grave? A. If Mr. Wilkeson communicates the impression that I ever wanted money from Henry Ward Beecher, it is false; Mr. Beecher has communicated, through Mr. Moulton requests that I be assisted by him, but I would not take a penny of Mr. Beecher's money if I suffered from hunger or thirst; and I said that if directly or indirectly he (Mr. Moulton) communicated to me any of his (Mr. Beecher's) money it would break out friendship; Wilkeson was very friendly to me; he is a sweet, lovable man, and it is an unaccountable thing that his memory is so bad; he is getting old; I have a letter in which he wants that apology delivered up.

Q. I will read to you from Mr. Wilkeson's testimony:—"His next complaint was that Mr. Beecher did not help him in his troubles." A. That's a lie; my complaint was that Mr. Beecher had been unjust to me, not that he had not helped me; I would not have taken his help.

By General Tracy—I ask you whether your relations and feelings toward Mr. Beecher, since January 1st, 1871, have not been friendly? A. Yes, sir; my relations and feelings toward him since January, 1871, when he made the apology, down to the time when the church began to put out its right and and take me by the throat, were friendly.

Q. They are not now friendly but they were friendly up to the beginning of the action of the church in this matter? A. Yes, sir; that is to say, they were friendly in the sense that we were not in collision with each other.

Q. Were they not those of friendship? A. No they were not.

Q. What did you mean by saying, after that apology was made, that you desired to see Mr. Beecher protected, rather than harmed, for his offence against you? A. So I did.

Q. Do you mean to say that that sentence expressed your real feelings toward a man who, you believed, had seduced your wife? A. Yes; I was under obligation; I had taken his apology and I had given my word that I would not have him exposed.

Q. Is it your sentiment that that is an offence for which one man can apologize to another? A. I know there is a code of honor among gentlemen that a man cannot condone such an offence; but I cannot see what offence a man cannot forgive, where an apology is made by the person committing it to the person against whom it is committed; if a man believes in the Christian religion he ought to; I sometimes forgave and sometimes I did not; I do know the line of difference.

Q. Is that your handwriting (showing a slip of paper on which was written "H. W. B.—Grace, mercy and peace. Sunday morning. T. T." A. I remember that; one morning Mr. Beecher met me in the street and told me how much pleasure it gave him; I have sent kindlier things than that to him.

Q. Did you feel as you spoke? A. I did; Mr. Moulton said two or three times, "Mr. Beecher is in great depression; can't you do something to cheer him?" One morning I walked to the church with him; in many circumstances I manifested feelings of kindness toward him; it would be a lie for me to say that I had a warm friendship for Mr. Beecher, and that I felt as kindly to him as if the offence had not been committed; if I had been a man morally great, I would have blotted it out and trodden it under foot; I was competent to forgive in a large degree; I forgave him in my best moods, but at other times I did not; I am not a very large man.

Q. You have quoted extensively the letters of your wife written prior to the time you say that she said this intercourse began—have you not her letters written to you also since that time and during that time? A. No; because at that time I came home to be editor of the *Union*, and have not lectured since.

Q. I ask you whether you have not letters from her written during the time that you say this was going on and since then? A. No, not written since; because I have not had occasion since to have letters; I have been at home.

Q. I understand you to say that these relations went on during your absence; have you any letters that were written by your wife at that time? A. No.

Q. Have you not letters from her that were written to you between 1868 and 1870? A. I think I have.

Q. Will you be kind enough to produce them to the committee? A. I do not know whether I will or not.

Q. Have you any letters from Mrs. Tilton complaining to you? A. Yes, I have.

Q. Have you not many letters from her stating forth her grievances? A. No she very rarely wrote such letters; she used occasionally to write to me letters begging intercession in regard to her mother and complaining of my views in theology.

Q. Did you never receive letters from her complaining in other respects? A. In what respects?

Q. Well in regard to people who were in the habit of frequenting your house at your solicitation? A. I have had letters from her mother, complaining of Susan Anthony and Mrs. Stanton; Mrs. Tilton thought Mr. Johnson and others were leading me astray; she is very orthodox; and she wrote me letters expressing strong and earnest hopes that I would be intensely orthodox.

Q. Did she ever complain of any female society on that ground, or in any way? A. No.

Q. Did she never complain of the presence of any ladies at your house? A. I do not think of any.

Q. Not of Mrs. Stanton nor Susan Anthony? A. She said she would consider it an insult if they came to the house; I do not remember of any others.

Q. Mrs. Woodhull came a great deal didn't she? A. She was three times in my house, once to meet Mr. Beecher and on two other occasions.

Q. Only three times? A. Three only.

Q. You say she came to meet Mr. Beecher? A. She did on Sunday afternoon at my house.

Q. Do you know when that was? A. I think Mr. Moulton made that interview; it must have been in 1871 or 1872, because my acquaintance with Mrs. Woodhull began in May, 1871; my impression is that it was warm weather; Mrs. Woodhull and her husband came; she always came with her husband.

Q. Did your wife complain of her being at your house? A. Yes; my wife came home, and Mrs. Woodhull and Mr. Moulton were sitting in the front parlor.

Q. What happened? A. Oh, nothing, except that Elizabeth expressed her indignation against the woman; I told Elizabeth that she was too dangerous a woman, and that too much of the welfare of our family depended on her; Elizabeth was wiser than I was.

Q. Did you excuse your acquaintance with Mrs. Woodhull to your wife by exciting her fears? A. I did not; I explained that acquaintance; I told her the way to get along with Mrs. Woodhull and prevent this coming out, was to keep friendly with her; it was a fatal policy, but then it seemed the only thing that we could do.

Q. Was the time that Mrs. Tilton expressed her indignation at Mrs. Woodhull's being at your house the first time that she had seen Mrs. Woodhull, to your knowledge? A. My impression is that she saw her in the *Golden Age* office once. It may have been before or after. I think Mrs. Woodhull came in to see me while Mrs. Tilton was there.

Q. With that exception, was the time when Mrs. Tilton expressed her indignation at Mrs. Woodhull's being at your house the first time that she had seen her? A. I do not know. Oh, no; Mrs. Woodhull and Colonel Blood had taken tea at our house.

Q. Before Mrs. Tilton came in and found her there? A. Yes.

Q. At whose invitation did they take tea there? A. At mine.

Q. Was it the first time Mrs. Tilton saw Mrs. Woodhull? A. I do not know.

Q. Mrs. Tilton always expressed indignation at her being there, did she not? A. Yes, she had a violent feeling against her; she had a woman's instinct that Mrs. Woodhull was not safe; the mistake was in not being friendly with Blood instead of Mrs. Woodhull; that was the blunder; I was at fault for that nobody else.

Q. Did Mrs. Tilton continue her expressions of indignation at your acquaintance with Mrs. Woodhull? A. Yes; Mrs. Tilton always felt that the policy was a mistaken one of undertaking to do anything with Mrs. Woodhull; Mrs. Tilton objected violently to my writing the sketch of Mrs. Woodhull; I read part of it to her; Mrs. Woodhull's husband wrote a biography about her, and wanted me to rewrite it, because my style was more vivid; Mrs. Tilton said she thought I would rue the day; she was far wiser than I was.

Q. Then you never succeeded in convincing your wife that it was necessary to placate Mrs. Woodhull? A. No, she had the opposite opinion; Mrs. Tilton had a strong repugnance to Mrs. Woodhull and to two or three other public women—Mrs. Stanton and Susan Anthony; she would not permit them to come into the house, and some of her letters were very violent against them; she was frequently with them for a long time and took part with them in women's meetings, and then she took a violent antagonism to them after her troubles came on.

Q. Did Mrs. Woodhull know of the antipathy of Mrs. Tilton to her? A. Yes; you could see it in the women's eyes; they flashed fire; the moment they saw each other their eyes flashed fire.

Q. It was perfectly evident, then, when the women came together, that they were thoroughly antagonistic? A. Oh, yes; thoroughly.

Q. Bitterly so? A. I cannot say that Elizabeth had bitterness; she had a certain moral and religious repugnance.

Q. Did not she discard Mrs. Woodhull's sentiments and denounce them? A. Mrs. Woodhull had not then expressed her sentiments.

Q. Not in 1872? A. This was not in 1872; when I wrote the sketch of Mrs. Woodhull she had never said anything on the subject of free love; her ideas were spiritualism and woman's suffrage.

By General Tracy—Q. Mr. Tilton, on page 51 of your manuscript, in subdivision X, you say, "In December 1870, differences arose between Theodore Tilton and Henry C. Bowen, which were augmented by the Rev. Henry Ward Beecher and Mrs. Beecher, in consequence whereof, and at the wish of Mrs. Elizabeth R. Tilton expressed in writing in a paper put into the hands of," etc., you do not state then in whose handwriting it was. A. It was Mrs. Tilton's.

Q. Was it not in your handwriting? A. It was not, sir.

Q. Did you not write that statement and get her to sign it? A. No, sir.

Q. Did you dictate it in any manner? A. I did not.

Q. Did you write the original? A. I did not.

Q. Was she well or sick at the time? A. She was neither one nor the other; she was ailing.

Q. Had she not suffered a miscarriage just previous? A. Well, I do not know how long before; I cannot tell the date; whether it came before or after I do not know; she was ill, I know.

Q. Was she not in bed? A. Most of the time.

Q. Was she not in bed at the time of the writing of this paper? A. I do not remember.

Q. Do you remember whether she wrote it in bed or not? A. I do not.

Q. Do you not know that she had suffered a miscarriage a few days before? A. No; I knew she had suffered a miscarriage before.

Q. Before the 24th day of December? A. I do not remember the date.

Q. Do you not know that she was very sick, and sick unto death? A. No, I do not know that she was sick unto death; she was ill, but not dangerously so.

Q. Who suggested to her the writing of that letter? A. She did it herself.

Q. Was she conversant with the particular state of your difficulty with Mr. Bowen from time to time and from day to day? A. It was not from day to day; I always informed her what troubles I had.

Q. You say this letter was written in consequence of the interference of Mr. and Mrs. Beecher? A. No, not precisely; I say that the letter was written through her desire that he and I should be reconciled.

Q. When you say that in "December, 1870, differences arose between Theodore Tilton and Henry C. Bowen, which were augmented by the Rev. Henry Ward Beecher and Mrs. Beecher; in consequence whereof, and at the wish of Mrs. Elizabeth R. Tilton, expressed in writing in a paper put into the hands of Mr. Francis D. Moulton," why do you say that it was in consequence of that difficulty being augmented by Mr. and Mrs. Beecher that this letter was written or this writing was made? A. Mrs. Tilton's confession to me was in the middle of the summer; she informed me shortly afterward that she had taken occasion to let Mr. Beecher know that she had made this confession, but she did not do that; I supposed that he knew of her confession, but he did not know of it. I met Mr. Beecher on the street, and he was about to speak to me; I did not speak to him; that excited my suspicion of the fact that he could not have known of Mrs. Tilton's confession; so I said to her, "Elizabeth, did not you tell me that Mr. Beecher knew what you had told me; to my mind he don't know it;" she then informed me that she could not bear to let him know that she had confessed; then, I think, her sickness came, though my recollection of dates, as I have said is very poor; towards the close of the year, or very near the close of the year, Mr. Bowen wanted to make a change in the editorship of the *Independent;* Mrs. Tilton was at Mrs. Morse's; she had gone to stay there a little while; Mr. Bowen sent me a notice or a letter, saying that he wanted the termination of my contract as editor of the *Independent* to take place six months subsequently; I said to myself instantly, "If Mr. Bowen wishes me to terminate the *Independent*, I must give him notice to terminate the *Union;* but before that I will send to Elizabeth to come to the *Union* office and state this proposition to her;" she came down and I informed her; I said, "Now, I cannot afford to edit only one of these papers; if I am to give up one I cannot keep the other;" when Mr. Bowen proposed that I should give up one and retain the other, I instantly said, "As he proposes that I shall give up the *Independent* I will give up the *Union*, and that will leave me free to lecture." After that, about the 23d or 24th of December, Mr. Bowen came to have a consultation with me and make new contracts, by which he should be editor of the *Independent* and I a special contributor of the *Independent* and for five years the editor of the *Union;* that contract was signed during the last week or ten days of 1870, and I published a valedictory in the *Independent* speaking well of Mr. Bowen, and he spoke well of me.

Somewhere about the 23d or 24th or 25th—between the publishing of that valedictory and the making of those two or three contracts—Mr. Johnson came to my house and said, "Mr. Bowen has heard something prejudicial concerning you; I think you had better go and see him." It was Saturday night. I went plump to his house and saw him, and said, "Mr. Bowen, Mr. Johnson says that you know something prejudicial to me." Mr. Bowen said, "I have my new editors in consultation and it is Saturday night; come on Monday." Monday was a holiday. Either Sunday was the actual Christmas or else Monday was, I do not remember which. I went on Monday with Mr. Johnson. I think this was on the 25th. We had a little talk. It was mentioned that some story had come to Mr. Bowen. I said, "Bring the person who told it into my presence and we will have the matter settled." I then went on talking about the new contract which I was to enter upon two or three days hence, as the editor of the *Union* for five years; he said that I ought to make more of Plymouth church and go to Plymouth church; Mr. Johnson said, "Perhaps this young man has a reason for not going to Plymouth church;" I gave him in a line to understand that I had lost my respect for Mr. Beecher, and could not, as a man maintaining my pride and self-respect, go there; at that, Mr. Bowen stated all the particulars that I chronicled of Mr. Beecher in that letter, only more vividly; at that Mr. Bowen made a challenge that Mr. Beecher would retire from the ministry, and said he would bear it and fortify it with facts, and I signed it and he carried it; in a few hours Mr. Moulton came in and I told him what I had done, and he said, "You are a damned fool, Mr. Bowen should have signed the letter as well as yourself;" the next morning I went to the *Union* office, and perhaps the morning after I wrote a little note to Mr. Bowen, the substance of which was that I was going to have a personal interview with Mr. Beecher; that I thought was the manly thing; Mr. Bowen, the next morning, after he had instituted this demand for the retirement of Mr. Beecher, and after saying that he would fortify it with facts, came to the *Union* office and said, "Sir, if you ever reveal to Mr. Beecher the things that I told you and Mr. Johnson I will cashier you;" it went through my blood; I said, "I will, at my discretion, utterly uninfluenced by you," and he was in a rage; then, after two or three days, and while I was writing my first article for the *Independent* under the new arrangement, as contributor instead of editor, there came (I guess it was the last night of the year) notices breaking my two contracts; those two contracts had been made within a week, and were not to take effect until the first of the year, and they were broken the last night of the year, or the night before; I went around to Frank with them, and showed them to him immediately; the next day I wrote my letter to Mr. Bowen; events came crowding together pell-mell so thick and fast that I do not know how to disentangle them.

Q. Why do you say that it was in consequence of the difficulty being augmented by Mr. and Mrs. Beecher? A. Elizabeth saw that Mr. Bowen and I were in collision; she was afraid that the collision would extend to Mr. Beecher and me, and she wished me, if possible, to make peace with him; that peace could be brought about only by his knowing what I knew of his relations with Mrs. Tilton; therefore, she wrote a womanly, kindly letter to him; I do not remember the phraseology; I remember only one phrase; it was peculiarly hers; she said she loved her husband with her maiden flame; Mr. Moulton will probably recall the whole phraseology.

Q. What was the substance of the letter? A. The substance of the letter I do not recall; the letter was returned to her; whether she has it or not I do not know; the object of the letter was to make peace; she felt that if Mr. Beecher and I could be reconciled, she herself and I would be more reconciled; there was a sort of mountain of clouds overcoming us.

Q. Who had reported to her the fact that your difficulty was being augmented by Mr. and Mrs. Beecher? A. I do not know; she reported it to me; it was through her that I learned that Mrs. Beecher was interfering with my affairs; it was through Mrs. Tilton that I learned of Mrs. Beecher's antagonism to me; I do not think Mr. Beecher was so largely involved in it as his wife was.

Q. Had you known of Mrs. Beecher's interference with your affairs prior to that? A. I cannot say with my affairs—not with my business affairs; with my domestic affairs; no, as I recollect. Elizabeth went sometimes to the Health Lift, and Mrs. Beecher came there and saw her one day.

Q. What date was that? A. I do not know; Mrs. Beecher, through Mrs. Morse, got the idea that I was Mr. Beecher's enemy; therefore Mrs. Beecher was very violently my enemy; Mrs. Beecher being my enemy, and feeling that I was bent on a battle against her husband, sought to make an alliance with Elizabeth, and, as I understand, wanted Elizabeth to go away from me and part company, and she would not do it—the trouble having hinged on the fact that Elizabeth had made me and Mrs. Morse a confession, but had not told Mr. Beecher that she had done so; I said there was only one way out of the difficulty, and that was that Mr. Beecher must know it.

Q. Did you say that to Elizabeth? A. I do not know about that.

Q. Had you said it previous to that? A. I do not know; I felt greatly chagrined at her not having told him, as she said she had; I could not understand why Mr. Beecher should speak to me on the street, and I instantly said, "He does not know it."

Q. You do not know when it was that he spoke to you on the street? A. My impression is that it could not have been much later than his first coming back from the country.

Q. When was that? A. All I can remember of that is the picture of the man with a kind of sunburn on him; if you will ask Elizabeth all of these things she can tell you; there was a large mass of complications that were afterward explained.

Q. Was not Mrs. Tilton sick on the evening of the 30th of December and in bed? A. I do not know whether she was or not.

Q. Do not you know that one of your allegations or complaints was that he obtained that retraction from her when she was sick in bed? A. I know that she was lying in bed.

Q. Did you not charge him with imposing upon her because she was sick? A. Yes.

Q. And was she not sick? A. I remember the picture of her lying ailing on the bed.

Q. What physician attended her? A. I think Dr. Parker; it may have been Dr. Stiles; he was subsequently our physician.

Q. This first letter which you quote from Mrs. Tilton, on page 35, in which she says:—"Love is praiseworthy, but to abuse the gift is sin; here I am strong; no temptations or fascinations," &c., what did you understand by that? A. I understood this—that she was in receipt of visits from him, and that she had once or twice felt that perhaps he was exercising an undue influence upon her; I know that once I was afraid she did not give me a correct account of his visits; there were a great many visits mentioned in her correspondence.

Q. Have you the letters here? A. No.

Q. I thought that you were to bring them? A. All the originals from which I have quoted I will carry before Judge Reynolds or any judge, in the presence of General Tracy; I have great confidence in you, gentlemen, but I do not propose to produce the originals here; if you will release one of your number to go with me before any magistrate, I will produce them; Mr. Moulton will, of course, be asked to produce his for examination, line for line; I do not suppose you would snatch them away or keep them, but at the same time I propose that if you would see the originals, General Tracy should go with me.

Q. Do you refuse to produce the originals before this committee? A. I do not refuse to produce them to the committee in the presence of some outside parties.

Q. Do you refuse to produce them to the committee alone? A. Yes, unless I can have some friend here with me.

Q. Why did you not take that position yesterday? A. Because yesterday we had only a chat.

Q. Yes, but did you not promise to produce them? A. Yes, and I do now.

Q. But you decline except in the presence of an officer? A.

I decline unless I can be perfectly certain that they will be returned to me; I don't want you to consider that as a disparagement; it is only a necessary element in this discussion; you shall see the originals, but I will only show them under safeguards.

Q. Why do you make that qualification? A. For this reason: you are six gentlemen, determined, if possible, not to find the facts, but to vindicate Mr. Beecher, and I am alone. There are eight of you and I am a single man, and if I should hand over to you now Mr. Beecher's apology perhaps you would not return it to me. Though I do not mean to make that implication, I do not mean to give you the chance. That is frank.

Mr. Hill—Let me say kindly, speaking on behalf of both of the counsel—the committee may speak for themselves—that the suggestion of such a theory is altogether groundless.

General Tracy—It is not only groundless, but outrageous.

Mr. Hill—I think you are unjust.

Mr. Tilton—I have been informed that this is a matter of life and death.

Mr. Claflin—This committee could not afford to take that position. It would not do to take those letters from you.

Mr. Tilton—I am perfectly willing to bring several friends of mine and make an examination of these letters; you shall see them; but under proper safeguards—that is all; if Mr. Tracy were in my position he would take the same ground.

General Tracy—No, he would not, I beg your pardon.

Q. At the beginning of the acquaintance of Mr. Beecher with your family—not with you or your wife, but with your family—did not you invite him frequently to your house? A. Yes, sir; and I was always very proud when he came.

Q. Did you not say to him often that you desired him to visit your house frequently? A. I did, and always scolded him because he did not come oftener; during the first part of our life we were in Oxford street, so far away that he very rarely came; the frequency of his visits took place after I purchased the house in Livingston street.

Q. When was that? A. I have forgotten the year; I should say it was seven, or eight, or nine, or ten years ago.

Q. Did not you say that there was a little woman at your house that loved him dearly? A. I did, many a time; I always wanted him to come oftener.

Q. You frequently spoke to him of the high esteem and affection that your wife bore to him, did you not? A. I did; he knew it and I knew it.

Q. You always knew it? A. I cannot say that I always did, because at first, during the early years of my married life, I felt that Mr. Beecher rather slighted my family; he was intimate with me, and I think loved me; but he did not use to come very often to my house, and it did not please me; I wanted him to come oftener.

Q. And it wounded you, did it not? A. I cannot say that I was wounded; I was a mere boy; it was a matter of pride to have him there; Elizabeth at first was modest and frightened; she did not know how to talk with him, or how to entertain him, and it was a slow process by which he obtained her confidence so that she could talk with him; it was the same with Mr. Greeley; he had great reverence for her, and had an exalted opinion of her; I do not think there was a woman that he had a higher regard for than Mrs. Tilton.

Q. And did she not have a high regard for him also? A. Yes.

Q. And that was known to you too? A. That was known to me, and I was very glad of it.

Q. Mr. Greeley came to your house often? A. He used to come and stay sometimes in the summer a week or two at a time; we kept bachelor's hall; yes, he came often; it was always a white day when Mr. Greeley came; he used to say that he never would come in my absence; he said it was not a good habit.

Q. Did you urge him to come when you were off lecturing? A. I did.

Q. Did not you impress upon Mr. Beecher the necessity and desire that you had, that he would call upon your family and see your wife frequently during your absence? A. I did.

Q. Now. Mr. Tilton, you have stated the religious character of your wife; will you describe it again? A. My wife's religious character I have, if you will pardon the allusion, undertaken to set forth in the book that I have spent a year in writing—a work of fiction called "Tempest Tossed"—a name strangely borrowed from my own heaving breast; in that novel is a character, Mary Vail; I do not want to say vainly before the public that I drew that character for Elizabeth, but I did; there is a chapter—the ninth, I think (I won't be certain about the number)—which is called "Mary Vail's Journal;" I know it is good because I made it up from Elizabeth's letters, and my heart was cleft in twain to find in these letters some of the same sentences that crept into this chapter; I changed them considerably to make them conform to the story; I had this feeling, that if in this novel I could, as a mere subordinate part of the story, paint that character, and have it go quietly, in an underhanded way, forth, that it was Elizabeth (for I think I drew it faithfully) it would be a very thorough answer, as coming from me, to the scandals in the community, and that people would say, "Theodore respects his wife," as I do to-day.

Q. Was it a truthful character of Elizabeth? A. It was; it was not drawn as well as the original would warrant.

Q. You say it was not drawn as well as the original would warrant; then her devotion and purity of life would warrant a higher character than you have given "Mary Vail" in that book? A. Yes, unless you attach a technical meaning to the word purity; she was made a victim.

Q. You say that the character in that book falls below the original? A. Yes, because I did not make it a prominent but a subordinate character.

Q. Are there any other persons that figure in this drama who are described in that book, "Tempest Tossed?" A. No, except by mere suggestions.

Q. Is not your true friend described there?

Mr. Tilton—You mean Mr. Moulton?

General Tracy—Yes. A. No; of the characters in "Tempest Tossed" Mary Vail is the only one that is true to life; the character of the colored woman was partly suggested by a colored woman that I knew.

Q. You have brought forward the letter of your wife where she describes herself as having received new light, as having read the character of Catherine Gaunt in "Griffith Gaunt;" have you read the character of Catherine Gaunt? A. Yesterday I said no, but I have an impression that I have; a friend of mine yesterday morning said that it is a singular result from "The Terrible Temptation;" Charles Reade has written a book called "The Terrible Temptation;" I have never read that book, but on second thought, I think I have read "Griffith Gaunt;" my impression is that I read it on a journey, and that I wrote something to Elizabeth about it and asked her to read it.

Q. Did you think that the guilt of "Catherine Gaunt" was that of adultery? A. I have no idea that I did.

Q. Has there been a change in your religious views since you were married? A. Yes, sir, very decided, I am happy to say; I think there is in every sensible man's.

Q. Do you know whether the change in your religious convictions was a source of great grief and sorrow to your wife? A. It was a great source of tears and anguish to her; she said to me once that denying the divinity of Christ in her view, nullified our marriage almost; and I think next to the sorrow of this scandal, it has caused that woman to sorrow more than any thing else she has suffered; because I cannot look upon the Lord Jesus Christ as the Lord God; I think her breast has been wrenched with it; she is almost an enthusiast on the subject of the divinity of her Savior.

Q. You think her a Christian, do you? A. Yes; she is the best Christian I know of, barring her faults; better than any minister.

Q. Well, on the whole, do you not think that she is about as white as most Christians? A. Yes, whiter than ourselves.

Q. Then you would not qualify the expression when you say that she is the best Christian you know, barring her faults? Do not you think that she is the best Christian you know with her faults? A. No. I would not say that, because there has been a strong deceit wrought out in Elizabeth that comes from the weakness of her character; she has had three strong persons to circulate among—Mr. Beecher, her mother and me; in sentiment she outdoes us all; her life is shipwrecked, but she is not to blame; I will maintain that to my dying day.

Q. Do not you know that in these exigencies she sought consolation from her pastor? A. I think she did; and he took advantage of her orthodox views to make them the net and the mesh in which he ensnared her, and for which I hold him in a contempt which no English words can describe.

Q. The change of your religious views has been the subject of a great deal of conversation and anguish and labor on her part, has it not? A. Oh, yes—of letters and prayers and tears and entreaties, many a time and oft.

Q. When you say that this has been the thing which has enabled her to be ensnared, do you mean by that, that you think that was the cause why, in some degree, her confidence in the judgment and advice of her pastor was increased, and why your influence over her was lessened? A. Oh yes; largely so; thoroughly so.

Q. Then when you found that she was leaning more strongly than formerly on the advice and consolation of her pastor, and less on your own, you attributed it naturally to your change in religious sentiments? A. Yes; at the same time I did not want Elizabeth to hold my view; I said that she might be a Catholic or a Mohammedan.

Q. Did she not feel that your views were a source of danger to the children? A. Yes; she would not let the children have playthings on Sunday; John G. Whittier came to our house (he appointed the time), and Mr. Greeley, and met Mr. Johnson; and it almost broke Elizabeth's heart to think that the best man in New England, whom she reverenced, should have appointed Sunday night; she never received visitors on Sunday

Q. Is it not a feature in her character that she has great reverence for those men whom she belives to be pure in life, and noble in thought and spirit? A. Yes; she would kiss the hem of their garments.

Q. That is a marked feature of her character, is it not? A. Uncommonly so.

Q. Does it not almost go to the extent of idolatry in one sense? A. Well, no; there are a great many women who look upon a man with a sense of worship; Elizabeth never did that; Elizabeth is the peer of any man; at the same time she reverences; it was not vanity—it was reverence; she never regarded Mr. Beecher as a silly woman regards him; she was not a silly woman taken captive; she was a wise, good woman taken captive; there are a great many people, particularly women, who, if President Grant should call on them, would feel greatly flattered; I do not think she would; but if she regarded President Grant as man of high religious nature, coming with the Gospel in his hand and devoted to the evangelical religion, then, whether he were famous or lowly, she would reverence him.

Q. So must there not be connected with her reverence the idea of absolute purity of life, as well as of religious character? A. Yes. I think Elizabeth regarded Mr. Beecher, in early days, as the essence of all that was religious, apostolic; I think she looked upon him very much as she would look upon the Apostle Paul.

Q. And you understood that? A. Yes, and in fact looked upon him so in my early life; I loved that man as well as I ever loved a woman.

Q. And is it not true that there is nothing that your wife so much abhors in man or woman as impurity? A. Exactly so.

Q. The fact that she believed that any persons were impure, however, if it were otherwise, she might reverence them, would destroy her respect and reverence for them would it not? A. It would in those days. [Here Mr. Tilton gave in illustration the instance of a gentleman who his wife felt had insulted her by saying that he sympathized with her, and hoped that she would lift up her head in self-respect, remarking that Tilton's chief temptation had been temptation to the sin of the sexes.] Mr. Tilton resuming: I do not think he did it vindictively, but the fact that he could have done it at all, burned in her blood.

Q. Was she not distressed at any suggestion of impropriety? A. She was particularly so; and she is more so now than ever, because in her early days such a thought was never in her mind; but when it had passed through her experience it came out with this contrition; I think that hers is one of the white souls; that is the truth of the case; she never ought to have been taken away from her home; you gentlemen did it; you did it, Mr. Tracy. "Thou art the man."

Q. Will you state more distinctly than you have done what you understand by that letter of February 3d, 1868, in which she says:—"Love is praiseworthy, but to abuse the gift is sin. There I am strong. No temptation or fascination could cause me to yield my womanhood?" A. I quoted that letter to show how strong her views were at that time.

Q. Did you quote it for the purpose of showing that at that time she was being tempted? A. I have heard her say the substance of that over and over again.

Q. When? A. I do not know when; a long time ago, years ago, when he (Mr. Beecher) used to go there; it was not because I had any suspicion of him then; Elizabeth always felt that when Mr. Beecher went to such and such a place there were women that would flatter him; I do not think she did at all; she has always been a stickler for the honor of her sex; she said to herself, "I will represent my sex."

Q. In other words, she wanted to show him purity of sentiment, and of communion of mind without passion? A. That is what she meant, I think.

Q. That is what you understood her to mean? A. That is exactly what I understood her to mean.

Q. For years? A. Yes, sir.

Q. That is the way you looked upon the relation between them for years? A. I ought to say for the earlier years.

Q. When did you first bring to your wife's attention the fact that you feared that there was something wrong? A. Elizabeth so blotted that out of my mind that I did not think of it again.

Q. How long ago was it? Years ago? A. Yes, as I recollect it, it must have been during the early years when we lived in Livingston street, in our present house.

Q. How long have you lived there? A. I do not know.

Mr. Winslow—About ten years, I remember.

General Tracy—It was a great many years ago? A. Yes.

Q. Was it before 1868? A. Long before.

Mr. Claflin—In '64, probably.

General Tracy—Was it before 1865? A. About 1862.

Q. Where did you live at the beginning of the war? A. I am very much ashamed that I am never able to answer such a question.

Q. You say that it was in the early years of your living at No. 174 Livingston street? A. Yes; pictures are vivid to me, and I remember where Elizabeth was sitting in the corner of my parlor; I spoke to her about it when we came home.

Q. How long since was it that you have mentioned that subject to any one until you put it in this communication? A. She blotted it out of my mind.

Q. Did you ever speak of it to any one? A. She blotted out all wrong as concerning her in the circumstance.

Q. You never mentioned it to Mr. Beecher? A. I was very young in those days and utterly unsuspicious of such things, and when I spoke to her about it she was a little confused and denied it; and then said it was so, but that she had said "You must not do that;" I had in those days something of the same reverence for Mr. Beecher that I have since so eminently lost.

Q. Do you know who was present besides your wife and Mr. Beecher? A. Nobody.

Q. There was nobody there but you three—you were looking at engravings? A. Yes.

By Mr. Winslow—Were you sitting on the floor? A. Not the whole of the time; I remember that those two were sitting down on the floor with the pictures; I am a restless sort of man, and I do not know where I was; it was a long time ago.

Q. Do you say that you saw it with your own eyes? A. With my own eyes.

Q. Do you remember whether Mr. Beecher looked at you first? A. No; he did not know that I noticed it; I was standing up, I think; I have to bring up the picture in my mind; I do not remember exactly whether I was standing or sitting; perhaps I was in a chair; I know that there was a kind of portfolio folded out and that the pictures were folded down (indicating with the hands); she was sitting on the floor or on a stool, and he on the floor.

Q. Were you where he could see you ? A. He was looking at the pictures.

Q. If he had looked up would he have seen you ? A. Yes.

By General Tracy—You were looking at some pictures in the room ? A. Yes; these things were on her lap.

Q. What part of her person did he touch ? A. Her ankles and lower limbs.

By Mr. Winslow—Not above the knee ? A. No. If he had he probably would have been struck; it was a question in my mind whether a minister could consider that a proper sort of caress.

Q. Was it done slyly ? A. Yes, very slyly; his right or left arm was under her dress.

By General Tracy—How were they sitting ? A. My impression is that she was sitting on some little stool and he on the floor by her side, and that some pictures were, perhaps, put up against the chair and folded, and that it was by an accidental brushing up of her dress that I saw his hand on her ankle.

Q. Do you know whether it was accidental or casual with him? A. I only know that I asked her.

Q. Could you know whether it was accidental or intentional ? A. I spoke of it to her; she at first denied it and then confessed it, and said that she had chidden him; I did not attach much importance to it after the explanation was made.

Q. You were in doubt whether it was intentional or accidental? A. It was merely a suspicion.

Q. How about the bedchamber scene ? A. That was a long while ago, and that was blotted out of my mind too.

Q. When was it? A. I do not remember the year; it was a good while ago.

By Mr. Winslow—Before or after the ankle scene? A. Before.

Q. How long? A. I do not know.

Q. Before 1868? A. I do not know.

Q. After you were living in Livingston street ? A. Yes; I remember the room; again, I identify it by the picture; it was in the left hand room; I have two front rooms on the second story, and it was the left hand of these two rooms; I knocked at the door and Elizabeth came; I was surprised that it was locked; she was surprised at finding me; Mr. Beecher was sitting in a red plush rocking chair—a sort of Ottoman chair—

with his vest unbuttoned; his face colored like a rose when I saw him.

Q. How long ago was that? A. I do not know.

Q. How long had you lived in Livingston street at this time? A. Do not remember.

Q. Had you lived there for two or three years? A. That I do not know; I should say I had lived there, perhaps, two years.

Q. Was it during the war? A. That I do not know.

Q. Do you know whether it was before or after your visit to Fort Sumter? A. No.

Q. The explanation was satisfactory to you on that occasion? A. Entirely so.

Q. So that you let it be, and attributed nothing to it? A. Yes, I attributed nothing to it; if the door had been simply shut, I should have thought nothing of it, but the door being locked I wondered at it.

Q. Was there more than one door leading to that room? A. One door comes in from the hall.

Q. Was there any other door leading into the room from the other room? A. There is a middle door communicating between the two rooms.

Q. Two sliding doors? A. Yes.

Q. And was there a door leading from the hall to the other room? A. Yes, that is the plan of the house.

Q. And the room that Mr. Beecher and your wife were in was a room communicating with another room with sliding doors? A. Yes.

Q. What was that room used for that Mr. Beecher was in? A. A bedroom.

Q. Was there a bed in it? A. Yes, sir.

Q. Is the other room a sitting room? A. It is.

Q. Did you try that door which led into the sitting room? A. No.

Q. Why? A. Because I came and knocked at the hall door.

Q. For aught you know, they had gone into the sitting room from the hall, and from there Mr. Beecher may have gone into the bedroom? A. Yes; I will give them the benefit of the doubt.

Q. Was it explained to your satisfaction? A. Yes.

Q. What was the explanation that satisfied you? A. The annoyance of the children; my wife said that our children and some of the neighbors' children were making a noise, and she wanted to have a quiet talk with Mr. Beecher, and so she locked herself in.

Q. That satisfied you? A. That satisfied me; it was entirely reasonable; I only quote it as a suspicion.

Q. Do you remember whether the sliding doors leading from this room to the sitting room were open? A. They were shut; I remember it because I looked in; I saw the two white doors coming together; the picture is distinct to my mind; I do not forget pictures.

By Mr. Claflin—Q. Was the door opened immediately? A. Yes; I do not want you to think that I thought there was anything wrong at that interview at all.

Q. The picture of the room was the only reason you have for believing that the sitting room door was shut? A. Yes, sir.

Q. Did the explanation so satisfy you that that thing was blotted from your remembrance? A. Yes.

Q. So you have never regarded that circumstance as evidence of wrong in any one? A. No.

Q. Have you ever mentioned that? A. I rather think I have.

Q. Why? A. Because afterwards there arose circumstances which made me feel that the explanation which she had given of these two events was not true.

By Mr. Winslow—To whom did you state it? A. I think to my mother; I do not recollect; I never made any blazonry of it, you know, abroad; I never thought, really, that there was any wrong in it until in the light of subsequent events; I do not say now that there was any wrong in it; Elizabeth always denied stoutly to me that anything wrong had taken place at that time.

Q. What kind of a room was that sitting room? A. It was the common sitting room of the house.

Q. The right hand part was the sitting room, and the left hand part was the bedroom communicating with it by sliding doors? A. Yes.

Q. That is, where you receive your intimate friends? A. Yes.

Q. If you had found Mr. Beecher with your wife in the sitting room you would have found him where you should have expected to find him, would you not? A. Yes.

Q. If the door had not been locked you would not have thought anything of it? A. No; I should have been happy to have seen him; we were in the best possible relations in those days; nobody was a more welcome guest at our house than he.

Q. Now, Mr. Tilton, can you say whether this scene was before the date of that letter of February 3d, 1868? A. Yes, it must have been a long time before that, I think; I won't be certain; it must have been a long time before 1868.

Q. You say that her letters informed you that Mr. Beecher had made twelve pastoral visits at your house in five weeks? A. I have those letters.

By Mr. Hill—You have all the letters from which you say you discovered that the twelve visits were made when you were away? A. Yes.

Q. And those you will produce? A. I think that perhaps I will.

By General Tracy—It was written here (in Mr. Tilton's communication) six and changed to five weeks—which is correct? A. (After some explanations.) It is correct as it is there.

Q. You say, Mr. Tilton, for a year after what you state as Mrs. Tilton's confession, she insisted to you that she had not violated her marriage vow? A. Yes; Elizabeth was in a sort of vaporous like cloud; she was between light and dark; she could not see that it was wrong; she maintained to her mother in my presence that she had not done wrong; she cannot bear to do wrong; a sense of having done wrong is enough to crush her; she naturally seeks for her own peace a conscientious verdict; she never would have had these relations if she had supposed at the time that they were wrong; Elizabeth never does anything that at the time seems wrong; for such a large moral nature, there is a lack of a certain balance and equipose; she has not a will that guides and restrains; but Elizabeth never does at any time that which does not have the stamp of her conscience at the time upon it.

Q. Do you say that she did or did not insist that she had violated her marriage vows? A. She always was saying that "it never seemed to her wrong;" and "Theodore, I do not see that I have wronged you."

Q. What do you understand her as meaning by "To love is praiseworthy, but the abuse of love is sin?" A. I rather think she meant carrying love to too great an extent.

Q. Would not that include criminal relations? A. Yes.

Q. Then you understand her, as early as 1868, as saying that the abuse of the gift of love by adultery would be a sin? A. Yes.

Q. She is a lady of intelligence, is she not? A. She is in

some respects a lady of extraordinary intelligence; she has a remarkable gift at times which anybody might envy; there is nothing low about Elizabeth.

Q. Is she a lady of large reading? A. There are very few ladies of larger reading; she was educated at the Packer Institute; I do not think she took quite a full course; she reads much to her blind aunt and to the children; I used to read a good deal to her; she was a good critic; Mr. Beecher carried to her sheets of his "Life of Christ" and many chapters of "Norwood; I used to read to her many things.

Q. What do you say about the "Life of Christ" and "Norwood"—that he carried them to her to criticise? A. Yes, or not exactly to criticise; she is not a critic in the sense that she can take a particular phrase and change the language of it; but she could tell whether a little speech put into Rose Wentworth's mouth was one a woman would be likely to say.

Q. He took those chapters to read to her for that purpose, having a high regard for her opinion in that matter—not as high regard for her opinion in a strictly critical sense? A. No; but in the sense whether it was womanly, and larger than that, whether it touched human sympathy or not. I remember that he took her the first sheet of the "Life of Christ; she wrote to me saying, "He said he had not read it to anybody else."

Q. When did he write "Norwood?" A. I do not know.

Q. When did he write his first volume of his "Life of Christ?" A. It was after "Norwood," I think.

Q. It was published after "Norwood?" A. I do not know about that.

Q. You know he took it to her to read? A. I know, because she wrote it in her letters; I believe she told the truth; you ask about "Norwood" and the "Life of Christ;" he had brought the opening part of the "Life of Christ" and I think also chapters of "Norwood."

Q. You understand that he brought them to her for the purpose of criticism? A. Yes.

Q. You yourself would regard her as an admirable critic? A. Oh, yes; I always liked to take everything I wrote to Elizabeth; sometimes when I thought I had written anything particularly nice I ran down and read it to her; she was one of the best of critics; she never praised an article because it was mine or his, but only when she liked it.

Q. You found her judgment not warped by her affections in

that? A. No, that is the particular feature of her character: if a lady were sitting at the piano and playing, and Elizabeth loved that lady very much, she would tell her about the playing—that it was good or that it was not—but she would not say that the playing was good because she loved the woman; she would not say so unless it was good; I was always quite certain that if Elizabeth liked what I wrote she did not like it on my account, though she was glad when I wrote a good thing; it was an honest criticism; if I had been a minister none of this trouble would have come; she was always in sorrow that I was not a minister—which is the only virtue that I possess; thank God that I do not belong to the priesthood or the church; it may not be an acceptable statement to the committee.

Q. Do you mean by that, Mr. Tilton, that the want of strong religious feature in your character was what she missed in you? A. No, Mr. Tracy, it was not that; because, though I should not like to say it of myself, yet I am a more religious man than most men of my acquaintance—that is, I am a man of religious sympathies who thoroughly hates and despises religious creeds; I do not believe in one of the thirty-nine articles, nor in either of the catechisms, nor in the divinity injunction of the Scriptures, nor in the divinity of Christ, in the sense in which it is held. I believe his writings to be enflooded by the Divine breath. It was not that I lack religious spirit. A man ought not to say that, perhaps, of himself, but I do not lack the religious spirit; I love God, and am fond of religious sentiment, but I hate the creeds; I was taught to hate them during the anti-slavery controversy; I saw the churches selling the negroes, and I despise a church; now put it down there (to a reporter); say that I despise the church, and generally despise ministers.

Q. Well, it was that lack of reverence for the church and its ordinances and your lack of belief in the divinity of Christ as she held it that she missed in you? A. Yes.

Q. And she grieved over it? A. Oh yes, indeed; grieved over it with tears.

Q. And what she found wanting in you she found in Mr. Beecher, did she not? A. Yes, she did, and he took advantage of it; that is why I say he ought to spend the rest of his life in penitence and anguish; if Mr. Beecher had held the same religious views that I hold, and gone to that house denying the divinity of Christ, he never could have made any approach to her, and the affection and love which she bore to him would never have existed—I mean the strong affection—it could not possibly have done so?

Q. The enthusiasm for him which she felt would never have existed in that case? A. No.

Q. You have no doubt that it was that feature in his character which roused her enthusiasm and made him to her a sort of poem, did it not? A. Yes, a sort of apostle; I think she regarded Mr. Beecher almost as though Jesus Christ himself had walked in; that is an extravagant expression, but you must not take it literally; I know that she wanted to make the children look upon the clergy with reverence; she ought to be an intense Roman Catholic, like Mme. Guion—a mystic; I think she certainly spends hours on her knees some days; I don't suppose a day ever passes over Elizabeth that the sun, if he could peep through the windows, would not see her on her knees, and my oldest daughter, Florence, though she looks like me, is like her mother; here has come this great calamity on my house; there was that publication last night; she saw it; and this morning what did she do? I heard a noise in the house, and found that she was down in the front parlor playing on the melodeon like a heroine, standing in the midst of this calamity like a rock in the sea; she gets that somewhat from me; I can stand all storms; she gets also from her mother the religious inspiration; Florence this morning had a genius for religion, when you would suppose that she would have been crushed; you (General Tracy) are not stronger in the court room than she was this morning at that musical instrument.

Q. You use the expression in regard to your daughter "genius for religion;" does not that express the character of your wife? A. Yes—even more so; my daughter is more intellectual; she is an abler and more stable woman, though not so sentimental, and less demonstrative; they are both great characters.

Q. Well, she is a character who could have an intimacy and reverence and enthusiasm for a man of Mr. Beecher's temperament and religious convictions and teachings, and carry it to an extreme length without the thought of passion or criminality? A. I do not think the thoughts of passion and of criminality were in her breast at all; I think they were altogether in his; I think she thought only of her love and reverence.

Q. Such a character would not excite the thought of jealousy as to her? A. Not in the slightest; I never had the slightest feeling of jealousy in regard to Elizabeth.

Q. The fact that she was manifesting this enthusiasm and all that, would not lead you to suspect her motives and purity originally? A. It would not; later it did.

Q. For how long a period? A. I do not know; I remember I wrote her some letters which, if she has kept them, would fix the date; there was a time when I felt that Mr. Beecher was using his influence greatly upon her.

Q. To control her in her domestic relations with you? A. No, but to win her; he was always trying to get her to say that she loved him better than me.

Q. She never would say it? A. I don't think she ever did.

Q. You do not believe she ever felt or believed it, do you? A. No; that is to say, in one sense she loved him; she loved his religious views, the loved him as an evangelical minister; but I don't think that on the whole he was as much to her as I was; still, of course, Mr, Tracy, I cannot question her motives; if she should say he was more to her than I was I cannot dispute it.

Q. You set out a letter that she wrote on the night of December 30th, after you returned to your house, referring to the retraction she had given to Mr. Beecher; did she write that letter or did you? A. She wrote it.

Q. Did you dictate it? A. No.

Q. Why did she write it? A. Because I asked her to make a calm statement of what she had designed in this letter to Mr. Beecher. She was in such a state of agony that she told me she could not recall her letter to him; she said she had given him this letter that he might fortify himself in a council of ministers; I asked her to take a pen at the end of the evening and give the exact circumstances and explain what she meant by it, and she wrote that letter; it was only the next day that the other letter came back, and then this one ceased to be of any importance; what struck me in that business as so damnable in Mr. Beecher, was that after coming and confessing to me and Mr. Moulton his criminal relations with Mrs. Tilton, and then asking to see her a few minutes, and going around the corner to see her, he should have come back again in half an hour, expressing his absolute heartbrokenness, whereas he had in his pocket this retraction from her; I say it was damnable and nefarious.

Q. Do you say that when you saw Mr. Beecher at Mr. Moulton's house Mr. Moulton was present? A. Yes, he was present in this way—I wanted a lengthy interview with Mr. Beecher alone, and when he came into the room I locked the door and put the key in my pocket, and narrated in order, Elizabeth's confession; it was a long one, and it would have been indelicate for me to touch it with any more elaboration than I have here; I do not wish to be questioned about it; it was a long story.

Q. Was Mr. Moulton present? A. Not at that part of the interview; after the door was opened he was; the interview that we three together had, was very short; I was on the stairs while Mr. Beecher talked with Mr. Moulton on the stairs; that interview was to bring me and Mr. Beecher together; the next time we all three had an interview.

Q. This retraction, you say in your communication, Mr. Beecher returned to you through Mr. Moulton; is that true? A. Yes, sir.

Q. Was that retraction ever delivered to you? A. I have got it now.

Q. Is it not in the possession of Mr. Moulton? A. Yes, but it belongs to me; Mr. Moulton had a safe place and I had not, and he has some of my papers.

Q. Do you mean to say that Mr. Moulton delivered that retraction to your actual keeping, and that you have had possession of it for any length of time? A. He did deliver it to me, and it was sent back to him.

Q. I ask you whether Mr. Moulton delivered that retraction to you and you kept it? A. Mr. Moulton put that retraction into my hand; exactly what I did with it—whether I carried it to my safe or not—I do not remember; I took a number of papers and put them in his keeping because I had no safe place.

Q. How long do you think you had possession of that paper? A. I do not remember; I never saw the retraction till it was brought back to me; then I read it; it may be that I never took it away from Mr. Moulton's house; it was sent back to me; it was put into my hand; I read it, and I made a copy of it.

Q. In short-hand? A. Yes.

Q. Did you ever have it longer than that? A. Yes; long enough to make forty copies in short-hand.

Q. But you returned it to Mr. Moulton, and he has kept it and has it now? A. Yes; unless he has been robbed.

Q. The letter which you say Mr. Beecher wrote Mrs. Tilton, with your permission, I see, as published, directs her to return it to him through your hands. A. Yes.

Q. Was it returned to him through your hands? A. It was returned to Mr. Moulton by me.

Q. Did you make a copy of it? A. I did.

Q. Then you took advantage of Mr. Beecher's direction to have that letter returned to him through your hands, to make a copy, and you made and preserved a copy of the letter? A. I did, exactly; and I have found a very good use for it in this late emergency.

Q. What you call the "apology"—is that in Mr. Beecher's handwriting? A. It is not.

Q. In whose handwriting is it? A. In Francis D. Moulton's, except the last sentence, which is Mr. Beecher's.

Q. "I trust this to Moulton in confidence," is in Mr. Beecher's handwriting, is not not? A. Yes.

Q. The words "in confidence" are underscored, are they not? A. I do not know.

Q. That document is written on how many half sheets of paper? A. I do not think on any; it is on sheets as big as that (legal cap).

Q. On how many—two or three? A. Yes, large sheets.

Q. Do you know whether the last sentence, "I trust this to Moulton in confidence," is separated by a wide space from the rest? A. I do not know; Frank can show it to you.

Q. Is it not separated by a wide space? No, not by a wide space.

Q. I ask you whether the last sentence of the letter is not here somewhere (indicating with the hand), and the line "I trust this to Moulton in confidence, H. W. Beecher," down there (indicating)? A. No, it is not.

Q. Is it not at the bottom of the page? A. It may be at the bottom of the page.

Q. Is it not away from the writing? A. No, it is not; it is a part of the letter.

Q. You were not present when it was written? A. No; otherwise it would not have been written.

Q. Because it would have been spoken? A. Yes; the substance was spoken to me a day or two afterwards in Mr. Moulton's bedchamber.

Q. You say if you had been present it would not have been written? A. Yes.

Q. That letter is not addressed to you, is it? A. It was addressed to Mr. Moulton, but it was brought to me on the authority of Mr. Beecher himself; it was brought to me greatly to my surprise; Mr. Moulton put it before me as evidence that I should maintain peace; I did not ask for it; it came unsolicited.

Q. You quote a letter dated on the 7th of January to you from Mr. Beecher. Was your suit with Bowen then pending? A. My suit with Bowen was pending from the 1st of January to the middle of the next year; I think it was in April, 1872; I never sued him; Mr. Moulton wanted to assume the management of my affairs with Mr. Bowen; Mr. Moulton, when sick, summoned us to him, and said, "I want to keep you on record and bind you to good will."

Q. You had a controversy? A. I had a controversy; I agreed not to do anything but at Mr. Moulton's discretion; Mr. Bowen owed me $7,000, and Frank said, "He has got to pay that; but I would rather pay it myself than that it should bring Mr. Beecher in collision, and I will agree that you shall have it, if I have to pay it myself; therefore, let this thing remain with me as long as I like—a year or ten years;" Frank was determined that peace should be kept.

Q. Were there any proceedings to perpetuate testimony taken? A. Frank thought Mr. Bowen ought to come to a settlement, and said, "I think I will put this in court;" and Mr. Ward instituted some proceedings; it was the mere suggestion of a suit, done without my knowledge; I think it was to perpetuate Mr. Johnson's testimony; I have forgotten.

Q. That was in 1872? A. Yes, it must have been in March.

Q. You say you put the management of your matter against Bowen in the hands of Moulton? A. I did.

Q. Did not he represent to you that it was absolutely indispensable or material that you and Mr. Beecher should keep on friendly terms in reference to this controversy with Bowen? A. No. The sum and essence of his management was the management of my relations to Mr. Beecher; he regarded Mr. Bowen as an incident; I could not afford to lose my office, and Mr. Moulton said, "You have got to keep peace with Mr. Beecher for the sake of yourself and family;" Mr. Moulton always made Mr. Bowen subsidiary to Mr. Beecher—and me also, till I revolted, after Dr. Bacon's letter.

Q. Do you mean to say that it was never regarded as important that friendly relations should be maintained between you and Mr. Beecher, having reference to your difficulty with Bowen? A. Not a particle: the more I quarreled with Mr.

Beecher, the better Mr. Bowen liked it; if, as a result of the controversy, Mr. Beecher should be dead, Mr. Bowen would not be one of the mourners, but one that would uplift the horn of gladness; he never wanted peace with Mr. Beecher; he is an enemy of Mr. Beecher, would rejoice in his downfall; perhaps I ought not to say that; it is speaking of the motives of people, but it is true.

Q. The triparite treaty was not signed until after February 7th, 1871? A. No.

Q. Was not your letter to Mr. Moulton of that date written for the purpose of calling out a reply from him? A. No; I wrote it because Frank insisted upon it; Frank had the idea that if I gave my word he would have me bound; he wanted me to write the utmost of what I could of good will in this letter.

Q. And did he get a corresponding answer from Mr. Beecher? A. Perhaps so; I do not think that he informed me that he was going to get an answer from Mr. Beecher.

Q. He informed you that he had got an answer from him afterwards, did he not? A. Yes, he showed it to me and I copied it.

Q. Do you say that your letter was not written in order to draw out an answer from Mr. Beecher? A. No, I wrote it to please Frank, because he wanted me to; perhaps there may be a sense in which I was to write what I could of good will, and Mr. Beecher what he could of good will; perhaps there may be correctness in your phrase; there was no collusion on my part with Mr. Beecher; It was Mr. Moulton's iron-like way of compelling things to go on in peace and harmony; he is a man of desperate strength of will.

Q. Now, will you produce all the letters which you quote on page 113 and 114 of your communication, beginning "My dear Frank, I am determined to make no more resistance. Theodore's temperament is such that the future, even if temporarily earned, would be absolutely worthless, and rendering me liable at any time of day?" etc. A. I cannot; Mr. Moulton can.

Q. Have you a copy of it? A. Yes, I think I am not wrong.

Q. Can you produce a copy? A. I do not know; I am sorry I cannot tell you; I have a mass of phonographic notes; whenever these letters came, whenever there was anything in them that Frank wanted me to see, he would read to me; whenever Mr. Beecher said anything that he thought, being read to me, would gratify my feelings and conduce to a compromise or peace between us, speaking of the kindness with which I treated him, or of his difficulties, Frank read them to me, and as I wrote short-hand, I always used to make a copy of them.

Q. And is that the only copy that you have of these papers? A. It is the only copy I have of Frank's papers.

Q. Copies in short-hand being read and never being compared with the originals? A. When Frank read to me three or four or five sentences I would write them down.

By Mr. Hall—Did you compare them with the originals? A. What do you mean by comparing them with the originals?

Q. Do you know that they are an exact transcript of the originals? A. Yes.

Q. You wrote them from your phonographic notes? A. You will find these extracts all perfectly correct—every one absolutely.

By Mr. Winslow—Do you remember the purport of what you left out? A. My impression is that this one of Mr. Beecher's letters to Frank was very long; it would certainly occupy four pages of foolscap; there was a long argument in it to show the difficulties that he was in; if I had quoted the whole it would have made this statement much stronger, but it would have made it a cumbered document.

Q. Is there something that you have not quoted? A. A great deal; but there is nothing in that quotation that violates the whole spirit of the letter.

Q. Had you no reason for omitting what you did, except to avoid length? A. No; only it alluded to interviews; for instance, in this way:—"I am greatly distressed with what the deacon said," or "The Brooklyn *Eagle* must not go on in this way;" many things might be added that are unimportant in this exhibit but were important at the time.

Q. On page 103, "No man can see the difficulties that environ me," etc., did you quote the whole of that letter? A. Only a fragment of it; there is not a whole letter in all these quotations.

Q. In making these quotations I see no stars? A. I do not know whether it is the omission of the printer; but I put in stars to show where the connection was broken off; where I took a paragraph which was long and it was continuous from beginning to end there is no need of stars.

Q. Your letter "To a Complaining Friend," that was published, to whom was that written? A. That was written to nobody; everybody was saying "You ought to answer the Woodhull scandal," and I put my wits together to frame a possible answer.

Q. Then you say that the letter "To a Complaining Friend" was a fiction? A. Yes, it was written on purpose as a public card.

Q. How long after the Woodhull scandal was that? A. It was published a long time after that date; not longer than two or three weeks I think, perhaps not ten days; my impression is that it was not published until a long time after; I thought I had written an ingenious card, but it did not amount to anything; Wendell Phillips said, "It is a fine thing but for one thing; you ought to have said that your wife was not guilty;" but I could not say that, and the card went for nothing; it was one of a number of ingenious subterfuges; I wrote it thinking that it would please Elizabeth; I read it to her before it was printed and she liked it; afterwards she spoke to me violently about it, and said it was another way of perpetuating the scandal.

Q. And charged you with publishing it for that purpose? A. No, not that.

Q. But did not she say that the effect of that publication would be to perpetuate the scandal and revive it? A. Yes, after it was published.

Q. The Woodhull scandal was dying out of the minds of the people, was it not, then, when that was published? A. I think not; I did not know the time when it was; it is a death of which I have had no notice yet; I thought I did a crafty thing in that card, but it failed.

Q. I asked whether the Woodhull scandal was not dying out of the minds of the people, and whether it would not have died out but for that? A. Well, I don't know; you are a better judge of that than I am; I think I heard less of it.

Q. Do you not know that the publication of that letter revived the talk and scandal? A. Yes, yes; everything revives the talk; the appointment of an investigating committee revived it in the same way, in general terms.

Q. What other publications have you made since the publication of the Woodhull scandal and the letter "To a Complaining Friend," and the Bacon letter, and the letters to the Council? A. The letter "To a complaining Friend" was put in the *Eagle* with a ferocious comment; if it had not been printed with a bad comment, I think it would have had a good effect; but that letter did harm.

Q. You mean to say that it revived or perpetuated the scandal instead of allaying it? A. It did harm in the sense that it purported to be a denial, looked as if it was meant for a denial which did not deny; and it left about this impression—that Mr. Tilton, a direct man, who knows what he means and could say it, if he could have denied this squarely would have done it; the impression was that it was written to deny, but that it did not deny.

Q. Did it not carry in it a strong implication of guilt? A. Well, perhaps in a sense you might inferentially say so; I think you might say that; I think if I had never said a word on the subject at all, from the beginning down, it would have been a great deal better.

Q. The scandal would have died out long ago, would it not? It has only been kept alive by your writings? A. I have acted like a fool, I admit.

By Mr. Tracy.—We all concede that, and do not need to call witnesses to prove it.

Q. Now, when the council was in session, that took the form, did it not, of an ecclesiastical controversy, in which the scandal proper dropped out of sight? A. There is no scandal proper.

Q. Well, this scandal itself dropped out of sight, and the controversy was over an ecclesiastical question, was it not? A. In a technical sense; but everybody said the council revived the business.

Q. Did not you know that your letters revived the scandal? A. Yes; or it did not need reviving—it had life in it.

Q. Did not your letters to the council largely call out the letters by Dr. Bacon? A. I think Dr. Bacon took a sublime indifference to my letters in the first place; he sent them back from the council; I do not now recollect that there was any extract from my letters to the council that were introduced at all by Dr. Bacon; perhaps there was; if he made any allusion at all to them it was a most unimportant one.

Q. You knew that the effect of your letters to the council would be to revive the scandal, did you not? A. No, I did not; I wrote to them to vindicate myself; I did not care whether they revived the scandal or not.

Q. Did not you know what the effect would be? A. I thought of vindicating myself; I had been attacked and I wrote a defence; the scandal had to take care of itself; I was not so tender toward the scandal that I should refrain from defending myself if it would revive it even.

Q. That is evident. Mrs. Tilton's letter to you quoted February 9th, 1868, and commencing, "Ah! did angel ever love so grandly as my beloved." In that letter, on page 164, this sentence occurs, "And the dear friends who love us." You originally wrote it, and you have erased "us" and put in "me." Do you know which is correct? What is the original? A. I think it is "me;" it is "me" (examining the first draft of the communication.)

Q. How came Mrs. Tilton to write that letter to Moulton, denying that she had ever thought of separating from you? A. Frank, as soon as he undertook to make the compromise between us, undertook to straighten out whatever was wrong; there was a story that Mrs. Morse set afloat about my being divorced, and Frank wrote a note to her or went to see her, and she wrote this note.

Q. Did not she write it at your suggestion? A. I do not think she did; I think she wrote it at Frank's suggestion; I had forgotten that letter until I found it among the papers.

Mr. Hill—Did not you make any suggestion to her about writing that letter? A. I do not recollect distinctly; it may be that I did; I do not know; I co-operated with Frank.

General Tracy—Has she not during this controversy signed letters that you have written for her? A. No; she wrote a letter to Dr. Storrs, a part of which I suggested the phraseology, of a delicate statement of her relations to Mr. Beecher, which, while it was not false, did not convey more than half of the truth; the remainder she wrote herself; she was going to state too much in it.

Q. Is there any other letter that she has ever written at your dictation, and signed after you had written it, in this controversy? A. Well, I do not know; I do not recollect any at present.

Q. Do you remember a letter that she wrote Mr. Moulton, commencing, "Dear Francis, I told you a falsehood last night?" A. I never saw it.

Q. Do you remember that Mr. Moulton reported to you, on any occasion, that she had made a statement that what you claimed was her confession she had made at your solicitation and instance, and at a time when you were also confessing to her, or anything of that description, and that you were angry about it, and took Moulton to your house to have him see whether she would make such a statement or not, and that Mr. Moulton coming in and repeating the statement in your presence, you asked her whether she had ever said so, and she said she had not, and you turned to Moulton and said, "Then you are the one who is the liar?" A. I do not remember an such phrase as that; Frank Moulton said to me, as nearly as I can recollect (his memory is better than mine), that Elizabeth, in a mood of severity on me (which she did not very often assume) said that I had made to her confession about myself corresponding with the confession which she had made to me against herself, which was not true; and Frank asked her squarely if it was so.

Q. Did he ask her or did you? A. I do not remember.

Q. What did she say? A. She said "No," and then Frank afterwards told me she said the opposite.

Q. Now did you not know that the very next morning she wrote to Mr. Moulton a letter beginning, "Dear Francis, I told you two falsehoods," and proceeded to say in substance, "The fact is that when I am in the presence of Mr. Tilton he has such a control over me that I am not responsible for what I say," or "I am obliged to say whatever he wills that I should say; but the truth is that I had reported the story just as you had heard it." A. I do not; I know that she had some conversation with him, which she reported to me as being greatly like a see-saw—saying one thing and unsaying it.

Q. Have you ever had doubts of her sanity? A. No.

Q. Never? A. No, sir.

Q. Have you ever threatened to put her in an asylum? A. No, sir.

Q. Have you ever circulated the story among her acquaintances or friends that she was becoming insane? A. No, but that her mother was; there was one time about then when she was a little delirious.

Q. When? A. I do not remember; her mind wandered a little in sickness; she has never had a taint of insanity; you know we have a customary phrase, "You say an extravagant being, my friend, you are insane;" that is the only possible way in which Elizabeth has been insane; she is not insane at all.

Q. Mr. Tilton you have quoted the letters of your wife here to prove what the character of your home was in the beginning of 1868 and through 1868? A. I quoted them to show what it was previous to her surrender to him.

Q. You have stated, Mr. Tilton, that there were acts of criminality, first at Mr. Beecher's house, and secondly, at your own house; do you pretend to have a personal knowledge of those acts? A. Only the knowledge of Mrs. Tilton's confession —that is all; I was absent at the time.

Q. Mr. Moulton was in college with you? A. Yes, sir.

Q. He has always been your friend from your college days? A. Yes, sir, and I hope he will be to the end of my life.

Q. Your novel is dedicated to him? A. Yes, but he has not done me the honor of reading it; I will never dedicate another.

Q. You say that you had not reported this scandal to the Woodhull women or woman; but you do not deny that you had frequently spoken harshly of Mr. Beecher to her? A. Oh, not harshly; I have spoken often critically of him, but always with a view to have her do no harm to him; I expressed my opinion about him.

Q. How came she and Mr. Beecher to have an interview? A. I do not remember the circumstances. I think Frank Moulton devised it; Mr. Beecher had a number of interviews with her at Frank's house and one at mine.

Q. Was not the object to get Mr. Beecher committed to her views of free love? A. No; to her views of the fourteenth and fifteenth amendments of woman's suffrage; Mr. Butler and I championed it, and we wanted Mr. Beecher to do the same.

Q. Was it not to get him to preside at Steinway Hall? A. That was not at my house, but at Frank's; I think at mine it was in regard to the fourteenth and fifteenth amendments.

Q. Well, an effort was made to get him to preside there and introduce her at Steinway Hall, and an exposition of this scandal was threatened if he did not preside there? A. Frank received a letter from Colonel Blood that he thought was a threat; it angered Frank a good deal.

By Mr. Winslow—Did you see the letter from Colonel Blood, in which it was threatened that this scandal would be exposed if Mr. Beecher did not preside at the Steinway Hall meeting; A. I do not think that is so; if it was I did not know it; I do not think there was any truth in it.

Q. Mr. Beecher had been importuned to preside, had he not? A. Yes; there came a note from Colonel Blood about the Woodhulls not being received in some hotel; they said it was because they were unpopular, and they wanted Mr. Beecher's help; there was something in the letter which Frank regarded as unhandsome, and I knew he was angry and expressed himself strongly about it, and said it looked like blackmail; it was one of the first indications of their attempting to use us.

Q. Do you not know that Mr. Beecher was threatened that in case he did not preside at that meeting this scandal should be published? A. It is the first time that I have ever heard it suggested.

Q. Was he not threatened by Mrs. Woodhull? A. Not that I have any knowledge of.

Q. Was not the very object of soliciting Mr. Beecher to preside at the Steinway Hall meeting on the part of you and Mr. Moulton in order to place Mrs. Woodhull under obligation, so that she should not make the publication? A. Precisely so; we did not know that there was to be a publication; we wanted to keep her on our side, and wanted to take every possible occasion to do it; her husband had spent a considerable length of time to devise this Steinway Hall speech; what is was about I do not know; she gave me and Frank the proofs, and he put them in his drawer; I never looked at them; it was our folly that we did not, for I might have known what was in that speech; she wanted Mr. Beecher to preside; I told Mr. Beecher that however unpopular she was he might go and preside, and I sketched a little sort of speech (and I think Frank sketched one) that, if he could see his way to do it, he might make:—"Fellow citizens—Here is a woman who is going to speak. She will probably speak on what you do not believe; but that is no reason why she should not be heard. It is bebecause I disagree with her that I would introduce her. I like free speech. I have the honor of presenting her." I said to him that he was able to carry a little speech of that sort and I felt that if he went and presided it would put her under the same obligation to him as I fancied that I had put her under to me in writing her biography; I considered that I had secured her good will by writing that and other things, and I thought that if Mr. Beecher would do some signal service of that kind, which he could do and which would be noted as such, it would fix her under gratitude, and we would all be fixed; Frank had done her some service; Frank had been very friendly to her; he had done her many services and he had great respect for her.

Q. You pressed that argument on Mr. Beecher? A. Yes, and Frank also.

Q. As a matter of safety? A. Yes; I said "Think it over, and if you find that you can, go and do it."

Q. Do you know whether the letter from Colonel Blood had been received at that time? A. I do not know.

Q. Mr. Beecher rejected your argument and refused to preside? A. He did not refuse, but said that if he saw his way clear he would come and let us know.

Q. But he did not let you know? A. He did not let us know.

Q. And you presided instead? A. I did not want to; but I had no idea of what the speech was going to be.

Q. Although the proofs were in your hands and you might have known? A. Yes; but I never did know; the proofs had been brought to Frank's study; I may have had the idea that they were for Mr. Beecher to see the speech; but it was not the printed speech that did the damage, it was the interjected remarks in response to the audience; she said violent things.

Q. Had you written her life at that time? A. Yes, I had; I am pretty certain of it.

Q. What other things had you done to put her under obligations? A. I will tell you what I did; I wrote that idea of the Fourteenth and Fifteenth amendments, and spent three of the solidest weeks of my life in working it into an argument and printing it into a tract; it was her idea, but she did not know how to expose it, and I worked it up in one of the most elaborate pieces of writing that I ever did; that was one of the great services; the second was the writing of a sketch; then, also, when Senator Carpenter attacked that proposition I made an elaborate reply.

Q. You went to the meeting yourself, and deliberately intended to go? A. No, I did not; Frank came to the *Golden Age* office; it rained and it was late, half-past seven o'clock, and I went to see who was to preside; there was no expectation that I would preside at all; we got there at ten minutes to eight o'clock, and the crowd was so great that we could not get in at the front way, and we went into a large anteroom, and there was Mrs. Woodhull, flushed and excited because there was not a brave man in the circle of the two cities to preside at her meeting; Mr. Beecher did not come, and one or two others that had been invited were not there; she felt that there was no courage in men, and she was going on alone, and I said, "I will preside at your meeting;" it was not more than ten minutes; I do not believe five minutes, forethought; I went on the platform and made a few remarks and introduced her; that was the way it came about.

[Here followed an examination (foreign to the inquiry) as to Mr. Tilton's relations to certain women, which is too indecent to reproduce.

Q. Did you ever express your attachment for —— in the presence of your wife? A. Ask my wife; take her answer; you may depend that I never said to ——, or any other lady, in the absence of my wife, what I would not have said in her presence; I have no secrets from Mrs. Tilton; I never had any, and should never have had any, but for this break up; I never had any secrets from Mrs. Tilton until within this last year or two, during which we have not harmonized as in former years.

Q. Have you ever admitted to her that you had committed adultery? A. I never admitted to her anything of the kind.

Q. But you don't mean to say that you have not, do you? A. Mr. Tracy, talk to me as one gentlemen to another.

General Tracy—You charge your wife with having committed adultery; I mean to ask you whether you have or not? A. I say, let my wife make the charge, if she wishes to.

Q. I ask you the question. A. You may ask it till doomsday.

Q. You decline to answer? A. I do not; I say I will take my wife's answer.

Q. How could she know that you had, if you had not confessed it to her? I ask you whether you have not been guilty of the crime? A. I decline to hold a conversation with you on such a subject.

Q. Have you not admitted to others your commission of adultery? A. Mr. Tracy, have you committed adultery?

General Tracy—I have not charged my wife with that crime.

Mr. Tilton—If I am to be charged with the crime of adultery in this business I wish to know it. I wish my wife, in whose interest you speak, to make the charge if she chooses. Now let her choose. If you, gentlemen, suppose that you are to fight this battle in reference to my character I will make it ten times harder than you see. Yesterday we were on the edge of peace; but if you mean to draw the sword, the sword shall be drawn.

Mr. Hill—Don't you think it is pretty well out?

Mr. Tilton—There is one thing that I was born for and that is war.

Q. Did you make the acquaintance of Mrs. Woodhull in the absence of ——? A. I don't remember whether she was absent or present.

Q. Don't you remember whether it was while she was at home or not that you were associating with Mrs. Woodhull? A. I knew Mrs. Woodhull a whole year.

Q. [After several questions interjected, involving reference to another woman.] Do you know whether or not information was communicated to your wife that you were living with Mrs. Woodull? A. I never lived with her.

Q. Do you remember whether your wife was told that you were living with her? A. I never heard of it till now; I saw something the day before yesterday in a salacious newspaper.

Q. The Chicago *Times?* A. Yes.

Q. Have you read it? A. Yes.

Q. Don't you know that information of precisely the character then published was communicated to your wife by the mother of Mrs. Woodhull during your intimacy with Mrs. Woodhull? A. I never heard of such a thing; I remember that Mrs. Morse was with Mrs. Claflin; the old, crazy woman came at the foot of her stairs one night and made a hideous racket of some sort of trash; Mrs. Morse quoted that, and got quite frightened about it.

General Tracy—I hope all the mothers of your friends are not insane. Don't you know that Mrs. Claflin at the same time communicated that to your wife? A. I did not know that she saw my wife; I understood that that woman made a visit at Mrs. Morse's; it may be, perhaps, that Mrs. Tilton's was there at the time.

Q. Don't you know that your wife's mind has been disturbed in regard to your own infidelity to her by your associations with public women? A. No, sir; if that pretence is made, Mr. Tracy, on your part, it is unmanly; if it is made on her part, it is false; I have never associated with public women.

General Tracy—I don't mean prostitutes; I mean reformers. A. Oh, yes; I said before that Elizabeth had been annoyed, over and over again, by my associations with all persons out of the realm of religious orthodox ideas.

Q. In that class of people whom among your lady acquaintances do you include? A. I include Mrs. Stanton and Miss Anthony, though I have not seen those people since Elizabeth ordered them out of the house; beyond those persons I don't know; Lucy Stone was one; she lived in Boston; she did not come very often; Elizabeth was a reformer at one time, and had the getting up of women's rights meetings, and had the children take the tickets; she arranged the campaign, but now she can't endure them.

In explanation of the above, Mr. Tilton, in the journals of July 28th, published a card, asserting that the cross-examination had been garbled, inasmuch as he had distinctly sworn that the several acts of criminality between Mr. Beecher and Mrs. Tilton were confessed by both of those parties to Mr. Tilton, as well as to Mr. Frank Moulton, the "Mutual Friend."

CHAPTER XIV.

A WEEK OF INTENSE EXCITEMENT.—THE WOMAN SUFFRAGE RAVENS GATHER ABOUT.—MRS. STANTON DECLARES THAT MR. TILTON ADMITTED TO HER THAT MR. BEECHER HAD SEDUCED MRS. TILTON, AND THAT MRS. TILTON CONFESSED THE SIN TO SUSAN B. ANTHONY.—COL. ANTHONY ASSERTS THAT HIS SISTER TOLD HIM THE SAME STORY.—MISS ANTHONY WILL NEITHER ADMIT NOR DENY THE ALLEGATIONS.—STARTLING STATEMENTS BY MR. CARPENTER.—THE CASE IN THE COURT AT LAST.—DISAPPEARANCE OF MR. MOULTON.

FOLLOWING close upon the publication of Mr. Tilton's cross-examination some startling revelations were made that, while making the mystery still deeper, were certainly damaging to Mr. Beecher's case. The following letters which appeared in the *Daily Graphic* over the signature of "Inquirer" created much comment:

"Please make room for the following points which may serve to throw a light upon the great scandal now agitating this community. In reciting them, I know fully whereof I speak;

"1. Tilton was not acquainted with Mrs. Woodhull until nearly a year after the difficulty in his family. His acquaintance with her was due to the fact that it came to his knowledge that she was in possession of his family secret. His famous life of that woman was written in the endeavor to placate her and prevent the publication of the scandal.

"2. The story of the scandal got to the public through the indiscretion of Miss Susan B. Anthony. She was a guest of the Tiltons when the alleged discovery was made by Mr. Tilton. Her story is that Mrs. Tilton came to her room one night complaining of the violence of 'Theodore,' and the matter was talked over fully at the breakfast-table the next morning.

"3. The first person who communicated the alleged facts to Mrs. Woodhull was Mrs. Elizabeth Cady Stanton, who had received them in confidence from Miss Anthony, and of course they were told in the same way to all the family acquaintances of those two distinguished reformers.

"4. It is understood that Mrs. Woodhull has in her possession a letter written by a brother of Miss Susan B. Anthony, a resident of Kansas, in which the whole story of the scene witnessed by his sister at the house of the Tiltons is told.

"5. Tilton really tried to save his wife from this scandal. He did not confess the fact even to his most intimate friends, and did all that a man could do to keep it secret until he was fairly driven to the wall.

"6. There is no doubt that at the time of this difficulty 'free-love' doctrines had a great deal to do with the catastrophe; that they were held in a measure by all the parties to this unhappy scandal. The celebrated 'free divorce' editorials in the *Independent* were written by Tilton subsequent to the discovery of the alleged scandal in his own family.

"7. There is no allegation on record of any infidelity on Tilton's part before the discovery of the supposed guilt of his wife. Whatever charges are against him date from a subsequent period.

"8. This was not a case of deliberate seduction on the part of Mr. Beecher, if the facts are as they are represented to me. She was angered at her husband for his self-sufficiency, his want of consideration for her, and what seemed to her jealous mind his probable infidelities. She went to Mr. Beecher for counsel, and in the prolonged interviews which ensued the intimacy occurred—if the facts are as Tilton supposes them to be.

"In closing, I venture the prediction that it will be found at the bottom of this whole affair, that Mr. Beecher held a sexual theory which he believes to be in advance of the present constitution of society, and that if the facts are as alleged he has fallen because of following out a higher law, as he supposed, than that which controls the conventions of our present society."

"Will you permit me to make a statement respecting this deplorable Tilton-Beecher business which may throw some light upon it? I should never have felt moved to utter a word on the subject, were it not that the facts have now become public property, and the incidents I am about to relate may help to form what is greatly needed, a coherent theory of this great scandal. The country is likely to be divided into earnest partisans of Tilton on the one hand, and Beecher on the other; —but surely there must be a large number of people who have no special partiality for either of those gentlemen, and who wish simply to get at the truth of the affair. The information came into my possession three years ago—how, it is needless to relate. My only object in giving it is to explain the relations of the parties to each other in a more judicial manner than would be the case if the *ex-parte* statements of either were taken as sole evidence.

"When Mr. Tilton and his wife were first married, they lived together with a tolerable degree of happiness. But the conditions changed greatly within eight or ten years. The wife, who was an intelligent and clever woman, bore children very rapidly; she has had seven, of whom four are now living. Immersed in maternal and household cares, Mrs. Tilton ceased to be attractive to her husband, over whom, in the meantime, a great change had come. From the obscurity of a reporter on the *Tribune* he had become the celebrated editor of the greatest religious newspaper in the country; he was moreover an admirable orator, and seemed to have a great and most brilliant career before him. With these changed conditions came changed deportment towards his wife. He manifested a remarkable degree of self-importance; he treated her, my informant says, with great want of consideration, and it is further hinted, that he was by no means faithful to his marriage vows. Led away by the flattery of women he failed to observe that moral code without which the marriage bond loses its sanctity. All this, of course, was extremely mortifying to the high-spirited wife and mother. She resented such treatment. And here let me remark that Mrs. Tilton is said to possess in an unusual degree, that craving for sympathy and tenderness which is the marked characteristic of her sex. It is even said that her exactions in this respect amount almost to selfishness.

"Thus, with extreme sensitiveness on both sides, the ill-feeling which Mrs. Tilton could not suppress was met on Mr. Tilton's part with a want of conciliation, which only tended to make matters worse. In this frame of mind Mrs. Tilton naturally turned for advice and sympathy to her pastor, to the friend of her husband, to the minister who had married her, to the man to whom she had always looked up with reverence and affection. It seems that Tilton had, about this time, been absent a great deal from home. It was in the winter, and he had seventy engagements for lectures, and consequently was traveling a great deal. Mrs. Tilton carried her bruised heart, her wounded pride, her unsatisfied longings to Mr. Beecher, and in him she found a warm sympathizer. Pity, as is well known, is near akin to love, and, if this theory is correct, it led the impulsive, warm-hearted preacher and the sympathetic, craving woman into an intimacy which it is alleged, became criminal. This was kept up for some time with the results that are known to the world.

"According to my information the explosion occurred in this wise: Miss Susan B. Anthony (through whom, it is alleged, the story subsequently became public, she relating it to all her female associates) was stopping at Mr. Tilton's house. Tilton had been unusually exasperating in his demeanor toward his wife, and it is said had given her renewed cause for jealousy. She was provoked beyond endurance, and, filled with a desire to humiliate him, in passionate utterances she told him, in the presence of the guest alluded to, that she had been as faithless to her marriage vows as he had been to his.

"A tremendous scene followed. Tilton was furious. Finally the whole story of her intimacy with her pastor came out. The circumstances, as I have depicted them, explain how the story got abroad. The secret, which should have been guarded by Theodore Tilton, Henry Ward Beecher, Mrs. Tilton, and their mutual friend, Frank Moulton, was first of all babbled about in the clique of woman suffragists, and finally found its way to the public.

"In justice to Mr. Tilton, however, it must be stated that up to the date of his last letter he invariably defended his wife. He had denied to everybody but Frank Moulton and Oliver Johnson that anything more occurred than an improper overture from Mr. Beecher to Mrs. Tilton.

"The way in which the public regard Tilton is very curious. Everybody admitted that he was a young man of great promise, a fine orator, an able journalist. But somehow he was always the subject of unfavorable comment on the part of the press. He never did anybody any harm; he never spoke unkindly of any of his contemporaries; he engaged in no cabals. But somehow he impressed the public and, I am told, the editors as a man who possessed a great deal of self-consciousness and as assuming a position he was not entitled to. At any rate, he failed to make that favorable impression on his contemporaries which his talents certainly seemed to entitle him to. He possibly lacked a sense of humor, and often a want of tact in dealing with the outside public. But the fact remains that while he has a strong case as against Mr. Beecher, the press of this city is almost unanimously against him.

"So here you have the story—the growing alienation between husband and wife, both of them strongly self-conscious, both craving sympathy, both failing to have due consideration for each other. Then comes the pastor, warm-blooded, exuberant, impulsive, and moreover, it is said, with an unhappy home of his own. Such a man dealing with such a woman—all parties being meanwhile infected more or less with the current sexual theories as to the right of individuals to bestow their affections on whom they please—such a man and such a woman, in such a frame of mind, are not at all unlikely to fall. How large a share the free-love doctrines had in this painful affair nobody will probably ever know; but that Henry Ward Beecher was deeply infected with these doctrines is no secret at all. Indeed, they were very plainly avowed by several members of his church to the writer as a positive defence of Mr. Beecher's slips when first this matter got into the papers; and I feel convinced that these pernicious doctrines have had much to do with this unhappy scandal.

"I give the statement with the accompanying hypothesis, as it may probably afford a solution of this very painful affair. That Mr. Beecher is the treacherous seducer which Mr. Tilton tries to prove him, very few people will believe. Mr. Beecher fell, if this story is true, through his sympathy with a woman in distress, whom he believed was alienated from her husband by the cruelty of the latter. All this is explicable, and the case affords another warning as to the misery which invariably results from the satisfaction of purely egotistic impulses."

Upon the appearance of these letters a reporter of the Brooklyn *Argus* visited Mrs. Stanton, who in answer to questions told the following story:—

"Some time—I think it was in the Fall of the year, though

I won't be positive—while Mrs. Bullard was still connected with the *Revolution*, Susan B. Anthony, Mr. and Mrs. Tilton, Mrs. Bullard, and myself, were in Brooklyn together. It was afternoon, and after calling at the office of the *Revolution*, Mr. Tilton and myself accompanied Mrs Bullard to her residence, and remained to dinner.

Through some misunderstanding, Miss Anthony went with Mrs. Tilton, and dined with her instead of us. There was some feeling on the part of Mrs. Tilton in regard to this, although it was quite unintentional on my part. Well, at the table—no one was present but Mrs. Bullard, Mr. Tilton, and myself—Theodore told the whole story of his wife's faithlessness. As I before observed, he did not go into the details; but the sum and substance of the whole matter he related in the hearing of Mrs. Bullard and myself. We were reformers. He gave us the story as a phase of social life."

"'This was the first you had heard of it?"

"'This was the first. The next evening, hearing that Miss Anthony was a little piqued at me for leaving her on the day before, I returned to my home in Tenafly. To my surprise, I found Susan awaiting my arrival. That evening, when we were alone, I said to her: 'Theodore related a very strange story to Mrs. Bullard and me, last evening.' Then I recounted to her all that he had told us. Miss Anthony listened attentively to the end. Then she said:

"'I have heard the same story from Mrs. Tilton. We compared notes, and found that by both man and wife the same story had indeed been told.'

"'What were the particulars of Mrs. Tilton's confession?'

"'I will tell you how it was made. When Mr. Tilton returned home that evening, some angry words—growing out of the separation in the afternoon—passed between him and his wife. Both became intensely excited. In the heat of the passion, and in the presence of Mrs. Anthony, each confessed to the other of having broken the marriage-vow. In the midst of these startling disclosures, Miss Anthony withdrew to her room. Shortly after she heard Mrs. Tilton come dashing up the stairs, and Mr. Tilton following close after. She flung open her bedroom door, and Elizabeth rushed in. The door was then closed and bolted. Theodore pounded on the outside, and demanded admittance, but Miss Anthony refused to turn the key. So intense was his passion at that moment that she feared he might kill his wife if he gained access to the room.

Several times he returned to the door, and angrily demanded that it be opened. "No woman shall stand between me and my wife," he said. But Susan, who is as courageous as she is noble, answered him with the words, "If you enter this room it will be over my dead body!" And so the infuriated man ceased his demands and withdrew. Mrs. Tilton remained with Susan throughout the night. In the excitement of the hour, amid sobs and tears, she told all to Miss Anthony. The whole story of her own faithlessness, of Mr. Beecher's course, of her deception, and of her anguish, fell upon the ears of Susan B. Anthony, and were spoken by the lips of Mrs. Tilton. The next morning, Mr. Tilton told Susan never to enter his house again. She told him she should enter whenever she chose; but I believe she did not go there again."

"By Mr. Tilton's cross-examination," observed the reporter, 'it appears that Mrs. Tilton was far from friendly to Miss Anthony. How could she have made this confession to her?'

"On the contrary, Mrs. Tilton thought a great deal of Miss Anthony, of Mrs. Bullard, and all those ladies. I was very intimate with her before Mrs. Woodhull's thunderbolt. At the time of our first knowledge of the affair, Mr. Wilkeson also heard of it. He besought the ladies not to make it public. To him it was a matter of money. He was a stockholder in Plymouth Church, in the *Christian Union*, and in "The Life of Christ." Now, the destruction of Mr. Beecher would be the destruction of all these. As Mr. Wilkeson expressed it, "It would knock the 'Life of Christ' higher than a kite." Hence his concern in keeping the matter secret.

This startling statement was followed by the following confirmation of Mrs. Stanton from Susan B. Anthony's brother. It is from a special dispatch to the Chicago *Tribune* from Leavenworth, Kansas:

"Col. Anthony, Susan B.'s brother, told your correspondent to-day that he first heard the scandal story from the lips of his sister, in Washington, one year ago. Susan B. Anthony told him that she was a guest at Tilton's house when a violent domestic scene occurred. She retreated to her room to avoid it, and was presently followed by Mrs. Tilton. The two women bolted the door, placing the bedstead against it, to keep Tilton on the outside. Tilton accused his wife of adultery with Beecher, and she replied with the accusation that he had procured an abortion for a young lady of Brooklyn, whom he had seduced, calling the lady by name. That night Miss Anthony and Mrs. Tilton slept together, and during a conversation the latter, in seeming mental distress, imparted the secret of a guilty intrigue with Beecher. Miss Anthony asked her how she came to yield to Beecher's advances; if he used force; to which Mrs. Tilton replied no force was used, she yielding without knowing why she did so. She averred that Beecher treated her with the kindness he would a child. She resolved many times to yield no more, but as often her good resolutions failed. This is the whole substance of Susan B. Anthony's story, as related to her brother. He is of the opinion that his sister will not testify in the case unless compelled to do so in court."

Several interviews followed with Miss Anthony, but she would neither contradict nor affirm the statements of Col. Anthony and Mrs. Stanton, alleging that she obtained the knowledge confidentially, and would only speak in a court of law. Mrs. Stanton was interviewed the second time and more fully explained matters in this fashion:

Reporter—You have no doubt in your mind but that Mrs. Tilton made a confession to Susan B. Anthony?

Mrs. Stanton—Not the slightest; not any more than though I had heard it myself. Susan always speaks the truth.

Reporter—And that confession was of a criminal intimacy with Henry Ward Beecher?

Mrs. Stanton—Yes; criminal as the word is generally understood. Mrs. Tilton did not look upon it in that way.

Reporter—But it was a confession of what Mr. Tilton has sinced charged.

Mrs. Stanton—Precisely.

Reporter—You know, beyond all doubt, that Theodore Tilton told to you and to Mrs. Bullard the story of his wife's infidelity?

Mrs. Stanton—Certainly. The main facts of the case he told us at the time I have specified. Many incidents related in the Woodhull statement I have never heard of; but the story itself I heard from his lips.

Reporter—After Mr. Tilton had told you this story did he ever deny it?

Mrs. Stanton—Yes. When the Woodhull thunderbolt had fallen, Mr. Wilkeson called upon Mr. Tilton and the latter flatly denied having made any such statement regarding his wife. As soon as I was informed of this I said to Miss Anthony, "I have proof of my story, and I want you to go straight to Mrs. Bullard's with me." We went there; and in an interview, lasting over an hour, I recalled to Mrs. Bullard Mr. Tilton's conversation to us on the Beecher matter, and she fully confirmed my statement to Miss Anthony, indignant at the message Mr. Wilkeson had communicated from Mr. Tilton, stated to Mrs. Bullard her interview with Elizabeth on that memorable night.

Reporter—To whom does this account, in the Chicago paper interview, refer?

Mrs. Stanton—To Mrs. Fernando Jones.

Reporter—What do you think of the statement credited to her?

Mrs. Stanton—Perhaps I ought to extend the same charity towards Mrs. Jones that she has towards me—I believe that the interviewer reported her words incorrectly. At the same time I readily understand how, not knowing that I had decided to make anything public, Mrs. Jones might have told her story out of simple friendship for me. That is, in order to hide the truth.

Reporter—Have you any idea what testimony Frank Moulton could render if he wished.

Mrs. Stanton—Nothing more than that he has been in the confidence of Mr. Beecher for many years. After a visit which the latter once made to Mr. Moulton, Frank said: "We have had Plymouth church on its knees here." Of course, his testimony ought to be had.

Reporter—Are you willing to appear before the committee, Mrs. Stanton?

Mrs. Stanton—No, not before that committee. When gentlemen who are in the confidence of its proceedings tell me that the integrity of every witness who appears against Mr. Beecher is to be impeached, I have no wish to give my testimony. I belong to a family of lawyers, and I have great respect for the law. When the case comes before a civil court I shall willingly appear if summoned. There is no stronger proof that the committee have a difficult case in sustaining Mr. Beecher than its understood determination to impeach the integrity of every witness against him, and no better proof of the strength of Mr. Tilton's position than its subterfuges in trying to undermine him by attacking the characters of all the ladies of his acquaintance. Can Mr. Beecher, in his circle, boast nobler, truer, purer women than those identified with the various reform movements in this country? Neither Mr. nor Mrs. Tilton need be ashamed of such acquaintances as Grace Greenwood, Celia Burleigh, Anna Dickinson, Lucy Stone, Susan B. Anthony or Paulina Davis, who have all been honored visitors at his house. It is beneath the dignity of any man or committee of men to attempt to shadow lives like these.

Reporter—Do you think Miss Anthony would be willing to testify before the committee?

Mrs. Stanton—I think not; but before the civil courts she undoubtedly would.

Reporter—Mrs. Stanton, do you believe in the doctrine of free love, as advocated by Mrs. Woodhull?

Mrs. Stanton—No; I believe in law. I have always been in favor of doing everything in harmony with law. In my address on "Marriage and Divorce," which was made in substance before the Legislature of New York, I gave my views on the whole social question. The speech is published. Any one can refer to it.

Reporter—The Chicago *Mail and Post* attributes to Mrs. Jones these words:—"Miss Anthony would not have revealed a confession of criminality made by Mrs. Tilton to any one—not even Mrs. Stanton." What have you to say on that?

Mrs. Stanton—Mrs Jones did not tell to the *Mail and Post* all that she might have told. Miss Anthony and I have been intimate friends for more than thirty years. When we met the evening after the confessions, both fresh with astonishment, it was perfectly natural that we should mutually confide. And we did so.

Reporter—Have you heard from Miss Anthony since the publication of your statement?

Mrs. Stanton—I have. She has been on a lecturing tour, and has been very unwilling to say anything about the matter. She considered it would be a breach of confidence.

Reporter—Did you read Mr. Carpenter's statement, published in the *Argus?*

Mrs. Stanton—I did, and in its confirmation I have to say that during my recent visit to Paulina Davis at Providence she told me that she had heard this story from Oliver Johnson's family long before I knew anything of it.

Reporter—What do you think of Mr. Tilton's arrest.

Mrs. Stanton—I was in hopes that it would bring the case into the courts, but I suppose some other means will have to be taken to accomplish that end.

At the conclusion of the interview, which had been pleasantly seasoned with a lunch and spiced with racy remarks on a variety of topics, Mrs. Stanton observed, "I don't like to be represented by the press as striking a blow at a woman; but when it comes to the women of the suffrage movement and Mr. Beecher, I prefer to let him kick the beam, though he may take some one woman with him."

Mr. Frank B. Carpenter, who figured as a friend of Mr. Tilton in all the negotiations with Rev. Dr. Bacon was interviewed by an *Argus* reporter on July 26th and thus described his connection with the case :—

"I was first brought actively into this case by Mr. Beecher. On Sunday, May 25th 1873, Mr. Beecher sent Mr. H. M. Cleaveland, his confidential friend and business partner, to my residence, in Forty-fifth street, with a horse and carriage. Mr. Cleaveland told me that Mr. Beecher wished me to come immediately to Brooklyn. On our way to Brooklyn, Mr. Cleaveland said that Mr. Beecher had learned that Mr. Bowen had reasserted to me the charges against him (Beecher) which he had formerly made to Mr. Tilton, but which he had retracted in a written covenant, in the possession of Mr. H. B. Claflin. Mr. Beecher had learned that Mr. Bowen had said to myself, and also in the presence of Mr. E. D. Holton, a citizen of Milwaukie (in an interview at the *Independent* office), that he did not wish us to understand that he had made a retraction. Mr. Cleaveland said Mr. Beecher wished me to confront Mr. Bowen on these points. He also said that the tripartite covenant was to be made public. Mr. Cleaveland drove me to Mr. Moulton's house, in Remsen street. Mr. Beecher was not there, but Mr. Moulton said it was Mr Beecher's wish that I should go to Mr. Bowen's house that evening, in company with Mr. Claflin and himself (Mr. M.), and repeat to them the substance of what Mr. Bowen had said to me. A few minutes later, Mr. Tilton came to Mr. Moulton's house; I told him about making the covenant public. Mr. Tilton said that if Mr. Beecher's friends made that covenant public, it would be a very dangerous thing. He protested against the publicity.

About eight o'clock Sunday evening, Mr. Moulton and myself went to Mr. Claflin's house, in Pierrepont street, where we found Mr, Claflin, and then all proceeded to Mr. Bowen's residence, corner of Clark and Willow streets. There I recounted to Mr. Bowen, in the presence of Messrs. Claflin and Moulton, the statements made by Mr. Bowen to myself concerning Mr. Beecher. Mr. Bowen admitted all that I said, and Mr Claflin expressed his astonishment that Mr. Bowen should have told those things after signing the covenant Mr. Claflin was the man who induced Bowen to sign that covenant. Mr. Bowen said he protested against giving publicity to the covenant. I said to Mr. Bowen: "The simplest justice to Mr. Beecher requires that, if your statements concerning Mr. Beecher are not true, you should make the most unqualified public denial. But if they are true, stand by your statements." Mr. Bowen had said to me that Mr. Beecher had made a confession on his knees to him. Mr. Tilton and Mr. Moulton had been told by Beecher that this was a lie. I said: "Mr. Bowen, there is a direct lie between you and Mr. Beecher, and for one, I want to know the truth."

Mr. Claflin said: "I think we had better have Mr. Beecher here, to-night."

I said I would be glad to have Mr. Beecher present.

Mr. Bowen said: "I am willing to have Mr. Beecher come here, and will confront him."

Mr. Claflin volunteered to go and get him, when Mr. Moulton started up and said:

"Mr. Claflin, I will go."

He went out, and was gone fifteen or twenty minutes. He returned without Mr. Beecher, saying that the house was closed and the windows darkened; that he rang the bell, but couldn't raise anybody. This was about 10:30 o'clock. Mr. Claflin then said:

"Well, I think it's very important that Mr. Bowen and Mr. Beecher should have a private interview before this matter goes any further."

Mr. Bowen pledged that he would be ready and willing to see Mr. Beecher the next day (Monday), any time between eight o'clock in the morning and ten o'clock at night.

Mr. Claflin said he would see Mr. Beecher the next morning and arrange such an interview, and, a few minutes later, we left Mr. Bowen's residence.

A few days after this I saw Mr. Claflin, who told me that he had seen Mr. Beecher the next day, and that Mr. Beecher said:

There isn't force enough in Brooklyn to draw me into a private interview with Henry C. Bowen."

At this time I had never seen the tripartite covenant, but Mr. Claflin had told me the paper was in his hands.

In my business relations with Mr. Bowen, we had frequent conversations in regard to his difficulty with Mr. Beecher. On one occasion, Mr. Bowen told me that they first wanted him to sign a much more sweeping document, declaring his charges against Mr. Beecher to be untrue. This, he said he had refused to do. Mr. Claflin then urged him to at least sign a paper withdrawing the charges, and he consented to do that. In regard to the second paper, Mr. Bowen subsequently said: "I made a mistake in signing that, but Mr. Claflin induced me to do it."

On the following Friday (May 30th, 1873), the tripartite covenant was made public in the New York morning papers. The following Sunday night I went to Plymouth Church, and after the services I went up to have some conversation with Mr. Beecher in regard to his sending Mr. Cleaveland for me the previous Sunday.

"Mr. Carpenter," says the interviewer, "here repeated to the writer the substance of the conversation which took place between Mr. Beecher and himself that evening. We can only say that the statements which Mr. Carpenter says Mr. Beecher made that evening are, if true, of the utmost significance and importance. Mr. Carpenter declares that he will not make public this conversation, unless he is called upon to testify before the proper tribunal. It was during this interview that Mr. Beecher told Mr. Carpenter that in case Theodore would make certain disavowals, he would share his fame and fortune with him, and pour in subscribers to the *Golden Age* by the thousands. The interview which Mr. Carpenter speaks of occurred on the evening of the same day, when Mr. Beecher wrote his touching letter, dated Sunday, June 1st, 1873. Great significance attaches to Mr. Carpenter's statement, from the fact that Mr. Beecher's card, exonerating Mr. Tilton from being his slanderer and defamer, was published the next day, June 2nd, 1873.

Reporter—How long have you been acquainted with Mr. Tilton?

Mr. Carpenter—Twenty years.

Reporter—Have you been intimate with him?

Mr. Carpenter—I have.

Reporter—Has he ever evinced, either by word or manner, vindictiveness or malice against Henry Ward Beecher?

Mr. Carpenter—No. I never knew a man to bear so much. One of the editors of the *Eagle* told me that Theodore Tilton had suffered more than any man since Jesus Christ. Tilton told me the night he put the Bacon letter to press that he would rather take thirty-nine lashes in the flesh, and draw blood every time, than have printed this thing against Mr. Beecher. Tilton further said: "Mr. Beecher has laid open his breast, and told me to smite. His pleading face is before me now. But Dr. Bacon has put me in the attitude of a knave and a dog, and I must place myself right before the world." He also said: "This is no impersonal newspaper attack. Dr. Bacon was my senior on the *Independent* He is a good and wise man, and if his statement goes forth uncontradicted, I am disgraced before Christendom." The morning that Dr. Bacon's speech was published, Mr. Beecher, Mr. Tilton, Mr. Moulton, and Mr. Thomas G. Shearman were together in Mr. Moulton's study. Mr. Tilton took out of his pocket a New York paper containing a report of Dr. Bacon's speech. That part of the speech referring to Beecher's magnanimity and to Tilton's being a knave and a dog, Mr. Tilton read to Mr. Beecher. He then said: "Mr. Beecher, you know that I have treated you with the utmost fairness, and that the statements of Dr. Bacon are untrue. I call upon you, as a simple act of justice, to make a correction of Dr. Bacon's charges. You have a newspaper of your own; you can do it without compromising yourself, and without damage to yourself. If you do not correct the impression which Dr. Bacon has given the public, I shall be compelled to do it myself; and if I do it, Mr. Beecher, it will be done with serious damage to you." Mr. Beecher made no reply.

Reporter—Have you regarded Theodore Tilton as a talebearer?

Mr. Carpenter—Theodore Tilton has striven to shield these parties. Dr. Storrs has frequently commented on his utter absence of vindictiveness, and the sorrow-stricken air and attitude with which Mr. Tilton came to him to ask his advice.

Reporter—What was the character of Mr. Tilton's home?

Mr. Carpenter—It was one of the most delightful homes I ever knew.

Reporter—Are you prepared to say, from your own knowledge, that Mr. Tilton was disinclined to publish the letter to Dr. Bacon?

Mr. Carpenter—I am, and do so say. After Dr. Bacon made that speech to the Divinity Class, Mr. Tilton wrote him a private letter, to correct the false impressions Dr. Bacon had formed up to three months after Mr. Tilton called Mr Beecher's attention to Dr. Bacon's open attack on him. Mr. Beecher had made no sign, had shown no intention, of replying. Then Tilton wrote the Bacon letter, as the least he could do in justice to his own good name, to his children, and to his friends. His intimate friends demanded that he should do it. They told Mr. Tilton that if he allowed such charges as Dr. Bacon had made, concerning him, to pass unrefuted, he would forfeit the respect of everybody. Mr. Tilton asked me if I would take his letter to Dr. Bacon. I said I would. At my request he accompanied me to New Haven, as I thought Dr. Bacon, upon reading that letter, would wish to ask questions which I couldn't answer. Mr. Tilton finally consented to go with me. Dr. Bacon received us with courtesy and kindness. Mr. Tilton said: "Dr. Bacon, I have come to you with my Statement. You have represented me before the world as a bad man. You have not had the facts in this case on which to form a correct judgment. I have come here, believing you to be a wise and good man—incapable of doing any man willful injustice. I do not want to make this case public, and I have come here with my friend, Mr. Carpenter, who bears this letter, in the hope that your wisdom may devise a course by which my good name may be saved, without giving publicity to the facts in this case." He then read the letter to Mr. Bacon, with scarcely an interruption. When he finished, Dr. Bacon said: "I have been thinking, Mr. Tilton, as you have been reading, whether this is a private communication?"

Mr. Tilton said: "All I want is justice. I hope you will suggest some way by which justice may be done without giving the case to the world."

A reference was then made to Mr. Bowen's part of the tripartite covenant, and Dr. Bacon said:

"I have observed that Mr. Bowen, in withdrawing his charges, does not say they are not true. He simply withdrew them."

Mr. Tilton spoke charitably and feelingly to Dr. Bacon with regard to Mr. Beecher, and did not show malice or vindictiveness. I call upon Dr. Bacon to testify to the truth of my statement. As we rose to take our leave, Dr. Bacon said he could not give advice on so important a matter without reflection. We bade him good-bye, and returned to New York the same evening. This was Friday, the 19th of last month.

The next evening, Mr. Tilton asked me to write a note to Dr.

Bacon, asking him if he could recommend any course by which publication could be avoided. In compliance with his request, I wrote this note:

NEW YORK, June 20th, 1874.

Rev. Dr. Bacon:

MY DEAR SIR—I was at Mr. Tilton's office to-day, and had a conversation with him concerning our recent interview at your study. The impression which you left on his mind was that of great fairness and candor towards his case and himself. This he expressed to me in still stronger terms than at first. He told me, furthermore, that, relying on your sense of justice, he would willingly forego the publication of his defence, if, in your judgment, the vindication of his course towards Plymouth Church could be accomplished in some other way than in making painful references to the pastor.

Mr. Tilton's respect for your opinion as to the wisest course for him to pursue is so strong that I am sure he will either publish or suppress his letter, according as you shall advise. He said, to-day, with great seriousness: "If I could see Dr. Bacon again, I would ask him this question: 'Is there any reason, either of morals or of expediency, which should forbid me to publish this letter?' In other words, is the injury which this publication will inflict on Mr. Beecher too great to warrant my resort to so extreme a measure in self-defence?

Mr. Tilton feels that the publication of his letter will strike a blow at Mr. Beecher from which he never can recover, and for this reason Mr. Tilton hopes you may be able to relieve him from his distressing public position without entailing distress upon Mr. Beecher. Mr. Tilton's continued silence, as you know, has been greatly misinterpreted by the public. The few who have stood faithfully through the storm of detraction, are now urgent that he should speak.

Any communication from you to myself will be considered confidential in its character, should you so desire.

I am, truly yours,

F. B. CARPENTER.

"This letter," said Mr. Carpenter, "I did not send, as I learned through Mr. C. C. Woolworth, of Brooklyn, that an esteemed mutual friend was going immediately to New Haven. I called on this friend (a Brooklyn gentleman esteemed for his piety and learning, whose name Mr. Carpenter desires to have suppressed for the present), and laid before him the points of my letter, asking him to have an interview with Dr. Bacon, and endeavor to arrange some settlement by which publicity could be avoided.

"No word came, and after waiting until Wednesday afternoon, the letter was printed. My friend saw Dr. Bacon, as he had promised, and, in the course of the interview, Dr. Bacon said: 'If Mr. Tilton publishes that letter, and Plymouth Church does not reply to it within twenty-four hours by a suit at law against Mr. Tilton, they will have no case before the Christian public.'"

Mr. Carpenter continued:—

"In the original letter, as read to Dr. Bacon, the charge against Mr. Beecher was in these words:—'Knowledge came to me, in 1870, that he (Mr. Beecher) had committed against me and my family a revolting crime.' After the letter was in type and the proof was being corrected, one of Mr. Beecher's intimate friends implored Tilton to change this language, and make the charge in the words: 'An offence which I forbear to name or characterize.' This gentleman said to Mr. Tilton, in my presence: 'If you will so change this language, Mr. Beecher will make a public acknowledgment of an offence.' Mr. Tilton at first refused to so modify the expression, but was overruled by the pleadings of Mr. Beecher's friends. I consider this another proof that Theodore Tilton has acted without malice in this matter."

Reporter—Did not Mr. Tilton think that Mr. Beecher's apology bound him to silence?

Mr. Carpenter—He never revealed that apology either to Dr. Storrs or myself until after Mr. Beecher wrote the letter of defiance calling for an investigating committee.

Reporter—In what terms was Mrs. Tilton referred to by her husband?

Mr. Carpenter—Always in the language of affection, and often with pride.

Reporter—Has Mr. Cleveland ever intimated to you that, in case of disclosure, other ladies would be involved?

Mr. Carpenter—He has repeatedly.

Reporter—Did he mention names?

Mr. Carpenter—He did.

Reporter—Will you state them?

Mr. Carpenter—I will not.

Reporter—Will you state them if called upon to give them before a court?

Mr. Carpenter—I might then be compelled to. I will not do it voluntarily.

Reporter—Did you ever have any conversation with Oliver Johnson in reference to this case?

Mr. Carpenter—Why do you ask this question?

Reporter—Mr. Johnson stated before the committee that Mr. Tilton had never, in conversation with him, accused Mr. Beecher of criminality. Did Mr. Johnson ever intimate to you that Mr. Tilton had charged criminality?

Mr. Carpenter—He has. Mr. Johnson and myself, as the friends of Mr. Theodore Tilton, have frequently talked over this matter. I had reason to consider Mr. Johnson Mr. Tilton's most intimate friend next to Mr. Moulton. Mr. Johnson and myself often conversed about Mr. Tilton with mutual interest and sympathy for him. Mr. Johnson gave me my first absolute conviction that there was something criminally wrong between Mr. Beecher and Mrs. Tilton. Mr. Johnson distinctly told me that Mr. Tilton had charged adultery between Mr. Beecher and Mrs. Tilton. This statement was made to me in July, 1873, at the foot of the stairs leading to the office of the *Christian Union*.

I can prove that Oliver Johnson used these words; "My lips are sealed by a solemn promise; but if I should disclose what I know, the roof of Plymouth Church would come right off." Another time, Mr. Johnson said to me, "I know a great deal more about this case than you do, and what you know is bad enough."

Reporter—Have you read Mrs. Tilton's statement?

Mr. Carpenter—I have.

Reporter—Has Mrs. Tilton ever made any admissions to you compromising Mr. Beecher?

Mr. Carpenter—Mrs. Tilton, in my presence, was asked by Mr. Tilton to put in writing something in reference to her relation with Mr. Beecher, that he could show to Dr. Storrs. This was in December, 1872, or January, 1873, Mrs. Tilton assented willingly, and, going to her room, returned in a few moments with a manuscript, on which was written, as near as I can remember, these words:

"On a certain occasion, Mr. Beecher solicited me to become a wife to him, with all that is implied in this relation. This proposition I communicated to my husband." Mr. Tilton took that writing to Rev. Dr. Storrs.

Reporter—How do know this?

Mr. Carpenter—I accompanied Mr. Tilton, and saw Theodore place this document in Dr. Storrs' hand.

Reporter—Why was Dr. Storrs called into this case?

Mr. Carpenter—Mr. Tilton knew Dr. Storrs as an intimate friend of Mr. Beecher's, and he went to him for counsel soon after the Woodhull letter appeared. He said: "Dr. Storrs I come to you for advice in regard to the proper action to be taken by myself in reference to the statements made in the Woodhull letter."

Dr. Storrs replied: "I have not read the statement made by Mrs. Woodhull, but if you think it is of sufficient importance to merit attention, I will do so.

Dr. Storrs read the remarkable Woodhull story, and a few days later, when Mr. Tilton visited him, said:

"Mr. Tilton, I have read this paper carefully, and if the statements are true, I draw from them four conclusions."

Mr. Tilton asked what the conclusions were.

Dr. Storrs then said:

First—That Mr. Beecher and Mrs. Tilton had criminal relations.

Second—That you discovered that.

Third—That Mr. Beecher received a paper from Mrs. Tilton denying that such relations had ever existed.

Fourth—That Mr. Moulton got that paper from Mr. Beecher.

Mr. Tilton said: "Dr. Storrs, what if those points can't be denied?"

Dr. Storrs replied: "If those points cannot be denied, I have no advice to give. An evasion would be worse than silence.

Reporter—Did Mr. Tilton tell Dr. Storrs all the facts in the case.

Mr. Carpenter—He did not. He told me he did not want to bring disgrace upon his wife, and, when he obtained from her the admission which he took to Dr. Storrs, he said he preferred that it should be made as delicate for Elizabeth as possible, but he could not bear to have the world think that he was attacking Mr. Beecher without just provocation, when the truth was exactly the opposite.

Reporter—Have you read Samuel Wilkeson's letter?

Mr. Carpenter—Certainly. Mr. Wilkeson has surely been misinformed. The idea that Theodore Tilton attempted to blackmail anybody, I can dispose of in about five minutes;

and I am glad you mentioned Wilkeson's communication. Mr. Bowen employed Mr. Tilton to edit the *Independent* and the *Union*, making a contract for five years. The contract provided that, in case Mr. Bowen should violate its terms, the forfeit should be six months' salary in advance. Mr. Tilton was discharged. He naturally expected that Mr. Bowen would, according to the contract, pay him six months' salary. The matter was left to arbitration. The gentlemen selected as arbitrators were James Freeland, Horace B. Claflin and Charles Storrs. Both Mr. Bowen and Mr. Tilton declared that they would abide by the finding of these arbitrators. Messrs. Freeland, Claflin and Storrs examined the contracts made between Mr. Tilton and Mr. Bowen, and, in a few moments, decided that Mr. Bowen ought to pay principal and interest to Mr. Tilton up to the last penny of the amount claimed. "This," said Mr. Carpenter, "is the truth about the so-called 'blackmailing' operation of Mr. Tilton's. It is just such abuse and misrepresentation of Tilton as this that has induced me to speak. I have felt and do feel very much as Frank Moulton does. Theodore Tilton is in the right in this matter. He should not be sacrificed. And I say this as an ardent admirer of Henry Ward Beecher. Frank Moulton was sincere when he said he loved Beecher, but beyond and above the love and admiration for that man, there is a controlling consideration of justice, and I know Frank Moulton too well to believe that he will think of shielding Henry Ward Beecher by wronging Theodore Tilton.

Reporter—Have you any statement or explanation to make concerning your affidavit charging that Mr. Beecher told you he would share his fame, fortune and honor with Mr. Tilton, in case Tilton would do certain things?

Mr. Carpenter—Only this: That I made that affidavit so that it would bear as lightly against Mr. Beecher as possible.

Reporter—Do you still refuse to give the substance of the conversation you had with Mr. Beecher on the evening of June 1st, 1873?

Mr. Carpenter—I do. No power save a legal tribunal shall oblige me to make public the statements in that interview.

Reporter—In alluding to Mr. Tilton's character, you stated that Horace Greeley and Charles Sumner had both alluded to Mr. Tilton's case.

Mr. Carpenter—Yes, Horace Greeley said to me: "Nobody can make me believe Theodore Tilton is a corrupt man—no matter what Mrs. Woodhull says." In March, 1873, when Sumner was sitting to me for his portrait, he spoke of Tilton in these words: "Theodore Tilton is a great writer. He is a man of genius. In reference to his domestic troubles, I doubt the propriety of longer silence on his part. I think the thunderbolt ought to fall."

I said: "How can you say that, when such interests are involved?"

Mr. Sumner replied: "I have been called into one such case, and I have seen the utter folly and futility of all measures to cover wrong."

Reporter—What is your opinion of Mrs. Tilton's statement?

Mr. Carpenter—I hesitate to express an opinion, for Mrs. Tilton has made such unaccountable statements to me. For instance, you remember I told you I was present when she put in writing the statement that Beecher had solicited her. Less than a year after, in conversation with her, she told me that her admission in that letter was untrue.

Reporter—Do you think Mr. Tilton published the Bacon letter because he thought it was Dr. Bacon's judgment that an investigation should be had?

Mr. Carpenter—I do. He appealed to Dr. Bacon for advice, but waited in vain for a single word of counsel. Dr. Bacon did say, however, to the friend who called on him in Theodore's behalf, that if Mr. Tilton did not make that letter public, he should be inclined to do it himself. Dr. Bacon had the utmost confidence in Mr. Beecher's innocence, and, in the face of such serious charges, he very naturally and wisely wanted to see an issue made, and have the scandal settled finally and forever.

Reporter—It has been stated that Mr. Beecher did not think he could consistently defend Mr. Tilton until the latter renounced Mrs. Woodhull and her associates.

Mr. Carpenter—That is true. Mr. Beecher told me that if Theodore would take the public position he wanted him to, on the Woodhull question, he would pour subscriptions into the *Golden Age* office by the thousands. Oliver Johnson, at one time, prepared a statement for Tilton to sign in regard to Woodhull, but Tilton declined. Mr. Tilton asked his intimate friends not to lose sight of the fact that Mr. Beecher addressed to him the letter of apology six months before he (Tilton) ever saw Victoria C. Woodhull.

Reporter—You said that the phrase in Mr. Tilton's original

letter to Dr. Bacon was one charging Mr. Beecher with a "revolting crime." You added that this phrase was modified so as to read, "an offense which I forbear to name or characterize." Who was the friend of Mr. Beecher who induced Mr. Tilton to modify the language of the charge?

Mr. Carpenter—He was a friend of both Mr. Beecher and Mr. Tilton.

Reporter—Was it Frank Moulton?

Mr. Carpenter—I decline to answer. But it was through his earnest pleading that the change was made. I remember he said:

"Theodore, don't put that word 'crime' in there—make it easy for Beecher to explain."

Mr. Tilton assented, with the assurance from this friend that the modification would bring from Mr. Beecher a public acknowledgment of an offense.

Reporter—If Mr. Beecher knew of the existence of these letters, why did he challenge investigation?

Mr. Carpenter—There are several reasons which will answer that question. You know he had previously been sustained to a remarkable degree by his Church. He may have known that Mrs. Tilton would sustain him, if it came to the worst. He may have supposed that the most important documentary evidence was destroyed, as did Mrs. Tilton. Or, driven to desperation, he may have courted the worst, for you remember he declared in one of his letters to Mr. Moulton: "Nothing can possibly be so bad as the power of great darkness in which I spend much of my time. I look upon death as sweeter far than any friend I have in the world."

Reporter—What is your estimate of Theodore Tilton, as a moral man?

Mr. Carpenter—I have scrutinized him for years, and I never could find in him, either in word or act, a suggestion of impurity. He is the cleanest man in his conversation I ever knew. Toward all women, Mr. Tilton is the most chivalrous of men. His references to his wife have invariably been of the most delicate and affectionate character. He has shielded her in every possible way.

Reporter—Mr. Carpenter, you have made some very important statements in regard to this scandal.

Mr. Carpenter—I have still more important ones in reserve. And in conclusion I want the *Argus* to understand that I am the friend of Theodore Tilton only so far as his position is one where he is fortified by truth. I have had an affection amounting to reverence for Henry Ward Beecher. But I am afraid this case has been taken out of Mr. Beecher's hands by his enthusiastic and over-zealous friends. The statements I have made I am prepared to make affidavit to. The dates and names I have quoted, I have mainly obtained from my written record, for I have kept a diary for many years.

In order to make his statement as complete and emphatic as possible, Mr. Carpenter sent the following telegram to the editor of the Brooklyn *Argus*, in which his interview was given:

HOMER N. Y., July 29th, 1874.

To the Editor of the Argus:—Please add to my statement to-day that Mr. Tilton told Rev. Dr. Storrs and myself, in December, 1872, that he had not told and could not tell us the whole truth.

Mr. Tilton never made a threat against Mr. Beecher.

He only spoke in self-defence, and as a wronged and suffering man.

In all references to Mr. Beecher's apology, Mr. Tilton always omitted the most important part of it—shielding his wife to Dr. Storrs, myself, and others.

FRANK B. CARPENTER.

The third week of the investigation ending August 1st, during which the above interviews occurred, developed little as to the doings of the committee. When Carpenter's statement appeared Oliver Johnson was interviewed and made general denials of the correctness of his statements. Members of the committee remained very reticent in their conversation with the gentlemen of the press who visited them by the score, but all seemed still disposed to shield Mr. Beecher. In the meantime Frank Moulton, the mediator between Messrs. Beecher and Tilton, had been summonsed before the committee to testify, as the committee declared they wanted his evidence before Mr. Beecher put in his final answer and the case was closed. Mr. Moulton, however, had disappeared.

While the reporters were chasing everybody in the country who was supposed to be able to throw new light on the scandal, and the committee were holding daily sessions, a very different scene was being enacted elsewhere. A reporter of the *Argus*, which throughout the investigation strongly championed Mr. Tilton's cause, went before a police justice and sued out a warrant for the arrest of Mr. Tilton for libelling Mr. Beecher. This extraordinary action created intense excitement. The complainant quoted the law justifying any citizen in making a complaint and the Justice held Mr. Tilton for examination on Monday, August 3d.

It may be mentioned in this connection that on Friday evening, July 31st, Mrs. Woodhull and Miss Claflin, accompanied by Mr. James McDermott went before the committee to testify; but were not admitted. They then handed in a written statement of the facts they would testify to, but it was returned to them and they were driven from the door. They had engaged passage to Paris on the steamer of the following day, but after this rebuff they changed their plans and abandoned the European trip. Thus closed one of the most exciting weeks in the recollection of Brooklynites, with (to all appearances) the committee no nearer a solution of the scandal than when they entered upon the investigation. It may, however, be incidentally stated here, that the Brooklyn *Eagle* published the following letter for the genuineness of which it vouched:—

MY DEAR MRS. TILTON:—I hoped that you would be shielded from the knowledge of the great wrong that has been done to you, and through you to universal womanhood. I can hardly bear to speak of it or allude to a matter than which nothing can be imagined more painful to a pure and womanly nature. I pray daily for you, "that your faith fail not." You yourself know the way and the power of prayer. God has been your refuge in many sorrows before. He will now hide you in His pavilion until the storm be overpast. The rain that beats down the flower to the earth will pass at length, and the stem, bent, but not broken, will rise again and blossom as before.

Every pure woman on earth will feel that this wanton and unprovoked assault is aimed at you, but reaches to universal womanhood.

Meantime your dear children will love you with double tenderness, and Theodore, against whom these shafts are hurled, will hide you in his heart of hearts.

I am glad that this revelation from the pit has given him a sight of the danger that was before hidden by specious appearances and promises of usefulness. May God keep him in courage in the arduous struggle which he wages against adversity, and bring him out, though much tried, like gold seven times fired.

I have not spoken of myself. No word could express the sharpness and depth of my sorrow in your behalf, my dear and honored friend. God walks in the fire by the side of those He loves, and in heaven neither you nor Theodore nor I shall regret the discipline, how hard soever it may seem now.

May He restrain and turn those poor creatures who have been given over to do all this sorrowful harm to those who have deserved no such treatment at their hands!

I commend you to my mother's God my dear friend! May His smile bring light in darkness and His love be a perpetual summer to you!
Very truly yours, HENRY WARD BEECHER.

HENRY SAGE.

CHAPTER XV.

MRS. TILTON'S CROSS-EXAMINATION—HER DESPERATE EFFORTS TO CLEAR THE CHARACTER OF THE ACCUSED PASTOR—A HIGHLY SEASONED PICTURE OF DOMESTIC INFELICITY AND BRUTAL TREATMENT OF ELIZABETH BY THEODORE—OUR "MUTUAL FRIEND MOULTON" HAS A SHARP CORRESPONDENCE WITH HENRY WARD, AND FINALLY AGREES TO MAKE A CLEAN BREAST OF ALL HE KNOWS—TILTON INSTRUCTS HIS COUNSEL TO BEGIN AN ACTION OF DAMAGES AGAINST BEECHER FOR THE SEDUCTION OF HIS WIFE—THE HUMOROUS SIDE OF THE SCANDAL—"SIR SINBAD'S ADVICE."

ON the afternoon of the 3d of August the Committee of Inquiry published a card, requesting all persons knowing anything of the case to go before said body and testify on the following (Tuesday) evening, which they intimated would be the last for receiving testimony. In the meantime, Mr. Carpenter had notified them of his determination not to appear. Mr. Moulton still kept away, and the criminal proceedings commenced by Mr. Gaynor in the court had been abandoned. The public began to surrender all hope of the facts coming out, and disappointment was the natural consequence on the part of those who relish so stupendous a scandal. On Tuesday morning Mrs. Tilton's cross-examination was published and the picture she drew of her home and the erratic life of Theodore read like a novel. It is not the purpose of the author to gratify the depraved tastes of any one by giving *all* the cross-examination, but he selects that portion telegraphed over the country by the Associated Press, as a readable and unobjectionable sketch of it. Mrs. Tilton opens her cross-examination thus:—

"I wish these gentlemen to understand that to a very large extent I take the blame upon myself of the indifference my husband has shown to me in all my life. At first I understood very well that I was not to have the attention that many wives had. I realized that his talent and genius must not be narrowed down to myself. That I made him understand. Also, to a very large extent, I attribute to that the later sorrows of my life. I gave him to understand that what might be regarded as neglect, under the circumstances would not be regarded by me as neglect in him, owing to his business and to his desire to make a name for himself and to rise before the world. At the birth of the first three children I had very severe and prolonged sickness, but when he saw me he never felt that I was sick, because on seeing him I always tried to feel well, I felt so desirous of his presence. It was charged upon me many a time by my mother and my brother, "When Theodore or the doctor comes you are never sick." They said of me, "She has never a genius for being sick."

Q. Will you state just what attention your husband bestowed upon you, in case of sickness during your confinement, or any other illnesses if you had them? A. Well, I had no attention whatever, I may truthfully say, from him, any more than a stranger would give. I do not think it was from neglect so much as from an inability on his part to understand that I was sick and suffering, though in fact I was very seriously ill.

In continuation, Mrs. Tilton stated that she was frequently sick, and her physician said there was care and trouble on her mind which he could not cure with medicine.

Q. What was the trouble, in point of fact? A. Well, any one of you gentlemen, I think, would have cared for my family as much as Theodore did. I was left entirely with my servants, and they were poor servants. I could not have my mother with me, because it was impossible for her to live with us on account of disagreement with Mr. Tilton. Tilton was dissatisfied with his home and with his wife's management, and was harsh in his criticisms.

Q. When did he begin to talk to you, if at all, in regard to your associations and friendship for Mr. Beecher? A. I think I had no visits from Mr. Beecher before 1866; that is the first that I remember seeing him very much.

Q. What was the criticism in regard to Mr. Beecher and yourself which Mr. Tilton made? A. I would like to go back a little here, for I think it will show you my manner with

Mr. Beecher when I lived in Oxford street. That was the first of this which Mr. —— filled my husband's mind, as early as 1865. Theodore then used to begin to talk to me about Mr. Beecher's wrong-doings with ladies, which he had heard from Mr. ——, and night after night, and day after day he asked me about Mr. Beecher. He seemed to be worried on that subject, so that when Mr. Beecher came to see me, Mr. Tilton immediately began to have suspicions, but, in order that I might be perfectly transparent to my husband with respect to my interviews with Mr. Beecher, whenever I was alone with him I used to make a memorandum and charge my mind with all the details of the conversation that passed between us, that I might repeat it to Mr. Tilton. It was so in regard to every gentleman who came to see me and with whom I sat alone. I was very closely watched and questioned, but especially in regard to Mr. Beecher. I attributed those criticisms from Theodore to Mr. ——'s criticisms. I never had a visit from Mr. Beecher that I was not questioned. Theodore would question me till I thought I had told him all we talked about, and perhaps a day or two afterwards I would throw out a remark which Mr. Beecher had made, and Theodore would say. "You did not tell me that yesterday." I would say "I forgot it." "You lie," he would say, "you didn't mean to tell me." "Oh, yes I did mean to tell you, but I forgot it." For two or three years I tried faithfully to repeat to my husband everything that I said and did until I found it made him more suspicious than ever. He believed I left out many things purposely, while I was conscious of never meaningly omitting anything. I wanted Theodore to know everything that passed between us. I often said if he would only come home and be there and know all.

Q. When did his complaints against you change from the form of criticism to that of accusation, or something more than criticism? A. In the latter part of the winter and early spring of 1869-70 he began to talk to me, assuming I had done wrong.

Q. In what respect? A. With Mr. Beecher.

Q. Criminally? A. Yes. I have been with him days and nights, talking this matter over, but I would like to have you know that these conversations lasted for years, and that the change of his thoughts from "the old to the new," as he called it, was gradual. I used to think his suspicions of me were caused by his not being at rest in his own mind.

Q. When he assumed you had been guilty of criminal intimacy with Mr. Beecher, how did you treat the subject? A. For a time I was very angry, and expressed myself to him as strongly as I possibly could. I became angry and said I would not be talked to in that way.

Q. State whether or not you invariably denied that you ever had any criminal intimacy with Mr. Beecher. A. I have indeed. I remember that he not only charged me with this in my presence, but often became so audacious as to write to me about it, and that seemed to me unpardonable.

Q. In making those offensive allegations what did he say? A. As often as any way, he said, "You will not deny that you have had criminal intercourse," and he tried to frighten me by saying that he had seen certain things.

Q. What things did he say he had seen? A. I remember that once or twice he pretended that he saw me sitting in Mr. Beecher's lap at home, in the red chair in the parlor. In reply to this I said "You didn't." I do not know what you gentlemen will think, but you certainly can see that such a continual talk, year in and year out, would have its influence upon me. I came to be quite indifferent, except in regard to my anxiety about him. It was a sort of morbid jealousy that he had. I was worn out and sick with it.

Q. Was it only in respect to Mr. Beecher that he made these accusations, or in respect to other people also? A. In respect to Mr. Beecher only, at that time. About 1870 I believe he began to think that I had great admiration for several people besides Mr. Beecher.

Q. Did he hesitate to mention names? A No, sir, he did not.

Q. How many different persons did he mention? A. Two or three gentlemen acquaintances.

Q. Did he ever make to you any charge or accusation, even with respect to Mr. Beecher, naming any definite time or place of any criminal act? A. Oh, no, never. He never connected any time with it.

Q. Did he ever pretend to you that you had been guilty of any impropriety with Mr. Beecher at his (Beecher's) house? A. No. He wondered why I went there on two or three occasions. I went on errands. I attended Mr. Burgess a great deal at the time of his death. He was a poor man and I went to Mr. Beecher two or three times to see him in regard to that man.

Q. Did you ever meet Mr. Beecher at other places by appointment? A. Never at all; not once.

Q. Did Mr. Tilton ever base any accusations against you upon any admissions which you had made to him, either with respect to an event at Mr. Beecher's or your house, or any other place? A. Yes; he based an accusation against me in his public statement, upon an interview which I had with Mr. Beecher in my second-story room, and I deny it in my public statement.

Q. In any conversation with you at any time did he accuse you of any wrong-doing with Mr. Beecher, based on any admission by you? A. No, sir.

Q. Is it true that in July 1870 you confessed to your husband any act or acts of impropriety with Mr. Beecher? A. No.

Q. Did you admit to him any wrongs of criminal intimacy with Mr. Beecher at other places? A. No, sir.

Mrs. Tilton was next questioned in reference to her letter about Catherine Gaunt. She said she had no reference therein to adultery or thought of it.

Q. What did you refer to? A. I will try to answer that question. The one absorbing feeling of my whole life has been Theodore Tilton. Neither Mr. Beecher, I assure you, nor any human being has ever taken away from me that one fact of my love for him. But I must say that I felt very great helpfulness in my own soul from having had the friendship of Mr. Beecher, and also of other people, as many women as men. I think that Theodore gathered up from all our talks in the summer of 1870 that I really found in Mr. Beecher what I did not find in him. He got that, I know. I gave it to him, but I often said, "Theodore, if you had given to me what you gave to others, I dare say I should find in you what I find in Mr. Beecher."

Q. In your Schoharie letter you spoke of your sin. What did you mean by that? A. Theodore's nature being a proud one I felt on reading that book that I had done him wrong—that I had harmed him in taking any one else in any way, although on looking it over I do not think but that I should do it again, because it has been so much to my soul.

Q. Taking any one else in what respect? A. I do not think if I had known as much as I do now of Mr. Tilton that I would *ever* have encouraged Mr. Beecher's acquaintance. I think I did wrong in doing it, inasmuch as it hurt Theodore.

I do not know as I can make myself understood, but do you know what I mean when I say that I was aroused in myself—that I had a self-assertion which I never knew before with Theodore? There was always a damper between me and Theodore, but there never was between me and Mr. Beecher. With Mr. Beecher I had a sort of consciousness of being more. He appreciated me. Theodore did not. I felt myself another woman. I felt that he respected me. I think Theodore never saw in me what Mr. Beecher did.

Mr. Sage—Do you mean to say that Theodore put down self-respect in you, while Mr. Beecher lifted it up?

Answer—Oh yes! I never felt a bit of embarrassment with Mr. Beecher, but to this day I never could sit down with Theodore without being self-conscious and feeling his sense of my inequality with him.

Witness continuing, said the sin she spoke of was nothing more than giving to another what was due to her husband,—that which he did not bring out. However, she did not feel now that there was any great sin about it. The sin was that she hurt her husband's pride by allowing any one else into her life at all. The wifely feeling she gave to her husband was pure. She gave Mr. Beecher nothing more than confidence and respect. She taught her daughters that if they gave their husbands what she had given to hers, they would do enough. Tilton frequently talked to her accusingly of the sensual effect of her presence upon gentlemen. His accusations were hard to live under. He seemed to be ashamed of her appearance, dress and bearings. On one occasion, in a company of his friends, he told her he would give $500 if she was not at his side. In hotels and public places on several occasions he said to her, "I wish you would not keep near me." It was evident to her that he did not want comparison made between them. It hurt very much. In 1870 she had a conversation with Tilton regarding his own habits and associates, in which he confessed criminality with other women. She did not confess adultery to him. It was the other way. He confessed to improper relations with several other women, and told her he wished her to understand that when he was away from home, lecturing or isiting, if he desired to gratify himself he would do it. The world was filled with slanders about him. He did not seem to know it. He thought everything came from her, and said so. He declared that she was the originator of all the talk about him, and insisted upon her correcting these impressions. He said on one occasion that a certain woman had been talking about him, and he wanted his wife to see her and put an end to it. She went to the woman and told her she should have avoided adding to the stories already afloat, for her sake, when she replied, "Mrs. Tilton, do you know why I didn't? because the night before, your husband had told stories about yourself to such and such persons that came to me directly, and I was not going to allow an accusation of that character to stand against you." Wherever she went she found that Tilton had not only made these accusations against her, but had recounted the details, which he has now published. Then he would deny to her that he had done so.

Mrs. Tilton's attention being called to her husband's allegation about the improper caress, she said there was no truth in it. She also denied the bedroom story, saying: Theodore had been with us that morning; he had gone out; Mr. Beecher was sitting in a large chair, and she had drawn up a smaller one. Beecher had in hand a little manuscript he was going to read. She did not remember what it was. The door from the bedroom to the hall was shut, and she had shut the door leading from the sitting-room to the hall, which was usually open. She had no sooner done that (which was to keep out the noise of the children playing in the hall), and sat down by the side of Beecher, when Theodore came to the other door. Not five minutes had elapsed since he went out. There was no hesitation in opening the door. The folding doors were wide open. The door leading to the hall from the bedroom was locked, but that was not uncommon. Her closing the other door, which was seldom closed, perhaps made Theodore suspicious.

Q. Was Mr. Beecher flushed when Theodore came in? A. Not at all.

Being next questioned as to the paper Tilton said she wrote to him in the latter part of 1870, stating that Beecher made improper approaches, witness said the paper she wrote was but a couple of lines, as far as she could remember. It was written at a time when nearly out of her mind, but what Theodore made her write she could not tell to this day; was conscious of writing many things under his dictation, or copying them off and giving them to him.

Q. Things that were false? A. Oh yes!

Q. What benefit did he tell you would come, if you would make these statements? A. He said this statement was to help him in the matter with Mr. Bowen. I did not understand how it was, but instead of going to Mr. Bowen with it he went to Mr. Moulton, and that quite startled me.

Q. Did Mr. Beecher make any improper suggestions or request to you? A. Why, no, sir. It was utterly false. I have done many things like signing that paper. There is a certain power Theodore has over me, especially if I am sick, and he hardly ever came to me while I was in any other condition to do anything of that sort. One or two letters I sent West will bear witness to that. I wrote a letter to Mrs. —— in one ten minutes, and in the next ten minutes wrote another letter to her with a statement contrary to that of the first. The first was written under Mr. Tilton's influence. After having written it I said to myself, "Why, I have stabbed Mr. Beecher," and I wrote in a second letter, "For God's sake don't listen to what I said in the first." I never have written a letter of my own in regard to this matter, except one very small letter in which I desire to confess. It was with regard to my mother. In that letter I gave her a very cruel stab. I wrote that, but the others are entirely of Mr. Tilton's concocting.

Mrs. Tilton admitted that she copied a note containing the words, "Mr. Beecher desired me to be his wife with all that it implies," which note was to be shown to Dr. Storrs. She at first refused, but he said he needed it because it would be a great deal better than anything he could write, and it was not anything after all. She replied, "It is not true, and what will Mr. Beecher say?" Frank Carpenter was present, but could not hear, as they spoke low. Mr. Tilton told her he had but fifteen minutes, and she sat down and wrote the note. It is absolutely false, but she wanted to make a strong statement. She thought it wickedly wrong, as it was. There was trouble, and she thought it would in some way serve Theodore and bring peace. He had said the whole affair was some scheme to get out of the Woodhull trouble.

Mrs. Tilton then related how, the week after the council of churches was called, she, without consulting Theodore, went to Dr. Storrs and told him that the letter was false; that she was not the author nor had she composed it in any way, and Dr. Storrs said he wished he had known it, for on that letter alone he had believed Beecher a wicked man. He asked her if she knew of the great sin she had done. She replied, she realized she had frequently done such things as that. She had no opportunity of explaining the circumstances, as the doctor was in a hurry and referred her to his wife.

Mrs. Tilton was asked if she ever saw the letter apparently from Beecher to herself dated February 7th, 1871. She replied never, until she saw it printed in Tilton's statement.

Q. Did you ever hear about it?

A. I was never willing to have anything to do with Moulton Mr. Tilton wanted her to treat Moulton as a mediator, but she would have nothing to do with a third party. She would be trusted as hitherto, and if Mr. Beecher or any one else had anything to say to her, it should not come through Moulton. Papers came to her through him, and she would not look at them. Moulton one day insisted on reading to her what he called a very important letter which she refused to receive, and it went in one ear and out the other, so she remembered nothing of it except that it urged her to treat Moulton as a confidant on some common ground, against which she rebelled.

Q. Do you recollect a letter beginning, "My dear husband, I desire to leave with you, before going to bed, a statement that Mr. Henry Ward Beecher called upon me this evening and asked me if I would defend him against any accusation in a council of ministers," and ending, "Affectionately, Elizabeth?" A. Yes, sir; but that is not my letter.

Q. How was it written? A. In the same way as those which I have already explained. I have no other explanation for any of them that were written in bed. Mr. Tilton wrote it first, and I sat on my sick bed and copied it.

Mr. Cleveland—Is that true of all the letters that have that signature? A. Yes, sir; so far as my authorship of them is concerned.

Mr. Winslow—Was he excited? A. He was always very much excited about his own public difficulties.

Q. Had he been out that evening? A. Yes; he had been to Frank Moulton's.

Mr. Hill—What time did he get home? A. My nurse had gone to bed and he found me in bed. I was very sick and my nurses were greatly disturbed.

Q. When he first came in, what did he say? A. I do not remember.

Mr. Winslow—What led you to this act? A. His bringing me pen and ink and paper. He had the letter already written.

Mr. Hill—What did he say about it? A. Really I positively tell you I cannot remember. I felt often at that time utterly despairing and miserable, and it mattered but little what I did.

Q. Was it when you were sick from a miscarriage? A. Yes.

Q. Do you recollect Mr. Beecher calling that evening? A. Yes.

Q. When? A. But a few hours before I wrote that letter.

Q. Can you remember that interview with Mr. Beecher? A. It was a very similar one to the other. I was half unconscious and was very ill-prepared to see either of them. My room was all darkened, and the nurse had gone to hers. She opened the door and said that Mr. Beecher wanted to see me. I certainly do not know what to tell you about that either.

Q. Do you remember writing some paper for Mr. Beecher? A. Yes.

Q. Can you recall the contents of that paper? A. No, I cannot. I think it was to do something for him because Theodore had done something against him.

Q. Is it true that he said anything to you about a council of ministers? A. I do not remember everything about it. I have tried very hard, dear friends, to get into mind those scenes, but they have utterly gone out of my brain. Witness never told Mrs. Anthony she had committed adultery or done wrong with Mr. Beecher, or anything to that effect.

Q. Did you ever tell any human being that you had been guilty of wrong doing with Mr. Beecher? A. I never voluntarily did so. Once my husband took me in Mrs. ——'s carriage to the house of a lady to whom he had been telling stories about me and Mr. Beecher. I went against my will, and when we got there he said, "I have brought Elizabeth herself to speak whether I have slandered her," and I did not deny him. It was the same thing as when I copied and signed letters which Theodore has prepared, and I am reminded of this. I do not know whether it was treachery, but many times he has said, "You have gone to Dr. Storrs and now he knows you are guilty." He found out that I had been to Dr. Storrs, and he was very angry.

Witness here recounted the scene at her house when Susan B. Anthony was present, much as heretofore published, except that she told Miss Anthony that Tilton accused her of adultery with Beecher, not that she had committed it. She told Miss Anthony that Tilton had charged her with infidelity with one and another, and that when he sat as his table many times he had said that he did not know who his children belonged to. She had spoken of it to another person besides Miss Anthony when she was aroused by Mrs. Woodhull's presence at her house, and by a visit from two of Mrs. Woodhull's sisters, whom she called the police to take away, but she had told these persons nothing more than what unjust accusations had been put upon her by her husband.

The committee had made strenuous efforts to induce Mr. Tilton to present to them the documents in the case, but he had not done so. "Our mutual friend Moulton" returned home the night before the publication of Mrs. Tilton's cross-examination, and it will be seen finally consented to appear before the committee. Mr. Tilton gives the following as his reasons for, at this stage of the case, ignoring the committee and beginning an action against Beecher for damages. On August 3d he wrote to the chairman of the committee, Mr. Sage:—

My Dear Sir:—I have just received your note of July 31st, four days after date. Unless you accidentally misdated it, the communication should have come to me several days ago. This leads me to recall a similar dilatoriness of the delivery of your original note first summoning me to your committee, which I received only four hours before I was to appear, and yet the summons bore the date of the day previous. But let these trifles pass. Your note just received surprises me by its contents, for you seem to have forgotten that on the last day of my appearance before your committee, I carried to your meeting not only all the documents which I quoted in my sworn statement (save those in Mr. Moulton's possession) but many more besides, making a double handful of interesting and important papers, vital to my case and destructive to yours. All these papers I proposed to lay before you, but no sooner had I begun to read them aloud in your presence than one of your attorneys stopped me in the reading and proposed that I should save the committee time by referring these papers to one of your members—the Hon. John Winslow, I acquiesced in this question and retired from your committee with the expectation of a speedy conference with Mr. Winslow. Perhaps it was my proper duty to have called on Mr. Winslow, but as the whole committee had previously set the example of calling in a body on one of the other parties to this controversy, I took it for granted that Mr. Winslow would repeat the precedent by doing me the honor to call at my house, at which he would have been a welcome guest. But while waiting for his coming I was called upon instead by a policeman, who arrested me and carried me, at thirty minutes' notice before Justice Riley's police court to answer the charge of libelling the Rev. Henry Ward Beecher, against whom I had spoken not a libel, but the truth. Up to the time of this arrest I had employed no lawyer, not needing any, but on finding myself before a police court and not understanding the motive of my arrest, nor the methods of courts, I requested my friend Judge S. D. Morris to answer for me in a technical proceeding in which I knew not how to answer properly for myself. Twice already I have been before this unexpected tribunal and may be called before it a third time Wednesday next. Meanwhile my counsel, to whom I have just shown your note, instructs me to lay no documents, papers, or remaining testimony before your committee, nor have further communication with you in any form, except to send you this present and final letter containing the reasons for this step. The reasons are as follows :—

First. You are a committee of Mr. Beecher's friends, appointed by himself; expected to act in his behalf; assisted by attorneys employed exclusively for his vindication; holding secret sessions inaccessible to the public; having no power to compel witnesses; having no opportunity for the opposite side to cross-examine such as voluntarily appear, publishing or suppressing their testimony as you see fit, and, so far as my own experience goes, asking no questions save such as were irrelevant to the case and omitting to publish in your imperfect and unjust report of my testimony all that was most pertinent to my own side of the controversy.

Second. The daily papers of Brooklyn and New York have been artfully fed day by day with crumbs of fictitious evidence against my own character, as if, not Mr. Beecher, but I alone, were the man on trial, and though I have little right, perhaps, to hold your committee responsible for this daily misrepresentation which may come through the malice of others, yet the result is the same to me as if you had deliberately designated it, and that result is this, namely: I expect no justice either from your tribunal, since you cannot compel witnesses to testify, nor from your reporters, since they do not give impartial reports.

Third. I cannot resist the conviction (though I mean no offence in expressing it) that your committee has come at last to be as little satisfactory to the public as to myself, and that your verdict (if you render one) could not possibly be based upon the full facts, since you have no power to compel witnesses, nor to verify their testimony by oath, nor to sift it by cross-examination.

For these reasons, which ought to have moved me earlier, I have at last instructed my counsel to proceeed at once at his discretion to carry my case from your jurisdiction to a court of law, and in view of this instruction from me he has in turn instructed me to hold no further communication with your committee except this present letter of courtesy, in which I have the honor to bid you farewell; in doing which allow me to add that the respect which I am unable to entertain for your committee as a tribunal, I cannot help expressing for you each and all as individuals.

Truly yours,

THEODORE TILTON.

To go back a stage in the narrative we will embody the following correspondence. On July 24th, Mr. Beecher wrote:—

MY DEAR MR. MOULTON:—I am making out a statement and I need the letters and papers in your hands. Will you send me by Tracy all the originals of my papers. Let them be numbered and an inventory taken, and I will return them to you as soon as I can see and compare, get dates, make extracts or copies, as the case may be.

Will you also send me Bowen's "Heads of Difficulty," and all letters of my sister if any are with you.

I heard you were sick—are you about again? God grant you to see peaceful times.

Yours gratefully,

F. D. Moulton. H. W. BEECHER.

Still there was no response, and on July 28th, Mr. Beecher wrote:—

MY DEAR FRIEND:—The Committee of Investigation are waiting mainly for you before closing their labors. I, too, earnestly wish that you would come, and clear your mind and memory of everything that can bear on the case. I pray you also to bring all letters and papers relating to it, which will throw light upon it, and bring to a result this protracted case.

I trust that Mrs. M. has been reinvigorated, and that her need of your care will not be so great as to detain you.

Truly yours, H. W. Beecher.

F. D. Moulton. Esq.

Mr. Moulton had in the meantime visited his counsel, General Butler, at Gloucester, Massachusetts, and on returning home responded:—

BROOKLYN, August, 4th, 1874.

MY DEAR MR. BEECHER:—I received your note of July 24th informing me that you are making a statement and need the letters and papers in my hands, and asking me to send them to you for the purpose of having extracts or copies made from them as the case may be, that you may use them in your controversy with Mr. Tilton.

I should be very glad to do anything that I may do, consistent with my sense of justice and right, to aid you; but if you will reflect that I hold all the important papers intrusted to me at the desire and request in the confidence of both parties to this unhappy affair, you will see that I cannot in honor give them or any of them to either party to aid him as against the other. I have not given or shown to Mr. Tilton any documents or papers relating to your affair, since the renewal of your controversy which had been once adjusted.

I need not tell you how deeply I regret your position as foes to each other after my long and as you, I have no doubt, fully believe, honest and faithful effort to have you otherwise.

I will sacredly hold all the papers and information I have until both parties shall request me to make them public, or to deliver them into the hands of either or both, or to lay them before the Committee, or I am compelled in a court of justice to produce them, if I can be so compelled.

My regret that I am compelled to this course is softened by belief that you will not be substantially injured by it in this regard, for all the facts are, of course, known to you, and I am bound to believe and assume that, in the statement you are preparing, you will only set forth the exact facts; and, if so, the documents, when produced, will only confirm, and cannot contradict, what you may state, so that you will suffer no loss.

If, on the contrary—which I cannot presume—you desire the possession of the documents in order that you may prove your statement in a manner not to be contravened by the façts set forth in them, to the disadvantage of Mr. Tilton, I should be then aiding you in doing that which I can not believe the strictest and firmest friendship for you calls upon me to do. With grateful recollections of your kind confidence and trust in me, I am very truly yours, F. D. MOULTON.

Rev. Henry Ward Beecher, Brooklyn, N. Y.

This letter evidently caused Mr. Beecher to lose faith in his "dear friend" Moulton for on the same day he wrote to Mr. Moulton thus:—

BROOKLYN, August 4th, 1874.

F. D· Moulton Esq.:

SIR—Your letter, bearing date August 4th, 1874, is this moment received Allow me to express my regret and astonishment that you refuse me permission even to see certain letters and papers, in your possession, relating to charges made against me by Theodore Tilton, and at the reasons given for the refusal.

On your solemn and repeated assurances of personal friendship, and in the unquestioning confidence with which you inspired me of your honor and fidelity, I placed in your hands for safe keeping various letters addressed to me from my brother, my sister and various other parties;

also memoranda of affairs not immediately connected with Mr. Tilton's matters. I also from time to time addressed you confidential notes relating to my own self, as one friend would write to another. These papers were never placed in your hands to be held for two parties, nor to be used in any way. They were to be held for me. I did not wish them to be subject to risk of loss or scattering, from my careless habit in the matter of preserving documents. They were to be held for me. In so far as these papers were concerned, you were only a friendly trustee, holding papers subject to my wishes.

Mr. Tilton has made a deadly assault on me, and has used letters and fragments of letters, purporting to be copies of these papers. Are these extracts genuine? Are they garbled? What are their dates? What, if anything, has been left out, and what put in?

You refuse my demand for these papers on the various pleas, that if I speak the truth in my statement I do not need them, that if I make a successful use of them it will be an injury to Mr. Tilton, and that you, as a friend of both parties, are bound not to aid either in any act that shall injure the other.

But when I demand a sight of the originals of papers of which you are only a trustee, that I may defend myself, you refuse, because you are the friend of both parties! Mr. Tilton has access to your depository for materials with which to strike me, but I am not permitted to use them in defending myself.

I do not ask you to place before the Committee any papers which Mr. Tilton may have given you. But I do demand that you forthwith place before the Committee every paper which I have written or deposited with you.

Truly yours,

H. W. Beecher.

Mr. Moulton's answer was very decided:—

No. 49 Remsen Street, Brooklyn, August 5th, 1874.

Rev. Henry Ward Beecher:

My Dear Sir—In all our acquaintance and friendship I have never received from you a letter of the tone of yours of August 4th. It seems unlike yourself, and to have been inspired by the same ill advisers who had so lamentably carried your private affairs before a committee of your church and thence before the public.

In reply let me remind you that during the whole of the past four years all the documents, notes, and memoranda which you and Mr. Tilton have intrusted to me have been so intrusted because they had a reference to your mutual differences. I hold no papers, either of yours or his, except such as bear on this case. You speak of "memoranda of affairs not immediately connected with the Tilton matter." You probably allude here to a memoranda of your difficulties with Mr. Bowen, but these have a direct reference to your present case with Mr. Tilton, and were deposited with me by you because of such reference. *You speak also of a letter or two from your brother and sister, and I am sure you have not forgotten the apprehension which we entertained lest Mrs. Hooker should fulfill a design which she foreshadowed, to invade your pulpit, and read to your congregation a confession of your intimacy with Mrs. Tilton.*

You speak of other papers, which I hold "subject to your wishes," I hold none such, nor do I hold any subject to Mr. Tilton's wishes. The papers which I hold, both yours and his, were not given to be subject to the wishes of either of the parties. But the very object of my holding them has been, and still is, to prevent the wish of one party being injuriously exercised against the other.

You are incorrect in saying that Mr. Tilton has had access to my "depository of materials;" on the contrary, I have refused Mr. Tilton such access. During the preparation of his sworn statement he came to me and said his case would be incomplete unless I permitted him to use all the documents, but I refused; and all he could rely upon were such notes as he had made from time to time from writings of yours which you had written to me to be read to him, and passages of which he caught from my lips in shorthand. Mr. Tilton has seen only a part of the papers in my possession, and would be more surprised to learn the entire facts of the case than you can possibly be.

What idle rumors may have existed in newspaper offices I know not, but they have not come from me. In closing your letter you say: "I do not ask you to place before the Committee any papers which Mr. Tilton may have given you; but I do demand that you forthwith place before the Committee every paper which I have written or deposited with you." In reply, I can only say that I cannot justly place before the Committee the papers of one of the parties without doing the same with the papers of the other, and I cannot do this honorably except either by legal process compelling me, or else by consent in writing, not only of yourself, but of Mr. Tilton, with whom I shall confer on the subject as speedily as possible. You will I trust, see a greater spirit of justice in this reply than you have infused into your unusual letter of August 4th.

Very respectfully,

FRANCIS D. MOULTON.

While this correspondence was being conducted Mr. Moulton was seeking by correspondence with Mr. Tilton, a way out of the difficulty which was successful, as will be seen by the correspondence below:—

BROOKLYN, August, 5th, 1874.

Theodore Tilton Esq:

MY DEAR SIR—I have received under date of July 25th, a letter from the Rev. Henry Ward Beecher, in which he expresses the wish that I would go before the Investigating Committee and "clear my mind and memory of everything that can bear on this case"—referring, of course, to the controversy between you and him.

I cannot, in view of my confidential relations with you, make any statement before the Investigating Committee, unless you release me, as Mr. Beecher has done, explicitly from my obligation to maintain your confidence.

If you will express to me clearly a request that I should go before the Investigating Committee and state any and all facts within my knowledge concerning your case with Mr. Beecher, and exhibit to them any or all documents in my possession relating thereto, I shall, in view of Mr. Beecher's letter, consider myseif at liberty to accede to the request of the Committee, to state such facts and exhibit such documents.

Very respectfully,

FRANCIS D. MOULTON.

BROOKLYN, August, 5th, 1874.

Francis D. Moulton Esq.:

MY DEAR SIR—In response to your note of this day mentioning Mr. Beecher's request that you should exhibit to the Committee the facts and documents hitherto held in confidence by you touching his difference with me, I hereby give you notice that you have my own consent and request to do the same.

Truly yours,

THEODORE TILTON.

Having thus secured the consent of both parties to the controversy to appear before the Committee with all the documents,Mr. Moulton addressed the Committee thus:—

MOULTON'S REPLY.

GENTLEMEN OF THE COMMITTEE:—I have received your invitation to appear before you. I have been ready, on any proper occasion, to disclose all the facts and documents known to me or in my possession relating to the subject matter of your inquiry, but I have found myself embarrassed because of my peculiar relations to the parties to the controversy. Friendly for years to all of them, and at the time of the outbreak of this miserable business having the kindest feeling toward each, I endeavored to avert the calamity that has now fallen upon all. Most fully and confidentially trusted by all parties, it became necessary that I should know the exact and simple truth of every fact and circumstance of the controversy, as I was made by mutual consent in some sort the arbiter of the affair, and, after, the estrangement, the medium of communication between the parties, each saying in writing to me such things as were desired to be said or written to the others; and in such case I gave the information or showed the communication to the person intended to receive or be affected by it. Under these circumstances I have not felt at liberty to give testimony or facts thus obtained in the sacredness of confidence before a tribunal not authorized by law to require them, however much otherwise I might respect its members and objects, without the consent of the parties from whom I received the disclosures and documents. With the consent or request of Mr. Beecher or Mr. Tilton. I have held myself ready, sorrowingly, to give all the facts, that I know about the objects of inquiry of the Committee, and produce whatever papers I have to the Committee, and leave copies of the same with them, if they desired it, with perhaps the one stipulation, that if I have to give my evidence orally or be cross-examined, I might bring with me a phonographic reporter, in order that I should have an exact copy of my testimony, for my own protection.

I am to-day in receipt, from Henry Ward Beecher and Theodore Tilton, of their consent and request, thus absolving me thereby from my confidential relations towards them, to appear before you, and to give you the facts and documents with reference to the difference between them.

It appears to me that, as Mr. Tilton has given his evidence, and Mrs. Tilton likewise, Mr. Beecher should be requested to add his own, in order that the three principal parties in the case shall have been independently heard on their own responsibility before I am called to adduce the facts in my possession derived from them all.

Nevertheless, since I am now fully released from my confidential relations with the parties involved in this sad affair, and since my only proper statement must consist of the truth, the whole truth, and nothing but the truth, I see no special reason why it may not be made at one time as well as at another; but as my statement will necessarily include a great multiplicity of facts and papers, I must ask a little delay to arrange and copy them. Accordingly, I suggest Saturday evening, August 8th, as an evening convenient for me to lay my statement before the Committee.

Yours truly,

FRANCIS D. MOULTON.

BROOKLYN, August 5th, 1874.

During the remainder of the week there were no important revelations beyond an attempt made by the Brooklyn *Eagle* to establish the insanity of Mr. Tilton, in the interest of Mr. Beecher, and a counter attempt on behalf of the friends of Mr. Tilton to impeach the damaging charges made by his wife. In support of the theory of Theodore's insanity the *Eagle* published alleged facts in connection with Tilton's family showing a tendency to insanity; but these publications were accepted by the public as an effort on the part of some of Mr. Beecher's ill-advised friends to direct attention from the real issue to matters entirely foreign to the inquiry. The other parties however were more successful, for a part of Mrs. Tilton's statements was most effectually impeached by a card from Rev. Dr. Storrs, a letter from Mr. Carpenter, and by the statements of Mrs. Woodhull, who clearly showed that the charge made by Mrs. Tilton that she had called the police to expel Mrs. W. from her house was false. The testimony of the latter, however, would not be accepted, were it not that Dr. Storrs' card clearly impeached her on other points, and public opinion reasoned that if this unfortunate lady would misrepresent in one matter she would in others, or all of her statements. It was expected that Mr. Moulton would present his statement, accompanied by all the correspondence, on Saturday, August 8th, but the day preceding that set forth for his appearance he was requested by the committee to defer its presentation until Monday evening, the 10th. In the meanwhile there had been ugly rumors in circulation to the effect that the committee were endeavoring to effect a compromise, and force was given to these rumors by this action of the committee.

Dropping the thread of our narrative for the nonce, we will speak of the excitement attending the publication of matters connected with the scandal. No event since the assassination of Abraham Lincoln attracted so much notice from the press. With the exception of four or five, the scandal found a place in all the leading journals of the country, and the illustrated papers' corps of artists united with the heavy writers of the daily press, in expressing in pictures what the editors expressed with the pen. Some of the cartoons were grossly indecent and uncalled for, at least until the pastor of Plymouth Church had been convicted. One of the most cruel was produced in the Cincinnati *Giglampz.* It represented Mr. Beecher driven outside the walls of a city, dressed as a leper, in a flowing robe, leaning upon a staff, the breast bare and branded with the letter A. Underneath the cartoon was the quotation :—

"Room for the leper! room!"—and as he came,
The cry passed on, "Room for the leper, room!"

The press was the vehicle for many clever criticisms at the expense of the parties to the scandal. One of the most reputable of the daily journals—the Chicago *Inter-Ocean*—collected and published them from time to time under the head of "Scandals." Here is a specimen :—

Susan stand up and shame the devil.

It is easier for a camel to skip through the eye of a needle than for a "nest-hider" to walk into heaven.

We find Mr. Tilton saying at one time that his wife is as pure as an angel; at another that she is as false as Lucifer.

The prevalent sentiment in the Southern press is that the gunning season in Brooklyn ought to have set in long ago.

Let us remember that neither religion, sects, nor virtue are touched by the scandal and infirmities involved in this Brooklyn exposition.

Susan B. Anthony was interviewed the other day concerning that about Beecher. Nothing was elicited, except that Susan's age is 55.

A "social cataclysm" is what they call it in the intellectual department of the New York *Tribune.* We should think it was at least that, if not more.

Suppose it should turn out simply that the man found the woman unduly attached to him, and cursed himself in that way for having been the cause of such a passion?

Miss Anthony who was present when Nathan put it to David about Mrs. Uriah, says she cannot remember anything that has so deeply affected her since that time as the present troubles in Brooklyn.

It is rumored that the Rev. Henry Ward Beecher has become involved in a rather awkward scrape with some woman or other in Brooklyn. If there is any truth in this, it is very strange that nothing is said about it in the newspapers.

"Is there nothing," exclaims a Brooklyn Journal, "to redeem Plymouth Church from this body of death?" Unless the case will yield to the marvelous influence of Hembold's buchu. it may be regarded as hopeless.

See here, where is George Francis Train? This is the first fight that he hasn't taken a hand in, and he hasn't fired a single pistol shot at the air or made a single speech. Come to the front, George, and wake snakes. Speak for Ireland, for Woodhull, the devil, or anybody. Otherwise there is a good chance for an unprofitable sleep.

That all may know the doubted foot
  That wears the dirty sandal,
Investigation boldly lit
  Investigation's candle.
And now it's groping for the nit
  That hatched the Plymouth scandal.
And soon a curious world may get
  The secret by the handle.

The newspaper offices were flooded with poems on the subject, which usually found a harbor in the waste baskets. One, however, we will give as it is after Mr. Tilton's poem "Sir Marmaduke's Musings :

SIR SINBAD'S ADVICE.

" Cling not to earth, there's nothing there,
However loved, however fair,
But on its features still shall wear
  The impress of mortality.

The voyager on the stormy deep,
Within his barque may smile and sleep—
But bear him on, he will not weep
  To leave its wild uncertainty.

Trust not to wealth—as well you may
Trust Asia's serpent's glittering play,
That dazzles only to betray
To death, or else to misery.

Trust not to Friendship—there may be
A word, a smile, a grasp for thee,
But wait the hour of need and see—
Nor wonder at its falsity.

Trust not to woman—she can smile,
And raise the d—l all the while:
Or, like 'Vic. Woodhull,' can beguile
With 'Free Love's new philosophy.'

Trust not to beauty! Like the rest,
She wears a lustre on her crest—
But short the hour, ere stands confest:
Her falsehood or her frailty!

Trust not to Fame! Her laurels wilt!
Watered by burning tears of guilt,
The Temple-altar Fame hath built,
In shattered ruin soon may lie!

Oh! trust to nothing here below,
In all this world of Sin and Woe;
And pray that women ne'er may know
'Vic. Woodhull's' nice morality.

Why bend your noble head in shame,
'Sir Marmaduke' of lofty name.
What cares the world for you, or fame;
It won't believe in Truth to-day!

O! cling not then, so fondly on
The flowers of earth around thee strewn—
Vic. says: they'll do to sport upon,
But never to love fervently."

CHAPTER XVI.

HISTORY OF PLYMOUTH CHURCH—PARTICULARS OF ITS EARLY ORGANIZATION—SOME STATISTICS OF ITS INCOME—EXCITING EVENTS CONNECTED WITH MR. BEECHER'S PASTORATE, AND THE DISTINGUISHED PERSONS WHO HAVE APPEARED IN THE EDIFICE.

NO work of this character would be complete that omitted a sketch of this Church, which has recently become so famous, and hence this chapter will be devoted to the Church, and some of the exciting incidents connected with it. The ground on which the present buildings of Plymouth Church stand comprises seven lots, 88 feet by 200 feet, and extends from Orange street to Cranberry street, forming a part of what is known to old Brooklynites as the "Hicks estate," the property at one time having belonged to John and Jacob M. Hicks, representatives of one of the oldest and wealthiest families of Brooklyn, Hicks street having been named after the family. In 1823 the First Presbyterian Church purchased the property of the Hickses, and erected thereon a church edifice, fifty-six by seventy feet, fronting on Cranberry street. At that period the little village of Brooklyn possessed a population of less than one thousand people, and the erection of a church on what was regarded and known as farm property, and in the midst of green fields, where cattle were wont to browse, was looked upon with feelings of doubt and distrust. But, notwithstanding the prophecies of a few timid members of the congregation, the society waxed strong and grew in grace and wisdom until the dimensions of the church edifice became so contracted that an addition of eighteen feet to the building could no longer be delayed. Accordingly, in 1831, a lecture room, including Sunday school rooms and a pastor's study, thirty-six feet by seventy-two feet, were added to the already prosperous little church.

Rev. Joseph Sanford was called to assume pastoral charge of the new congregation, and continued in that capacity from 1823 to 1829, a period of five years, when he was superseded by the Rev. Daniel L. Carroll, D.D., who was succeeded in turn in 1837 by the Rev. Samuel H. Cox, D.D., a name familiar to old church goers of this city. The Rev. Dr. Cox continued in charge of the congregation even after the society had removed, in 1847, to their new church edifice on Henry street, near Clark.

Among all these churches, and in a city with a population of 60,000 souls, there was but one Congregational Church (the Rev. R. M. Storrs, Jr., Church of the Pilgrims). The necessity for an additional Congregational Church was therefore felt and demanded. Accordingly Messrs.

John T. Howard, Henry C. Bowen, and Seth B. Hunt, of the Church of the Pilgrims, and Mr. David Hale, of the Broadway Tabernacle, held a consultation with a view to establishing a new Congregational Church. And inasmuch as the congregation of the Rev. Dr. Cox, known as the First Presbyterian Church, were about removing to their new edifice on Henry street, near Clark, the property which they had heretofore occupied on Cranberry street was offered for sale at $25,000. The locality and purchase money asked for the Cranberry street church property seemed to impress the foregoing gentlemen as a favorable spot for the establishment of a new church organization, and after due deliberation Mr. Howard was authorized, on behalf of the committee, to purchase the property on the following terms :—$20,000; $9,500 payable in cash, and the residue, $10,500, to remain on mortgage. In June, 1846, the sale was consummated, and, according to the manual of Plymouth Church, Messrs. Charles Rowland, David Hall, Jira Payne, David Griffin, Henry C. Bowen, and John T. Howard held a meeting on Saturday evening, May 9th, 1847, at the residence of Henry C. Bowen, having for its object the formation and establishment of a new Congregational Church in Brooklyn :—"The meeting was opened by prayer, after which David Hale made some statements in relation to the property now held by the Plymouth Church, and then, in behalf of himself and the other owners, offered the use of said property for purposes of religious worship as soon as the premises should be vacated by the First Presbyterian Church." Whereupon it was

Resolved, That religious services shall be commenced, by Divine permission, on Sunday, the 16th day of May, that being the first Sabbath after the house was to be vacated.

Rev. Henry Ward Beecher, at that time pastor of the Second Presbyterian Church, of Indianapolis, Ind,, and a young man, thirty four years old, happened to be in the city, having, through the influence of Mr. William P. Cutter, of New York, an intimate friend of the rising young Congregational preacher, been invited to deliver an address before the American Home Missionary Society in May, 1847. Mr. Beecher accepted the invitation, but for some reason delivered the address before the Foreign Missionary Society, instead of the society to which he was originally invited to speak. Some of the members of the new Congregational Church heard Mr. Beecher's effort, and were so well pleased, that he was invited to preach the opening sermon of the Cranberry street Congregational Church.

The pew rents for such years as records have been kept were as follows :—

1853	$11,157	1860	$28,682	1867	$49,000
1854	11,729	1861	28,750	1868	58,335
1855	12,053	1862	18,100	1869	54,970
1856	12,595	1863	23,396	1870	54,840
1857	14,340	1864	31,000	1871	56,744
1858	16,300	1865	39,642	1872	60,318
1859	26,052	1866	42,782	1873	59,114

Out of the pew rents of the last five years alone the sum of $78,950 has been applied to strictly mission purposes, exclusive of all expenditure upon the church or its own Sunday school.

The collections of the church for benevolent objects of all kinds (exclusive of pew rents, but including contributions in the schools), so far as any records remain, have been as follows:—

Year	Amount	Year	Amount	Year	Amount
1850	$1,873	1858	$ 5,148	1866	$20,742
1851	2,863	1859	6,340	1867	18,564
1852	1,815	1860	9,584	1868	39,712
1853	4,339	1861	11,980	1869	11,520
1854	5,116	1862	18,106	1870	18,938
1855	6,088	1863	no record.	1871	27,033
1856	no record.	1864	11,144	1872	19,788
1857	6,306	1865	14,572	1873	33,221

These figures do not include any contributions not taken under the immediate supervision of officers of the church or society, and represent only a very small part of the donations of the congregation. Recently, an effort was made to ascertain the contributions of members outside of the church collections; and it was found that over $300,000 had been given in one year, for charitable purposes, by the public subscriptions of a small portion of the members. Concerning the private charities of these members, and the general donations of all the rest of the church, no trustworthy estimate can be made.

The officers of the church, at the present time, are as follows:—

Pastor—Henry Ward Beecher, installed November 11, 1847.

Pastoral Helper—Samuel B. Halliday.

Clerk of the Church—Thos. G. Shearman.

Treasurer—Stephen V. White.

Deacons—John T. Howard, Charles M. Morton, Reuben W. Ropes, Elmer H. Garbutt, Benoni G. Carpenter, Samuel E. Belcher, Robert R. Raymond, John B. Hutchinson, Henry W. Sage.

Deaconesses—Mrs. Mary W. Halliday, Mrs. Frances L. Pratt, Mrs. Julia P. Hawkins, Mrs. Mary L. Thalheimer, Mrs. Isabella P. Beecher, Mrs. Mary A. Fanning.

Examining Committee—Pastor, Pastoral Helper and Clerk (*ex-officio*), Daniel W. Talmadge (clerk), Lysander W. Manchester, Thomas J. Tilney, George H. Day, David H. Hawkins, Henry M. Cleveland.

Music Committee—Pastor (*ex-officio*), Rossiter W. Raymond, John A. Fowle, Wallace E. Caldwell, Samuel E. Belcher, Horatio C. King, Henry N. Whitney.

Committee on Church Work—Pastor (*ex officio*), George A. Bell, Elmer H. Garbutt, Reuben W. Ropes, John T. Howard, Augustus Storrs, John B. Hutchinson, Assistant Clerk, Daniel W. Talmadge.

Auditors—Lorin Palmer, Moses K. Moodey.

Treasurer Deacons' Fund—E. H. Garbutt.

Within the walls of this structure, rich and sacred with the memories of famous orators, legislators, statesmen, gifted women, literateurs and divines, has been heard the voices of the agitators of anti-slavery, when it was almost dangerous to speak the words aloud. The silvery-tongued Wendell Phillips, the scholarly and eloquent Sumner, the gifted and erudite William Lloyd Garrison, the radical and impassioned Gerrit Smith, the brilliant Curtis, the statesman shoemaker Henry Wilson, John B. Gough, and scores of the greatest and ablest expounders of anti-slavery have given utterance to their views, and made the grand old edifice fairly ring with their eloquence and the magnetism with which they pronounced their convictions. It is here that Chapin, with glowing imagery and majestic and elegant English, has spoken "Woman's

Work" and the "Roll of Honor." Here Mrs. Livermore, Elizabeth Cady Stanton, Susan B. Anthony, Lucy Stone, Julia Ward Howe, Mrs. Tracy Cutler (the Western female lawyer), Lucy Harper, Henry B. Blackwell and Colonel T. W. Higginson, have explained and expounded the nature of their peculiar views, generally preceded by the late David Coombes, dressed in revolutionary costume, who, taking his stand in front of the platform, would proceed to unroll sundry mathematical problems, proving beyond a doubt his claims on certain families, to whom he had loaned money some thirty years ago, until he was ejected from the building, in spite of withering glances which he cast at the disturber of what he called "free speech." Here it was that the world-famed Casta Diva, Adelina Patti, sang her sweetest notes, in "Moses in Egypt," and thrilled the hearts of thousands by her rendition of the "Last Rose of Summer." Here Parepa has filled the building with her melody, and moved her audience to tears. Here Theodore Thomas and his orchestra have performed the inspired oratorios, symphonies and sonatas of Handel, Beethoven, Mozart and Gluck. Here poor Harry Sanderson, Mills and Rubenstein "the great," have made the piano speak, and Ole Bull has evoked, by the aid of his magical bow, the poetry of sound. Charles Dickens, in the winter of 1867, told of "Tiny Tim," "Bob Crachit," "Boots at the Holly Tree Inn," and "Poor Jo," and drew such crowds that carriages lined both sides of the street for blocks, while many encamped outside of the church on the previous night of the reading, by the light of bonfires, in order that they might secure seats. Here the famous Plymouth Organ concerts have been held on Saturday afternoons, and the great church organ (the largest, with one exception, in America) has pealed forth on Sunday mornings and evenings, its tidings of great joy. Here the Prince of Wales, and Presidents Lincoln and Grant have attended Divine service. It is here that Congregational singing is heard at the best, and, perhaps, in the history of no church has it been carried to such a high state of perfection. The visitor to Plymouth for the first time will probably never forget the inspiration incited by the vast assemblage rising, and literally singing with all their heart and soul, "The Shining Shore," "Jesus, Lover of My Soul," or "Homeward Bound."

Probably no church in the United States has experienced so many anxious, exciting and memorable Sunday services as has Plymouth. It was on Sunday evening, June 8, 1856, that the services were of a peculiar exciting nature, it having been reported by the New York papers of that day that a gang of New York roughs expected to visit the church in the evening and create a general disturbance. The Mayor of Brooklyn and the Chief of Police were notified, and a large posse of police were detailed in citizens' dress to watch the evening services, while a number of the regular attendants of the church armed themselves with revolvers, and prepared to give the ruffians a good warm Congregational reception in case they should attempt to demolish the church building or disperse the congregation. As the hour for the evening service drew nigh, crowds and gangs of rough-looking men from the worst localities of New York and Brooklyn formed in front of Musical Hall, at Fulton and Orange streets, and on adjacent corners, and when the church was opened, a number of them walked in, but behaved with great decorum when they observed the immense crowd in attendance. After remaining awhile they passed out, muttering as they did so a few ill-chosen remarks about "damned abolitionists and negro worshippers." Finally, as the audience were listening with almost breathless attention to Mr. Beecher, something struck one of the windows to the east of the pulpit, rattled against the glass, causing considerable excitement among the ladies and other persons present who sat near the windows, and then dropped on the window sill. For a few minutes the excitement was intense, but after a time quiet was restored, and the equanimity of the congregation regained. It was subsequently discovered that the object thrown against the window was a bullet, evidently used by some mischievous person with a view of creating a sensation, or for the purpose of raising a prodigious excitement in the neighborhood.

On Sunday morning, February 5, 1860, a little mulatto slave girl, ten years old, and valued at $900, occupied a seat by Mr. Beecher on the platform. She was brought to Brooklyn from Washington, D. C., by Rev. Bishop Falkner, then a member of Plymouth Church, but now pastor of the Mediator Congregational Church, Rochester avenue and Herkimer street. The reverend gentleman having obtained permission from her master, and determining to secure her freedom if possible, he introduced her to Mr. Beecher, by whom she was presented during the services of that memorable Sunday morning to his congregation, accompanied by a statement of the object in view, and a request for a liberal contribution of money, in order that she might be rescued from slavery. The collection taken up that morning in the church, together with a collection taken up for the same purpose by the Sunday school in the afternoon, amounted in the aggregate to $1,000. The interest manifested by the congregation in the morning was very great, one of the ladies in the audience, Miss Rose Terry, a sister of Major General Terry, dropping a gold ring in the contribution box as it passed. This ring was afterward placed by the pastor on the finger of the little slave girl with the remark that it was her freedom ring. She was then named after Mr. Beecher and Miss Terry, Rose Ward.

On Sunday, June 1, 1861, a similar incident transpired at Plymouth Church, when Mr. Beecher called upon his congregation to witness a "live slave woman," and introduced a young girl about twenty years old, named Sarah. who had been told by her master that if she could raise her freedom money among her white abolition friends he would be willing to release her from slavery. Accordingly, with her owner's permission, she was brought North, with the promise that if the money was not raised she would be returned. Three hundred dollars of the freedom money had already been collected when she was brought to Brooklyn. When the announcement was made to the congregation of Plymouth Church that the sum of $800, exclusive of jewelry, had been raised by collection in the church, the applause that followed lasted for several minutes.

On a Sunday in April, 1861, during the stirring and exciting period of early rebellion days, Mr. Beecher preached a sermon to the First Long Island (infantry) Volunteers, better known as the "Brooklyn Phalanx," and of which one of his sons was an officer. On the same day the congregation contributed at the conclusion of the morning services, the sum of $3,000, to aid in equipping the regiment for service in the field.

In the autumn of 1862, the church played its part well in providing accommodations for the defenders of the Union, a regiment of Maine volunteers, "on its way to the front," occupying the building, and sleeping for two nights on its cushioned seats

On April 12, 1865, a large number of the members of Plymouth Church and Mr. Beecher celebrated the fourth anniversary of the surrender of Fort Sumter, by Major Anderson, the steamer Quaker City conveying the Plymouthites to the fort, where Mr. Beecher delivered the address. On their return, while stopping at Fortress Monroe, the excursionists were grieved to hear that the fourteenth President of the United States, Abraham Lincoln, had suffered death at the hands of the assassin John Wilkes Booth, and when the party reached Brooklyn it was publicly announced that Mr. Beecher would preach a sermon on the martyred President on the following Sunday morning, April 24, 1865. The services on that memorable morning in spring will never be forgotten by those who participated in them. They are vividly portrayed in *Harper's Magazine*, by an eye-witness, as follows:—

"Presently the seats were all full. The multitude seemed to be solid above and below, but still the newcomers tried to press in. The platform was fringed by the legs of those who had been so lucky as to find seats there. There was loud talking and scuffling, and even occasionally a little cry at the doors. One boy struggled desperately for his life or breath. The ushers, courteous to the last, smiled pitifully upon their own efforts to put ten gallons into a pint pot. As the hour of service approached, a small door under the choir, and immediately behind the mahogany desk upon the platform opened quietly, and Mr. Beecher entered. He stood looking at the crowd for a little time without taking off his outer coat, then advanced to the edge of the platform and gave some directions about seats. He indicated with his hands that the people should pack more closely. The ushers evidently pleaded for the pewholders who had not arrived; but the preacher replied that they could not get in, the seats should be filled that the service might proceed in silence. He turned and opened the door. Then he removed his coat, sat down, and opened the hymn book, while the organ played. The impatient people meantime had climbed up to the window sills from the outside, and the great white church was like a hive, with the swarming bees hanging in clusters upon the outside.

The service began with an invocation. It was followed by a hymn, by the reading of a chapter in the Bible, and a prayer. The congregation joined in singing, and the organ, skilfully and firmly played, preventing the lagging which usually spoils congregational singing. The effect was imposing The vast volume filled the building with solid sound. It poured out at the open windows, and filled the still morning air of the city with solemn melody Far upon every side those who sat at home in solitary chambers heard the great voice of praise. Then amid the hush of the vast multitude, the preacher, overpowered by emotion, prayed fervently for the stricken family and the bereaved nation. There was more singing, before which Mr. Beecher appealed to those who were sitting to sit closer, and for once to be incommoded, that some more of the crowd might get in; and as the wind blew freshly from the open windows, he reminded the audience that a handkerchief laid upon the head would prevent the sensitive from taking cold. Then, opening the Bible, he read the story of Moses going up to Pisgah, and took the verses for his text. The sermon was written, and he read calmly from the manuscript. Yet at times, rising upon the flood of feeling, he shot out a solemn adjuration, or asserted an opinion with a fiery emphasis that electrified the audience into applause. His action was intense, but not dramatic, and the demeanor of the preacher was subdued and sorrowful. He did not attempt to speak in detail of the President's character or career. He drew the bold outline in a few words, and, leaving that task to a calmer and fitter moment, spoke of the lessons of the hour. The way of his death was not to be deplored; the crime itself revealed to the dullest the ghastly nature of slavery; it was a blow, not at the man, but at the people and the government; it had utterly failed, and finally, though dead, the good man yet speaketh. The discourse was brief, fitting, forcible and tender with emotion. It was a manly sorrow and sympathy that cast its spell upon the great audience, and it was good to be there.

"There was another hymn, a peal of pious triumph, which poured out of the heart of the congregation, and seemed to lift us all up, up into the sparkling, serene, inscrutable heaven."

One of the most interesting events was the visit of New England's Quaker poet, John G. Whittier. The poet had not been in Brooklyn for many years, and being a very warm friend of the pastor, he attended the morning services. Mr. Beecher noticed the poet in the audience. This fact was shown by the selection of one of Mr. Whittier's hymns from the Plymouth Church Collection. And at the end of the services Mr. Beecher sent one of the ushers to the seat occupied by the gifted stranger inviting him forward to the platform. With much hesitation Mr. Whittier reached the altar, where he was most warmly welcomed by Mr. Beecher, who evinced his great pleasure at the honored presence of the great Quaker, by presenting him with a beautiful basket of flowers. Mr. Beecher then introduced the poet to several ladies and gentlemen, and then, in company, followed the modest stranger to his carriage.

CHAPTER XVII.

SOMETHING ABOUT THE BEECHER FAMILY——DR. LYMAN BEECHER—HARRIET BEECHER STOWE, AND OTHER MEMBERS OF THE FAMILY WHO HAVE COINED REPUTATIONS IN RELIGION AND LETTERS.

PERHAPS in speaking of the Beechers it is safe to say that no American family has become so distinguished in religion and letters, nor is there anywhere,at this period of American history,a family more widely known, more generally despised by some, more warmly appreciated by others, or more universally complimented for their rare and varied talents by others who have become accustomed to accept anything they give utterance to, as strictly orthodox. The progenitor of the present generation, Dr. Lyman Beecher, was in his day one of the most gifted lights of the American pulpit—a man of original thought,whose greatest delight was when engaged with the pen or voice in controversaries with rivals of the *white cravat.* Thrice married he had as issue, thirteen children, nearly all of whom in the various walks of life adopted by them, became more or less renowned. All the sons are,or have been,ministers,—an unusual thing for sons of a minister—and the daughters were equally distinguished, Every school child has become familiar with Catharine Beecher as the authoress of school books, and her experience as a teacher,and a writer on domestic economy was varied, indeed. Harriet Beecher Stowe won a world-wide reputation by her "Uncle Tom's Cabin" and

"Dred," ana later a great deal of criticism from her ill-timed reference to the domestic affairs of Lord Byron. Many, many years ago, the author received his first impressions of the horrors of the slave system from reading Uncle Tom's Cabin, and young as he was, he recollects distinctly that the impression of the author left upon his mind, was that of a woman whose sympathies issued forth from a warm heart as the waters flowed when Moses smote the rock. Another daughter is Isabella Beecher Hooker, who of late has taken an active part in the Woman's Rights movement, and who figures more or less conspicuously in this great, disgusting and unfortunate religious scandal. In our narrative of the great sensation of the past five years, frequent reference is made to this lady, who however, it man be said, has never taken the ultra ground upon which Mrs. Woodhull stands, although recognizing and bearing testimony to the correctness of the ostracised and maligned priestess of the new social revolution. Of the sons, Henry Ward stands pre-eminently as the ablest representative and the widest known. Several of the brothers in a more limited sphere of Christian usefulness have achieved fame and the love of all with whom they have been brought in contact both within the pale of the congregations over which they presiue and among the worldly minded who have learned to admire them for their generous qualities of mind and heart. Dr. Edward Beecher for many years located at Galesburg, Illinois, was recognized as the peer of the clergy of that State. He was the author of a number of radical theological works that encountered severe criticism, chief among which, perhaps, may be classed the Conflict of Ages.

Then there is the popular, eccentric Thos. K. Beecher of Elmira, N. Y., who, in his way is as ultra and sensational as his more noted brother, Henry Ward. It is related of him that during the Fremont campaign in 1856, the Rev. Thomas declared that he would not shave or be shaved until John C. Fremont was elected President of the United States. It is not necessary to add that *he wears a full beard to this day.*

Rev. Chas. Beecher, of Owego, N. Y., is another of the same stamp, but younger and not so well known.

There are several others, but enough have been sketched to justify the statement that the Beechers are a remarkable family—as remarkable as they are talented.

CHAPTER XVIII.

A BRIEF SKETCH OF HENRY WARD BEECHER—HIS SCHOOLBOY DAYS—PREACHING TO NEGROES—HIS EARLY MINISTERIAL LABORS IN THE WEST—SOMETHING ABOUT HIS THEOLOGICAL VIEWS—PERSONAL APPEARANCE AND ANECDOTES OF THE MAN.

HENRY WARD BEECHER, the central figure in this volume, first saw the light on June 24th, 1813, and is now in his sixty-second year. He is the issue of Dr. Lyman Beecher's second wife, who died during the infancy of this afterwards-famous divine, and, of course, in early childhood he was not blessed with the maternal devotion that does so much to mould the character of the future man. Yet he had a step-mother possessing many excellent characteristics. His boyhood differed but little from that of other children, yet early in life he betrayed an enthusiastic love for nature, and he was never happier than roaming the fields or forests gathering wild flowers and admiring everything beautiful in nature. Possessed of a high degree of vitality, he was often subject to severe discipline for overstepping the Puritanic idea of propriety. It was observed that he preferred to collect his lessons from nature's open book rather than from the duller teachings of the trained pedagogue, and still he is remarkable for that striking characteristic. He was graduated, we learn, from Amherst College in 1834, and then entered Lane Seminary, Cincinnati, of which Dr. Lyman Beecher was President, for a theological course.

He first began his ministry while taking this course. In the suburbs of Cincinnati was a colored church without any regular pastor, and the congregation were only too happy to listen to the eloquence of the young student from Lane Seminary. In this colored church Henry Ward Beecher made his *debut* as a teacher of the truths of his Master, and probably it was to this circumstance that he owes the love he has ever since displayed for his fellow-creatures and human freedom. His first regular settlement as pastor was at Lawrenceburgh, Indiana, in charge of a Presbyterian church. It was about this time he married Miss Eunice Leighton of Hill Farm, Massachusetts—a lady who has certainly up to this time well sustained the position of wife to one of the most distinguished divines that the nineteenth century has produced. Of his career at Lawrenceburgh we are told more minutely elsewhere. There he remained from 1837 until 1839, when he was called to Indianapolis as pastor of the First Presbyterian Church, which he had charge of for eight years. The fame of the young minister, however, had extended beyond the confines of the then little town of Indianapolis, and the great tidal wave of his popularity began to set in. He was very radical for the old staid Presbyterian church, and showed a desire to be independent, to accept the truth wherever found, whether within or without the Presbyterian faith. His sermons were oftener drawn from the fruits and flowers, the forests and hills, the birds and the beasts, than from the catechism and the laws and the prophets. "It was," says a biographer, "during his residence here that he delivered and published a series of 'Lectures to Young Men,' which were at the time very popular and were sold and read extensively at the East as well as in the vicinity where published. He was also editorially connected with an agricultural paper. In 1847 he received a call to become the Pastor of the Plymouth Congregational Church at Brooklyn, which was accepted and for nearly twenty-seven years he has held the position, and it is safe to say that no clergyman in America has ever so quickly attained, or so long retained such a hold upon the masses as Mr. Beecher. He has been praised, flattered, and almost deified by some, and villified, misrepresented and lied about by others. No man has ever preached to such congregations, for the hundreds who crowd his church are but a drop in the bucket compared to the thousands who hear his sermons, prayers and talks, through the medium of the press. Reporters attend his Sunday services, and his sermons are reported and printed in full, formerly in the *Independent*, but now in pamphlet form called "The Plymouth Pulpit." The New York *Herald* reports and prints his weekly Lecture Room talks, and for years a Boston daily has, in its Saturday evening issue, published one of his sermons. But the Church is not the only avenue through which he reaches the public. He has, for many years been one of the most popular lecturers in the country; and he is now the *great star* of the lecture room. Like Cushman, Booth or Jefferson of the stage, he can dictate his own terms, and managers will "see him" for they know he is sure to draw. He has also been a prominent stump speaker in all the more exciting political campaigns for years, and it may be said in this connection, that many of his so-called sermons were very like political harangues. He has also been connected with the press for a long time. Was one of the most popular writers for the *Independent*, his contributions being signed with an asterisk, became popularly known as the "Star Papers," and were subsequently published in book form under that title. He was at one time the reputed editor of the *Independent*, but was really little more than a contributor; the editorial labors being performed by the late Joshua Leavitt and others, but it was a good card, and the publishers knew it would win."

He has also for years written for the *New York Ledger*, his first contribution being a serial for which Bonner paid a very large price, and it was doubtless a very good investment; yet the same story written by an unknown author, probably would

18

not have brought a hundred dollars. Mr. Beecher still writes short sketches and squibs for the *Ledger*. In addition to all these labors he has, until recently, been the ostensible editor of the *Christian Union* from its foundation, and his name has undoubtedly been one of the principal levers which have hoisted that publication into popularity. He also compiled and edited what is known as the "Plymouth Collection of Hymns and Tunes," and later he wrote the "Life of Christ," which has had a very large sale, and was very highly complimented by the critics. Mr. Beecher made one venture in imitation of Mrs. Stowe in the field of fiction, under the title of "Norwood," which, however, was not characterized by extraordinary vigor or originality of plot and design, and the fact that he had ever written it would probably soon have been forgotten had Theodore Tilton not recalled during his cross-examination attention to it, by remarking that Mr. Beecher used to bring the proofs of "Norwood" to Mrs. Tilton for her criticism and suggestion.

From the foregoing sketch of his various occupations it will be readily seen that Mr. Beecher has been anything but a drone in the human hive; on the contrary he has been "abundant in labors." Not one in a thousand could have endured half so much, and yet to-day, not one man in five thousand is, at the age of sixty-two, so well preserved.

In personal appearance Mr. Beecher shows that he has lived a life of activity, and given full development alike to mind and body—that, as one writer says, "he has realized to the fullest extent all the benefits which Macbeth invokes for his guests when he says:—

"And now may good digestion wait on appetite, and health on both."

His head is large, and his face full, round and ruddy; eyes large, full and expressive; lips and chin heavy and suggestive of an epicure. Tilton reports him a voluptuary, but he has certainly a keen appreciation of the good things of this life, but his healthy, robust frame clearly shows that he has never so far abused the generous gifts of Providence as to make the acquaintance of dyspepsia. Certainly his general physique exhibits a highly animal organization, such as one would expect to find in the make-up of a well-fed butcher. Yet one look at his expressive face tells one that it is that of a man of no common character. One writer in sketching him and drawing a comparison between Beecher and Dr. Storrs of Brooklyn, said :—"Mr. Storrs has no lack of veneration; Mr. Beecher has no lack of the want of it." A more recent one says, "He looks like a man who loves the entire race of Adam, and would like to gather them to his bosom as a hen gathereth her young brood to shield them from the storm or threatened danger."

It is reported of him that some years ago in discussing theology with his friend Rev. E. H. Chapin, (confessedly the ablest Universalist preacher in the country,) the latter remarked, "Well, after all, there is not very much difference in our belief." "Yes there is Chapin, a *Hell* of a difference," was the characteristic response of Beecher, and yet, not long after, he declared that no one could really believe the old Calvinistic doctrine of hell, and retain their reason for a fortnight. One week you would imagine him to be a Spiritualist, and the next he would inveigh against it in no measured terms. Consistency and uniformity are no elements in his character. Possibly his beliefs do not vary so much as one would suppose, but his want of method and system in the preparation of his sermons fosters a loose mode of expression which makes him liable to be misunderstood. He does not sit down in his library on Monday, and build up his sermons according to the schools from "firstly" to "finally" but often selects his theme half an hour before going to church and relies upon his impulses, and the inspiration of the hour; drawing from the storehouse of memory, or perhaps upon some incident of the moment for his illustrations. One anecdote on this point, which is probably untrue, and which the author learns Mr. Beecher has denied, is too good however to pass over here. The story goes that one very hot

Sabbath morning he entered his pulpit and when ready to begin his sermon, slowly arose, drew his handkerchief across his face, and casting his eyes over his congregation, exclaimed, "It is damned hot!'" The congregation were startled, but when he finished the sentence, "were the words I heard when I entered this church," and then preached one of the best sermons of his life on "Profanity," they were in ecstacies. This is the story, but whether true or false the author has no personal knowledge.

His manner in his pulpit delivery is in such utter disregard of church decorum that the holy sanctuary is sometimes called "Beecher's Circus." As we have already said he deals largely in metaphors or illustrations drawn from nature, or real life, or books. In the habits of a snail, the flight of a bird, the mechanism of a steam engine, the babbling of the brooks; either will give him the groundwork for one of his inimitable sermons. At times he walks up and down the platform terribly in earnest, like a well-schooled actor gesticulating wildly until fear seems to settle down upon his hearers. The next moment he will strike a vein of pathos in which his hearers are entranced, then he will suddenly run into the comic "and his queer conceits will be enforced and vivified," says a biographer by the most comical gestures, and grotesque facial contortions, and the listener or observer must be more than ordinarily well anchored who can refrain from a good hearty laugh "right out in meeting" and the mental exclamation will involuntarily arise, "What a rare comedian."

"In his illustrations he frequently uses some most beautiful figures, and whether studied and wrought out for the occasion or not, they always *seem* to be spontaneous. For instance, once discussing upon the loving kindness, and forgiving mercy of the Great Father, he stopped, was silent for a moment, an almost heavenly smile came over his face, and with a voice subdued and modulated as very few are capable of doing, he said, "God forgives as a mother, who kisses away into everlasting forgetfulness the faults of her erring, but penitent child."

"As previously remarked, Mr. Beecher is not a Theologian, and cannot be claimed by any school, although he has been for twenty-five years the foremost preacher in the country, and his church *is called* "Congregational;" yet he is not in accord with that denomination, and it is almost certain, that if he were a young, and unknown man, and should present himself before an association of Orthodox Congregational Ministers, as a candidate for ordination and installation, as a Pastor, and should while under examination, avow a tithe of his disregard for the accepted doctrines of that organization, which he so freely and boldly preaches to his own people, he would be unanimously rejected as unsound and dangerous. Or if he should succeed by his wonderful magnetic power, in so mesmerizing a staid body of Puritan Clergymen, as to secure their indorsement, we think the bones of Cotton Mather, Edwards, Hopkins, Tyler, and others of the departed New England Fathers would rattle in their graves.

"What is Orthodoxy?" he asks. "I will tell you. Orthodoxy is *my* doxy—and Heterodoxy is *your* doxy, that is if *your* doxy is not like *my* doxy.' What is terribly and dangerously heterodox this year, may be accepted as the very essence of orthodoxy next year.

"His idea of the true mission of the church and its ministry is *not* to dig among the dead dogmas of the past, or to choke his people with the dust from the mummies of a theology which might have been good centuries ago, but is now obsolete. But rather this, that Christianity, if valuable at all, is only so, when applied to the living issues of the day, and that its forms of presentation and application must change with advancing civilization. As well think of compelling the full grown, brawny man, to wear the bands and swaddling clothes of his infancy, and be fed on pap, as to demand that this generation shall be restricted to the theologic limits of the centuries which have passed into history. Every art, every science, and every profession have made, and will continue to make rapid strides with each succeeding generation, and there is no reason why theology should be an exception. Such are Mr. Beecher's ideas, although not expressed in his own words.

"Mr. Beecher is a better demolisher than builder. He has done much to weaken and pull down the old walls of religious superstition, and in doing so may not have been very cautious in avoiding to pull down and weaken faith in some doctrines that were still valuable. Like Theodore Parker and other radical demolishers of old and musty creeds, he has not evinced much constructive talent, and yet, there can be little question that while he has done much to unsettle the faith of thousands in the theology of their ancestors, he has at the same time accomplished a good work in diffusing more liberal ideas throughout the land, and all denominations (perhaps unconsciously) have modified and softened not only their beliefs, but their manner of teaching them, and few ministers now would dare to preach to an intelligent congregation, the doctrines of "Infant Damnation" and that God the Father *had before the foundation of the world elected* unborn millions to suffer the fiery tortures of *Eternal Hell.*

"Mr. Beecher's appearance upon the platform of the Lecture Room is not much different from what it is in the church. There are the same general characteristics, but more abandon and a broader humor. His lectures are generally upon Political, National or Social topics, and as in his sermons, he is profuse in the use of illustrations. He so utterly ignores in his dress and manners, the conventionalities of the clergy, that one who was ignorant of the fact, would never suspect him of belonging to the fraternity. He not only ignores, but most heartily despises, the traditional peculiarities and deportment so generally adopted by his brethren in the ministry."

"Once in the course of a lecture he alluded to the severe criticisms which had been so freely made by both the secular and religious press upon his taking such an active part in political affairs, (this was in the winter following the Fremont campaign, during which he not only took the stump, but preached politics in his church, and sent out his burning sarcasms, weekly, through the columns of the *Independent*). He said :—' Did I when I became a minister cease to be a man and a citizen? No! A thousand times no! Have I not as much interest in our government as though I were a lawyer, a doctor, a merchant, a banker, a farmer, a ditch digger or a wood sawyer?' 'Out upon this idea that a minister must *dress* minister, *walk* minister, *talk* minister, *eat* minister, and wear his ministerial badge as a convict does his stripes.' 'I have the same rights, privileges, and responsibilities as any other citizen, and I intend to claim them always and everywhere, and I ask no exemptions or privileges on the ground that *I am a minister*.' In the delivery of the above, his mimickry of the conventional minister was one of the finest pieces of comedy acting it has ever been the privilege of the author to witness, and he has seen Sothern, Jefferson, Warren, Clarke and nearly all the great comedians of the age. Another instance of his wonderful power in the use of illustration.

"He, in the course of a lecture, managed to bring in trout fishing; and he at once threw himself into the attitude of an expert angler; he threw his fly, (an imaginary one of course) and presently hooked his finny game, and then for five minutes (it seemed fifteen) he dodged from one side of the rostrum to the other, up and down, giving line and reeling in, until the entire audience (nearly two thousand) leaned forward with expectant eyes and open mouths, until, finally after many attempts and feints he landed the speckled beauty, when there was a sigh of relief all through the hall, and one particularly excited man exclaimed : "By —— he's got him." Now there was no water, no trout, no rod, no line, no fly, and yet there was all the excitement there could have been, had the audience really seen Seth Green or George Dawson hook and land a three pounder.

"Socially Mr. Beecher is as pleasing and interesting as in his public efforts; always genial and hearty, brim full of life and running over with humor, abounds in anecdote, and tells a good story, enjoys a hearty laugh after a hearty dinner. His fund of magnetism, like the widow's cruse is, never exhausted, no matter how frequent or large drafts are made upon it. The men admire him, the woman adore him, and the children all love him. He is very fond of children and pets of all kinds. A good horse is his delight, and he enjoys hugely a ride behind one who goes in *two and a small fraction*, and probably would not object, if he had the means, to emulate his friend Bonner in his stables, stud and equipage; and no man is a more ardent lover of the beautiful in nature. The rocks and rills, the vales and hills, woods, brooks and rivers all find in him an enthusiastic worshiper.

Mr. Beecher's profession never prevents him from having his "little joke" for which he has a keen relish. The late T. Starr King, (in many respects the most brilliant genius that ever adorned the American pulpit, or lecture hall) related the following characteristic anecdote of Mr. Beecher. Mr. King, as those who have seen him will remember, was a thin, spare man with an almost bloodless face, and it seemed a marvel how such a frail physical structure could sustain such a colossal brain, heart and soul. One cold, winter morning he was walking across Boston Common; the east wind was sweeping through the mall and walks, and he said it seemed as though the very marrow in his bones had turned to ice, his lips were blue, and his whole frame shivering, when suddenly a pair of strong arms were thrown around him from behind, and he was lifted up bodily; turning his head he saw the round, jolly face of Mr. Beecher, his cheeks in a ruddy glow, and glistening with perspiration. "How is it (asked King) that you are glowing with warmth while I am nearly chilled to death?" "Easily accounted for, Bro. King," responded Beecher. "What right have you who are not orthodox, to expect to have warm blood coursing through your veins? It is simply orthodoxy, or the lack of it, that makes the difference. You must be orthodox, my brother if you want to be warm and vigorous."

"Mr. Beecher and Rev. E. H. Chapin have for many years been warm personal friends, and have been co-workers in the temperance cause. Chapin has suffered occasional attacks of gout, and has at times been confined for some weeks and suffered intensely from its effects. During one of his attacks, the author called upon him at his house, and found him in his easy chair, with his game foot swathed and resting upon a cushion in the genuine old aristocratic style. After disposing of the business which occasioned the visit, a little time was spent in familiar chat. "By the way," said Chapin, "Beecher was over to see me yesterday, and hit me a good one. Ah!" said he, "this *preaching* temperance is all very fine, and possibly may be productive of great good to our fellow creatures, but if one wants to enjoy the blessed fruits of temperance in his own body, he must *practice* as well as preach."

The above, the author believes, is a just sketch of this great divine. In compiling it he has liberally quoted from another writer whose views concide so nicely with his own that he has felt constrained to use them here. Of course, no attempt is here made to sketch Mr. Beecher's eventful career, that alone would fill this volume, the only aim being to give sufficient to enable the reader with the assistance of the portrait of Plymouth's pastor, to form an intelligible opinion of him.

The author cannot resist the temptation to embody here a criticism of Mr. Beecher, written in 1868, it is said by Chauncy Burr,—not to endorse it, but rather to give the reader the opinion of one so well known as Mr. Burr:—

Of the cleverness of Henry Ward Beecher, both as a writer and speaker, there can be no question. Even in a profession for which he is least of all fitted, he has made a sensation, partly because of a natural genius which would have given him pre-eminence anywhere, and partly because he pressed into its practice those tricks which would have given him success in the profession for which he was best fitted by nature. He has managed in his ministry to mingle the pulpit and the playhouse as no other man living could have done, and to bring the buffoonery of the stage, with a very thin varnish over it, into the services of the conventicle. His sermons are always exceedingly clever—not as sermons, but as things to amuse and entertain an audience. They solve no difficulties of doctrine, they remove no doubts of the troubled Christian, they comfort no soul anxious to be relieved of its sin, they show no road to salvation—for all practical purposes, and with but a few changes of words, they might answer for the debating club, the stump, or the mock-court of the cider-cellar; but as specimens of word-weaving—of words with little original thought, they are almost marvellous. And for those who are jaded with novels, and surfeited with flash newspapers, it will be pleasant news to learn that forty-six of Beecher's sermons, revised by the author, and considered by him to be his best and wittiest, and least tainted with piety, have been issued in two large and handsome volumes, and may be placed in the library alongside of the Chevalier de Faublas, and Fredoniad, and be read and enjoyed at any time by the lover of light literature. Yet there is a slight fault in the compilation. The book is an incongruous mixture. After each sermon we have a copy of those public instructions to the Almighty, in regard to the latter's conduct of affairs, which Mr. Beecher, like a chaplain of Congress, is in the habit of giving weekly, in the shape of prayer. That these instructions are wise, there can be no doubt. So long as Mr. Beecher remains in a state of anxious doubt as to whether he did or did not create the Creator, their utterance may be a relief to the preacher. But why put them in a book? They are strictly a private affair between the Almighty and the Deity of Plymouth Church, and they occupy space which might have been better filled by two or three entertaining and comic sermons. In a future edition, we hope that Mr. Beecher will cut these out, and thus add another to the many favors he has conferred upon his devout worshippers.

CHAPTER XIX.

SKETCH OF THEODORE TILTON—HIS CAREER AS A REPORTER, EDITOR, LECTURER, NOVELIST AND POET—HIS PERSONAL APPEARANCE—HIS DEVOTED ADMIRATION OF THE FAIR SEX—A MAN WHOSE ADONIS-LIKE APPEARANCE WOULD CARRY THE CITADEL OF ANY SUSCEPTIBLE HEART—MR. SAMUEL BOWLES' SKETCH OF HIM.

MR. TILTON occupies the second place in importance in this work, and we shall do no more than endeavor to give a hurried sketch of his career and labors since attaining his majority. It may be said, however, that he was educated in the public schools of New York, selected the journalistic profession became a stenographer and general reporter on the *Tribune*, was a protege of Horace Greeley, and finally rose through all the grades of journalism until he became editor of the Brooklyn *Union* and the *Independent*, in the service of Henry C. Bowen.

"His personal appearance, says a gifted biographer, is almost remarkable. Nature must have been in a kindly mood when she arranged the mould in which the physical Theodore Tilton was cast; and his mental abilities and characteristics are in sweet accord with his physical symmetry. Mr. Tilton is emphatically what Trowbridge's "Vagabond" said he was in his early manhood, "One of your handsome men."

He is rather tall, neither slim, nor stout, but of elegant form and proportion. His hair (worn long) is in color between a brown and auburn, and is inclined to curl, is always neatly arranged, and combed back, hanging in heavy masses over his collar. His eyes are very expressive, piercing, yet with an almost dove-like softness and tenderness. His features come nearer to the pure Grecian type than any American whom we have met; always cleanly shaved, his dress faultlessly neat, rich and becoming, and his linen immaculate in its whiteness. In fact his whole appearance would indicate that he fully accepted the truth of the proverb that "cleanliness is akin to Godliness." The reader may think we are drawing the portrait of a perfect Adonis; and perhaps we may as well admit it, for we have rarely, if ever, met a man who approximates so nearly to our standard of the ideal Adonis, as does Theodore Tilton; and we should think that any woman of sentiment and refinement would not only admire him, but fall in love with him. Socially, he is not only interesting, but fascinating; *almost irresistible;* always the refined gentleman; a first class conversationalist, and an evening spent with him, listening to his converse, or hearing him read poetry, with his soft, rich voice, is something to remember with pleasurable emotion; and yet he is a radical of the most ultra type.

"Mr. Tilton is about thirty-seven years of age, and has during his whole manhood life, been connected with Journalism. In his early career as a journalist, he was a stenographer and reporter, but he first became prominently known to the public through his connection with the *Independent*, of which he was for several years the responsible, managing editor, and in his editorials, no one can gainsay that he was in all respects what the title of that paper indicates, for he was emphatically *independent* in the full significance of that word. In his expressions of his views, political, social or religious, he as utterly ignored the old beaten tracks and long accepted formulas, as did his pastor, Mr. Beecher, in his ministrations at Plymouth Church. As a radical he fairly out-distanced those who had been pioneers in the cause before he had ever written a paragraph.

"The *Independent*, as the reader is aware, was started as a professedly religious publication, but has really been quite as much devoted to political, social and commercial interests as to purely religious topics, and under the management of Mr. Tilton, politics seemed to be the dominant feature in that sheet; and while Mr. Tilton was professedly a republican, he never hesitated to score any leader in that party who failed to come up to his ideas of the true mission of radical republicanism. He was, prior to the act of emancipation, a most ultra and uncompromising advocate of freedom for all, and as soon as the abolition of slavery had become a fixed fact he turned his artillery upon the real or supposed wrongs of woman, and the columns of his paper fairly teemed with appeals and arguments in behalf of woman's rights, and female suffrage, and we question if the cause has ever had a more enthusiastic advocate among the "Lords of creation" than Theodore Tilton. He not only wrote for it, but spoke for it; and was sneered at and made the target for all sorts of ridicule by the conservative press the country through.

"From the initiatory of woman's rights and female suffrage, to the extreme and revolutionary social-freedom platform of Mrs. Woodhull and her disciples, the road was an easy and natural one, and Mr. Tilton was ere long found standing side by side with her, and openly indorsing her particular doctrines. Thus we find him November 20th, 1871, at Steinway Hall, New York city, presiding at an immense meeting, and introducing Mrs. Woodhull to the audience before whom she delivered her celebrated speech defining for the first time *publicly* the principles of social freedom as held by her; and whatever may be his position *now*, the part he assumed *then* was virtually a public indorsement of, and declaration of adhesion to, the bold platform launched on the waves of public opinion on that occasion. He also wrote (or allowed his name to go forth to the public as the author of) a biography of Mrs. Woodhull, and eulogized her as one of the *purest women on earth;* and she at that time, no doubt, counted upon him, as one who would stand in the front rank as an advocate and exemplar of her social doctrines, and as a founder and sustainer of the Utopia, to the establishment of which she had pledged her "fortune," her "life" and her "sacred honor."

After his dismissal from the service of Mr. Bowen, Mr. Tilton founded the *Golden Age* which supplied a new field for the journalist. The *Age* took very radical and independent ground on all public questions, and when the Liberal Republican movement was inaugurated Tilton was one of its most earnest supporters, throwing his pen and voice into the campaign in support of its principles and Horace Greeley. A few weeks ago he temporarily retired from the *Age* but still owns it.

As a lecturer Theodore was no less brilliant than as a journalist. Though not so popular on the rostrum as Beecher, he was decidedly attractive, and rarely did he fail to secure crowded houses when announced to appear. As a delver in the field of fiction he has won success in his first effort, and his book "Tempest Tossed" shows that many of the characters are ably drawn. Indeed, it is as a novel admitted to be superior to Beecher's "Norwood." "Mary Vail," one of the characters in "Tempest Tossed," it is admitted, represents Mrs. Tilton. We regret that we have not space to quote from the work in this connection. As a poet Mr. Tilton has shown considerable genius. Two of the most noted ones are "Sir Marmaduke's Musings," given elsewhere, and "A Faith Confession." The latter is as follows:—

As other men have creeds, so I have mine;
I keep the holy faith in God, in man,
And in the angels ministrant between.

I hold to one true church of all true souls;
Whose churchly seal is neither bread nor wine,
Nor laying on of hands, nor holy oil,
But only the anointing of God's grace.

I hate all kings, and caste, and rank of birth;
For all the sons of men are sons of God;
Nor limps a beggar but is nobly born;
Nor wears a slave a yoke, nor Czar a crown,
That makes him less or more than just a man.

I love my country and her righteous cause:
So dare I not keep silent of her sin;
And after Freedom, may her bells ring Peace!

I love one woman with a holy fire,
Whom I revere as priestess of my house;
I stand with wondering awe before my babes,
Till they rebuke me to a nobler life;
I keep a faithful friendship with my friend,
Whom loyally I serve before myself;
I lock my lips too close to speak a lie;
I wash my hands too white to touch a bribe;
I owe no man a debt I cannot pay—
Except the love that man should always owe.

Withal, each day, before the blessed Heaven,
I open wide the chambers of my soul,
And pray the Holy Ghost to enter in.

Thus reads the fair confession of my faith,
So crossed with contradictions by my life,
That now may God forgive the written lie!
Yet still, by help of him, who helpeth men,
I face two worlds, and fear not life nor death!
O Father! lead me by Thy hand! Amen.

The course he has seen fit to pursue in regard to the scandal which so deeply affects his domestic relations, has been variously commented upon; his reticence for years, has been severely condemned by some of his friends, and as heartily commended by others. Whether he has acted wisely or not, is neither the purpose or province of the writer to attempt to decide.

One thing, however, is certainly very sure, and that is, he deeply regrets his association with, and frequent public indorsement of the champions of free love, and social revolution, and has doubtless found it as dangerous an occupation as holding a wolf by the ears, *neither safe to hold on or let go.* The details of his experience in this character will hereinafter more fully appear.

The author while preparing this imperfect sketch of Mr. Tilton, found in the *Springfield* (*Massachusetts*) *Republican*, edited by Mr. Samuel Bowles, who has long known Mr. Tilton, the following article:—

Forty years ago, this summer, young Henry W. Beecher graduated from Amherst college. The next year, was born Theodore Tilton in New York city. People yet in their youth may remember the brilliancy of Tilton's debut. In the ten years succeeding the attainment of his majority, he worked upon the *Independent*, and became the idol and the weekly teacher of a vast constituency of readers. He was young, handsome and full of heart. He had the physique of the natural man and a head and face like Goethe's in that bust of him in his youth, and such as a pagan would have called god-like. He was a man of impulses and affections no less ardent and broad than Mr. Beecher's, and in his writing he added to these a style trenchant and vigorous. He loved humanity in the abstract and he loved it in his friends having for his intimates even of his own sex a fraternal embrace that smacked of the Gallic habit. He was a man whose heart was great, and it was a time when heart was needed. It was a time when dormant natures had to be roused, when the discouraged and the weary had to be nerved again to the conflict. It was no time for logic, but for battle, and we all pressed on, grateful for any impetus, impatient of reason. In the great anti-slavery war, Theodore Tilton did his share.

After the war, we fell upon times which demanded considerable cold calculation, and we slid back into the old materialistic "horse-sense" ways of looking at things. Our Donatello, (for he strongly reminds us of Hawthorne's "Marble Faun"), seemed out of place with his sentiment, which by that time we had come to call gush. In our cynical mood, he seemed an overgrown boy rather than a mature man. Spoiled by the flatteries that had been heaped upon him and soured by business disappointments, we see him at length plunged into a domestic difficulty of an appalling character. A Sickles would have shot the supposed intruder, a selfish man would have settled it "for a consideration," but Tilton forgave. He undertook to save his wife and Mr. Beecher; the smart became too sore, and he sought advice, and little by little he proved quite inadequate in cunning to carry out the plan which his heart dictated.

CHAPTER XX.

SKETCH OF MRS. THEODORE TILTON *nee* ELIZABETH RICHARDS. —HER DEEPLY RELIGIOUS TURN OF MIND.—THE DELICATE COMPLIMENTS PAID HER BY THE HUSBAND WHO CHARGES HER WITH A GREAT SIN.

WITHOUT some facts descriptive of the above named lady—who in this disgraceful and nauseating scandal, has certainly suffered more acute anguish than any of the parties to it; yet who we are told, has maintained a calmness such as only women in affliction know how—this volume would be very incomplete. The author has never met her, and must depend upon those who have, for a biographical and personal sketch. He will, therefore, be excused for extracting from the writings of others. The *Daily Graphic* in describing her remarks:—

"Mrs. Elizabeth R. Tilton, whose name has become unfortunately conspicuous in connection with the great Brooklyn Scandal, is a lady of about forty years of age. She is under medium height, with black hair and eyes, a face that is interesting though not beautiful, with an expression that indicates unusual sensibility and sentimentality rather than intellectual force or refinement. Her appearance is modest and her air peculiarly sincere and confiding. Her manners are easy and natural, with a simple grace which is more pleasing than what passes for elegance in polite society. Her prevailing mood is profoundly serious, lit up with occasional gleams of joy and sometimes breaking into a beautiful playfulness. At times, when her feelings are pleasantly excited and her face glows with expression, she appears really handsome; at other times, when depressed or wearied or unexcited, her eye is lustreless and her face is dull and unattractive. She is a good housekeeper and an excellent mother, devotedly fond of her children, and doing more for them and spending more time in reading to them and talking with them than most mothers. Her tastes and habits are domestic, sentimental, and religious rather than æsthetic or literary; her reading has not been extensive, and her favorite pictures are valuable for their sentiment rather than artistic excellence or imaginative power. She has had seven children, four of whom are living. The eldest is a daughter of more than ordinary maturity of mind and force of character. She resembles her father much more than the other children—so much that she would be recognized as his daughter by those who are familiar with his features. Her home, on Livingston Street, was once peculiarly attractive and charming by affection that filled its rooms with a climate of summer and a fragrance as of blooming roses; it was tastefully furnished, graced with exquisite pictures, made poetic by the disposition and arrangement of its contents, and the ideal element visible and palpable in every apartment. It seemed to realize the ideal of home.

"Of Mrs. Tilton's married life it is obviously indelicate and unbecoming to say much. She was naturally religious, and united with the church when young and had a class in the Sunday-school. She was attached to all persons of a religious cast of mind, and particularly friendly to her pastor, to whom she seems to have gone for counsel, and on whom she leaned perhaps more than was well for either. The last evidence of her religious sincerity is furnished by the fact that her husband has defended her so long, and by his emphatic statements before the committee. If she has sinned, he contends, that was through the blinding of her conscience and the misleading of her mind, and he acquits her of guilt while he accuses her of crime. 'I have taken pains to say that she was a devoted Christian woman,' said Mr. Tilton on examination; 'a tender, delicate, kindly Christian woman. Her's is one of the white souls.'

"'There are a great many women who look upon a man with a sense of worship; Elizabeth never did that; Elizabeth is the peer of any man; at the same time she reverences; it was not vanity—it was reverence; she never regarded Mr. Beecher as a silly woman regards him; she was not a silly woman taken captive; she was a wise, good woman taken captive. Elizabeth was in a sort of vaporous-like cloud. She was between light and dark. She could not see that it was wrong. She maintained to her mother in my presence that she had not done wrong; she cannot bear to do wrong; a sense of having done wrong is enough to crush her; she naturally seeks for her own peace a conscientious verdict; she never would have had these relations if she had supposed at the time that they were wrong; Elizabeth never does anything that at the time seems wrong; for such a large moral nature, there is a lack of a certain balance and equipoise; she has not a will that guides and restrains; but Elizabeth never does at any time that which does not have the stamp of her conscience at the time upon it. I think she certainly spends hours on her knees some days; I don't suppose a day passes over Elizabeth that the sun, if he could peep through the windows, would not see her on her knees.'"

"Testimony like this," says the *Graphic*, "from an accusing husband invests the character of the wife with peculiar interest, if not with mystery. It is hard for a majority of people to comprehend such complexity. But it is not difficult to see that such a woman as he has described, could hardly enjoy his eccentricities of belief, his intimate relations with reformers of all kinds. his severe criticisms of the church she regarded as so sacred. She naturally recoiled from much that he loved, and wanted to hide her face from the pictures he hung on the wall. His friends she looked upon as the foes of religion, and the more firmly he set his face towards freedom the more resolutely she hid hers in the tradition of her childhood. He says: 'She would not let the children have playthings on Sunday. John G. Whittier came to our house one Sunday night, and Mr. Greeley, and met Mr. Johnson; and it almost broke Elizabeth's heart to think that the best man in New England, whom she reverenced, should have appointed Sunday night; she never received visitors on Sunday." His change of religious views "was a great source of tears and anguish to her; she said to me once that denying the divinity of Christ in her view nullified our marriage almost; and I think next to the sorrow of this scandal it has caused that woman to sorrow more than anything else; she has suffered because I cannot look upon the Lord Jesus Christ as the Lord God; I think her breast has been wrenched with it."

Whether this lady be guilty or innocent of the damaging charges alleged against her, every womanly heart must admire the delicate manner in which the author of those charges speaks of her. It is evident that Theodore Tilton still loves her as he loves his God, or he would never have resorted to such subterfuges as he did to shield her reputation. Another writer thus pictures her:

"A most dominating wealth of silken brown hair; soft and soulful eyes of richest hazel; a face of exquisite sweetness and tenderness, and ripe with culture and character; a mouth carved by the gods, and lips full, warm and suggesting robustness of modest passion; a chin indicating a gentle, firm and abundant will; a shapely neck and graceful shoulders, and a finely developed bust—all harmony; all beauty; all the vigor and tenderness of young life and fascination. The witching eyes seemed to brighten when looked into; a smile so very sweet as to thrill me appeared upon that face when I involuntarily fixed my gaze upon it."

Of her early life there is little to say. In early life she resided with her widowed mother in New York. The family subsequently removed to Brooklyn, where she attended several private schools, and finally completed her education at the Packer Institute, which is more noted for the superiority of the education imparted, than for the inculcation of religious principles. Of these times a recent writer says:—

"She was a strangely earnest little brunette, that inspired the kindest regards in her teachers, and a kind of awe in her schoolmates. She graduated at the age of eighteen, and at once came to the aid of her mother, who was then keeping a boarding house on Livingston street, a little below the pleasant frame cottage where she so lately lived, with the same energy and self-devotion that she had displayed in conquering her school tasks. It was here that she met Mr. Tilton. He was a *protegé* of Mr. Beecher, and hence came to her with the best of earthly recommendations. Mr. Beecher had known her from a child. She had sat upon his knee; and when she at last became acquainted with the tall, handsome, enthusiastic young writer, who carried his indorsement, she was not disinclined to receive his attentions. He became a boarder at her mother's house. When she was twenty-two years old they were married. This was in 1855. Her life now became wholly domestic, a part of it devoted to her three children, and the remainder to the supervision of a large and fashionable boarding house."

CHAPTER XXI.

SKETCH OF MRS. VICTORIA CLAFLIN WOODHULL—HER PERSONAL APPEARANCE—A GLANCE AT HER PECULIAR SOCIAL THEORIES—A DANGEROUS ANTAGONIST, EITHER IN CONVERSATION OR AS A WRITER.

HER late devoted admirer having reserved so much space to a sketch of this remarkable woman's early trials, victories and misfortunes, extracts from which we give elsewhere, it is hardly necessary for us to say much in addition. She is now about thirty-six years of age, is of medium height, has a good form, erect and firm in her carriage; her features are regular and of the aquiline type; eyes dark blue and very expressive, and when in speaking she gets thoroughly roused, they are flashingly eloquent. She is rather inclined to paleness, except when excited in conversation or speaking to an audience there comes a flush upon her cheeks which is of the hectic order; her hair, which is a light brown, is worn short and carelessly arranged; her forehead is high and broad, and her whole head and face indicate more than ordinary intellectuality and mental power. When not engaged in speaking she has a sad and decidedly thoughtful expression, and in her general appearance what the French term *spirituelle*. There is nothing masculine or sensual in her looks, and if she is the sensual, depraved woman that she is charged withal, her whole physiognomy is a glaring lie. Her manners are refined and lady-like. When strangers are presented to her, she greets them with a winning cordiality which at once sets them at ease; she is a good conversationalist, and never wearies one with worn out platitudes, but is original in her modes of expression, every now and then startling her auditors with some bold and novel proposition. She is apt to call things by their right names, speaks out boldly what she thinks, and we should infer that she had adopted as her own, the motto of the Knight of the Garter. A close observer spending an hour in her company, and witnessing her greetings to one and another, speaking briefly to a half dozen different persons, and perhaps on as many different topics, will readily understand the secret of her wonderful power over both men and women. We do not wonder that so many love her, and others fear her, for no one can long be placed within the charmed circle of her presence and remain insensible to the almost irresistible power of her fascinations. But it is on the platform that her particular talents are most vividly exhibited.

As a rule, female declaimers are not a success, and Mrs. Woodhull is not altogether an exception to the rule, and yet there is a something about her that will not only attract, but hold an audience; she is a radical of the radicals, and boldly, nay, defiantly launches forth her most ultra and advanced doctrines of free love, and, as we think, ofter shocks her hearers by preaching extremes of social and sexual freedom.

She has a pleasant voice, and ordinarily speaks with deliberation, enunciating clearly and distinctly; is at times quite logical, but often mistakes sophistry for logic. She appears best when she is broken up in her discourse by hisses, or other uncomplimentary interruptions; they seem to evoke all the latent powers of her whole nature, and leaving her desk and manuscript, she pours forth a perfect torrent of fiery eloquence, freely using (and effectively too) invective, sarcasm, or ridicule, as the occasion demands; she is never at a loss for a ready and apt retort on such occasions. Her perorations at the close of a long and carefully written speech, *seem* to be impromptu, and the ideas, and words wherewithal to clothe them, to come from the inspiration of the moment; and even an unbeliever in

Spiritualism can almost believe that what she claims is really true; that she is controlled and guided by the spirit of Demosthenes, who, as she says, has for years been her special guardian, and that she not only draws her inspiration from him, but also many of her ideas and expressions; she most assuredly has all the appearance of one so wholly rapt and absorbed by some invisible influence as to be hardly conscious of her own identity. She is very pointed and often personal in her speeches; and to use a pugilistic simile, "hits from the shoulder" and has no hesitation in hitting "below the belt." She is merciless; sparing neither friend or foe; truth, as she claims, is what she is seeking, no matter where it may lead, or how many previously accepted opinions, or former friends and associates are sacrificed. Nothing is sacred or inviolate with her, if it stand in the way she has marked out. She says "wherever I find a social carbuncle I shall plunge my surgical knife of reform into it, *up to the hilt.*" As it regards consequences personal to herself, she declares she never takes them into the account; she may be shut up in prison, or even led to the stake, but she will not turn one hair's breadth to the right or left from the course marked out for her by her own conscience, and the teachings of her guardian spirit. In a speech in Chicago she said, "I am charged with seeking notoriety, but who among you would accept any notoriety and pay a tithe of its cost to me? Driven from my former beautiful home, reduced from affluence to want, my business broken up and destroyed, dragged from one jail to another, and in a short time am again to be arraigned before the courts and stand trial for telling the truth. I have been smeared all over with the most opprobrious epithets, and the vilest names, am stigmatized as a bawd and a blackmailer. Now until you are ready to accept my notoriety, with its conditions—to suffer what I have suffered and am yet to suffer—*do not dare to impugn my motives;* as to your approval or dissent, your applause or your curses, they have not a feather's weight with me, I am set apart for a high and sacred duty, and *I shall perform it without fear or favor.*"

As a writer she wields a caustic and eloquent pen, and especially does she shine as such in responding to an attack upon her. Whenever she "strikes back" her blows fall with telling effect upon her adversaries, who are invariably carried off wounded. She has written much upon the financial questions agitating the country from time to time, and wrote so well that many of her essays were honored with a place in the New York *Herald*. One of her best known works is "The Principles of Government." Her social theories are most revolting and find but few indorsers, for their adoption would sap the foundations of domestic life, and bring man down to the status of the brute creation.

COL. BLOOD.

CHAPTER XXII.

SKETCH OF COL. JOHN H. BLOOD.—THE "BREVET" HUSBAND OF VICTORIA WOODHULL.—WHAT MRS. WOODHULL SAYS OF HIM.

THIS man was originally, we believe, from Missouri. During the war he held the rank of Colonel of a Missouri regiment. He was at one time one of the leading spiritualists of St. Louis, and for some time filled a responsible government office; there he was married, but secured a divorce that he might marry "the Woodhull."

Col. Blood is about thirty-seven years of age, rather below the average height, and, as will be seen by his portrait, rather good looking. His hair is a dark brown, and his face is adorned with a heavy mustache, and side whiskers approximating in length the Dundreary style. He has a pleasing countenance, and is a good talker, has a pleasant voice, but rarely speaks in public. When making an announcement, or speaking a few words upon any subject under discussion, he impresses one as having clear ideas, and at least a fair capacity for expressing them, and is in appearance what would be generally termed a "good fellow." It has been said, and is by many believed that he is the "power behind the throne," or the "Warwick" of the Woodhull kingdom, and that he writes the speeches, editorials, etc., of Victoria and Tennie. But we have personal assurance that such a suspicion is not well founded. This however is a matter of opinion rather than knowledge. But we do believe him to be a valuable, and important spoke in the business wheel of the firm.

In regard to his peculiar relations with Mrs. Woodhull, no better authority can be quoted than that of Mrs. Woodhull, who in a speech, at Vineland, New Jersey, a few years ago, (pointing to Col. Blood,) exclaimed: "There stands my lover, but when I cease to love him, *I shall leave him;* yet I hope that time will never come."

TENNIE C. CLAFLIN.

CHAPTER XXIII.

SKETCH OF TENNIE C. CLAFLIN.—HER PERSONAL APPEARANCE. —THE BUSINESS "MAN" OF THE BROKERAGE FIRM.—EXTRACTS FROM HER WRITINGS.—HER POWER AS A CLAIRVOYANT, AND A REMARKABLE TEST OF IT.

WE propose to say but little of Miss Tennie C. Claflin, as she has not figured very prominently in connection with the charges. Nevertheless her life has been so intimately entwined with that of Victoria, that an attachment has grown up between them that is lasting. In Mr. Tilton's Life of Woodhull, Tennie's career is sketched, but we will give a few facts regarding her in this chapter. In her youth she was a clairvoyant and so-called medium, as was also her sisters Victoria and Mary (Mrs. Dr. Spar). Tennie is about twenty-nine years of age, is quite handsome, compared with the other sisters, and is rather below medium height, and while she is not stout, she has a plump, well-rounded form, and in both form and features singularly free from anything approximating to angularities; her complexion is light, almost to paleness, and her skin is fair as that of an infant; hair, light brown, worn short, and inclined to curl; eyes blue, sparkling, and very expressive. When engaged in conversation upon any topic which interests her, she is all animation; talking not only with her tongue, but with eyes, face, hands, and *all over;* and one would think her whole physical structure was inlaid with a thousand sensitive spiral springs. She is all nerve and vivacity; full of magnetism and excitability, very free in her modes of expression, and seemingly never stops to think how any sentence is going to sound to another, or that by her careless freedom she is liable to be misapprehended, and notwithstanding she has since her girlhood been much around the world, and has mingled largely and freely with men of the world, she will say and do the most *outre* things, but with an air of the most childlike and unsophisticated innocence.

"Her face" says a writer, "does not wear the sad expression of her sister, nor is it like hers sicklied o'er with the pale cast of thought." We should judge that as a broker she would be of more service to the firm as a drummer up of business, and in entertaining patrons, than in attending to details which require patience and consecutive thought, and that as one of the late stock brokerage firm of Woodhull & Claflin, Tennie was the Jim Fisk and Victoria the Jay Gould; and as publishers of the *Weekly* Victoria's sphere was the editorial sanctum and Tennie's that of outside business *man!* to get subscribers and secure paying advertisements. Like her sister she is an ardent spiritualist, and sees visions, and dreams dreams; both developing a strong hereditary superstition of this peculiar form. Tennie sometimes is heard upon the platform as a speaker, and while quite as enthusiastic as her sister, is not as argumentative or effective. She also wields a ready pen, and has issued quite a large book under the title of "Constitutional Equality of the Sexes." She has also written more or less for the *Weekly*, and has given to the public through its columns free utterance to her free social theories; her strongest points however are made on the subject of the social equality or the sexes—maintaining that if the woman who violates the laws of social purity is ostracised by society, her male partner in guilt should suffer the same penalty, or if the libertine and seducer be received into, and petted by society, his female victim be equally well received—that if female chastity be the condition of social recognition, the same condition be inexorably required of the man; that if Hester Pryne be compelled to wear the "scarlet letter" in the market place, her reverend seducer shall stand by her side, wearing the same red insignia of shame; or to use an old and trite maxim, "Sauce for goose, sauce for gander."

While it is not our intention to give endorsement in any manner to the peculiar views of Miss Claflin, we will make some extracts from her published writings that the reader may see the advanced views on social questions:

"Whatever may be your ideas as to whether individuals should, or should not, be permitted to think upon social freedom, and to advocate their views regarding it, none of you will, I dare say, presume to deny my sister and myself the right to advocate whatever religious views we may hold; and I further presume you will not object to our changing those views (at any time) according to any new light that may shine upon us.

"Herein, I shall not hesitate to say that in religion we are most thorough, and I trust devout spiritualists; and that whether we are deceived, insane, or whatever else may be conceived of, all our movements are largely the result of spirit influence, and often of positive direction. And we are proud to proclaim at all times and in all places that we yield willing obedience to all such requirements, because through a long series of years we have learned from frequent trial to trust them.

"We know, as well as any of you know what you are engaged in, that we are engaged in introducing new social views to the notice, and for the consideration of the general public; and that these views look to radical and sweeping changes in the present system, which everybody knows must be changed before anything like the millenium, in which all Christians pretend to believe, can be realized. Step by step we have been led on, from one thing to another, sometimes ourselves even, fearing the results which might come, but ever being justified by what has come, until we now stand on the very brink of what we know, is to be a social earthquake. What this earthquake may destroy, who may be swallowed up in its yawning chasm, or whether we ourselves may be swept away, we do not know; but that great good to the human family will come of it, we feel assured. Our course has not always brought us peace, happiness and comfort; on the contrary we have suffered almost all the terrors to which human life is subject. Even now we stand under two criminal indictments, upon both of which, if present public opinion, under the manipulations of the church and press, could have its way, whether according to law we are, or are not guilty, we should be so adjudged; yet we rely upon truth as against all other powers that may be conjured up to oppose it, and we know that it shall triumph, even if we are crushed in the process.

"You must remember that many, if not most of you, today worship One, who in doing His duty to His Father, died upon the cross. None of you imagine that it was a pleasant duty He performed in thus yielding up His life. He did not live selfishly for Himself, as I fear most of those who profess Him so loudly, live for themselves. He was despised of the authorities in government, in philosophy and in religion. His associates were Magdalens, sinners and lowly fishermen; and yet you now exalt Him to the throne of the Universe, and pretend *weekly at least*, to bow in homage before His shrine.

"I would not have it understood from this reference that my sister and I presume to place ourselves as Christs of the present generation. On the contrary we wish it to be distinctly understood, that we lay claim to nothing, except this: that without fear or favor, we do what we believe to be right to do; that we live the life which is the best we can live, and which we are willing the whole world shall know, and that we obey the directions of those whom we know to be wiser than we are. Again I say you may credit us with insanity, if you will; but I pray you, along with it, to also give us credit for honesty of purpose.

"It has been freely circulated through the press, that we are simply notoriety seekers. Now let me ask you to consider calmly for a moment the probabilities of such a thing. Do people usually invoke upon themselves continuous persecution, merely to obtain notoriety? Do they consciously invoke the terrible power of the press to crush them, to brand them before the world by every vile and detestable epithet known to language; do they seek the hoots and jeers of the common multitudes, and the sneers, and upturned noses of the select few wherever they go; do they purposely, render themselves friendless, and homeless and distressed in all possible and conceivable ways merely to become simply notorious? Nay, my friends! none of you can honestly say you believe this. It requires stern convictions of duty; unflinching allegiance to purposes; undying devotion to principles, and an unswerving faith to enable any one, and especially frail women, to endure unto the end under all these trials.

* * * * * * * * * * *

"If one half that had been charged against us, had even a shadow of foundation in fact, we should have been long ere this, and justly too, in the Penitentiary.

"Early in this course, which has been marked out to us, we sometimes almost fainted by the way-side. It was almost a greater sorrow than we could endure, to see the whole public press teeming with the most outrageous and debasing items about us. Every woman knows what it requires to endure even the shadow of a reflection upon her private social life, to say nothing about sweeping charges, destroying in the minds of those, who from them alone, gather their information, and form their conclusions, every sentiment of respect, and making room for utter detestation and hate.

"It has been said that we are utterly insensible to these things; but if the public knew what it has cost us in sleepless nights, in heart-aches and laceration of soul, to be able to perform our duties, under the heavy hand, that has at times been laid upon us, you would wonder, not that we have maintained ourselves, but that we could ever presume to think of living at all.

* * * * * * * * * *

"There are thousands upon thousands in this country, who hate us with the most inveterate hatred; who think us the personification of every thing that is bad, who honestly believe that no fate could be too cruel for us to endure, and yet not one of these people, *of their own knowledge*, know a single fact to justify their convictions.

* * * * * * * * * *

"Man proposes, but God disposes; and we are very willing to act our part as best we may, and trust the rest to Him who 'maketh even the wrath of man to praise Him.' We have cast ourselves into the gap broken in social despotism, and there we shall stand firmly and proudly, until the war shall be ended and the victory secured, even if it brings death to us. And I say here and now: We shall be justified!

"Thus through storm and sunshine alike, we have steadfastly pursued our way, halting at nothing, but shoulder to shoulder, battling together, for what we believe to be the right and the truth."

Miss Claflin was once married, but secured a divorce. For several years she lived in the West and followed, under the name of Tennessee Claflin, the calling of clairvoyant and medium, and the files of the Cincinnati papers in 1864 will exhibit her card. The author has never placed any faith in the powers of clairvoyants; but there is certainly possessed by this young woman some power of sight-seeing that he cannot explain, and he proposes to give an instance of it here. After the battle of Resacca, Ga., in 1864, while examining the deserted rebel works, the author was shot in the foot by a concealed rebel, who had remained hid in the woods and desired to test his musket before surrendering to the "Yanks." He went back to Cincinnati to recuperate from the wound. While at the hotel he became restless and wearied by confinement, and asked the clerk where he could go to pass an hour pleasantly. A visit to Tennessee Claflin, the seeress, was recommended. Calling a coach he was soon put down at her door and "hobbled in on crutches." After receiving her fee, the fair seeress told him much in his past life that he knew to be true and only known to himself; but the most remarkable statement was this:

"Why, Captain," said she, "you were not wounded in battle."

"How then did I receive it?" he asked in great astonishment.

"When the rebels evacuated their works and the Federal army moved forward in pursuit, you lingered behind to look at the works and was shot by a rebel concealed in a tree."

The author was thunderstruck. This woman at Cincinnati, two weeks after the battle, had correctly described an event certainly only known to him and the concealed rebel who drew his "bead" upon him that morning. This is mentioned here merely as proof that the woman has some means of "guessing" correctly. The author has never spoken to her since that day in 1864, but has frequently seen her in the metropolis dodging into brokers' offices and newspaper sanctuaries, and discovered in that vivacious little creature "Tennessee Claflin, the Cincinnati Clairvoyant."

CHAPTER XXIV.

HENRY C. BOWEN, HIS MERCANTILE CAREER AS THE SENIOR MEMBER OF THE FIRM OF BOWEN, MCNAMEE & CO.—HIS CAREER AS AN EDITOR AND PUBLISHER—THE CHARGE THAT HE WAS THE FIRST PERSON TO CIRCULATE CHARGES AGAINST THE PASTOR.

THE gentleman who, throughout the entire excitement, figured more or less prominently in it, and who it is alleged was the first to circulate rumors of his pastor's criminality, is about sixty-four years of age. "He was," says a writer, "formerly one of the foremost dry goods merchants in New York, being the senior partner of the house of Bowen, McNamee & Co., who many years ago did business down Broadway, below the Astor House, afterward in a splendid block erected on the site of the old Broadway Theatre. He was from its foundation one of the pillars of Plymouth church, and probably was more largely instrumental than any other one man, in securing the services of Mr. Beecher, as its pastor. He was always a radical abolitionist, having received his business, political and religious training from the Tappans, who were among the pioneers in the anti-slavery movement in New York. His house at one time had a large southern trade, but when sectional strife was at its flood, the names of Bowen, McNamee & Co. were among the first to be put upon what was called the "black list," and southern merchants were emphatically warned not to patronize them. They accepted the situation, and boldly unfurled a banner bearing the following inscription "*Our Goods and not our Principles, for sale.*" Mr. Bowen was one of the founders of the *Independent* and it is not too much to say that no paper in this country in its inception, ever had such a brilliant array of talent, editorial, and as stated contributors as this. Its responsible editors were, Rev. Joshua Leavitt, Rev. Geo. B. Cheever, D. D., Rev. Leonard Bacon, D. D. and Rev. R. S. Storrs, Jr. D. D. Among its stated contributors were Henry Ward Beecher, Harriet Beecher Stowe, Chas. L. Brace, Rev. F. D. Huntington, (at that time a popular Unitarian clergyman in Boston,) Edna Dean Proctor, and many others. Mr. Bowen was the commercial editor, and furnished, or was responsible for the "sinews of war." During the financial storm of 1857, "a feature" in the business department of the *Independent*, was the publication weekly, of a list of failures. Many commercial and mercantile houses protested against this feature, but the commercial editor with characteristic firmness adhered to the plan, until one fine day the old, and as was supposed, wealthy firm of Bowen, McNamee & Co., had to "walk the plank" whereupon it was suddenly discovered that the publication of the list of failures was not expedient. It came to pass, in the course of human events that Bowen abandoned mercantile pursuits, and finally became (after the retirement of Mr. Richards) the publisher of the *Independent*, and is now publisher, proprietor, and, in name at least, editor. He is a shrewd, sharp, business man, but some of his transactions, in relation to the Beecher scandal, and his summary dismissal of Mr. Tilton from his position as editor of the *Independent* and the "*Brooklyn Union*," are, to say the least a little questionable.

Some two years ago Mr. Bowen disposed of his interest in the *Brooklyn Union* and now devotes his entire attention to the *Independent*.

LADIES BRINGING BOUQUETS TO MR. BEECHER

CHAPTER XXV.

MR. BEECHER UNBOSOMS HIMSELF TO THE COMMITTEE—HIS VERY REMARKABLE EXPLANATION OF HIS RELATIONS TO TILTON AND HIS FAMILY, ALLEGES THAT HE WAS BLACKMAILED BY TILTON AND MOULTON, DENIES ANY CRIMINALITY WITH MRS. TILTON AND GIVES MOST ASTOUNDING EXPLANATIONS OF THE LETTERS CONFESSING SOME SIN IN THE PREMISES.

THE evening Mr. Moulton's statement was being read in New York and Brooklyn for the first time, there was a busy scene at the residence when the examination was held. That evening thirty or forty stenographers were engaged in preparing for the press Mr. Beecher's statement in defense, which is given here. It was published on the ensuing morning:—

Gentlemen of the Committee: In the statement addressed to the public on the 22d of July last I gave an explicit, comprehensive and solemn denial to the charge made by Theodore Tilton against me. That denial I now repeat and reaffirm. I also stated in that communication that I should appear before your committee with a more detailed statement and explanation of the facts in the case. For this the time has now come. Four years ago Theodore Tilton fell from one of the proudest editorial chairs in America, where he represented the cause of religion, humanity and patriotism, and in a few months thereafter became the associate and representative of Victoria Woodhull and the friend of her strange course. By his follies he was bankrupt in reputation, in occupation and in resources. The interior history of which I am now to give a brief outline, is the history of his attempts to so employ me as to re-instate him in business, restore his reputation, and place him again upon the eminence from which he had fallen. It is a sad history, to the full meaning of which I have but recently awakened, Entangled in a wilderness of complications, I followed, until lately, a false theory and delusive hope, believing that the friend who assured me of his determination and ability to control the passionate vagaries of Mr. Tilton, to restore his household, to rebuild his fortunes and to vindicate me, would be equal to that promise. His self-confessed failure has made clear to me what for a long time I did not suspect. The real motive of Mr. Tilton. My narrative does not represent a single standpoint, only as regards my opinion of Theodore Tilton. It begins at my cordial intimacy with him in his earlier career, and later my lamentation and sorrowful but hopeful affection for him during the period of his initial wanderings from truth or virtue. It describes my repentance over evils befalling him, of which I was made to believe myself the cause, my persevering and friendly despairing efforts to save him and his family by any sacrifice of myself not absolutely dishonorable, and my growing conviction that his perpetual follies and blunders rendered his recovery impossible. I can now see that he is and has been from the beginning of the difficulty, a selfish and reckless schemer, pursuing a plan of mingled good and hatred, and weaving about me a network of suspicious misunderstandings, plots and lies to which my own innocent words and acts, nay even my thoughts of kindness toward him have been made to contribute. These successive views of him must be kept in mind to explain my course through the last four years. That I was blind so long, as to the real motive of the intrigue going on around me was due partly to my own overwhelming public engagements, and partly to my complete surrender of this affair and all papers and questions connected with it into the hands of Mr. Moulton, who was intensely confident he could manage it successfully. I suffered much, but I inquired little, Mr. Moulton was chary to me of Mr. Tilton's confidences in him, reporting to me occasionally in a general way Mr. Tilton's words and outbreaks of passion only as an element of trouble which he was able to control, and as additional proofs of the wisdom of leaving it to him. His command of the situation seemed to me at the time complete, immersed as I was in incessant cares and duties, and only too glad to be relieved from considering the detail and wretched complications, the origin and fact of which remained, in spite of all friendly intervention, a perpetual burden to my soul. I would not read in the papers about it, I would not talk about it, I made Moulton for a long period my confidant, and my only channel of information. From time to time suspicions were aroused in me by indications that Mr. Tilton was acting the part of an enemy, but the suspicions were rapidly allayed by his own behavior towards me in other moods, and by the assurances of Mr. Moulton, who ascribed the circumstances to misunderstanding or to malice on the part of others.

It is plain to me now that it was not until Mr. Tilton had fallen into disgrace and lost his salary that he thought it necessary to assail me with charges which he pretended to have had in mind for six months. The domestic offense which he alleged was very quickly and easily put aside, but yet in such a way as to keep my feelings stirred up in order that I might, through my friends, be used to extract from Mr. Bowen $7,000, the amount of a claim in dispute between them. A check for that sum in hand, Mr. Tilton signed an agreement of peace and concord, not drawn by me, but accepted by me as sincere. The *Golden Age* had been started, he had the capital to carry it on for a while. He was sure that he was to head a great social revolution.

With returning prosperity he had apparently no griefs which could not be covered by his signature to the articles of peace, yet the change in that covenant, made by him before signing it, and represented to me as necessary merely to relieve him from the imputation of having originated and circulated certain old and shameless slanders about me, were made, as now appears, to leave him free for future operations upon me and against me.

So long as he was or thought he was on the road to a new success, his conduct toward me was as friendly as he knew how to make it. His assumption of superiority and magnanimity, and his patronizing manner were trifles at which I could afford to smile, and which I bore with the greater humility, since I still retained the profound impression made upon me, as explained in the following narrative: That I had been a cause of overwhelming disaster to him, and that his complete restoration to public standing and household happiness was a reparation justly required of me, and the only one which I could make; but with a peculiar genius for blunders, he fell almost at every step into new complications and difficulties, and in every such instance it was his policy to bring coercion to bear upon my honor, my conscience and my affections, for the purpose of procuring his extrication at my expense. Theodore Tilton knew me well. He has said again and again to his friends that if they wished to gain any influence over me they must work upon the sympathetic side of my nature. To this he has addressed himself steadily for four years, using as a lever without scruples my attachment to my friends, to my family, to his own household, and even my old affection for himself. Not blind to his fault, but resolved to look on him as favorably and hopefully as possible, and ignorant of his deep malice. I labored earnestly, even desperately, for his salvation. For four years I have been trying to make the man as great as he conceived himself to be, to restore to prosperity and public confidence one who, in the midst of my efforts in his behalf, patronized disreputable people and doctrines, refused, when I besought him to separate himself from them, and ascribed to my agency the increasing ruin which he was persistently bringing upon himself, and which I was doing my utmost to avert. It was hard to do anything for such a man. I might as well have tried to fill a seive with water.

In the latter stages of the history he actually incited and created difficulties, apparently for no other purpose than to drive me to fresh exertions. I refused to endorse his wild views and associates. The best I could do was to speak well of him, mention those good qualities and abilities which I still believe him to possess in his higher moods, and keeping silence concerning the evil things which I was assured and believed had been greatly exaggerated by public report. I would not think him so bad as my friends did. I trusted to the germs of good which I thought still lived in him.

On the appearance of the first attack from Tilton, I immediately called for a thorough examination by a committee of my church. I am not responsible for delays in the publicity of the details. All the harm I have so long dreaded has come to pass. The time has arrived when I can freely speak in vindication of myself. During four years singularly burdened with labor, I find myself in a position where I know my innocence without being able to prove it. Mr. Beecher says Tilton was first known to him as a reporter of his sermons, and he gives his history up to the time when Tilton became his assistant editor of the *Independent*, in which relation he, Beecher, became greatly attached to him. During vacations, while my family were at my farm, I became so familiar with the families of my friends and their children, that I went in and out daily as in my own house. Mr. Tilton urged me to do the same at his house, speaking extravagantly of his wife's esteem for me. On returning from England I paved the way for him to become the sole editor of the *Independent*. The violent assault on me by Tilton in 1866, on account of my Cleveland letter, broke off my connection with the *Independent*. The social relations with Tilton continued very kindly until 1868 and 1869, but on political matters there was a coolness.

During all the time of the visits to Tilton's house there never was the slightest hint from him or any member of his family of any dissatisfaction with my familiar relations to his household. I gave copies of my books to Mrs. Tilton, sent flowers from my farm to a dozen families, which she occasionally shared, and only once gave her a present, a brooch of little value, as one of the souvenirs of my European trip. Beecher refers to the affection shown him by the children of Tilton, and Mrs. Tilton seemed an affectionate mother, a devoted wife looking up to her husband. So far from supposing that my presence and influence was alienating Mrs. Tilton from her family relations, I thought on the contrary that it was giving her strength and encouraging her to hold fast upon a man evidently sliding into dangerous associations and liable to be immersed by unexampled self-conceit. I regarded Mr. Tilton as in a very critical period of his life, and used to think it fortunate he had good home influences about him. During the late years of our friendship Mrs. Tilton spoke very mournfully to me about the tendency of her husband to great laxity of doctrine in religion and morals. She gave me to understand that he denied the divinity of Christ, the inspiration of the scriptures and most articles of the orthodox faith, while his views as to the sanctity of the marriage relation were undergoing constant change in the direction of free love. In the latter part of July, Mrs. Tilton was sick, and at her request I visited her. She seemed much depressed, but gave me no hint of any trouble having reference to me. I cheered her as best I could, and prayed with her just before leaving. This was our last interview before the trouble broke out in the family. I describe it because it was the last, and its character has a bearing upon a latter part of my story. Concerning all my other visits, it is sufficient to say that at no interview which ever took place between Mrs. Tilton and myself did anything occur which might not have occurred with perfect propriety between a brother and sister, between a father and child, or between a man of honor and the wife of his dearest friend, nor did anything ever happen which she and I sought to conceal from her husband.

After giving reasons for the removal of Tilton from the editorial chair of the *Independent*, Mr. Beecher, proceeded: After Mr. Tilton's return from the West in December, 1870, a young girl whom Mrs. Tilton had taken into the family, educated and treated like her own child, (her testimony I understand is before the committee) was sent to me with an urgent request that I would visit Mrs. Tilton at her mother's. She said that Mrs. Tilton had left her home and gone to her mother's in consequence of the ill-treatment of her husband. She then gave me an account of what she had seen, of the cruelty and abuse on the part of the husband that shocked me; and yet more, when with downcast look she said that Mr. Tilton had visited her chamber in the night, and sought her consent to his wishes. I immediately visited Mrs. Tilton at her mother's, and received an account of her home life and the despotism of her husband, and of the management of a woman whom he had made housekeeper, which seems like a nightmare dream. The question was whether she should go back or separate forever from her husband. I asked permission to bring my wife to see them, whose judgment in all domestic relations I thought better than my own, and accordingly a second visit was made. The result of that interview was that my wife was indignant toward Mr. Tilton, and declared no consideration on earth could induce her to remain an hour with a man who had treated her with an hundreth part of such insult and cruelty. I felt as strongly as she did, but hesitated as I always do at giving advice in favor of a separation. It was agreed that my wife should give her final advice at another visit. The next day, when ready to go, she wished a final word, but there was company, and the children were present, and so I wrote on a scrap of paper, "I incline to think your view is right, and that a separation and settlement of support will be the wisest, and that in his present desperate state her presence near him is far more likely to produce hatred than her absence." Mrs. Tilton did not tell me that my presence had anything to do with this trouble, nor did she let me know that on the July previous he had extorted from her a confession of exces-ive affection for me. On the evening of December 27th, 1870, Mr. Bowen, on his way home, called at my house and handed me a letter from Mr. Tilton. It was as nearly as I can remember in the following terms:

Henry Ward Beecher: For reasons which you explicitly know, and which I forbear to state, I demand that you withdraw from the pulpit and quit Brooklyn as a residence.

[Signed] THEODORE TILTON.

I read it over twice and turned to Bowen and said, "This man is crazy, this is sheer insanity," and other like words. Bowen professed to be ignorant of the contents, and I handed him the letter to read. We at once fell into a conversation about Mr. Tilton, during which Bowen stated that Tilton had been reduced from an editor of the *Independent* to a contributor, because his religious and social views were ruining the paper, the conversation resulting in the opinion that Bowen could not retain relations with Tilton. Bowen derided Tilton's letter and promised his friendship to Beecher, and Tilton was subsequently removed from the *Union*. Beecher says he felt unhappy at Tilton's disaster, as his affairs did not promise that sympathy and strength which makes one's house as mine has been in times of adversity, a refuge and tower of defence.

Mr. Beecher continues: On the 29th of December, 1870, Mr. Tilton having learned that I had replied to his threatening letter by expressing such an opinion of him as to set Mr. Bowen finally against him and bring him face to face with immediate ruin, extorted from his wife, then suffering from a severe illness, a document incriminating me and prepared an elaborate attack upon me. On Tuesday evening, Dec. 30th, 1870, about seven o'clock, Francis D. Moulton called at my house, and, with intense earnestness, said, "I wish you to go with me and see Mr. Tilton." I replied that I could not then, as I was just going to my prayer meeting. With the most positive manner he said, "You must go; somebody else will take care of the meeting." I went with him, not knowing what trouble agitated him, but vaguely thinking that I might now learn the solution of the recent threatening letter. On the way I asked what was the reason of this visit, to which he replied that Mr. Tilton would inform me, or words to that effect. On entering his house, Mr. Moulton locked the door, saying something about not being interrupted. He requested me to go into the front chamber over the parlor. I was under the impression that Mr. Tilton was going to pour out upon me his anger for colleaguing with Bowen and for the advice of separation given to his wife. I wished Mr. Moulton to be with me as a witness, but he insisted I should go by myself. Mr. Tilton received me coldly, but calmly. After a word or two, standing in front of me with a memorandum in his hand, he began a set oration. He charged me in substance with acting for a long time in an unfriendly spirit, that I had sought his downfall, had spread injurious rumors about him, was using my place and influence to undermine him, had advised Mr. Bowen to dismiss him, and much more that I cannot remember. He then declared that I had injured him in his family relations, had joined with his mother-in-law in producing discord in his house, advised a separation, and alienated his wife's affections from him, had led her to love me more than any living being, had corrupted her moral nature, and had taught her to be insincere, lying and hypocritical, and ended by charging that I had made wicked proposals to her. Until he reached this I had listened with the same contempt, under the impression that he was attempting to bully me. But with the last charge he produced a paper purporting to be a certified statement of a previous confession made to him by his wife of her love for me, and that I had made proposals to her of an impure nature. He said that this confession had been made to him in July, six months previous, that his sense of honor and affection would not permit any such document to remain in existence, that he had burned the original and should now destroy the only copy, and he then tore the paper into small pieces. If I had been shocked at such a statement, I was absolutely thunderstruck when he closed the interview by requesting me to repair at once to his house, where he said Elizabeth was waiting for me, and learn from her lips the truth of his stories, in so far as they concerned her. This fell like a thunderbolt upon me. Could it be possible that his wife, whom I had regarded as a type of moral goodness, should have made such false and atrocious statements, and yet if she had not how would he dare to send me to her for confirmation of his charges? I went forth like a street walker; I believe Moulton went with me to the door of Tilton's house. The houskeeper (the same woman of whom Mrs. Tilton has complained) seemed to have been instructed by him, for she evidently expected me, and showed me at once to Mrs. Tilton's room. Mrs. Tilton lay upon her bed, white as marble, with closed eyes as in a trance, and with her hands upon her bosom, palm to palm, like one in prayer. She made no motion and gave no sign of recognition of my presence; I sat down near her and said, "Elizabeth, Theodore has been making very serious charges against me and sent me to you for confirmation." She made no reply or sign, yet it was plain she was conscious and listening. I repeated some of his statements, that I had brought discord to the family, had alienated her from him, had sought to break up the family, usurped his influence, and then as well as I could I added he said that I had made improper suggestions to her, and that she had admitted the fact to him last July. I said "Elizabeth, have you made such statements to him?" She made no answer. I repeated the question. Tears ran down her cheeks and she very slightly bowed her head in acquiescence. I said you cannot mean you have stated all that he has charged. She opened her eyes and began in a slow and feeble manner to explain how sick she had been, how wearied out with importunity, that he had confessed his own alien loves and said he could not bear to think that she was better than he, that she might win him to reformation if she would confess that she had loved me more than him, and that they would repent and go on with future concord. I cannot give her language, but only the tenor of her representations. I received them impatiently. I spoke to her in the shortest language of her course. I said to her, have I ever made any improper advances to you? She said no. Then I asked "Why did you say so to your husband? She seemed deeply distressed; "my friend (by that designation she almost always called me) I am sorry, but I could not help it. What could I do?" I told her she could state in writing what she had now told me. She beckoned for her writing materials, which I handed from the secretary standing near by, and she sat up in bed and wrote a brief counter statement in a sort of postscript. She denied explicitly that I had ever offered any improper solicitations to her, that being the only charge made against me by Mr. Tilton, or sustained by the statement about the confessions which he had read to me. I dreamed of no worse charge at that time. The mere thought that he could make it and could have extorted any evidence on which to base it was enough to take away my senses. Neither my consciousness of its utter falsehood nor Mrs. Tilton's retraction of her part in it could remove the shock from my heart and head. Indeed her admission to me that she had stated under any circumstances to her husband so wicked a falsehood, was the crowning blow of all. It seemed to me as if she was going to die, that her mind was overthrown, and that I was in some dreadful way mixed up in it and might be left by her death with this terrible accusation hanging over me. I returned like one in a dream to Moulton's house, where I said very little and soon went home. It has been said that I confessed guilt and expressed remorse. This is utterly false. Is it likely that with Mrs. Tilton's retraction in my pocket I should thus stultify myself? On the next day at evening, Mr. Moulton called at my house and came up into my bedroom. He said that Mrs. Tilton, on her husband's return to her, after our interview, had informed him what she had done and that I had her retraction. Moulton expostulated with me, and said the retraction, under the circumstances, would not mend matters, but only awaken fresh discord between husband and wife, and do great injury to Mrs. Tilton without helping me. Mrs. Tilton, he said, had already recalled in writing the retraction made to me, and, of course, there might be no end to these contradictions. Meanwhile Tilton had destroyed his wife's first letter, acknowledging the confession, and Mr. Moulton claimed that I had taken a mean advantage and made dishonorable use of Theodore's request that I should visit her, in obtaining from her a written contradiction to the document not in existence. He said all difficulties could be settled without any such papers, and that I ought to give it up. He was under great excitement. He made no verbal threats, but he opened his overcoat, and with some emphatic remarks, showed a pistol, which afterwards he took out and left on the bureau near which he stood. I gave the paper to him, and after a few moments talk he left.

Beecher then refers to the great distress of mind caused to him by the action of Mrs. Tilton in this matter, but finally supposed she had been overborne by sickness, shattered in mind and no longer responsible for her acts. His soul went out to her in pity. He blamed himself for imprudence and want of foresight, for he thought it was the result of her undue affection for him, and he could have borne any punishment if that poor child could but emerge from this cloud. He judged from Tilton's anger and fury that the charge made by him and supported by the accusation of his wife, was to be publicly pressed against him, which might result in great disaster, if not absolute ruin. He considered his name, his church, everything connected with him involved. He says, "My earnest desire to avoid public accusation and the evils necessarily flowing from it has been one of the leading motives that must explain my action during these three or four years." Moulton visited Beecher at this time, finding him in a sore and distressed condition. Moulton seemed convinced that Beecher had been seeking Tilton's downfall; had leagued with Bowen against him, and by advice had nearly destroyed his family. Beecher says he needed no arguments to induce him to do or say anything to remedy the injury of which he believed he had been the active cause. Moulton assured Beecher of Tilton's purity and faithfulness to his wife. Beecher felt convicted of slander in its meanest form, became intensely excited, felt his mind in danger of giving away, and pouring forth his heart in unrestrained grief and bitterness of self-accusation, but denying any intentional wrong. Moulton said if Tilton could feel assured of Beecher's friendliness, there would be no trouble in making reconciliation. I gave him leave to state to Theodore my feelings. He proposed that I should write a letter. I declined, but said that he could report our interview. He then prepared to make a memorandum of the talk, and sat down at my table and took down, as I supposed, a condensed report of my talk, for I went on still pouring out my wounded feelings over this great desolation in Tilton's family. It was not a dictation of sentence after sentence, he a mere amanuensis and I composing for him. Mr. Moulton was putting into his own shape part of that which I was saying in my own manner with profuse explanations. This paper of Mr. Moulton's was a mere memorandum of points to be used by him in setting forth my feelings. That it contains matter and points derived from me is without doubt, but they were put with sentences by him and expressed as he understood them, not as my words, but as hints of my figures and letters, to be used by him in conversing with Mr. Tilton. He did not read the paper to me, nor did I read it, nor have I ever seen it or heard it read that I remember, until the publication of Mr. Tilton's recent documents, and now reading it I see in it thoughts that point to the matter of my discourse, but it is not my paper, nor are those my sentences; nor is it a correct report of what I said. It is a mere string of hints, hastily made by an unpractised writer as helps to his memory in representing to Mr. Tilton how I feel toward his family. If more than this be claimed, if it be set forth as in any proper sense my letter, I then disown it and denounce some of its sentences, and particularly that in which I am made to say that I had obtained Mrs. Tilton's forgiveness. I never could have said that, even in substance. I had not obtained nor asked any forgiveness from her, and nobody pretended that I had done so. Neither could I ever have said that I humbled myself before Tilton as before God, except in the sense that both to God and to the man I thought I had deeply injured I humbled myself, as I certainly did; but it is useless to analyze a paper prepared as this was. The remainder of my plain statement concerning it will be its best comment. This document was written upon three separate half sheets of large letter paper. After it was finished Mr. Moulton asked me if I would sign it. I said no. It was not my letter. He replied that it would have more weight if I would in some way indicate that he was authorized to explain my sentiments. I took my pen and at some distance below the writing and upon the lower margin, I indicated that I had committed the document in trust to Mr. Moulton. I signed the line thus written by me. A few words more as to its future fate. Mr. Moulton of his own accord said that after using it he would in two or three days bring the memorandum back to me, and he cautioned me about disclosing in any way that there was a difficulty between Mr. Tilton and me, as it would be injurious to Tilton to have it known that I had quarrelled with him as well as to me to have rumors set afloat. I did not trouble myself about it until more than a year afterwards, when Tilton began to write up his case, (of which hereafter,) and was looking up documents. I wondered what was in the old memorandum and desired to see it for greater certainty. So one day I suddenly asked Moulton for that memorandum and said, "You promised to return it to me." He seemed confused for a moment and said, "Did I?" "Certainly," I answered. He replied that the paper had been destroyed, and on my putting the question again, "that paper was burnt up long ago."

During the next two years, in various conversations of his own accord, he spoke of it as destroyed. I had never asked for nor authorized the destruction of this paper, but I was not allowed to know that that document was in existence, until a distinguished editor in New York within a few weeks past assured me that Mr. Moulton had shown him the original, and that he had examined my signature to be sure of its genuineness. I know there was a copy of it since this statement was in preparation. While I reject this memorandum as my work, or an accurate condensation of my statements, it does undoubtedly represent that I was in profound sorrow and that I blamed myself with great severity for the disasters of Tilton's family, and I had not then the light I now have. There was much that weighed heavily on my heart and conscience, which now weighs only on my heart. Soon after this I met Tilton at Moulton's house. Either Moulton was sick, or was very late in rising, for he was in bed. The subject of my feelings and conduct towards Tilton was introduced. I made a statement of the motives under which I had acted in counseling Bowen of my feelings in regard to Tilton's family, disclaiming with horror the thought of wrong, and expressing my desire to do whatever lay in human power to remedy any evil I had occasioned, and to reunite his family. Tilton was silent and sullen. He played the part of an injured man, but Moulton said to Mr. Tilton with intense emphasis, that is all that gentleman can say, etc. You ought to accept it. It is an honorable basis of reconciliation. This he repeated two or three times, and Tilton's countenance cheered up under Moulton's strong talk. We shook hands and parted in a friendly way. Not very long afterwards Tilton asked me to his house, and said that he should be glad to have the good old times renewed. I do not remember whether I ever took a meal after this under his roof, but I certainly was invited by him to renew my visits as formerly. I never resumed my intimacy with the family, but once or twice I went there soon after my reconciliation with Tilton, and at his request. Beecher gives an account of a reconciliatory scene at Tilton's house in the presence of Tilton's wife, which Beecher now thinks was for effect in order that he (Beecher) could be used to get money out of Bowen for Tilton, which the latter claimed was due him. Moulton lost no opportunities of presenting the kindest views of Tilton, but complained that Mrs. Tilton did not trust her husband nor Moulton, and the latter urged Beecher to inspire confidence in Mrs. Tilton in Moulton and lead her to take kinder views of Theodore. A letter with such intent was accordingly written to her Feb. 17th, 1871. A copy was furnished the committee. Beecher said he had no recollection of seeing or hearing read a letter of Tilton's of Feb. 7th, 1872. In explanation of saying in a letter to Mrs. Tilton that he did not expect to be alive many days, Beecher states he felt as if he would be struck with apoplexy for the past fifteen years. Tilton dropped from the church roll. Beecher then details the action of the church relative to expunging Tilton's name from the rolls, and said that in the *Woodhull Advertiser* of May, 1871, was an article shadowing an account of a disturbance in Tilton's family, but the full account was delayed till November, 1872, ostensibly by Tilton's influence. During this time both Moulton and Tilton made a heroine of Woodhull, and invited her to their houses. Beecher had three interviews with Woodhull, at the last of which she threatened him because he declined presiding at one of her lectures in Steinway Hall, and both Tilton and Moulton made most strenuous exertions to induce Beecher to identify himself with her. She was denounced heartily by Beecher as the centre of everything that was foul or vile, and he persistently resisted all efforts to identify himself with her. Beecher says he gave a letter to Moulton which Mrs. Tilton wrote him, in which she states that her husband and herself were going West, and expresses the hope that the proposed interview between Tilton and Beecher would be productive of good. This letter Moulton would not allow Beecher to see. Beecher then gives the account of the tripartite treaty of concord, peace and amnesty between them, Bowen paying Tilton $7,000, claimed. Subsequently when the Woodhulls had endeavored to obtain money out of Beecher and his wife, that woman published her version of the Tilton scandal, with which Tilton was believed to be in connivance. Beecher refers to letters written to him, one of which was to Moulton, in which he refers to the approach of death. He says it has been printed by Tilton in garbled form. The tripartite treaty was against Beecher's judgment, and was a patched-up peace. He continues: That I have previously erred in judgment with this perplexed case, no one is more conscious than I am. I chose the wrong path and accepted disastrous guidance in the beginning, and have indeed traveled on a rough and ragged edge in my prolonged efforts to suppress this scandal which has at last spread so much desolation through the land. I cannot admit that I erred in desiring to keep these matters out of sight. In this respect I appeal to you and to all Christian men to judge whether almost any personal sacrifice ought not to have been made rather than suffer the morals of an entire community, especially the young, to be corrupted by the filthy details of scandalous falsehood daily iterated and amplified for the gratification of the impure curiosity, and the demoralization of every child that is old enough to read. The full nature of this history requires that one more fact should be told, especially as Mr. Tilton has invited it. Money has been obtained from me in the course of these affairs in considerable sums, but I did not at first look upon the suggestions that I should contribute to Mr. Tilton's wants as savoring of blackmail. This did not occur to me until I had paid perhaps $2,000. Afterwards I contributed at one time $5,000. After the money had been paid over in five $1,000 bills, to raise which I mortgaged the house I live in, I felt very much dissatisfied with myself about it. Finally a square demand and threat made to me by my confidential friend, that if $5,000 were not paid, Tilton's charges would be laid before the public. This, I saw at once, was blackmail in its boldest form, and never paid one cent of it; but challenged and requested the fullest exposure. But, after the summer of 1873, I became inwardly satisfied that Tilton was an inherently and inevitably ruined man. I no longer trusted either his word or his honor. I came to feel that his kindness was but a snare, and his professions of friendship treacherous. He did not mean well by me nor by his own household; but I suffered all the more on this account, as he had grown up under my influence and my church, and I could not free myself from a certain degree of responsibility for his misdoings, such as visits a father. Beecher then gives the action of the church relative to the proceedings of the examining committee. Beecher states he wrote a letter of resignation, but did not send it in, as he considered it a self-sacrifice which would not stop the trouble, but he showed it to Mr. Moulton, and thinks possibly Moulton copied it. Beecher has the original. Beecher concludes as follows:

Gentlemen of the Committee:—In the note requesting your appointment I asked that you should make a full investigation of all sources of information. You are witnesses that I have in no way influenced or interfered with your proceedings or duties. I have wished the investigation to be so searching that nothing could unsettle its results. I have nothing to gain by any policy of suppression or compromise. For four years I have borne and suffered enough. I will not go a step further. I will be free. I will not walk under the rod or yoke. If any man would do me a favor let him tell all he knows now. It is not mine to lay down the law of honor in regard to the use of other persons' confidential communications, but, in so far as my own writings are concerned, there is not a letter or document which I am afraid to have exhibited, and I authorize and call upon all living persons to produce and print forthwith whatever writings they have of mine. It is time, for the sake of decency and public morals, that this matter should be brought to an end. It is an open pool of corruption, exhaling deadly vapors. For six weeks the nation has risen up and sat down upon scandal. Not a great war or revolution could have filled the newspapers more than this question of domestic trouble, magnified a thousandfold, and, like a sore spot on the human body, drawing to itself every morbid humor in the blood.

Whoever is buried with it, it is time that this abomination be buried below all touch or power of resurrection.

The following are the most interesting parts of Mr. Beecher's cross-examination:

Question.—Can you tell how you came to write that letter of despondency dated Feb. 5th, 1872, to Moulton? Answer.—I would come back from a whole week's lecturing and would be perfectly fagged out, and the first thing on getting home there would be some confounded development opening on me. In this state of mind, in which I had no longer any resistancy or rebound in me, I would work the whole week out, and in this way it happened time and time and time again. On one of these occasions I went to Moulton's store. Moulton had always treated me with the greatest personal kindness. He treated me as if he loved me. On this occasion I went down to the store to see him and his face was cold toward me.

I proposed to walk with him, and he walked with me in such a way that it seemed to me as though it was irksome to him to have me with him, as though he wanted to shake me off. Now anything like that all but kills me. I don't wish to push myself upon any body, to feel that I have pushed myself upon any human being who does not want me, is enough to kill me, and to be treated so by him at that time made it seem to me as though the end of the world had come, for he was the only man on the globe I could talk with on this subject. I was shut up to every human being. I could not go to my wife. I could not go to my children. I could not go to my church. He was the only one person to whom I could talk, and when I got that rebuff from him it seemed as though it would kill me, and the letter was the production of that mood into which I was thrown.

Q.—Do you suppose that you or the community would have heard anything of the trouble of Tilton with his family had he been a successful man? A.—I am morally certain that the thing would have been deeper buried than the bottom of the sea if Mr. Tilton had gone right on to a prosperous career and he had had the food which he had been accustomed to; but Mr. Tilton is a man who starves for want of flattery, and no power on God's earth can make him happy when he is not receiving some incense.

With reference to his first acquaintance with Moulton, Mr. Beecher said he only had a casual acquaintance with him until he came to his (Beecher's) house on this business.

Q.—Did Moulton say anything when the so-called apology was written, to the effect that there was nothing about the case but what an apology might cover? A.—He made the impression on my mind not only that Tilton had been greatly injured, but that Tilton was saturated with conviction that I was using my whole powers against him. When any disclosure of my real feelings was made to him he treated it with a kind of incredulty as if I was acting a part. But when I shed tears, and my voice broke, and I walked up and down the room with unfeigned distress, he seemed to be touched, and finally he said, "Now if that is the way you feel, if Mr. Tilton could be made to see it, this whole thing could be settled.

Q.—If you used these words, "He would have been a better man in my circumstances than I have been," what did you mean by them? A.—I do not know, I'm sure. The conversation was hypothetical in respect to the betrayal of friends in an hour of emergency, in respect to undermining Tilton just at the time when Bowen and all the world were leaving him, in respect to want of fidelity, and there is one thing that you are to bear in mind, a thing that I have never mentioned to any of you, and that had a very strong influence upon me. I never can forget a kindness done to me. When the war broke out my son went into a Brooklyn regiment, and, after being seven months in a camp at Washington, he played a series of pranks on some of the officers, and got himself into great trouble, and Col. Adams recommended him to resign, and he came to me. Well, it broke my heart. I had but one boy that was old enough to go, that I could offer to my country, and I told Theodore, who was in the office with me. He made the case his own. Mr. Tilton has a great deal in his upper nature. If he could be cut in two, and his lower nature separated from his upper, there is a great deal in his upper nature capable of great sweetness and beauty. At any rate, he took up my case. He suggested himself that the thing to do would be to get him transferred into the regular army. He said that he knew Sam Wilkeson, a correspondent of the *Tribune*, who was at that time in Washington, and had great influence, and that he would go right on that very night and secure this thing. He did, without a moment's delay, start and go to Washington, and he secured, through Sam Wilkeson, from Simon Cameron, then secretary of war, the appointment of Henry as second lieutenant in the fourth artillery service. I have felt ever since, that in the doing of that thing he did me a most royal service. I have felt it exquisitely and there has not been a time when I have done anything that hurt Tilton that that thing has not come back to me, and when it seemed as though I had in an hour of his need and trouble stepped aside and even helped to push him down.

Q.—What was in your mind when you wrote these words, "When I saw you last I did not expect ever to see you again, or be alive many days?" A.—Just what I have stated in my statement already. Q.—Nothing else? A.—No. I know I frequently said, "I wish I were dead," and Theodore Tilton he came in and said he wished he was dead, and Moulton was frequently in a state in which he wished he was dead, and Mrs. Moulton said, "I am living among friends, every one of whom wishes he was dead," or something like that. I do not know but it was smarter than that, but she put it in a way that was very ludicrous. Every one of us used to be echoing that expression. We were vexed and plagued together, and I used the familiar phrase "I wish I were dead."

Q.—The outside gossip is that you referred in that line to contemplated suicide.

Mr. Beecher—How do you propose to cure the gossip?

Mr. Winslow—I cannot say, but I want to know if anything of that kind was in your mind? A.—It was not. My general purpose in the matter of this whole thing was this: and I kept it as the motto of my life, by patient continuance in well doing to put to shame those who falsely accused me. Of course in my dismal moods I felt as though the earth had come to an end. Now, in interpreting these special letters everybody is irresistibly tempted to suppose that everything I said was said narrowly in regard to their text, instead of considering the foregoing state of my mind. Whereas my utterances were largely to be interpreted by the past, as well as by the present or the future. I cannot interpret them precisely as I can a note of hand or a check. A man that is practical, a man that is oftentimes extravagant, a man that is subject to moods such as make me such as I am, can't narrowly measure his words.

Q.—In view of all that has happened, what is your present feeling as to the conduct of Moulton—his sincerity? A.—I have no views to express.

Q.—Has Moulton any secret of yours in papers, in documents, or a knowledge of any act of yours that you would not have see the light in this house? A.—Not that I am aware of

Q.—Have you any doubt? A.—I have none.

Q.—Do you now call upon him to produce all he has and tell all he knows? A.—I do.

By Mr. Cleveland—Have you reason, in the light of recent disclosures, to doubt his fidelity to you during those four years? A.—The impression made by him during the four years of friendship and fidelity was so strong that my present surprise and indignation do not seem to rub it out. I am in that kind of divided consciousness that I was in respect to Elizabeth Tilton, that she was a saint and chief of sinners, and Mr. Moulton's hold upon my confidence was so great that all that has come now affects me as a dream.

By Mr. Winslow—In your letter of Feb. 5th, 1872, you speak of the possibility of a ruinous defense of you breaking out. How could there be any ruinous defense of you? A.—A defense of me conducted by ignorant people, full of church zeal and personal partizan feeling, knowing nothing of the facts, and compelling this whole avalanche of mud to descend on the community, might have been ruinous. I think now as I then felt.

Q.—You speak of remorse, fear and despair? A.—I suppose I felt them all. Whether I was justified in so feeling is a question. When I lived in Indianapolis there was an old lawyer there named Calvin Fletcher, a New England man, of large brain, who stood at the head of the bar. He was a Methodist Christian man. He took a peculiar fancy to me, and he used to come and see me often when I was a young minister, and I would see him a great deal. He would make many admirable suggestions, one of which was that he never admitted anybody was to blame except the party who uttered the complaint. Says he, "I hold myself responsible for having every body do right by me, and if they do not do right, it is because I do not do my duty. And now," said he, "in preaching during your life do you take blame upon yourself, and don't you be scolding your church and blaming everybody. It is your business to see that your folks are right." Well, it sank down into my heart and became a spring of influence from that day to this. If my prayer meetings do not go right it is my fault. If the people do not come to church, I am the one to blame for their not coming. If things go wrong in my family, I find the reason in myself. I have foreseen quarrels in the church, and if I had left them alone they would burst and break out, but acting under the advice thus given, and doing my own duty I have had no difficulty in my church.

As to his relations with Mrs. Woodhull Mr. Beecher answered:—

Q. Are you clear in your recollection that you never met the Woodhull more than three times? A. I am perfectly clear, that is, to speak to them.

Q. State the times, the places. A. On one occasion I was walking with Mr. Moulton in the general direction of Tilton's house, when he said that Mrs. Woodhull was going to be there. I at first hesitated, and he said come in and just see her. I said, very well. I went in, and after some conversation down in the parlor I went up stairs into the famous boudoir-room, where she sat waiting, and, like a spider to a fly, she rushed to me on my entrance and reached out both her hands with the utmost earnestness, and said how rejoiced she was to see me. I talked with her about five minutes and then went down stairs. My second interview with her was on an occasion when I had been with some twenty or thirty gentlemen to look at the warehouse establishment of W. Robinson. We were on the steamer that had been chartered for this occasion, and when I came up, Moulton said: "Come with me to town." He never told me there was to be any company. When I came there I learned there was to be something in New York in the evening, and that there were to be there a number of literary ladies, among whom was Mrs. Woodhull. I was placed at the head of the table near Mrs. Moulton, I think on her left. Mrs. Woodhull was next to me, or else she was first and I was next; I do not remember which. At that table she deigned to speak to me. I addressed a few words to her for politeness sake during the dinner, but there was no sort of enthusiasm between us. My third and last interview was at Mr. Moulton's house. She had addressed a letter to me saying that she would open all the scandal if I did not preside at Steinway Hall; and in reply to that Mr. Moulton advised that, instead of answering her letter, I should see her and say without witnesses what I had to say. She brought with her, her great subject. It was in type, and my policy was to let her talk, and say little, which I did; and she went on saying: "You know," "you believe," "so and so," and I said nothing, and so on from point to point, until I said at last: "Mrs. Woodhull, I do not understand your views. I have never read them thoroughly. As far as I do understand them I do not believe in them, and though I am in favor of free discussion, this presiding at meetings is a thing I seldom ao for anybody, and I shall not do it for you, because I am not in sympathy with your movement.

Q. Has Mrs. Woodhull any letters of yours in her possession? A. Two, I suppose, unless she has sold them.

Q. Upon what subject? A. She inclosed a letter to me with one from my sister, Mrs. Isabella Hooker, inviting me to be present at the suffrage convention at Washington. To that letter I replied briefly in the negative, but made a few statements in respect to my ideas of woman's voting. The other letter was just before her scandalous publication. She wrote to me a whining letter, saying that her reformatory movements had brought upon her such odium that she could not procure lodgings in New York, and that she had been turned out of the Gilsey House, I think, and asking me, in a very significant way, to interpose my influence or some other relief for her. To that letter I replied very briefly, saying I regretted when anybody suffered persecution for the advocacy of their sincere views; but that I must decline to interfere.

By Mr. Claflin—These are two letters, the signatures of which he showed to Mr. Bowen and myself. It was reported that by these letters you were to be sunk 40,000 fathoms deep. I told Bowen before I went there that I knew of the existence of letters, and that was all they contained. Mr. Bowen made the journey clear down from Connecticut on purpose to go up there.

On other points the examination showed this result:—

Q. Now as to what occurred in your library and in his bed-chamber. I refer to the occasion in which he said you touched his wife's ankle and were found with a flushed face in the bed-chamber of his house? A. I do most emphatically deny that either of these scenes ever occurred.

Q. Did you ever admit at any time to Mr. Moulton or Mr. Tilton, or to any other person, that you ever had any relations with Mrs. E. R. Tilton, or ever committed any act to or with her, or said any word to her which would be unfit for a Christian man to hold, do or say with the wife of a friend; or for a father to hold, do or say with his daughter; or a brother with his sister? Did you ever admit this in any form, or in any words? A. Never.

By Mr. Tracy—Q. Did you ever, in fact, hold any such relations, do any such act or utter any such word? A. Never.

By Mr. Cleveland—Q. In your statement you have alluded

to one payment of $5,000. Have you furnished any other money to those parties? A. I have furnished at least $2,000 beside the $5,000.

Q. To whom did you pay that money? A. To Mr. Moulton.

Q. In various sums? A. In various sums, partly in cash and partly in checks.

Q. Have you any of those checks? A. I have several. I don't remember how many.

Q. Where are they? A. I have some of them here. One of June 23d, 1871, drawn on the Mechanics' Bank to the order of Frank Moulton and indorsed in his handwriting, and one of May 29th, 1872, to the order of F. D. Moulton and also indorsed in his handwriting. Each of these that are marked "for deposit" across the face have been paid.

Q. As nearly as you can recollect, how much money went into the hands of Mr. Moulton? A. I should say I have paid $7,000.

Q. To what use did you suppose that the money was to be appropriated? A. I supposed that it was to be appropriated to extricate Mr. Tilton from his difficulties in some way.

Q. You did not stop to inquire how or why? A. Mr. Moulton sometimes sent me a note saying, "I wish you would send me your check for so much."

Q. Did you usually respond to the demands of Mr. Moulton for money during these months? A. I always did.

Q. Under what circumstances did you come to pay the $5,000 in one sum? A. Because it was represented to me that the whole difficulty could be now settled by that amount of money, which would put the affairs of the *Golden Age* on a secure footing; that they would be able to go right on; that with the going on of them the safety of Tilton would be assured, and that would be the settlement of the whole thing. It was to save Tilton pecuniarily.

Q. Were there any documents shown you by Moulton? and what did he show you before you made the payments? A. It was the result of inclination and general statements, and I finally said to him: "I am willing to pay $5,000." I came to do it in this way:—There was a discussion about that paper. Mr. Moulton was constantly advancing money, as he said to me, to help Mr. Tilton. The paper was ready. One evening I was at his house. We were alone together in the back parlor, and Moulton took out of his pocket a letter from "Blank." It was read to me. In it the writer mentioned contributions which the writer had made to Theodore. I understood from him the writer of this letter had given him some thousands of dollars down in cash, and then taking out two checks or drafts, which, as I recollect, were on bluish paper, although I am not sure of that. There were two checks, each of them amounting to one or two thousand more, and I should think it amounted in all to about $6,000, although my memory about quantities and figures is to be taken with great allowance. But it produced the impression on me that the writer had given him $1,-000 or $2,000 in cash down, and, as the writer explained in the letter, it was not convenient to give the balance in money at that time, but that the writer had drawn time drafts, which would be just as useful to him as money, and Mr. Moulton slapped the table and said that is what I call friendship, and I was stupid and said yes, it was. Afterward, when I got home, and thinking about it in the morning, "why," said I, what a fool! I never dreamed what he meant." Then I went to him and said: "I am willing to make a contribution and put the thing beyond a controversy." Well, he said something like this: that he thought it would be the best investment that ever I made in my life. I then went to the Savings Bank and put a mortgage of $5,000 on my house. I took a check which was given me by the bank's lawyer, and put it into the bank, and on Moulton's suggestion that it would be better than to have a check drawn to his order, I drew the money in $500 or $1,000 bills, I have forgotten which, but I know that they were large, for I carried the roll in my hand, and these I gave into his hands. From time to time he spoke in the most glowing terms, and said he was feeding it out to Theodore, and he said that at the time of the first installment he gave Theodore $500 at once, and that he sent with it a promissory note for Theodore to sign, but that Theodore did not sign it and sent it back, saying that he saw no prospect in the end of paying the loans, and that he could not honorably, therefore, expect them, and refused to sign any note, and Moulton laughed significantly and said that Tilton subsequently took the money without giving any note.

Q. Did you receive any note or security whatever, or evidence of debt, from Mr. Moulton, or has there been any offer to return the money to you? A. Nothing of the kind. It was never expected to be returned by either party.

Q. Has Moulton said anything to you about money in a comparatively recent period? A. About the time of the publication of the Bacon letter, I think, I had been given to understand that he had offered $5,000 in gold to Mr. Tilton if he would not publish that letter, and that at the then stage of affairs Moulton felt profoundly that Tilton could not come out with a disclosure of all this matter without leaving Moulton in an awkward position, and that he offered $5,000 in gold if Tilton would not publish that letter. It led to some little conversation about a supply of money, and he said that I had better give him my whole fortune than have Tilton go on in his course.

Q. That you had better give your whole fortune to Mr. Tilton? A. Yes, rather than have Tilton go into this fight.

Q. Was that before or after the publication of the Bacon letter? A. I can't be certain. It was about that time.

Q. Did Mr. Moulton ever question you in regard to this matter, whether you had ever spoken on that to any one, or expressed any anxiety in your mind about it? A. He did; not many weeks ago, among the last interviews I had with him.

Q. Since the publication of that Bacon letter? A. Yes; I think it was on the Sabbath day after the appointment of this Committee. I had preached but once on that day, and on the afternoon of that day he saw me, and said to me in a conversation: "You have never mentioned about that $5,000?" I said yes; I had to one or two persons; mentioned it to Oliver Johnson for one, because he was saying something to me one day about what some of Tilton's friends were saying and I incidentally mentioned that to him, which he never repeated, I suppose to anybody.—Mr. Moulton said: "I will never admit that; I shall deny it always.

Q. Have you any objections to state what Tilton's friends were saying to Oliver Johnson and others? what did Oliver Johnson say to you? A. On one occasion he reported to me that among the friends of Tilton he had heard reproaches made against me; that I neither was endeavoring to help Theodore in reputation or in any other way, and that the expression was this: That I had been the instrument of his being thrown off the track in life, and that I would not reinstate him. I replied, in substance, that so far as reputation was concerned, I not only longed and tried to do what I could for Tilton, but that his association with the Woodhull was fatal to him, and I could not make any head against it. And with regard to the other, I said to him that I had been willing to help him materially, and that recently I paid five thousand dollars to him.

Q. Did you see and have a conversation with Tilton soon after the payment of the five thousand dollars? A. On the Sunday morning following the payment of the five thousand dollars, as I was going to church in the morning, I met Mr Tilton standing right opposite the house.—He put his arm through mine and was in his most beatific mood. While walking along down to the church he was talking all the way of grace, mercy and peace to me, and at that time I recollect thinking that five thousand dollars is very mollifying.

By Mr. Claflin—Q. Did you at any time receive the note which the Committee have in evidence, as follows:

H. W. B.—Grace, mercy and peace. T. T. Sunday morning.

A. Yes. He sent it on Sunday morning, by his wife, who had laid it on my pulpit stand.

By Mr. Cleveland—If your mortgage was dated about May 1st, 1873, the money was of course paid to Mr. Moulton after your mortgage was made? A. Yes, sir. I did not keep the money an hour. I went with it directly from the Mechanics' Bank, where I drew it, and put it into Moulton's hands on the same day, and within a few days.

Q. At his house? A. I do not know.

Q. Here is a letter dated May 1st, 1874, in which Tilton refers to some story of Carpenter's about your offering money. Did you receive that letter? A. I did, sir. It was a magnificent humbug. I knew that Mr. Tilton knew that he had been tinkling my gold in his pockets for months and years, and he wrote that letter to be published for a sham and mask.

Q. What did you understand by Carpenter's relations to the money matter? A. My first knowledge of Mr. Carpenter was that he was putting his nose into this business, which did not concern him. That was also Mr. Moulton's impression. I asked Moulton, one day, what under the sun is Carpenter doing around here and meddling with this matter? He summarily damned him and represented him as a good-natured and well-meaning busy-body. I suggested, why didn't he tell him distinctly that his presence was not wanted? He said, "Well, he serves us some useful purpose. We hear of things going on in the clubs or any place in New York. We put Carpenter on the track, and he fetches all the rumors, and so we use him to find out what we could not get otherwise." And I did find that he not only did that, but that Mr. Carpenter was one of those good-natured men whose philanthropy exhibited itself in trying to settle quarrels and difficulties by picking up everything he could hear said by, for, or against a man, and carrying it to the parties where it would do the most harm possible. He was a kind of good-natured fool, and in all this matter he has been a tool more than a helper. He has never once done anything, except in the kindest way, and never once done anything in the whole of this matter, from beginning to end, that was not a stupid blunder. I made up my mind from the beginning that if I was silent to everybody in this matter, I would be especially silent to him (Carpenter). I recollect but one interview with him that had any particular significance. He came to see me once when the Council was in session, and our document was published. There was a phrase introduced into it that Tilton thought pointed to him, and Tilton, that night, was in a bonfire flame and walked up and down the street with Moulton. I was in at Freeland's and in comes Carpenter with his dark and mysterious eyes. He sat down on the sofa, and in a kind of sepulchral whisper, told me of some matters. Says I, "That is all nonsense," that it meant "blank," and Carpenter was rejoiced to hear it, and then went out. On another occasion he came to me and in a great glow of benevolence said there was to be a newspaper established in New York, and that I was to take the editorship, and a half million was to be raised almost by the tap of a drum—I was amused, but said to him gravely:—"Well, Carpenter, if I should leave the pulpit, I think it very likely I should go into journalism. It would be more natural to me than anything else." That was the amount of the conversation.

One other conversation I have some recollection of, in April last, and that was when Mr. Moulton had a plan on foot to buy the *Golden Age* of Tilton, and send him to Europe, and Carpenter came in and talked with me about it. I recollect very distinctly that conversation. My eyes were beginning to be enlightened. My education was beginning to tell on me a little, and I said to Mr. Carpenter, distinctly: "Mr. Carpenter, that is a matter which I can have nothing to do with. I don't know but that if Tilton wishes to go to Europe with his family, and live there for some time, that his friends would be willing to raise that amount of money, but that it is a matter you must talk with somebody else, and not with me."

Q. Did you say that if Tilton printed his documents you would never ascend that pulpit again? A. I never said that, and I should never talk about the thing with such a weak man as he.

Q. Who introduced the subject of going to Europe when Carpenter came to see you? A. He did.

The following are the letters referred to in the statement of Mr. Beecher. The first one was written by him to Mrs. Tilton for the purpose of disposing her more kindly toward her husband and Mr. Moulton, whom she distrusted:

BROOKLYN, Feb. 7th, 1871.

MY DEAR MRS. TILTON:—When I saw you last I did not expect ever to see you again or to be alive many days. God was kinder to me than were my own thoughts. The friend whom God sent to me, Mr. Moulton, has proved above all friends that ever I had, noble and willing to help me in this terrible emergency of my life. His hand it was that tied up the storm that was ready to burst upon our heads. I am not the less disposed to trust him from finding that he has your welfare most deeply and tenderly at heart. You have no friend, Theodore excepted, who has it in his power to serve you so vitally, and who will do it with so much delicacy and honor. I beseech of you, if my wishes have yet any influence, let my deliberate judgment in this matter weigh with yours. It does my sore heart good to see in Mr. Moulton an unfeigned respect and honor for you. It would kill me if I thought otherwise. He will be as true a friend to your honor and happiness as a brother could be to a sister. In him we have a common ground on which you and I may meet. The past is ended, but is there not a future, no wiser, higher, holier future? May not this friend stand as a priest in the new sanctuary of reconciliation and mediate and bless you, Theodore and my most unhappy self. Do not let my earnestness fail of its end. You believe in my judgment. I have put myself wholly and gladly in Moulton's hands and there I must meet you. This is sent with Theodore's consent, but he has not read it. Will you return it to me by his hands! I am very earnest in this wish, for all our sakes, for such a letter ought not to be subject to even a chance of miscarriage.

Your unhappy friend,

H. W. BEECHER.

The same day he wrote as follows to Mr. Moulton:-

FEBRUARY 7TH, 1871.

MY DEAR MR. MOULTON:—I am glad to send you a book which you will relish or which a man on a sick bed ought to relish. I wish I had more like it, and that I could send you one every day, not as a repayment of your great kindness to me, for that never can be paid; not even by love, which I give you freely. Many, many friends has God raised up to me, but to no one of them has he ever given the opportunity and the wisdom so to serve me as you have. My trust in you is complete. You have also proved yourself Theodore's friend and Elizabeth's. Does God look down from heaven on three unhappy creatures that more need a friend than these? Is it not an intimation of God's intent of mercy to all that each one of these has in you a tried and proved friend, but only in you are we three united! Would to God, who orders all hearts, that by your kind mediation Theodore, Elizabeth, and I could be made friends again. Theodore, will have the hardest task in such a case, but has he not proved himself capable of the noblest things? I wonder if Elizabeth knows how generously he has carried himself towards me. Of course I can never speak with her again, except with his permission, and I do not know that even then it would be best. My earnest longing is to see her in the full sympathy of her nature at rest in him once more trusting her and loving her with even a better than the old love. I am always sad in such thoughts. Is there any way out of this night? May not a day star arise?

Truly yours always, and with trust and love,

HENRY WARD BEECHER.

When Tilton and Moulton appeared to look upon Mr. Beecher as the author of all the trouble that had fallen upon the former, Mr. Beecher wrote the following letter to Mr. Moulton, from which Mr. Tilton gave extracts in his statement.

MONDAY, Feb. 5th, 1872.

MY DEAR FRIEND:—I leave town to-day and expect to pass through from Philadelphia to New Haven. Shall not be here until Friday. About three weeks ago I met T. in the cars going to B. We talked much. He told me to go on with my work, without the least anxiety in so far as his feelings and actions were the occasion of apprehensions. On returning home from New Haven, where I am three days in the week delivering a course of lectures to the theological students, I found a note from E., saying that T. felt hard towards me, or was going to see or write to me before leaving for the West. She kindly added, "Be not cast down. I bear this almost always, but the God in whom we trust will deliver us all safely. I know you do and are willing abundantly to help him, and I also know your embarrassments." There were added words of warning, but also of consolation, for I believe E. is beloved of God, and that her prayers for me are sooner heard than mine for myself or for her. But it seems that a change has come to T. since I saw him in the cars. Indeed, ever since he has felt more intensely the force of feeling in society and the humiliations which environ his enterprise. He has growingly felt that I had a power to help which I did not develop, and I believe that you have participated in the feeling. It is natural you should. T. is dearer to you than I can possibly be. He is with you. All his trials lie open to your eye daily. But I see you but seldom, and my personal relations, environments, necessities, limitations, dangers and perplexities you cannot see or imagine. If I had not gone through this great year of sorrow, I would not have believed that any one could pass through my experience and be alive or sane.

I have been the centre of three distinct circles, each of which require clear mindedness and peculiarly inventive or originative power, viz: First—The great Church; Second—The newspaper; Third—The book. The first I could neither get out of nor slight; the sensitiveness of so many of my people would have made any appearance of trouble or any remission of force an occasion of alarm and notice and have excited where it was intended that rumors should die and everything be quiet. The newspaper I did roll off my mind, did but little except give general directions and in so doing I was continually spurred and exhorted by those in interest. It could not be helped.

The "Life of Christ," long delayed, had locked up the capital of the firm, and was likely to sink them. Finished it must be. Was ever book born of such sorrow as that was? The interior history of it will never be written. During all this time you literally were all my stay and comfort. I should have failed on the way but for the courage which you inspired and the hope which you breathed. My vacation was profitable. I came back hoping that the bitterness of death was passed, but T's. troubles brought back the cloud with even severe sufferings. For all this fall and winter I have felt that you did not feel satisfied with me, and that I seemed both to you and T. as contenting myself with a cautious or sluggish policy, willing to save myself, but not to risk anything for T. I have again and again probed my heart to see whether I was truly liable to such feeling and the response is unequivocal that I am not.

No man can see the difficulties then environing me, unless he stands where I do. To say that I have a church on my hands, is simple enough, but to have the hundreds and thousands of men present eyeing me, each one with his keen suspicion or anxiety, or zeal; to see tendencies, which, if not stopped, would break out in a ruinous defence of me; to stop them without seeming to do it; to prevent any one questioning me; to meet and allay prejudices against T., which had their beginning years before his; to keep serene, as I was not alarmed or disturbed; to be cheerful at home and among friends, when I was suffering the torments of the damned; to pass sleepless nights after, and yet to come up fresh and full for Sunday

—all this may be talked about, but the real thing cannot be understood from the outside, nor its wearing and grinding on the nervous system.

God knows I have put more thought and judgment and earnest desire into my efforts to prepare a way for T. and E. than ever I did for myself a hundredfold. As to the outside public, I have never lost an opportunity to soften prejudices, to refute falsehoods, and to excite a kindly feeling among all whom I met. I am thrown among clergymen, public men and generally the makers of public opinion, and I have used every rational endeavor to repair the evils that have been visited upon T., and with increasing success, but the roots of this prejudice are long.

The catastrophe which precipitated him from his place only disclosed feelings that had existed long. Neither he nor you can be aware of the feelings of classes in society on other grounds than later rumors. I mention this to explain why I know with absolute certainty that no mere statement, letter, testimony or affirmation will reach the root of affairs and reinstate them. Time and work will, but chronic evils require chronic remedies.

If my destruction would place him all right that shall not stand in the way. I am willing to step down and out. No one can offer more than that. That I do offer. Sacrifice me without hesitation if you can clearly see your way to happiness and safety thereby. I do not think that anything would be gained by it. I should be destroyed; but he would not be saved. Elizabeth and the children would have their future clouded. In one point of view I could desire the sacrifice on your part· Nothing can possibly be so bad as the horror of the great darkness in which I spend much of my time.

I look upon death as sweeter-faced than any other friend I have in the world. Life would be pleasant if I could see that rebuilt which is scattered; but to live on the sharp, ragged edge of anxiety, remorse, fear, despair, and yet to put on all appearances of serenity and happiness, cannot be endured much longer, I am well nigh discouraged.

If you, too, cease to trust me, to love me, I am alone. I have not a another person in this world to whom I could. go. Well, to God I commit all; whatever it may here, it shall be well there. With sincere gratitude for your heroic friendship, and with sincere affection, even though you love me not, I am yours though unknown to you.

H. W. B.

The letter of Mrs. Tilton, which is here partly quoted, is as follows:—

I leave for the West, Monday next. How glad I was to hear you were your own self on Sunday morning. Theodore's mind has been hard toward you of late, and I think he proposes an interview with you by word or note before leaving home. If so be not cast down. I fear this almost always, but the God in whom we trust will deliver all safely. I know you do and are abundantly willing to help him, and I also know your embarrassments. I anticipate my Western trip, where I may be alone with him, exceedingly.

After the Woodhull story was published and while Mr. Tilton seemed really desirous for a short time of protecting his wife, Mr. Beecher sent through him the following letter to her:—

My Dear Mrs. Tilton:—I hoped that you would be shielded from the knowledge of the great wrong that has been done to you and through you to universal womanhood. I can hardly bear to speak of it or allude to a matter than which nothing can well be more painful to a pure, womanly nature. I pray daily for you, that your faith fail not. You yourself know the way and the power of prayer. God has been your refuge in many a sorrow before. He will now hide you in His pavilion until the storm be overpast. The rain that beats down the flower to the earth will pass at length and the stem bent but not broken, will rise again and blossom as before. Every pure woman on earth will feel that this wanton and unprovoked assault is aimed at you, but reaches to universal womanhood. Meantime your dear children will love you with double tenderness, and Theodore, at whom the shafts are hurled, will hide you in his heart of hearts. I am glad that revelation from the pit has given him a sight of the danger that was hidden by specious appearances and promises of usefulness, May God keep him in courage in the arduous struggle which he wages against adversity and bring him out though much tried, like gold seven times refined. I have not spoken of myself. No words could express the sharpness and depth of my sorrow in your behalf, my dear and honored friend. God walks in the fire by the side of those He loves, and in Heaven neither you nor Theodore, nor I shall regret that discipline how hardsoever it may seem now. May He restrain and turn those poor creatures who have been given over to all this sorrowful harm to those who have deserved no such treatment at their hands. I commend you to my mother's God, my dear friend; may His smile bring light in darkness, and His love perpetual summer to you.

Very truly yours,

Henry Ward Beecher.

Mr. Beecher gives in full the letter written to Mr. Moulton after the unauthorized publication of the tripartite covenant, of which Mr. Tilton made garbled extracts. It is as follows :—

SUNDAY MORNING, June 1st, 1873.

MY DEAR FRANK :—The whole world is tranquil and the heaven is serene, as befits one who has about finished this world life, I could do nothing on Sunday. My head was confused, but a good sleep has made it like crystal. I have determined to make no more resistance. Theodore's temperament is such that the future, even if temporarily earned, would be absolutely worthless, filled with abrupt changes and rendering me liable at any hour of the day to be obliged to stultify all the devices by which we saved ourselves. It is only fair that he should know the publication of the card which he proposes, would leave him far worse off than before. The agreement was made after my letter through you was written. He had it a year. He had condoned his wife's fault. He had enjoined upon me with the utmost earnestness and solemnity not to betray his wife, nor leave his children to a blight. I had honestly and earnestly joined in the purpose. Then this settlement was made and signed by him. It was not my making. He revised his part so that it should wholly suit him, and signed it. It stood unquestioned and unblamed for more than a year. Then it was published. Nothing but that which he hid in private, when made public, excited him to fury, and he charged me with making him appear as one graciously pardoned by me.

It was his own deliberate act, with which he was perfectly content, till others saw it, and then he charges a grievous wrong home on me. My mind is clear. I am not in haste. I shall write for the public a statement that will bear the light of the Judgment Day. God will take care of me and mine. When I look on earth it is deep night; when I look to the heavens above I see the morning breaking; but oh! that I could put in golden letters my deep sense of your faithful, earnest, undying fidelity, your disinterested friendship. Your whole life, too, has been to me one of God's comforters.

It is such as she that renews a waning faith in womanhood. Frank would not have wasted any more energy on a hopeless task with such a man as Theodore Tilton. There is no possible salvation for any who depend upon him. With a strong nature he does not know how to govern it; with generous impulses, the undercurrent that rules him is self; with ardent affections, he cannot love long that which does not repay him with admiration and praise; with a strong theatric nature, he is constantly imposed upon with the idea that a position, a great stroke, a *coup d'etat* is the way to successs. Besides these he has abundant good things about him, but these traits are made absolutely unreliable. Therefore there is no use in further trying.

I have a strong feeling upon me, and it brings great peace with it, that I am spending my last Sunday, and preaching my last sermon. Dear God, I thank Thee. I am indeed beginning to see rest and triumph. The pain of life is but a moment, the glory of the everlasting emancipation is wordless, inconceivable, full of becoming glory. Oh, my beloved Frank, I shall know you there and forever hold fellowship with you, and look back and smile at the past. Your loving

H. W. BEECHER.

To this letter it will be remembered Mr. Moulton wrote a reply in Mr. Beecher's presence. It is in the following words:—

MY DEAR FRIEND:—Your letter make this first Sabbath of summer dark and cold like a vault, You have never inspired me with courage or hope, and if I had listened to you alone, my hands would have dropped helpless long ago. You don't begin to be in the danger to-day that has faced you many times before. If you now look it square in the eyes, it will cower and sink away again. You know that I have never been in sympathy with, but that I absolutely abhor the unmanly mood out of which your letter of this morning came. This mood is a reservoir of mildew. you can stand it if the whole case were published to-morrow. In my opinion it shows only a selfish faith in God to go willing into heaven if you could, with a truth that you are not courageous enough, with God's help and faith in God, to try to live on earth. You know that I love you; and because I do I shall try, and try, and try, as in the past. You are mistaken when you say that "T. charges you with making him appear as one graciously pardoned by you." He said the form in which it was published in some of the papers made it so appear; and it was from this that he asked relief. I do not think it impossible to frame a reply which will cover the case. May God bless you. I know He will protect you.

Yours,

FRANK.

That Mr. Beecher's defence gave a plausible explanation of the scandal, the public generally admitted, but there were many, very many, who could not accept a mere simple statement like this as of more weight than the affidavit of Tilton, the explicit charges of Moulton, and the declarations of Carpenter. The people of Plymouth church, however, accepted it as a complete vindication of their beloved pastor, and on the evening of its publication a meeting was held in Plymouth church, devoted to prayer and praise to God for the delivery of the accused from the hands of his enemies. It was a Jubilee in fact, in which many of the lights of the Congregation poured out their souls in prayer. At the business meeting that followed, a resolution was adopted requesting the examining Committee to report "at as early a day as is consistent with truth and justice." When the proceedings in the church had closed the congregation, by invitation of Rev. Mr. Halliday, assistant pastor, repaired to the pastor's residence. The scene that ensued is thus described by a reporter:—

The first to arrive at Mr. Beecher's house was an old member of the church, and one between whom and the pastor there exists a strong affection. Mr. Beecher was lounging in careless ease on the front stoop, his head thrown back on the door. As the gentleman approached Mr. Beecher glanced up with a flush of satisfaction on his countenance.

"What, have you come to see me," Mr. Beecher said in a jocular tone.

"Why not, Mr. Beecher?" returned the equally delighted gentleman.

"Oh I didn't know," said Mr. Beecher, smiling, "that you cared to have anything to do with me," and then he rose and strained his friend to his arms.

"There'll be a thousand more here in a minute, Mr. Beecher."

"Come in," said the dominie "I'm ready for them," and he led the way into the library. Mrs. Beecher and Captain Beecher were there. The door was wide open. In a moment the people began streaming in. They came in with a rush, a crush, and a bustle. It looked as if they were going to fill the house from roof to cellar. Mr. Beecher, with a countenance lighted with joy, but with eyes filling with tears, stood with Mrs. Beecher in the centre of the room. A dozen hands were outreached to him at once. He took as many of them as he could conveniently hold, right and left. The ladies went up to Mrs. Beecher and kissed her. She was powerfully affected and could scarcely return their kind attentions. There was a flood of congratulations poured upon the pastor and his wife, sympathy, love and confidence was expressed on every side.

Mr. Beecher's fatigue seemed to wear away under the kindnesses of his friends. There were not only Plymouth people, but many strangers. They alike felt the warmth of the preacher's hands, and shared in his cheery words. To one, a stranger who was profuse in his expressions of regard, Mr. Beecher said: "Yes, I have had a severe trial, but I have tried to bear it patiently, conscious of my integrity." Allusion was made to his assailants, when he said: "I have been sadly deceived in those whom I implicitly trusted."

The public now looked for every utterance from Messrs. Moulton and Tilton, with great anxiety. Mr. Moulton suddenly disappeared from the city and reappeared at Portland, Maine, but the week, pregnant with anxiety and excitement, closed without any response from "Our Mutual Friend" to the damaging charge of blackmailing his pastor. Not so with Mr. Tilton. To a reporter of the *Herald* he took occasion to declare as follows:—

"I think," replied Mr. Tilton, "that probably nowhere else in the civilized world was there a more dastardly act committed than yesterday—no, not by any member of the human race—than Henry Ward Beecher's attack on Frank Moulton as a blackmailer. Mr. Moulton is rich enough to pay Mr. Beecher's salary as a bagatelle. He is, moreover, the most faithful friend that Mr. Beecher ever had, or ever will have again, though he should live to be a hundred years old. Frank Moulton's services to that man—the way he has put a shield over him and guarded him, year by year, for the last four years, from the exposure of his guilty secret—the zeal and care with which he has striven to keep public ruin from overtaking him in the pulpit, and disgrace from shadowing his children and grandchildren—services like these are rarely rendered by one man to another, and I know of no instance of such baseness of ingratitude as the desperate minister of Plymouth church has exhibited in thus striking a man, whose shoe latchet he is unworthy to unloose. I care nothing for this pitiful pretext of blackmailing, except so far as it affects Mr. Moulton—if it can affect him at all, which it will not, for he is too proud a man to be wounded by such a stab—he will simply be filled with scorn. So far as I myself am concerned, the only money which I know of Mr. Beecher's paying is in a case which is one of the many proofs of his guilt. A young girl, a servant in my house, overheard, four years ago, a conversation between Mrs. Tilton and me concerning her intimacy with Mr. Beecher. This conversation was repeated by the listener to the family relatives and to some friends. Her disposition to repeat the story was dangerous for the actors in it, and accordingly it was deemed best to send her to the West to a boarding school. She remained there three years, and the bills were paid by Mr. Beecher. Perhaps he regards this as blackmail. As to his contributing money to the *Golden Age*, it is the first time that any person connected with the *Golden Age* has ever heard of it. If the capital of that paper, which a number of friends made up, contained a secret and silent contribution from Henry Ward Beecher the knowledge of that fact was carefully withheld from me and my associates in that journal. If Mr. Beecher did contribute this money unbeknown to me, and if he procured it by a mortgage on his house, or in any other difficult way, then this fact alone, without any other evidence added, is enough to convict him of every charge that I have made. Mr. Beecher's crime against me and mine was enough of a sin to answer for, but in adding to this baseness his audacious and desperate attacks on Mr. Moulton and Mr. Carpenter as blackmailers, to say nothing of myself, whom he includes in the accusation, he bids fair to sink as low as he once stood high."

FRANK MOULTON.

CHAPTER XXVI.

"MUTUAL FRIEND MOULTON'S" CRUSHING MANIFESTO.—HE TELLS ALL HE KNOWS.—MR. BEECHER AND MRS. TILTON HAD ADMITTED TO HIM THEIR ACTS OF ADULTERY.—BOWEN'S MACHINATIONS.—ELIZABETH'S CONFESSION, RETRACTION, AND ADMISSION THAT SHE IS INCAPABLE OF UTTERING THE TRUTH.—HOW BEECHER USED MOULTON TO COVER HIS TRACKS.—ISABELLA BEECHER HOOKER'S FREE LOVE FANCIES.—REV. THOS. K. BEECHER SEES NO HOPE FOR HENRY, AND EXCLAIMS: "HANDS OFF UNTIL HE IS DOWN."—A FEARFUL PICTURE OF LYING, PREVARICATION, AND PLOTTING.—THE BLACKMAIL STORY EXPLODED.—PLYMOUTH CHURCH DRIVEN INTO SILENCE.

WHEN the events recorded in the last chapter had been made public, and the people had learned that Mutual Friend Moulton had returned to the city, and was preparing a statement in defence of himself, additional interest centered in the case. The press of the country, with few exceptions, had accepted Mr. Beecher's defence as an earnest of his innocence of adultery. The change in public sentiment gave courage to the Plymouth Church Committee and lawyers, and it was semi-officially announced that on Friday night, the 21st of August the Committee would report to the Church a vindication of their pastor. "The best laid plans of mice and men" etc., were disarranged when it became mooted about that Moulton's supplementary statement that the Committee had suppressed, would appear in the *Daily Graphic* of that afternoon. The Committee were alarmed, for they knew that the publication of Moulton's statement would render a vindication of Mr. Beecher *on the evidence,* impossible. The Committee consequently met and adjourned, after deciding upon the postponement of the presentation of their report in vindication of Henry Ward Beecher. The first edition of the *Graphic* appeared at noon, containing several pages of *fac similes* of letters very damaging to the pastor, and the announcement that the half past two o'clock edition would contain an exclusive copy of Moulton's statement. Excitement ran high. Orders for extra copies poured in from all quarters; newsboys were alive to the importance of the document, and when the hour arrived for the appearance of the extra, the scene about the office of the *Graphic* and its branches reminded one of war times. An immense number was sold, and on the following day a special edition was put to press to supply the demand for orders of the previous day that the publishers were unable to fill. Many of the other evening journals issued extras made up from the *Graphic,* to whom the document was given exclusively by Mr. Moulton.

The following is the letter of Mr. Moulton, issued as a preface to the statement he had supplied to the Committee, days before, and which they had suppressed:—

To the Public:—I became a party almost accidentally in the unhappy controversy between Mr. Beecher and Mr. Tilton. I had been a friend of Mr. Tilton since my boyhood, and for Mr. Beecher I had always entertained the warmest admiration.

In 1870 I learned for the first time that Mr. Beecher had given Mr. Tilton so grave a cause of offence that if the truth should be made public a great national calamity would ensue. I believed that the scandal would tend to undermine the very foundations of social order, to lay low a beneficent power for good in our country, and blast the prospects and blight the family of one of the most brilliant and promising of the rising men of the generation. This disaster—as I deemed it and still regard it—I determined to try and avert.

For nearly four years I have labored most assiduously to save both of these men from the consequences of their acts, whether of unwisdom or passion—acts which have already seriously involved them in a needless and disastrous quarrel, which is made the pretext of pouring on the community a flood of impurity and scandal deeply affecting their own families, and threatening like a whirlpool, if not stifled, to draw into its vortex the peace of mind and good repute of a host of others. More than all, I saw that, because of the "transgression of another," innocent children would be burdened with a load of obloquy which would weigh most heavily and cruelly on their young lives.

All these considerations determined me to take an active part in the transactions which have since become so notorious.

This decision involved me in great anxiety and labor, for which the hope of saving these interests could be my only compensation. Even that reward has now failed me, and instead of it an attempt is made to throw on me a part of the shame and disgrace which belongs to the actors alone.

One of them, whom I have zealously endeavored to serve, has seen fit, with all the power of his vast influence and matchless art as a writer, to visit on me the penalties of his own wrong doing, at the same time publicly appealing to me to make known the truth, as if it would justify his attack on me.

I feel that the failure of my exertions has not been owing to any fault of mine. I worked faithfully and sincerely, under the almost daily advice and direction of Mr. Beecher, with his fullest approbation, confidence and beaming gratitude, until, as I think, in an evil hour for him, he took other advisers. I have failed, and now, strangely enough, he seems to desire to punish me for the sad consequences of the folly, insincerity and wickedness of his present counselors.

Mr. Beecher, in his statement, testifies that he brought on this investigation without my knowledge or advice.

Even while mourning what seemed to me the utter unwisdom of this proceeding, I have done all I could honorably do to avert this catastrophe. I have kept silent, although I saw with sorrow that this silence was deeply injuring the friend of my boyhood.

Prompted by a sense of duty—not to one only but to all the parties involved—I denied the united and public appeals made to me by Mr. Beecher and Mr. Tilton to produce the evidence in my possession; partly because I felt that the injury thereby done to Mr. Tilton was far less calamitous than the destruction which must come on all the interests I had for years tried to conserve, and especially on Mr. Beecher himself, if I should comply with this request.

But I stated clearly that in one emergency I should speak—namely, in defence of my own integrity of action if it should be wantonly assailed.

I left Mr. Beecher untrammeled by the facts in my hands, to defend himself, without the necessity of attacking me.

By the published accusations of Mr. Beecher affecting my character, my own self-respect, the advice of friends and public justice make it imperative that "the truth, the whole truth and nothing but the truth" should now be fully declared.

I give to the public, therefore, the statement I had prepared to bring before the committee, without the alteration or addition of a sentence and scarcely a word—certainly without the change of a single syllable—since I read Mr. Beecher's statement and evidence, or because of it.

This paper I withdrew from the committee when before it in a last despairing effort for peace, at the earnest solicitation of some of Mr. Beecher's friends, and with the approval also of some of the most valued of my own.

I do not now give it to the committee, but to the public, because its production concerns myself rather than the principals in the strife. It is made for my own protection against public accusation and not to aid either party to the controversy.

For the needless and cruel necessity that now so imperatively compels its production I have the most profound grief—for which there is but a single alleviation—namely, that the disclosure of the facts at this time can scarcely work more harm to him whom I at first tried to befriend by withholding them from the public, than they would have caused him in January, 1871, when, but for my interference, the public most assuredly would have been put in possession of the whole truth.

This publication, to which Mr. Beecher forces me renders fruitless four years of constant and sincere efforts to save him. It leaves him and Mrs. Tilton in almost the same position in which I found them, excepting in so far as their own late disingenuous untruthfulness in their solemn statements may lower them in the estimation of the world.

I reserve to myself the right hereafter to review the statements of Mr. Beecher in contrast with the facts as shown by the documents herewith subjoined and others which I have at my hand—the production of which did not seem to be necessary until some portion of the published evidence of Mr. Beecher demanded contradiction.

FRANCIS D. MOULTON.

STATEMENT OF FRANCIS D. MOULTON.

GENTLEMEN OF THE COMMITTEE:—I need not repeat to you my great, very great sorrow to feel obliged to answer your invitation, and, with the permission of the parties, to put before you the exact facts which have been committed to me or come to my knowledge in the unhappy affair under investigation. In so doing I shall use no words of characterization of any of them or of inculpation of the parties, nor shall I attempt to ascribe motives, save when necessary to exactly state the fact, leaving the occurrences, their acts of omission and commission, to be interpreted by themselves. In giving conversations or narrative I, of course, can in most cases give only the substance of the first and will attempt to give words only when they so impress themselves upon my mind as to remain in my memory, and of the latter only so much as seems to me material.

I have known Mr. Theodore Tilton since 1850 intimately, in the kindest relations of social and personal friendship. I have known Rev. Henry Ward Beecher since 1869, and then casually as an acquaintance and an attendant upon his ministrations up to the beginning of the occurrences of which I shall speak.

Since Mr. Tilton's valedictory, as editor of the *Independent*, on the 22d of December, 1870, I inferred that there had been some differences between himself and Mr. Henry C. Bowen, the proprietor, but learning that Tilton had been retained as contributor to that journal and editor of the Brooklyn *Union*, of which Bowen was also proprietor, I supposed that the differences were not personal or unkind. Up to that time, although I had been a frequent visitor at Tilton's house and had seen himself and Mrs. Tilton under all the phases of social intercourse, I had never heard or known of the slightest disagreement or unkindness existing between them, but had believed their marital relations were almost unexceptionally pleasant. On the 26th of December, 1870, being at Mr. Tilton's house, he came home from an interview with Mr. Bowen, and told me with some excitement of manner that he had just had a conference with Bowen, and that in that interview Bowen had made certain accusations against Beecher, and had challenged him (Tilton), as a matter of duty to the public, to write an open letter, which Bowen was to take to Beecher, of which he showed me the original draft, which is as follows :—

[FIRST DRAFT—MARKED "A."]

December 26th, 1870—BROOKLYN.

HENRY WARD BEECHER :—

SIR :—I demand, that for the reasons which you explicitly understand, you immediately cease from the ministry of Plymouth Church, and that you quit the city of Brooklyn as a residence.

(Signed) THEODORE TILTON,

Tilton explained that the words "for reasons which you explicitly understand" were interlined at the request of Bowen, and he further stated that he told Bowen that he was prepared to believe his charges because Beecher had made improper advances to Mrs. Tilton. Surprised at this I asked him, "What?" when he replied, "Don't ask me; I can't tell you." I then said, "Is it possible you could have been so foolish as to sign that letter on the strength of Bowen's assertion and not have Bowen sign it too, although, as you say, he was to carry it to Beecher?" He answered, "Mr. Bowen gave me his word that he would sustain the charges and adduce the evidence to prove them whenever called upon." I said, "I fear you will find yourself mistaken. Has the letter gone?" He answered, "Bowen said he would take it immediately." I afterwards learned from Beecher that Bowen had done so, because on the 1st of January following Beecher gave me the copy he received, as I find by a memorandum made at the time on the envelope, and I find by a later memorandum on the envelope that the original draft was given to me by Tilton on the 5th of the same month. I insert here the following memorandum of the facts above stated, made at the time, giving the hour when it was made:—

BROOKLYN, Dec. 26th, 1870.

Theodore Tilton informed me to-day that he had sent a note to Mr. Beecher, of which Mr. H. C. Bowen was the bearer, demanding that he (Beecher) should retire from the pulpit and quit the city of Brooklyn. The letter was an open one. H. C. Bowen knew the contents of it, and said that he (Bowen) would sustain Tilton in this demand.

3.45 P. M.

In a day or two after that Mr. Tilton called on me at my house and said that he had sent word to Bowen that he was going to call on Beecher within half an hour or shortly; that Bowen came up into the office with great anger and told him if he should say to Beecher what he (Bowen) had told him concerning his (Beecher's) adulteries he would dismiss him from the *Independent* and the *Union*. Tilton told him that he had never been influenced by threats and he would not be in the present case, and he subsequently received Bowen's note of dismissal.

What those charges were and the account of the interview will appear in the following letter addressed to Bowen by Tilton, bearing date the 1st of January, 1871, which also gives in more substance and more detail what Tilton had said to me in the two conversations which I have mentioned:—

BROOKLYN, Jan. 1st, 1871.

MR. HENRY C. BOWEN:—

SIR—I received last evening your sudden notice breaking my two contracts—one with the *Independent*, the other with the Brooklyn *Union.*

With reference to this act of yours I will make a plain statement of facts.

It was during the early part of the rebellion (if I recollect aright) when you first intimated to me that the Rev. Henry Ward Beecher had committed acts of adultery for which, if you should expose him, he would be driven from his pulpit. From that time onward your references to this subject were frequent, and always accompanied with the exhibition of a deep-seated injury to your heart.

In a letter which you addressed to me from Woodstock, June 16th, 1868, referring to this subject, you said:—"I sometimes feel that I *must break silence*, that I *must* no longer suffer as a *dumb man*, and be made to bear a load of grief *most unjustly*. One word from me would make a *revolution* throughout Christendom, I had almost said—and *you know it.* * * * You have just a little of the evidence from the great volume in my possession. * * * I am not pursuing a phantom, but solemnly brooding over an awful reality."

The underscorings in this extract are your own. Subsequently to the date of this letter, and at frequent intervals from then till now, you have repeated the statement that you could at any moment expel Henry Ward Beecher from Brooklyn. You have reiterated the same thing not only to me but to others.

Moreover, during the year just closed your allusions to the subject were uttered with more feeling than heretofore, and were not unfrequently coupled with your emphatic declaration that Mr. Beecher ought not to be allowed to occupy a public position as a Christian preacher and teacher.

On the 26th, of December, 1870, at an interview in your house at which Mr. Oliver Johnson and I were present, you spoke freely and indignantly against Mr. Beecher as an unsafe visitor among the families of his congregation. You alluded by name to a woman, now a widow, whose husband's death you have no doubt was hastened by his knowledge that Mr. Beecher had maintained with her an improper intimacy. You avowed your knowledge of several other cases of Mr, Beecher's adulteries. Moreover, as if to leave no doubt on the mind of either Mr. Johnson or myself, you informed us that Mr. Beecher had made to you a confession of his guilt, and had with tears implored your forgiveness. After Mr. Johnson retired from this interview you related to me the the case of a woman whom you said (as nearly as I can recall your words) that * * * * * * *

During your recital of the tale you were full of anger toward Mr. Beecher, You said with terrible emphasis, that he ought not to remain a week longer in his pulpit. You immediately suggested that a demand should be made upon him to quit his sacred office. You volunteered to bear to him such a demand in the form of an open letter, which you would present to him with your own hand and you pledged yourself to sustain the demand which this letter should make—namely, that he should for reasons which he explicitly knew, immediately cease from his ministry of Plymouth Church and retire from Brooklyn.

The first draft of the letter did not contain the phrase "for reasons which he explicitly knew," and these words (or words to this effect) were incorporated in a second, at your motion. You urged furthermore (and very emphatically) that the letter should demand not only Mr. Beecher's abdication of his pulpit, but cessation of his writing for the *Christian Union*, a point on which you were overruled. This letter you presented to Mr. Beecher at Mr. Freeland's house. Shortly after its presentation you sought an interview with me in the editorial office of the Brooklyn *Union*, during which, with unaccountable emotion in your manner, your face livid with rage, you threatened with a loud voice that if ever I should inform Mr. Beecher of the statements which you had made concerning his adultery, or should compel you to adduce the evidence on which you agreed to sustain the demand for Mr. Beecher's withdrawal from Brooklyn, you would immediately deprive me of my engagement to write for the *Independent* and to edit the Brooklyn *Union*, and that in case I should ever attempt to enter the offices of those journals you would have me ejected by force. I told you that I should inform Mr. Beecher or anybody else, according to the dictate of my judgment, uninfluenced by any threat from my employer. You then excitedly retired from my presence. Hardly had your violent words ceased ringing in my ears when I received your summary notices breaking my contracts with the *Independent* and the Brooklyn *Union*. To the foregoing narrative of facts I have only to add my surprise and regret at the sudden interruption, by your own act, of what has been on my part towards you, a faithful friendship of fifteen years.

Truly yours,

THEODORE TILTON.

In this letter I have omitted the sentence quoted as the

words of Mr. Bowen, after the words, "as nearly as I can recall your words, that"—simply desiring to say that it contained a charge of rape, or something very nearly like ravishment, of a woman other than Mrs. Tilton, told in words that are unfit to be spread upon the record, but, if desired, the original is for the inspection of the committee.

On Friday evening, the 30th of December, being the night of the Plymouth Church prayer meeting, Tilton came to me and said, in substance, that by his wife's request he had determined to see Beecher, in order to show to Beecher a confession of his wife of the intercourse between them, which he (Tilton) had never up to that time mentioned to him (Beecher), and the fact of the confession, of which his wife had told him that she had never told Beecher, although her confession had been made in July previous in writing, which writing he (Tilton) had afterwards destroyed; but that his wife, fearing that, if the Bowen accusations against Beecher were made public, the whole matter would be known and her own conduct with Beecher become exposed, had renewed her confession in her own handwriting, which he handed to me to read, which was the first knowledge I had of its existence.

Tilton did not tell me how his wife came to make the confession in July, nor did I at that time or ever after ask. Indeed, I may state here, once for all, that I refrained from asking confessions of the acts of all the parties further than they chose to make them to me voluntarily for the purpose for which I was acting.

Tilton wanted me to go down and ask Beecher to come up and see him at my house, which I did. I said to Mr. Beecher, "Mr. Tilton wants you to come and see him at my house immediately." He asked, "What for?" I replied, "He wants to make some statement to you in reference to your relations with his family." He then called to some one in the back room to go down and say that he should not be at the prayer meeting, and we went out together.

It was storming at the time, when he remarked, "There is an appropriateness in this storm," and asked me, "What can I do? What can I do?" I said, "Mr. Beecher, I am not a Christian, but if you wish I will show you how well a heathen can serve you." We then went to my house, and I showed him into the chamber over the parlor, where Mr. Tilton was, and left them together. In about an hour Mr. Beecher came down and asked me if I had seen the confession of Elizabeth.

I said I had. Says he, 'This will kill me," and asked me to walk out with him. I did so, and we walked to Mr. Tilton's house together, and he went in. On the way he said, "This is a terrible catastrophe; it comes upon me as if struck by lightning."

He went into Tilton's house and I returned home. Within an hour he returned to my house, and we left my house again together and I walked with him to his house. Tilton remained at my house while Beecher was absent at Tilton's house, and when he returned there was no conversation between them. When we arrived at Beecher's house he wanted me to stand by him in this emergency, and procure a reconciliation if possible. I told him I would, because the interests of women, children and families were involved, if for no other reason. That ended the interview that night. During this evening nothing was said by Mr. Beecher as to the truth or falsity of Mrs. Tilton's confession, nor did he inform me that he had obtained from her any recantation of the confession, which I afterwards learned he had done.

I returned to my house and had some conversation with Tilton, in which he told me that he had recited to Beecher the details of the confession of his wife's adulteries, and the remark which Beecher made was, "This is all a dream, Theodore," and that that was all the answer that Beecher made to him. I then advised Tilton that for the sake of his wife and family and for the sake of Beecher's family, the matter should be kept quiet and hushed up. The next morning, as I was leaving home for business, Tilton came to my house and with great anger said that Beecher had done a mean act; that he had gone from that interview of last night to his house and procured from Elizabeth a recantation and retraction of her confession. He said, for that act he would smite him; that there could be no peace. He said, "You see that what I have told you of the meanness of that man is now evident." Tilton said that Beecher, at the interview of last night, had asked his permission to go and see Elizabeth, and he told him he might go, which statement was confirmed by Beecher himself, and Beecher left him for that purpose. I said to Tilton, "Now, don't get angry; let us see if even this cannot be arranged. I will go down and get that retraction from him."

I was then going to my business, so that I was unable to go that morning, but went that evening, saw Beecher, and told him that I thought he had been doing a very mean and treacherous act—treacherous, first toward me, from whom he wanted help, in that he did not tell me on our way to his house last night what he had procured from Mrs. Tilton, and that he could not expect my friendship in this matter unless he acted truthfully and honorably toward me. I further said : "Mr. Beecher, you have had criminal intercourse with Mrs. Tilton; you have done great injury to Tilton otherwise. Now, when you are confronted with it, you ask permission of the man to again visit his house, and you get from that woman who has confessed you have ruined her, a recantation and retraction of the truth for your mere personal safety. That won't save you.

At that interview he admitted with grief and sorrow the fact of his sexual relations with Mrs. Tilton, expressed some indignation that she had not told her husband, and that in consequence of being in ignorance of that fact he had been walking upon a volcano—referring to what he had done in connection with Bowen and with reference to Tilton's family. He said that he had sympathized with Bowen, and had taken sides with him as against Tilton, in consequence of stories which were in circulation in regard to him, and especially of one specific case where he had improper relations with a woman whom he named, and to whom a letter from his wife will make a part of this statement, and had so stated to Bowen. And he told me that he would write to Bowen and withdraw those charges, and gave me the rough draft of a letter which he wrote and sent to Bowen, which letter is here produced, marked "C.":—

BROOKLYN, Jan. 2d, 1871.

MY DEAR MR. BOWEN :—Since I saw you last Tuesday, I have reason to think that the only cases of which I spoke to you in regard to Mr. Tilton were exaggerated in being reported to me, and I should be unwilling to have anything I said, though it was but a little, weigh on your mind in a matter so important to his welfare. I am informed by one whose judgment and integrity I greatly rely, and who has the means of forming an opinion better than any of us, that he knows the whole matter about Mrs.——, and that the stories are not true, and that the same is the case with other stories. I do not wish any reply to this. I thought it only due to justice that I should say so much. Truly yours,

(Signed) H. W. BEECHER.

Mr. Beecher told me that Mrs. Beecher and himself, without knowing of the confession of Mrs. Tilton to her husband, had been expressing great sympathy toward Mrs. Tilton and taken an active interest with her against her husband. I said, "Mr. Beecher, I want that recantation; I have come for it." "Well," said he, "what shall I do without it?" I replied, "I don't know. I can tell you what will happen with it." He asked, "What will you do if I give it you?" I answered, "I will keep it as I keep the confession. If you act honorably I will protect it with my life, as I will protect the other with my life. Mr. Tilton asked for that confession this morning, and I said, 'I will never give it to you; you shall not have it from my hands until I have exhausted every effort for peace.'" Mr. Beecher gave me back the paper, the original of which I now produce in Mrs. Tilton's handwriting, marked "D," as follows:—

December 30th, 1870.

Wearied with importunity and weakened by sickness, I gave a letter inculpating my friend Henry Ward Beecher, under assurances that that would remove all difficulties between me and my husband. That letter I now revoke. I was persuaded to it, almost forced, when I was in a weakened state of mind. I regret it and recall all its statements.

(Signed) E. R. Tilton.

I desire to say explicitly Mr. Beecher has never offered any improper solicitations, but has always treated me in a manner becoming a Christian and a gentleman.

(Signed) Elizabeth R. Tilton.

Afterward Mr. Tilton left with me another letter, dated the same night of the recantation, December 30th, bearing on the same topic, to be kept with the papers, which was in his wife's handwriting. It is here produced and marked "E," as follows:—

December 30th, 1870—Midnight.

My Dear Husband—I desire to leave with you before going to sleep a statement that Mr. Henry Ward Beecher called upon me this evening, asked me if I would defend him against any accusation in a council of ministers, and I replied solemnly that I would in case the accuser was any other person than my husband. He (H. W. B.) dictated a letter which I copied as my own, to be used by him as against any other accuser except my husband. This letter was designed to vindicate Mr. Beecher against all other persons save only yourself. I was ready to give him this letter because he said with pain that my letter in your hands addressed to him, dated December 20th, "has struck him dead and ended his usefulness."

You and I are pledged to do our best to avoid publicity. God grant a speedy end to all further anxieties. Affectionately,

(Signed) ELIZABETH.

When I went home with the recantation I found Tilton there and showed it to him. He expressed his surprise and gratification that I should have been able to get it, and I then showed to him how very foolish it would have been in the morning to have proceeded angrily against Beecher. I made another appeal for peace, saying that, notwithstanding great difficulties appeared in the way, if they were properly dealt with they could be beaten out of the way. He expressed his willingness and desire for peace.

When I saw Beecher I made an agreement, at his request, to go and see him on Sunday, January 1st. I went to his house in accordance with the engagement. He took me into his study, and then told me again of his great surprise that Elizabeth should have made the confession of his criminal commerce with her to her husband without letting him (Beecher) know anything about it, making his destruction at any moment possible, and without warning to him. He expressed his great grief at this wrong which he had done as a minister and friend to Theodore, and at his request I took pen and paper and he dictated to me the following paper, all of which is in my handwriting except the words, "I have trusted this to Moulton in confidence," and the signature, which latter are in Mr. Beecher's. It is here produced and marked "F.":—

BROOKLYN, Jan. 1st, 1871.

[In trust with F. D. Moulton].

MY DEAR FRIEND MOULTON:—I ask through you Theodore Tilton's forgiveness, and I humble myself before him as I do before my God. He would have been a better man in my circumstances than I have been. I can ask nothing except that he will remember all the other hearts that would ache. I will not plead for myself. I even wish I were dead; but others must live and suffer.

I will die before any one but myself is implicated, All my thoughts are running toward my friends, toward the poor child lying there and praying with her folded hands, she is guiltless—sinned against; bearing the transgression of another. Her forgiveness I have. I humbly pray to God that he may put it into the heart of her husband to forgive me.

I have trusted this to Moulton in confidence.

(Signed) H. W. BEECHER.

This was intrusted to me in confidence, to be shown only to Tilton, which I did. It had reference to no other fact or act than the confession of sexual intercourse between Beecher and Mrs. Tilton, which he at that interview confessed, and denied not, but confessed. He also at other interviews subsequently held between us in relation to the unfortunate affair unqualifiedly confessed that he had been guilty of adultery with Mrs. Tilton, and always in a spirit of grief and sorrow at the enormity of the crime he had committed against Mr. Tilton's family. At such times he would speak with much feeling of the relation he had sustained toward them as pastor, spiritual adviser and trusted friend. His self-condemnation at the ruin he had wrought under such circumstances was full and complete, and at times he was so bowed down with grief in consequence of the wrong he had done that he threatened to put an end to his life. He also gave to me the letter, the first draft of which, marked "A," is above given, in reference to which he said that Bowen had given it to him; that he had told Bowen that Tilton must be crazy to write such a letter as that; that he did not understand it, and that Bowen said to him, "I will be your friend in this matter." He then made a statement which Tilton had made to me at my house of the charge that Bowen had made to him (Tilton); said that Bowen had been very treacherous toward Tilton as well as toward himself, because he (Beecher) had had a reconciliation with Bowen, of which he told me the terms, and that Bowen had never in his (Beecher's) presence spoken of, or referred to any allegation of crime or wrong-doing on his part with any woman whatever. He gave me, in general terms, the reconciliation, and afterwards gave me two memoranda, which I here produce, which show the terms of the reconciliation. The first is in the handwriting of Bowen, containing five items, which Beecher assured me were the terms which Bowen claimed should be the basis of reconciliation. It is as follows, and is marked "G":—

First—Report and publish sermons and lecture-room talks.

Second—New edition Plymouth Collection and Freeland's interest.

Third—Explanations to church.

Fourth—Write me a letter.

Fifth—Retract in every quarter what has been said to my injury.

The second paper is a pencil memorandum of the reconciliation with Bowen in Beecher's handwriting, giving an account of the affair. It is marked "H," as follows:—

About February, 1870, at a long interview at Mr. Freeland's house, for the purpose of having a full and final reconciliation between Bowen and Beecher, Mr. Bowen stated his grievances, which were *all* either of a business nature or of my treatment of him *personally* (as per memorandum in writing).

After hours of conference everything was adjusted. We shook hands. We pledged each other to work henceforth without jar or break. I said to him:—"Mr. Bowen, if you hear anything of me not in accordance with this agreement of harmony do not let it rest. Come straight to me at once, and I will do the same by you.

He agreed. In the lecture room I stated that all our differences were over, and that we were friends again. This public recognition he was present and heard, and expressed himself as greatly pleased with. It was after all this that I asked Mr. Howard to help me carry out this reconciliation, and to call on Mr. Bowen and to remove the l ttle difference between them.

Mr. Howard called, expressed his gratification.

Then it was that without any provocation he (Mr. Bowen) told Mr. Howard that this reconciliation did not include one matter, that he (Bowen) "knew *that* about Mr. Beecher which if he should speak it would drive Mr. Beecher out of Brooklyn." Mr. Howard protested with horror against such a statement, saying:—"Mr. Bowen this is terrible. No man should make such a statement unless he has absolute evidence." To this Mr. Bowen replied that he had this evidence, and said, pointedly, that he (Howard) might go to Mr. Beecher, and *that Mr. Beecher would never* give his consent that he (Bowen) should tell Mr. Howard this secret.

Mr. Bowen *at no time* had ever made known to Mr. Beecher what this secret was, and the hints which Mr. Beecher had had of it led him to think it was *another matter*, and not the slander which he now finds it to be.

In that interview Beecher was very earnest in his expression of regret at what had been done against Tilton in relation to his business connection with Bowen, and besought me to do everything I could to save him from the destruction which would come upon him if the story of his (Beecher's) intercourse with Mrs. Tilton should be divulged. In compliance with the directions of Beecher, January 1st, 1871, I took the paper marked "F," which he had dictated to me, to Tilton, detailed to him Beecher's expressions of regret and sorrow, spoke to him of his agony of mind, and again appealed to him to have the whole matter kept quiet, if for no other reason, for the sake of the children. To this Tilton assented. I found him writing the letter to Bowen of that date, which I have before produced marked "B." He told me also of the contracts he had with Bowen with a penalty, when he left the *Independent*, to be editor of the Brooklyn *Union* and special contributor to the *Independent*, at a salary of $100 per week, with another salary of equal amount for his editorship of the Brooklyn *Union* and a portion of the profits. Copies of these contracts I cannot produce, because both papers were delivered to Bowen after the arbitration of the controversy of which I am about to speak. These contracts provided that they could be terminated by mutual consent or upon six months' notice, or upon the death of either party, or at once by the party who wished to break or annul them paying to the other the sum of $2,500. Tilton insisted that that sum, with his arrears of salary, was justly due him, and that he should bring suit against Bowen unless he settled, and he gave me an authorization to settle his affairs with Bowen, which paper I gave to Mr. Bowen when I went down to treat with him, retaining this copy, marked "I":—

BROOKLYN, JAN. 2d, 1871.

MR. H. C. BOWEN:—

SIR— I hereby authorize Mr. Francis D. Moulton to act in my behalf in full settlement with you of all my accounts growing out of my contracts for services to the *Independent* and the Brooklyn *Daily Union.*

(Signed) THEODORE TILTON.

Acting in the interest of Beecher. I told Tilton that this controversy with Bowen, if possible, should be peacefully settled lest it might reopen the other matters relating to Beecher's conduct in Tilton's family and the charges made by Bowen against Beecher. To this Tilton assented, giving me the authorization above quoted.

At my earliest convenience I called upon Bowen at his office upon this business, telling him that I wanted him to settle with me, as I was authorized by Tilton by this letter (handing him the letter) to settle for the breaking of the contract with Tilton as contributor to the *Independent*, and as editor of the Brooklyn *Union*. I also handed him an article written by Tilton for the *Independent*, which he (Tilton) claimed was in part performance of his contract, which article was subsequently returned to Tilton by Bowen through me. Bowen said that he did not consider that he owed Tilton any money at all for breaking the contracts—that he had terminated them, having, in his opinion, sufficient reasons for so doing. "Well," I said, "Mr. Bowen, your contracts are specific." He said he "knew they were, but they provided for arbitration in case of any differences between the parties." I replied, in substance, that the arbitration only referred to differences between the parties as to the articles to be published as editor and contributor by Tilton and as to Bowen's conduct as publisher, and that there was a fixed sum as penalty for breach of the contracts. The interview terminated with his refusal to settle the claim I demanded, which refusal I reported to Tilton, advising him still not to sue Bowen.

The following correspondence is with reference to my meeting Mr. Bowen on this business. The letter marked "J 1" is my note to Mr. Bowen, and his reply, marked "J 2":—

BROOKLYN, Jan. 9th, 1871.

MR. HENRY C. BOWEN:—

DEAR SIR—Referring to a recent interview with you, I would state that in consequence of illness I have been detained at home, and I deem it of great importance to the interest of all concerned in the affairs about which we talked, that you and I should meet at an early moment. If you will call at my house, No. 143 Clinton Street, I shall be glad to see you at any hour convenient tó youself to-morrow.

Truly yours,

F. D. MOULTON.

90 WILLOW STREET, BROOKLYN, Jan, 10th, 1871.

SIR:—I am not very well but will try to call at your house Thursday evening at eight o'clock. I am engaged to-morrow evening. I can go this evening if you will inform me that it will be convenient for you to see me. Unless I learn from you to the contrary I will see you on Thursday evening.

Very respectfully,

HENRY C. BOWEN.

MR. F. D. MOULTON.

In pursuance of this correspondence we met at my house and entered into negotiations about the settlement of the contract with Tilton. At that time, during the interview, I showed Bowen the letter of January 1st, of Tilton, (which he, Tilton, had placed in my hands to use in accordance with my own discretion), heretofore given, marked "B." Bowen, during the reading of the letter, seemed to be much excited, and at only one point of the letter questioned the accuracy of its statements, which states as follows: "that alluding by name to a woman, now a widow, whose husband's death no doubt was hastened by his knowledge that Mr. Beecher had maintained with her an improper intimacy." To that he said, "I didn't make that allusion; Mr. Tilton made it." I went on to the close of the letter and finished it, when Bowen said to me, "Has Tilton told Beecher the contents of this letter?" I replied, "Yes, he has." Said he, "What shall I do? What I said at that interview was said in confidence. We struck hands there, and pledged ourselves to God that no one there present would reveal anything there spoken." I said to him, "It would be an easy matter to confirm what you say or prove that what you say is false. Mr. Oliver Johnson was there, and I have submitted this letter to Mr. Johnson, in Mr. Tilton's presence, and he tells me that there was no obligatory confidence imposed on any of the parties concerning anything said at this interview, save a special pledge, mutually given, that nothing should be said concerning Mr. Beecher's demonstrations toward Mrs. Tilton. Mr. Johnson also says—and this confirms what you say in regard to one point—namely, that the allusion to the widow was made by Theodore Tilton, and that you said you had no doubt that her husband's death was caused by his knowledge of her improper intimacy with Mr. Beecher. Quoting your language, he says that you said, 'I have no doubt about it whatever.' Mr. Johnson also says that your statements in regard to Beecher were not intimations of his adulteries, but plain and straightforward charges of the same. He says that you said that you knew of four or five cases of Mr. Beecher's adulterous intercourse with women. Mr. Johnson says also that you at that interview plainly declared that Mr. Beecher had confessed his guilt to you." I also said to him:—"Mr. Tilton states that you said, 'I can't stand it any longer. You and I owe a duty to society in this matter. That man ought not to stay another week in his pulpit. It isn't safe for our families to have him in this city.'" I also said to him:—"Mr. Johnson also states that at the interview of December 26th, at your house, Willow Street, you voluntarily pledged your word to Mr. Johnson that you would take no further measures in regard to Mr. Tilton, without consultation with him (Mr. Johnson), and that you had said substantially the same thing to him previously, during private conversations between you and him." I then said to Bowen that I thought he was a very treacherous man, and for this reason that I knew he had had a reconciliation with Beecher—or rather I was informed of it—which was perfected in the house of God, and that within forty-eight hours from that time he had avowed to Mr. Howard that he could if he chose drive Mr. Beecher out of town. I told him, further, that I was also informed that, prior to that reconciliation, he had made no charge against Beecher's character to Beecher, but only behind his back, and I said, "Mr. Bowen, I have the points of settlement between you and Beecher in your own handwriting, and there is no reference to any charge of crime of any kind against Beecher." Mr. Bowen made no denial of these assertions of mine, but seemed, on the contrary, abashed and dejected, and in reply to my question, "What do you say to these charges which you have made against Beecher?" he declined to say anything about them, but repeated the question, "What can I do?" I answered, "I am not your adviser; I cannot dictate to you what course you should pursue, but you have done great injustice to Mr. Tilton and to Mr. Beecher and you ought to take the earliest means of repairing the injury. I should think it would be but just for you to restore Tilton to the *Independent*, but I don't believe he would go back if you should offer it to him." His reply was, "How can I do that now?" I told him I didn't know; he must find a way to settle his own difficulties. He again expressed his willingness to arbitrate the question of money between himself and Tilton growing out of the contract. I told him that I would not arbitrate; that a plain provision of the contract provided that he should pay what I demanded, and he must fulfill it. Mr. Bowen rose to leave, and said before leaving, whenever I wanted to see him he would be happy to come to my house and confer on this subject; and he did, on several subsequent occasions, visit me at my house whenever I sent for him to consult on this matter. The means I have of giving so accurately the conversation between myself and Bowen as to the conversations had with Tilton and Oliver Johnson are that prior to my meeting with Bowen, as I told him, I had an interview with Oliver Johnson in the presence of Tilton, where the whole matter was discussed, and a memorandum of Oliver Johnson's statement, in which he gave his recollection of the interview of December 26th, when Tilton and Johnson were present, was taken by Tilton in short-hand in my presence, and copied out at the time in Johnson's presence, which memorandum has been in my possession ever since, and from which I read each statement, one after the other, to Mr, Bowen. I here produce it, marked "K":—

At the interview of December 26th, (Willow Street, No. 90), Mr. Bowen voluntarily pledged his word to Mr. Johnson that he (H. C. B.) would take no further measures in regard to Mr Tilton, without consultation with Mr. Johnson. Mr. Bowen likewise had said substantially the same thing to Mr. Johnson previously during private conversations between these two persons.

There was no obligatory confidence imposed on any of the parties concerning anything said at this interview save a special pledge, mutually given, that nothing should be said concerning Mr. Beecher's demonstration toward Mrs. Tilton.

Mr. O. J. says that Mr. Bowen's statements in regard to H. W. B. were not intimations of H. W. B.'s adulteries, but plain and straightforward charges of the same. H. C. B., stated that he knew four or five cases of Mr. B.'s adulterous intercourse with women.

O. J. says that H. C. B. at this interview plainly declared that H. W. B. had confessed his guilt to H. C. B.

H. C. B.—I cannot stand it any longer. You and I owe a duty to society in this matter. That man ought not to stay another week in his pulpit. It is not safe for our families to have him in this city.

The allusion to the widow was made by T. T., and H. C. B. said he had no doubt that her husband's death was caused by his knowledge of her improper intimacy with H. W. B. "I have no doubt about it whatever."

To make an end of the statement as to the controversy between Tilton and Bowen, I further state that various negotiations were had between Bowen and myself, which resulted finally in an arbitration in which H. B. Claflin, Charles Storrs and James Freeland were referees; that there was very considerable delay arising from my own absence South in the early spring on account of sickness, Mr. Bowen's absence during the summer, and Tilton's absence during the fall and winter on his lecturing tour; so that the arbitration did not terminate until the 2d of April, 1872. This arbitration was determined upon by me, and my determination given to Mr. Claflin in the following note which I sent, marked "K 2":—

BROOKLYN, April 1st, 1872.

MY DEAR MR. CLAFLIN:—After full consideration of all interests other than Theodore's, I have advised him to arbitrate on grounds which he will explain to you, and which I hope will accord with your judgment and kind wishes toward all concerned. Cordially yours,

FRANCIS D. MOULTON.

Tilton and Bowen and myself appeared before the arbitrators, and all made statements. In Tilton's statement was included the letter marked "B," before given, which he had put into type, which fact influenced me to consent to the arbitration in order to do away with the necessity for its publication. After full hearing—nothing having been submitted to the arbitrators except the business differences of Tilton and Bowen the arbitrators made an award that Mr. Bowen should pay Tilton the sum of $7,000 for which he (Mr. Bowen) drew his check upon the spot and the contracts were given up to him.

After the above settlement a paper, which has since been called the "tripartite agreement," was signed by Bowen and Tilton, Beecher signing it subsequently. The inducing cause to this arbitration was the fact that Tilton had commenced a suit against Bowen and prepared an article for the *Golden Age*, in which he embodied his letter (marked "B") to Mr. Bowen and a statement of the circumstances. He submitted that article to me, and I begged him to withhold it from publication. I also brought Beecher and Tilton together, and Beecher added his entreaties to mine. To prevent its publication and close the suit, which might work injury to Beecher and others, I agreed to submit Mr. Tilton's claim to arbitration, to which I had been invited before by Mr. Bowen, but which I had refused, as before stated. In this interview between Beecher, Tilton and myself I said, "Perhaps we can settle the whole matter if I can see Mr. Claflin, for Claflin knows Bowen well, and understands the importance of all these interests." Beecher said he would send Claflin to me, and I might confer with him upon the matter. In consequence of this Mr. Claflin called on me and we conferred upon the matter, and subsequently the arbitration was agreed upon. At the conclusion of the arbitration the parties signed the "tripartite covenant," which was drawn up (as I understand) by Mr. Samuel Wilkeson. It was first signed by Bowen. In the form in which it was first drawn it bound the parties to say nothing of any wrong done or offence committed by Beecher, and fully exonerated him therefrom. After Bowen had signed it, it was handed to Tilton to sign, and he refused. He was willing to sign an agreement never to repeat again the charges of Bowen, saying that if for no other reason, if the matter should thereafter ever come to light, it would appear that there had been something between Beecher and Mrs. Tilton, and it might be used as evidence to the injury of himself and family, as well as of Beecher, and, therefore, it was not for the interest of either Tilton or Beecher to sign it in the form first proposed. No copy of that "tripartite covenant" was confided to me. Appended to this covenant and made, a part of it was a copy of the proof sheet article for the *Golden Age*, so that it might be known exactly to what scandal it referred. How that "tripartite covenant" came to be published I know not. As a part of that settlement it was arranged that Tilton should write a letter to Bowen, to be published in the *Independent*, with certain comments to be made by Bowen. The original draft of these, in full recantation and withdrawal of all charges and matters of difference between Tilton and Bowen, is herewith produced and marked "L":—

THEODORE TILTON:

We have received the following note from an old friend:—

OFFICE OF THE "GOLDEN AGE,"
(Original date blotted).
NEW YORK, April 3d, 1872.

HENRY C. BOWEN, Esq:—

MY DEAR SIR—In view of misapprehensions which I lately found existing among our mutual friends at the West, touching the severance of our relations in the *Independent* and the Brooklyn *Union*, I think it would be well, both for your sake and mine, if we should publicly say that, while our political and theological differences still exist, and will probably widen, yet that all other disagreements (so far as we ever had any) have been blotted out in reciprocal friendliness and good will.

Truly yours,
THEODORE TILTON.

It is so long since Mr. Tilton's pen has contributed to the *Independent* that we give to his brief note his old and familiar place at the head of these columns. While we never agreed with some of his radical opinions (and quite likely, as he intimates, we never shall, yet we owe to his request as above printed the hearty response which his honest purposes, his manly character, and his unstained integrity elicit from all who know him well. The abuse and slanders heaped upon him by some unfriendly journals have never been countenanced by the *Independent.* Regretting his opposition to the present Administration, we nevertheless wish abundant prosperity to the *Golden Age* and its editor. H. C. B.

The above proposed card was subsequently and voluntarily changed by Mr. Bowen into a still stronger and more friendly notice of Mr. Tilton.

After the tripartite covenant was signed it came to the knowledge of Beecher, as he informed me, that Bowen was still spreading scandals about him, at which he was angered and proposed to write Bowen a letter stating the points that had been settled in their reconciliation and agreement and the reason why Mr. Bowen's mouth should be closed in regard to such slanders. I find among my papers a pencil and ink memorandum of the statements intended to be embodied in that letter, which was submitted to my judgment by Beecher. It is in his handwriting and is produced, marked "M." It reads as follows:—

I. That he allowed himself to listen to unfounded rumors.

II. That he never brought them either (1) to me (2) nor in any proper manner to the church; (3) that he only whispered them, and even that only when he had some business end in view.

III. That he did not himself believe that anything had occurred which unfitted me for the utmost trust shown.

(1) By continuing for twelve to fifteen years a conspicuous attendant at Plymouth church.

(2) By contracts with me as editor of the *Independent.*

(3) By continued publications of my sermons, &c., making the privilege of doing so—even as late as the interview at Freeland's—one of these points of settlement.

(4) By a settlement of *all difficulties* at Freeland's (and a reconciliation which was to lead to work together), in which *not a single hint* of any *personal* immorality, but every *item was business.*

IV. As a result of such agreement—

(1) I was to resume my old familiarity at his house.

(2) To write him a letter that he could give his family to show that I had restored confidence.

(3) To endeavor to remove from him the coldness and frowns of the parish, as one who had *injured me.*

(4) A *card* to be published, and which was published, giving him the right to put in the *Independent* sermons and lecture room talks, &c.

(5) I was invited to go to Woodstock and be his guest, as I was at Grant's reception.

V. Of the settlement by a committee whose record is with Mr. Claflin I have nothing to say. I did not see Mr. Beecher during the whole process, nor do I remember to have spoken with him since.

VI. Now the *force of the statement that he did not himself believe* that I had done *anything immoral* which should affect my standing as a *man*, a *citizen* and a *minister*, illustrated by the foregoing facts, is demonstrated by his conduct when he *did* believe that Theodore Tilton committed immoralities, his dispossession of *Independent* his ignominious expulsion from B. *U.*, his refusal to pay him the salary and forfeit of contract.

As a part of this transaction Beecher sent me the following note, marked "N":—

MONDAY.

MY DEAR FRIEND—I called last evening, as agreed, but you had stepped out. On the way to church last evening I met Claflin. He says B. *denies* any such treacherous whisperings, and is in a right state.

I mentioned my proposed letter. He liked the idea. I read him the draft of it (in lecture room). He drew back, and said better not send it. I asked him if B. had ever made him statement of the very *bottom* facts; if there were any charges I did not know. He evaded and intimated that if he had he hardly would be right in telling me. I think he would be right in telling *you*—ought to. I have not sent any note and have destroyed that prepared.

The real point to avoid is, to an appeal to church and then a council.

It would be a conflagration, and give every possible chance for *parties*, for hidings and evasions, and increase an hundred-fold this scandal, without healing anything.

I shall see you as soon as I return.

Meantime I confide everything to your wisdom, as I always have, and with such success hitherto that I have full trust for future.

Don't fail to see C. and have a full and confidential talk.

Yours, ever

From the time of the tripartite covenant nothing occurred to disturb the relations between Beecher, Tilton and Bowen, or either of them, so far as I know, until the publication in *Woodhull & Claflin's Weekly* of an elaborate story concerning the social relations between Beecher, Tilton and Mrs. Tilton. After that publication appeared it again came to the knowledge of Beecher that Bowen was making declarations derogatory to his character. This was followed by the publication of the "tripartite covenant," which Beecher informed me was done by Mr. Samuel Wilkeson, and also that Beecher was not a party to its publication nor knew anything about it. There afterward appeared an account of an interview between Bowen, H. B. Claflin and Mrs. Woodhull, published in the Brooklyn *Eagle*, in which an attempt was made to obtain from her any letters which she might have showing that Beecher was guilty of criminal conduct, which attempt failed. Whereupon Beecher addressed me the following note, which I here produce, marked "N 2":

I need to see you this evening any time till half past ten. Can you make appointment? Will you call at 124, or shall I? At what hour? I send Claflin's letter. Keep it. Answer by telegraph. H. W. B.

I shall take tea at Howard's, 74 Hicks, and should you call, let it be there. Or I will go round to your rooms. I want to show you a proposed card.

I also produce a letter of Claflin to Beecher of June 28th, 1873, which was enclosed with the above, marked "N 3":—

NEW YORK, June 28th, 1872.

MY DEAR MR. BEECHER—I have yours. It was distinctly understood that the call on Woodhull was entirely private and not to be reported. I told Bowen, Woodhull had no letters from you of the least consequence to him or anybody else, and I was entirely satisfied after the interview that I was entirely right. I went there at Bowen's earnest solicitation, knowing it could not harm you and might satisfy him, as I think it did. It was in bad faith to publish the meeting. All present must have been disgusted at the utter lack of what Woodhull professed to have, but could not produce. Truly your friend, H. B. CLAFLIN.

P. S.—Wish you would call and see me if you pass the store. I am always in at about eleven A. M. H. B. C.

Beecher, when we met in pursuance of his note, produced to me a memorandum of a card which he proposed to publish in the *Eagle*, and which he submitted to my judgment and gave me leave to alter the same as I thought fit. That paper is herewith produced, marked "N 4":—

BROOKLYN, June, 1873.

I have seen in the morning papers that application has been made to Mrs. Victoria Woodhull for certain letters of mine supposed to contain information respecting certain infamous stories against me. She has two business letters, one declining an invitation to a suffrage meeting and the other declining to give her assistance solicited.

These, and all letters of mine in the hands of any other persons, they have my cordial consent to publish. I will only add in this connection that the stories and rumors which have for a time been circulated about me are grossly untrue, and I stamp them in general and in particular as utterly false.

I saw the editor of the Brooklyn *Eagle* at his office, and after consultation with him the card was published as follows:—

TO THE EDITOR OF THE BROOKLYN EAGLE :—

SIR—In a long and active life in Brooklyn it has rarely happened that the *Eagle* and myself have been in accord on questions of common concern to our fellow citizens. I am for this reason compelled to acknowledge the unsolicited confidence and regard of which the columns of the *Eagle* of late bear testimony. I have just returned to the city to learn that application has been made to [Mrs.] Victoria Woodhull for letters of mine supposed to contain information respecting certain infamous stories against me. [I have no objection to have the *Eagle* state, in any way it deems fit, that Mrs. Woodhull] or any other person or persons who may have letters of mine in their possession have my cordial consent to publish them. In this connection [and at this time] I will only add that the stories and rumors which have, for some time past, been circulated about me are untrue, and I stamp them in general and in particular as utterly untrue. Respectfully,

(Signed) HENRY WARD BEECHER.

In order that the emendations made by myself and Mr. Kinsella may be observed at a glance, I have enclosed in brackets the words which are not in the original. It will be thus seen how much of this card was the composition of Mr. Beecher, and how much he relied upon the judgment of others in its preparation.

I would have submitted this card to Beecher before publication, but he was absent. For obvious reasons I held myself excepted from this call for publication, *as was well* understood by Beecher. I know nothing further of the relations of Bowen and Beecher in this connection which is of importance to this inquiry. I have traced them thus far because that controversy at each stage of it continually threatened the peaceful settlement of the trouble of Tilton and Beecher, an account of which I now resume.

Another curious complication of the relations of the parties arose from the publication by Mrs. Woodhull of the story in her journal. It is a matter of public notoriety that Mrs Isabella Beecher Hooker, the sister of Beecher, had espoused the cause of Mrs. Woodhull on the question of woman suffrage, and had been accused still further of adopting her social tenets.

Beecher's relation to Mrs. Tilton had been communicated to her. This had been made a subject of communication from Mrs. Hooker to her brother, and, after the publication by Mrs. Woodhull, Mrs. Hooker addressed the following note to her brother, which contains so full and clear an exposition of all the facts and circumstances that I need not add a word of explanation. I produce Mrs. Hooker's letter to Beecher under date of November 1st, 1872, marked "N 5":—

HARTFORD, Nov. 1st, 1872.

DEAR BROTHER—In reply to your words, "If you still believe in that woman," &c., let me say that from her personally I have never heard a word on this subject; and when, nearly a year ago, I heard that when here in this city she said she had expected you to introduce her at Steinway, I wrote her a most indignant and rebuking letter, to which she replied in a manner that astounded me by its calm assertion that she considered you as true a friend to her as myself.

I enclosed this letter to Mr. Tilton, asking him to show it to you if he thought best, and to write me what it all meant. He never replied nor returned the letter to me as I requested, but I have a copy of it at your service. In the month of February, after that, on returning from Washington, I went to Mrs. Stanton's to spend Sunday. At Jersey City I met Mrs. W., who had come on in the same train with me, it seemed, and who urged me in a hasty way to bring Mrs. Stanton over on Monday for a suffrage consultation as to spring convention. Remembering her assertion of the friendship between you, and of her meeting you occasionally at Mr. Moulton's house (I think this is the name), I thought I would put this to test, and replied that if I could be sure of seeing you at the same time I would come. She promised to secure you if possible, and I fully meant to keep my appointment, but on Sunday I remembered an appointment at New Haven, which I should miss if I stopped in New York, and so I passed by, dropping her a letter by the way. Curiously enough sister Catherine, who was staying at your house at this time, said to me here, casually, the latter part of that same week, "Belle, Henry went over to New York to see you last Monday, but couldn't find you." Of course my inference was that Mrs. W. either had power over you, or you were secretly friends. During that Sunday Mrs. Stanton told me precisely what Mr. Tilton had said to her, when in the rage of discovery he fled to the house of Mrs. ——, and before them both narrated the story of his own infidelities as confessed to his wife and of hers as confessed to him. She added that not long after she went to Mr. Moulton's and met you coming down the front steps, and on entering met Tilton and Moulton, who said:—"We have just had Plymouth Church at our feet and here is his confession," showing a manuscript. She added that Mrs. Tilton had made similar statements to Miss Anthony, and I have since received from Miss A. a corroboration of this, although she refused to give me particulars, being bound in confidence, she thinks. From that day to this I have carried a heavy load, you may be sure. I could not share it with my husband, because he was already over-burdened and alarmingly affected brain-wise, but I resolved that if he went abroad, as he probably must, I would not go with him, leaving you alone as it were, to bear whatever might come of revelation. I withstood the entreaties of my husband to the last, and sent Mary in my stead, and at the last moment I confided to her all that I knew and felt and feared, that she might be prepared to sustain her father should trial overtake them. By reading the accompanying letters from them you will perceive that from outside evidence alone he had come to the conclusions which I reached only through the most reliable testimony that could well be furnished in any case and against every predisposition of my own soul. Fearing that they would hasten home to me and thus lose all the benefit of the journey (for, owing to this and other anxieties of business, John had grown worse rather than better up to that very time, though the air of the high Alps was beginning to promote sleep and restoration), I telegraphed by cable, "No trouble here—go to Italy," and by recent letters I am rejoiced to hear of them in Milan in comfortable health and spirits. From the day those letters came the matter has not been out of my thoughts an hour, it seems to me, and an unceasing prayer has ascended that I might be guided with wisdom and *truth*. But what is the truth I am farther from understanding this morning than ever. The tale as published is *essentially* the same as told to me—in fact, it is impossible but that Mr. Tilton is the authority for it, since I recognize a verisimilitude, and, as I understand it, Mrs. T. was the sole revelator. The only reply I made to Mrs. Stanton was that if true, you had a philosophy of the relation of the sexes so far ahead of the times that you dared not announce it, though you consented to live by it; that this was in my judgment wrong, and God would bring all secret things to light in his own time and fashion, and I could only wait. I added that I had come to see that human laws were an impertinence, but could get no further, though I could see glimpses of a possible new science of life, that at present was revolting to my feelings and my judgment; that I should keep myself open to conviction, however, and should converse with men, and especially women, on the whole subject, and as fast as I *knew* the truth I should stand by it, with no attempt at concealment. I think that Dr. Channing probably agrees with you in theory, but he had the courage to announce his convictions before acting upon them. He refused intercourse with an uncongenial wife for a long time, and then left her and married a woman whom he still loves, leaving a darling daughter with her mother, and to-day he pays photographers to keep him supplied with her pictures as often as they can be procured. I send you the article he wrote when, abandoned by all their friends, he and his wife went to the West and stayed for years. Crushed by calumny and abuse, to-day they are esteemed more highly than ever, and he is in positions of public trust in Providence.

You will perceive my situation, and, by all that I have suffered and am willing to suffer for your sake, I beg you to confide to me the whole truth. Then I can help you as no one else in the world can. The moment that I can know this matter as God knows it He will help you and me to bring everlasting good out of this seeming evil. If I could say truthfully that I believe this story to be a fabrication of Mr. and Mrs. Tilton's imposed upon a credulous woman—mere medium, whose susceptibility to impressions from spirits in the flesh and out of it is to be taken into account always—the whole thing dies. But if it is essentially true there is but one honorable way to meet it, in my judgment, and the precise method occurred to me in bed this morning, and I was about writing you to suggest it when your letter came.

I will write you a sisterly letter, expressing my deep conviction that this whole subject needs the most earnest and chaste discussion; that my own mind has long been occupied with it, but is still in doubt on many points, that I have observed for years that your reading and thinking has been profound on this and kindred subjects, and now the time has come for you to give the world, through your own paper, the conclusions you have reached and the reasons therefor. If you choose, I will then reply to each letter, giving the woman's view—for there is surely a man's and a woman's side to this beyond everywhere else—and by this means attention will be diverted from personalities and concentrated on social philosophy—the one subject that now ought to occupy all thinking minds.

It seems to me that God has been preparing me for this work, and you also, for years and years. I send you a reply I wrote to Dr. Todd long ago, and which I could never get published without my name (which for the sake of my daughters I wished to withhold) although Godkin, of the *Nation*; Holbrook, of the *Herald of Health*; Ward, of the *Independent*, and every mother to whom I have read it all told me it was the best thing ever written on the subject, and the men said they would publish if they dared, while Mrs. —— urged me to give my name and publish, and said she would rather have written it than anything else of its length in the world, and if it were hers she would print it without hesitation. I send also a copy of a letter I wrote John Stuart Mill on his sending me an early copy of his "Subjection of Women," and his reply. I am sure that nearly all the thinking men and women are somewhere near you and will rally to your support if you are bold, frank, and absolutely truthful in stating your convictions. Mrs. Burleigh told Dr. Channing she was ready to avow her belief in social freedom when the time came; she was weary now and glad of a reprieve, but should stand true to her convictions when she must. My own conviction is that the one radical mistake you have made is in supposing that you are so much ahead of your time, and in daring to attempt to lead when you have anything to conceal. Do not, I pray you, deceive yourself with the hope that the love of your church, or any other love, human or divine, can compensate the loss of absolute truthfulness to your own mental convictions. I have not told you the half I have suffered since February; but you can imagine, knowing what my husband is to me, that it was no common love I have for you and for the truth, and for all mankind, women as well as men, when I decided to nearly break his heart, already lacerated by the course I had been compelled to pursue, by sending him away to die, perhaps, without me at his side.

I wish you would come here in the evening some time (to the Burton cottage) or I will meet you anywhere in New York you appoint, and at any time. Ever yours, BELLE.

Read the letters from John and Mary in the order I have placed them. I will send these now and the other documents I have mentioned another day, waiting till I know whether you will meet me.

On the 3d of the same month Mrs. Hooker addressed a letter to her brother, the Rev. Thomas K. Beecher, which I produce, marked "N 6":—

[Please return this letter to me when you have done with it.]

HARTFORD, SUNDAY, Nov. 3d, 1872.

DEAR BROTHER TOM:—The blow has fallen, and I hope you are better prepared for it than you might have been but for our interview. I wrote H. a single line last week, thus, "Can I help you?" And here is his reply—"If you still believe in that woman you cannot help me. If you think of her as I do you can, perhaps, though I do not need much help. I tread the falsehoods into the dirt from which they spring, and go on my way rejoicing. My people are thus far heroic and would give their lives for me. Their love and confidence would make me willing to bear far more than I have. Meantime the Lord has a pavilion in which He hides me until the storm be overpast. I abide in peace, committing myself to Him who gave Himself for me. I trust you give neither countenance nor credence to the abominable coinage that has been put afloat. The specks of truth are mere spangles upon a garment of falsehood. The truth itself is made to lie. Thank you for love and truth and silence, but think of the barbarity of dragging a poor dear child of a woman into this slough. Yours truly."

Now, Tom, so far as I can see, it is he who has dragged the dear child into the slough and left her there, and who is now sending another woman to prison who is innocent of all crime but a fanaticism for the truth as revealed to her, and I, by my silence, am consenting unto her death.

Read the little note she sent me long ago, when, in a burst of enthusiasm over a public letter of hers which seemed wonderful to me, I told her how it affected me, and mark its prophetic words :—

NEW YORK, August 8th, 1871.

MY DEAR, DEAR FRIEND :—I was never more happy in all my life than I am this morning, and made so by you whom I have learned to love so much. From you, from whom I had expected censure, I receive the first deep, pure words of approval and love. I know my course has often been contrary to your wishes, and it has been my greatest grief to know that it was so, since you have so nobly been my defender. But all the time I knew it was not I for whom you spoke, but all womanhood, and I was the more proud of you that your love was general and not personal. I am often compelled to do things from which my sensitive soul shrinks, and for which I endure the censure of most of my friends. But I obey a Power which knows better than they or I can know, and which has never left me stranded and without hope. I should be a faithless servant, indeed, were I to falter now when required to do what I cannot fully understand, yet in the issue of which I have full faith. None of the scenes in which I have enacted a part were what I would have selfishly chosen for my own happiness. I love my home, my children, my husband, and could live a sanctified life with them and never desire contact with the wide world. But such is not to be my mission. I know what is to come, though I cannot yet divulge it. My daily prayer is that heaven may vouchsafe me strength to meet everything which I know must be encountered and overcome. My heart is, however, too full to write you all I wish. I see the near approach of the grandest revelation the world has yet known, and for the part you shall play in it, thousands will rise up and call you blessed. It was not for nothing that you and I met so singularly. Let us watch and pray, that we faint not by the wayside before we reach the consummation. We shall then look back with exceeding great joy to all we have been called upon to suffer for the sake of a cause more holy than has yet come upon the earth. Again I bless you for your letter, Affectionately and faithfully yours,

VICTORIA C. WOODHULL.

Oh, my dear brother, I fear the awful struggle to live according to law has wrought an absolute demoralization as to truthfulness, and so he can talk about "spangles on a garment of falsehood," when the garment is truth and the specks are the falsehood.

His first letter to me was so different from this. I read it to you, but will copy it lest you have forgotten its character:—

April 25th, 1872.

"MY DEAR BELLE:—I was sorry when I met you at Bridgeport not to have had longer talk with you about the meeting in May. I do not intend to make any speeches on any topic during anniversary week. Indeed, I shall be out of town. I do not want you to *take any ground this year except upon suffrage.* You know my sympathy with you. Probably you and I are nearer together than any of our family. I cannot give reason now. I am clear; still, you will follow your own judgment. I thank you for your letter. Of some things *I neither talk, nor will I be talked with.* For love and sympathy I am deeply thankful. The only help that can be grateful to me or useful is *silence* and a silencing influence on all others. A day may come for converse. It is not now. Living or dead, my dear sister Belle, *love me*, and do not talk about me or suffer others to in your presence. God love and keep you. God keep us all. Your loving brother,

H. W. B."

The underscoring is his own, and when I read in that horrible story that he begged a few hours' notice that he might kill himself, my mind flew back to this sentence, which suggested suicide to me the moment I read it: "Living or dead, my dear sister Belle, *love me*," and I believed even that.

Now, Tom, can't you go to brother Edward at once and give him these letters of mine, and tell him what I told you; and when you have counseled together as brothers should, counsel me also, and come to me if you can. It looks as if he hoped to buy my silence with my love. At present, of course, I shall keep silence, but truth is dearer than all things else, and if he will not speak it in some way I cannot always stand as consenting to a lie. "God help us all." Yours in love,

BELLE.

If you can't come to me, send Edward. I am utterly alone, and my heart aches for that woman even as for my own flesh and blood. I do not understand her, but I know her to be pure and unselfish and absolutely driven by some power foreign to herself to these strange utterances, which are always in behalf of freedom, purity—truth, as she understands it—always to befriend the poor and outcast, and bring low only the proud, the hypocrites in high places. The word about meeting at Mrs. Phelps' house I have added to the copy. If you see Henry tell him of this.

The reply to this letter by the Rev. Thomas K. Beecher to his sister is as follows, and needs but a single remark—the thought of a good man as to the value of testimony in this case. I refer to the last sentence of the postscript. This is produced, marked "N 7:"—

ELMIRA, NOV. 5, 1872.

DEAR BELLE:—To allow the devil himself to be crushed for speaking the truth is unspeakably cowardly and contemptible. I respect, *as at present advised*, Mrs. Woodhull, while I abhor her philosophy. She only carries out Henry's philosophy, against which I recorded my protest some years ago, and parted (lovingly and achingly) from him, saying, "We cannot work together." He has drifted, and I have hardened like a crystal till I am sharp cornered and exacting. I cannot help him, except by prayer. I cannot help him through Edward. In my judgment Henry is following his slippery doctrines of expediency, and, in his cry of progress and the nobleness of human nature, has sacrificed clear, exact ideal integrity. Hands off until he is down, and then my pulpit, my home, my church and my purse and heart are at his service. Of the two, Woodhull is my hero and Henry my coward, *as at present advised*. But I protest against the whole batch and all its belongings. I was not anti-slavery; I am not anti-family. But, as I wrote years ago, whenever I assault slavery because of its abominations I shall assail the Church, the State, the family and all other institutions of selfish usage.

I return the papers. *You* cannot help Henry. You must be true to Woodhull. I am out of the circle as yet, and am glad of it. When the storm-line includes me I shall suffer as a Christian, saying, "Cease ye from man."

Don't write to me. Follow the truth, and when you need me cry out.

Yours lovingly,

(Signed) TOM.

P. S.—I am so overworked and hurried that I see upon review that my letter *sounds* hard—because of its sententiousness. But believe me, dear Belle, that I see and suffer with you. You are in a tight place. But having chosen your principles I can only counsel you to be true and take the consequences. For years, you know, I have been apart from all of you except in love. I think you all in the wrong as to anthropology and social science. *But* I honor and love them who suffer for conviction's sake. My turn to suffer will come in due time. In this world all Christians shall suffer tribulation. So eat, sleep, pray, take good aim and shoot, and when the ache comes say even hereunto were we called. But I repeat—you can't help Henry at present.

P. S.—I unseal my letter to enclose print and add :—You have no *proof* as yet of any offense on Henry's part. Your testimony would be allowed in no court. Tilton, wife, Moulton & Co. are witnesses. Even Mrs. Stanton can only declare *hearsay*. So if you move remember that you are standing on uncertain information, and we shall not probably ever get the facts, and I'm glad of it. If Mr. and Mrs. Tilton are brought into court, nothing will be revealed. Perjury, for good reason, is, with advanced thinkers, no sin.

It will be observed in the letter of Mrs. Hooker that she speaks of having refused to go to Europe with her husband, and that she remained at home in order to protect her brother in this emergency of his life.

A letter came into my hands with the others from Mr. Hooker to his wife, under date of Florence, Italy, November 3d, 1871, which tends to show that all this matter had been discussed between Mr. Hooker and his wife long before the publication by Mrs. Woodhull. I extract so much from the letter as refers to this subject. The remainder is a kindly communication of an absent husband to a loved wife, about wholly independent matters which have nothing to do with this controversy. It is produced, marked "N 8":—

FLORENCE, Sunday, Nov. 3d, 1872.

MY PRECIOUS WIFE :—I hope you were not pained by what I wrote on Friday about the H. W. B. matter. I am getting much more at peace about the matter, but I cannot look upon it in any other light, and it is a relief to me to speak my mind right out about it and then let it rest. I could not have been easy till I had sworn a little. The only mitigation of the concealment of the thing that I can think of is this—and it seems to me that some excuse, or at least explanation, may be found here—viz. that a consideration of the happiness of both Mr. T. and his wife required it, or seemed to, and the very possible further fact that he preferred to disclose it, but took the advice of a few of his leading friends in the church and was overruled by them, they agreeing to take the responsibility of the concealment. This would take off somewhat from the hypocrisy of the thing, but leaves the original crime as open to condemnation as ever. But enough of this. Only let me request you to keep me informed of all that occurs, and do not rely upon my getting the news from the papers. I see by an extract from the Boston *Advertiser* that Mrs. W. has employed two Boston lawyers (it gives their names) to bring suit against the *Republican* and *Woman's Journal*, so that it looks as if the exposure is near at hand. I want to say one word more, however. Can you not let the report get out after the H. matter becomes public, without being exactly responsible for it, that you have kept up friendship with Mrs. W. in the hope of influencing her not to publish the story, you having learned its truth—and that is substantially the fact as I have understood it—and that you gave up going to Europe with me so as to be at home, and comfort H. when the truth came out, as you expected it to do in the course of the summer? This will give an appearance of self-sacrifice to your affiliation with her, and will explain your not coming abroad with me—a fact which has a very unwife-like look. I know that you will otherwise be regarded as holding Mrs. W.'s views, and that we shall be regarded as living in some discord, and probably (by many people) as practising her principles. It would be a great relief to me to have your relations to Mrs. W. explained in this way, so creditable to your heart. There is not half the untruth in it that there has been all along in my pretended approval of Mrs. Woodhull's course, and yet people think me an honest man. I have lied enough about that to ruin the character of an average man, and have probably damaged myself by it. * * *

After Beecher had seen these letters of his sister, Mrs. Hooker, he came to me, in trouble and alarm, and handed me all the letters, together with one under the date of November 27th, which I herewith produce, with the enclosure, cut from the Hartford *Times*, to which it alludes. It is marked "N 9":—

HARTFORD, Wednesday, 27th, 1872.

DEAR BROTHER:—Read the enclosed, clipped from the *Times* of this city last evening. [See enclosure below.] I can endure no longer. I must see you and persuade you to write a paper which I will read, going alone to your pulpit and taking sole charge of the services. I shall leave here on eight A. M. train Friday morning, and unless you meet me at Forty-second street station, I shall go to Mrs. ——'s house, opposite Young Men's Christian Association, No. — Twenty-third street, where I shall hope to see you during the day. Mrs. —— kindly said to me, when last in New York, "My daughter and I are now widows, living quietly in our pleasant home, and I want you to come there, without warning, whenever you are in New York, unless you have other friends whom you prefer to visit."

So I shall go as if on a shopping trip, and stay as long as it seems best.

I would prefer going to Mrs. Tilton's to anywhere else, but I hesitate to ask her to receive me.

I feel sure, however, that words from her should go into that paper, and with her consent I could write as one commissioned from on high.

Do not fail me, I pray you; meet me at noon on Friday as you hope to meet your own mother in heaven. In her name I beseech you, and I will take no denial. Ever yours, in love unspeakable, BELLE.

[Enclosure mentioned in above letter.]

"Eli Perkins," of the New York *Commercial*, a prominent republican paper, has this to say:—

"Nast's very boldness—his terrible aggressiveness— is what challenges admiration and makes *Harper's Weekly* a success.

"When I asked him if he didn't think it a great undertaking to attack Mr. Greeley, he said:—

"'Yes; but I knew he was an old humbug. I knew I was right, and I knew right would win in the end. I was almost alone, too. The people were fooled with Greeley, as they are fooled with Beecher, and he will tumble further than Greeley yet.'

"We had a talk about Beecher and Tilton, and putting this with other conversations with personal friends of Mr. Tilton and with newspaper men in New York, I am satisfied that a terrible downfall surely awaits the one who has erred and *conceals* it."

Beecher then informed me of his apprehension that his sister, in her anxiety that he should do his duty in presenting this truth as she understood it, and in protecting Mrs. Woodhull from the consequences of having published the truth, from which she was then suffering, would go into his pulpit and insist upon declaring that the Woodhull publication was substantially true; and he desired me to do what in me lay to prevent such a disaster. I suggested to him that he should see Mrs. Hooker, speak to her kindly, and exhort her not to take this course, and that Tilton should see her and so far shake her confidence in the truth of the story as to induce her to doubt whether she would be safe in making the statement public. In this course Beecher agreed, and such arguments and inducements were brought to bear upon Mrs. Hooker as were in the power of all three of us, to prevent her from doing that which would have certainly brought on an exposure of the whole business. During the consultation between Beecher and myself as to the means of meeting Mrs. Hooker's intentions, no suggestion was ever made on the part of Beecher that his sister was then or had been at any other time insane.

All these letters I received from Beecher, and they are those to which he alludes in his communication of the 4th instant as the letters of his sister and brother delivered to me, and which I did not believe that I could honorably give him up, because I thought—and I submit to the committee I was right in thinking—that they form a part of this controversy, and were not, as he therein alleged, simply given to my keeping as part of his other papers, which he could not keep safely on account of his own carelessness in preserving documents.

Beecher was exceedingly anxious that Tilton should repudiate the statement published by Woodhull, and denounce her for its publication, and he drew up, upon my memorandum book, the form of a card to be published by Tilton over his signature; and asked me to submit it to him for that purpose, which I here produce, marked "N 10:"—

In an unguarded enthusiasm I hoped well and much of one who has proved utterly unprincipled. I shall never again notice her stories, and now utterly repudiate her statements made concerning me and mine.

Beecher told me to say to Tilton, substantially:—"Theodore may for his own purpose, if he choose, say that all his misfortune has come upon him on account of his dismissal from the *Union* and the *Independent*, and on account of the offence which I committed against him; he may take the position against me and Bowen that he does; yet the fact is that his advocacy of Mrs. Woodhull and her theories has done him the injury which prevents his rising. Now, in order to get support from me and from Plymouth Church, and in order to obtain the sympathy of the whole community, he must publish this card; and unless he does it he cannot rise." He also said the same thing to Tilton in my presence. To this Tilton answered in substance to Beecher:—"You know why I sought Mrs. Woodhull's acquaintance. It was to save my family and yours from the consequences of your acts, the facts about which had become known to her. They have now been published, and I will not denounce that woman to save you from the consequences of what you yourself have done."

To resume:—After I had carried to Mr. Tilton the paper of apology which had reference to Beecher's adultery, and had received assurances that all between Tilton and Beecher should be kept quiet, I immediately conveyed the information to Beecher. He was profuse in his professions of thankfulness and gratitude to me for what he said were my exertions in his behalf. Soon after that I was taken sick, and while on my sick bed, on the 7th of February, I received the following letter from Beecher, marked "O:"—

February 7th, 1871.

My Dear Mr. Moulton:—I am glad to send you a book which you will relish, or which a man on a sick bed *ought* to relish. I wish that I had more like it, and that I could send you one every day, not as a repayment of your great kindness to me—for that can never be repaid, not even by love, which I give you freely.

Many, many friends has God raised up to me; but to no one of them has he given the opportunity and the wisdom so to serve me as you have. My trust in you is implicit. You have also proved yourself Theodore's friend and Elizabeth's. Does God look down from heaven on three unhappy creatures that more need a friend than these?

Is it not an intimation of God's intent of mercy to all, that each one of these has in you a tried and proved friend? But only in you are we three united. Would to God, who orders all hearts, that by your kind mediation Theodore, Elizabeth and I could be made friends again. Theodore will have the hardest task in such a case; but has he not proved himself capable of the noblest things?

I wonder if Elizabeth knows how generously he has carried himself toward me? Of course, I can never speak with her again, except with his permission, and I do not know that even then it would be best. My earnest longing is to see her in the full sympathy of her nature at rest in him and to see him once more trusting her and loving her with even a better than the old love. I am always sad in such thoughts. Is there any way out of this night? May not a day star arise? Truly yours always, with trust and love,

Henry Ward Beecher.

On the same day there was conveyed to me from Beecher a request to Tilton that Beecher might write to Mrs. Tilton, because all parties had then come to the conclusion that there should be no communication between Beecher and Mrs. Tilton or Beecher and Tilton, except with my knowledge and consent, and I had exacted a promise from Beecher that he would not communicate with Mrs. Tilton or allow her to communicate with him unless I saw the communication, which promise, I believe, was, on his part, faithfully kept, but as I soon found, was not on the part of Mrs. Tilton.

Permission was given to Beecher to write to Mrs. Tilton, and the following is his letter, here produced, marked "P":—

BROOKLYN, Feb. 7th, 1871.

MY DEAR MRS. TILTON:—When I saw you last I did not expect ever to see you again or to be alive many days. God was kinder to me than were my own thoughts. The friend whom God sent to me (Mr. Moulton) has proved above all friends that ever I had, able and willing to help me in this terrible emergency of my life. His hand it was that tied up the storm that was ready to burst upon our head. I am not the less disposed to trust him from finding that he has our welfare most deeply and tenderly at heart. You have no friend (Theodore excepted) who has it in his power to serve you so vitally, and who will do it with so much delicacy and honor. I beseech of you, if my wishes have yet any influence, let my deliberate judgment in this matter weigh with you. It does my sore heart good to see in Mr. Moulton an unfeigned respect and honor for you. It would kill me if he thought otherwise. He will be as true a friend to your honor and happiness as a brother could be to a sister's. In him we have a common ground. You and I may meet in him. The past is ended. But is there no future?—no wiser, higher, holier future? May not this friend stand as a priest in the new sanctuary of reconciliation, and mediate and bless you, Theodore, and my most unhappy self? Do not let my earnestness fail of its end; you believe in my judgment. I have put myself wholly and gladly in Moulton's hands, and there I must meet you. This is sent with Theodore's consent, but he has not read it. *Will you return it to me by his hands?* I am very earnest in this wish for all our sakes, as such a letter ought not to be subject to even a chance of miscarriage.

Your unhappy friend, H. W. BEECHER.

This was a letter of commendation, so that Mrs. Tilton might trust me, as between her and her husband, as fully as Beecher did. In the meanwhile Mr. Beecher's friends were continually annoying him and writing him about Tilton and the rumors that were afloat with regard to both, and on the 13th of February, Beecher received the following letter from his nephew, F. B. Perkins, which he (Beecher) handed me, with a draft of a reply, on the 23d of the same February, which he sent without showing me again and upon that draft I made the following note. I herewith produce these documents, marked "Q," "R" and "S" respectively:—

BOX 44, STATION D,
NEW YORK, February 13th, 1871.

MY DEAR UNCLE:—After some consideration I decide to inform you of a matter concerning you. Tilton has been justifying or excusing his recent intrigues with women by alleging that you have been detected in the like adulteries, the same having been hushed up out of consideration for the parties. This I *know*.

You may, of course, do what you like with this letter. I suppose such talk dies quickest unanswered. I have thought it best to let you know what is being said about you, and by whom, however; for, whether you act in the matter or not, it has been displeasing to me to suppose such things done without your knowledge. I have thought other people base, but Theodore Tilton has in this action dived into the very sub-cellar of the very backhouse of infamy. In case you should choose to let him know of this, I am responsible and don't seek any concealment. Very truly yours,

To Rev. HENRY WARD BEECHER. F. B. PERKINS.

P. S.—I cannot say Tilton said "adulteries." He was referring to his late intrigues with Mrs. —— and others, however he may have described them. What I am informed of is the excuse by implicating you in "similar" affairs. F. B. P.

FEBRUARY 23d, 1871.

MY DEAR FRED:—Whatever Mr. Tilton formerly said against me—and I know the substance of it—*he has withdrawn* and frankly confessed that he had been misled by the statements of one who, when confronted, backed down from his charges.

In some sense I am in part to blame for his indignation. For I lent a credulous ear to reports about *him*, which I have reason to believe were exaggerated or wholly false. After a full conference and explanation there remains between us no misunderstanding, but mutual good will and reconciliation have taken the place of exasperation. Of course, I shall not chase after rumors that will soon run themselves out of breath if left alone. If my friends will put their foot silently on any coal or hot embers and crush them out, *without talking*, the miserable lies will be as dead in New York in a little time as they are in Brooklyn. But I do not any the less thank you for your affectionate solicitude and for your loyalty to my good name. I should have replied earlier; but your letter came when I was out of town. I had to go out again immediately. If the papers do not meddle, this slander will fall still-born—dead as Julius Cæsar. If a *sensation* should be got up, of course there are enough bitter enemies to fan the matter and create annoyance, though no final damage. I am your affectionate uncle, H. W. B.

[Note by Moulton in relation to the above.]

H. W. Beecher agreed to hold this letter over for consideration, but sent it before seeing me again. I at first approved of the letter, but finally concluded to consult with T. T., who offered a substitute, the substance of which will be found in pencil on copy of H. W. B.'s reply to P.

Following is a copy of the substitute referred to:—

An enemy of mine, as I now learn, poisoned the mind of Theodore Tilton by telling him stories concerning me. T. T. being angered against me because I had quoted similar stories against him, which I had heard from the same party, retaliated. Theodore and I, through a mutual friend, were brought together, and found upon mutual explanations that both were victims of the same slanderer.

No further correspondence was received from Perkins in this connection to my knowledge except the following note to Tilton, herewith produced and marked "T":—

May 20th, 1871.

Mr. Tilton:—If there had not been others by I would have said to you at meeting you this noon what I say now:—Our acquaintance is at an end, and if we meet again you will please not recognize me.

F. B. Perkins.

Meanwhile Mrs. Morse, the mother-in-law of Mr. Tilton, who was from time to time an inmate of his family in Livingston street, had, as I was informed, both by Mr. and Mrs. Tilton, learned from her daughter the criminal relationship heretofore existing between Beecher and herself, and who could not understand why that matter had been settled, and who had not been told how it had been adjusted, and who had had a most bitter quarrel with Tilton, accusing him of not having so carried his affairs as to keep what fortune he had, and who had called upon Beecher about the relations between Tilton and Mrs. Tilton, and who had, as Beecher had informed me, filled the minds of Mrs. Beecher and himself with stories of Tilton's infidelity and improper conduct to his wife, wrote the following letter to Beecher, under date of January 27th, 1871, which he delivered to me the next day, as appears by my memorandum thereon, together with the draft of an answer which he said he proposed to send to Mrs. Morse. Her letter is herewith produced, marked "U" and Mr. Beecher's draft of reply marked "V," and are as follows:—

[Received January 27th, 1871; received from H. W. B. January 28th, 1871.]

Mr. Beecher;—As you have not seen fit to pay any attention to the request I left at your house now over two weeks since, I will take this method to inform you of the state of things in Livingston street. The remark you made to me at your own door was an enigma at the time, and every day adds to the mystery. "Mrs. Beecher has adopted the child." "What child," I asked. You replied, "Elizabeth."

Now, I ask what earthly sense was there in that remark? Neither Mrs. B., yourself nor I can have done anything to ameliorate her condition. She has been for the last three weeks with one very indifferent girl. T. has sent ****** with the others away, leaving my sick and distracted child to care for all four children night and day, without fire in the furnace or anything like comfort or nourishment (sic) in the house. She has not seen any one. He says, "She is mourning for *her sin.*" If this be so, one twenty-four hours under his shot, I think, is enough to atone for a lifelong sin, however henious (sic). I know that any change in his affairs would bring more trouble upon her and more suffering. I did not think for a moment when I asked Mrs. B. as to your call there, supposing she knew it, of course, as she said you would not go there without her.

I was innocent of making any misunderstanding if there was any. You say, "Keep quiet." I have all through her married life done so, and we now see our eror (sic). It has brought him to destruction, made me utterly miserable, turned me from a comfortable home and brought his own family to beggary. I don't believe if his honest debts were paid he would have enough to buy their breackfast (sic). This she could endure and thrive under, but the publicity he has given to this recent and most *crushing of all trouble* is what's taken the life out of her. I know of twelve persons whom he has told, and they in turn have told others. I had thought we had as much as we could live under from his neglect, and ungovernable temper. But this is the death blow to us both, and I doubt not Florence has hers. Do you know when I hear of you cracking your jokes from Sunday to Sunday, and think of the misery you have brought upon us, I think with the Psalmist, "There is no God." Admitting all he says to be the invention of his half-drunken brain, still the effect upon us is the same, for all he's told believe it. Now he's nothing to do, he makes a target of her night and day. I am driven to this extremity—to pray for her release from all suffering by God's taking her to Himself, for if there's a heaven I know she'll go there.

The last time she was in this house she said:—"Here I feel I have no home, but on the other side I know I shall be more than welcome." Oh, my precious child! how my heart bleeds over you in thinking of your sufferings. Can you do anything in the matter?

Must she live in this suffering condition of mind and body with no aleviation? (sic.)

You or any one else who advises her to live with him when he is doing all he can to kill her by slow torture is anything but a friend.

I don't know if you can understand a sentence I've written, but I'm relieved somewhat by writing. The children are kept from me, and I have not seen my dieing (sic) child but once since her return from this house.

I thought the least you could do was to put your name to a paper to help reinstate my brother (in the Custom House). Elizabeth was as disappointed as myself. He is still without employment, with a sick wife and five children to feed, behind with rent, and everything else behindhand.

If your wife has adopted Lib (sic) or you sympathize with her, I pray you do something for her relief before it is too late. He swears so soon as her breath leaves her body he will make this whole thing public, and this prospect, I think, is one thing which keeps her living. I know of no other. She's without nourishment (sic) for one in her state, and in *want*—actual want. They would both deny it, no doubt, *but it's true.*

Mrs. Judge MORSE :—

MY DEAR MADAM :—I should be very sorry to have you think I had no interest in your troubles. My course toward you hitherto should satisfy you that I have sympathized with your distress. But Mrs. Beecher and I, after full consideration, are of one mind—that, under present circumstances, the greatest kindness to you and to all will be, in so far as we are concerned, to leave to time the rectification of all the wrongs, whether they prove real or imaginary.

It will be observed that in the letter of Mrs. Morse she says Tilton had sent * * * * * * with the others away. I purposely omit the name of this young girl. There was a reason why it was desirable that she should be away from Brooklyn. That reason, as given me by Mr. and Mrs. Tilton, was this :—She had overheard conversations by them concerning Mrs. Tilton's criminal intimacy with Beecher, and she had reported these conversations to several friends of the family. Being young, and not knowing the consequences of her prattling, it seemed proper, for the safety of the two families, that she should be sent to a distance to school, which was accordingly done. She was put at a boarding school at the West, and the expenses of her stay there were privately paid through me by Beecher, to whom I had stated the difficulty of having the girl remain in Brooklyn; and he agreed with us that it was best that she should be removed and offered to be at the cost of her schooling. The bills were sent to me from time to time as they became due, a part of them through Mrs. Tilton. Previous to her going away she wrote the following letters to Mrs. Tilton—marked "W" and "X"—and they were sent to me by Mrs. T. as part of these transactions:—

BROOKLYN, Jan. 10th, 1871.

MY DEAR MRS. TILTON:—I want to tell you something. Your mother, Mrs. Morse, has repeatedly attempted to hire me, by offering me dresses and presents, to go to certain persons and tell them *stories* injurious to the character of your husband. I have been persuaded that the kind intentions shown me by Mr. Tilton for years were dishonorable demonstrations. I never, at the time, thought that Mr. Tilton's caresses were for such a purpose. I do not want to be made use of by Mrs. Morse or any one else to bring trouble on my two best friends, you and your husband. Bye by.

******

These notes are in Mrs. Tilton's handwriting and on the same paper used by her in correspondence with me.

JANUARY 12th.

MY DEAR MRS. TILTON:—The story that Mr. Tilton once lifted me from my bed and *carried* me screaming to his own, and attempted to violate my person is a wicked lie. Yours truly, ******

While this young lady was at school she did inform a friend of Mrs. Tilton, Mrs. P., of the stories of the family relations. These stories were written to Brooklyn, and came to the knowledge of my friends, creating an impression upon their minds unfavorable to Mr. Tilton, and might possibly lead to the reopening of the scandal. I therefore took pains to trace them back, and found that they came from Mrs. P., to whom the schoolgirl had told them. I therefore called upon Tilton and asked if these stories could not be stopped. Soon afterward he produced to me a letter, dated the 8th of November, 1872, written by Mrs. Tilton, with a note to me on the back thereof, to disabuse Mrs. P.'s mind as to the girl's disclosures. The letter is here produced, marked "Y:"—

BROOKLYN, Nov. 8th, 1872.

MY DEAR MRS. P.:—I come to you in this fearful extremity, burdened by my misfortunes, to claim your promised sympathy and love. * * * I have mistakenly felt obliged to deceive ****** these two years, that my husband had made false accusations against me *which he never has to her or any one.*

In order that he may not appear on his defence, thus adding the terrible exposure of a lawsuit, will you implore silence on her part against any indignation which she may feel against him; for the one only ray of light and hope in this midnight gloom is his entire sympathy and co-operation in my behalf.

A word from you to Mr. D*** will change any unfriendly spirit which dear mother may have given him against my husband.

You know I have no mother's heart, that will look charitably upon all, save you. Affectionately, your child, ELIZABETH.

Of course you will destroy this letter.

TUESDAY, Jan. 18th, 1872.

DEAR FRANCIS:—Be kind enough to send me $50 for ******. I want to enclose it in to-morrow's mail. Yours gratefully, ELIZABETH.

Also, I produced—out of the order of time—a letter of Mrs. Tilton, marked "Y 2," sent to me a year afterwards for money for the purpose of paying this young person's school expenses, and also a statement of accounts and letters of transmission, and note acknowledging receipt for quarter ending June, 1871, from the principal of that school, marked "Z 1" and "Z 2." All these sums were paid by Beecher, and I forwarded the money to settle them through Mrs. Tilton, or sent the money directly to the principal of the school at her request:—

STATEMENT OF ACCOUNT.

——— FEMALE SEMINARY.

Miss ****** ******

To ******		Dr.
For boarding		$76 50
For tuition, primary class		10 80
For washing		7 23
For fire (two months)		4 00
For music (double lessons), $36; use piano, $4 50		40 50
For advanced items—		
Books and stationery	$4 14	
Music	5 10	
Physician and medicine	6 00	
Seat in church	1 00—	16 24
Amount		$155 27

June, 1871.

———, June 8th, 1871.

MRS. TILTON:—I send you with this a statement of Miss ******'s bill for the past half school year.

****** is doing very well in her studies, and is quite a favorite with us.

Sometimes she is not very well, but I think, on the whole, her health is improving.

Could you not come and make us a visit and bring Mr. Tilton with you? A little rest would do you both good. Very respectfully yours,

——— ———.

****** is making very good progress in music and in some of her common branches, as arithmetic, geography and spelling.

——— SEMINARY, Dec. 18th, 1873.

F. D. MOULTON, Esq. :—

DEAR SIR :—Yours containing check for $200 in full for Miss ******'s school bill is received. This pays all her indebtedness to this date. Very truly yours, ——— ———.

Beecher was very anxious to ascertain, through me, the exact condition of Tilton's feelings towards him, and how far the reconciliation was real, and to get a statement in writing that would seem to free him (Beecher) from imputation thereafter. I more than once applied to Tilton to get a statement of his feelings towards Beecher, and received from him, on the 7th of February, 1871, the following letter, which I produce, marked "A A:"—

BROOKLYN, Feb. 7th, 1871.

MY VERY DEAR FRIEND :—In several conversations with me you have asked about my feelings toward Mr. Beecher, and yesterday you said the time had come when you would like to receive from me an expression of them in writing. I say, therefore, very cheerfully, that, notwithstanding the great suffering which he has caused to Elizabeth and myself, I bear him no malice, shall do him no wrong, shall discountenance every project (by whomsoever proposed) for any exposure of his secret to the public, and (if I know myself at all) shall endeavor to act toward Mr. Beecher as I would have him in similar circumstances act toward me.

I ought to add that your own good offices in this case have led me to a higher moral feeling than I might otherwise have reached. Ever yours affectionately, THEODORE TILTON.

TO FRANK MOULTON.

From that time everything was quiet. Nothing occurred to mar the harmony existing between Tilton and Beecher, or the kindly relations between Tilton and Mrs. Tilton, during the summer of 1871, except idle gossip which floated about the city of Brooklyn, and sometimes was hinted at in the newspapers, but which received no support in any facts known to the gossiper or the writer, or through any communication of Mr.

or Mrs. Tilton or Mr. Beecher. And I received no letters from Beecher alluding to this subject upon any topic until his return, on the 30th September, from his vacation, showing that in fact the settlement was enabling him to regain his health and spirits. I produce this note, marked "B B:"—

SATURDAY, September 30th, 1871.

MY DEAR FRIEND:—I feel bad not to meet you. My heart warms to you, and you might have known that I should be here, if you loved me as much as I do you. Well, it's an inconstant world! Soberly, I should be glad to have you see how hearty I am, ready for work and hoping for a bright year.

I have literally done *nothing* for three months, but have "gone to grass." Things seem almost strange to come back among men and see business going on in earnest.

I will be here on Monday at ten A. M. I am, my dear Frank, truly and gratefully yours, HENRY WARD BEECHER.

Taking advantage of this lull in the controversy it may be as convenient here as anywhere to state the relations of Mrs. Tilton to the matter and her acts toward the several parties. I shall be pardoned if I do it with care, because my statement, unhappily for us both, must be diametrically opposite to one published as hers. I had been on terms very familiar, visiting at Mr. Tilton's house. I had seen and known Mrs. Tilton well and kindly on my part, and I believed wholly so on hers, and, as I have before stated, I had never known or suspected or seen any exhibition of inharmony between her and her husband during those many familiar visits, and of course I had no suspicion of infidelity upon the part of either toward the other. The first intimation of it which came to me was in the exhibition of her original confession, of which I have before spoken. The first time I saw that confession was on the 30th of December, 1870. The first communication I had from Mrs. Tilton after I had read her confession on the Friday evening, as before stated, was on the next morning, the 31st of December, 1870, the date being fixed by the fact cited in her letter showing that she gave her retraction to Beecher on the evening previous. The letter from her is as follows, marked "C C:"—

SATURDAY MORNING.

MY DEAR FRIEND FRANK:—I want you to do me the greatest possible favor. My letter which you have and the one I gave Mr. Beecher at his dictation last evening ought both to be destroyed.

Please bring both to me and I will burn them. Show this note to Theodore and Mr. Beecher. They will see the propriety of this request. Yours truly, E. R. TILTON.

I could not, of course, accede to this request of Mrs. Tilton, because I had pledged myself to Beecher that her retraction on the one side and her confession to Tilton on the other—which are the papers she refers to as "my letter which you have and the one I gave Mr. Beecher"—should not be given up, but should be held for the protection of either as against the other.

I learned in my interview with Beecher on the 1st day of January, 1871, that he had been told by his wife and others that Mrs. Tilton desired a separation from her husband on account of his supposed infidelities to her, and that Mrs. Tilton had applied to Mrs. Beecher for advice upon that subject. This being the first I had heard of asserted infidelity of Tilton to his marriage vows, either the next day or second day after I asked Mrs. Tilton if it were so and if she had ever desired a separation from her husband on that or any other account—wishing to assure myself of the facts upon which I was to act as mediator and arbitrator between the parties. She stated to me that she had not desired a separation from her husband, but that application had been made to Mr. and Mrs. Beecher through her mother, upon her own responsibility, to bring it about, and on the 4th day of January she sent me the following letter, which, although dated January 4th, 1870, was actually written January 4th, 1871, and dated 1870, as is a common enough mistake by most persons at the beginning of a new year. But it bears internal evidence of the time of its date, and also I know that I received it at that time, it being impossible that it should have been a year previous. I produced it, marked "DD:"—

No. 174 LIVINGSTON STREET,
BROOKLYN, Jan. 17th, 1870 (?).

Mr. FRANCIS D. MOULTON:—

MY DEAR FRIEND:—In regard to your question whether I have ever sought a separation from my husband, I indignantly deny that *such was ever the fact*, as I have denied it a hundred times before. The story that I wanted a separation was a deliberate falsehood, coined by my poor mother, who said she would bear the responsibility of this and other statements she might make, and communicated to my husband's enemy, Mrs. H. W. Beecher, and by her communicated to Mr. Bowen. *I feel outraged* by the whole proceeding, and am now suffering in consequence more than I am able to bear. I am yours, very truly,

ELIZABETH R. TILTON.

As bearing upon this topic of her husband's infidelity and her desire for separation, I produce another letter, dated January 13th, 1871, written by Mrs. Tilton, and addressed to the person whose name I have hitherto and still suppress, as the one with whom Bowen had alleged an improper connection with Tilton, and because of which improper connection Beecher had been informed Mrs. Tilton was unhappy and desired the separation. It is marked "EE":—

174 LIVINGSTON STREET,
BROOKLYN, Jan. 13th, 1871.

MY DEAR FRIEND AND SISTER:—I was made very glad by your letter, for your love to me is most grateful, and for which I actually hunger. You, like me, have loved and been loved, and can say with Mrs. Browning:—

"Well enough I think we've fared,
My heart and I."

But I find in you an element to which I respond; when or how I am not philosopher enough of the human mind to understand. I cannot reason—only feel.

I wrote to you a reply on the morning of my sickness, and tinged with fears of approaching disaster, so that when mail day arrived I was safely over my sufferings, with a fair prospect of returning health. I destroyed it lest its morbid tone might shadow your spirit. I am now around my house again, doing very poorly what I want to do well. All these ambitions and failures you know, darling, and when, in your last letter to Theodore—those good, true letters—you tell indirectly of your life with your parents, I caught and felt the self-sacrifice, admired and sincerely appreciated your rare qualities of heart and mind. I am a more demonstrative and enthusiastic lover of *God* manifested in his children than you will believe, and my memories of you fill me with admiration and delight. I have caught up your card picture which we have, in such moments and kissed it again and again, praying, with tears, for God's blessing to follow you and to perfect in us three the beautiful promise of our nature. But, my sweet and dear ——, I realize in these months of our acquaintance how almost impossible it is to *bring out* these blossoms of our heart's growth—God's gifts to us—to human eyes. Our pearls and flowers are caught up literally by vulgar and base minds that surround us on every side, and so destroyed or abused that we know them no longer as our own, and thus God is made our only hope.

My dear, dear sister, do not let us disappoint each other. I expect much from you—you do of me. Not in the sense of draining or weariness to body or spirit—but trust and faith in human hearts. Does it not exist between us? I believe it! My husband has suffered much with me in a cruel conspiracy made by my poor suffering mother, with an energy worthy of a better cause—to divorce us by saying that *I* was seeking it because of Theodore's infidelity, making *her* feelings *mine*.

These slanders have been sown broadcast. I am quoted everywhere as the author of them. Coming in this form and way to Mr. Bowen they caused his immediate dismission from both the *Independent* and *Union*. Suffering thus, both of us, so unjustly—(I knew nothing of these plans)—anxiety night and day brought on my miscarriage; a disappointment I have never before known—a *love babe* it promised, you know. I have had sorrow almost beyond human capacity dear ——. It is my mother! That will explain volumes to your filial heart. Theodore has many secret enemies, I find, besides my mother, but with a faithfulness renewed and strengthened by experience *we* will, by silence, time and patience, be victorious over them all. My faith and hope are very bright, now that I am off the sick-bed, and dear Frank Moulton is a friend indeed. (He is managing the case with Mr. Bowen.) We have weathered the storm, and, I believe, without harm to our *Best*. "Let not your heart be troubled," dear sweet—I love you. Be assured of it. I wish I could come to you. I would help you in the care of your loved ones, for *that* I can do. "My heart bounds toward all." Then your spirit would be free to write and think.

But hereunto I am not called. My spirit is willing. My dear children are all well. Floy, on her return at the holiday vacation, found me sick, and we concluded to keep her with us, and she has entered the Packer. Our household has, indeed, been sadly tossed about, and the children suffer with the parents; but *the end has come*, and I write that you may have joy and not grief, for that is past! I am glad you love Alice. I have kissed her for you many times. I will teach all my darlings to love you and welcome your home-coming. Ralph is a fine, beautiful boy, and to be our only baby—very precious, therefore. Carroll is visiting Theodore's parents at Keyport. I hope your mother is now better and that you have reached the sunshine. Our spirits cannot thrive in nature's gloom. Give much love to your parents. I am yours, faithfully and fondly,

SISTER ELIZABETH.

This letter requires a word of explanation. It will be observed that in the course of the correspondence between Bowen and Beecher there had been claimed infidelities on the part of Tilton with a certain lady whose name is not disclosed, although well known to all the parties, and much of the accusations against Tilton connected him with that lady, and it was averred that they came from his wife. The above letter was written to that lady long after the accusations had been made against Tilton, and after they had been communicated to his wife, and I bring it in here as bearing on the question whether Mrs. Tilton desired a separation from her husband, as had been alleged, on account of his infidelities with this lady.

I have already stated that I had, as a necessary precaution to the peace of the family and the parties interested, interdicted all the parties from having communication with each other—except the husband and wife—unless that communication was known to me, and the letters sent through me or shown to me. Mr. Tilton and Mr. Beecher, as I have before stated, both faithfully complied with their promise in that regard, so far as I know, I was away sick in the spring of 1871, as before stated, and went to Florida. Soon after my return Beecher placed in my hands an unsigned letter from Mrs. Tilton, in her handwriting, undated, but marked in his handwriting, "Received March 8th, 1871." I here produce it, marked "FF."

WEDNESDAY.

MY DEAR FRIEND:—Does your heart bound *towards all* as it used? So does mine! I am myself again. I did not dare to tell you till I was sure; but the bird has sung in my heart these *four* weeks, and he has covenanted with me never again to leave. "Spring has come."* Because I thought it would gladden you to know this, and not to trouble or embarrass you in *any way* I now write. Of course I should like to share with you my joy; but can wait for the Beyond!

When dear Frank says I may once again go to old Plymouth, I will thank the dear Father.

Such a communication from Mrs. Tilton to her pastor, under the circumstances and her promise, seemed to me to be a breach of good faith. But desirous to have the peace kept, and hoping if unanswered it might not be repeated, I did not show it to Tilton or inform him of its existence.

On Friday, April 21st, 1871, Mr. Beecher received another letter, of that date, unsigned, from Mrs. Tilton, which he gave to me. It is here produced, marked "GG," as follows:—

FRIDAY, April 21st, 1871.

MR. BEECHER:—As Mr. Moulton has returned will you use your influence to have the papers in his possession destroyed? My heart bleeds night and day at the injustice of their existence.

As I could not comply with this request, for reasons before stated, I did not show this letter to Tilton, nor did I call Mrs. Tilton's attention to it.

On the 3d of May, Mr. Beecher handed me still another letter, unsigned, but in Mrs. Tilton's handwriting, of that date, which is here produced. marked "HH":—

BROOKLYN, May 3d, 1871.

MR. BEECHER:—My future either for life or death would be happier could I but feel that you *forgive* while you forget me. In all the sad complications of the past year my endeavor was to entirely keep from *you* all suffering; to bear myself alone, leaving you forever ignorant of it. My weapons were love, a large untiring generosity and *nest hiding!* That I failed utterly we both know. But now I ask forgiveness.

The contents of this letter were so remarkable that I queried within my own mind whether I ought not to show it to Tilton; but as I was assured by Beecher, and verily believed, and now believe, that they were unanswered by him, I thought it best to retain it in my own possession, as I have done until now. But, from the hour of its reception, what remained of faith in Mrs. Tilton's character for truth or propriety of conduct was wholly lost, and from that time forth I had no thought or care for her reputation only so far as it affected that of her children.

After this I do not know that anything occurred between myself and Mrs. Tilton of pertinence to this inquiry, or more than the ordinary courtesies or civilities when I called at her house, and I received no other communication from her until shortly before the question of the arbitration of the business between Bowen and Tilton was determined upon. I had learned that Mrs. Tilton had been making declarations which were sullying the reputation of her husband, and giving it to be understood that her home was not a happy one, because of the want of religious sympathy between herself and her husband, and because he did not accompany her to church as regularly and as often as she thought he ought to do, and she thought it would be well for the children to do, and sometimes speaking of her unhappiness, without defining specially the cause, thus leaving for the busybodies and intermeddlers to infer causes of unhappiness which she did not state. I thought it my duty to the parties to caution her in that regard, and I said to her that I thought she ought not, in the presence of others, to upbraid her husband with their differences in religious feeling or opinions, and that it was not well for her to make any statement which should show her home unhappy, or that she was unhappy in it, because it might lead to such inquiries as might break it up, as well as the settlement, which she was so desirous to maintain for the sake of both families—Mrs. Beecher's and her own.

This conversation drew from her the following letter, marked "H":—

SUNDAY MORNING, Feb. 11th, 1872.

MY DEAR FRIEND FRANCIS:—All the week I have sought opportunity to write you, but as I cannot work in the cars as Theodore does, and the time at our stopping places must be necessarily given to rest, eating and sight-seeing, saying nothing of lecture-going, I have failed to come to you before.

It was given to you to reveal to me last Sabbath evening two things (for which God bless you abundantly with his peace). First, the truth that until then I had never seen nor felt, namely, *whenever* I remembered *myself* in conversing with others to the shadowing of Theodore I became his *enemy!* And the second truth was that *I* hindered the *reconstruction more than any one else.*

Whenever I become convinced I know I am immovable. Henceforth silence has locked my lips and the key is cast into the depths. Theo. need fear me no longer, for I would be the enemy of no one.

I have not been equal to the great work of the past year. All I have done is to cause the *utter misery* of those I love best—my mother, husband, Mr. B. and my dear children.

But how greatly I prize your counsel and criticisms you will never know. You do not at all terrify me, only convince, and I bless you.

Pardon this hasty line, which I'm sure you'll do, since you forgive so much else. Good night. Affectionately, ELIZABETH.

After the signing of the tripartite covenant, April 2d, 1872, Tilton desired that I should return him the paper containing his wife's confession, in order, as he said, to relieve her anxiety as to its possibly falling into wrong hands, and she was very desirous that this paper should be destroyed. As I held it solely for her protection, and under pledge to him, I gave it to him, and he told me afterwards that he gave it into her hands and that she destroyed it. She also confirmed this statement.

Some time after that—it is impossible for me to fix the date precisely—I learned from Beecher that Mrs. Tilton had told him that when she made her confession to her husband of her infidelity with him (Beecher) her husband had made a like confession to her of his own infidelities with several other women. This being an entirely new statement of fact to me, and never having heard Mrs. Tilton, in all my conversations with her, although she had admitted freely her own sexual intercourse with Beecher, make any claims that her husband had confessed his infidelity, or that he had been unfaithful to her, I was considerably surprised at this intimation made at so late a period, and I brought it to the attention of Tilton, in the form of a very strong criticism of his course towards me, that he had kept back so important a fact, which might have made a great difference as to the course that ought to be taken. Tilton promptly, and with much feeling, denied that he had ever made any such confession, or that his wife ever claimed that he had, and desired me to see Mrs. Tilton, and satisfy myself upon that point; and he went immediately with me to his house, that I might see Mrs. Tilton before he should have the opportunity to see her, after he had learned the alleged fact. We went to the house together and found her in the back parlor. On our way to the house Tilton said to me:—"Frank, what is the use of my trying to keep the family together when this sort of thing is being all the time said against me? You are all the time telling me that I must keep the peace, and forget and forgive, while these stories are being circulated to my prejudice." On arriving at the house I asked Mrs. Tilton to step into the front parlor, where we two were alone. I then put the question to her:—"Elizabeth, did you tell Mr. Beecher that when you made your confession to your husband of your infidelity with Beecher, your husband at the same time made a confession to you of his own infidelity with other women?" I said, "I want to know if this is true for my own satisfaction." She answered, "Yes." I then stepped with her into the back parlor, where her husband was waiting, and I said to him, "Your wife says that she did tell Beecher that you confessed your infidelity with other women, at the time she made her confession to you." Elizabeth immediately said, "Why, no, I didn't tell you so. I could not have understood your question, because it isn't true that Theodore ever made any such confession, and I didn't state it to Mr. Beecher, because it is not true."

I was very much shocked and surprised at the denial, but of course could say nothing more, and did say nothing more upon that subject, and left and went home. The next morning I received the following letter from Mrs. Tilton without date, so, that I am unable to give the exact date of this transaction; but I know it was after the tripartrite covenant. The letter is here produced and marked "JJ.":—

DEAR FRANCIS:—I did not tell you *two* falsehoods at your last visit. At first I entirely misunderstood your question, thinking you had reference to the interview at your house the day before. But when I intelligently replied to you, I *replied falsely*. I will now put myself on record truthfully.

I told Mr. B. that at the time of my confession T. *had* made similar confessions to me himself, *but no developments as to persons*. When you then asked, for your own satisfaction, "Was it so?" I told my second lie. After you had left I said to T., "You know I was obliged to lie to Frank, and I now say, rather than make others suffer as I *now do*, I must lie; for it is a physical impossibility for me to tell the truth."

Yet I do not think, Francis, had not T.'s angry, troubled face been before me, I would have told you the truth.

I am a perfect coward in his presence, not from any fault of his, perhaps, but from long years of timidity.

I implore you, as this is a side issue, to be careful not to lead me into further temptation.

You may show this to T. or Mr. B. or any one. An effort made for truth. Wretchedly, ELIZABETH.

This letter was wholly unsatisfactory to me, because nothing had occurred the day previous in which she could possibly have referred. After the publication, on the 2d day of November, 1872, in *Woodhull and Claflin's Weekly*, of the story of Tilton and Beecher's conduct in relation to Mrs. Tilton, and as my name was mentioned in the article as one possessing peculiar knowledge upon the whole subject, I was continually asked by my acquaintances, and even by strangers, upon their ascertaining who I was, whether that publication was true; and I found great difficulty in making an answer. A refusal on my part to answer would have been taken to be a confession of the truth of the charges. Therefore, when people inquired who had no right to my confidence, I answered them in such phrase as, without making a direct statement, would lead them to infer that the charges could not be sustained.

In some cases I doubt not that the inquirers supposed that I, in fact, denied their truth; but upon that point I was very studious not directly to commit myself. Finding that my very silence was working injury to the cause of the suppression of the scandal, I told Tilton that I wished to be authorized by his wife to deny it.

I thought it certainly could not possibly be true to the extent, and in the circumstances with the breadth, in which it was stated in that newspaper. Soon after I received the following paper, without date, from Mrs. Tilton, which is produced and marked "KK":—

Mr. Moulton:—

My Dear Friend:—For my husband's sake and my children's, I hereby testify, with all my woman's soul, that I am innocent of the crime of impure conduct alleged against me. I have been to my husband a true wife; in his love I wish to live and die. My early affection for him still burns with its maiden flame; *all the more* for what he has borne for my sake—both private and public wrongs. His plan to keep back scandals long ago threatened against me I never approved, and the result shows it unavailing; but few would have risked so much as he has sacrificed for others ever since the conspiracy began against him, two years ago.

Having had power to strike others, he has forborne to use it, and allowed himself to be injured instead. No wound is so great to me as the imputation that he is among my accusers. I bless him every day for his faith in me, which swerves not, and for standing my champion against all my accusers.

Elizabeth R. Tilton.

Upon the strength of that I thereafterwards said that Mrs. Tilton denied the story. About the 16th of December, 1872, Mr. Carpenter and Dr. Storrs undertook to look up the reports, with the intention, as I understood, of advising some public statement, or as being concerned in some investigation of the matter, and Mrs. Tilton wrote for them the following paper bearing that date, which I produce marked "LL":—

December 16th, 1872.

In July, 1870, prompted by my duty, I informed my husband that Mr. H. W. Beecher, my friend and pastor, had solicited me to be a wife to him, together with all that this implied. Six months afterwards my husband felt impelled by the circumstances of a conspiracy against him, in which Mrs. Beecher had taken part, to have an interview with Mr. Beecher.

In order that Mr. B. might know exactly what I had said to my husband, I wrote a brief statement (I have forgotten in what form), which my husband showed to Mr. Beecher. Late the same evening Mr. B. came to me (lying very sick at the time) and filled me with distress, saying I had ruined him, and wanting to know if I meant to appear against him. This I certainly did not mean to do, and the thought was agonizing to me. I then signed a paper which he wrote, to clear him in case of a trial. In this instance, as in most others when absorbed by one great interest or feeling, the harmony of my mind is entirely disturbed, and I found on reflection that this paper was so drawn as to place me most unjustly against my husband and on the side of Mr. Beecher. So in order to repair so cruel a blow to my long suffering husband, I wrote an explanation of the first paper and my signature. Mr. Moulton procured from Mr. B. the statement which I gave to him in my agitation and excitement, and now holds it.

This ends my connection with the case. ELIZABETH R. TILTON.

P. S.—This statement is made at the request of Mr. Carpenter, that it may be shown confidentially to Dr. Storrs and other friends with whom my husband and I are consulting.

This paper was delivered to me, and the theory of the confession then was that Mr. and Mrs. Tilton should admit no more than the solicitation; but that endeavor to make an explanation of the business fell through, and after it was shown to those interested, as I was told, the paper remained with me.

I received no further communication from Mrs. Tilton until the 25th of June of this year (1874), and that communication came to me in this wise. When Tilton showed me his Dr. Bacon's letter I most strongly and earnestly advised against its publication, and said to him in substance, that, while I admitted the wrong and injustice of Dr. Bacon's charges, that he (Mr. T.) had lived by the magnanimity of Beecher, and that he was a dog and a knave, when I believed he had acted a proper and manly part in endeavoring to shield his family, yet that its publication would so stir the public mind that an investigation would be forced upon him and Beecher in some manner which I could not then foresee, and that the truth would in all probability have to come out, or so much of it that Mrs. Tilton and Beecher would be dishonored and destroyed, and he himself be subjected to the severest criticism. Notwithstanding my advice, he was so wrought up with the continued assaults upon him by the friends of Beecher that he determined on the publication of the letter.

He said to me, in substance, that as the course I had advised in the matter in regard to the church investigation had been so completely set aside by Beecher's friends, and they had so far ignored all propositions coming from me as to the best mode of disposing of the matter, they evidently did not any longer intend to be guided by my counsel or wishes; and if Beecher and his friends set me aside in the matter, he (Mr. T.) could see no reason why he should any longer yield to my entreaties or follow my lead. The only modification that I was able to get of the Bacon letter was this:—It originally read that Beecher had committed against him and his family "a revolting crime.

I insisted that that should be changed into "an offence committed against me," which was done, and the letter was published in that form.

The reasons which actuated me to require this change by Tilton in his letter were in the hope that reconciliation and peace might still be possible. As the letter as amended would state an offence only, and also that an apology sufficient in the mind of Tilton had been made for that offence, if Beecher, in reply to the Bacon letter, should come out and state that it was true he had committed an offence against Tilton for which he had made the most ample apology, which had been accepted by Tilton as satisfactory, and as the matter was nobody's business but that of the parties interested, he would never become a party to any investigation of the subject, and that Tilton had acted not unjustly or unfairly toward him in what he had done; that in such case the affair might possibly have been quieted and peace maintained. But if the words "revolting crime" remained in the letter all hope of reconciliation or escaping the fullest investigation would be impossible. After the publication of that letter I so advised Mr. Beecher, his friends and counsel, but that advice was unheeded; and I also gave Mr. Beecher the same advice at a consultation with him for which he asked in a letter, which will hereafter in its proper place be produced. Some days subsequent to this advice of mine to Tilton, I received the following letter, of date June 25th, 1874, from Mrs. Tilton, which is the last communication I have had with or from her on the subject. It is herewith produced, and marked "MM":—

June 25th, 1874.

MR. MOULTON:—It is fitting I should make quick endeavor to undo my injustice toward you.

I learned from Theodore last night that you greatly opposed the publication of his statement to Dr. Bacon. I had coupled you with Mr. Carpenter as advising it.

Forgive me, and accept my gratitude. ELIZ. R. TILTON.

Having now placed before the committee my statement of the facts concerning Mrs. Tilton and the documentary evidence that I have to support them, and as they are diametrically opposed to nearly all that Mrs. Tilton appears to declare in her published statement, I deem it my duty to myself and my position in this terrible business to say that during this affair Mrs. Tilton has more than once admitted to me and to another person to my knowledge—whom I do not care to bring into this controversy—the fact of her sexual relations with Beecher, and she never has once denied them other than in the written papers prepared for a purpose which I have already exhibited; but, on the contrary, the fact of such criminal intercourse being well understood by Beecher, Tilton and Mrs. Tilton to have taken place, my whole action in the matter was based upon the existence of that fact, and was an endeavor, faithfully carried out by me in every way possible, to protect the families of both parties from the consequences of a public disclosure of Mrs. Tilton's admitted infidelities to her husband.

I now return to the documentary evidence, and the necessary explanations thereof, which I have of the condition of the affair as regards Beecher himself, after the fall of 1871, as disconnected with the affair of Bowen, which I have already explained. At about this time I received the following letter, marked "MM 2":—

NO. 15 EAST THIRTY-EIGHTH STREET, 19th, 11th, 1871.

REV. H. W. BEECHER:—

DEAR SIR:—For reasons in which *you* are deeply interested as well as myself, and the cause of truth, I desire to have an interview with you, without fail, at some hour to-morrow. Two of your sisters have gone out of their way to assail my character and purposes, both by the means of the public press and by numerous private letters written to various persons with whom they seek to injure me and thus to defeat the political ends at which I aim.

You doubtless know that it is in my power to strike back, and in ways more disastrous than anything that can come to me; but I do not desire to do this. I simply desire justice from those from whom I have a right to expect it; and a reasonable course on your part will assist me to it. I speak guardedly, but I think you will understand me. I repeat that I must have an interview to-morrow, since I am to speak to-morrow evening at Steinway Hall, and what I shall or shall not say will depend largely upon the result of the interview. Yours very truly,

VICTORIA C. WOODHULL.

P. S.—Please return answer by bearer.

The foregoing letter occasioned Mr. Tilton much anxiety lest Mrs. Woodhull, in proceeding against Mr. Beecher and his sisters, would thereby involve Mrs. Tilton.

Accordingly, knowing that Mr. Beecher and Mrs. Woodhull were to have an interview at my house on the next day, he came to it uninvited, and urged Mr. Beecher to preside on that evening at Steinway Hall. After Mrs. W. left Tilton repeated this urgency to Beecher.

On that evening I went to Steinway Hall with Tilton, and, finding no one there to preside, Tilton volunteered to preside himself, which, I believe, had the effect of preventing Mrs. Woodhull's proposed attack on the Beecher family at that time. On the 30th of December, 1871, Mrs. Woodhull also sent a letter to Beecher desiring that he would speak at a woman's suffrage convention in Washington, to be held on the 10th, 11th and 12th of January following. That letter Beecher forwarded to me, with the following note of date the 2d of January, 1872, herewith produced and marked "NN:"—

BROOKLYN, TUESDAY EVENING, January 2d, 1872.

MY DEAR MOULTON:—1. I send you V. W.'s letter to me and a reply which I submit to your judgment. Tell me what you think. Is it too long? Will she use it for publishing? I do not wish to have it so used. I do not mean to speak on the platform of *either* of the two suffrage societies. What influence I exert I prefer to do on my own hook; and I do not mean to *train* with either party, and it will not be fair to press me in where I do not wish to go. But I leave it for *you*. Judge for me. I have leaned on you hitherto, and never been sorry for it.

2. I was mistaken about the *Ch. Union* coming out so early that I could not get a notice of *G. Age* in it. It was *just the other way*, to be delayed, and I send you a rough proof of the first page, and the *Star* article.

In the paper to-morrow a line or so will be inserted to soften a little the touch about the *Lib. Christian.*

3. Did you think I ought to keep a *copy* of any letters to V. W.? Do you think it would be better to write it again, and not say so much? Will you keep the letter to me, and send the other if you judge it wise?

4. Will you send a line to my house *in the morning* saying what you conclude?

I am full of company.

Yours truly and affectionately, H. W. B.

There is a paragraph in this note which needs a word of explanation. I had advised Beecher, in order that he might show that there was no unkindly feeling between him and Tilton, to publish in the *Christian Union* a reference to the *Golden Age*. He agreed to do so; but instead of that he had a notice which I thought was worse than if he had said nothing, and the allusion in the second paragraph of this letter is to a letter which I had written to Beecher upon the two topics—this and Mrs. Woodhull.

A retained copy of my letter I herewith submit, marked "OO:"—

My Dear Sir:—First with reference to Mrs. Woodhull's letter and your answer; I think that you would have done better to accept the invitation to speak in Washington, but if lecture interferes your letter in reply is good enough, and will bear publication.

With relation to your notice of the *Golden Age* I tell you frankly, as your friend, that I am ashamed of it, and would rather you had written nothing. Your early associations with and present knowledge of the man who edits that paper are grounds upon which you might have so written that no reader would have doubted that in your opinion Theodore Tilton's public and private integrity was unquestionable. If the article had been written to compliment the *Independent* it would receive my unqualified approval.

On the 5th of February, 1872, I received from Mr. Beecher the letter which I here produce, of that date, and marked "PP:"—

Monday, Feb. 5th, 1872.

My Dear Friend:—I leave town to-day, and expect to pass through from Philadelphia to New Haven. Shall not be here till Friday.

About three weeks ago I met T. in the cars going to B. He was kind. We talked much. At the end he told me to go on with my work without the least anxiety, in so far as his feelings and actions were the occasion of apprehension.

On returning home from New Haven (where I am three days in the week, delivering a course of lectures to the theological students), I found a note from *E.* saying that *T.* felt hard toward me, and was going to see or write me before leaving for the West.

She kindly added, "Do not be cast down. I bear this almost always, but the God in whom we trust will *deliver us all safely*. I know you do and are willing abundantly to help him, and I also know your embarrassments." These were words of warning, but also of consolation, for I believe E. is beloved of God, and that her prayers for me are sooner heard than mine for myself or for her. But it seems that a change has come to T. since I saw him in the cars. Indeed, ever since he has felt more intensely the force of feeling in society, and the humiliations which environ his enterprise, he has growingly felt that I had a power to help which I did not develop, and I believe that you have participated in this feeling. It is natural you should. T. is dearer to you than *I* can be. He is with you. All his trials are open to your eye daily. But I see you but seldom, and my personal relations, environments, necessities, limitations, dangers and perplexities you cannot see or imagine. If I had not gone through this great *year of sorrow*, I would not have believed that any one could pass through my experience and be *alive* or *sane*. I have been the centre of three distinct circles, each one of which required clearmindedness and peculiarly inventive or originating power, viz :—

1.—The *great* church.

2.—The *newspaper*.

3.—The *book*.

The first I could neither get out of nor slight. The *sensitiveness* of so many of my people would have made any appearance of trouble or any remission of force an occasion of alarm and notice and have excited, when it was important that rumors should die and everything be quieted.

The newspaper I did roll off, doing but little except give general directions, and in so doing I was continually spurred and exhorted by those in interest. It could not be helped.

The "Life of Christ," long delayed, had locked up the capital of the firm, and was likely to sink them—finished it *must* be. Was ever book born of such sorrow as that was? The interior history of it will never be written.

During all this time, *you*, literally, were all my *stay and comfort*. I should have fallen on the way but for the courage which you inspired and the hope which you breathed.

My vacation was profitable. I came back, hoping that the bitterness of death was passed. But T.'s troubles brought back the cloud, with even severer suffering. For all this fall and winter I have felt that you did not feel satisfied with me, and that I seemed, both to you and T., as contenting myself with a cautious or sluggish policy, willing to save myself but not to risk anything for T. I have again and again probed my heart to see whether I was truly liable to such feeling, and the response is unequivocal that I am not. No man can see the difficulties that environ me, unless he stands where I do.

To *say* that I have a church on my hands is simple enough; but to have the hundreds and thousands of men pressing me, each one with his keen suspicion, or anxiety, or zeal; to see tendencies which, if not stopped, would break out into ruinous defence of me; to stop them without seeming to do it; to prevent any one questioning me; to meet and allay prejudices against T. which had their beginning years before this; to keep serene, as if I was not alarmed or disturbed; to be cheerful at home and among friends, when I was suffering the torments of the damned; to pass sleepless nights often and yet to come up fresh and full for Sunday. All this may be talked about, but the real thing cannot be understood from the outside, nor its wearing and grinding on the nervous system.

God knows that I have put more thought and judgment and earnest desire into my efforts to prepare a way for T. and E. than ever I did for myself a hundredfold. As to the outside public, I have never lost an opportunity to soften prejudices, to refute falsehoods and to excite kindly feeling among all whom I met. I am thrown among clergymen, public men and generally the makers of public opinion, and I have used every rational endeavor to repair the evils which have been visited upon T., and with increasing success.

But the roots of this prejudice are long. The catastrophe which precipitated him from his place only disclosed feelings that had existed long. Neither he nor you can be aware of the feelings of classes in society, on other grounds than late rumors. I mention this to explain why *I knew* with *absolute* certainty that no mere statement, letter, testimony or affirmation will reach the root of affairs and reinstate them. *Time* and *work will.*

But chronic evil requires *chronic remedies.* If my destruction would place him all right, that shall not stand in the way. I am willing to step down and out. No one can offer more than that. That I do offer. Sacrifice me without hesitation, if you can clearly see your way to his safety and happiness thereby. I do not think that anything would be gained by it. I should be destroyed, but he would not be saved. E. and the children would have their future clouded. In one point of view I could desire the sacrifice on my part. Nothing can possibly be so bad as the horror of great darkness in which I spend much of my time. I look upon death as sweeter faced than any friend I have in the world. Life would be pleasant if I could see that rebuilt which is shattered. But to live on the sharp and ragged edge of anxiety, remorse, fear, despair, and yet to put on all the appearance of serenity and happiness, cannot be endured much longer.

I am wellnigh discouraged. If you, too, cease to trust me—to love me—I am alone; I have not another person in the world to whom I could go.

Well, to God I commit all. Whatever it may be here, it shall be well there. With sincere gratitude for your heroic friendship, and with sincere affection, even though you love me not, I am yours (though unknown to you),

H. W. B.

This letter was to let me know that Elizabeth had written him, contrary to her promise, without my permission, and also to inform me of his fears as to the change in Tilton's mind, and its clear statement of the case as it then stood, cannot be further elucidated by me. On the 25th of March I received a portrait of Titian as a present from Mr. Beecher, with the following note, as a token of his confidence and respect. It is produced, and marked "QQ:"—

My Dear Friend:—I sent on Friday or Saturday a portrait of Titian to the store to you. I hope it may suit you.

I have been doing ten men's work this winter—partly to make up lost time, partly because I live under a cloud, feeling every month that I may be doing my last work, and anxious to make the most of it. When Esau sold his birthright he found "no place for repentance, though he sought it carefully with tears." But I have one abiding comfort. I have known you, and found in you one who has given a new meaning to friendship. As soon as warm days come I want you to go to Peekskill with me.

I am off in an hour for Massachusetts, to be gone all the week.

I am urging forward my second volume of "Life of Christ," for "the night cometh when no man can work."

With much affection and admiration, yours truly, H. W. B.

March 25th, 1872. Monday morning.

After Tilton had written a campaign document against Grant's administration, and in favor of Mr. Greeley's election, Beecher discussed with me the position taken by Tilton. Beecher also gave me a copy of his (Beecher's) speech opening the Grant campaign in Brooklyn. After the speech was delivered he sent me the following note of May 17th, 1872, which I here produce, marked "R R:"—

May 17th, 1872.

My Dear Frank;—I send you the only copy I have of my speech at the Academy of Music on Grant, and have marked the passage that we spoke about last night, and you will see just what I said, and that I argued then just as I do now.

Pray send it back, or I shall be left without a speech!

I read Theodore's on Grant. I do not think it just. It is ably written; it is a case of *grape shot*. *Yet*, I think it will overact; it is too strong—will be likely to produce a feeling among those not already intense, that it is excessive. Yours sincerely and ever, H. W. B.

Don't forget to send back my *speech*.

About the time of this occurrence Beecher and Tilton met at my house on friendly terms. In fact I cannot exhibit better the tone of Tilton's mind in the winter and spring of 1871-72 than to produce here a letter, written to me at that time without date, but I can fix the date as early as that. It is here produced, and marked "S S:"—

HUDSON RIVER RAILROAD, Monday Morning.

MY DEAR FRANK:—I am writing while the train is in motion—which accounts for the apparent drunkenness of this shaken chirography. Mrs. Beecher sits in the next seat. We are almost elbow to elbow in the palace car. She is white haired and looks a dozen years older than when I last had a near view of her. My heart has been full of pity for her, notwithstanding the cruel way in which she has treated my good name. Her face is written over with many volumes of human suffering. I do not think she has been aware of my presence, for she has been absorbed in thought—her eyes rooted to one spot.

A suggestion has occurred to me which I hasten to communicate. She is going to Florida and may never return alive. If I am ever to be vindicated from the slanders which she has circulated, or which Mr. Bowen pretends to have derived from her and Mrs. Morse, why would it not be well to get from her and Mrs. Morse a statement under oath (by such a process as last evening's documents make easy and harmless) of the exact narrations which they made to him and to others.

It would be well to have *them* say what they said before *he* gets a chance to say what they said to *him*. Speak to Mr. Ward about it. Of course I leave the matter wholly to you and him.

I am unusually heavy hearted this morning. My sullen neighbor keeps the dark and lurid past vividly before my mind. If she actually knew the conduct which her priestly husband has been guilty of, I believe she would shed his blood—or perhaps, saving *him*, she would wreak her wrath on his *victims*. There is a look of desperation in her eye to-day as if she were competent to anything bitter or revengeful. But perhaps I misjudge her mind. I hope I do.

I shall not be home till Thursday afternoon instead of morning, as I said—leaving for Washington at nine P. M. that evening. Ever yours,

THEODORE.

On the 3d of June, 1872, Beecher received from Mrs Woodhull the following letter of that date, which I here produce, marked "T T:"—

44 BROAD STREET, June 3d, 1872.

REV. HENRY WARD BEECHER:—

MY DEAR SIR:—The social fight against me being now waged in this city is becoming rather hotter than I can well endure longer, standing unsupported and alone, as I have until now. Within the past two weeks I have been shut out of hotel after hotel, and am now, after having obtained a place in one, hunted down by a set of males and females, who are determined that I shall not be permitted to live even, if they can prevent it.

Now, I want your assistance. I want to be sustained in my position in the Gilsey House, from which I am ordered out and from which I do not wish to go—and all this simply because I am Victoria C. Woodhull, the advocate of social freedom. I have submitted to this persecution just so long as I can endure to; my business, my projects, in fact everything for which I live suffers from it, and it must cease. Will you lend me your aid in this? Yours very truly, VICTORIA C. WOODHULL.

The above letter was sent to me enclosed in note from Beecher of the same date, which is here produced, and marked "UU:"—

MONDAY EVENING, June 3d, 1872.

MY DEAR MR. MOULTON:—Will you answer this? Or will you see that she is to understand that I can do nothing! I certainly shall not, at any and all hazards, take a single step in that direction; and if it brings trouble—it must come.

Please drop me a line to say that all is right—if in your judgment all is right. Truly yours, H. W. B.

This letter of Mrs. Woodhull, together with those before produced asking Beecher to speak at a suffrage convention, are all the letters I have from her to Beecher. To this letter no reply was made.

After the publication of the tripartite covenant by Mr. Wilkeson, which I believe was on the 29th of May, 1873, the story of the troubles between Beecher and Tilton was revived, with many rumors, and those claiming to be friends of Beecher were endeavoring, as Tilton thought, to explain the terms of that covenant in a manner prejudicial to him. Some enemies of Beecher were endeavoring to get some clew to the proofs of the facts at the bottom of these scandals.

After the publication of this "tripartite covenant" was

made, Tilton deemed, from the comments of the press, that the statement reflected upon him, and he desired that in some way Beecher should relieve him from the imputation of having circulated slanderous stories about him without justification, for which he had apologized, and by advice of friends he prepared a card for me to submit to Beecher to have him sign and publish in his vindication. The original card I herewith produce, marked "UU 1":—

A letter written by Theodore Tilton to Henry C. Bowen, dated Brooklyn, January 1st, 1871, narrating charges made by Mr. Bowen against my character, has been made public in a community in which I am a citizen and clergyman, and thrust upon me, by no agency of my own, what I could not with propriety invite for myself—namely, an opportunity to make the following statements:—

1. By the courtesy of Mr. Tilton, that letter was shown to me at the time it was written, and before it was conveyed to Mr. Bowen, two and a half years ago. By legal and other advisers, Mr. Tilton was urged to publish it then, without delay, or a similar statement explaining his sudden collision with Mr. Bowen, and his unexpected retirement as editor of the *Union* and contributor to the *Independent*. But although Mr. Tilton's public standing needed such an explanation to be made, and although he had my free consent to make it, yet he magnanimously refrained from doing so, through an unwillingness to disclose to the public Mr. Bowen's aspersions concerning myself. Mr. Tilton's consideration for my feelings and reputation, thus evinced from the beginning, has continued to the end, and I have never ceased to be grateful to him for an uncommon manliness in accepting wounds to his own reputation for the sake of preventing aspersions on mine.

II. The surreptitious and unauthorized publication last Sunday of Mr. Tilton's letter—a publication made without the knowledge of Mr. Tilton or myself—gives me the right to say that Mr. Bowen long ago retracted his mistaken charges in the following words, under his own hand and seal, dated —— ——, namely:—

III. In addition to Mr. Bowen's voluntary statement above given, I solemnly pronounce the charges to be false, one and all, and to be without any color of reason or foundation in fact.

IV. All my differences with Mr. Bowen, and all temporary misunderstandings between Mr. Tilton and myself, growing out of these, were long ago settled justly, amicably and in the spirit of mutual good will.

HENRY WARD BEECHER.

Beecher felt much aggrieved at this claim upon him by Tilton, feeling that the matter had been all settled, and adjusted, and he answered Tilton's application in this regard by the letter herewith produced, under date of June 1st, marked "UU 2:"—

SUNDAY MORNING, June 1st, 1873.

MY DEAR FRANK:—The whole earth is tranquil and the heaven is serene, as befits one who has about finished his world-life. I could do nothing on Saturday—my head was confused. But a good sleep has made it like a crystal. I have determined to make no more resistance. Theodore's temperament is such that the future, even if temporarily earned, would be absolutely worthless—filled with abrupt charges, and rendering me liable at any hour or day to be obliged to stultify all the devices by which we have saved ourselves. It is only fair that he should know that the publication of the card which he proposes would leave him far worse off than before.

The *agreement* was made after my letter through you was written. He had had it a year. He had condoned his wife's fault. He had enjoined upon me with the utmost earnestness and solemnity not to betray his wife, nor leave his children to a blight. I had honestly and earnestly joined in the purpose. Then this settlement was made and signed by him. It was not my making. He revised his part so that it should wholly suit him, and signed it. It stood unquestioned and unblamed for more than a year. *Then it was published.* Nothing but that. That which he did in private when made public excited him to fury, and he charges me with *making him appear* as one *graciously pardoned by me!* It was his own deliberate act, with which he was perfectly content till others saw it, and then he charges a grievous wrong home on me!

My mind is clear. I am not in haste. I shall write for the public a statement that will bear the light of the judgment day. God will take care of me and mine. When I look on earth it is deep night. When I look to the heavens above I see the morning breaking. But, oh! that I could put in golden letters my deep sense of your faithful, earnest, undying fidelity, your disinterested friendship! Your noble wife, too, has been to me one of God's comforters. It is such as she that renews a waning faith in womanhood. Now, Frank, I would not have you waste any more energy on a hopeless task. With such a man as T. T. there is no possible salvation for any that depend upon him. With a strong nature, he does not know how to govern it. With generous impulses, the undercurrent that rules him is self. With ardent affections, he cannot love long that which does not repay him with admiration and praise. With a strong, theatric nature, he is constantly imposed upon with the idea that a position, a great stroke, a *coup d'état*, is the way to success.

Besides these he has a hundred good things about him, but these named traits make him absolutely unreliable.

Therefore there is no use in further trying. I have a strong feeling upon me, and it brings great peace with it, that I am spending my *last Sunday*, and preaching my last sermon.

Dear, Good God, I thank Thee I am indeed beginning to see rest and triumph. The pain of life is but a moment; the glory of everlasting emancipation is wordless, inconceivable, full of beckoning glory. Oh, my beloved Frank, I shall know you there, and forever hold fellowship with you, and look back and smile at the past. Your loving H. W. B.

Meanwhile charges were preferred against Tilton for the purpose of having him dismissed from Plymouth church. This action, which seemed to threaten the discovery of the facts in regard to the troubles between Beecher and Tilton, annoyed both very much; and I myself feared that serious difficulty would arise therefrom. Upon consultation with Beecher and Tilton I suggested a plan by which that investigation would be rendered unnecessary, which was in substance that a resolution should be passed by the church amending its roll; alleging that Tilton, having voluntarily withdrawn from the church some four years before, therefore the roll should be amended by striking off his name. This course had been suggested to me by Mr. Tilton about a year and a half before in answer to a letter by Beecher, dated December 3d, 1871, marked "UU 3:"—

My Dear Friend:—There are two or three who feel anxious to press action on the case. It will only serve to raise profitless excitement, when we need to have quieting.

There are already complexities enough.

We do not want to run the risk of the complications which, in such a body, no man can foresee and no one control. Once free from a sense of responsibility for *him*, and there would be a strong tendency for kindly feeling to set in, which now is checked by the membership, without attendance, sympathy, or doctrinal agreement.

Since the connection is really formal, and not vital or sympathetic, why should it continue, with all the risk of provoking irritating measures? Every day's reflection satisfies me that this is the course of wisdom, and that T. will be the stronger and B. the weaker for it.

You said that you meant to effect it. Can't it be done promptly? If a letter is written it had better be very short, simply announcing withdrawal, and perhaps with an expression of kind wishes, &c.

You will know. I shall be in town Monday and part of Tuesday. Shall I hear from you?

DECEMBER 3d, 1871.

But when the meeting of the church was held for that purpose it was charged there that Tilton had slandered the pastor. Tilton therefore took the stand and said, in substance, that if he had uttered any slanders against Beecher he was ready to answer them as God was his witness. Beecher thereupon stated that he had no charges to make, and the matter dropped. But when the resolution was passed, instead of being put so as to exonerate Tilton, it was declared in substance that, whereas certain charges had been made against him, and as he pleaded to those charges non-membership, his name be dropped from the roll.

This action of the church very much exasperated Tilton, who thought that Beecher should have prevented such a result, and that he might have done so if he had stood by him fully and fairly as agreed. In that, however, I believe Tilton was mistaken, because Mr. William F. West, who preferred the charges against Tilton, did it against the wish of Beecher and without any consultation with him, as appears by the following letter of June 25th, 1873, produced here, and marked "VV."

NEW YORK, June 25th, 1873.

REV. H. W. BEECHER:—

DEAR SIR:—Moved by a sense of duty as a member of Plymouth Church, I have decided to prefer charges against Henry C. Bowen and Theodore Tilton, and have requested Brother Halliday to call a meeting of the Examining Committee in order that I may make the charges before them.

Thinking that you would perhaps like to be made acquainted with these facts I called last evening at Mr. Beach's house, where I was informed that you had returned to Peekskill.

I therefore write you by early mail to-day. Yours very truly,

WM. F. WEST.

Meanwhile, through the intervention of Dr. Storrs and others, as I understood, an ecclesiastical council had been called. The acts of this council in attempting to disfellowship Plymouth Church were very displeasing to Beecher, and caused him much trouble, especially the action of Dr. Storrs, which he expressed to me in the following letter, dated March 25th, 1874, which is here produced and marked "WW":—

[Confidential.]

My Dear Frank:—I am indignant beyond expression. Storrs' course has been an unspeakable outrage. After his pretended sympathy and friendship for Theodore he has turned against him in the most venomous manner—and it is not sincere. His professions of faith and affection for me are hollow and faithless. They are merely *tactical*. His object is plain. He is determined to *force* a conflict, and to use one of us to destroy the other if possible. That is his game. By stinging Theodore he believes that he will be driven into a course which he hopes will ruin me. If ever a man betrayed another he has. I am in hopes that Theodore, who has borne so much, will be unwilling to be a flail in Storrs' hand to strike at a friend. There are one or two reasons, emphatic, for *waiting* until the end of the council before taking any action.

1. That the attack on Plymouth Church and the threats against Congregationalism were so violent that the public mind is likely to be absorbed in the ecclesiastical elements and not in the personal.

2. If Plymouth Church is *disfellowshipped* it will constitute a blow at me and the church, far severer than at him.

3. That if council does *not disfellowship* Plymouth Church, then, undoubtedly, Storrs will go off into Presbyterianism, as he almost, without disguise, *threatened* in his speech, and in that case the emphasis will be *there*.

4. At any rate, while the fury rages in council it is not wise to make any move that would be *one* among so many, as to lose effect in a degree, and after the battle is over one can more exactly see what ought to be done. Meantime I am *patient* as I know how to be, but pretty nearly used up with inward excitement, and must run away for a day or two and hide and sleep, or there will be a funeral.

Cordially and trustingly yours, H. W. B.

March 25th, 1874.

No one can tell under first impressions what the effect of such a speech will be. *It ought to damn Storrs.*

While these proceedings were pending Rev. Mr. Halliday, the assistant of Beecher, called upon him and upon me to endeavor to learn the facts about the difficulties between Beecher and Tilton. I stated to Halliday that I did not think that either he or the church were well employed in endeavoring to reopen a trouble which had been adjusted and settled by the parties to it, and that it was better, in my judgment, for everybody that the whole matter should be allowed to repose in quiet. The result of the interview between Halliday and Beecher was communicated to me in the following letter, undated and unsigned, so that I cannot fix the date, but it is in Beecher's handwriting, and is here produced and marked "XX."

SUNDAY—A. M.

MY DEAR FRIEND—Halliday called last night. T.'s interview with him did not satisfy but disturbed. It was the same with Bell, who was present. It tended directly to unsettling.

Your interview last night was *very beneficial*, and gave confidence. This must be looked after.

It is vain to build if the foundation sinks under every effort.

I shall see you at 10:30 to-morrow—if you return by way of 49 Remsen.

The anxiety which Beecher felt about these stories and the steps he took to quiet them, together with the trust he reposed in me and my endeavors to aid him in that behalf, may perhaps be as well seen from a letter headed "25, '73," which I believe to be June 25th, 1873, and directed "My dear Von Moltke," meaning myself, and kindly complimenting me with the name of a general having command of a battle. It is here produced and marked "YY:"—

25th, '73.

MY DEAR VON MOLTKE:—I have seen Howard again. He says that it was not from Theodore that Wilkeson got the statement, but from Carpenter.

Is he reporting that view? I have told Claflin that you would come with Carpenter if he could be found, and at any rate by nine to-night (to see Storrs), but I did not say anything about Storrs.

I sent Cleveland over with my horse and buggy to hunt Carpenter.

Will you put Carpenter on his guard about making such statements?

From him these bear the force of coming from head-quarters. Yours truly and ever,

H. W. BEECHER.

Meanwhile Halliday had an interview with Tilton, the result of which as unsettling the matter between Tilton and Beecher, was very anxiously awaited by Beecher, who communicated to me, and who was also quite as anxious that Tilton should take no steps by which the matter between them should get into the newspapers or be made in any manner a matter of controversy. With this view he stated the situation on the same night of the interview of Halliday and Tilton in the following letter, which is without date and was written in pencil in great haste, and is here produced, marked "ZZ":—

SUNDAY NIGHT.

MY DEAR FRIEND:—

1. The *Eagle* ought to have nothing to-night. It is *that* meddling which stirs up our folks. Neither *you* nor Theodore ought to be troubled by the side which you served so faithfully in public.

2. The deacon's meeting I think is adjourned. I saw Bell. It was a friendly movement.

3. The only near, next danger is the women—Morrill, Bradshaw, and the poor, dear child.

If papers will hold off a month we can ride out the gale and make safe anchorage, and then when once we are in deep, tranquil waters we will all join hands in a profound and genuine *laus Deo!* for through such a wilderness only a Divine Providence could have led us undevoured by the open-mouthed beasts that lay in wait for our lives.

I go on twelve train after sleepless night. I am anxious about Theodore's interview with Halliday. Will you send me a *line* Monday night or Tuesday morning, care of M. P. Kennard, Boston, Mass.

I shall get mails there till Friday.

I have now produced to the committee all the letters and documents bearing upon the subject matter of this inquiry which I have in my possession, either from Beecher, Tilton or Mrs. Tilton, previous to the Bacon letter, and there is but one collateral matter of which I desire to speak.

I saw questions put in the cross-examination of Tilton, as published in the Brooklyn *Eagle*, and also published in the newspapers—with how much of truth I know not—that Mr. Samuel Wilkeson had charged that Tilton's case (in controversy with Bowen) was for the purpose of blackmailing him and Beecher, and that he (Wilkeson) knew that there had been no crime committed against Tilton or his household by Beecher. Beecher never intimated to me that he thought there was any desire on Tilton's part to blackmail him; and as I had the sole management of the money controversy between Tilton and Bowen, which I have already fully explained, I know there was no attempt on Tilton's part to blackmail or get anything more than what I believed his just due from Bowen To that I am certain that Mr. Wilkeson is wholly mistaken in that regard.

The question whether Wilkeson knew or believed that any offence had been committed will depend upon the fact whether he knew of anything that had been done by Beecher or Tilton's wife which called for apology at the time he wrote the tripartite covenant. It will be remembered that the tripartite covenant was made solely in reference to the disclosures which Bowen had made to Tilton and Tilton had made to Bowen, and Tilton's letter sets forth that the only disclosure he made to Bowen of Beecher's acts towards himself were of improper advances made to his wife, and that he so limited his charge in order to save the honor of his wife. These questions will be answered by the production of the letter of April 2d, 1872, written by Samuel Wilkeson, which are marked "AAA":—

NORTHERN PACIFIC RAILROAD COMPANY,
SECRETARY'S OFFICE, 120 BROADWAY,
NEW YORK, April 2d, 1872.

MY DEAR MOULTON:—Now for the closing act of justice and duty.

Let Theodore pass into your hand the written apology which he holds for the improper advances, and do you pass it into the flames of the friendly fire in your room of reconciliation. Then let Theodore talk to Oliver Johnson.

I hear that he and Carpenter, the artist, have made this whole affair the subject of conversation in the clubs. Sincerely yours,

SAMUEL WILKESON.

This letter, it will be observed, contains no protest against blackmailing, either on Tilton's part or my own, upon Beecher or Bowen, and is of the date of the tripartite covenant. Wilkeson also, hearing of Tilton's troubles, kindly offered to procure him a very lucrative employment in a large enterprise with which he was connected, as appears from a letter dated January 1st, 1871, which I herewith produce, marked "BBB 1:"—

NORTHERN PACIFIC RAILROAD COMPANY,
January 11th, 1871.

DEAR TILTON:—You are in trouble. I come to you with a letter just mailed to Jay Cooke, advising him to secure your services as a platform speaker to turn New England, Old England or the great West upside down about our Northern Pacific.

Pluck up heart! You shan't be trampled down. Keep quiet. Don't talk. *Don't publish.* Abide your time and it will be a very good time. Take my word for it. SAMUEL WILKESON.

It will be observed that this letter was dated after the letter of apology and after the letter of Tilton to Bowen, and Wilkeson could hardly have desired to employ in so grave an enterprise one whom he then knew or believed to be attempting to blackmail his employer. And, besides, his kindly expressions and advice to Tilton seemed to me wholly inconsistent with such an allegation.

I think it just, in this connection, to state a fact which bears in my mind upon this subject. On the 3d of May, 1873, I knew that Tilton was in want of money, and I took leave, without consulting him, to send him my check for $1,000 and a due bill for that amount to be signed by him, enclosed in a letter which I here produce, marked "BBB2," all of which he returned to me with an indorsement thereon. The following is the document:—

NEW YORK, May 3d, 1873.

DEAR THEODORE:—I enclose to you a check for $1,000, for which please sign the enclosed. Yours, F. D. MOULTON.

[Endorsement on above by Tilton.]

DEAR FRANK:—I can't borrow any money, for I see no way of returning it. Hastily, T. T.

After the above paper was returned to me, on the same day I sent him the $1,000, leaving it to be a matter as between ourselves, and not a money transaction.

I know, to the contrary of this, so far as Beecher is concerned, that Tilton never made any demand on him for money or pecuniary aid in any way or form. He asked only that Beecher should interpose his influence and power to protect him from the slanders of those who claimed to be Beecher's friends, while Beecher himself, with generosity and kindness toward Tilton, which had always characterized his acts during the whole of this unhappy controversy, of his own motion insisted, through me, in aiding Tilton in establishing his enterprise of the *Golden Age*, for which purpose he gave me the sum of $5,000, which I was to expend in such manner as I deemed judicious to keep the enterprise along, and if Tilton was at any time in need personally to aid him. It was understood between myself and Beecher that this money should go to Tilton as if it came from my own voluntary contributions for his benefit, and that he should not know—and he does not know until he reads this statement, for I do not believe he has derived it from any other source—that this money came from Beecher, or thinks that he is in any way indebted to him for it. I annex an account of the receipt and expenditure of that sum, so far as it has been expended, in a paper marked "CCC:"—

STATEMENT OF ACCOUNT.

1873.	
May 2d, received	$5,000
May 3d, paid	$1,000
July 11th, paid	650
August 15th, paid	250
September 12th, paid	500
September 30th, paid	500
December 16th, paid	200
1874.	
February 24th, paid	500
March 30th, paid	400
May 2d, paid	250
May 26th, paid	300
Total	$4,550

I also annex two letters of March 30th, 1874, from the publisher of the *Golden Age*, which will tend to vouch the expenditure of a part of the above amount. They are marked "DDD" and "EEE" respectively:"—

THE GOLDEN AGE, NEW YORK, March 30th, 1874.
[Private.]

DEAR MR. MOULTON:—We are in a tight spot. Mr. —— is away and we have no money and no paper. Can't get the latter without the former. We owe about $400 for paper, and the firm we have been ordering from refuse to let us have any more without money. Haven't any paper for this week's issue. Truly yours, O. W. RULAND.

If you can do anything for us I trust you will, to help us tide over the chasm.

THE GOLDEN AGE, NEW YORK, March 30th, 1874.

DEAR MR. MOULTON:—I am more grateful than I can tell you for the noble and generous way you came to the rescue of the *Golden Age* this afternoon. Truly your friend, O. W. RULAND.

I think proper to add, further, that Tilton more than once said to me that he could and would receive nothing from Beecher in the way of pecuniary assistance. I remember one special instance in which the subject was discussed between us. Beecher had told me that he was willing to furnish money to pay the expenses of Tilton and his family in traveling abroad, in order that Tilton might be saved from the constant state of irritation which arose from the rumors he was daily hearing. I rather hinted at than informed Tilton of this fact, and he repelled even the intimation of such a thing with the utmost indignation and anger. Therefore I only undertook the disbursement of this sum at the most earnest and voluntary request of Beecher.

As I have brought before the committee the somewhat collateral matter of the letters of Mrs. Woodhull to Beecher to influence him into the support of her doctrines and herself socially, which I thought but just to him, it seems but equally just that I should make as a part of my statement a letter, that came into my possession at the time it was written, from Tilton to a friend in the West—and not for the purpose of publication—explaining his position in regard to Mrs. Woodhull and the injurious publication made against him and his family and Mr. Beecher. This letter I here produce, marked "FFF 1:"—

No. 174 Livingston Street, Brooklyn, Dec. 31st, 1872.

My Dear Friend:—I owe you a long letter. I am unwell and a prisoner in the house, leaning back in leather-cushioned idleness and writing on my chair board before the fire. Perhaps you wonder that I have a fire, or anything but a hearthstone broken and crumbled, since the world has been told that my household is in ruins. And yet it is more like your last letter—brimful of love and wit and sparkling like a fountain in midwinter.

Nevertheless you are right. I am in trouble, and I hardly see a path out of it,

It is just two years ago to-day—this very day, the last of the year—that Mr. Bowen lifted his hammer, and with an unjust blow smote asunder my two contracts—one with the *Independent* and the other with the Brooklyn *Union*. The public little suspects that this act of his turned on his fear to meet the consequences of horrible charges which he made against Henry Ward Beecher. I have kept quiet on the subject for two years through an unwillingness to harm others, even for the sake of righting myself before the public. But, having trusted to time for my vindication I find that time has only thickened my difficulties, until these now buffet me, like a storm.

You know that Bowen long ago paid to me the assessed pecuniary damages which grew out of his breaking of the contracts, and gave me a written vindication of *my* course, and something like an apology for *his*. This settlement, so far as I am concerned, is final.

But Bowen's assassinating dagger drawn against Beecher has proved as unable as Macbeth's to "trammel up the consequence." And the consequence is that the air of Brooklyn is rife with stories against its chief clergyman, not growing out of the Woodhull scandal merely, but exhaled with ever fresh foulness, like mephitic vapors, from Bowen's own charge against Beecher.

Verily, the tongue is a wild beast that no man can tame, and like a wolf it is now seeking to devour the chief shepherd of the flock, together also with my own pretty lambs.

For the last four or five weeks, or ever since I saw the Woodhull libel, I have hardly had a restful day; and I frequently dream the whole thing over at night, waking the next morning unfit for work.

Have you any conception of what it is to suffer the keenest possible injustice? If not, come and learn of me.

To say nothing of the wrong and insult to my wife, in whose sorrow I have greater sorrow, I have to bear the additional indignity of being misconstrued by half the public and by many friends.

For instance, it is supposed that I had a conspirator's hand in this unholy business, whereas I am as innocent of it as of the Nathan murder.

It is hinted that the libelous article was actually written by me; whereas (being in the north of New Hampshire) I did not know of its existence till a week after it had convulsed my own city and family. My wife never named it in her letters to me lest it should spoil my mood for public speaking. (You know I was then toiling day and night for Mr. Greeley's sake).

Then, too, it is the sneer of the clubs that I have degenerated into an apostle of free love; whereas the whole body of my writings stands like a monument against this execrable theory.

Moreover, it is charged that I am in financial and other relations with Mrs. Woodhull; whereas I have not spoken to, nor met, nor seen her for nearly a year.

The history of my acquaintance with her is this :—In the spring of 1871, a few months after Bowen charged Beecher with the most hideous crime known to human nature, and had slammed the door of the *Independent* in my face, and when I was toiling like Hercules to keep the scandal from the public, then it was that Mrs. Woodhull, hitherto a stranger to me, suddenly sent for me and poured into my ears, not the Bowen scandal, but a new one of her own—namely, almost the same identical tale which she printed a few weeks ago. Think of it! When I was doing my best to suppress *one* earthquake Mrs. Woodhull suddenly stood before me portentous with another. What was I to do? I resolved at all hazards to keep back the new avalanche until I could securely tie up the original storm. My fear was that she would *publish* what she told to me, and, to prevent this catastrophe, I resolved (and, as the result proves, like a fool, and yet with a fool's innocent and pure motive) to make her such a friend of mine that she would never think of doing me such a harm. So I rendered her some important services (including especially some labors of pen and ink), all with a view to put and hold her under an obligation to me and mine.

In so acting toward her I found to my glad surprise and astonishment that she rose almost as high in my estimation as she had done with Lucretia Mott, Elizabeth Cady Stanton, Isabella Beecher Hooker, and other excellent women. Nobody who has not met Mrs. Woodhull can have an adequate idea of the admirable impression which she is capable of producing on serious persons. Moreover, I felt that the current denunciations against her were outrageously unjust, and that, like myself, she had been put in a false position before the public, and I sympathized keenly with the aggravation of spirit which this produces. This fact lent a zeal to all I said in her defence.

Nor was it until after I had known her for a number of months, and when I discovered her purposes to libel a dozen representative women of the suffrage movement, that I suddenly opened my eyes to her real tendencies to mischief; and then it was that I indignantly repudiated her acquaintance, and have never seen her since.

Hence her late tirade.

Well, it is over, and *I* am left to be the chief sufferer in the public estimation.

What to do in the emergency (which is not clearing, but clouding itself daily) I have not yet decided.

What I *could* do would be to take from my writing desk and publish to-morrow morning the prepared narrative and vindication, which, with facts and documents, my legal advisers pronounce complete.

This would explain and clarify everything, both great and small (including the Woodhull episode, which is but a minor part of the whole case); but if I publish it I must not only violate a kind of honorable obligation to be silent, which I had voluntarily imposed upon myself, but I must put my old friend Bowen to a serious risk of being smitten dead by Beecher's hand.

How far Bowen would deserve his fate I cannot say, but I know that all Plymouth Church would hunt him as a rat.

Well, perhaps the future will unravel my skein for me without my own hand; but whatever happens to my weather-beaten self, I wish to you, O prosperous comrade, a happy New Year. Fraternally yours,

THEODORE TILTON.

P. S.—Before sending this long letter (which pays my debt to you) I have read it to my wife, who desires to supplement it by sending her love and good will to the little white cottage and its little red cheeks.

The first intimation of the insanity of Tilton arose in this wise:—Prior to Sunday, March 29th, 1874, a publication was made of a statement by a reporter of the Brooklyn *Union* purporting to be the result of an interview with Mr. Thomas G. Shearman, clerk of Plymouth church, to the effect—I quôte from memory—that Tilton was insane, and that he stated that Mrs. Tilton had mediumistic fits—whatever disease that may be—in which she had stated matters affecting the character of Beecher, and to the statement of neither of them, for that reason, was any credit to be given. This publication, as it tended not only to excite Tilton to a defence of his sanity, but also, as coming from the clerk of Plymouth Church, might be supposed to be an authoritative expression of its pastor, annoyed Beecher very much, and he wrote the following letter, marked "FFF 2," which I herewith produce:—

SUNDAY NIGHT, March 29th, 1874.

MY DEAR FRANK:—Is there to be no end of trouble? Is wave to follow wave in endless succession? I was cut to the heart when C. showed me that shameful paragraph from the *Union*. Its cruelty is beyond description. I felt like lying down and saying, "I am tired—tired—tired of living, or of trying to resist the devil of mischief." I would rather have had a javelin launched against me a hundred times than against those that have suffered so much. The shameful indelicacy of bringing the most sacred relations into such publicity fills me with horror.

But there are some slight alleviations. The paragraph came when the public mind was engaged with the council and with Theodore's letters. I hope it will pass without further notice. If it is *not taken up* by other papers it will sink out of sight and be forgotten; whereas, if it be assailed, it may give it a conspicuity that it never would have had. But I shall write Shearman a letter and give him my full feeling about it. I must again [be]; as I have heretofore been, indebted to you for a judicious council on this new and flagrant element. My innermost soul longs for peace; and if that cannot be, for death, that *will* bring peace. My fervent hope is that this drop of gall may sink through out of sight and not prove a mortal poison. Yours ever, H. W. BEECHER.

I have written strongly to Shearman and hope that he will send a letter to T. unsolicited. I am sick, head, heart and body, but must move on! I feel this morning like letting things go by the run.

The letter of retraction, as proposed by Tilton, not being forthcoming, I felt it my duty, in his interest, to take such measures as should result in an apology from Shearman to Tilton. I accordingly carried to him a copy of the paper having the article, and laid it upon his desk in his office, and said to him that if the statements in this article were not actually made by him he ought to retract them. Although it lay on his desk he said to me that he had not seen the article and did not mean to see it. I told him that he must see it, and if it was not true that he must say so. He said he didn't want to read it and wouldn't read it. I then left him. Afterwards I saw Tilton and told him what I had done, and he said, "we will go up together," which we did, and met Mr. Shearman. Mr. Tilton called his attention to the statement in the Brooklyn *Union* as having come from him (Shearman), concerning himself and his wife, that one was crazy and the other subject to mediumistic fits. Said he, "Mr. Sherman, this is untrue, and if you are not correctly reported your simple duty is to say so; and if you have made such a statement I demand that you retract and apologize. If you do not, I shall hold you responsible in any way I can for such injurious statement." Shearman then read the paragraph in the *Union*, and made an explanation in this wise:—That he might probably have repeated to somebody a story which Tilton had told him of the mediumistic states of Mrs. Woodhull, and perhaps have made the mistake of using Mrs. Tilton's name instead of Mrs. Woodhull's. Tilton said to him, "Mr. Shearman, you know that you are deliberately uttering falsehoods, and I won't allow you to think even that you can deceive me by such a statement as you are making now. You must make such an explanation of this statement in the *Union* as shall be satisfactory to me, or, as I said before; I shall hold you responsible." During the first part of the conversation Mr. Shearman called in a witness from his outer office, but when the conversation became earnest and Tilton began charging him with an untruth, Shearman bid the witness retire, which he did. Tilton and I then left the office.

Within a few days of this interview Tilton procured the affidavit of the reporter of the *Union* that the statement that Shearman had been reported as making he did, in fact, make. On, March 20th Shearman sent to me, for delivery to Tilton, a note of which I produce a copy under that date, marked "GGG," The original was delivered up to Shearman afterwards:—

BROOKLYN, March 30th, 1874.

DEAR SIR:—My attention has been called to a newspaper paragraph which I have not seen, but which I am told is to the effect that I stated to a reporter that you had described Mrs. Tilton as having, in a mediumistic or clairvoyant state, made some extraordinary statements of a painful nature.

I have for some years past made it a rule never to send corrections to newspapers of anything relating to myself, no matter how erroneous such statements may be.

But I have no objection to saying to you personally that this story, if correctly quoted here, appears to be an erroneous version of the one and only statement which I had from you over a year ago, viz., that Mrs. Woodhull did exactly the thing here attributed to Mrs. Tilton.

I do not know that I ever repeated that story in the presence of any reporter for the paper in question, but I have done so in the presence of others, and I may, of course, by an unconscious mistake, have used your wife's name in the place of another and wholly different person. If so I beg that you will assure Mrs. Tilton of my great regret for such an error.

Yours obediently,

T. G. SHEARMAN.

When I took this note to Tilton he refused to receive it, saying:—"I will not receive any such note from Shearman. He knows it contains a falsehood and I cannot take it from him. You may carry it back to him." I did so, and stated to him Tilton's answer. Afterwards he substituted for that note another, under the date of April 2d, 1874, which is here produced, marked "HHH":—

BROOKLYN, April 2d, 1874.

DEAR SIR:—Having seen a paragraph in the Brooklyn *Union* of Saturday last containing a report of a statement alleged to have been made by me concerning your family and yourself, I desire to assure you that this report is seriously incorrect, and that I have never authorized such a statement.

It is unnecessary to repeat here what I have actually said upon these subjects, because I am now satisfied that what I *did* say was erroneous, and that the rumors to which I gave some credit were without foundation. I deeply regret having been misled into an act of unintentional injustice, and am glad to take the earliest occasion to rectify it.

I beg, therefore, to withdraw all that I said upon the occasion referred to as incorrect (although then believed by me), and to repudiate entirely the statement imputed to me as untrue and unjust to all parties concerned.

Yours obediently,

T. G. SHEARMAN.

THEODORE TILTON, Esq.

In no part of that negotiation did Mr. Shearman suggest to me that there were any doubts as to Tilton's sanity, and denied both to me and to him that he had ever said anything to the contrary, or that Mrs. Tilton was in any way incapacitated from telling the truth by reason of mediumistic fits or other physical disability. Shearman's action was communicated to Beecher; but meanwhile it had come to be spread about that Beecher had made a similar accusation as to the sanity of Mr. and Mrs. Tilton to that of Shearman.

A member of your committee, Mr. Cleveland, communicated the fact to Beecher, to which Beecher made an indignant denial, as appears by his note to Mr. Cleveland, who communicated a copy of it to me in a note under date of April 2d, which I here produce, marked "III":—

[Copy.]

My Dear Cleveland:—You say that I am supposed to have reported to some members of the council substantially the same story that is attributed to Shearman.

How can any human being that knows me believe any such impossibility? I never opened my lips to any human being on the subject. I will defy any man to face me and say that by word, look or intimation I ever alluded to it. I have been as dumb as the dead. They that dare to say I have spoken of it are liars, if they mean to themselves, and the bearers of lies if they received it from others.

I have a feeling too profoundly sacred to make such sacrilege possible.

April 2d, 1874. H. W. Beecher.

Frank Moulton, Esq.:—

Dear Sir:—Herewith you have copy of a note received from Mr. Beecher respecting the matter of which it speaks.

Not seeing you when I called this A. M., and leaving the city, I send by Mr. Halliday. Mr. Beecher wants to see you *before* or *after* the meeting this evening. Truly yours, H. M. Cleveland.

Having retained the friendship of the principal parties to this controversy down to to-day, I have not thought it proper to produce herewith any letters that I have received from either of them excepting the single one exonerating me from blame and showing Mrs, Tilton's confidence in me, which I thought was due to myself to do because of the peculiar statement attributed to her; nor have I produced any papers or proposals for a settlement of this controversy since it has broken out afresh and since the publication of Tilton's letter to Dr. Bacon and the call of Beecher for a committee; nor have I since then furnished to either party, although called upon by both, any documents in my posession that one might use the same against the other. I have endeavored to hold myself strictly as a mediator between them, and my endeavor has been, even down to the very latest hour, to have all the scandals arising out of the publication of the facts of their controversies and wrongs buried out of sight, deeming it best that it should be so done, not only for the good of the parties concerned and their families, but that of the community at large.

If any evidence were needed that, in the interest of the parties, and especially of Beecher, I was endeavoring to the latest hour to prevent the publication of all these documents and this testimony, and that I retained the confidence of at least one of the parties in that endeavor, I produce a letter of July 13th, 1874, being a note arranging a meeting between myself and Beecher in regard to this controversy. It is marked, " JJJ " :—

JULY 13th, 1874.

MY DEAR FRANK :—I will be with you at seven, or a little before. I am ashamed to put a straw more upon you, and have but a single consolation —that the matter cannot distress you *long*, as it must soon end—that is, there will be no more anxiety about the *future*, whatever regrets there may be for the past. Truly yours and ever, H. W. BEECHER.

If there is any paper or fact supposed by either of the parties, or by the committee, to be in my posession which will throw any further light upon the subject of your inquiry, I shall be most willing to produce it if I have it, although I do not believe that there is any such ; and I am ready to answer any proper question which shall be put to me in the way of cross-examination by any of the parties concerned or their counsel, as fully as my memory or any data I have will serve, so that all the facts may be known ; for, if any part of them be known, I deem it but just to truth and right that all should be known. As, however, controversy has already arisen as to the correctness of the reports of evidence taken before the committe, I must ask leave, if any cross-examination is to be had orally, to be accompanied by my own stenographer, who shall take down the evidence I may give as a necessary measure for my own protection.

Leaving to your committee, without comment, the facts and documents herewith presented, I have the honor to remain, yours, truly, FRANCIS D. MOULTON.

Before closing this compilation, however, justice to the committee and the reader requires that the conclusions of the jury of inquiry should be embodied. Discarding the studied argument used to justify their verdict of "not guilty," as too absurd, the gist of the report is given in the verdict attached to the document that will ever stand as a reproach to its authors:—

First—We find from the evidence that the Rev. Henry Ward Beecher did not commit adultery with Mrs. Elizabeth R. Tilton, either at the time or times, place or places set forth in the third and fourth subdivisions of Mr. Tilton's statement, nor at any other time or place whatever.

Second—We find from the evidence that Mr. Beecher has never committed any unchaste or improper act with Mrs. Tilton, nor made any unchaste or improper remarks, proffer or solicitation to her of any kind or description whatever.

Third—If this were a question of errors of judgment on the part of Mr. Beecher it would be easy to criticise, especially in the light of recent events. In such criticism, even to the extent of regrets and censure, we are sure no man would join more sincerely than Mr. Beecher himself.

Fourth—We find nothing whatever in the evidence that should impair the perfect confidence of Plymouth church or the world in the Christian character and integrity of Henry Ward Beecher.

And now let the peace of God that passeth all understanding rest and abide with Plymouth church and her beloved eminent pastor, so much and so long afflicted.

HENRY W. SAGE,
AUGUSTUS STORRS,
HENRY M. CLEVELAND,
HORACE B. CLAFLIN,
JOHN WINSLOW,
S. V. WHITE,
Committee of Investigation.

Dated BROOKLYN, August 27th, 1874.

Several days passed after the publication of Mr. Moulton's statement before the committee appointed by Mr. Beecher made their official report. The public, however, had come to understand just what it would be, from a "brief" supplied to the

Herald and telegraphed over the country. This report was as expected a vindication of Mr. Beecher, or as many journals, and a large part of the community styled it "whitewash." The document was a cunningly worded legal argument in which the authors sought to render the *entire* evidence of the prosecutor and his witnesses useless, inasmuch as a part of this evidence had been impeached by Bessie Turner, and other witnesses for the defence. The committee came to the *Sage* conclusion that if the prosecution was "tipped up" on a few points their entire charges must fail, and hence *Mr. Beecher was vindicated (?) by a committee of his own choice, composed of gentlemen who had a pecuniary interest in Plymouth church*, as Mr. Samuel Wilkeson—according to Mrs. Elizabeth Cady Stanton—had in "The Life of Christ," that he feared, "would be knocked higher than a kite." The compiler does not consider the report of this committee of sufficient importance to embody in this work. He may, however, be permitted to say that with every desire to fill the position of an impartial historian, he can but regret that the gentlemen who have conducted the inquiry should resort to the "pettifogging" mode of *trying the witnesses for the prosecution* rather than the accused. Mr. Tilton made specific charges, reduced them to writing, and made affidavit to them in legal form. Mr. Moulton sustained Mr. Tilton's most damaging charges, and supplemented his testimony with letters of a most damaging character, that, critically examined, gave force to the charges. No effort was made by the committee and its tricky legal advisers to prove these letter forgeries; no attempt was made to have Mr. Tilton indicted for perjury. The policy of this biased committee apparently was to paint Mr. Beecher as a pure and spotless minister, by blackmailing the character of every person who had been known to have given currency to the reputed crimes of the pastor. These "chivalrous" gentlemen in their desire to do their work *well* had the exceedingly bad taste to stab the reputation of Miss Susan B. Anthony, whose private character until Bessie Turner testified, stood as before the world as that of any wife or maiden in the city of churches. This despicable subterfuge was easily pierced by the eye of the public, and when Mr. Beecher's committee put it in force, the general exclamation, outside the Plymouth coterie was "shame! shame!" It would be a charity to throw the responsibility for this heartless mode of conducting the investigation upon the counsel for the defence; but the gentlemen composing the committe are persons of intelligence, familiar with the routine of courts of law, and the author can find no excuse for their action, and hence they must bear all the odium attaching to such irregular procedure.

While saying this much by way of criticism of the committee the reader will please remember that the compiler still adheres to the neutral position he takes in the preface to this edition, and does not wish to give expression to any individual opinion upon the guilt or innocence of Mr. Beecher. He will however, venture the opinion that the grossly partizan course pursued by the committee has done more to injure Mr. Beecher in the estimation of the reading public, than all the utterances of the Woodhull-Claflin women, and the affidavits and "gush" of Mr. Theodore Tilton the accomplished novelist and poet. The vindication will pass for naught and in closing a compilation, the object of which is to enable the reader to form conclusions of his own from an unbiased standpoint, the compiler will express the hope that the court of law, to which the inquiry now goes, will throw such barriers about the legal lights who figure in it, that will prevent the opening of the sluice gates and the free passage of a sea of scandal that threatens to swamp the characters of the innocent as well as the guilty.

Since the foregoing compilation was brought to a close supplementary statements have been published by Messrs. Moulton and Tilton. Much of that made by the former gentleman is so very obscene that the author is compelled to pass it over with the remark that the document as a whole, while very able, clearly convicting Mr. Beecher of misrepresentation, or willful falsehood, certainly exonerated Mr. Moulton from the charge of blackmailing the pastor. Mr. Moulton gives letters, and makes detailed reports of conversations with Mr. Beecher, in which that gentleman admitted his adultery, that if sustained in a court of law must result in Mr. Beecher's conviction. The statement of Mr. Tilton is a strong one, calculated to strengthen the views of those who, from reading all the evidence *pro* and *con*, have come to the conclusion that he is guilty. He clearly shows that the committee's report, (that until recently Tilton had not charged Beecher with adultery,) is untrue, and he does this by embodying a copy of the speculations filed against him, when he was placed on trial before Plymouth Church for slandering Mr. Beecher. The third specification accuses him of charging Beecher with the commission of adultery. Mr. Tilton also quotes a letter from Mrs. Tilton to her mother (Mrs. Morse), in which language is used that can scarcely be construed into anything else than an admission on the part of Mrs. Tilton of adultery. The compiler does not believe that the cause of morality and religion would be advanced by the reproduction of these two sub-statements in full, or that it is necessary for a clear understanding of the deplorable controversy; hence they are omitted in this compilation. It is probable that before the second edition is put to press a competent court of law will pass upon the case, and therefore, for the present this compilation is here brought to a close.

THE END.

www.ingramcontent.com/pod-product-compliance
Lightning Source LLC
LaVergne TN
LVHW021225110826
845150LV00002B/250